Margaret Barker is an independent scholar, a Methodist local preacher and a former President of the Society for Old Testament Study. She has developed 'Temple Theology' as a new approach to biblical studies, and was given a DD for her work on the temple and the origins of Christian liturgy. For many years, she was a member of the Ecumenical Patriarch's Symposium on Religion, Science and the Environment, and has made Temple Theology the basis for her work on the environment. She was a co-founder of the Temple Studies Group, www.templestudiesgroup.com.

Her recent books include *Temple Mysticism* (2011), *Temple Themes in Christian Worship* (2008), *Christmas: The Original Story* (2008), *The Hidden Tradition of the Kingdom of God* (2007), *Temple Theology* (2004), *An Extraordinary Gathering of Angels* (2004), *The Great High Priest* (2003) and *The Revelation of Jesus Christ* (2000).

# KING OF THE JEWS

## Temple Theology in John's Gospel

MARGARET BARKER

First published in Great Britain in 2014

Society for Promoting Christian Knowledge
36 Causton Street
London SW1P 4ST
www.spckpublishing.co.uk

Copyright © Margaret Barker 2014

All rights reserved. No part of this book may be reproduced or transmitted in any form or by any means, electronic or mechanical, including photocopying, recording, or by any information storage and retrieval system, without permission in writing from the publisher.

SPCK does not necessarily endorse the individual views contained in its publications.

Unless otherwise noted, Scripture quotations are taken from the Common Bible: Revised Standard Version of the Bible, copyright © 1973 by the Division of Christian Education of the National Council of the Churches of Christ in the USA. Used by permission. All rights reserved.
Extracts marked AV are taken from the Authorized Version of the Bible (The King James Bible), the rights in which are vested in the Crown, and are reproduced by permission of the Crown's patentee, Cambridge University Press.
Extracts marked GNB are taken from the Good News Bible published by The Bible Societies/HarperCollins Publishers Ltd UK, and are copyright © American Bible Society, 1966, 1971, 1976, 1992, 1994.
Extracts marked NEB are taken from the New English Bible, copyright © The Delegates of the Oxford University Press and The Syndics of Cambridge University Press, 1961, 1970. Used by permission.

*British Library Cataloguing-in-Publication Data*
A catalogue record for this book is available from the British Library

ISBN 978–0–281–06967–5
eBook ISBN 978–0–281–06968–2

Typeset by Data Standards Ltd, Frome, Somerset

eBook by Data Standards Ltd, Frome, Somerset

*For*
*Timothy Wilton MA (Oxon), MBBS (Lon), FRCS (Eng)*

# Contents

| | |
|---|---|
| *Preface* | ix |
| Introduction | 1 |

## Part 1
## THE BACKGROUND TO JOHN'S GOSPEL

| | |
|---|---|
| 1  The Jews in John's Gospel | 23 |
| 2  Who was Moses? | 34 |
| 3  The king in the Old Testament | 62 |
| 4  The king in the New Testament | 105 |

## Part 2
## TEMPLE THEOLOGY IN JOHN'S GOSPEL

| | |
|---|---|
| Introduction to Part 2 | 147 |
| John 1 | 159 |
| John 2 | 188 |
| John 3 | 198 |
| John 4 | 214 |
| John 5 | 222 |
| John 6 | 247 |
| John 7 | 262 |
| John 8 | 269 |
| John 9 | 288 |
| John 10 | 300 |
| John 11 | 317 |
| John 12 | 339 |

| | |
|---|---|
| John 13 | 376 |
| John 14 | 398 |
| John 15 | 423 |
| John 16 | 447 |
| John 17 | 481 |
| John 18—19 | 516 |
| John 20 | 564 |
| John 21 | 596 |
| *Index of canonical and deuterocanonical texts* | 607 |
| *Index of other texts* | 625 |
| *Index of names and subjects* | 632 |

# Preface

I had intended to write a short book about John's Gospel, but soon realized that this was not possible. Many people have written on John's Gospel, and I have learned from their labours. I have not, however, written a book that discusses their work. Rather I have sketched an outline of how John's Gospel can be read in the light of Temple Theology. This is only a beginning; there is much still to do.

The contrast between the first and second temples is very clear in John's Gospel, as are the roots of Christianity in the older temple. I suggest that many of the 'problems' encountered in studying John's Gospel are due to the unrecognized presuppositions of those asking the questions. I brought different presuppositions to the task, and the results were very interesting indeed.

I should like to thank all those who make my work possible: my family, especially my husband Richard who lives with the inevitable piles of paper that accumulate when a book is being written, and my daughter Katy who understands both her mother and computers; the ever-helpful staff of the Cambridge University Library; and my friends in the Temple Studies Group who send me all sorts of information they have found in their own reading.

This book is dedicated, with my thanks, to the orthopaedic surgeon who literally put me back on my feet.

*Margaret Barker*
*Advent 2013*

# Introduction

At the beginning of his great work *The Interpretation of the Fourth Gospel* (1953), C. H. Dodd wrote this:

> I propose to take soundings here and there, in the religious literature of that time and region ['the varied and cosmopolitan society of a great Hellenistic city such as Ephesus under the Roman empire'] with a view to reconstructing in some measure the background of thought which the evangelist presupposed in his readers.[1]

He listed the five areas he thought important for background to the writings of John:

- the higher religion of Hellenism: the Hermetic literature;
- Hellenistic Judaism: Philo of Alexandria;
- Rabbinic Judaism;
- Gnosticism;
- Mandaeism.

The result was a massive and massively learned book, but it was flawed by the assumption that John was reflecting the situation *in which* he wrote, and not that *of which* he wrote. This was part of a long-established debate about the Johannine community and its relationship to Gnosticism; and about the sources of the Gospel, which invariably meant how it related to the incidents described in the synoptic Gospels; and overshadowing much of it was the figure of Rudolf Bultmann.

Then the implication of the Qumran texts (discovered from 1947 onwards) began to be felt, namely that the religious scene in Palestine in the time of Jesus was very different from anything that had been imagined. Scholars began to ask where 'John' fitted into this newly discovered situation. The debate about origins was no longer between Judaism and Hellenism, but rather within the variety of Jewish sects that existed in the time of Jesus. It was assumed that Judaism was the norm, and that anything different within the 'Jewish' spectrum must have been the result of syncretism. The problem peculiar to the study of the Gospel

---

[1] C. H. Dodd, *The Interpretation of the Fourth Gospel*, Cambridge: Cambridge University Press, 1953, p. 9.

of John was the fact that where it was most 'Jewish' it was also most anti-Jewish. John used the Jewish Scriptures against the Jews. After the discovery of the Nag Hammadi texts (in 1945) it also became clear that John had known and used a 'Wisdom myth' that was central to Gnostic systems. It was also clear that John shared with the Gnostics his attitude to 'the Jews'. Some 40 years ago, Quispel wrote thus of the origin of the Gnostics:

> It seems to me that the real issue is this: Most Gnostics were against the Jewish God who created the world and gave the Law. Is it possible that this doctrine is of Jewish origin? ... Even those who do accept that many Gnostic views are to be derived from Judaism seem to have avoided this theme.[2]

The debate about the origins of John's Gospel became very detailed and very complex. John was assumed to be well down a long line of development. Dunn, for example, concluded as late as 1991: 'Having looked at the beginnings and earliest forms of the tradition which the fourth evangelist used, it remains for us to remind ourselves how extensive his reworking and elaboration of tradition could be.' He also said: 'John's gospel is probably best regarded as an *example* of how elaboration of the Jesus tradition did (or might) happen, rather than as a basis for further elaboration.'[3]

My proposal is simpler. The 'background' to the Fourth Gospel is temple tradition and the memories and hopes of those who longed for the true temple to be restored. The 'Jews' were a group within Palestinian society, one among many groups who were the heirs of first-temple tradition in some way or another. These others may be classed together as 'Hebrews'. The Johannine community were non-Jewish but nevertheless temple-rooted Hebrews in Palestine who became the Church. They could have had links to the community at Qumran, or to the Magharians, people so called because their writings were found in a cave. Of these Quispel observed:

> As far as I know, only one Jewish text attests that there were Jews who taught a highest God and an inferior creator of the world. This is Al-Qirqisani's *Account of the Jewish Sects* ... The Magharians in Palestine distinguished between God, who is beyond anthropomorphism, and one of his angels, who is responsible for all the anthropomorphic features

---

[2] G. Quispel, *Gnostic Studies I*, Istanbul: Nederlands Historisch-Archaeologisch Instituut in het Nabije Oosten, 1974, p. 213.
[3] J. D. G. Dunn, 'John and the Oral Gospel Tradition', in *Jesus and the Oral Gospel Tradition*, ed. H. Wansbrough, Sheffield: Sheffield Academic Press, 1991, pp. 351–79, pp. 373, 379.

contained in the Old Testament, and who is creator of the world ... Moreover, it seems impossible that the author refers to members of the Qumran community ... [because] in the Dead Sea Scrolls, this curious concept cannot be found.[4]

The public teaching in John's Gospel is a stylized summary of Jesus' many debates with the Jews, and the teaching after the last supper is a summary of what Jesus taught his disciples privately during his ministry, when the embryonic Christian community was sharing meals and using the words of the *Didache*. The wine was taken in thanks for the holy vine of David made known through Jesus the Servant, and the broken bread was thanksgiving for the life and knowledge made known through Jesus the Servant. The community was the broken bread gathered together again into one loaf, which represented those scattered after the destruction of the original temple who came together again as the new temple.[5] In other words, Jesus taught about the Davidic kingship, which had been at the heart of the original temple, and about life and knowledge, which sounds very like 'Gnosticism', but the life and knowledge was linked to eating bread, which sounds very like the 'Wisdom myth' of the first temple.

The incipient 'Gnosticism' that so many have detected in the Fourth Gospel shows that 'Gnosticism' was a part of Jesus' teaching even though later forms were declared to be heretical and so excluded from church teaching. Gnosticism in its earliest forms was pre-Christian, but not Jewish; it was Hebraic and an heir to temple tradition. The Christians adopted this teaching, and John's Gospel shows it was remembered as the teaching of Jesus himself. As we shall see, some books found at Nag Hammadi, and believed to represent the earliest stages of 'Gnosticism', are evidence of this: the *Gospel of Truth* reads very like an exposition of Jesus' teaching after the last supper, especially his teaching about the Name, and it shows how the present state of error is due to people forgetting the Father – which is what happened in the post-Josian changes.[6] *Eugnostos the Blessed* is the Hebraic pre-Christian form of the *Wisdom of Jesus*, the latter being the Christianized version of the text that attributes this teaching to Jesus. Further, it was teaching given after his resurrection. Philip asked Jesus to teach them about the origin of the creation and the divine plan, and Jesus then spoke about the invisible heavenly powers,

---
[4] Quispel, *Gnostic Studies I*, n. 2 above, p. 215.
[5] *Didache* 9, 10.
[6] See below, p. 70.

that is, the world of the holy of holies. Thomas then questioned Jesus and was told that Jesus had come from the Boundless One to teach about the invisible world and to give his disciples power over the spiritually blind. The disciples were the sons of light, and both Philip and Thomas were key figures in the Gospel of John.

The rest of the teaching in *Eugnostos* and the *Wisdom of Jesus* could well have been derived from an aspect of the mysterious *raz nihyeh* ('the mystery of becoming') which the people at Qumran were exhorted to study. This seems to have been the knowledge symbolized by the holy of holies of the temple; no definition of the term is known. In temple symbolism, the holy of holies represented the source of all life, and so the *raz nihyeh* included the secrets of the holy of holies. It was also beyond time, and on its veil all history was depicted, so the *raz nihyeh* included knowledge of all history past, present and future. One of the Enoch books[7] described how Rabbi Ishmael[8] was shown the veil, on which he saw all history, but this belief was ancient. The LORD reminded the Second-Isaiah that he had seen 'in the beginning', that is, in the holy of holies, how the enemies of his people would be brought to nothing (Isa. 40.21–24); the Psalmist sang that when he entered the sanctuary, he saw what would happen to evil people (Ps. 73.16–20); and John was summoned to enter heaven to see what would take place in the future (Rev. 4.1). All this was part of the mystery.

The Qumran *Community Rule*, thought to be one of the oldest documents of the collection, sets out the rules, ideals and ceremonies of the group, and ends with a poem about the role of their Master and his duty to teach about the *raz nihyeh*. Vermes observed:

> There are, to my knowledge, no writings in ancient Jewish sources parallel to the *Community Rule*, but a similar type of literature flourished among Christians between the second and fourth centuries, the so-called 'Church Orders' represented by such works as the *Didache*, the *Didascalia*, the *Apostolic Constitution*.[9]

The Master of the Qumran group had to 'conceal the teaching of the Law from men of injustice, but impart true knowledge and righteous

---

[7] *3 Enoch*, a Hebrew text incorporating much ancient material that probably reached its present form in the sixth century CE. The passage referred to here is *3 Enoch* 45.
[8] He taught in Palestine in the early second century CE, and was called 'the high priest' although this must have meant he was from a high-priestly family, since he lived after the destruction of the temple in 70 CE.
[9] G. Vermes, *The Complete Dead Sea Scrolls in English*, London: Penguin, 1997, p. 98.

judgement to those who have chosen the Way'.[10] This teaching, then, was not open to all, just as Jesus said about his parables:

> To you has been given the secret of the kingdom of God, but for those outside everything is in parables; so that they may indeed see but not perceive, and may indeed hear, but not understand; lest they turn again and be forgiven. (Mark 4.11–12, quoting Isa. 6.9–10)

John reflects on this same passage from Isaiah at the end of his account of Jesus' public ministry: some people just did not receive his teachings (John 12.39–40). The poem at the end of the Qumran *Rule* seems to be the words of the Master: 'I will conceal/impart knowledge with discretion', where the original 'conceal' has been changed to 'impart', a correction that has interesting implications. The poem continues with the words of the Master, and these words could well have been spoken by John's Jesus, of whom the Baptist said: 'He who comes from heaven is above all. He bears witness to what he has seen and heard, yet no one receives his testimony' (John 3.31b–32). These are the words of the Master at Qumran:

> For from the spring of my knowledge comes my light,
> and my eyes have seen his wonderful works ...
> knowledge hidden from a man,
> a skilful plan hidden from the sons of Adam ...
> God has given them as an eternal possession,
> And made them inherit the lot of the holy ones.[11]

Many fragments of a similar Rule, the *Damascus Document*, were found at Qumran. The name comes from the self-description of the group, 'members of the new covenant in the land of Damascus'. To this group was revealed 'the hidden things in which all Israel had gone astray' and they were waiting for the glory of God to be revealed to Israel.[12] This community was preserving the older ways from which the rest of 'Israel' had departed; and they regarded themselves as the Chosen Ones and also as angels, since they were to 'inherit the portion of the holy ones'.

In their worship they stood with the angels, and in one of their hymns they sang:

> An iniquitous spirit you have purified from great transgression,
> That it might take its place with the host of the holy ones,

---

[10] *Community Rule*, 1QS IX.
[11] *Community Rule*, 1QS XI.3, 6, 7, my translation.
[12] *Damascus Document*, CD III, VIII.

*Introduction*

And enter into community with the sons of heaven.[13]

They prayed that their priests would stand in the holy of holies:

> May you be as an angel of the presence in the abode of holiness ... May you attend upon the service in the temple of the kingdom and decree destiny in company with the angels of the presence ...[14]

This could easily be the picture of worship in the Book of Revelation, where the servants of the LORD, with his Name on their foreheads, stand before the throne of the Lamb and worship him. The sign of the Name was an X and it indicated two things: being a high priest; and Christian baptism and anointing. In the early Church it meant both.

Those at Qumran who learned about the *raz nihyeh* and worshipped as/with the angels in heaven cannot have been very different from those who wrote and read John's Gospel and the Book of Revelation. The latter were the Hebrew-Christian community who saw themselves as the heavenly throng in the Book of Revelation. Their Lamb on the throne opened a sealed book – secret teaching – and they were originally people chosen from all the 12 tribes of Israel to receive the Name of the LORD on their foreheads (Rev. 7.3–4).[15] This vision was set in the early days of the first temple, before the kingdom divided, and it had become the hope for the future. The chosen ones became the ritually pure army of the Lamb (Rev. 14.1–5), riding out from heaven to fight with the Logos in order to establish a pure new Jerusalem (Rev. 19.11–16; 21.9–27). The Qumran community also saw themselves as the army of the sons of light,[16] ritually pure and accompanied by high priests clad in their white linen garments. The Qumran army was led by the Prince of Light and fought under war banners bearing names such as 'Truth of God', 'Justice of God', 'Glory of God'. The Logos who led his army from heaven in Revelation 19 bore the names 'Faithful' and 'True', with 'King of kings' and 'LORD of Lords' on his banner (Rev. 19.11, 16).[17]

There are obvious similarities between the teachings outlined in the Qumran Rules and the more detailed expositions of the heavenly world

---

[13] *Hymns*, 1QH XI.22–23, my translation.
[14] *Blessings*, 1QSb IV.
[15] Later the Hebrew community was joined by Gentile converts (Rev. 7.9).
[16] *War Scroll*, 1QM I, VII, XIII, IV respectively.
[17] 'On his robe and on his thigh' (Rev. 19.16) shows a mistranslation of a Hebrew original, in which *deghel*, 'war banner', has been read as *reghel*, usually 'foot', but also 'leg', e.g. 1 Sam. 17.6. The letters *d* and *r* look very similar in Hebrew.

*Introduction*

found in the Nag Hammadi texts *Eugnostos the Blessed* and the *Wisdom of Jesus Christ*. The shorter text, *Eugnostos*, was linked to the longer with:

> All these things that I have just said to you, I have said in the way that you can accept, until the one who does not need to be taught is revealed among you, and he will say all these things to you joyously and in pure knowledge.[18]

In the *Wisdom of Jesus Christ* Jesus taught his disciples on a mountain top in Galilee, where he appeared as an angel of light,[19] something familar in the synoptic Gospels as the Transfiguration. He had come to reveal the divine name (cf. John 17.6) 'and the complete will of the mother of the holy angels', in other words, the teaching of Wisdom. This would remove their blindness.[20] The thought-world of *Eugnostos* (and so, by implication, of Jesus) was the holy of holies in the first temple, and thus of the origin of creation. The ranks of angels proceeding from their divine source are familiar from the Psalms and from Revelation (e.g. Ps. 104.1–4; Rev. 4.1– 5.14). There is no way of knowing whether the similarities to the New Testament, and especially to the writings of John, were due to Gnostic texts drawing on Johannine writings, or John writing within this same temple tradition.

In the light of Vermes' observation that the Qumran *Community Rule* resembled certain early Christian texts, there must have been some link between the temple traditions preserved at Qumran and those in 'Gnostic' Christianity. The New Testament also shows the link, when familiar lines are set in this context: Saul was sent to arrest *followers of the Way in Damascus*, one of the ways that the Qumran community described themselves (Acts 9.2), and later, as the Christian Paul, he preached about the Way in Ephesus (Acts 19.23). He then sent to the Christian community in Ephesus a letter beginning:

> He has made known to us in all wisdom and insight the mystery of his will, according to his purpose which he set forth in Christ, as a plan for the fullness of time, to unite all things in him, things in heaven and things on earth. (Eph. 1.9–10)

The theme here is Christ restoring the unity which, as we shall see, was represented by the holy of holies, the place of light. Writing to Corinth, he described Jesus as 'the Power of God and the Wisdom of God' (1 Cor.

---

[18] *Eugnostos*, Coptic Gnostic Library (hereafter CG) III.3.90.
[19] *Wisdom of Jesus Christ*, CG III.4.91.
[20] *Wisdom*, CG III.4.118.

1.24, my translation), a very Gnostic-sounding phrase. In the *Gospel of Thomas*, also found at Nag Hammadi, Jesus taught his disciples that they had come from the light and so were children of the light, the chosen ones of the Living Father,[21] just as the people of Qumran described themselves as the sons of light. John exhorted a Christian community to 'walk in the light' (1 John 1.7).

The Qumran Rules reveal a community led by people who believed themselves to be the faithful guardians of the older ways, the heirs of the ancient high priests, a community separated from the 'men of injustice' and led by 'the sons of Zadok, the priests who keep the covenant'.[22] They believed that the God of Israel had created the spirits of light and darkness, and that they were the sons of light. The ruler of the darkness was Melchi-Resha', who looked like a dark snake and was in conflict with the ruler of light. We assume that the ruler of light was Melchi-Zedek, although the text is broken at this point.[23] Both these ruling angels had three names, but those names have not survived either. Melchi-Zedek, however, appears in another text which tells more about him: he was expected to appear at the start of the tenth jubilee, to rescue his own people from the power of Belial (which must have been one of the three names of the Angel of Darkness) and to make the great atonement.[24] The early Christians identified Jesus as Melchi-Zedek, as we shall see, which means that they also thought of him as the angel/messenger of light, in conflict with the ruler of darkness.

The ways of the two spirits are described in two early Christian texts: the *Didache* and the *Letter of Barnabas*.[25] *Barnabas*, for example, describes the two ways of teaching – one of light, the other of darkness – over which are set the light-bearing angels of God led by the LORD of all eternity, or the angels of Satan led by the ruler of this present evil age.[26] The two lifestyles are described, so that the Christian could recognize the presence of the spirits and and their effect. John used distinctive terms for the two spirits:

- The Counsellor, *paraklētos*, often translated 'the Advocate', 'the helper' (14.16, 26; 16.7), described also as the spirit of truth (14.17; 16.13) and as the holy spirit who would teach them all things (14.26). This spirit

---
[21] *Gospel of Thomas* 50.
[22] *Community Rule*, 1QS V.
[23] *Testament of Amram*, 4Q543–8.
[24] *Melchizedek*, 11QMelch.
[25] *Community Rule*, 1QS III–IV; *Didache* 1—6; *Letter of Barnabas* 18—20.
[26] *Barnabas* 18.

appears as the angel of Jesus (Rev. 1.1) who revealed the meaning of the visions to John, and as the spirit that Jesus handed on (translating literally) when he died (19.30).

- The devil, Satan, who entered the heart/mind of Judas (13.2, 27), described also as the ruler of this world who was cast out (12.31), and in Revelation he was 'that ancient serpent, who is called the Devil and Satan, the deceiver of the whole world' (Rev. 12.9). His role was to fight against the children of the Lady, who kept the commandments of God and bore witness to Jesus (Rev. 12.17).

John summarized the ways of the two spirits in his first letter: 'He who loves his brother abides in the light ... he who hates his brother is in the darkness' (1 John 2.10–11).

These two opposing angels appear in another early Christian text, the *Shepherd of Hermas*.

> There are two angels with man, one of righteousness and one of wickedness.
> The angel of righteousness is delicate and modest and meek and gentle ...
> he speaks to you of righteousness, of purity, of reverence, of self control, of every righteous deed and of all glorious virtue.
> [The angel of wickedness] is ill-tempered and bitter, and foolish, and his deeds are evil, casting down the servants of God.[27]

This is a Greek text, but the imagery is from the Hebrew-thinking first Christians, for whom '*the angel* of righteousness' and '*the angel* of wickedness' would have sounded very similar to 'the king of righteousness' and 'the king of evil'. The Hebrew for 'king of' is *melek*, and for 'angel of' is *mal'ākh*. This world of conflicting spirits seems far removed from the later attempts to formulate a tidy Trinity, and the *Paraklētos*, as we shall see, may not have been the Holy Spirit who spoke to Jesus at his baptism.

The old-style priests at Qumran with their knowledge of the *raz nihyeh*, and the people who wrote *Eugnostos* with their knowledge of the angel world, were all members of the same temple family. The strange life-forms that appear in later Gnostic texts are no more bizarre than the beings around the heavenly throne described by Ezekiel, a first-temple priest (e.g. Ezek. 1.4–25), and Dionysius the Areopagite reminded his readers that such creatures were not to be understood literally:

> We cannot, as mad people do, profanely visualise these heavenly and godlike intelligences as actually having numerous feet and faces ... The Word of

---

[27] *Shepherd of Hermas*, Mandate 6.2.

*Introduction*

God makes use of poetic imagery when discussing these formless intelligences ... as a concession to the nature of our own mind.[28]

Dionysius, whenever he was writing,[29] was deeply rooted in the traditions of the holy of holies which break the surface in some of the Qumran texts with their enigmatic references to the *raz nihyeh*, and in the hierarchies of the early Gnostic texts. He gives the fullest exposition of this heavenly world, and shows that it was the fundamental world-view of the Church. It is often assumed that his system was derived from Neo-Platonism, and this may have influenced some of his choice of language, but Platonism itself derived ultimately from the world view of the first temple[30] and so Dionysius' immediate source in no way excludes the possibility that his deepest roots lay in temple tradition.

There is a direct line from Ezekiel and the world of the first-temple priesthood to Dionysius, his understanding of the heavenly hierarchy and the Christian liturgy of which he wrote. The Qumran community with their *Community Rule* and their *Hymns* and *Blessings* lie close to this line, as does *Eugnostos*. So too do the gospels of Thomas and Philip, and, most significantly for our enquiry, the Gospel of John. It would, however, be difficult to place the synoptic Gospels on this line. The fact that these latter are taken as the norm, that is, as the basis from which to assess the authenticity of John's Jesus and the sources of John's Gospel, is the root of many self-made problems in understanding John's Gospel such as trying to work out where it originated and the identity of that elusive 'Johannine community' with its Gnostic tendencies.

Christianity was an heir to temple tradition, and the gospels of Thomas and Philip, which were never a part of the New Testament, are deposits of this very early Hebrew-Christian teaching, as is the Book of Hebrews. Thomas and Philip are prominent disciples in John's Gospel but not in the synoptic Gospels, and, even if the gospels attributed to them are pseudepigrapha, there must have been a reason for that style of teaching to be preserved under the names of Johannine disciples. Had there been a different set of Gospels in the New Testament, say Mark, John, Philip and Thomas, there would have been a very different basic picture of the teaching of Jesus, and scholars would have discussed 'the problem of

---

[28] Dionysius, *Celestial Hierarchy* 137AB.
[29] He was traditionally identified as Dionysius the Areopagite, whom Paul converted in Athens (Acts 17.34), but scholars now place him in fifth/sixth-century Syria.
[30] See my books *The Great High Priest. The Temple Roots of Christian Liturgy*, London: T&T Clark, 2003, pp. 262–93 and *The Mother of the Lord*, vol. 1, London: T&T Clark, 2012, pp. 270–305.

Mark' and wondered where a Marcan community, so deprived of Jesus' most profound teaching, could have existed. But we have Matthew, Mark, Luke and John, and as a result, there is a 'problem' with John; with the origin of Gnosticism; with how the Qumran community related both to Judaism and to Christianity; and, as we shall see, in identifying certain early hymns as Christian.

For centuries, there was a 'hidden tradition' within the Church, passed down orally from the original disciples and not committed to writing. There had been a hidden tradition in the temple, guarded by the high priests and described in the Old Testament as the exclusive right of the sons of Aaron to matters 'within the veil' (Num. 18.7). Presumably this hidden tradition was oral, because Enoch, who represents the older priesthood, blamed the invention of writing on the fallen angels,[31] and the fallen angels in the Enochic tradition were a thinly disguised reference to the new-style priests of the second temple. The puritanical writers of Deuteronomy discouraged interest in such secret matters, but did not deny that they existed:

> The secret things belong to the LORD our God: but the things that are revealed [that is, the law of Moses] belong to us and to our children for ever, that we may do all the words of this law. (Deut. 29.29)

The older priesthood in the period before Moses and the Aaronite priests was represented by such figures as Melchi-Zedek and Enoch, both of whom received heavenly knowledge. The broken *Melchizedek* text found at Qumran depicts him as the divine high priest who would bring the teachers/?teachings that had been kept hidden and secret;[32] a fragmented *Melchizedek* text found at Nag Hammadi deals with the role of the great high priest and keeping revealed knowledge secret: 'These revelations do not reveal to anyone in the flesh, since they are incorporeal'.[33] Jesus was proclaimed as the Melchi-Zedek priest (Heb. 7.1–28), and the writer of Hebrews was not able to write about the details of the holy of holies (Heb. 9.5). Presumably s/he knew about them. Enoch, who was another high-priestly figure, entered the holy of holies where he stood with the angels round the throne and was taught 'all the hidden things'.[34]

---

[31] *1 Enoch* 69.9–10.
[32] *Melchizedek*, 11QMelch. Translation in *Qumran Cave 11. Discoveries in the Judaean Desert* XXIII, ed. F. Garcia-Martinez, Oxford: Oxford University Press, 1998, p. 229.
[33] *Melchizedek*, CG IX.1.27.
[34] *1 Enoch* 40.2.

Origen knew about the unwritten traditions and told Celsus about them; he linked the oral tradition to Ezekiel the first-temple priest but also to John:

> Our prophets did know of greater things than any in the Scriptures, which they did not commit to writing. Ezekiel, for example, received a scroll written within and without ... but at the command of the Logos he swallowed the book in order that its contents might not be written and so made known to unworthy persons [Ezek. 2.9—3.3]. John is also recorded to have seen and done something similar [Rev. 10.9]. Paul even heard unspeakable things which it is not lawful for a man to utter [2 Cor. 12.4]. And it is related of Jesus, who was greater than all these, that he conversed with his disciples in private, and especially in their secret retreats concerning the gospel of God; but the words he uttered have not been preserved because it appeared to the evangelists that they could not be adequately conveyed to the multitude in writing or speech.[35]

Luke records that 'a great many of the priests' joined the Christian community in Jerusalem (Acts 6.7), and we can only assume that they brought their learning with them.

That the temple and the early Church each had a secret tradition does not necessarily mean that the content of both was identical. Temple imagery is, however, found in most references to the secret tradition in the Church, and so it is likely that the secret things not recorded in the Old Testament became the secret things not recorded in the New Testament. In early Christian texts, a characteristic of the 'secret tradition' was that Jesus taught it to his disciples after his resurrection. Eusebius, quoting a lost work of Clement of Alexandria, wrote: 'James the Righteous, John and Peter were entrusted by the Lord after his resurrection with the higher knowledge. They imparted it to the other apostles, and the other apostles to the seventy, one of whom was Barnabas.'[36] In temple tradition, as we shall see, resurrection was not a post-mortem experience but rather the moment of *theōsis*, when the human king, or rather, the priest-king, became the divine son and was shown the secret things of the holy of holies.[37] The teaching of Jesus, as set out by John, extended this temple privilege to his disciples: 'To all who received him, who believed in his name, he gave power to become children of God' (1.12); and thus resurrection for Christians

---
[35] Origen, *Against Celsus* 6.6.
[36] Eusebius, *History of the Church* 2.1.
[37] See below, pp. 75-6, 87.

was not a post-mortem event but rather the moment when they had been baptized into Christ (Gal. 3.27; Col. 3.1–3). Jesus was resurrected at his baptism,[38] and this was re-enacted at every baptism. The resurrected Christians were 'in Christ', so were collectively the high priest, and they had learned the secrets of the high priesthood. In the synoptic Gospels this is indicated by the saying that so often follows an enigmatic saying or a parable: 'He who has ears to hear, let him hear' (e.g. Matt. 11.15; 13.9, 43 and parallels). It is found also at the end of each of the seven letters from the risen (post-resurrection) LORD in Revelation: 'He who has an ear, let him hear what the Spirit says to the churches' (e.g. Rev. 2.7); and after the revelation about the beast: 'This calls for wisdom; let him who has understanding reckon the number of the beast ...' (Rev. 13.18).

Post-resurrection teaching was the private teaching given after Jesus' baptism. Eusebius again:

> Paul ... committed nothing to writing but his very short epistles; and yet he had countless unutterable things to say, for he had reached the visions of the third heaven, had been caught up to the divine paradise itself and had been privileged to hear there unspeakable words. Similar experiences were enjoyed by the rest of the Saviour's pupils ... the twelve apostles, the seventy disciples, and countless others besides.[39]

What has happened to all these experiences? 'Was Eusebius writing fiction at this point, or is there a major element of early Christianity missing from our present understanding of its origins? There is certainly a great difference between how the Christians in the middle of the fourth century described their origins and how those origins are commonly described today.'[40]

The imagery associated with Christian secret tradition was drawn from the temple: from the holy of holies and from the oil that transformed the Davidic kings into sons of God and opened their eyes to receive the hidden knowledge. This is apparent in the seven letters in Revelation, where all the teaching is given in temple symbolism: the lampstands, the tree of life, the two-edged sword, the seven spirits and the seven stars, the Name on a white stone, the white garments and the oil to open eyes. So too in the very early texts from Ignatius, bishop of Syrian Antioch at the beginning of the second century. When he wrote letters to several

---

[38] See below, p. 116.
[39] Eusebius, *History* 3.24.
[40] From my article 'The Secret Tradition', in my *The Great High Priest*, pp. 1–33, p. 22.

*Introduction*

churches on his way to a martyr's death under Trajan,[41] he used the language of the temple and clearly knew a fuller version of Christian teaching (the secret tradition?) than is apparent in the New Testament.

> Do not allow yourselves to be anointed with the foul-smelling chrism of the prince of this world's doctrines.[42]

> Even though I myself ... for all my ability to comprehend celestial secrets and angelic hierarchies and the dispositions of the heavenly powers, and much else both seen and unseen, am not yet on that account a real disciple.[43]

> The priests of old, I admit, were estimable men; but our own High Priest is greater, for he has been entrusted with the Holy of Holies, and to him are the secret things of God committed.[44]

Clement of Alexandria, writing a century or so after Ignatius, knew the secret teaching. He described authentic Christian teaching as 'gnosis', not to imitate a currently fashionable genre, but because authentic Christian teaching was 'gnosis' and it was being abused by heretical imitations. Cardinal Daniélou was correct when he observed: 'The later Gnostics who wanted their bizarre teachings to be accepted as genuine, presented them as the secret teachings of Jesus, showing that such a genre did exist.'[45] Clement wrote:

> [Christian teachers] preserving the tradition of the blessed doctrine derived directly from the holy apostles Peter, James and John, the son receiving it from the father (but few were like their fathers), came by God's will to us also to deposit those ancestral and apostolic seeds.
>
> [This knowledge] has descended by transmission to a few, having been imparted unwritten by the apostles ... Thus the Lord allowed us to communicate of the divine mysteries, and of that holy light, to those who were able to receive them. He certainly did not disclose to the many what did not belong to the many ... But the secret things are entrusted to speech, not to writing ...
>
> [Some people make] a perverse use of divine words ... neither themselves entering in to the kingdom of heaven, nor permitting those they have deluded to attain the truth. But not having the key to enter ... but only a

---

[41] He was emperor from 98 to 117 CE.
[42] Ignatius, *To the Ephesians* 17.
[43] Ignatius, *To the Trallians* 5.
[44] Ignatius, *To the Philadelphians* 9.
[45] J. Daniélou, 'Les traditions secrètes des Apôtres', *Eranos Jahrbuch* 31 (1962), pp. 119–207, p. 203.

false counterfeit key, by which they do not enter in as we enter in, through the tradition of the Lord, by drawing aside the curtain, but bursting through the side door and digging secretly through the wall of the Church, stepping over the truth, they set themselves up as guides to the mysteries ...[46]

Entering the holy of holies was entering the light of the divine presence. Receiving the knowledge of the holy of holies – 'the secrets of the kingdom' – was enlightenment, seeing the light. The people who had been walking in darkness saw a great light when the divine son was born as their king (Isa. 9.2, 6–7). Perhaps this vivid imagery was drawn from an actual temple ceremony, when the newly 'born' king emerged from the holy of holies and thus the light in the holy of holies that represented the presence of God shone into the relatively dark *hêkhāl* of the temple. So too, the suffering Servant saw the light after his trials. Jesus understood this as the servant entering his glory (Luke 24.26), and the knowledge he was given there enabled him to set others on the right path: 'After the suffering of his soul, he will see light and be satisfied, and through his knowledge shall his servant, the Righteous One, make many righteous ...' (Isa. 53.11).[47] The Servant/Lamb on the throne in heaven had 'seven horns and ... seven eyes, which are the seven spirits of God ...' (Rev. 5.6). This meant that the One on the throne had been given the sevenfold spirit (Isa. 11.2) and his 'horns' were in fact rays of light – it is the same word in Hebrew. This was the King who had received the sevenfold spirit and was shining with the sevenfold light of complete knowledge which he taught to his people. The unknown voice at Qumran could sing:

> Through me you have illumined the faces of many,
> And you have increased them beyond number.
> For you have given me knowledge of your wonderful mysteries,
> And in your wonderful council you have shown yourself strong to me.[48]

The early Christians described their baptism/resurrection as enlightenment, according to Justin who was writing towards the middle of the second century:

> As many as are persuaded that what we teach and say is true ... are brought by us where there is water, and are born again in the same way in which we

---

[46] Clement, *Miscellanies* 1.1; 6.7; 7.17.
[47] This is translated from the pre-Christian text in the great Isaiah scroll from Qumran, 1QIsa$^a$. The later text, from which our Old Testament is translated, is shorter, possibly changed or damaged.
[48] *Hymns*, 1QH XII.28–29, my translation.

ourselves were born again. For [in the name of the Trinity] they then receive washing with water ... This washing is called illumination, because they who learn these things are illuminated in their understandings.[49]

And what they learned, according to Dionysius, was the hidden tradition: 'This is the kind of divine enlightenment into which we have been initiated by the hidden tradition of our inspired teachers, a tradition at one with Scripture.'[50]

The Church preserved the world view of the temple, and two of the early leaders were described as high priests. James the brother of Jesus[51] used to enter the holy place wearing linen garments and pray for forgiveness of the people's sins, which is immediately recognizable as the role of the high priest on the Day of Atonement. James was also called 'the Righteous One', as was Jesus (Acts 3.14), and this had been a title of the ancient high priests. 'Zadok' meant 'the righteous one'. This information about James was recorded in the early fourth century by Eusebius in his *History of the Church*, but he was quoting from Hegesippus 'who belonged to the first generation after the apostles'.[52] Epiphanius, writing later in the fourth century, also used Hegesippus and said that James wore the *petalon*, the golden plate worn by a high priest on his forehead, inscribed with the Name.[53] John also had been a high priest, according to Polycrates, bishop of Ephesus at the end of the second century. When he wrote to Victor, bishop of Rome, he said that John was buried in Ephesus and he too had worn the *petalon*.[54] Thus Hegesippus and Polycrates, writing in the second century, were describing the great church leaders of the previous century as high priests. Their work survives only in quotations in other writers, one small indication of how much has been lost.

In early Christian writings there are several references to an unwritten tradition of teaching, something that could not be put into writing for just anybody to read. It concerned the meaning of the holy of holies, what Jesus described as the secrets of the kingdom which he did not teach openly, but only privately to his disciples (e.g. Mark 4.11). The early Christians knew the secret teachings about the holy of holies, but did not

---

[49] Justin, *Apology* 1.61.
[50] Dionysius, *On the Divine Names* 592B.
[51] Mentioned in Mark 6.3 and remembered as the son of Joseph, who was a widower when he married Mary.
[52] Eusebius, *History* 2.23.
[53] Epiphanius, *Panarion* 1.29.4.
[54] Eusebius, *History* 3.31.

## Introduction

reveal them, as can be seen from Hebrews 9.3–5. A writing attributed to Clement of Rome in the late first century records a saying of Jesus not found in the New Testament: 'Peter said: "We remember that our Lord and teacher, commanding us, said: 'Keep the mysteries for me and the sons of my house.'" Wherefore he also explained to his disciples privately the mysteries of the kingdom of heaven.'[55] This is a fuller version of '[Jesus] said to them [when they were alone], "To you has been given the secret of the kingdom of God, but for those outside, everything is in parables"' (Mark 4.11). Clement of Alexandria also knew the longer form of the saying in a gospel he did not name: 'It is for only a few to comprehend these things. It was not out of envy that the Lord said in one of the gospels: "My mystery is for me and the sons of my house".'[56]

The saying seems to be Jesus' version of Isaiah 24.16, which English versions translate: 'I pine away, I pine away' (RSV) or 'My leanness! My leanness!' (AV), which make no sense, but the Targum translated *rzy* as 'my mystery' and so read the original Hebrew as 'My mystery for me! My mystery for me!' The context is an apocalypse: Isaiah had described the collapse of all creation when people had broken the everlasting covenant. Then he described the judgement and the LORD being established (again) as King in Zion, manifesting his glory (Isa. 24.23). The 'mystery' line marks the transition to his description of the coming judgement:

> From the ends of the earth we hear songs of praise,
> Of glory to the Righteous One.
> But I say, 'My mystery is for me, My mystery is for me! ...' (Isa. 24.16)

The meaning of the original is probably lost beyond recovery, but the context is the coming of the Righteous One to bring judgement and to establish the kingdom again in Zion. Knowledge of the future must have been part of the mystery.

The Christians sang about the secret tradition in their hymns, but these were not recognized as Christian hymns until quite recently, largely due to their singing about the mystery and about God-given knowledge. The *Odes of Solomon*[57] were variously identified as Jewish and Gnostic, but Charlesworth declared in the Preface to his critical edition that they were the earliest Christian hymn book.[58] This is what the early Christians were

---

[55] *Clementine Homilies* 19.20.
[56] Clement, *Miscellanies* 5.10.
[57] A collection of 42 hymns, of which one survives in Coptic, one is missing, and the rest are known in Syriac.
[58] J. H. Charlesworth, *The Odes of Solomon*, Oxford: Oxford University Press, 1973, p. vii.

singing, the first and third of these extracts being words attributed to Christ:

> Keep my secret, ye who are kept by it: keep my faith, ye who are kept by it: and understand my knowledge, ye who know me in truth ...[59]

> He has caused his knowledge to abound in me ...[60]

> I imparted my knowledge without grudging ... and transformed them into myself.[61]

These hymns, which some have dated to the first century, but most to the second or third, lie close to that line between Ezekiel and *Eugnostos*, but scholars hesitated to accept them as Christian because the synoptic picture of Jesus was assumed to be the norm.

The 'sons of my house' who guarded the mystery were those who had received the LORD's full teaching, according to Origen. He explained that many customs and practices in Christian worship were not described in the Scriptures, but were part of the secret tradition:

> Bending the knee, facing east, the ritual of the Eucharist, the rites and ceremonies of baptism ... [are all done] according to the way in which they have been revealed and entrusted to us by the great high priest and his sons.[62]

Since Christians were the new royal priesthood, they were worthy to see the Word of God and the mysteries of Wisdom. The temple furnishings represented knowledge, and so were kept from general view, just as Aaron and his sons, said Origen, had to cover the furnishings of the tabernacle before the Levites carried them through the desert (Num. 4.1–5). 'If one is a priest to whom the sacred vessels, that is, the secrets of mysterious Wisdom, have been entrusted, he must keep them veiled and not produce them easily for the people.'[63] Now the items that were missing from the second temple and would be restored by the Messiah were all linked to the holy of holies, the place of the Lady, and Origen knew that the temple vessels represented the 'secrets of mysterious Wisdom'.

The elusive 'Johannine community' were the Hebrew disciples of Jesus who saw themselves as the true high priesthood restored, destined to stand in the holy of holies bearing the Name on their foreheads and

---
[59] *Odes of Solomon* 8.11–13, tr. J. H. Bernard, Cambridge: Cambridge University Press, 1912.
[60] *Odes* 12.3a.
[61] *Odes* 17.12a, 13b.
[62] Origen, *On Numbers*, Homily 5.
[63] Origen, *On Numbers*, Homily 4.

*Introduction*

worshipping the Lamb. They were the spiritual – and perhaps the literal – heirs of those for whom the Third-Isaiah spoke centuries earlier, when he promised an unknown group that they would (again?) be called the priests of the LORD, and inherit their land.

> For I the LORD love justice,
> I hate robbery and wrong;
> I will faithfully give them their recompense,
> And I will make an everlasting covenant with them.
> (Isa. 61.8)

This was part of the the passage that Jesus read in the synagogue at Nazareth, and announced that he was its fulfilment (Luke 4.21). This was the Johannine community, a priestly group, who had received the heavenly knowledge when they were baptized/resurrected, as John reminded the recipients of his first letter: 'You have been anointed by the Holy One and you know all things [or 'all know'] … the anointing which you have received from him abides in you, and you have no need that anyone should teach you …' (1 John 2.20, 27, my translation).

*****

In this book I shall first address the question of names: who were the Jews and who were the Hebrews; then I shall show how the older ways of the royal high priests, the Melchi-Zedek priests, were almost lost when the Moses traditions came to dominate during the second-temple period; and finally I shall show how the original temple teachings were restored by Jesus, who was proclaimed as 'a great high priest' (Heb. 4.14), as 'another priest raised up in the likeness of Melchi-Zedek' (Heb. 7.15, my translation), and also as 'the King of the Jews' (John 19.19).

# Part 1
# THE BACKGROUND TO JOHN'S GOSPEL

# 1

# The Jews in John's Gospel

The identity of 'the Jews' is the perennial problem in studying John's Gospel. The book is most Jewish when it is anti-Jewish, and John's use of the Hebrew Scriptures is very different from that in the synoptic Gospels. The Gospel is steeped in Old Testament imagery, and it used to be said that John had 'caught the sense of the Old Testament and then worked it up into a new and original Christian form'.[1] We should not use those words today, although Barrett's conclusion suggested that he had glimpsed something of the real origin of John, despite the fashionable assumptions of scholarship with which he was hindered.

> For [John] the OT was itself a comprehensive unity ... It was not (in general) his method to bolster up several items of Christian doctrine and history with supports drawn from this or that part of the OT; instead, the whole body of the OT formed a background, or framework, upon which the new revelation was rested.[2]

We now know that the whole body of the Old Testament is in no way a unity, and the theme of my book is that, far from being a new revelation, John presented Jesus as the original revelation restored. The immediate background to John's Gospel is the turmoil and hopes in Palestine at the end of the second-temple period, but the deep background is the entire second-temple period, the violent events that preceded the destruction of the first temple in 597 and 586 BCE, and the divided society that emerged after some of the exiles had returned from Babylon to build the second temple. In the writings of the Third-Isaiah we glimpse the beginning of the troubles: the servants of the LORD (Who were they? The priests whom Jesus restored?) found themselves rejected from the new temple, and the prophet condemned their persecutors: 'You shall leave your name to my chosen for a curse, and the Lord GOD [Yahweh] will slay you, but his servants he will call by a different name [What name?]' (Isa. 65.15).

---

[1] Thus C. K. Barrett, 'The Old Testament in the Fourth Gospel', *Journal of Theological Studies* 47 (1947), pp. 155–69, p. 164.
[2] Barrett, 'The Old Testament in the Fourth Gospel', p. 168.

We also glimpse their hopes: for the light and the glory of the LORD to dawn upon them and for their sons and daughters to return home. A Messiah would bring the Jubilee, they would be recognized again as priests with a double portion in their land, and the city and the Lady it represented would no longer be abandoned and desolate.

> Say to the daughter of Zion,
> 'Behold your salvation comes;
> Behold his reward is with him,
> And his recompense before him.'
> And they shall be called The holy people,
> The redeemed of the LORD;
> And you shall be called Sought out,
> A city not forsaken.     (Isa. 62.11b–12)

The persecutors were those now known as 'the Jews', but the new name for the chosen ones is not known. This division within the heirs to the temple is the deep root of the division apparent in John's Gospel and explains the fragment in the *Gospel of Philip*: 'No Jew [was ever born] to Greek parents, and Christians [were not born] from the Jews ... but another ... named the chosen people.'[3] Philip is an important figure in John's Gospel, and some of the enigmatic sayings included in 'his' gospel are best understood in the light of John.

So, we ask, who were the Jews in the time of Jesus? John used the name 68 times, whereas Mark used it 6 times, and Matthew and Luke each 5 times. The 'Jews' must have been a major theme of John's Gospel, even though all the Gospels agree that the title on the cross read 'The King of the Jews'. Why?

It is all too easy to assume that in the time of Jesus everyone in Palestine who was not a Samaritan or a Gentile was a Jew, but this may not be a valid assumption. There were many groups and sects in Palestine at that time who claimed roots in the Hebrew tradition, but there is no certain definition of Hebrew tradition either. Nor will accepting and using the Hebrew Scriptures serve as a definition, since these were not defined until after the destruction of the Jerusalem temple in 70 CE. There was no fixed canon of Hebrew Scriptures when the New Testament was written: the Jews in Alexandria were using texts that never became part of the Hebrew canon but were included in the Septuagint translation of the Scriptures, the largely pre-Christian Greek; and the first Christians quoted as Scripture texts such as *1 Enoch* that are in neither the Hebrew nor the

---

[3] *Gospel of Philip*, CG II.3.75.

Greek canon. How the various texts were read and understood is not certain either: the Hebrew texts evolved into several distinct forms, and the meaning of the official Jewish form was not fixed until later, when the vowels were added to the consonantal texts. It is therefore simplistic to think that there was an 'Old Testament' or a 'Hebrew Bible' in the time of Christian origins, and that it had a true meaning from which all other interpretations were sectarian deviations.

The Samaritans, for example, accepted as Scripture only the Books of Moses (Genesis, Exodus, Leviticus, Numbers and Deuteronomy), in a form slightly different from the present form of the Hebrew Scriptures, but they had other holy books whose date and origin is not known. People who assume that 'the Jews' were the norm speak of the separation of Jews and Samaritans as 'the Samaritan schism' – although nobody can say exactly when this happened or why. Scholars have been wary for a long time of assuming any norm, but this has survived in popular understanding of the Bible.

> It may indeed be the case that the regular use of [the word 'schism'] in describing Samaritan origins is itself an example of the remarkable success of anti-Samaritan polemic and the way in which it has affected the interpretation of Old Testament material. For the whole idea of a schism ... requires an orthodox norm, and such a norm was not established in Judaism until the Christian era. In these circumstances, no one group within the rich complex of Judaism should be regarded as schismatic.[4]

What group, then, called themselves Jews? Josephus, himself a Jew and writing at about the same time as John the Evangelist, said this: '[Jews] is the name they are called by from the day that they came up from Babylon, which is taken from the tribe of Judah ...'[5] In the early part of his *Antiquities*, where he dealt with the ancient genealogies, he explained that those called Jews were originally called Hebrews,[6] and his own use of the two names confirms this. In *Antiquities* 11—20, which deal with the period after the return from Babylon, he used 'Jew' many times, whereas in the pre-exilic section he used the word only 28 times. In Book 11, for example, which covers the period from Cyrus to Alexander the Great, he mentioned 'the Jews' 91 times.

---

[4] R. J. Coggins, *Samaritans and Jews. The Origins of Samaritanism Reconsidered*, Oxford: Basil Blackwell, 1975, p. 163; quoting P. R. Ackroyd, *Israel under Babylon and Persia*, Oxford: Oxford University Press, 1970, p. 185.
[5] Josephus, *Antiquities* 11.173.
[6] Josephus, *Antiquities* 1.146.

## The background to John's Gospel

It is not easy to know when the name *Ioudaios* = Jew became current in Greek. The original Hebrew is literally 'a man of Judah', but the literal meaning of a word is not so important for our quest as how it was actually being used when John wrote his Gospel.[7] The Hebrew 'man of Judah' was sometimes translated literally into Greek in the Septuagint (LXX) (e.g. Zech. 8.23), and at other times as *Ioudaios*, 'Jew' (e.g. Jer. 52.28, 30), but this passage is missing from several texts of the LXX and may be a later insertion. It cannot be used to show when the name *Ioudaios* began to be used. It is found in Esther (e.g. Esth. 2.5), and throughout John's Gospel. The problem is, as Meeks observed, that 'the Fourth Gospel is most anti-Jewish just at the points where it is most Jewish', and John used 'Jew' to distance himself from them.[8]

The Qumran texts suggest that the community who wrote the *Damascus Document* and the *War Scroll* regarded themselves as exiles, a priestly group who had withdrawn from Judah and so, presumably, from the people of Judah, the Jews. They saw themselves as the faithful priests described by Ezekiel, the sons of Zadok who kept guard over/preserved the LORD's sanctuary when the people of Israel went astray (Ezek. 44.15, my translation). They had departed from the land of Judah.[9] The *Damascus Document* has an enigmatic outline of the history of this community: the founders were a remnant who had survived in the age of wrath, when others had forsaken the LORD, and he had handed them over to enemies.[10] The conquest by Nebuchadnezzar occurred during the age of wrath, but not necessarily at the beginning. The enemies of the community were identified as 'the princes of Judah', and they fulfilled the prophecy of Hosea 5.10: 'the princes of Judah have become like those who remove the landmark; upon them I will pour out my wrath like water'.[11] The focus of this group, who had withdrawn from what Judah had become, was the original temple.

Others in the region identified themselves to foreigners as Hebrews but not Jews, and it may be that the Qumran community thought of themselves in the same way – not a part of the new-style religious community that had been established in Jersualem in the fifth century

---

[7] The word 'British' in contemporary English as spoken in England means something very different now from what it meant 100 or even 50 years ago.
[8] W. A. Meeks, '"Am I a Jew" – Johannine Christianity and Judaism', in *Christianity, Judaism and Other Greco-Roman Cults*, ed. J. Neusner, Leiden: Brill, 1975, pp. 163–86, pp. 172, 181.
[9] *Damascus Document*, CD IV; and VI is similar, as is the *War Scroll*, 1QM I.
[10] *Damascus Document*, CD I.
[11] *Damascus Document*, CD VIII.

BCE, and certainly not as 'sectarian Jews', which is how the Qumran community is sometimes described. In the fourth century BCE, said Josephus, the Samaritans explained to Alexander the Great that they were Hebrews but not Jews.[12] In the New Testament, Hebrews were distinguished from Hellenists among the Jerusalem Christians (Acts 6.1), and it is usually assumed that this meant converts who spoke Hebrew and those who spoke Greek. But there may have been more to the distinction than just language. Nobody knows how the book came to have its title, but 'To the Hebrews' was known to Clement, who was bishop of Rome in the 90s CE, so it represents the situation in the earliest years of the Church.[13] Now 'To the Hebrews' is written in *Greek*, and scholars recognize that it does not read like a translation. If there were Greek-speaking 'Hebrews', as this text implies, the definition of 'a Hebrew' cannot have been the language s/he normally spoke. 'To the Hebrews', therefore, raises an important question: why this title, and not 'To the [Greek-speaking] Jews'? And why does this text use imagery from the first temple, such as the ark and the cherubim (Heb. 9.4), and emphasize the priesthood of Melchi-Zedek (Heb. 7.1–25), when none of these was in the second temple? The focus of the Hebrews was the original temple.

Paul claimed that he had been a zealous Jew (Gal. 1.13), but also that he was by birth a Hebrew of the Hebrews and a Pharisee (Phil. 3.5). Elsewhere, when confronting a dispute within the Christian community, after some people had been preaching 'another Jesus', he demanded: 'Are they Hebrews? So am I. Are they Israelites? So am I. Are they descendants of Abraham? So am I.' As further evidence of his good standing, he recalled what he had suffered for his new faith: 'Five times I have received *at the hands of the Jews* the forty lashes less one' (2 Cor. 11.22, 24). Paul, identifying himself as a Hebrew, was whipped by people he identified as Jews. One hypothesis compatible with this evidence is that Jews, when they became Christians, identified themselves as Hebrews, and this implies there was something implicit in the contemporary definition of a Jew that was incompatible with Christianity. On the other hand, Paul, in a moment of anger, described Peter as a 'Jew' (Gal. 2.14).

It used to be the custom to call people of Hebrew ancestry who became Christians 'Jewish-Christians', but the problem of identities within the heirs of ancient Israel is now recognized as complex, and not helped by referring to 'varieties of *Judaism*' or 'many *Judaisms*' as though the 'Jews'

---
[12] Josephus, *Antiquities* 11.344.
[13] *1 Clement* 36 quotes Heb. 1.4.

were the majority, the norm, or at any rate a privileged group. Robert Murray observed long ago:

> In the period under discussion [the period of Christian origins], it is misleading to use 'Jewish' and 'Judaism' for all the heirs of ancient Israel; these terms are really appropriate for those who looked to Jerusalem as their focus of identity, while a distinct term is needed for those who were hostile to the Jerusalem of the Second Temple.[14]

Those who came from Babylon and built the second temple were the ones Josephus identified as 'the Jews', and the biblical texts from this period show that new names were being given. The Third-Isaiah, condemning the attitudes adopted by the people who built the second temple and established its cult, declared: 'You shall leave your name to my chosen for a curse, and the LORD God will slay you; but his servants he will call by a different name' (Isa. 65.15). We do not know that name.

After his conversion Paul went to Arabia (Gal. 1.17), and when he returned he went to Syria and Cilicia. This would have included the time in Syrian Antioch (Acts 13.1–3), whence he was sent on his first missionary journey with Barnabas. Shortly after this, he wrote the letter to the Galatians, and outlined the position he would later develop fully in Romans: that the roots of Christianity lay in the faith of Abraham, 430 years before the law of Moses was given (Gal. 3.16–18). It is possible that this is what he had learned in 'Arabia', which Jews still remembered as the place where the young priests of the first temple had settled after the destruction of the Jerusalem temple in 586 BCE. The Jerusalem Talmud, where this is mentioned,[15] was written as late as the fourth century CE, but incorporated older material. Had Paul been in contact with the descendants of those priestly exiles who retained the ways of the first temple? It is possible.

The non-biblical accounts of the history of Jerusalem found in *1 Enoch*, which was quoted as prophecy by Jude (Jude 14) and treated as Scripture by a first-generation Christian writer,[16] describe those who returned from Babylon as 'an apostate generation'.[17] These are the people Josephus called 'the Jews'. The *Apocalypse of Weeks* in *1 Enoch* is a stylized history with each period described as a week. In the first week, a key event was

---

[14] R. Murray, 'Jews, Hebrews and Christians. Some Needed Distinctions', *Novum Testamentum* 24.3 (1982), pp. 194–208, p. 195.
[15] Jerusalem Talmud *Ta'anit* 4.5.
[16] The *Letter of Barnabas* 16 paraphrases *1 Enoch* 89.56 as Scripture.
[17] *1 Enoch* 93.9.

the birth of Enoch, in the second the story of Noah, in the third the choosing of Abraham. In the fifth week, the temple was built. So much is clear; but in the fourth week, between Abraham and the building of the temple, where we should expect to find Moses, the exodus and Sinai, there is no mention of them, but only of visions of holy and righteous ones and, apparently, the law being given.[18] *This Enoch text tells the history of 'Israel' without mentioning Moses, but emphasizes the figures of Enoch, Noah and Abraham.*

There is something similar in *Jubilees*, a longer and different account of the stories in Genesis and Exodus as far as Sinai. *Jubilees* answers the question: how could Moses have known all the earlier history of his people, as recorded in the first book of Moses (Genesis), and the answer is: he saw it all in his vision on Sinai. What he saw, however, does not correspond exactly to what is implicit in Genesis and Exodus. Several laws that the biblical account attributes to Moses, for example those for firstfruits and the Sabbath year, were apparently observed by Noah long before they had been revealed to Moses. According to *Jubilees*, they had been given to Enoch and passed on by Methuselah and Lamech.[19] Abraham in turn passed on to Isaac the laws he had received from Enoch and Noah, laws about idolatry, pollution and consuming blood, and about offering sacrifices in the correct way and with the prescribed words.[20] Isaac passed the laws on to his grandson Levi.[21] *According to this line of tradition, the Levitical priesthood received their laws from Enoch, not from Moses.*

Fragments of the original Hebrew of *Jubilees* have been found at Qumran, showing that the community who distanced themselves from second-temple Jerusalem knew and preserved an alternative history that attributed important laws and customs to the same ancient figures as appear in the *Apocalypse of Weeks*: Enoch, Noah and Abraham. The account in *Jubilees* may be a fiction, but anyone attributing ancient customs to the patriarchs before the time of Moses was saying that Moses was a latecomer to the laws and customs of his people. The Jews in John's Gospel are identified as disciples of Moses, and 'Jews' may imply more than just 'people of Judea'. It may indicate the newcomers who followed Moses.

---

[18] *1 Enoch* 93.3–7.
[19] *Jubilees* 7.34–39.
[20] *Jubilees* 21.1–26.
[21] *Testament of Levi* 9.1–14.

The line of patriarchs – Enoch, Noah, Abraham – represented the priesthood of the first temple, and this also included Melchi-Zedek. There are two versions of his story: he was Noah's son Shem;[22] or he was Noah's nephew, the son of his brother Nir who is not mentioned in the biblical story.[23] Add to this the fact that Moses is not mentioned at all in the earliest Hebrew Scriptures. In the early canonical prophets there is one passing reference in Micah (Mic. 6.4); nothing in Isaiah until the latest post-exilic material (Isa. 63.11–12); one passing reference in Jeremiah (Jer. 15.1); and nothing in Ezekiel or the other pre-exilic prophets. Moses is not mentioned in the earlier psalms, the first reference being in Book III of the Psalter which is thought to be the psalms used after the destruction of the first temple. Moses appears in Psalm 77.20 and in a few later psalms (in the title of Ps. 90 and in Pss. 99.6; 103.7; 105.26; 106.16, 23, 32). In contrast, he is mentioned 647 times in Exodus–Deuteronomy.[24] Absence of evidence is not evidence of absence, but the non-appearance of Moses in the earlier writings does raise questions as to his importance at that time. One possible construction upon this evidence is that Moses grew in importance during the second-temple period. After the demise of the monarchy, he took over the roles of the ancient Davidic kings, and aspects of the first-temple cult that had originally been the role of the king were absorbed into the Moses saga.

Take Sinai, for example. The *Apocalypse of Weeks*, which has neither Moses nor the exodus, does include an event in the fourth week that seems to be a lawgiving with angels present. Now there is an ancient poem that describes how heavenly instruction was given when the LORD appeared with a host of angels. It is now called the *Blessing of Moses* and included at the end of Deuteronomy (Deut. 33.2–29), but it looks as though something has been changed in this poem, since Moses does not fit easily here. One possibility is that a single line – 'when Moses commanded us a law' (v. 4a) – has been inserted between two existing lines of text in order to relocate it in the familiar Moses-on-Sinai story; or it could be that the person named Moses had formerly been someone else.[25] There are problems with almost every Hebrew word in the opening verses of this poem; for example, none of the 11 Hebrew words in verse 3

---

[22] Targums *Pseudo-Jonathan* and *Neofiti* to Gen. 14.8 and *Leviticus Rabbah* XXV.6.
[23] *2 Enoch* 70—73.
[24] Figures from F. Brown, S. R. Driver and C. A. Briggs, *A Hebrew and English Lexicon of the Old Testament*, Oxford: Clarendon Press, (1907) 1962, p. 602.
[25] See below, p. 133.

is clear. It may once have described the LORD coming in judgement from Sinai to give his law:

> His anger smote the people,
> All his holy ones were with him,
> And they humbled themselves and received his words.
> (Deut. 33.3, my reconstruction and translation)

The line about Moses follows. This poem, without the Moses line, fits well into the fourth week of the *Apocalypse of Weeks*: the LORD giving the law in the presence of the angels, but not in the context of the exodus.

Then there was an Ezekiel (not the prophet) who lived in Egypt in the early part of the second century BCE and wrote a Greek-style play about the exodus. He knew that when Moses went up Sinai, he not only saw the heavenly throne, as described in Exodus 24.9–10; he was also invited to sit on it, just as Psalm 110 says of the Davidic prince:

> The LORD says to my lord:
> 'Sit at my right hand,
> Till I make your enemies
> Your footstool.'
> The LORD sends forth from Zion
> Your mighty sceptre. (Ps. 110.1–2)

In this play, Moses on Sinai has taken over the role of the king in the holy of holies, where there was the cherub throne of the LORD.

> Methought upon Mount Sinai's brow I saw
> A mighty throne that reached to heaven's high vault,
> Whereon there sat a man of noblest mien
> Wearing a royal crown, whose left hand held
> A mighty sceptre; and his right to me
> Made sign, and I stood forth before the throne.
> He gave me then the sceptre and the crown,
> And bade me sit upon the royal throne
> From which himself removed.[26]

Two centuries later, Philo described Moses in the same way: '[Moses] was named god and king of the whole people and entered, it is said, into the darkness where God was.'[27] Thus, in the time of Jesus, some learned people such as Philo – and maybe others, who can know? – considered

---

[26] Extant in Eusebius, *Preparation of the Gospel* 9.29, tr. E. H. Gifford, Oxford: Oxford University Press, 1903.
[27] Philo, *Life of Moses* I.158.

Moses to be the king of the Jews, and further, that the king of the Jews was also divine.

The Moses saga complements the *Apocalypse of Weeks*, which does not mention Moses but does have a lawgiving, whereas the earliest versions of the exodus story do not mention the lawgiving on Sinai. The two halves of the familiar story had separate origins. The old poem in Exodus 15, for example, describes the dramatic parting of the waters and the destruction of Pharaoh's chariots, but the people are led straight from Egypt to the holy mountain and established there. No Sinai. The same is true of all the exilic accounts (e.g. Deut. 6.20–24, 26.5–9; Josh. 24.2–13; Ps. 136) and it was not until the post-exilic Nehemiah that the two stories were fused (Neh. 9.9–15). The Sinai story was also inserted into the story of Moses in Exodus–Leviticus–Numbers when the present Pentateuch was compiled. The Israelites moved to Kadesh after crossing the sea, made a long detour to Sinai, and then returned to Kadesh where the journey resumed. There are Kadesh narratives (Exod. 17—18 and Num. 10—14) enclosing Sinai material (Exod. 19—24 and 32—34). These observations were published by Julius Wellhausen in 1883, and further explored by Gerhard von Rad in 1938.[28] The date when the Moses of the exodus first went to Sinai has been a puzzle for a long time.

Even so brief a sketch as this shows that, far from being a unity, there are two streams in the Old Testament. One is the Moses and exodus stream which became the story of the people in the promised land under kings who were mostly failures. The other is the story of the temple and its priest-kings who entered heaven, but who ceased to function when their temple cult was destroyed. 'The Jews' were the disciples of Moses who built the second temple. They were very influential in creating the present form of the Hebrew Scriptures, and their work has long dominated the way the Hebrew Scriptures have been read. The 'others' were those who remembered the temple and the anointed priest-kings, the people the Third-Isaiah called the rejected servants of the LORD, his chosen ones who would be called by a new name (Isa. 65.15). He spoke of one anointed by the Spirit of the LORD who would restore what they had lost and rebuild the temple ruins (Isa. 61.1–4). They would once again be recognized as priests of the LORD, with the everlasting covenant restored (Isa. 61.6). It was these rejected people who called the Jews 'the apostate

---

[28] The English translation of G. von Rad's 'The Form-Critical Problem of the Hexateuch' is in *The Problem of the Hexateuch and Other Essays*, tr. E. W. Trueman Dicken, London: Oliver and Boyd, 1966, pp. 1–78, citing Wellhausen on p. 14.

generation', and in the time of Jesus, it seems that the rejected people were known as the Hebrews.

The Gospel of John shows the turbulence when these two streams came together. Those the Evangelist described as Jews no longer understood the ways of the original temple, and John used irony to emphasize just how much had been lost. On the other hand, John provided the *Hebrew* place names for his readers, who clearly distanced themselves from 'Jews': Bethesda (5.2); Gabbatha (19.13); Golgotha (19.17). The synoptic Gospels only give Golgotha.

Before looking at the Gospel of John, we must first look briefly at the way the exodus and Moses group told their story, then at what can still be recovered of the temple world of the ancient Davidic kings, and last at the emphasis on kingship in the rest of the New Testament.

# 2

# Who was Moses?

The search for Moses does not begin in Exodus on the banks of the Nile. It begins in Jerusalem in the reign of King Josiah, about 623 BCE. The Hebrew Scriptures as we know them did not exist, but someone was preserving the records of the kings of Jerusalem: for Solomon there had been 'the book of the acts of Solomon' (1 Kings 11.41); 'the history of Nathan the prophet', 'the prophecy of Ahijah the Shilonite' and 'the visions of Iddo the seer' (2 Chron. 9.29). There were collections of ancient poems and sagas, such as the 'Book of Jashar' (2 Sam. 1.18). None of these books has survived, or at any rate not under any of those titles. Someone was also preserving the sayings of the prophets, and some of these have survived although we can never know what has been lost. Isaiah, almost a century before the time of Josiah, had told his disciples to bind up the testimony and seal the teaching (Isa. 8.16); and presumably the priests had deposits of temple teaching, sacred law and genealogies.

In the time of King Josiah a lawbook was discovered in the temple, and this prompted him to purge both the temple and the land. The account of the purges in 2 Kings 23 wants the reader to conclude that the lawbook was Deuteronomy, or at any rate, an early form of it. Josiah did what Deuteronomy prescribed. A comparison of Deuteronomy 12.1–14 and 2 Kings 23.8–20 shows how closely his actions implemented the commands of Deuteronomy. Since Deuteronomy was set in the time of Moses, before the temple was built, there is nothing in Deuteronomy about the purge of the temple which is described in 2 Kings 23.4–7, but the pattern is the same. There was to be only one centre of worship; Jerusalem was not named, but described as the place where the LORD would make his name dwell (Deut. 12.5; 2 Kings 23.11). There was to be no God but the LORD, no image of any sort and no altars, no sacred pillars or holy trees (Asherahs) (Deut. 12.2–3). Josiah had an Asherah removed from the temple (2 Kings 23.6) and he destroyed it with great fury: he burned it, beat it to ashes and then scattered the ashes on common graves. He also removed from the temple the 'things' made for Baal, for Asherah and for the host of heaven, and burned them too (2 Kings 23.4). English translations say he removed the 'vessels', but the Hebrew word means any sort of equipment, not just bowls and flagons.

He removed from the temple any furnishings that were part of the older cult – and here we see the writer's agenda. By mentioning Baal – 'the vessels made for Baal, for Asherah, and for all the host of heaven' – he wants the reader to understand that everything removed from the temple was an import from the forbidden religions of 'the nations whom you shall dispossess' (Deut. 12.2). This is how the text was read until the ancient city of Ugarit was rediscovered in 1929,[1] and with it, a mass of tablets that told the myths of a neighbouring culture destroyed about 1200 BCE. These people had worshipped Baal, but their equivalent of Asherah, who was the great sun deity and mother of the gods, was not associated with him. In other words, it seems very likely that 'Baal' was inserted into the account of Josiah's temple purges in order to discredit by association Asherah and the (her?) host of heaven.

The 'host of heaven' had been part of the original temple and its worship. Isaiah, for example, had seen a vision of 'the King, the LORD of Hosts' (Isa. 6.5), and yet Josiah removed all trace of the hosts from the temple, and Deuteronomy forbad worshipping them: 'And beware lest you lift up your eyes to heaven, and when you see the sun and the moon and the stars, all the host of heaven, you be drawn away and worship them and serve them ...' (Deut. 4.19). Writers influenced by the ideals of Deuteronomy (the 'Deuteronomists', hereafter D) removed this title if they found it in earlier source material when they were compiling the history of their people. For example, the disciples of Isaiah composed a linking passage between two collections of oracles (Isa. 36—39), in which they had King Hezekiah pray to the 'LORD of Hosts, God of Israel ... enthroned above the cherubim' (Isa. 37.16), exactly as Isaiah had seen in his vision. The writer influenced by Deuteronomy incorporated this passage into his history as 'O LORD the God of Israel, who art enthroned above the cherubim ...' (2 Kings 19.15). The hosts were removed.

Something similar happened to 'Asherah', or rather, to her symbols that were removed from the temple in the purge. She had been the Lady of Jerusalem in the temple, but her name was either changed within the text or edited out of it, and the process of recovering her is complex. Suffice it to say that where the name is found in ancient graffiti (that is, in writing that has not been edited), it has the form Ashratah, and she is associated with the LORD. Most scholars have declared that she was the

---

[1] On the Mediterranean coast, opposite Cyprus.

consort of the LORD, but the evidence makes it more likely that she was his mother. We shall return to this in the next section.

One of her symbols was a great tree. In the myth and poetry of the Hebrew Scriptures it appears as the tree of life, and in the sagas and histories it is the various great trees that were in the oldest places of worship: the LORD appeared to Abram at the oak of Moreh (Gen. 12.6–7), and there was an oak tree in the sanctuary of the LORD at Shechem (Josh. 24.26). In the temple it was represented by the fiery tree, the menorah, but this also represented the host of heaven – sun, moon and the five known planets – who were the Lady's children. In the Gnostic text the *Wisdom of Jesus Christ*, Jesus taught his disciples 'the whole will of the mother of the holy angels',[2] and, since one of her names was Wisdom, this was a reference to Wisdom's teachings. In the first temple, though, the Lady had been Ashratah, the 'Asherah' that was removed from the temple by her enemies and burned. The Deuteronomist writer, when he described Solomon's temple in detail, did not mention any menorah, but Zechariah, a prophet when the people came from Babylon to build the second temple, saw a menorah in one of his visions (Zech. 4.1–3, 10–14; the text seems to be disordered at this point). He must have remembered a menorah in the original temple since the second temple was not yet built.

Another of Ashratah's symbols was the sun, just as the great lady of Ugarit had been represented by the sun. Josiah removed from the temple precincts the horses that had been dedicated to the sun, and the chariots of the sun (2 Kings 23.11), presumably the chariot throne and the four horses that Zechariah saw in his temple vision riding out onto the earth (Zech. 1.7–11; also 6.1–8 where they appear with chariots), and the four horses that John saw riding out onto the earth (Rev. 6.1–7). Their role in the temple is not known, but Josiah removed them.

The furnishings Josiah removed were remembered for centuries. There is a clue in the Hebrew text of Haggai, Zechariah's contemporary, who was exhorting the people from Babylon to build the temple: 'Thus says the LORD of Hosts: "... build the house that I may take pleasure in it and that I may *appear in my glory*, says the LORD"' (Hag. 1.7–8, c.f. John 17.19). The words in italics are literally 'be glorified', but there is one letter missing compared with the regular form of the word as found in e.g. 2 Samuel 6.22, where David says '... I shall be held in honour' – the same word but with a final letter *h*. Now the Hebrew letter *h* was also the number 5, and so the short form of 'glory' in Haggai was said to remind

---

[2] See below, p. 549.

the reader that the LORD's glory was diminished in the second temple by five items.³ Later texts gave lists of those five missing items. One is found in the *Numbers Rabbah*:⁴

> When the Temple was destroyed, the candlestick was stored away. It was one of the following five things that were so stored away: the ark, the candlestick, the fire, the Holy Spirit and the cherubim. When the Holy One, blessed be He, in His mercy will again build His Temple and His Holy Place, he will restore them to their position in order to gladden Jerusalem ...⁵

Another list says that the missing items included the anointing oil, the manna and Aaron's rod that blossomed,⁶ and Hebrews mentions these items in the temple, along with the ark that housed them (Heb. 9.4).

There is, however, a problem with the menorah. The arch of Titus in Rome, which shows the loot that was taken when the Romans destroyed the temple in 70 CE, depicts a huge seven-branched lampstand. There must have been a menorah in the later temple, but there was something about this object that was not acceptable to the people who remembered the original temple and longed for its restoration. It may be that the menorah in the original temple had had a different form and a different meaning, and it may even have been set in a different place. The original had probably been in the holy of holies, whereas the tabernacle associated with the Moses tradition set the lamp in the outer part of the tabernacle, outside the veil (Exod. 40.24–25). In the Deuteronomist's account of Solomon's temple the single menorah is not mentioned; there are instead ten golden lampstands in the *hêkhāl*, outside the holy of holies, presumably to give light (1 Kings 7.49). Whatever the detail, the menorah was a golden almond-like tree bearing seven lamps (Exod. 25.31–39). In other words, it was a fiery tree, which is how later writings describe the tree of life.

When Enoch visited paradise in one of his visions, he saw this tree of life in the midst of the garden: beautiful and fragrant, with wide-spreading branches and looking like gold and crimson fire. Enoch said it was a tree that looked like no known tree, but had 'something of every tree and every fruit'.⁷ The date and origin of this particular Enoch text is not known for certain, but another, known from Qumran,⁸ describes a fragrant tree

---

³ Babylonian Talmud *Yoma* 21b.
⁴ Compiled in the thirteenth century CE from earlier material.
⁵ *Numbers Rabbah* XV.10, tr. J. J. Slotki, London, 1939.
⁶ Babylonian Talmud *Horayoth* 12a.
⁷ *2 Enoch* 8.4.
⁸ The fragrant tree is described in *1 Enoch* 25; fragments of an Aramaic version of chapter 27 have been found: 4QEnᶜ, 4QEnᵉ.

which Enoch saw on his heavenly journey to the south. The archangel Michael, who was travelling with him, said that after the day of judgement, the tree would be transplanted northwards to a holy place in the house of the LORD, where its fruit would give life to the chosen ones.[9] In the Book of Revelation, the tree was restored to the temple, and the LORD promised his faithful followers access to the fruit (Rev. 2.7; 22.14). The restored tree was not in the outer part of the temple, as prescribed for the tabernacle, but in the holy of holies, 'the tree of life with its twelve kinds of fruit' (Rev. 22.2). Since the tree did not replicate any one type of tree, tracing references is not easy. Ben Sira's great poem about Wisdom compares the great height of her tree to many kinds of tall trees and her spreading branches to a terebinth. She was also like a vine, and some texts at this point compare the vine to a mother: 'I am the mother of beautiful love, of fear, of knowledge, and of holy hope. Being eternal, I therefore am given to all my children, to those who are named by him.'[10]

Whatever the detail of the items missing from the second temple and where they went – this may be lost beyond recovery – the gist is clear enough: certain items that disappeared from the temple in the time of Josiah would be restored in the time of the Messiah. This meant more than restoring the sacred objects,[11] since the temple furnishings symbolized the most holy teachings of the temple, as Origen knew, and so the restoration of the temple furnishings meant the restoration of first-temple theology. These would have been the teachings from the time of the Lady, what the *Wisdom of Jesus Christ* described as 'the whole will of the mother of the holy angels'. The items that can be located belonged in the holy of holies: the ark and the cherubim formed the throne, the manna and Aaron's rod were in the ark, and the anointing oil had been kept in the holy of holies.[12] This, together with Wisdom describing herself in Proverbs 8.23 as *hidden away* from eternity,[13] before the beginning of the earth, suggests that the Lady had been in the holy of holies – and the Christians knew this.

The missing items, and so presumably the teaching they represented, were restored in the early Church: John the Baptist said Jesus would baptize with the Holy Spirit and with fire (Matt. 3.11; Luke 3.16, which

---

[9] *1 Enoch* 25.3–5.
[10] The poem is Ben Sira 24; the vine is v. 17 and the mother v. 18.
[11] See above, p. 18.
[12] Tosefta *Kippurim* 2.15.
[13] The Hebrew has 'hidden away', *nskty*, but the LXX has 'established me', reading the Hebrew as *nwsdty*. The letters *k* and *d* can look very similar.

happened at Pentecost, Acts 2.1-4); the ark reappeared in the temple (Rev. 11.19), as did the cherubim, that is, the heavenly throne; and before the throne burned the seven torches of fire, the menorah (Rev. 4.2-8). This appears in the final vision as the tree of life set by the throne (Rev. 22.1-2). In this Christian text, the restored menorah was in the holy of holies, not in the outer part of the temple. The Lady of the temple also reappeared in the holy of holies, as the Woman clothed with the sun, crowned with stars and with the moon beneath her feet. This was Ashratah returning, and in the vision she gave birth in the holy of holies to a male child who was taken up to the throne of God while she herself fled away into the wilderness (Rev. 12.1-6). Here was the mother of the LORD, the King, whom the Christians recognized in Mary. Jesus' debates with 'the Jews' in John's Gospel show just how much of this temple teaching had been forgotten or abandoned, but there are also glimpses of how much passed into Christian teaching.

John recorded the visions in the Book of Revelation, but the opening title makes clear who originally received them: it was Jesus.

> The revelation of Jesus Christ, which God gave him to show his servants what must soon take place; and he made it known by sending his angel to his servant John, who bore witness to the word of God and to the testimony of Jesus Christ, even to all that he [i.e. Jesus] saw.

John collected the visions and their meanings (the angel 'made it known') and then compiled the Book of Revelation. The visions are set in the original, true temple, and were originally written down in a Semitic language. Word patterns and sentence forms show this very clearly, for example in the great number of sentences in Revelation that begin with 'and'. This is not good Greek style, but is normal in Hebrew. The Greek text in the New Testament is a poor translation, and should not be compared with the much better Greek of John's Gospel, which also was a translation. It is unlikely that Jesus taught his disciples in Greek, and so the teaching in, for example, chapters 13—17 must have been translated by John or someone else before it reached the form in which we know it.

The years that followed Josiah's purges were a time of turmoil for the kingdom of Judah. Josiah himself was killed in battle, which was not the expected reward for one who had so faithfully implemented the requirements of Deuteronomy. It was said that Jeremiah wrote a lament for Josiah that was written in 'the Laments' (2 Chron. 35.25), perhaps Lamentations 3, and perhaps this was the material added to the scroll after Jehoiakim his son had burned the prophet's words (Jer. 36.27-32).

So little can be known for certain. Jeremiah had found good in Josiah, who was a just king unlike his extravagant and violent heir Jehoiakim (Jer. 22.13–19). The words of repentance from a disillusioned king could well have had some basis: 'We have transgressed and rebelled, and thou hast not forgiven' (Lam. 3.42). Many remembered the purges in the time of Josiah as the sin for which Jerusalem was destroyed, and the refugees in Egypt blamed the disaster on rejecting the Lady from the temple (Jer. 44.16–19).

The turmoil that preceded the destruction of the kingdom of Judah in 597 BCE and later the destruction of the city and temple in 586 BCE has obscured so much of what happened after the purges in the time of Josiah. It is not known what books survived, where or how. It is assumed that the books which now form the Hebrew Bible – or an earlier form of them – were compiled at this time. The oracles of the first-temple prophets were collected and in some cases set within a prose framework for a context. The records of the kings, both written and oral, were compiled into 1–2 Samuel and 1–2 Kings, but these collections were written with a clear agenda: to show how the kings who had not implemented the ideals of Deuteronomy had been the disaster that eventually caused the destruction of Jerusalem. The Deuteronomic histories, as they are generally known, have invariably been the primary source for reconstructing the history of Jerusalem under the Davidic kings, and so many of the real antecedents of Christianity – 'the King of the Jews' – have been overshadowed and even obscured by the different agenda in this presentation of history.

A few examples from the D histories will illustrate this point. When the Philistines began to threaten them, the elders of Israel asked Samuel to find them a king. He gave a long warning against kings – how much they would cost, how they would demand servants and taxes, 'and in that day you will cry out because of your king' (1 Sam. 8.18). But a king they had, and the rest of the D histories demonstrate that this had been a great mistake. The temple was also a mistake: Solomon spent far too much money on it and had had to sell part of his kingdom to pay for it (1 Kings 9.10–14); he even used forced labour from his own people to build it (1 Kings 5.13–18). Then the kingdom split because of the arrogance of Solomon's son Rehoboam (1 Kings 12.1–20). The kings of both kingdoms failed to live up to the ideals of the Deuteronomists and so were condemned. Abijam of Jerusalem 'walked in all the sins which his father did before him' (1 Kings 15.3). The next king, Asa, was deemed good because he removed the 'male cult prostitutes' from the land, along with all the idols his fathers had made, and he also banished his own mother because she had made an 'Asherah', an abominable image that he cut down and burned (1 Kings 15.9–15).

This pattern continues throughout the histories. Those who promoted a Deuteronomic style of worship were commended; those who did otherwise were condemned. There was no other criterion. Omri, who reigned for 40 years, the most famous and influential of the kings of Israel, was dismissed in four verses as evil (1 Kings 16.25–28); whereas Hezekiah, who purged the temple, removed the Asherah and embarked on an unwise rebellion against the superpower of Assyria, was commended (2 Kings 18.1–8). The great prophet Isaiah had a different view of him; initially he condemned him and said he would not survive his serious illness, but when the king repented, the prophet said he would live another 15 years (2 Kings 20.1–7). Ahaz his father had followed the other religion: he sacrificed and burned incense at high places, and even offered his son as a sacrifice (2 Kings 16.1–4). Enoch 'saw' Jerusalem at this time on one of his heavenly journeys. He saw the holy mountain over the Gihon spring, with its water flowing to the south, that is, before Hezekiah built the tunnel to bring the water into the city. He also saw trees in the holy place that were branches sprouting again from a tree that had been cut down.[14]

Isaiah, who was active during Ahaz's reign too, did not condemn the king for his religious practices; he only condemned him for failing to trust in the LORD and he prophesied that the royal house would survive. The Virgin would conceive and bear a son, who would be the future king (Isa. 7.1–14). Using the religion of Ugarit to illuminate otherwise disconnected texts, we can see that Jerusalem had a great Lady whose title was 'the Virgin', the mother of the sons of god (that is, the angels), and she was regarded as the heavenly mother of the crown prince. There are several places in the Hebrew Scriptures with traces of a Lady who was the mother of the kings in Jerusalem, and it is interesting that the name of the king's (human) mother is invariably included in the little information that is recorded about him (e.g. 1 Kings 15.2; 22.42; 2 Kings 12.1; 14.2). Her title, when it appears, is often translated 'queen mother' but it was literally 'the great lady', $g^e bhîrâ$ (1 Kings 15.13; 2 Kings 10.13; Jer. 13.18; 29.2).

Deuteronomy had a clear picture of who a king should be and how he should behave. With the wisdom of hindsight, Deuteronomy ruled that there should never (again) be a king like Solomon, one who traded horses with Egypt and had many wives and accumulated great wealth. The ideal

---

[14] *1 Enoch* 26.1–2.

king had to rule with a copy of Deuteronomy by his side in order to ensure a long reign and heirs to follow him (Deut. 17.14–20). This is very different from the divine priest-kings we glimpse in the Psalms: '... the processions of my God, my King, into the sanctuary' (Ps. 68.24), those Davidic princes who could claim at their enthronement:

> I will tell of a decree of the LORD:
> He said to me, 'You are my son,
> Today I have begotten you.'
> (Ps. 2.7)

*These, however, are the real kings of Jerusalem whom we seek in order to understand John's Gospel, not the ones proposed by Deuteronomy.*

According to the Chronicler (the D historian does not have this information), Josiah began his purges in the twelfth year of his reign (2 Chron. 34.3), and Jeremiah was called to be a prophet in the thirteenth year of his reign (Jer. 1.2). His family were country priests (Jer. 1.1), and would have been among those whom Josiah dispossessed. Jeremiah was called to resist 'the kings of Judah, its princes, its priests, and the people of the land' (Jer. 1.18). Now the words of Jeremiah show more signs of D editors than any other prophetic book, presumably because he was an eyewitness of their purges, but underneath their easily identified layers and additions we can still glimpse the original prophet who was called to resist them. He saw the branch of an almond tree, *šāqēdh*, and was assured that the LORD was watching over, *šōqēdh*, his work (Jer. 1.11–12). The tabernacle menorah was an almond-like tree (Exod. 25.31–39), and so this could well be an assurance to Jeremiah that the threatened menorah/Ashratah would not be completely destroyed by Josiah's purges.

Many scholars agree that the Mosaic form of a covenant does not appear in Hebrew literature before the time of Josiah. Ever since the great nineteenth-century German scholar Julius Wellhausen, scholars have been aware that many things changed in the time of Josiah, and one of them was the nature of covenant. It was Deuteronomy and then the later prophets who regarded 'covenant' as a contract, a series of rules to keep. This was the Mosaic form of covenant that is usually regarded as the norm, or even as the only form for a covenant. The earlier writings, however, had a different idea about covenant, one that reappeared in Christianity; it was the bonds of creation, the system established by the Creator to hold secure both the natural order and human society. This was the covenant maintained by the high priests, and this was the covenant that Jesus renewed at the last supper.[15] It is the covenant implied in the story of Noah, where it is called the everlasting covenant (Gen. 9.12–17); and vividly described by Isaiah when he said that contemporary disasters were proof that this covenant was collapsing due to human sin (Isa. 24.4–6). The covenant with Abraham was a promise to give the land to him and his descendants, and not a conditional contract (Gen. 15.1–21). Abraham 'believed the LORD; and he reckoned it to him as righteousness' (Gen. 15.6). This is the verse to which Paul appealed when he said that the basis of the Christian faith was not with Moses, but older than Moses (Gal. 3.6, one of his earlier writings, and also Rom. 4.3, his last). Deuteronomy, on the other hand, said that the land was not given by promise; its possession was conditional on keeping the commandments. This was the new style of covenant (Deut. 11.8–9).

Deuteronomy itself reveals many of the ways in which the new emphasis on Moses changed the older forms of thought and worship. Some are still clearly visible in the text; others have to be deduced from the changed meanings of words such as 'covenant'. In the text, Deuteronomy says that the statutes and ordinances taught to the people by Moses were to be their wisdom (Deut. 4.5–6). This implies that there had been another form of Wisdom, and, as we shall see, this was the case. Jeremiah condemned this change:

> How can you say, 'We are wise,
> And the law of the LORD is with us?'
> But, behold, the false pen of the scribes
> Has made it into a lie.
> The wise men shall be put to shame,
> They shall be dismayed and taken;
> Lo, they have rejected the word of the LORD,
> And what wisdom is in them?   (Jer. 8.8–9)

Deuteronomy says that the laws revealed to Moses were all that the people needed; there had been 'secret things', but these were not for the people who followed Moses: 'The secret things belong to the LORD our God; but the things that are revealed belong to us ... that we may do all the words of this law' (Deut. 29.29). Set this alongside another passage, which asks why anyone is needed to go up to heaven or to cross the sea in order to bring down commandments, when they have all they need already, and it is clear that some secret teaching, wisdom, was being replaced. Moses said:

---

[15] See my book *Temple Themes in Christian Worship*, London: T&T Clark, 2007, pp. 173–99.

> For this commandment which I command you this day is not too hard for you, neither is it far off. It is not in heaven that you should say, 'Who will go up for us to heaven, and bring it to us, that we may hear it and do it?' Neither is it beyond the sea that you should say, 'Who will go over the sea for us, and bring it to us, that we may hear it and do it?' (Deut. 30.11–13)

Deuteronomy says the Sabbath must be observed so that everyone, including servants and animals, can rest. This is because the people have a common memory of being slaves in Egypt, from which the LORD delivered them, and so they in turn must set their servants and animals free from work (Deut. 5.15). The other (and older) version of the Sabbath commandment says that everyone must rest because the LORD made heaven and earth in six days and then rested on the seventh day, and so that day became sacred (Exod. 20.11). The Deuteronomist's explanation was drawn from the Moses story, as we should expect, but the other (and older) explanation was drawn from observing the process of creation. Now the teaching drawn from observing nature was 'wisdom', and there is ample evidence for this style in earlier texts and also in *1 Enoch*.

> Does a lion roar in the forest, when he has no prey …
> Does evil befall a city unless the LORD has done it? (Amos 3.4, 6)

> Even the stork in the heavens knows her times;
> And the turtledove, swallow and crane
> Keep the time of their coming;
> But my people know not the ordinance of the LORD. (Jer. 8.7)

> As a hart longs for flowing streams,
> So longs my soul for thee, O God. (Ps. 42.1)

> Observe ye everything that takes place in the heaven, how they do not change their orbits …
> But ye – ye have not been steadfast, nor done the commandments of the LORD.[16]

This is consistent with Deuteronomy 4.6: the law of Moses was to replace Wisdom, and it did.

There is also a significant omission. The Deuteronomists' calendar has no place for the Day of Atonement, which had been the most important temple festival. In the second temple, the ritual was performed by the high priest as prescribed in Leviticus 16, a (now) confused Priestly text which attributes the Day of Atonement prescriptions to Moses. Two goats were

---

[16] *1 Enoch* 2.1; 5.4.

chosen by lot, one to represent Azazel, the leader of the fallen angels, and this goat was banished to the wilderness, bearing away all the people's sins. The other goat represented the LORD, and this goat was sacrificed, and its blood used to purify and consecrate the tabernacle/temple. This text has usually been misread, since the Hebrew preposition $l^e$ can mean either 'for' or 'as'. Here in Leviticus 16.8 it meant 'as'. Each goat represented a divine being in the rite of atonement, and the sacrificed goat 'was' the LORD whose blood cleansed and consecrated the creation.[17]

Deuteronomy 16 sets out the calendar of festivals, each of which had to be kept in the temple, 'the place which the LORD your God will choose' (v. 6): the year began with Passover, then after seven weeks, Weeks, and then, after an unspecified interval, Tabernacles. The priestly calendars (Lev. 23; Num. 28—29), in their revised second-temple form, included other festivals: the New Year and the Day of Atonement. The festival they describe as 'trumpets' was a vestige of the ancient New Year, but in these calendars was prescribed for the first day of the *seventh* month (Lev. 23.24; Num. 29.1). The ancient New Year festival was described in the older Exodus calendar as the 'ingathering at *the end* of the year' (Exod. 23.16), as is implied by the Gezer calendar which begins the year with the months of ingathering.[18] In the second-temple calendar, there had been a six-month shift, so that the new year was celebrated with Passover, the great festival of the pro-Moses group. Deuteronomy had no place for the festivals of the original temple which marked the building and reconsecrating of the temple, itself a symbol of the whole creation. As Moses took over the key roles from the first temple, so the very possibility of the Day of Atonement was denied, as we shall see.

The calendar remained a matter of dispute as can be seen from the *Damascus Document*, the manifesto of the faithful sons of the Righteous One (the sons of Zadok, Ezek. 44.15). They held fast to the commandments of God, and God had revealed to them the hidden things in which the rest of Israel had gone astray, including the calendar – 'the glorious feasts'.[19] Their community kept the ancient solar calendar of 364 days which Josiah had abandoned when he drove the Lady from the temple,[20] and in this calendar of exactly 52 weeks the festivals fell on the same day of the week each year: Passover was on a Tuesday and the

---

[17] Origen, the great Christian biblical scholar who died in 253 CE, read the text this way, *Against Celsus* 6.43.

[18] The Gezer calendar has been dated anywhere between the eleventh and sixth centuries BCE.

[19] *Damascus Document*, CD III.

[20] See my book *The Mother of the Lord*, vol. 1, London: T&T Clark, 2012, pp. 45, 49.

## The background to John's Gospel

Day of Atonement on a Friday. The new year always fell on the fourth day of the week, presumably because this was when the lights of heaven were created to be 'signs and for seasons and for days and years' (Gen. 1.14).[21] The Qumran community ordered their worship in accordance with 'the great light of heaven'.[22] This eclipsing of the ancient autumn festivals – New Year, Day of Atonement and Tabernacles – in favour of Passover marked the transition to the pro-Moses era, and a theme that runs through John's Gospel is Jesus restoring the autumn festivals to their dominant position. Three Passovers are mentioned in the Gospel, and, as we shall see, at each one Jesus shows how his teaching based on the Day of Atonement supersedes that of Passover.

- At the first Passover (2.23), Nicodemus came to Jesus, and John shows that Nicodemus, a representative of second-temple teaching, simply did not understand the beliefs of the old temple. The Man had to be lifted up like Moses' serpent – the link to exodus and Passover – and then Jesus spoke of the Son being given for the life of the world, and his judgement being a time of salvation. These, as we shall see, were Day of Atonement themes.
- At the second Passover (6.4), Jesus fed the 5,000 and then spoke of the manna – the link to exodus and Passover – and taught that this food perished and did not give eternal life. In contrast, the Day of Atonement sacrifice – the goat that represented the LORD – was consumed by the officiating priests. The *Letter of Barnabas* shows that the first Christians understood the death of Jesus as this sacrifice, and 'the prophet' is quoted: 'Let them eat of the goat which is offered for their sins at the fast, and (note this carefully) let all the priests, but nobody else, eat of its inward parts, unwashed and with vinegar.' A token part of the offering was consumed with its blood and with vinegar, and Barnabas explains that when Jesus drank vinegar before he died, he was preparing himself as that sacrifice.[23] 'The prophet' cannot be identified, but in the Mishnah there is an allusion to eating the raw sin offering on the Day of Atonement.[24]
- At the third Passover (19.31–37), Jesus died at exactly the time when the Passover lambs were being sacrificed in the temple. John emphasized the similarity between Jesus and the Passover lambs but

---

[21] See J. Maier, *The Temple Scroll*, Sheffield: JSOT Press, 1985, pp. 71–6.
[22] *Hymns*, 1QH XX.5.
[23] *Letter of Barnabas* 7.
[24] Mishnah *Menaḥoth* 11.7.

also the vinegar that characterized the Day of Atonement. Hebrews too understood the death of Jesus as fulfilling the Day of Atonement sacrifice: 'not the blood of goats and calves, but his own blood' (Heb. 9.12).

With the second-temple calendar, Passover could have fallen on any day of the week, and Jesus waiting for the right time (e.g. 2.4, 'My hour is not yet come') meant that *he was waiting for the year when Passover fell on a Friday, so as to replace the Passover sacrifice with the Day of Atonement sacrifice.*

Deuteronomy also gave a different version of the Sinai story, which took place on a mountain they called Horeb. The older version in Exodus 24 says that Moses and the others who went up the mountain with him had a vision of the God of Israel, with a sapphire pavement beneath his feet (Exod. 24.9–10). This is very like the description given by Ezekiel, a first-temple priest (Ezek. 1.3), who had a vision of the heavenly throne leaving Jerusalem and going to Babylon. He saw a sapphire throne and, upon it, a fiery human form (Ezek. 1.26–28). This must have been how the people of the first temple described the throne. Deuteronomy would have none of this. At the holy mountain '... the LORD spoke to you out of the midst of the fire; you heard the sound of words, but saw no form; there was only a voice. And he declared to you his covenant, which he commanded you to perform ...' (Deut. 4.12–13). And as we have already seen, Deuteronomy forbad the worship of the hosts of heaven.

There was a new basis for action in Deuteronomy, best illustrated by changes to the meaning of some words. In the older ways, the verb *dābhaq* meant 'to cleave' in the old sense of that word: to stay close to, keep close to, be joined to. Thus in the story of Ruth, Orpah left her mother-in-law but Ruth *clung* to her (Ruth 1.14); or in Eden 'Therefore a man leaves his father and his mother and *cleaves* to his wife ...' (Gen. 2.24). For Deuteronomy, relationship with the LORD was based not on union but on obedience: 'You shall fear the LORD your God; you shall serve him and *cleave* to him ...' (Deut. 10.20). Key words from the old ways disappeared: 'grace' and 'graciousness' do not appear in Deuteronomy; 'trust' appears once, in a negative sense: 'your ... fortified walls, in which you trusted' (Deut. 28.52); 'truth' once, but only in the sense of apportioning blame (Deut. 13.14); and 'kindness' not at all. Deuteronomy had a very different world-view from that of the Psalmist, and a very different idea of the ways of God. Thus John made his comparison: 'The law was given through Moses; grace and truth came through Jesus Christ' (John 1.17).

The heirs of the Deuteronomists were responsible for preserving and compiling many of the Hebrew Scriptures. There is no agreement as to who were the final editors of the first five books of the Hebrew Scriptures, the Pentateuch. They might have been the heirs of the Deuteronomists, or they might have been second-temple priests, who were Aaronite priests and therefore of the same basic outlook as the Moses and Deuteronomy group. As far as Enoch was concerned, they were all an apostate generation, but Josephus called them 'the Jews'. This was the era of Moses.

Certain interesting points do emerge, however, from close inspection of their work, especially in the light of later traditions and social memories. The religion of Abraham, Isaac and Jacob as described in Genesis had various El names for God: e.g. El Elyon (Gen. 14.18); El Ro'i (Gen. 16.13); and El Shaddai (Gen. 17.1; 28.3; 35.11; 43.14; 48.3; 49.25). Now El simply means 'God', and these titles mean respectively 'Most High God', 'God who sees' and 'God with breasts'. This latter is the most natural way to translate El Shaddai, and the later convention that it meant God Almighty is a good example of how things were changed after Josiah had purged the temple of the Lady. The patriarchs worshipped at sacred trees (e.g. Abraham at Moreh where the LORD appeared to him, Gen. 12.6–7); at sacred stones and pillars (e.g. Jacob at Bethel, Gen. 28.18), and at altars wherever the LORD appeared (e.g. to Abraham at Moreh, Gen. 12.8; to Isaac at Beersheba, Gen. 26.23–25; to Jacob at Bethel, Gen. 35.1–7). Abraham also thought he should sacrifice his son, as did King Ahaz in the time of Isaiah (2 Kings 16.3), but the reworked story had Isaac saved. Genesis 22.11–14 reads like a modifying insertion, especially as Genesis 22.19 does not mention Isaac returning to Beersheba with his father, and later traditions told of Isaac going to heaven and then being resurrected.[25] Now all these ways of the patriarchs are the very practices that Josiah stamped out: he broke in pieces the pillars, he cut down the Asherim, the sacred trees (2 Kings 23.14); he destroyed the altar at Bethel, set up by Jacob (2 Kings 23.15); and he destroyed the place where children were sacrificed (2 Kings 23.10). Deuteronomy prescribed the purges thus: 'You shall tear down their altars, and dash in pieces their pillars, and burn their Asherim [sacred trees] with fire ...' (Deut. 12.3).

The implication of these comparisons was noticed long ago: the religion depicted in Genesis as the religion of the patriarchs was in fact *the religion practised in Israel and Judah in the late seventh century BCE, the*

---

[25] E.g. Targum *Pseudo-Jonathan* Gen. 22.

*religion purged by Josiah.*²⁶ The next stage of the history was the story of Moses, and so his saga was joined to that of the patriarchs at the beginning of Exodus. It was marked by the revelation to Moses from the burning bush. Now a burning bush is very similar indeed to a fiery tree, and so the incident in Exodus 3 is in effect the Lady passing over her people to Moses who superseded her. In Exodus 3.14 the name revealed from the bush was to be used by all future generations: *'ehyeh ᵃšer 'ehyeh* (Exod. 3.13–15), a name with a first-person form and thus with no obvious gender. The second account reveals more: the LORD explained to Moses that he had been revealed to the patriarchs as El Shaddai, 'God with breasts', but was in future to be known as *yhwh*, the LORD (Exod. 6.2–3).

There are other traces in the Pentateuch of the faith that Josiah purged. Later tradition assigned special roles to the children of Amram: Miriam, Moses and Aaron. Moses, it was said, became the king, Aaron the high priest, and Miriam 'took' wisdom. 'It was from her that Bezalel descended, from whom in turn David who was a king.'²⁷ In the Pentateuch, Miriam and Aaron challenged the authority of Moses who had *married a foreign wife*. Miriam was smitten with leprosy as a punishment and disappeared from the story (Num. 12). She died at Kadesh, and then the people had no water (Num. 20.1–2). Moses had to provide a new source of water by striking a rock. The people left Kadesh and wandered for 38 years in the desert until they crossed the brook Zered and their wanderings were over (Deut. 2.14). We have seen how Moses became the king; Miriam, Moses' older sister, *was ousted by her younger brother who provided a new source of water, that is, knowledge*; but Aaron the high priest survived alongside Moses. Miriam/Wisdom was the ancestor of Bezalel who designed the tabernacle and also of David, the first king in Jerusalem. The familiar stories encode the turbulence that engulfed both the ancient temple and the monarchy, from which the religion of Moses emerged as the dominant influence. The mother of Jesus was Miriam/Mary.

There is also the story of Eden. Adam was told he could eat from any tree in the garden except the tree of the knowledge of good and evil. He was intended to eat from the tree of life. This is a temple story, since the temple represented Eden (decorated with cherubim, palm trees and flowers, 1 Kings 6.29), and Adam was the original high priest. He was set

---

²⁶ First suggested by J. van Seters, 'The Religion of the Patriarchs in Genesis', *Biblica* 61 (1968), pp. 220–33.
²⁷ *Exodus Rabbah* XLVIII.4.

in the garden 'to lead the worship and to preserve the teachings', which is the other meaning of the Hebrew words translated 'to till ... and keep' (Gen. 2.15). Then the human pair listened to a snake who persuaded the woman that the other tree was exactly like the tree of life, 'good for food ... a delight to the eyes ... to be desired to make one wise ...' (Gen. 3.6). So they ate, and soon after were driven from the garden. Why was there a snake in the temple garden? Isaiah had seen snake-like beings in the temple because the seraphim were, literally, fiery serpents. One of them brought a coal in his hand to cleanse Isaiah's mouth, so the snake was one of the LORD's temple servants (Isa. 6.6). The Psalmist said there were fiery servants in the temple, but we have no idea how he imagined them: '[O LORD], who makes winds his angels and flames of fire his servants' (Ps. 104.4, my translation). In Eden, this was Satan's first deception, appearing as a temple servant.

When Revelation described his downfall, he was 'that ancient serpent, who is called the Devil and Satan, the deceiver of the whole world' (Rev. 12.9). Within the temple context, we should expect the deceiver to have taken a familiar and acceptable form, and so he appeared as a fiery minister in the temple, offering another tree instead of the tree of life and making it seem identical. Recall that the lawbook was 'found' in the temple in the time of Josiah; nobody knows how it came to be there, and the same is true of the forbidden tree in the Genesis Eden. Nobody knows how it came to be in the Eden/temple. This story, set as the Preface to the Pentateuch but not mentioned anywhere else *in this form* in the Hebrew Scriptures, decodes itself. Adam, the original priesthood, lost his temple and found instead a world of thorns, thistles and toil. The forbidden tree represented the new law-based ways, which cut Adam off from the tree of life. This was long remembered: the early Christian text, the *Acts of John*, describes Jesus singing a hymn with his disciples before he was arrested by 'the lawless Jews who were governed by the lawless serpent'.[28] There are many such examples, where, reading just below the surface text, the turmoil of the early second-temple period can be found.

These are but two of many examples. Further evidence of the older faith can be found in ancient biblical texts that differ from those used for most English translations. Concealing what could not be mentioned was a well-known characteristic of the scribes who transmitted the texts. We do not know why the material was not simply omitted. Sometimes, the scribes were able by subtle changes to incorporate their own opinion into

---

[28] *Acts of John* 94, thought to be an early second-century text.

the text. Isaiah, for example, prophesied that there would be five cities in Egypt where people would worship the LORD of Hosts, and one would be called the City of the Sun (Isa. 19.18), presumably a reference to the Lady, who was symbolized by the sun. The present text says it would be called the city of *destruction*, the scribes' opinion of the Lady. One letter was changed into another that looked almost the same: 'sun', *ḥeres*, became 'destruction', *heres*. The letters look and sound just as similar in Hebrew as they are in the English transliteration.

The results of this scribal activity were called the 'restorations of the scribes', *tiqqûnê sôpherîm*.[29] The changes were a deliberate departure from the earlier text to avoid what was later perceived as blasphemy and they were made according to strict rules: certain letters could be exchanged or repositioned, or similar-sounding letters could be substituted so that the word was changed. Every effort was made to ensure that the resulting text had the same number of letters as the original. Sometimes the letters were not changed, but the words were pronounced differently, which is easy to do in Hebrew where only the consonants are written and the reader supplies the appropriate vowels. Sometimes the groups of letters were divided differently, making different words from the same consonants. This work was attributed to Ezra and the men of the great synagogue, the legendary group (and their heirs) who returned from Babylon to restore the Scriptures and to teach their meaning. Tradition said that their work began when Ezra and the Levites read the law in Jerusalem: 'And they read from the book, from the law of God, clearly; and they gave the sense, so that the people understood the reading' (Neh. 8.8). There were rules for the temple scribes, who even altered existing scrolls. During the minor days of a festival for example, 'they may not ... correct a single letter even in the scroll of the Temple Court'.[30]

These were the people that Enoch called the apostate generation – the Moses people – but, at the end of their allotted time, sevenfold wisdom and knowledge, he said, would be given (restored?) to the righteous.[31] This was the fruit of the tree of life, which Jesus promised to his faithful followers (Rev. 2.7; 22.14). He himself was the Lamb with seven eyes and seven horns; in other words, he was anointed with the Spirit and had received sevenfold knowledge and illumination.[32]

---

[29] See, for example, D. Barthélemy, 'Les tiqquné sopherim et la critique textuelle de l'Ancien Testament', Supplements to Vetus Testamentum IX (1963), pp. 258–304.
[30] Mishnah *Moʻed Katan* 3.4.
[31] *1 Enoch* 93.10.
[32] See below, p. 244.

Enoch also knew that the Scriptures were being changed. The date of these changes is not so important as the fact that changes had been made.

> Woe to you who set at nought the words of the righteous ... Woe to you who write down lying and godless words ...
> Woe to them who pervert the words of uprightness, and transgress the eternal law ...
> ... sinners will alter and pervert the words of righteousness in many ways, and will speak wicked words and will lie, and practise great deceits, and write books concerning their words.[33]

Behind all these accusations of apostasy and of rewriting the records, we try to find the Davidic priest-kings in Jerusalem.

The first disciples of Jesus prayed the words in the *Didache* during his ministry to give thanks that the ways of the Davidic priest-kings had been restored. Jesus the Servant of the LORD had made known to them the vine of the house of David and the bread that symbolized life and knowledge. Presumably this means that Jesus had been teaching the ways/knowledge of the priest-kings, reminiscent of the cryptic line in the Qumran *Melchizedek* text, that when Melchi-Zedek returned, the teachers who had been kept hidden and secret would return.[34] This teaching is not obviously in the synoptic Gospels, but there is much in John's Gospel that points to it.

The eucharistic prayers in the *Didache* may be a rare glimpse of Jesus' life before his baptism, and then of time he spent alone with his disciples (e.g. Mark 4.10, 34). If the *Didache* prayers had been the customary table prayers of Jesus' disciples during his ministry, then a reflection upon them at the last supper would explain the form of the high-priestly prayer in John 17.

This is the first *Didache* prayer, the italics showing the links to John 17:

> About the Thanksgiving, give thanks like this:
>
> First, concerning the cup:
> We thank you, our Father, for the holy vine of your servant David, which you have made known to us through Jesus your servant.
> To you be glory for ever.
> Concerning the broken [bread]:
> We thank you, our Father, for the *life and knowledge which you have made known to us through Jesus your servant*.

---

[33] *1 Enoch* 98.14, 15; 99.2; 104.10.
[34] *Melchizedek*, 11QMelch.

> To you be glory for ever.
> *Just as this broken [bread] was scattered on the mountains and was gathered and became one, so may your assembly\* be brought together from the ends of the earth into your kingdom.*
> To you be glory and power for ever through Jesus Christ.[35]

\*The Greek word *ekklēsia* does not necessarily mean 'Church'. In the Septuagint it was used for the assembly of Israel (e.g. Deut. 31.30; 1 Chron. 29.1) and for the host of angels (e.g Ps. 89.6), and it means, literally, 'those called out'.

This is the second prayer:

> After you have been filled, give thanks like this:

> We thank you, holy Father, for *your holy Name, which you have made to tabernacle in our hearts.*
> And for the *knowledge* and faith and *immortality which you have made known to us through Jesus* your servant.
> To you be glory for ever.
> You, Almighty Lord, created all things for the sake of your Name,
> And you gave food and drink to humans for enjoyment so that they would thank you.
> But to us you have graciously given spiritual food and drink and eternal life through your servant.
> Above all, we thank you for your power.
> Glory to you for ever.
> Remember, O Lord, to *deliver your assembly from all evil, and to bring it to completion in your love*. From the four winds *gather what you have consecrated into your kingdom which you have prepared for it.*
> For yours is the power and the glory for ever.
> May grace come and may this world pass away.
> Hosanna to the God of David.
> If anyone is holy, let him approach. If anyone is not, let him repent.
> Maranatha. Amen.[36]

It is unlikely that these prayers were composed after the last supper, but the fact that they were preserved at all shows they had had an important place in the life of the early Christian community. The prayers have been compared to Jewish table prayers of the form 'Blessed art thou, Lord God ...', but the *Didache* prayers have the form 'We give thanks ...' which is a very important difference. These *Didache* table prayers were

---

[35] *Didache* 9.1–4, my translation.
[36] *Didache* 10.1–7, my translation.

used by people looking for the restoration of the Davidic priest-kings, and Jesus, whom they called 'the Servant', became their teacher. When they told the story of his birth they described the birth of the new Davidic king: 'the Anointed One, the LORD' (Luke 2.11, translating literally) whom wise men came *to worship* (Matt. 2.2).

Jesus recognized at his baptism that he was the Servant, as we shall see,[37] and so he was called to fulfil the hopes of those looking for the Davidic priest-king. He had to become, and indeed had already become, the Lamb of the throne visions in Revelation 4—5. He was the Anointed One, the LORD, 'who was and is and is to come' (Rev. 4.8). Hence the prayer in the *Didache*: '*Maranatha*', 'Come, LORD', but preceded by 'Let grace come ... Hosanna to the God of David' which means 'Save us!' as in Psalm 118.25: 'Save us, we beseech thee, O LORD!' These cries did not originate as prayers for the second coming of Jesus: they had long been the cries of the LORD's people in time of distress. Psalm 80, to which we shall return, calls on the LORD of Hosts:

> Come to save us!
> Restore us, O God;
> Let thy face/presence shine, that we may be saved.
> (Ps. 80.2–3)

There are many examples. They pictured the LORD coming in judgement, to punish his (i.e. their) enemies and to heal the land (Deut. 32.43). These words from Deuteronomy became a key text to identify Jesus, cited in Hebrews 1.6, although the present Hebrew text of Deuteronomy has lost this particular line. The Firstborn, said the writer of Hebrews, had come into the world; the LORD had appeared to save his people. The Baptist spoke of the 'one who comes after me who was before me' (John 1.30, my paraphrase), and he identified himself as the voice preparing the way of the LORD (John 1.23). This was not a rereading of a text about the LORD, applying it to Jesus: people were expecting the LORD to come, and just as he had once been present with his people in the Davidic king, so too the Christians believed that he was present in Jesus, the restored Davidic king. According to the *Didache* prayers, Jesus had been teaching about the holy vine of David, the Servant, and about the bread that imparted life and knowledge, faith and immortality.

The words of the prayers reveal some important roots of Christianity that are right on that line between Ezekiel, the Book of Revelation, John's

---

[37] See below, p. 386.

Gospel and the early Gnostic texts. In particular, Jesus' teaching about the true vine (John 15.1–6)[38] and his high-priestly prayer in John 17 seem to be an expansion of the *Didache* prayers.

- *Didache* 8: 'Deliver us from the Evil One'; cf. 'keep them from evil' (John 17.15);
- *Didache* 9: 'Life and knowledge made known to us'; cf. 'This is eternal life, that they know thee the only true God, and Jesus Christ whom thou hast sent' (John 17.3);
- *Didache* 9: 'As this broken [bread] ... was gathered and became one, so may your assembly be brought together from the ends of the earth into your kingdom'; cf. 'that they may be one' (John 17.11, 21);
- *Didache* 10: 'Holy Father'; cf. 'Holy Father, keep them in thy name ...' (John 17.11);
- *Didache* 10: 'Your Holy Name which you have made to tabernacle in our hearts'; cf. 'I have disclosed/given them knowledge of your Name' (John 17.6, 26, my translation), 'Keep them in your Name' (John 17.11, my translation).
- *Didache* 10: 'The Church you have consecrated' (Greek *hagiazō*); cf. 'Consecrate them in the truth' (John 17.17, my translation); 'consecrated in truth' (John 17.19).
- *Didache* 10: 'From the four winds gather what you have consecrated into your kingdom which you have prepared for it'; cf. 'Father, I desire that they also, whom thou hast given me, may be with me where I am, to behold my glory which thou hast given in thy love for me before the foundation of the world' (John 17.24). This is the vision of gathering into the kingdom: the four angels restraining the four winds until the faithful have been marked with the Name (Rev. 7.1–8), and the final vision of the consecrated servants, marked with the Name, standing in the presence of the Lamb who is enthroned in the light of divine glory (Rev. 22.3–5).

If the *Didache* prayers had been the customary table prayers of Jesus' disciples during his ministry, then the high-priestly prayer at the last supper was a reflection upon them.

Psalm 80 gives part of the context. Written after the destruction of the first temple and kingdom, the psalm mourns for the vine that has been cut down and burned. The text is not always clear, and there is no text of

---

[38] See below, pp. 400–1.

this psalm from Qumran to help with clarification, but the prayer for restoration is unmistakable:

> Turn again, O God of Hosts!
> Look from heaven and see; give your attention to this vine.
> Strengthen what your right hand planted
> [And heed] the son you have made strong for yourself.
> [The vine] was burned with fire and cut down,
> May they perish at the rebuke of your face/presence.
> May your hand be upon the man of your right hand,
> Upon the son of man whom you have strengthened for yourself.
> Then we will never turn back from you,
> Give us life and we will call on your Name.
> Restore us, O LORD God of Hosts,
> Make your face/presence shine and we shall be saved.
> (Ps. 80.14–19, my translation)

In the earlier part of this psalm, the vine represents the people – 'a vine out of Egypt' (Ps. 80.8) – and Jeremiah also described the people as a vine (Jer. 2.21). In this section, however, the vine is the origin of the son whom the LORD has made strong. This is the vine imagery in Ezekiel where it, or rather *she*, since 'vine' is a feminine noun, was uprooted and stripped of her fruit. Her strong stem withered, and she was burned. This was a lament for the mother of the Davidic house, not for one particular queen, but for the heavenly Mother who gave birth to all the Davidic kings. She was Wisdom, also known as the Spirit. Ezekiel was lamenting for the princes of Israel who had several human mothers but one heavenly Mother: 'Your mother was like a vine ... [Her] strongest stem became a ruler's sceptre ...' Once the vine was uprooted, stripped of its fruit and burned, 'there remains ... no strong stem, no sceptre for a ruler' (Ezek. 19.10, 11, 14), and, we assume, no more fruit, which was true Wisdom teaching.

In the companion lament, Ezekiel described the Queen Mother as a lioness who had lost her cubs (Ezek. 19.1–9), which explains a title given to Jesus in Revelation: 'the lion of Judah'. The royal imagery of lion and vine is implicit in the titles for Jesus in the Book of Revelation: 'the Lion of ... Judah, the Root of David' (Rev. 5.5); 'the Root and Offspring of David, the Bright Morning Star' (Rev. 22.16, my translation).[39] The earliest example of the two royal images together, however, is the *Blessing of Jacob*, an ancient poem in Genesis.

---
[39] Morning Star, see below, p. 75.

> Judah is a lion's whelp ...
> The sceptre shall not depart from Judah ...
> Until he comes to [Shiloaḥ] ...[40]
> Binding his foal to the vine
> And his ass's colt to the choice vine,
> He washes his garments in wine,
> And his vesture in the blood of grapes ...
> (Gen. 49.9, 10, 11)

The foal and the ass's colt are familiar from Zechariah's royal prophecy:

> Rejoice greatly, O daughter of Zion,
> Shout aloud, O daughter of Jerusalem!
> Lo, your king comes to you;
> He is the Righteous One and Saviour,
> Humble and riding on an ass,
> on a colt, the foal of an ass.
> (Zech. 9.9, my literal translation)

Zechariah's prophecy became the crowd's acclamation on Palm Sunday (John 12.15); and in the time of Jesus, royal Shiloaḥ was known as Siloam, where Jesus gave sight to a man who had been born blind (John 9.1–7). In the *Blessing of Jacob*, the Davidic prince was bound to the vine at Shiloaḥ and he washed his garments in wine, the blood of the vine. Doubtless this was a memory of royal ritual: the Davidic kings were anointed at the Gihon spring (1 Kings 1.38–40), which flowed out and became the Shiloaḥ. It is possible that the prayer in the *Didache* gives thanks for the restoration of the Davidic vine and the stem to be a king: 'We give thanks to thee, our Father, for the holy vine of thy servant David, which thou hast made known to us through thy servant Jesus.'

Ben Sira described Wisdom as a vine, the mother. The text of his 'Praise of Wisdom' exists in several forms, but the imagery is clear enough.

> [17]Like a vine I put forth buds of grace,
> and my flowers are the fruit of glory and wealth.
> [18]*I am the mother of the love of beauty,*
> *of fear and knowledge and of holy hope;*
> *I give these to all my children,*
> *eternal [love] for those who are chosen by him.*
> (Ben Sira 24.17, 18, my translation)[41]

---

[40] The text has 'Shiloh', which makes no sense, but the very similar 'Shiloaḥ' does.
[41] Verse 18 is not found in most texts.

Who could have written this? The vine of David in the *Didache* could have meant Wisdom, the mother, as is also suggested by the prayer over the bread.

The *Didache*'s thanksgiving over the bread was 'for the life and knowledge thou hast made known through thy servant Jesus' and also derives from the royal cult. Two very early sources – the *Didache* and Justin[42] – said that the bread of the Eucharist was the pure cereal offering prophesied by Malachi to replace the polluted bread[43] of the second-temple offering (Mal. 1.11). Cyril of Jerusalem in the mid-fourth century taught that the bread of the Eucharist had replaced the bread of the Presence.[44] All witness to a much neglected aspect of Christian symbolism: the bread of the Eucharist as the new bread of the Presence.[45] Tradition remembered it as the bread of Wisdom's table, which she fed to her disciples so that they could live:

> Come, eat of my bread
> And drink of the wine I have mixed.
> Do not be deceived[46] but live
> And walk in the way of insight.
> (Prov. 9.5–6, my translation)

The Septuagint knew a longer text:

> Come, eat from my loaves
> And drink wine which I have mixed for you;
> Leave foolishness and live
> So that you may reign for ever;
> Seek prudence so that you may live
> And in your state of knowledge join things together correctly.
> (LXX Prov. 9.5–6, my literal translation)

Wisdom's food nourished the royal house – 'that you may reign for ever'.

The bread of the Presence is one of the many unexplained aspects of temple ritual. It had been the most holy[47] food of the high priests, that is, it nourished them with holiness (Lev. 24.5–9), and it was set out on a golden table in the tabernacle/temple, along with wine and incense (Exod.

---

[42] *Didache* 14; Justin, *Trypho* 41.
[43] The polluted offering in Mal. 1.7. is *leḥem*, 'bread', as in AV, but more recent translations of the Old Testament have 'food'.
[44] Cyril, *Catecheses* 22.5.
[45] See my book *Temple Themes in Christian Worship*, London: T&T Clark, 2007, pp. 209–19.
[46] The word implies someone who has been deceived.
[47] 'Most holy' means 'imparting holiness'.

25.23-30). Nothing more is said about it in the Hebrew Scriptures. The rest has to be reconstructed from later sources:

- The bread represented a presence, and refugees in Egypt after the destruction of Jerusalem said they had worshipped the queen of heaven with small loaves that represented her (Jer. 44.19, my literal translation);
- Wisdom met her disciples like a mother or like a wife, offering them the bread of understanding and the water of wisdom (Ben Sira 15.2-3); those who ate *her* would hunger for more, and those who drank her would thirst for more (Ben Sira 24.21).
- Jewish tradition remembered that the bread and wine which Melchi-Zedek offered Abraham (Gen. 14.18) were the bread of the Presence and the wine that was set with it; and that he was instructing Abraham in the priesthood (the secret knowledge?). This account also linked Melchi-Zedek's hospitality to Wisdom's table in Proverbs 9.[48]
- According to the *Testament of Levi*, when the seven angels made Levi a priest, presumably when the older priesthood passed to the house of Levi the ancestor of Aaron, they vested him using an otherwise unknown ritual. It was very different from the blood smearing and sacrifices used to consecrate the high priests of the house of Aaron (Lev. 8—9), but very similar indeed to the earliest known Christian rites of baptism. He was *anointed with oil* and given a staff, *washed with water and fed bread and wine, dressed in white linen* and girded with purple, given an olive branch and *a wreath for his head*, before finally he was crowned with the priestly circlet (possibly bearing the Name, as in Exod. 28.36-38), and his hands were filled with incense.[49]

Nobody knows the origin of the detail in *Genesis Rabbah* about Melchi-Zedek offering Abraham the bread and wine when he made him a priest, or of the seven angels in the *Testament of Levi* giving Levi bread and wine when they made him a priest, but it can no longer be assumed that they were just the product of later imaginations. The consistency in these 'later' stories suggests that they were a social memory of the older ways, of Melchi-Zedek handing over his high priesthood to Abraham, and the seven angels (or the sevenfold angel, as in Rev. 15.6) passing it to Levi. What is important for our quest is that bread to impart life and

---
[48] *Genesis Rabbah* XLIII.6.
[49] *Testament of Levi* 8.1-11. The italics show which elements were also part of Christian baptism.

knowledge was *linked to the older ways*, to Melchi-Zedek and so to the Davidic king who was 'priest for ever after the order of Melchi-Zedek' (Ps. 110.4, my translation).

The eucharistic prayers in the *Didache* originated in the community (communities?) among whom Jesus grew up. They reflect the hopes of people who were looking for the destruction of Herod's temple in Jerusalem and for the restoration of the true temple and the Davidic kings. This is the cultural context of the songs in Luke's nativity story: turning the disobedient to the wisdom of the righteous ones;[50] the Son of the Most High to sit on the throne of David; remembering the mercy promised to Abraham and his seed; a horn of salvation in the house of his servant David; the oath sworn to Abraham (Luke 1.17, 32, 54–55, 69, 73). *Moses is not mentioned*; the hope was for Abraham – or whatever he represented – and for the royal house of David. The people who cherished these hopes were drawn from all 12 tribes and they were waiting for the angel of the sunrise to mark them with the sign of the Name of the LORD (Rev. 7.1–12). This had been Ezekiel's vision too: before the destruction of Jerusalem and its polluted temple in his time, the LORD had sent his angel to mark those who 'sigh and groan over the abominations ... committed [in Jerusalem]' (Ezek. 9.4). The mark of the LORD was, translating literally, the letter *tau*, an X, which became the mark of Christian baptism, the 'seal of the living God'. When the Church began to include Gentiles, so the vision was widened to include the great multitude from every nation (Rev. 7.9).

At his baptism, Jesus saw the heavens open and felt the Spirit come upon him (Mark 1.10 and parallels). The Baptist also recognized the sign of the resting Spirit (John 1.32). This was Isaiah's oracle of the new branch from the house of David on whom the Spirit would rest, so that he could teach with wisdom and understanding, counsel and might, knowledge and the fear of the LORD (Isa. 11.2). The Christians remembered that Jesus had had a throne experience at his baptism – the vision that became Revelation 4—5 – and that he had wrestled with its implications during his time in the desert.[51] His community recognized him as the Servant, hence his title in the *Didache* prayers and the frequent use of 'Servant' texts in the New Testament.[52]

---

[50] Wisdom here is *phronēsis*, 'prudence', 'good sense'.
[51] See below, p. 125.
[52] See below, pp. 90–4; also my book *Temple Mysticism. An Introduction*, London: SPCK, 2011, pp. 133–69.

*Who was Moses?*

The eucharistic prayers in the *Didache* suggest that Jesus the Servant was restoring – 'making known' – the ways of the Davidic kings and the bread of the Presence; in other words, he was restoring the temple as it had been under the Melchi-Zedek priests, before the temple became the place of the sons of Aaron in the era of Moses.

# 3
# The king in the Old Testament

Moses, speaking in Deuteronomy, taught the people of Israel that when the law was given, the LORD was not seen, and that there was no need for secret teaching brought from heaven since they had the commandments. In addition, the spiritual heirs of the Deuteronomists in effect wrote the monarchy out of their histories and left the reader of the Old Testament with many problems. What is the context for some of the mysterious and even opaque patches of Hebrew text that are found from time to time in the Hebrew Scriptures? Which layer of the text do we read? What vowels do we put to words that could have more than one meaning? *It is becoming increasingly clear that the final form of the Hebrew text is not the text that is relevant to Christian origins, and that it may even have been shaped in reaction to Christian claims.*

## The temple context

To rediscover the world of the kings in Jerusalem, and thus the background to John's Gospel, it is important to try to recover the temple, which was a 'map' of their world. This has to be reconstructed largely from later memories and echoes, but a picture does emerge from many texts written over a long period of time. The process is like trying to reconstruct a wrecked ship using pieces that have been washed up on many shores. There is not enough to assemble a complete vessel, but sufficient to have a good idea of what it was like.

Any reconstruction of the world of the first temple is fraught with problems. The description of the desert tabernacle made at Sinai was written after the first temple had been destroyed. Since the two were intended to be similar – the temple being the larger and permanent version of the tabernacle – memories of the temple almost certainly coloured the description of the tabernacle, and so what is said of the tabernacle can, in most cases, be used for the temple also.[1] But the

---
[1] There were differences. The cherubim, for example, faced each other in the tabernacle (Exod.

## The king in the Old Testament

description of the tabernacle in Exodus and the description of Solomon's temple in 1 Kings were both compiled after Josiah's purges, and so certain features are likely to have been left out in these post-exilic pro-Moses accounts. For example, only the Chronicler mentions the cherub throne in the holy of holies (1 Chron. 28.18),[2] but Ezekiel in his vision saw it leave and so it must have been in Solomon's temple. This suggests that the throne and the teaching it represented were unacceptable to the pro-Moses group. The throne was not, however, forgotten; the cherubim of the chariot throne over the ark were represented by the cherubim of the mercy seat over the ark, where the LORD spoke to Moses and appeared to the high priest (Exod. 25.17–22; Lev. 16.2; 1 Kings 8.6–7), but the Christians still knew about the original throne in the holy of holies – it is described in Revelation 4—5 – where the LORD had appeared in/as the Davidic king. Early Christian beliefs and teachings about the first temple and the Davidic king were based on much more than is apparent in a simple reading of the current Hebrew Scriptures.

Remnants of the pattern of temple symbolism can still be discerned in Exodus 40, where Moses began to assemble the tabernacle on the first day of the first month, and so it was probably a new year ritual which re-enacted the process of creation as described in Genesis 1. Ginzberg assembled a huge number of later Jewish texts that were based on this system of correspondences between the account of the creation and the form of the tabernacle/temple; in detail they differ from each other, but the overall pattern is consistent.[3] In the Old Testament, the Greek and Hebrew of Exodus 40 differ;[4] there is dislocation around the fifth act, setting up the altar for incense, and there is no real place in the six-act/six-day scheme for the external altar for sacrifice. This may reflect the broken pattern in Genesis 1, where there are two distinct acts of creation on the third day and the sixth day (Gen. 1.9–13, 24–31). Either the six-day pattern was once an eight-day pattern, or extra material was incorporated into a six-day temple scheme. The 'extra' in Genesis 1 is the creation of fish, birds and

---

25.20), but in the temple looked out into the *hêkhāl*, since their wings were spread and touched both sides of the holy of holies (2 Chron. 3.10–13).

[2] 1 Kings 6.23–28 mentions the cherubim, but not that they were the throne.

[3] L. Ginzberg, *Legends of the Jews*, vol. 1, Philadelphia: Jewish Publication Society of America, 1909, pp. 51–3.

[4] The LXX does not mention the bronze sea where the priests washed before entering the tabernacle or approaching the altar; Exod. 40.7, 11, 30–32 are not in the LXX.

animals, corresponding to the altar of sacrifice that dislocates the account in Exodus 40.[5]

Each stage in the summary at the end of Exodus is marked by the words: 'as the LORD commanded Moses' (Exod. 40.19, 21, 23, 25, 27, 29, 32). This corresponds to the LORD's revelation to David of the temple plan (only recorded in 1 Chron. 28.19), and is an example of Moses taking over the role of the king. The first four stages of the construction and the last represent the first four days of creation and the sixth: Day One (not 'the first day') was the separation of light from darkness; the second day was the veil to represent the firmament separating what is above from what is below; the third day was the table for bread, wine and incense to represent the earth and its plants; the fourth day was the seven-lamp menorah to represent the lights of heaven (the sun, moon and five known planets); and the sixth day was the laver of water to purify the high priests, representing the creation of the male-and-female human being.[6] In this scheme the menorah is outside the veil, but the early Christian vision of

---

[5] The reason for this speculation – and like so much else in biblical studies, it can only be speculation – is that the original pattern may have been for a temple that did not offer the Mosaic-style animal sacrifice and so had no need of a great altar for animal and bird sacrifices. There had been animals offered as a substitute for human sacrifice, notably as a substitute for the king on the Day of Atonement, and there had been child sacrifice that Isaiah did not condemn. The Melchi-Zedek priests offered bread and wine; the Hebrew temple at Yeb in southern Egypt offered only cereal offerings, libations and incense until blood sacrifices were introduced and this prompted the local population to burn the temple in 411 BCE (see my book *The Mother of the Lord*, vol. 1, London: T&T Clark, 2012, pp. 20–1); and there is an alternative account of the consecration of a high priest in the *Testament of Levi* 8.2–11, a late second-temple text preserved by Christians, which does not involve the animal sacrifices prescribed in the law of Moses (Lev. 8.1–36), but only the holy oil, the holy food and the holy vestments. A good case can be made for the cereal offerings that are now part of the law of Moses having originated as a distinct and older system that was incorporated into the Mosaic system of blood sacrifices but retained a position of precedence (A. Marx, *Les offrandes végétales dans l'Ancien Testament*, Leiden: Brill, 1994). This would explain a cryptic passage in Hosea, a contemporary of Isaiah:

> I desire steadfast love, *ḥesedh*, and not sacrifice,
> The knowledge of God, *ᵉlohîm*, rather than whole burnt offerings,
> Like Adam they transgressed the covenant,
> There they were treacherous against me.
> (Hos. 6.6–7, my translation)

This implies that there had been a covenant with Adam based on loving kindness and heavenly knowledge, superseded by a cult of blood sacrifices. The Christians believed that the death of Jesus had been the last human sacrifice, and not offered with substitutes, and their later worship used wine and bread to represent the blood offerings.

[6] A summary of later Jewish legends about the days of creation and the tabernacle can be found in Ginzberg, *Legends of the Jews*, pp. 50–1.

the restored temple had the menorah within the veil, set by the throne in the holy of holies (Rev. 4.5).

This position of the menorah is implied in the *Song of the Three Young Men* (the Benedicite)[7] which summons all creation, in the traditional order, to worship the LORD on his throne. The *Song* begins by calling on the creation within the veil – the angels, the powers, the weathers – and then calls to the creation outside the veil – the earth, the land, the plants, the waters, fish, birds, animals, people. The creation within the veil corresponds to the list of powers in *Jubilees*, a text that in other respects, as we shall see, seems to preserve material from the pre-Moses stratum.[8] In the Benedicite the sun, moon and stars are listed among the creation within the veil, and so in that pattern, the menorah would have been in the holy of holies, where the first Christians saw it.

Two elements of the biblical pattern are important for understanding the role of the king. First, that 'Adam' was created to be the high priest; and second, that the holy of holies within the veil represented the beginning of creation and housed the chariot throne/mercy seat where the Davidic king sat 'as' the LORD. In Genesis this is called Day One, not 'the first day', to remind readers that this state was not part of the temporal process. It was outside time and beyond time, yet still somehow in the midst of the creation. It was the pre-created light that was separated from the darkness. The 'light' and 'darkness' of John's Gospel presuppose this temple setting. Everything outside the veil represented the material world of time, matter and darkness; but everything within the veil was light, limited neither by time nor by matter. It was the hidden world of God and the angel powers that Isaiah glimpsed when he saw the LORD enthroned (Isa. 6.1–5). The angels and the throne are not mentioned in Genesis 1, because this book was for public reading, and information about the angels and the throne within the veil was secret knowledge. It was only for the high priests (Num. 18.7), but much of it seems to be preserved in the Enochic writings and similar books such as *Jubilees*.

Day One also indicated unity. Rabbi Judan, a teacher in fourth-century CE Palestine, said that Day One was the state when the Holy One was One with his universe;[9] in other words, it was the state of Unity underlying all the distinct and separated parts of the visible world. It was the state of light before the material creation, and was

---

[7] In the LXX of Daniel 3, after v. 23, but not in the Aramaic text.
[8] *Jubilees* 2.2. See below, p. 154.
[9] *Genesis Rabbah* III.8.

separated from the darkness that needed the sun, moon and stars for light. It was the source of light and life. Although this evidence is from a later period, Day One as the unity of the pre-created state explains much in John's Gospel and is therefore likely to have been known to the early Christians. In the temple, the holy of holies was a golden cube (1 Kings 6.20), which in John's vision became the huge golden cube of the heavenly city (Rev. 21.15–18). This was the state where the LORD reigned, and so was the kingdom. Here John saw the throne and all the servants of the LORD who worshipped him. They had his Name on their foreheads because they had been baptized, but in this temple context, wearing the Name also indicated that they were all high priests. They were standing where the LORD God was enthroned in the pre-created light, and they too *reigned* for ever and ever. They were kings (Rev. 22.1–5). Hence Jesus' high-priestly prayer: 'Father, I desire that they also, whom thou hast given me, may be with me where I am, to behold my glory which thou hast given me in thy love for me before the foundation of the world' (John 17.24).

## The secret things

Like the Christians in the vision, so too the temple mystics ascended in their visions and stood before the throne, where they could watch the process of creation and learn its secrets. Since they were outside time, they had an overview of all time. This knowledge, as we have seen, was concealed behind the temple veil and was known as 'the hidden things'. In the Qumran texts it is called the *raz nihyeh* which may mean the secrets of becoming, of how things come to be. The fact that we cannot translate this key term with certainty shows how little is really known about temple teaching in the time of Jesus. There are hints of this secret teaching in the Hebrew Scriptures, but Deuteronomy discouraged it, and this is why so little survives in biblical sources. Isaiah, for example, had been told 'in the beginning' – in the holy of holies, the beginning of creation – what the future of his people would be (Isa. 40.21–23). Habakkuk stood in the tower – the holy of holies was often called the tower – and waited for what the LORD would show him (Hab. 2.1–3).

The Enochic *Parables* are three accounts of what Enoch saw in the holy of holies, and these are important for reconstructing what was meant by 'the secret things'. Enoch stood among the angels and was shown 'the hidden things': the secrets of the heavens and how the kingdom was divided, that is, how the unity of Day One became the diversity of the visible creation.[10] Jesus' high-priestly prayer (John 17) describes the reverse of this process: how the many of the material world would become the One, and how this would be proof of their divine origin.[11] Enoch also saw a Man figure, a Righteous One, who brought his blood into heaven along with the prayers of the righteous on earth. The Man was then 'named', that is, given the Name Yahweh and then enthroned. He was the anointed one and afterwards gave much wise teaching.[12]

As we have also seen, Ignatius, bishop of Antioch at the end of the first century CE, knew that Jesus had taught about the secret things of the holy of holies, because he had restored the high priesthood of the first temple together with its secret knowledge. The writer of Hebrews explained that Jesus was not an Aaronite high priest. He was a Melchi-Zedek high priest, and this was central to the exposition. Now there are no certain references to Aaronite priests in first-temple writings, nor in the texts from the Yeb temple community in southern Egypt, which must be significant. With a change in the high priesthood, the writer of Hebrews explained, came a change in the law (Heb. 7.11–25). The Aaronite high priests had naturally been associated with the law of Moses, which implies that Melchi-Zedek had had another law and that this had been the way of the original temple. Melchi-Zedek had been associated with Abraham, and so Paul's argument that the roots of Christianity lay deeper than Moses was being expressed in another way: the Christians also had the older high priesthood.

## The second God

Not only had there been another high priesthood in the first temple, but before the influence of the Deuteronomists the Hebrews had known of more than one divine being. The other nations had other gods, but they also recognized more than one divine being in their own Jerusalem temple. There was God Most High (El Elyon) who had sons, the Firstborn of whom was the LORD (Yahweh) the God of Israel, and the Mother of the LORD was the Lady of the temple.

In the earlier texts, the deities of other nations were regarded as less powerful, and the God of the Hebrews was the Firstborn, the LORD. There are triumphant claims for the superiority of Israel's God(s) in early texts,

---

[10] *1 Enoch* 40.2; 41.1.
[11] See below, pp. 513–14.
[12] *1 Enoch* 47.1–3, 10; 48.2; 51.3.

for example in Exodus 15.11, 'Who is like thee, O Lord, among the gods?', or '... in the midst of the gods he holds judgement' (Ps. 82.1). There were also fallen or hostile deities, who had temporary power and would be judged and punished by the God of the Hebrews. We glimpse them in Psalm 58, where the righteous pray for their defeat and punishment; and in Psalm 82, where they are 'the sons of the Most High' (v. 6) facing judgement. In this psalm, the angelic state was linked to the possession and right use of secret knowledge, and those expelled from this state lost their knowledge and had to live in darkness as mortals.

> They have no knowledge, no understanding, they walk about in darkness ...
> You are *elohim*, all of you sons of Elyon,
> But like Adam you shall die, and like one of the princes you shall fall.
> (Ps. 82.5, 6–7, my translation)

In exilic texts the other gods were dismissed as non-existent, for example, in the Second-Isaiah. The test was the possession of that secret knowledge, in this case, of the future:

> Tell us what is to come hereafter,
> That we may know that you are gods;
> Do good, or do harm,
> That we may be dismayed and terrified.
> Behold, you are nothing,
> And your work is naught;
> An abomination is he who chooses you.
> (Isa. 41.23–24)

In some post-exilic texts, however, the old gods still appear as the angel princes of the nations, and with them there is the Lord, the God of Israel, who is the second God. A fiery Man appeared to Daniel, for example, and told him the future: he would have to fight for his people against the Prince of Persia, and after that the Prince of Greece would come against him. The fiery Man, clothed in linen and wearing a sash of gold, was a high priest (Dan. 10.4–21). All the priests wore linen and a coloured sash, but only the high priest wore a sash interwoven with gold.[13] This fiery Man dressed as a high priest was the Lord, the guardian of Israel. John saw him too, a fiery Man clothed in linen with a golden girdle round his breast (Rev. 1.12–16), and he recognized him as the risen Lord. John was then summoned to stand before the throne and learn about the future, the

---

[13] Josephus, *Antiquities* 3.159.

secret knowledge: 'Come up hither and I will show you what must take place after this' (Rev. 4.1).

The present Book of Daniel was compiled in the mid-second century BCE, during the war led by the Maccabees against the Syrians, but it was a reworking of much older material. The Man ascending to heaven and being enthroned was a vision from the time of the Davidic kings (Dan. 7.9–14), and the angel princes were the gods of the other nations as they were being described in the mid-second century BCE. The Man in Daniel's vision went up to the 'Ancient of Days', another God. He was *offered* before him, but 'offered' here has the technical sense of a temple offering. When he had been offered, the Man was enthroned. It was recognized long ago that this vision had much in common with the myths of ancient Ugarit, where the god Baal ascended with clouds,[14] and with Psalm 2, where the Davidic king was enthroned.[15]

There are signs that this text has been reworked to obscure the original meaning. The interpretation given after the vision is that the Man figure represents the 'people of the saints of the Most High' (Dan. 7.25, 27), but the Aramaic is awkward in both verses, making 'Most High' into a plural form. The Man did not originally represent the people, but was the ancient Davidic king, who perhaps – we can only guess – had had the title: 'the Holy One of the Most High'. Collective sonship was a characteristic of the Deuteronomic reuse of the older material, as in 'You are the sons of the LORD your God' (Deut. 14.1) addressed to the whole people, and not just to the king. So too the Holy One became *the holy ones*, the saints, of the Most High. The argument implied here continued well into the Christian era, for example in the writings of Aphrahat in the early fourth-century Syrian church. The Man in Daniel's vision could not have been the Jewish people, he argued, because they had never come upon the clouds of heaven. The Christians had inherited the worldly kingdom (he was writing not long after Constantine became the Roman emperor), but the Jews had not.[16]

Eissfeldt pointed out many years ago[17] that there is no rivalry in the Hebrew biblical texts between El and Yahweh, and that a small group of early texts survives, many in Genesis, where El is clearly a separate deity from Yahweh. Now *'el* can mean simply 'a god', but in many texts it is a

---

[14] J. A. Emerton, 'The Origin of the Son of Man Imagery', *Journal of Theological Studies* 9 (1958), pp. 225–42.
[15] A. Bentzen, *King and Messiah*, English translation London: Lutterworth, 1955.
[16] Aphrahat, *Demonstrations* 5.21, 23.
[17] O. Eissfeldt, 'El and Yahweh', *Journal of Semitic Studies* 1 (1956), pp. 25–37.

name, and this group of early texts 'name El as the only, or at least the highest, god, without mentioning a relationship between this god and Yahweh or Israel'.[18] 'We thus see that Genesis retained more or less distinct memories that the pre-Mosaic Hebrews, or at least certain groups of them, were connected with the god El ...'[19] In the exilic period, El and Yahweh coalesced, and the prophet who proclaimed this was the Second-Isaiah. There are verses such as 'Oracle of Yahweh: You are my witnesses, and I am El. And from henceforth I am He' (Isa. 43.12–13, my translation) and 'Turn to me and be saved, all the ends of the earth! For I am El and there is no other' (Isa. 45.22, my translation). The most natural way to read them is as a declaration that Yahweh is El, not that Yahweh is a god.

This coalescence of El and Yahweh after the time of Josiah is consistent with other changes at that time. Van Seters, as we have seen, argued that the religion of the patriarchs was in fact the religion of seventh-century Judah that Josiah purged. He drew this conclusion about the occurrence of El names in the stories of the patriarchs:

> Consequently, if one begins, as I have done, with the view that the stories of the patriarchs in Genesis, even in their Yahwistic form, date from the time of the exile, it is still possible to explain such features as the *'el* epithets and the references to sacred trees, pillars and altars as consistent with the theological concerns and religious practices of that period. They are not archaic remnants of a distant or primitive stage of Israelite religion ...[20]

The religion of Jerusalem in the time of the kings, then, distinguished between El and Yahweh, and this distinction accounts for the two figures in Daniel's vision. The One who went with clouds to be enthroned was the Davidic king who became divine. This distinction between El and Yahweh is important for understanding John's Gospel, since it was Yahweh the Son of El Elyon who became the Davidic priest-king and was therefore incarnate as the King of the Jews. Jesus' teaching about Father and Son has its roots in the first temple.

## Melchi-Zedek

The mysterious figure of Melchi-Zedek is an important aspect of the quest for the second God. Genesis says Melchi-Zedek was the priest of El Elyon (God Most High) in Salem (Jerusalem) (Gen. 14.18), and other texts show

---

[18] Eissfeldt, 'El and Yahweh', p. 28.
[19] Eissfeldt, 'El and Yahweh', p. 35.
[20] J. van Seters, 'The Religion of the Patriarchs in Genesis', *Biblica* 61 (1980), pp. 220–33, p. 232.

that *the Melchi-Zedek high priest was Yahweh, the son of El Elyon when he was in human form*. There are two texts in the Hebrew Scriptures that have information about Melchi-Zedek and both have been corrupted. This will prove to be the case with many passages that are evidence for the first temple. The correcting scribes had reason to change them, because Melchi-Zedek is evidence for the divine priest-king in the older royal cult.

First, there is the incomprehensible passage in the *Song of Moses* (not a Melchi-Zedek text) which is an ancient poem attached to the end of Deuteronomy that originally described Yahweh as one of the sons of God:

> Remember the days of old,
> Consider the years of many generations;
> Ask your father and he will show you;
> Your elders and they will tell you.
> When the Most High gave to the nations their inheritance,
> When he separated out the sons of Adam,
> *He fixed the boundaries of the peoples*
> *According to the number of the sons of Israel.*
> For the LORD's allocation was his people,
> Jacob was his allotted portion. (Deut. 32.7–9, my translation)

The Septuagint translation here is so very different that it invites investigation. In the Greek, the words in italics are:

> He established the boundaries of the nations
> According to the number of the angels of God.

A fragment of this passage was found among the Dead Sea Scrolls,[21] just enough to see that the pre-Christian Hebrew had been 'according to the number of the sons of God'. The visible letters are *bny 'l*, and there may have been more letters that have broken off. Those letters are enough, though, to establish that a pre-Christian Hebrew text read 'sons of El'. Yahweh was one of the sons of El, and he received Israel as his people. *Whoever wrote and used this Qumran text of Deuteronomy knew of El and Yahweh as Father and Son*. Someone changed this text and obscured evidence for the two divine beings.

The key verse for showing that Yahweh, the Son of El Elyon (God Most High), was present on earth as the priest-king Melchi-Zedek is the Hebrew of Genesis 14.22: 'I have sworn by Yahweh God Most High ...' Here, Yahweh is identified as God Most High, El Elyon, but this form of the name only occurs here in the post-Christian Hebrew text and in the

---

[21] 4QDeut[j].

## The background to John's Gospel

Targums derived from it. In all the other ancient texts Melchi-Zedek's God is simply God Most High. The Septuagint and the *Genesis Apocryphon* found at Qumran have only 'God Most High'.[22] Josephus has no detail; Melchi-Zedek was simply a priest of God.[23] *Jubilees* has a gap where Melchi-Zedek should be. The evidence suggests that Melchi-Zedek's God was a sensitive issue for post-Christian Jews, since other texts imply that Melchi-Zedek was in fact Yahweh the priest-king appearing to Abram. By giving Melchi-Zedek's God the name Yahweh-El-Elyon, this removed the possibility that Melchi-Zedek himself was Yahweh.

Three other texts support the view that Yahweh appeared as Melchi-Zedek. First, the *Apocalypse of Abraham*, a Palestinian-Jewish text from perhaps the late first century CE. This is an expansion of Genesis 15; in other words, it tells what happened immediately after Abram had met Melchi-Zedek. Genesis says the Lord Yahweh spoke to Abram in a vision, and told him to prepare three animals and two birds for a sacrifice. At sunset, a mysterious fire pot and a flaming torch passed between the prepared sacrifices, and Yahweh promised to give the land to Abram and his descendants. In the *Apocalypse of Abraham*, the figure who appeared to Abram immediately after he met Melchi-Zedek was named Yahwehel. He told Abram he had been appointed to guard him and his heirs, and to *reveal secret things*. Yahwehel was a glowing human figure dressed as a high priest with turban, purple garments and a golden staff. The radiant figure then led Abram up into heaven to receive a vision of the future.[24] Now the form of the name Yahweh*el* suggests he was an angel, like Gabri*el*, Rapha*el* or Micha*el*; and his glowing appearance confirms this. He was the angel Yahweh.

The second example is an early Christian text that tells the same story about Abram. The *Clementine Recognitions*, attributed to Clement bishop of Rome at the end of the first century, says that an angel stood by Abram in a vision and taught him about God and about the future. Other stories about Abraham in this book have the Yahweh of the Hebrew Scriptures called either the 'True Prophet' or the 'Righteous One', that is, Zadok.[25]

The third example is the fragmented text about Melchi-Zedek found at Qumran.[26] This describes the events of the 'tenth jubilee' when Melchi-Zedek would appear and there would be the final great Day of

---

[22] *Genesis Apocryphon*, 1Q20.22.
[23] Josephus, *Antiquities* 1.180.
[24] *Apocalypse of Abraham* 9—32.
[25] *Clementine Recognitions* 1.32–4.
[26] *Melchizedek*, 11QMelch.

*The king in the Old Testament*

Atonement. The text incorporates several prophecies about Melchi-Zedek: he was the unnamed person anointed with the Spirit (Isa. 61); he was the God who would preside at the judgement (Ps. 82); and he was the one who would fulfil Isaiah 52.7: 'Your God reigns'. In his time, teachers/teaching that had been kept 'hidden and secret' would be restored.[27] This Melchi-Zedek was a divine figure, and could well have been the angel high priest described in the *Apocalypse of Abraham*. Three texts of seemingly different origin have the same picture of Melchi-Zedek.

Philo also has interesting information about Melchi-Zedek which points to his being Yahweh. Melchi-Zedek was high priest of God Most High,[28] he said, the priest-Logos who offered Abram bread and wine (Gen. 14.18), unlike the inhospitable Ammonites and Moabites who did not even offer bread and water (Deut. 23.3–4).[29] Here we must note that Philo used the term Logos to describe the Image of God, *seen in human form*. When Moses was on Sinai, for example, he *saw* the most holy Logos;[30] when Hagar ran away, Philo says she met an angel who was the divine Logos, whereas Genesis says she met the angel of the LORD (Gen. 16.7–14).[31] At the end of this story, the Hebrew text is unreadable, but the Septuagint has Hagar say, 'I truly *saw* him face to face when he appeared to me' (Gen. 16.13, my translation). When Balaam's ass saw the angel of the LORD (Num. 22.24), Philo says she *saw* the Logos.[32] Philo also described the Logos as: 'High Priest and King';[33] 'High Priest, his Firstborn';[34] 'God's Man, the Logos of the Eternal'.[35] Above all, the Logos was *seen*. Philo also knew that some people in his time were mistakenly confusing and conflating God Most High and the Logos. Those who could not look in the sun, he said, but could only see the *parhelion*, were saying that this was the sun itself: 'So some regard the Image of God, his Angel the Logos, as his very self.'[36] These must have been the people who added Yahweh to the name of Melchi-Zedek's God, thus conflating Yahweh and El Elyon. These people had lost the distinction between Father and Son.

---

[27] F. Garcia-Martinez, ed., *Qumran Cave 11. Discoveries in the Judaean Desert XXIII*, Oxford: Oxford University Press, 1998, p. 229.
[28] Philo, *Abraham* 235.
[29] Philo, *Allegorical Interpretation* III.82.
[30] Philo, *Confusion of Tongues* 97.
[31] Philo, *Cherubim* 3.
[32] Philo, *Cherubim* 35.
[33] Philo, *On Flight* 118.
[34] Philo, *On Dreams* I.215.
[35] Philo, *Tongues* 41.
[36] Philo, *On Dreams* I.239.

## The birth of the king

Psalm 110 describes how a Davidic prince became the Melchi-Zedek priest in the temple ritual for enthroning the new king and giving him his royal power. This psalm became one of the two most-used proof texts in the New Testament,[37] a fact that must be significant for recovering the role of the Davidic kings in the New Testament, but the Hebrew text in parts is so damaged that some cannot be read at all. Melchi-Zedek and his heavenly birth must have been a problem for the correcting scribes.

The beginning of the psalm is fairly clear: the LORD invited the Davidic prince to sit at his right hand and promised him power to rule in the midst of his foes. Then the Hebrew text becomes almost unreadable. The most opaque passage is translated thus by the RSV:

> Your people *will offer themselves freely*
> On the day *you lead your host*
> *Upon the* holy *mountains.*
> From the womb *of the morning*
> *Like dew your youth will come to you.*
> (Ps. 110.3)

The words in italics show where there are problems in the Hebrew, and those underlined are where the Septuagint seems to have come from a different Hebrew text. The Septuagint is:

> With you is rule on a day of your power
> Among the splendours of the holy ones.
> From the womb before Morning-star, I brought you forth.[38]

This shattered verse describes how the Davidic prince became Melchi-Zedek when he was enthroned. It probably had details of how a human prince became a divine being, and although the process is complicated, the verse is so important that an attempt must be made to reconstruct the original.

The Greek seems to have the best sense for line 2: 'among the splendours of the holy ones.' This indicates a ritual in the holy of holies, among the angels, and the Hebrew can be read that way if the *r* which gives the reading 'mountains' is read as the very similar-looking *d*, which gives 'splendours'. On the other hand, the Hebrew has 'holy one' singular, not the plural of the Greek text, and 'holy one' may conceal one of the

---
[37] The other is Isa. 52.13—53.12.
[38] Tr. A. Pietersma in A. Pietersma and B. G. Wright, *A New English Translation of the Septuagint*, Oxford: Oxford University Press, 2007.

names of the heavenly Mother of the king. In a birth oracle, we should expect to find a mother, and two of the Hebrew words here look like names: 'holy one', Hebrew *qdš*, could have been a vestige of Qudshu; and 'womb', Hebrew *rḥm*, could have been a vestige of Rahmay, both of which were names for the goddess in neighbouring Ugarit who was the heavenly mother of their crown princes. This may not be just coincidence.

With different vowels, the Hebrew consonants for 'your youth will come to you' become 'I have begotten you'. The Hebrew consonants translated 'host' or 'power' can also mean 'birth' because there are two Hebrew roots, both written *ḥûl*, one meaning 'to writhe', as in giving birth, and the other meaning 'be firm/strong'. The presence of 'I have begotten you' favours the meaning 'birth'. There remain 'the dawn/Morning Star', and 'the dew', which is not in the Greek. Now Morning Star was one of the royal titles claimed by Jesus in the Book of Revelation: 'I am the Root and the Offspring of David, the bright Morning Star' (Rev. 22.16, my translation); and a morning star was a great angel, a son of God. Job 38.7 has the two titles in parallel, to describe the angels who were present at the creation. 'Root and Offspring of David' is an allusion to Isaiah's prophecies of the anointed Davidic king:

> There shall come forth a shoot from the stump of Jesse,
> And a branch, *nezer*,[39] shall grow out of his roots.
> (Isa. 11.1)

> For he shall grow up before him like a young plant
> And like a root out of dry ground.
> (Isa. 53.2, my translation)

The shoot/branch image is drawn from the tree of life which was a symbol for Wisdom (Prov. 3.18), and 'dew' was the fragrant oil extracted from the tree of life. 'Dew' was a well-known way of describing the anointing oil: it was on Aaron's beard like the dew of Hermon (Ps. 133.2–3); and in Enoch's description of his own anointing: 'the appearance of that oil is greater than the greatest light, and its ointment like sweet dew, and its fragrance myrrh …'.[40] Enoch then said that this oil transformed him into one of the glorious ones, an angel. Anointing was, in effect, the sacrament of Wisdom, and the king-making imagery was all linked to Wisdom, the mother figure, and her tree.

The latter part of the damaged verse was originally something like this:

---

[39] This was the basis of Matthew's wordplay: Jesus was a *nezer* from Nazareth (Matt. 2.23).
[40] *2 Enoch* 22.9–10.

## The background to John's Gospel

> On the day of your birth
> In the glory of Qudshu/the Holy One(s)
> From Raḥmay/the Womb I have begotten you,
> With dew as the Morning Star.

The psalm continues:

> You are a priest for ever,
> After the order of Melchi-Zedek.

The ritual described in this verse appears also in the *Gospel of Philip*:

> Is it permitted to utter a mystery? The father of everything united with the virgin who came down and a fire shone for him on that day. He appeared in the great bridal chamber. Therefore his body came into being on that very day. It left the bridal chamber as one who came into being from the bridegroom and the bride.[41]

This is the double Incarnation which Paul described as 'the Power of God and the Wisdom of God' (1 Cor. 1.24, my translation). The human king who emerged from the holy of holies was the son of both the LORD and the Lady, and the Lady was also the Mother of the LORD. So too in Revelation the Woman clothed with the sun gives birth to the male child, who is enthroned, but then rides out from heaven as the Bridegroom of the Bride (Rev. 12.1–6; 19.6–16). The Lady gave birth to her son through anointing him with her oil, which Philip describes as 'the fire'.[42]

There was a rich web of symbolism surrounding the oil, and this too must be significant in recovering the role of the Messiah, the Anointed One. First, it could not be used outside the temple/tabernacle (Exod. 30.33), which was understood both literally and also in the sense that its meaning could not be understood outside the temple world-view.[43] According to an early Christian text, the perfumed temple oil was only a copy of the perfumed heavenly oil that exuded from the tree of life. The Son had been anointed with this oil in the reality that the holy of holies represented; in other words, he was anointed in eternity with oil from the tree of life, and the temple priests made their perfumed oil as an imitation. 'God anointed [the Son of God] with oil taken from the wood of the tree of life ... and [the Son] anoints with similar oil every one ... when they

---

[41] *Gospel of Philip*, CG II.3.71.
[42] *Gospel of Philip*, CG II.3.67.
[43] This was explained and expanded by Dionysius, *The Ecclesiastical Hierarchy* 472C–485B. English translation by C. Luibheid, *Pseudo-Dionysius. The Complete Works*, New York: Paulist Press, 1987. English translations call the perfumed oil the 'ointment'.

## The king in the Old Testament

come to his kingdom.' The oil that anointed Aaron was therefore an inferior imitation of the true oil that anointed the Son.[44]

According to Eusebius, a bishop in Palestine in the early fourth century, Moses had seen in a vision all heavenly realities that he had to imitate in tabernacle/temple worship. He had seen the true High Priest of God, of whom Aaron was but an imitation. He had seen the *raz nihyeh*:

> And Moses himself, having first been thought worthy to view the divine realities in secret, and the mysteries concerning the first and only Anointed High Priest of God, which were celebrated before him in his theophanies, is ordered to establish figures and symbols on earth of what he had seen in his mind in visions.

Eusebius found this set out in Psalm 45, which he translated:

> Thy throne, O God, is for ever and ever,
> Wherefore God, thy God, has anointed thee ...
> (Ps. 45.6, 7)

This is one of the many instances of the Christians recognizing the Son, the second God, in the Hebrew Scriptures. Eusebius continued:

> The Anointer, being the Supreme God, is far above the Anointed, he being God in a different sense. And this would be clear to anyone who knew Hebrew ... Therefore in these words you have it clearly stated that God was anointed and became Christ ... And this is he who was the beloved of the Father, and his Offspring, and the eternal priest, and the being called the Sharer of the Father's throne.[45]

The eternal priest was begotten in the holy of holies by the oil: 'With oil I have begotten you ... You are an eternal priest after the order of Melchi-Zedek' (Ps. 110.3b–4, my translation).

There are two other passages about the royal 'birth': the first was the words heard at Jesus' baptism, according to the earliest texts of Luke.

> 'I have set my king on Zion, my holy hill.'
> I will tell of a decree of the LORD:
> He said to me, 'You are my son, today I have begotten you.
> Ask of me, and I will make the nations your heritage,
> And the ends of the earth your possession.
> You shall break them with a rod of iron,
> And dash them in pieces like a potter's vessel.'    (Ps. 2.6–9)

---

[44] *Clementine Recognitions* 1.44–8.
[45] All from Eusebius, *Proof of the Gospel* IV.15. For more detail, see my book *The Great Angel. A Study of Israel's Second God*, London: SPCK, 1992, pp. 198–201.

The Davidic king was the 'son' of the LORD, as explained in the oracle to David: 'I will raise up your offspring after you ... I will be his father, and he shall be my son' (2 Sam. 7.12, 14). The son was born to rule and to judge.

The second is the prophecy later woven into Gabriel's words at the Annunciation (Luke 1.32–33):

> For to us a child is born, to us a son is given;
> And the government will be upon his shoulder,
> And his name will be called
> 'Wonderful Counsellor, Mighty God, Everlasting Father,* Prince of Peace.'
> Of the increase of his government and of peace
> There will be no end,
> Upon the throne of David, and over his kingdom,
> To establish it, and to uphold it
> With justice and righteousness.
> From this time forth and for evermore.                (Isa. 9.6–7)

*The same Hebrew letters, *'by'd*, can also be read as 'Father of Booty', in other words, 'the Warrior', and this seems more appropriate here.

The king is 'born' in the glories of Qudshu/the Holy One(s), and the angels sing 'Unto us a child is born' to celebrate the new Davidic king who would rule his kingdom. The four throne names of the Hebrew text became just one in the Greek: the Messenger/Angel of Great Counsel. It seems that the newborn king was remembered as an envoy of Wisdom, and it was Wisdom that enabled kings to rule: 'Honour Wisdom, that you may reign for ever' (Wisd. 6.21).

Now we encounter two questions: 'motherhood' and 'sonship'. There are so many familiar but largely unexamined texts in the Hebrew Scriptures that mention a mother figure. The female figure in Isaiah's oracle, which the Jewish community in Egypt remembered as *the Virgin*[46] and not as *a young woman* (Isa. 7.14), was the heavenly Mother of the LORD. The only pre-Christian Hebrew text of Isaiah is the great Isaiah scroll from Qumran, which has an astonishing title in Isaiah 7.11: 'Ask a sign from the *Mother of the LORD your God.*' The difference from the Hebrew text that underlies the English translations is only one letter, but that letter is clear. Isaiah's contemporary Micah also spoke of the woman who was about to give birth to the great Shepherd of Israel, in whose time the scattered brethren would return to Israel (Mic. 5.3). Both these are

---

[46] This is how they translated the Septuagint at Isa. 7.14.

familiar texts, and yet the 'mother' in them has been filtered from how they are usually read. There are many examples. When Philo, an older contemporary of John, was explaining the hidden meaning of the words of Scripture, he wrote this:

> We say that the high priest is not a man but a divine Logos ... his father being God, who is father of all, and his mother is Wisdom through whom [fem.] the universe came to be. Further, his head has been anointed with oil, which means that [his mind] has been illuminated with brilliant light.[47]

Wisdom as the Mother again.

Sonship did not mean literally what it means today. The relationship between God and the angels was one of 'sonship'. They were described as 'sons of God', and the LORD, as we have seen, was the Firstborn of the sons of God. In the oldest Hebrew texts they are 'sons of *'ēlîm*, gods' (e.g. Ps. 29.1 and possibly the Qumran Hebrew of Deut. 32.8, but the text is broken, and they may be 'sons of *'el*'). They are *'ēlîm*, gods (Ps. 58.1) and also *ᵉlohîm*, sons of *'el 'elyon*, meaning angels/gods, sons of God Most High (Ps. 82.6). But *ᵉlohîm*, a plural form, is also translated 'God' (e.g. Gen. 1.1), which raises interesting possibilities of other translations, and the distinct possibility that 'God' was understood as being a plurality within the unity. Since the 'sons' had been part of the unity, this explains Jesus' teaching about unity in his high-priestly prayer (John 17).

Although 'emanations' are held to be a later Gnostic phenomenon, this is the best way to describe the unity and plurality of the angel state in Day One as the heavenly powers emerged into the material creation. This characteristic of temple thought was long remembered and became a feature of the much later Kabbalah. Very roughly, the scheme was this: the invisible Father, God Most High, had 'sons' who could become visible (cf. Col. 1.15), and they in turn had 'sons' who were their human/material manifestation. Thus the sons of God Most High were angels, one of whom was Yahweh, and *the sons of Yahweh were those human beings in whom he was present*. Since the angels were all One with/in the Father, so too the human 'sons' were drawn into that unity. They were described as 'sons' rather than as created beings, since they shared the same nature. They were 'begotten not created'. In the royal rituals, Yahweh, the son of God Most High, became present in the king through the anointing, and so the king was the son of the LORD. The LORD, the son of God Most High, spoke to the human David:

---

[47] Philo, *On Flight* 109–10.

> I have found David, my servant;
> With my holy oil I have anointed him ...
> He shall cry to me, 'Thou art my Father,
> My God, and the Rock of my salvation.'
> And I will make him the firstborn,
> The highest of the kings of the earth.
> (Ps. 89.20, 26–27)

And the people saw processions of their God, their King, going into the temple (Ps. 68.24). The divine king, the son of God Most High and also the son of Yahweh, was not just a figure expected to appear in the future; he had been present in Jerusalem with his people: Immanuel, God with us.

The Deuteronomist's description of a coronation has no suggestion that the king was ritually born in the temple as the divine Son, nor that he was worshipped by his people. When the boy-king Jehoash was made king, after hiding from the murderous hands of his grandmother Athaliah:

> Then [Jehoiada the priest] brought out the king's son, and put the crown, *nēzer*, upon him, and gave him the testimony, *'ēdûth*; and they proclaimed him king, and anointed him; and they clapped their hands, and said, 'Long live the king!' (2 Kings 11.12)

The boy-king was brought out from the place where he had been hidden and was made to stand by the pillar according to the custom (v. 14), and the trumpets sounded. The interesting words in this account are 'crown', *nēzer*, and 'testimony', *'ēdûth*: 'crown' is literally 'consecration', as used of the high priest in 'the *consecration* of the anointing oil of his God is upon him' (Lev. 21.12), and so Psalm 89 may describe the anointing; and 'testimony' was used to describe the tables of the law: '[The LORD] gave to Moses ... the two tables of the testimony, tables of stone ...' (e.g. Exod. 31.18); and this would correspond to Deuteronomy's prescription for a king:

> When he sits on the throne of his kingdom, he shall write for himself in a book a copy of this law, from that which is in the charge of the Levitical priests; and it shall be with him, and he shall read in it all the days of his life ... (Deut. 17.18–19).

But what might the 'testimony' have been before the time of Josiah and the law of Deuteronomy? Presumably it would have been whatever writing preceded Deuteronomy in the temple. Since the ancient kings had been the LORD, we can ask what Isaiah had in mind when he said that his oracles of judgement were all in the *Book of the* LORD (Isa. 34.16); and we can also ask about the sealed book that the Lamb was worthy to open once he had been enthroned (Rev. 5.1–10) and which inaugurated the judgement.

## The Righteous One

By the time of Josephus and Philo,[48] Melchi-Zedek was thought to be a name, but Genesis 14, Psalm 110 and the *Melchizedek* text from Qumran have it as two words, suggesting that it was a title, *malkî-ṣedheq*. It meant something like 'Righteous King'. The problem is the form of the word *malkî*, which naturally means 'king of', and so the title/name would have been 'king of righteousness'. This is how Hebrews understood it (Heb. 7.2). The idea of *ṣedheq*, 'righteousness', was fundamental to the identity of ancient Jerusalem, but it is not always clear how the letters should be pronounced: as *ṣedheq*, 'righteousness', or as *ṣadhōq*, more familiar as the English form Zadok. The name Zadok means Righteous One – 'the one made righteous' – and the other form of the name was Zaddik, meaning 'the one who makes righteous' as in 'By his knowledge shall Zaddik my servant make many righteous' (Isa. 53.11, my translation). The Preface to Isaiah mourns the corrupted state of the city where *ṣedheq* ('righteousness' or 'the Righteous One'?) used to lodge (Isa. 1.21); and the same question can be asked of Jeremiah's predicted future blessing for the abode of *ṣedheq*, the hill of the Holy One: 'The LORD bless you, O habitation of righteousness, O holy hill' (Jer. 31.23),[49] which could also be read: 'The LORD bless you, abode of Zadok, hill of the Holy One.' A pre-Davidic ruler of Jerusalem had been named Adonizedek, 'the Lord *ṣedheq*' (Josh. 10.1, 3), the same form of name as Melchi-Zedek. There had been a high priest named Zadok, who anointed Solomon, and whose son also was (high) priest (1 Kings 1.38–39; 4.1–4, but the latter is not a clear text). The community described in the *Damascus Document* considered themselves the true sons of Zadok who had not gone astray and who claimed for themselves the prophecies in Ezekiel, that they would serve in the true temple when it was restored (Ezek. 44.15–16).[50] The Righteous One, then, was associated with the original temple priesthood in

---

[48] Josephus, *Antiquities* 1.180; Philo, *Allegorical Interpretation* III.82.
[49] Also Jer. 50.7, where RSV renders 'abode of *ṣedheq*' as 'true habitation'.
[50] *Damascus Document*, CD III–IV.

Jerusalem, and it was a title that the first Christians gave to Jesus (Acts 3.14).

There is only one detailed account of the king-making ritual in the temple, and this is the enthronement of Solomon. In view of Psalm 110, we should expect this account to include a reference to becoming Melchi-Zedek. Solomon, we are told, sat on the throne of the LORD as king (1 Chron. 29.23), and Psalm 110 is sometimes set in this context: David composing a psalm for his son's enthronement. The passage in 1 Chronicles, invariably altered in translation, gives the clearest biblical picture of the divine king. 'Then David said to all the assembly, "Bless the LORD your God". And all the assembly blessed the LORD, the God of their fathers, and bowed their heads and worshipped the LORD and the king' (1 Chron. 29.20). That is a literal translation of the Hebrew. The people worshipped[51] the LORD-and-the-king. There is no second verb 'did obeisance' as in some English versions. Whatever the assembly did before the LORD was also for the king.

Then there was sacrificing and feasting before the LORD, presumably meaning before the king who was seated on the throne of the LORD, and Solomon was anointed. Here the Hebrew has lost two letters, and reads 'they anointed', and then the text is confused. The usual translation inserts 'him' – derived from the Greek – and becomes 'they anointed *him* as prince for the LORD, and Zadok as priest' (1 Chron. 29.22b). The present Hebrew text, without 'him', could be referring to two people: Solomon the prince and Zadok the priest. But the Hebrew read in the light of the Greek could also imply a double anointing of one person rather than two people being anointed: Solomon was anointed to two roles and 'Zadok' here would then have been a title rather than the name of a second person. The problem is the meaning of the preposition $l^e$, which occurs at the beginning of each of the four vital words: $l^e$Yahweh, $l^e$prince, and $l^e$Zadok $l^e$priest. Yahweh/prince and Zadok/priest are two parallel pairs. This is a late text, so the word could be an influence from Aramaic, but this would then leave the question: why was Yahweh anointed?

Now in this context of anointing, a change in status is implied, and so the regular Hebrew meaning would be appropriate, as in: 'The LORD sent me to anoint you as, $l^e$, king' (1 Sam. 15.1, my translation). The description of Solomon's anointing may then have been: 'they anointed

---

[51] Or however one chooses to translate the Hithpa'lel of *šḥh*. The point is that whatever they did to the LORD, they did also to the king.

## The king in the Old Testament

[Solomon] as the LORD as prince and as Zadok as priest.' The text makes clear that Solomon had become Yahweh, for Solomon sat on the throne of the LORD as, $l^e$, king (1 Chron. 29.23). We should expect a similar construction for the pair Zadok/priest, and when the temple was dedicated, Solomon did act as priest: he led the prayers, gave the blessing, and offered the sacrifices (2 Chron. 6.1–3, 12–13; 7.5). He also consecrated additional space in the temple court, to accommodate the huge number of sacrifices (2 Chron. 7.7). The confused state of the Hebrew text probably conceals the true nature of the ancient kings and is thus another opaque Melchi-Zedek text. Here Solomon became the LORD, the king, exactly as Isaiah had seen in his call vision: 'My eyes have seen the King, the LORD of Hosts' (Isa. 6.5). He also became Zadok/Zaddik the priest, Zadok being a title rather than a name, and so held by more than one person. The account of Solomon's enthronement in 1 Chronicles 29 originally described how he became the human presence of the LORD, the king ('I have begotten you with dew', Ps. 110.3) and also the high priest ('a priest for eternity', Ps. 110.4, my translations). He became Melchi (king) – Zedek (righteous one).

Jeremiah, in the dark days after Josiah's purges, looked forward to the return of such a king:

> Behold the days are coming, says the LORD, when I will raise up for David a righteous branch, and he shall reign as king and be wise, and he shall do justice and righteousness in the land ... And this is the name by which they will call him: 'Yahweh our $ṣdq$'. (Jer. 23.5–6, my translation)

We do not know how the second part of the Yahweh name should be read; it could be 'the one who makes us righteous', or 'our Righteous One': Yahweh our Righteous One. Zechariah had a similar hope. He assured the Lady of Jerusalem that her king would return:

> Rejoice greatly, O Daughter of Zion!
> Shout aloud, O Daughter of Jerusalem!
> Behold, your king comes to you,
> He is a Righteous One and a Victor.
> (Zech. 9.9, my translation)

Isaiah, in an obscured text about the mystery, looked forward to the coming of the Righteous One. The present Hebrew text is read:

> From the ends of the earth we hear songs of praise,
> Of glory to the Righteous One.
> But I say, 'I pine away, I pine away. Woe is me!

For the treacherous deal treacherously,
The treacherous deal very treacherously.'

(Isa. 24.16)

The text must have been difficult for a long time, because the Septuagint is very different. The Targum, however, shows that some people understood the word *raz* as 'mystery', which was its meaning in later Hebrew. The Targumist read the Hebrew as 'My mystery for me, my mystery for me', which s/he expanded as 'The mystery of the reward of the righteous has been shown to me, the mystery of the punishment of the wicked has been revealed to me.' The Righteous One revealed a mystery, and it seems that Jesus applied this text to himself.

There are two places where an *agraphon*[52] has Jesus cite this text. A book attributed to Clement of Rome has Peter say this: 'We remember that our Lord and teacher commanding us, said: "Keep my mysteries/secrets for me and the sons of my house." Wherefore also he explained to his disciples privately the mysteries of the kingdom of heaven.'[53] Clement of Alexandria also knew this *agraphon*.[54] The first Christians sang this as the words of the LORD: 'Keep my mystery, you who are kept by it … ',[55] and the *Acts of John* has Jesus saying this to his disciples in Gethsemane: 'Keep silence about my mysteries.'[56] These mysteries were the secret teaching that distinguished Jesus' disciples from those outside their community: 'To you has been given the secret of the kingdom of God, but for those outside everything is in parables' (Mark 4.11). This was the knowledge that the Righteous One was given so that he could make many righteous (Isa. 53.11).

Jesus also spoke of the teaching/knowledge being in a place, and how some people had barred access to this place. When he was in dispute with some experts in the law of Moses, he accused them of killing the prophets and building their tombs, a reference to the Deuteronomists and their heirs suppressing prophecy unless it had been fulfilled or was in accordance with the law of Moses (Deut. 18.15–22). Wisdom had sent her prophets and envoys, Jesus said, and they had killed and persecuted them. 'Woe to you lawyers! for you have taken away the key of knowledge; you did not enter yourselves, and you hindered those who were entering' (Luke 11.52). Here the two traditions were set side by side and in conflict:

---

[52] A saying attributed to Jesus that is 'not written' in the canonical Gospels.
[53] *Clementine Homilies* 19.20.
[54] *Miscellanies* 5.10.
[55] *Odes of Solomon* 8.10.
[56] *Acts of John* 96.

the law of Moses and the knowledge which the Righteous One brought from heaven.

## Wisdom from heaven

The priest-king brought this knowledge down from heaven. The scorn in Deuteronomy – 'Who will go up for us to heaven, and bring it to us, that we may hear it and do it?' (30.11) – was directed against this claim. Solomon was proverbially wise; he went to the great high place at Gibeah to offer sacrifice and, presumably, to seek revelation there. Solomon asked for an understanding mind to govern well, and the LORD promised him both a wise and understanding mind and also great wealth (1 Kings 3.3–14). This is one of the few surviving traces of the temple-wisdom of the kings. Most of what remains in the Hebrew Scriptures is now secularized proverbs attributed to Solomon (Prov. 1.1; 10.1), and preserved by Hezekiah (Prov. 25.1), with nothing to suggest that this wisdom had once been the secrets of creation and history revealed in the holy of holies.

The ancient wisdom was not forgotten; it survived elsewhere, beyond the new ways of the Deuteronomists and their heirs. Some traces can still be found in the Hebrew texts, but, lacking a context, they are not recognized for what they are. Isaiah's Servant, for example, was exalted and lifted up and became wise, and the knowledge he received in his ascended state enabled him to restore others to righteousness. He became the Righteous One (Isa. 52.13; 53.11).

There is one passage in Proverbs which shows how the king received secret knowledge in the holy of holies, but its context has been altered and the opening lines are almost unreadable. Proverbs 30.1–4 is now listed in Hebrew as 'The words of Agur son of Jakeh of Massa', but the Septuagint read the letters as 'Son, fear my words and when you have received them repent', suggesting that Agur son of Jakeh may be a fiction. Another opaque line follows: 'The man says to Ithiel, to Ithiel and Ucal ...' of which it has been said: 'In such a verse there is hardly a glimmer of light.'[57] Using the rules of the correcting scribes, in this case rearranging the letters, a comprehensible sentence reappears. Ithiel, rather than being a name, is from the verb *'th* meaning 'come', and 'To Ithiel', *l'yty'l*, rearranged becomes *'tytyl'l*, 'I came to God'. Ucal, rather than being a name, is from the verb *ykl* meaning 'to be able' or 'to have power', as in: 'You are *able to* [do] all things' (Job 42.2); 'I am not *able to* endure iniquity' (Isa. 1.13); or

---
[57] W. McKane, *Proverbs*, London: SCM Press, 1970, p. 644.

## The background to John's Gospel

'The king is not *able* [to do] anything against you' (Jer. 38.5, my translations).

The first line is then 'I came to God, I came to God and endured [his presence]'; cf. 'For destruction from God was a terror to me, and by reason of his highness I could not *endure*' (Job 31.23, AV). The context of this terror, but not these precise words, is found in Isaiah's description of standing before the throne:

> Who among us can dwell with the devouring fire?
> Who among us can dwell with everlasting burnings?
> He who walks righteously [from the word *ṣdq*] and speaks uprightly ...
> Your eyes will see the king in his beauty ... (Isa. 33.14, 15, 17)

Then the unknown figure in Proverbs 30 describes his former state and how he was transformed from being *ba'ar* to being wise. The key word here, *ba'ar*, was used to describe people who lacked wisdom, especially about the work of the Creator, and the words used to translate it are indicated in italics:

> How great are thy works, O LORD !
> Thy thoughts are very deep!
> The *dull* man cannot know,
> The stupid cannot understand this ...
> (Ps. 92.5–6; also Ps. 94.8)

The people who possessed this knowledge were, proverbially, the sons of ancient kings. Thus Isaiah said:

> The princes of Zoan are utterly foolish;
> The wise counsellors of Pharaoh *give stupid* counsel.
> How can you say to Pharaoh,
> 'I am a son of the wise,
> A son of ancient kings'? (Isa. 19.11)

The disordered lines in Proverbs 30 were once something like:

> For I was more stupid than a Man
> And I did not have the discernment of Adam.
> (Prov. 30.2)

Then we follow the Septuagint, whose translators must have known this text before the 'corrections' were made. Instead of reading *l'*, 'not' – 'For I have not learned wisdom' – we undo the work of the correcting scribes and invert the letters to *'l*, 'God'. The line then becomes: 'And God has taught me wisdom ...', which is the Septuagint text, and must have been the Hebrew that the translators had before them. The whole section was originally:

> I came to God, I came to God and endured [his presence];
>
> For I was more stupid than a Man
> And I did not have the discernment of Adam.
> And God has taught me wisdom,
> I learned the knowledge of the holy ones. (Prov. 30.1b–3)

'Man' is written with a capital letter because the Man was a significant figure in the world of the temple: a Man (or Son of Man, which is just idiomatic Hebrew for the same thing) was a divine being, whereas an animal indicated a mortal. Adam was the original Man, created to eat from the tree of life and to be wise, and, as the Image of the Creator, to uphold the creation. Luke described Adam as the son of God (Luke 3.38).

Becoming a Man in temple tradition meant becoming divine: *theōsis*. In the dream histories of *1 Enoch* (one of the later parts of the Enochic collection) Noah and Moses both began life as animals and were transformed by acquiring knowledge: Noah was born a white bull, but one of the archangels instructed him in a secret and he became a Man;[58] Moses was born a sheep, but after he had been instructed on Sinai he became a Man.[59] Heavenly knowledge transformed a mortal into a Man, and the angels were also Men. The Man Gabriel flew to Daniel: 'He made me understand and he said to me, "O Daniel, I have now come to make you wise with discernment"' (Dan. 9.21–22, translating literally), and he then revealed the future. John saw 'a Man, that is, an angel', measuring the golden city (Rev. 21.17). Pilate presented Jesus to the Jews: 'Behold the Man' (John 19.5, my translation). Jesus was dressed as the king.

The unknown speaker in Proverbs 30 described what he learned from God as wisdom, the knowledge of the holy ones (the Hebrew word is plural). This could mean either 'the knowledge that the angels possessed', as in Psalm 82.5, where the sons of God Most High were to be made mortal for abusing their knowledge; or it could mean knowledge about the angels, which in temple tradition meant knowing their names. Josephus said that the Essenes were sworn to preserve (secrecy about) their writings and the names of the angels;[60] and there is a broken text in *1 Enoch* that describes how an evil angel tried to learn the great hidden

---

[58] *1 Enoch* 89.1.
[59] *1 Enoch* 89.36.
[60] Josephus, *War* 2.142.

Name so as to have power over the creation.⁶¹ What follows in Proverbs 30 suggests that the latter meaning was intended here. This is the Septuagint text, with the Hebrew in italics for comparison:

> Who has ascended to heaven and come down?
> Who has gathered the wind in his bosom [*fists*]?
> Who has wrapped the waters in his garments?
> Who has taken control of [*established*] all the ends of the earth?
> What is his name?
> Or the name of his children [*his son*] that you may know?
> (Prov. 30.4)

Finally, the context of the passage has been changed in the Hebrew text, and the wisdom saying is now attributed to Agur son of Jakeh. In the Septuagint, however, this passage appears after a version of Proverbs 24.22 that is much longer than the Hebrew text and describes the words of a king:

> The tongue of a king is a short sword and not flesh,
> Whoever is handed over will be destroyed.
> If his anger is sharpened, it takes people with leather cords.
> It devours the bones of men and burns like a flame,
> So that they cannot be eaten by young eagles.
> (LXX Prov. 24.22cde)

The picture, though strange, is somehow familiar: these were the traditional images for the powerful teaching given by the divine king. This is how Isaiah, who knew the divine kings in Jerusalem, described the Anointed One from the house of David:

> With righteousness he shall judge the poor,
> And decide with equity for the meek of the earth;
> And he shall smite the earth with the rod of his mouth,
> And with the breath of his lips he shall slay the wicked.
> (Isa. 11.4)

The LORD made the mouth of his Servant like a sharp sword (Isa. 49.2), and John described a sharp sword coming from the mouth of the risen LORD when he saw him robed as a high priest, and again when he rode out to fight the armies of the beast (Rev. 1.16; 19.15). Familiar too, by now, is the fact that a text about the anointed kings – yet another text – is no longer readable.

---

⁶¹ *1 Enoch* 69.13–15; see below, pp. 511–12.

Scholars have suspected for a long time that the dislocation and muddle in this passage did not happen by accident.[62] McKane wrote this in his commentary on Proverbs:

> It is impossible to believe that [this state of the text] can have happened by accident. It can only have happened as a deliberate process of mystification, in which case one has to look for a motive. Why should such a riddle be constructed? ... If then we are to think in terms of deliberate mystification, we should look for an original which has the appearance of being theologically scandalous.[63]

Now theological scandal was precisely what the correcting scribes set out to remove from the sacred Hebrew texts, and so we suspect their work here. A righteous king went up to heaven and there learned the secrets of the creation and of history. Then he returned to teach what he had learned. Hence the Baptist's words about Jesus: 'He who comes from heaven is above all. He bears witness to what he has seen and heard, yet no one receives his testimony' (John 3.31b–32).

Only a few traces of these wise kings remain in the Hebrew Scriptures: Solomon had 'wisdom and understanding beyond measure'; he uttered 3,000 proverbs, and 1,005 songs. 'He spoke of trees, from the cedar that is in Lebanon to the hyssop that grows out of the wall; he spoke also of beasts, and of birds, and of reptiles, and of fish. And men came from all peoples to hear the wisdom of Solomon ...' (1 Kings 4.29, 33, 34). The Jewish community in Egypt, however, the spiritual descendants of those who kept the ways of the original temple, attributed rather more to Solomon's wisdom.

> For it is he who gave me unerring knowledge of what exists,
> To know the structure of the world and the activity of the elements;
> The beginning and end and middle of times,
> The alternations of the solstices and the changes of the seasons,
> The cycles of the years and the constellations of the stars,
> The natures of animals and the tempers of wild beasts,
> The powers of spirits and the reasonings of men,
> The varieties of plants and the virtues of roots.
> I learned both what is secret and what is manifest
> For Wisdom, the fashioner of all things, taught me.
>
> (Wisd. 7.17–22)

---

[62] See C. C. Torrey, 'Proverbs, chapter 30', *Journal of Biblical Literature* 73 (1954), pp. 93–103.
[63] McKane, *Proverbs*, p. 644.

The biblical texts give nothing of the hidden knowledge taught by Wisdom: the structure of the world, for example, or astronomy and the calendar, but all this and more is found in *1 Enoch* as the knowledge revealed to Enoch in the holy of holies.[64] A Jewish text from the early second century CE, *2 Baruch*, attributes all this knowledge to Moses, as we should expect, since he took over the roles of the ancient king.[65] On Sinai he had been shown what Enoch had learned in the holy of holies.

## The Servant

This role of the Davidic king and his heavenly knowledge is seen most clearly in Isaiah's fourth Servant song. The figure of the Servant is central to John's writings, both the Gospel and Revelation, where the Servant appears as the Lamb due to wordplay, as we shall see. There are four passages in the Second-Isaiah that seem to be quotations from earlier poetry about a suffering figure, presumably the later disciple reinterpreting material from the original Isaiah. Three of the four are used of Jesus in the New Testament: Isaiah 42.1–4, which was quoted at Jesus' baptism; Isaiah 49.1–6, alluded to in the Song of Simeon (Luke 2.29–33); [Isaiah 50.4–9]; and Isaiah 52.13—53.12, the fourth Servant song, which, together with the Melchi-Zedek psalm, is the most quoted text in the New Testament. The fourth Servant song is also another text in which the pre-Christian Hebrew from Qumran is significantly different from the later Hebrew text.[66] The Servant was an important figure for understanding Jesus.

In the fourth Servant song, the LORD spoke through his prophet, and so the poem begins: 'My Servant ...' The Targum, however, has 'My Servant *the Anointed One*', which is not in the present Hebrew text. It is, however, in the pre-Christian Qumran text, which has one more letter on the word 'marred' (Isa. 52.14) which makes it 'anointed'. The Servant was the Anointed One, and the people who used the *Didache* prayers would have known this when they described Jesus as the Servant. The Servant would be *śkl*, which the RSV translates 'shall prosper', but the Hebrew word can also mean 'shall have insight/understanding', and this is how the Septuagint understood the word: he 'shall understand'. The first part of the song was:

---

[64] Mainly in the *Parables of Enoch*, cc. 37—71, but there is also a long astronomy section, cc. 72—82.
[65] *2 Baruch* 59.4-12.
[66] The Isaiah scroll, 1QIsa$^a$.

> Behold my Servant shall have understanding,
> He shall be exalted and lifted up and shall be very high.
> As many were astonished at him [Heb. has 'you'],
> He was anointed more than a man in his appearance,
> And his form from beyond the sons of Adam.
> (Isa. 52.13–14, my translation)

'Exalted and lifted up' are the words Isaiah used to describe the LORD whom he saw in his vision (Isa. 6.1); and 'anointed beyond human appearance' implies the transfiguration that Enoch described when he was anointed. The Targum knew this too, but has the line in another place, after 53.2: 'His appearance shall not be that of a common man, but his countenance shall be a holy brightness, *zyw*.' Maybe there was a different text, but whatever the original, this was the exalted king, anointed, transfigured and given heavenly knowledge. He had become an angel, and two of his titles are known: he was the Angel of Great Counsel, and he was the Man/Son of Man.

He also performed the atonement ritual. The Qumran *Melchizedek* text expected Melchi-Zedek to bring the great Day of Atonement at the end of the tenth jubilee, and the fourth Servant song links atonement to the role of the exalted Anointed One. The original poem shows signs of being an interpretation of contemporary events, most likely the near-fatal illness of Hezekiah, from which he recovered (Isa. 38.1–8).[67] The key word here is *yazzeh*, which means 'sprinkles' (as in Lev. 16.14), and this was the action of the high priest on the Day of Atonement, sprinkling the blood (Isa. 52.15). Both AV and RSV translate the word 'startles', thus obscuring the context of the song. This has happened in many other places in the song, maybe the result of wordplay that was characteristic of temple discourse, or maybe the work of the scribes.

- 'To whom has the arm of the LORD been revealed' could also be read: 'to whom has the seed/son of the LORD been revealed?' (Isa. 53.1). So too 'he shall see his offspring' can be read as: 'he shall be revealed as the son' (Isa. 53.10).
- 'Young plant' can also mean 'suckling child' as in the Septuagint 'little child'. 'A root from dry ground' (Isa. 53.2) would then allude to the royal title claimed by Jesus in Revelation 22.16 ('I am the Root and the Offspring of David, the Bright Morning Star', my translation); and 'dry

---

[67] See my article 'Hezekiah's Boil', *Journal for the Study of the Old Testament* 95 (2001), pp. 31–42.

ground' in Hebrew looks very like the word for 'Zion'. This was the crown prince in Zion.
- The Servant suffered. 'Upon him was the chastisement that made us whole, and with his stripes we are healed' (Isa. 53.5) can also be read: 'the covenant bond of our peace was upon him, and by his joining us together we are healed'.[68]
- 'They made his grave with the wicked, and with a rich man in his death' (Isa. 53.9) can also be read: 'He gave the goats for his offering and the goat for his death', a reference to the two goats which were used as substitutes for the high priest in his symbolic self-offering on the Day of Atonement; cf. the emphasis in Hebrews 9.11–12, where Jesus' death was the true atonement offering, and not made with substitute animals.

The Servant's self-offering was an *'āšām* sacrifice (Isa. 53.10), offered for sacrilege against holy things or violation of the covenant,[69] further evidence that this was the Day of Atonement sacrifice. 'He poured out his soul to death' (Isa. 53.12) refers to the blood pouring at the end of the atonement ritual, when any blood that remained after the sprinkling was poured under the great altar (cf. Phil. 2.7).[70]

This ritual was not favoured by the Deuteronomists: there was no Day of Atonement in their calendar, as we have seen, and they included in the Sinai story an emphatic denial that atonement was possible. When Moses came down from the mountain with the tablets of the law and he saw the golden calf, he smashed the tablets and destroyed the golden calf (Exod. 32.1–12). Then he offered himself to the LORD as atonement for their sin. ' "If thou wilt forgive their sin – and if not, blot me, I pray thee, out of thy book which thou hast written." But the LORD said to Moses, "Whoever has sinned against me, him will I blot out of my book" ' (Exod. 32.32–33). This shows clearly that the law of Moses meant individual responsibility for sins, with no possibility of atonement by another person. The role of the royal high priest on the Day of Atonement had no place in the era of Moses.

In the Qumran Hebrew, there is one more word in Isaiah 53.11, 'light', which is also in the Septuagint, giving the line: 'After the sorrow/trouble of his soul he will see light and be satisfied/filled [presumably with the light].' Then we discover the purpose of the knowledge: 'And by his

---
[68] For detail, see my book *Temple Mysticism. An Introduction*, London: SPCK, 2011, pp. 152–7.
[69] J. Milgrom, *Leviticus 1—16*, New York: Doubleday, 1991, p. 347.
[70] Mishnah *Yoma* 5.6.

knowledge shall the Righteous One, my Servant [here Zaddik, which implies action – 'the one who makes righteous'], make many righteous, and he shall bear their iniquities.' This was the double role of the high priest: to uphold the covenant bonds by removing the effects of the sin that had broken them, that is, making everything righteous again; and to give right teaching – heavenly knowledge about the creation – so that the covenant was not broken again. Zechariah sang of his son John who would be a prophet of the Most High, giving his people the 'knowledge of salvation in the forgiveness of their sins' (Luke 1.77). This was more than just the message of forgiven sin; it was the Servant's knowledge – the knowledge that led to salvation – that caused many to be restored to 'righteousness', and so the Baptist, born a priest, would herald the restoration of the ancient ways. During the second-temple period, Malachi had complained bitterly that his fellow priests had not taught true knowledge, and so the covenant had been broken. A priest, he said, was a messenger/angel of the LORD of hosts (Mal. 2.7), and others would describe Malachi's contemporaries as fallen angels.

The other Servant songs reveal more about the Davidic king. The first (Isa. 42.1–4) shows that his role was to give right judgement, *mišpaṭ*, often translated 'justice', meaning the teaching that promoted righteousness. He had to bring forth *mišpaṭ*, which suggests that he brought it out *from* somewhere, the most likely place being the holy of holies.

> I have put my Spirit upon him, he will bring forth *mišpaṭ* to the nations …
> He will faithfully bring forth *mišpaṭ*
> … till he has established *mišpaṭ* in the land … (vv. 1, 3, 4)

The Servant is compared to a damaged branch of the menorah.[71] When the words are read with different vowels, the Servant himself is described as a damaged branch of the lamp who would not be broken off or extinguished.

> A bruised lamp branch, he will not be broken,
> A spluttering wick, he will not be quenched,
> He will faithfully bring forth justice. (Isa. 42.3)

Since the menorah was the symbol of the Lady's tree, the Servant was one of her branches that had been damaged, but would not be broken off, nor would his light be put out.

---

[71] A 'reed', *qāneh*, was also the hollow branch of the lamp (Exod. 25.32).

The second song has the Servant appointed from the womb and named from his mother's body, which is the parallelism of Hebrew poetry. This could mean simply that he was chosen before he was born; or it could refer to the king-making in the holy of holies, which in Psalm 110 is described as birth from the womb and naming: 'from the womb/Raḥmay I have begotten you as the Morning Star ... as Melchi-Zedek ...' His Mother was the Lady. The Servant's mouth was made like a sharp sword, and he was the one who would show forth the glory of the LORD. The third song describes the Servant as a teacher, but the Hebrew of Isaiah 50.4 is far from clear, and one wonders what it was about the Servant's teaching that necessitated this confusion.

It looks as though the First-Isaiah gave three birth oracles about the king:

- the Virgin who would bear a son (7.14);
- the child named as Wonderful Counsellor, Mighty God, Father of Booty, Prince of Peace, which the Septuagint summarized as the Angel of Great Counsel, the Messenger of Heavenly Wisdom (9.6–7);
- the effect of the Spirit upon him when he was anointed – wisdom, understanding, counsel, might, knowledge and the fear of the LORD. These gifts resulted in righteousness and faithfulness, and the whole land full of the knowledge of the LORD (11.1–9).

The First-Isaiah had also given the four Servant oracles, which described the role of the king: to bring forth *mišpaṭ* from the holy of holies, to show the glory of the LORD, to teach, and to be raised up and given the knowledge that would restore many to righteousness. This he effected by making himself the atonement offering that revealed him as the son of the LORD, his human presence. The First-Isaiah has left the fullest contemporary picture of the Davidic king, and it is no coincidence that his writings are the most frequently quoted texts in the New Testament.

All the king's throne names are incorporated into the fourth Servant song, showing that the birth oracles and the songs were all about the same royal figure:

- He had understanding and knowledge (Isa. 52.13; 53.11); a reference to the Wonderful Counsellor.
- He was anointed, exalted and transfigured, causing kings to marvel (Isa. 52.13–15); a reference to the Mighty God.
- He divided the spoils as a victorious warrior (Isa. 53.12); a reference to the Father of Booty.

- He restored the covenant of peace with the *'āšām* sacrifice, making many righteous (Isa. 53.5, 10, 11); a reference to the Prince of Peace.

Isaiah, and sometimes perhaps his disciples, gave many glimpses of the Davidic kings, or rather, the high ideals which were the myth of the monarchy. One, in Isaiah 32, shows how the righteousness of the king affected the whole creation, and not just the well-being of his people. Perhaps this was prompted by disillusionment with the reality of certain kings; we cannot know. The same themes appear in Psalm 72:

> Give the king thy justice, *mišpaṭ*, O God,
> And thy righteousness, *ṣᵉdhāqâ*, to the King's son
> So that he judges your people with righteousness, *ṣedheq*,
> And your poor with justice, *mišpaṭ* ...
> So that the mountains bring peace, *šālōm*, to the people,
> And the hills bring righteousness, *ṣᵉdhāqâ*.
> (Ps. 72.1–3, my translation)

The psalm continues with hopes for righteousness and peace during the king's reign. He will be a mighty warrior whose foes bow at his feet, and to whom kings bring tribute; but he will also care for the poor and the oppressed.

Isaiah 32.1 looks forward to a time when the king will rule with righteousness, *ṣedheq*, and the princes with justice, *mišpaṭ*. The lines that follow differ considerably in the Septuagint. The Hebrew is:

> Each will be like a hiding place from the wind,
> A covert from the tempest,
> Like streams of water in a dry place,
> Like the shade of a great rock in a weary land.
> (Isa. 32.2)

The Greek is: 'And the man will be hiding his words, and will be hidden as from rushing water. And he will appear in Zion like a rushing river, glorious in a thirsty land.' This text must have been opaque when it reached the translator, but there are some clues: 'dry place' is written in the same way as 'Zion', so this may have been about someone who was like streams of water in Zion. The Greek has neither 'shade' nor 'rock', and read the Hebrew *kbd* as 'glorious' rather than 'great'.

This may once have been the LORD appearing as the King, especially in the light of what follows. The gifts of perception granted to the Anointed One by Wisdom are restored: the eyes of those who see will no longer be smeared over, and the ears of those who hear will pay attention; the mind of the hasty will discern knowledge, and the tongue of the hesitant will be quick to speak clearly (a literal paraphrase of Isa. 32.4). This looks very like the removal of the punishment proclaimed in Isaiah 6.10, when Wisdom had been rejected: 'Make the heart/mind of this people fat, make their ears heavy and smear over their eyes; lest they see with their eyes and hear with their ears, and its mind discerns, and repents and is healed' (my translation). The punishment for rejecting Wisdom was to live with what they had chosen, and this is an important theme in John's Gospel. When those gifts of perception were restored, there would be no more false values: the fool called noble, the poor ruined with lying words; and no more devastation in the land: no more barren fields and vineyards, with the soil producing only thorns. All this would end when the Spirit was poured out again, so that there was justice, *mišpaṭ*, in the wilderness and righteousness, *ṣᵉdhāqâ*, in the fruitful field.

> And the effect of righteousness will be peace, *šālôm*,
> And the result of righteousness, quietness and trust for ever.
> (Isa. 32.17)

If the Spirit poured out was the return of Wisdom, then Wisdom was another name for the Spirit. This can be seen also in Proverbs 1.23, where Wisdom calls out to those who have rejected her: 'Give heed to my reproof; behold I will pour out my Spirit on you; I will make my words known to you' (my translation).

## Seeing the LORD

The Davidic king was the visible presence of the LORD, and John emphasized that the glory of the LORD had been seen. Seeing the presence of the LORD was another aspect of the monarchy that became controversial, but exactly how the presence was seen is not known. The Deuteronomists emphasized that no form of the LORD was seen when the commandments were given (Deut. 4.12), but Isaiah said he saw the King, the LORD of Hosts, enthroned in the holy of holies (Isa. 6.5). A vestige of this survived with the second-temple high priests, who were vested with garments made 'for glory and for beauty' (Exod. 28.2). Ben Sira described Simon the high priest on the Day of Atonement:

> How glorious was he when the people gathered round him,
> As he came out of the house of the veil.
> Like the morning star among the clouds ...
> When he put on his glorious robe

### The king in the Old Testament

And clothed himself with superb perfection
And went up to the holy altar,
He made the court of the sanctuary glorious.
(Ben Sira 50.5, 6, 11, my translation)

The high priests in their blessing prayed that people would see the presence of the LORD.

> The LORD bless you and keep you:
> The LORD make his face/presence to shine upon you,
> and be gracious to you:
> The LORD lift up his countenance/presence upon you,
> and give you peace. (Num. 6.24–26)

The people responded with a similar prayer: 'When I call, answer me, my God, my Righteous One ... *Lift up* the light of your face/presence upon us, O LORD ...' (Ps. 4.1, 6, my translation), but there is a problem with the verb in verse 6 and the reference to the blessing has been obscured.[72] There are many other indications that the words of the high-priestly blessing, which must once have been the greatest blessing for Israel, had become controversial: by the end of the second-temple period, the text could not be explained, and some said it could not even be spoken.[73] Targum *Neofiti* did not translate the blessing into Aramaic but left the text in Hebrew; Targum *Pseudo-Jonathan*, however, said that seeing the face of the LORD meant illumination of the mind.

> May the LORD make the graciousness of his countenance shine upon you in the study of the Torah, and reveal to you obscure things and protect you.
> May the LORD show the graciousness of his countenance to you in your prayer and give you peace in all your space.

This was also how the Qumran community understood the blessing:

> May he bless you with all good, and keep you from all evil,
> May he illuminate your heart with the wisdom of life, and grant you knowledge of eternal things,
> May he show the presence of his mercy to you for eternal peace.[74]

Now enlightenment, life-giving wisdom and eternal knowledge are very like the gifts given to the ancient kings, and perhaps passed on by them. An unknown voice at Qumran could sing:

---

[72] The verb is *nsh*, 'test', when *nś'* (which is pronounced in the same way), 'lift up', is expected and makes more sense.
[73] Mishnah *Megillah* 4.10.
[74] *Community Rule*, 1QS II.3–4, my translation.

> You have revealed yourself to me in your power as perfect light ...
> Through me you have illumined the faces of many,
> and you have increased them beyond number,
> For you have given me knowledge of your wonderful mysteries.[75]

It may be that this was how 'seeing the face of the LORD' had always been understood; that encountering the LORD - or whoever was his visible presence - was illumination and revelation.

There are many examples in the Psalms: *Hallelujah*, the most familiar word that survives from the ancient temple, is usually translated 'Praise the LORD', but the Hebrew could also mean: 'Shine, LORD!'[76] People called on the LORD to shine forth: 'Thou who art enthroned upon the cherubim, shine forth' (Ps. 80.1); 'O LORD ... shine forth ...' (Ps. 94.1). The LORD came from Sinai, according to the old poem, and he shone forth with his host of angels when he became king and the heads of the tribes were assembled for his blessing (Deut. 33.2–5).[77] Seeing the glory was seeing the face/presence, hence the words of the blessing: 'I shall behold thy face' (Ps. 17.15), where 'behold' is the verb *ḥzh* that implies seeing in a vision. Isaiah knew that the upright would see the King in his beauty (Isa. 33.17). The Psalmist sang: 'Let thy face shine on thy servant ...' (Ps. 31.16).

> The LORD is my light and my salvation;
> Whom shall I fear? ...
> Thou hast said, 'Seek ye my face.'
> My heart says to thee,
> 'Thy face, LORD, do I seek.'
> Hide not thy face from me.
>                                         (Ps. 27.1, 8–9)

Seeing the face/presence of the LORD became a sensitive matter. At some stage, changes were made in the biblical texts themselves to divert the reader from this idea, and Aramaic translations opted for other words. The problem may have been anthropomorphism, describing the LORD in a human form that was seen. But the original Hebrew texts *did* describe the LORD visible in human form, and the later 'sensitivity' must have been prompted by some development.

First, the Hebrew texts. The most ancient calendars in the Pentateuch list three pilgrimage feasts each year: Unleavened Bread, Harvest and

---

[75] *Hymns*, 1QH XII.28, my translation.
[76] The Hebrew root *hll* can be either 'praise' or 'shine'.
[77] Deut. 33.4 is probably an addition, to adapt the poem for the era of Moses. The verse detaches easily, and the poem makes better sense without it.

## The king in the Old Testament

Ingathering (Exod. 23.14–17; 34.18–23; Deut. 16.1–17). Each says: 'Three times a year shall all your males *appear* before the Lord Yahweh', or something similar. The word 'appear' *yr'h* is given vowels that produce the meaning 'appear', but it could equally well be read with different vowels as 'see'. In these examples, both readings are possible. There are other examples, however, where the text is naturally read as 'see', and to translate 'appear' is simply *not possible for the text*. It is, nevertheless, given as the meaning. Thus Exodus 34.24, 'when you go up to appear before the LORD', would need different letters from those in the text, which actually says: 'when you go up *to see* the face of the LORD'. The same is true of Deuteronomy 16.16 and Isaiah 1.12. The Hebrew Lexicon notes these problems and says that the vowels were changed 'to avoid the expression "see the face of the LORD" '.[78]

Second, there are the Targums, the Aramaic translations of the Hebrew texts. Here, there are three approaches:

- The translations of the old calendars adopted the meaning imposed by the 'new' vowels and had people appearing before the LORD.
- The translation of the Psalms kept the 'appearance', but the way in which the LORD appeared was changed. The 'face/presence' became:
  - the Shekinah, in e.g. Tg. Ps. 22.24;
  - the Brightness, in e.g. Tg. Ps. 11.7;
  - the Splendour, in e.g. Tg. Ps. 13.1;
  - the Glory, in e.g. Tg. Ps. 17.15.
- Most difficult of all was the introduction of the word *memra*, whose meaning is uncertain.

*Memra* is usually translated 'word', and is 'at once the best known and the most problematic of all the distinctive phrases' found in the Targums.[79] Many scholars saw in the *memra* the Aramaic equivalent of the Word in John's Gospel, indicating a mediator between God and the world, a second divine person, but about a century ago a counter-argument began which said that mainstream Rabbinic Judaism had no place for such a second God: *memra* was just a characteristic of Targum translation, meaning something like 'voice, command'. It was never used to translate the Hebrew 'word of the LORD'. This confident statement, made from the point of view of later Rabbinic Judaism, did not take into account the fact

---

[78] F. Brown, S. R. Driver and C. A. Briggs, *A Hebrew and English Lexicon of the Old Testament*, Oxford: Clarendon Press, (1907) 1962, pp. 816, 908.

[79] R. Hayward, *Divine Name and Presence. The Memra*, Totowa, NJ: Allanheld, Osmun and Co., 1981, p. 1.

## The background to John's Gospel

that there were heirs of the original temple who were not Rabbinic Jews and who did have a place for plurality within the divine unity, as we have seen.

When another Targum (*Neofiti*) was identified in 1956, which had far more examples of the term *memra*, there was increased interest in its meaning, and one of the detailed studies of *memra* prompted by the new discovery concluded, interestingly, that the term had originally indicated a sophisticated theological insight *that had been lost over the years*. There had been

> a change and development in the meaning of *Memra* in the course of the Targum tradition. Originally a term bearing a particular and distinctive theology of the Divine Name and Presence, it was used sparingly in carefully chosen contexts. To distinguish *Memra*, the Divine *ehyeh* of God's self designation, from the Tetragram YHWH, the Name by which men address Him, the formula *Name of the Memra* was used, while the *Voice of the Memra* indicated the active divine presence in God's speech, commandments, and statutes ... But at some point in the tradition, the content of *Memra* was lost; how or why we do not clearly know ... Thus strangely, one of the richest and most fertile ideas of Jewish exegesis faded away.[80]

This is the conclusion of a very complex and technical investigation, from which a few key points will be given below. Important for our quest is that *memra* was thought to have been originally a way of describing the divine presence. This was something that became controversial with the Deuteronomists, who emphasized that the LORD was not seen when the commandments were given; there was only a voice (Deut. 4.12). They also emphasized that the presence of the LORD in the temple was his Name dwelling there, and presumably this Name was spoken (Deut. 12.5, 11). In earlier times, the presence of the LORD in the temple had been the royal high priest, who was seen.

The crucial texts for establishing the meaning of *memra* were the accounts of Moses learning the new name, stories that mark the transition, as we have seen, from the religion of the patriarchs to the religion of Moses, and with that transition came a new significance for the name Yahweh. In the first temple Yahweh had been the Son of God Most High, but after the influence of the Deuteronomists, Yahweh and God Most High had coalesced. The prophet who proclaimed this was the Second-Isaiah. The form of the divine Name found most frequently in the Hebrew

---

[80] R. Hayward, 'The Memra of YHWH and the Development of Its Use in Targum Neofiti 1', *Journal of Jewish Studies* 25 (1974), pp. 412–18, p. 418.

Scriptures is Yahweh, meaning 'He who causes to be'; but in the 'transition' story of the burning bush, there is the different and unique form *'Ehyeh*, meaning 'I who cause to be', usually translated 'I AM THAT I AM' or 'I AM WHO I AM' (Exod. 3.14, AV, RSV). This form is the one used by the LORD of himself, since the form Yahweh is, strictly speaking, used by others to address him: 'You who cause to be'. The form *'Ehyeh* shows that the LORD himself is present (and speaking), present in his spoken Name. In the Targums, *memra* was used to represent *'Ehyeh*, even when the Hebrew Scriptures do not suggest it is a divine name, e.g. Exodus 3.12:

- Hebrew: 'And he said, because I will be with you …'
- Targum *Neofiti*: 'And he said, because I, my *memra*, will be with you …'

Further, the divine descent becomes the revelation of the *memra*, e.g. Exodus 3.8:

- Hebrew: 'I have come down to deliver them …'
- Targum *Neofiti*: 'I have been revealed in my *memra* …'
- Targum *Pseudo-Jonathan*: 'I have been revealed to you today because of my *memra*.'

The *memra* was the divine presence, expressed through the personal form of the Name as it is spoken.

In the history of Jerusalem, these changes prompted by the Deuteronomists (no visible presence, the LORD present in his uttered Name) happened during and after the time of Josiah, with the purges and the new emphasis on Moses that marked the end of the first temple. This may account for the second-temple custom on the Day of Atonement: in the temple, and only in the temple, the high priest called out the actual Name, not a substitute such as was used out of reverence on other occasions and in other places. This was the Presence. 'In the temple they pronounced the Name as it is written, but in the provinces by a substituted word.'[81] The Name was called out at the moment when the cleansing of the temple, that is, the renewal of the creation, was completed. As in the *Prayer of Manasseh*,[82] the Name was the seal that secured the creation:

---

[81] Mishnah *Sotah* 7.6.
[82] *Prayer of Manasseh* 3: '[You who] have made heaven and earth and all their order … and sealed it with thy terrible and glorious name …' The *Prayer* is a prayer of penitence, and its context is most likely the Day of Atonement.

> When the priests and the people which stood in the Temple Court [on the Day of Atonement] heard the expressed name come forth from the mouth of the high priest, they used to kneel and bow themselves down on their faces and say 'Blessed be the name of the glory of his kingdom for ever'.[83]

Reconstructing the older temple is always a problem, but Ezekiel, a priest whose family must have served in the first temple (he himself would have been too young) described a heavenly high-priest figure in his jewelled vestments who was cast down from the mountain garden because he corrupted his wisdom, and his temple was burned (Ezek. 28.12–19). He was described as a 'seal of *measurement*' or 'seal of *plan*', two words that look similar in Hebrew, the latter also meaning 'knowledge' in the Qumran *Blessings*.[84] The important word is clear: the heavenly high priest was himself the *seal* (of creation), the role that in the second temple was given to the spoken Name of the LORD, rather than to his visible presence in the high priest.

This new Name *'Ehyeh* as the Presence can be seen in the Second-Isaiah.

- 'That you may know and believe me and understand that *I am He* ...' (Isa. 43.10);
- '... *I am He*; there is none who can deliver from my hand ...' (Isa. 43.13);
- 'I, I am He who blots out your transgressions ...' (Isa. 43.25);
- 'Hearken to me ... *I am He*, I am the first and I am the last ...' (Isa. 48.12).

The Hebrew here is not *'Ehyeh*, but *'anîhû'* (or a variant of it), which means literally, 'I am he'. Deuteronomy has the same expression:

> See now that I, *I am he*,
> And there is no god besides me.
> I kill and I make alive;
> I wound and I heal; and there is none that can deliver out of my hand.
> (Deut. 32.39)

In the Targum, this was expressed by means of *memra*.

> When the *Memra* of the LORD shall be revealed to redeem his people, He will say to the nations, See now that I am He who is there and He who was there

---

[83] Mishnah *Yoma* 6.2. For detail see Hayward, 'The Memra of YHWH', n. 80 above.
[84] *tabhnîth*, 4QBer[a] 1.2.

## The king in the Old Testament

and He who will be there, and there is no other God besides Me. I, in my *Memra*, kill and make alive ...[85]

It seems that when the Deuteronomists denied the visible presence of the LORD and said that he was only heard, the older belief in the 'appearance' of the LORD was changed among the heirs of the Deuteronomists into 'hearing' the LORD, but not among all the heirs of Hebrew tradition. Most of the reverent circumlocutions used in the Targums to avoid saying that the LORD appeared have clear counterparts in the Hebrew text: the Glory of the LORD (Lev. 9.6; Isa. 60.1; Ezek. 1.28); the Name of the LORD (Ps. 8.1; Isa. 30.27); the Presence of the LORD (Exod. 33.14; Isa. 63.9). There is no counterpart in the Hebrew text for *memra*, since it does not, as we have seen, translate 'the word of the LORD'.

So too with Philo, a near contemporary of John. He had many titles for the Logos, sometimes thought to be the Greek equivalent of *memra*. He was, however, quite clear that the Logos was the second God, something denied by scholars on the basis of evidence in Rabbinic texts: 'For nothing mortal can be made in the likeness of the Most High One and Father of the Universe, but (only) in that of the second God who is his Logos.'[86] Philo's Logos was King, Shepherd, High Priest, Firstborn Son, Angel, Man, Seal, all of which show that Philo's Logos was drawn from the original temple and the royal cult.[87] All but 'seal' are images of a human being, whereas the Targum's circumlocutions – Glory, Presence, Name – are abstractions that do not suggest a human form. But, said Philo, *the Logos was seen*: Moses and the elders on Sinai *saw* the Logos,[88] something that Deuteronomy specifically denied in favour of hearing the voice. Philo knew of a visible second God, and one of John's great claims was that he had heard, seen, looked upon and touched the Logos (1 John 1.1).

The second God made visible, according to Ezekiel, was his 'appearance'. This is how Ezekiel distinguished between the sequence of emanations by which the invisible world of the holy of holies emerged and became a material form in the visible creation. His language is consistent and seems to be technical terms. When he attempted to describe his vision of the throne chariot leaving the temple, he distinguished between the invisible 'form', $d^e m\hat{u}th$, which was the

---

[85] Targum *Pseudo-Jonathan* Deut. 32.39; see Hayward, *Divine Name and Presence*, n. 79 above, p. 29.
[86] *Questions on Genesis* II.62.
[87] High Priest, Firstborn, Man, *On Dreams* I.215; High Priest and King, *On Flight* 118; Archangel, *Heir* 215; Seal, *On Flight* 12.
[88] *Tongues* 96.

heavenly reality, and the visionary appearance that he actually saw, *mar'eh*. This pair of words, *dᵉmûth* and *mar'eh*, is found throughout the visions, but only the AV translates the words consistently as likeness = *dᵉmûth* and appearance = *mar'eh* (Ezek. 1.5, 13, 16, 26, 28; 8.2; 10.1, 22). In particular, consider his (now confused) description of the LORD in human form.

> And above the firmament that was over their heads there was the *dᵉmûth* of a throne and its *mar'eh* was like sapphire stone, and upon the *dᵉmûth* of the throne was a *dᵉmûth* as the *mar'eh* of Adam upon it ... Like the *mar'eh* of the bow that is in the cloud on a day of rain, this was the *mar'eh* of the glory round about. This was the *mar'eh* of the *dᵉmûth* of the glory of the LORD ...
> (Ezek. 1.26, 28, my literal translation)

What Ezekiel actually saw was the *mar'eh* of the LORD, and presumably this was how other first-temple priests described the Presence of the LORD in a vision. In material form, however, as the royal high priest, he was the 'likeness', *ṣelem*, of God, just as Adam had been created as the image, *ṣelem*, according to the likeness, *dᵉmûth*, of God.

When such a vision of the Presence was denied and replaced by the divine voice of the Presence, there was wordplay again. Only the Aramaic word has survived, and the *memra*, the divine presence as the Name *'Ehyeh*, replaced the Hebrew *mar'eh*, the vision of the LORD. Philo's visible Logos, drawn from the royal cult, was Logos in the sense of 'correspondence', the visible that corresponded to the invisible form. The Davidic king was the presence corresponding to the heavenly reality of the LORD; he was the high priest, the Servant, and he had been given the heavenly knowledge so as to rule as the LORD, the king.

This was the King of the Jews, the original Davidic priest-king of the first temple. Thus when Matthew wrote that the magi came to worship the newborn king, this was not the later Christian community reading their own worship practices back into the original story. The king of the Jews had been worshipped, as the Chronicler wrote: 'They worshipped the LORD and the king' (1 Chron. 29.20, my literal translation).

# 4

# The king in the New Testament

The New Testament begins with Matthew's genealogy of Jesus, traced back through the kings of Judah and Jerusalem to Solomon and David, and then back to Abraham. It ends with John's vision of the throne in the holy of holies and the servants of God-and-the-Lamb worshipping before him, reminiscent of the Chronicler's account of Solomon's enthronement (Rev. 22.1–5). The conclusion of the Book of Revelation is a collection of early prophecies, which are the words of Jesus as the divine King: 'I AM coming soon', 'I AM the first and the last', 'I AM the Root and the Offspring of David, the Bright Morning Star' (Rev. 22.12, 13, 16, 20, my translations). Thus the New Testament begins and ends with the Davidic kings in the temple, and to this important aspect of the New Testament we now turn.

Before considering John's Gospel in detail, it is important to see how the 'royal' texts and themes in the Hebrew Scriptures were used by the early Christians, since their writings were the public presentation of the royal mysteries in the Book of Revelation. First, we ask, what did the early Christians understand by resurrection, since the ancient kings had been 'resurrected' when they were anointed and transformed. The Messiah was, by definition, resurrected, sent forth from the holy of holies to be the presence of the LORD with his people on earth. Paul said that the resurrection body was not physical; it was spiritual, and it was not necessary to die in order to attain that state (1 Cor. 15.44, 51, 53). Jesus was to change our lowly state into his glorious state (Phil. 3.21), and Paul was emphatic that what he taught was what he had learned, presumably from those who instructed him after his conversion (1 Cor. 15.3–4). This implies the co-existence of both physical and spiritual, just as the disciples saw Jesus at the Transfiguration: the radiant heavenly being who was at the same time the man with whom they shared their days. The *Hymns* of Qumran show that some contemporaries of the first Christians lived and worshipped in a state of 'realized eschatology', believing that the final state of living in heaven was possible for some people before they died. They sang of 'enter[ing] into community with the congregation of the sons of heaven', and of standing as an angel of the Presence, 'in the company of the angels'.[1] Presumably they believed that they were already living the angelic life, as did the divine priest-kings of old.

Some of the early Christians were visionaries who ascended to heaven. John in the Book of Revelation is the most obvious example, but there were others too. Paul had reached the third heaven and there learned things he could not reveal in a letter, presumably the secret knowledge (2 Cor. 12.1–4). Stephen, the first martyr, saw the heavens open and the Son of Man standing at the right hand of God (Acts 7.55–56). Outside the New Testament, there is the *Ascension of Isaiah*, in which 'Isaiah' and a group of others who had taken the names of the ancient prophets left Jerusalem and its wicked rulers, and went to live in the desert. This is a thinly veiled account of the early Christian community in Jerusalem. These people were 'many of the faithful who believed in the ascension into heaven', and they recorded the ascent of their leader 'Isaiah'. 'His eyes were open, but his mouth was silent, and the mind in his body was taken up from him.' He was taken by an angel on a heavenly journey in which he saw history unfold before him, including the descent of Yahweh the Anointed One to become incarnate as Jesus.[2] 'Isaiah' here was probably James, the leader of the Jerusalem church.[3] He had been an ascetic and, apparently, had the status of a high priest, since he entered the holy of holies.[4] He also received visions of the throne, and a book used by the Ebionites was called the *Ascents of James*, and so presumably he was remembered as a mystic who ascended.[5]

## As it is written

The ascending priest-kings reappear in the Hebrew Scriptures if the texts are read without the usual presuppositions:

> Of old thou didst speak in a vision to thy faithful one and say:
> 'I have set the crown[6] on one who is mighty,

---

[1] *Hymns*, 1QH III; *Blessings*, 1QSb IV.
[2] *Ascension of Isaiah* 2.7–11; 7.11; 10.7.
[3] See my book *The Revelation of Jesus Christ*, Edinburgh: T&T Clark, 2000, pp. 193–4.
[4] Thus Eusebius, *History of the Church* 2.25, quoting Hegesippus, a Christian writer in the mid-second century.
[5] 'Ebionites' was the Greek-speaking Christians' name for the Hebrew Christians, derived from their self-designation 'the poor', *'ebhyōnîm*. The term was used at Qumran, and Epiphanius (died 403 CE) included extracts from their writings in his *Heresies* 30.16.
[6] Reading *nēzer*, 'consecrating crown', for *'ēzer*, 'help'.

> I have raised up high one chosen from the people.
> I have found David my servant;
> With my holy oil I have anointed him ...'
>
> (Ps. 89.19–20, my translation)

Or in the last words of David:

> The oracle of David the son of Jesse,
> The oracle of the man whom God *raised up*,[7]
> The Messiah of the God of Jacob ...
> The delight of the psalms of Israel ...
> The spirit of the LORD speaks in me,
> His word is on my tongue. (2 Sam. 23.1–2, my translation)

'Raised up' here is the word that also means 'resurrect' (Job 14.12; Ps. 88.10; Isa. 26.14, 19).

This image of 'raising up' was used of Jesus, but Acts suggests that this raising up happened before Jesus' public life. 'God, having raised up his servant, sent him to you first ...' (Acts 3.26; the verb here is *anistēmi*, whence *anastasis*, 'resurrection'). Earlier, Peter has shown how closely this raising up was linked to ascent and enthronement:

> [David] foresaw and spoke of the raising up of Christ, that he was not abandoned in Hades, nor did his flesh see corruption. This Jesus God raised up, and of that we are all witnesses. Being therefore exalted at the right hand of God ... (Acts 2.31–33, my translation)

This understanding of 'raising up/resurrection' as ascent is seen in the comparison of Jesus and Melchi-Zedek.

> Now if perfection had been attainable through the Levitical priesthood ... what further need would there have been for another priest to *rise up* after the order of Melchi-Zedek, rather than one named after the order of Aaron?
>
> This becomes even more evident when another priest *rises up* in the likeness of Melchi-Zedek, who has become a priest not according to a legal requirement concerning bodily descent, but by the power of an indestructible life.
>
> For it is witnessed of him: 'Thou art a priest for ever, after the order of Melchi-Zedek.' (Heb. 7.11, 15–17, my translation)

The contrast here is between the hereditary Aaronite priesthood, who came to office through the deaths of their fathers, and the Melchi-Zedek priest who rose up and became a priest through indestructible, perhaps

---

[7] Reading with the Qumran text and the LXX.

we could say eternal, life. The contrast is between descent and ascent, between the priesthood of the Moses era and the priesthood of the original temple.

The proof texts for Jesus' resurrection are not those in the Hebrew Scriptures that deal with physical, post-mortem, resurrection, such as:

> Thy dead shall live, their bodies shall rise.
> O dwellers in the dust, awake and sing for joy!
> (Isa. 26.19)

Or 'And many of those who sleep in the dust of the earth shall awake, some to everlasting life, and some to shame and everlasting contempt' (Dan. 12.2).

The Christians chose their proof texts from the psalms and prophecies of the royal cult, and so described Jesus in terms of the resurrection of the Davidic priest-king. Confusion has come into the reading of these texts because the older, pre-Deuteronomic belief that the king was Yahweh has been all but lost.[8]

The most frequently quoted texts in the New Testament are Psalms 2 and 110, and Isaiah 53, all royal texts. The words and themes of these psalms, and the royal oracles and Servant songs of Isaiah, are woven into many different contexts, showing how much these texts shaped the discourse of the early Christians.

Psalm 2 was frequently quoted: the rulers conspiring against the LORD and his anointed, verses 1–2 being fulfilled when Pilate and Herod co-operated in the arrest of Jesus (Acts 4.25–26; cf. Luke 23.12). At Jesus' baptism, the voice from heaven said, 'This is/Thou art my beloved Son', which is Psalm 2.7a, combined with words from Isaiah 42.1, 'my Chosen One, in whom my soul delights'; or, in some versions, it was quoted in full '... today I have begotten you'. Similar words were heard from the cloud at the Transfiguration, with the same difficulty in identifying the precise source of the quotation – if it was intended to be a quotation (Matt. 17.5; Mark 9.7; Luke 9.35; also 2 Pet. 1.17). The words could have been a fusion of both Psalm 2 and Isaiah 42, by those who considered that these two texts naturally belonged together and referred to the same person. Paul, speaking in the synagogue at Pisidian Antioch, said that these words were fulfilled in the raising up of Jesus (Acts 13.33), showing that raising up meant being born as a divine Son. This verse was also the first proof text in Hebrews (Heb. 1.5), and was set with Psalm 110.4 to show that Jesus

---

[8] See my book *The Great Angel. A Study of Israel's Second God*, London: SPCK, 1992, *passim.*

was the Son of God and also Melchi-Zedek the priest-king of Jerusalem (Heb. 5.5–6). The Book of Revelation cites Psalm 2.8–9 several times: in the letter to Thyatira the Son of God promises to his faithful followers that they, like him, will rule the nations with a rod of iron (Rev. 2.26–27); the child of the Woman clothed with the sun was taken to the throne of God to rule the nations with a rod of iron (Rev. 12.5); and the warrior Word of God rode from heaven to rule the nations with a rod of iron, and with his teaching which was the sharp sword from his mouth (Rev. 19.15).

Psalm 110.1 is quoted at Mark 12.36 (and its parallel passages Matt. 22.44 and Luke 20.42–43), showing that 'The LORD said to my Lord, sit at my right hand …', and the debate about its meaning, came from the very earliest memories of Jesus. Jesus alluded to the verse again at his trial (Mark 14.62//Matt. 22.46//Luke 22.69), and this too must have been fundamental to the memories of who Jesus claimed to be. The verse was set by Luke into Peter's address at Pentecost (Acts 2.34); it was alluded to by Paul when he was explaining the resurrection (1 Cor. 15.25), and he linked this verse to both resurrection and Ascension (Eph. 1.20–22). He also extended the application of the verse to include all Christians: 'If then you have been raised with Christ, seek the things that are above, where Christ is, seated at the right hand of God' (Col. 3.1). This must mean resurrection in the sense of ascent and transformation, since Paul reminds these still-living Christians that they *have been raised* with Christ. The verse is mentioned twice in the first chapter of Hebrews (Heb. 1.3, 13) and also at Hebrews 10.12–13; 12.2. The latter is the heavenly vision to inspire Christians, but the examples in Hebrews 1 link this verse to what must have been its original context: the role of the priest-king on the Day of Atonement: 'When he had made purification for sins, he sat down at the right hand of the Majesty on high …' and 'But when Christ had offered for all time a single sacrifice for sins, he sat down at the right hand of God, there to wait until his enemies should be made a stool for his feet'. Psalm 110.4 is also quoted several times in Hebrews: 'You are a priest for ever, after the order of Melchi-Zedek' (my translation) is found at Hebrews 5.6, 10; 6.20; 7.11, 15, 21.

Isaiah's royal texts are also used frequently in the New Testament. Several individual verses of Isaiah 53, the fourth Servant song, are quoted or alluded to, but some seem to be no more than a passing turn of phrase. This suggests that the early community was familiar with this chapter, and the words came easily to mind. 'LORD, who has believed our report?' is quoted at John 12.38 and Romans 10.16, and Luke found an allusion to verse 12, 'he was reckoned with transgressors', when Jesus spoke of his

*The background to John's Gospel*

disciples carrying swords (Luke 22.37). Peter wove a homily about Christian conduct around verses 5, 6, 9 (1 Pet. 2.21–25), in the manner of Paul exhorting the Christians at Philippi to model their conduct on the suffering and humility of Jesus (Phil. 2.5–11). Matthew linked verse 4, 'Surely he has borne our griefs and carried our sorrows', to Jesus' ministry of healing (Matt. 8.17); and when Philip met the Ethiopian (Acts 8.26–39), he was reading verses 7–8:

> As a sheep led to the slaughter,
> Or a lamb before his shearer is dumb,
> So he opens not his mouth.
> In his humiliation, justice was denied him.
> Who can describe his generation?
> For his life was taken up from the earth.[9]

Philip related the words to Jesus.

Of the other Servant passages, the first song is quoted in full by Matthew after Jesus refused to be drawn into controversy with the Pharisees over his healings (Matt. 12.9–21). 'I have given you as ... a light to the nations' (Isa. 42.6)[10] is part of Simeon's song, and so he must have recognized Jesus as the Servant (Luke 2.32). Paul and Barnabas used the verse to justify preaching to Gentiles (Acts 13.37) as did Paul before Agrippa (Acts 26.23). Paul alluded to the second song in his letter to the Galatians, 'he who had set me apart before I was born' (Gal. 1.15; Isa. 49.1), and possibly in his letter to the Philippians, 'I did not run in vain or labour in vain' (Phil. 2.16; Isa. 49.4); and Simeon's 'light to the nations' occurs also in Isaiah 49.6. Paul alludes to the third song, 'Who shall bring any charge against God's elect?' (Rom. 8.33; Isa. 50.8), and Hebrews 1.11 quotes from it: 'they will all grow old like a garment' (Isa. 50.9). These examples do not point to the use of royal traditions, but they do show, by the variety of contexts in which the Servant songs are quoted, that the early Christians were familiar with these texts and wove them into their writings.

The same is also true of the royal oracles earlier in Isaiah. The oracle to Ahaz was quoted by Matthew: 'Behold, the Virgin shall conceive and bear a son ...' (Matt. 1.23; Isa. 7.14).[11] The opening of the second royal oracle, 'the people who walked in darkness have seen a great light', is woven into the song of Zechariah (Luke 1.79; Isa. 9.2), and Matthew saw Jesus'

---

[9] The text in Luke's Acts is an exact quotation from the Septuagint.
[10] Assuming the longer version of this song; some say it is 42.1–4, others 42.1–9.
[11] Matthew has the Hebrew correctly, '*the* Virgin', not '*a* virgin' as in AV and RSV.

## The king in the New Testament

ministry in Galilee fulfilling the prophecy that Zebulon, Naphtali and Galilee would see the light (Matt. 4.15–16; Isa. 9.1–2).

Given the vast amount of the Hebrew Scriptures that is not quoted or alluded to in the New Testament, the use of these royal texts – psalms and prophecies – must be significant. The texts are not always used in an obviously 'royal' context, but their frequent use shows how familiar the early Christians were with these texts. So too with the Book of Revelation. The strangeness of this text must not distract us from the fact that this too is a royal text, possibly a glimpse of part of the royal mysteries, or at any rate inspired by them.

The visions John recorded in Revelation were originally the visions of Jesus that he had been authorized to interpret.[12] The opening lines of Revelation make this clear:

> The revelation of Jesus Christ, which God gave to him to show to his servant what must soon take place; and he made it known by sending his angel to his servant John, who bore witness to the word of God and to the testimony of Jesus Christ, even to all that he saw. (Rev. 1.1–2)

What Jesus saw were the visions that form the main part of the book, chapters 4—22. The setting for all these visions was the temple, and the action centred on the throne and the figure upon it. In other words, these were visions set within the old royal cult, visions of the LORD, the King, and they were either already known to Jesus or else first received by him. Traces of them break the surface in the Gospels: the events that would precede the destruction of the temple (Mark 13 and near parallels in Matt. 24 and Luke 21) are a summary of the vision of the seven seals (Rev. 6); the angel reapers (Matt. 13.36–43) are the angel reapers in the vision (Rev. 14.14–16); Satan's fall from heaven (Luke 10.18) is the fall of Satan in the vision (Rev. 12.9), and Jesus describing the Son of Man enthroned in glory, with his disciples also on 12 thrones, is the final judgement scene (Matt. 19.28, cf. Rev. 20.4).[13] This suggests that Jesus knew the throne visions and that they shaped his ministry. Given the cultural context of the visions, it is likely that they were 'thought' in Hebrew. They offer a way into the Gospels of Matthew, Mark and Luke, who show the importance of the royal tradition in each of their distinctive ways of telling the story of Jesus. This was already woven into what they received from their sources, and was not their own characteristic interpretation.

---

[12] See my book *The Revelation of Jesus Christ*.
[13] For more examples, see my book *The Revelation of Jesus Christ*.

## The enthronement

The first vision of the main part of Revelation is the throne, with the LORD upon it (Rev. 4.2–11). The hosts of heaven were worshipping the one on the throne 'who was and is and is to come', this being a reference to the Targumic (Aramaic) way of expressing the Name (Rev. 4.8). Then the Lion of Judah, the Root of David, approached the throne to take the sealed book, and, despite many who translate this differently, the word is 'book', *biblion*, written within and without, that is, on both sides of the page. The Lion of Judah and Root of David was then described as the Lamb, this being an example of characteristic temple wordplay on the royal title 'Servant'. In Aramaic, 'Servant' and 'Lamb' can be the same word *talya'*, literally 'young one', and this gives scope for the visionaries' custom of describing the angel characters in their visions as 'men' and the human characters as various clean or unclean animals. In this case, the Servant entered the holy of holies and approached the throne as the Lamb, a human being. In temple ritual, a human being entered the holy of holies only on the Day of Atonement, when the royal high priest offered a substitute for his own life/blood in the holy of holies.[14]

Then the Lamb was enthroned and he prepared to sit in judgement. In the vision seen by Jesus or John, the Lamb/Servant who had been offered was enthroned, and as he opened the sealed book, so the judgement came from the holy of holies to the earth. This was the scene in Daniel, where the One who had been presented/offered was given 'dominion and glory and kingdom' (Dan. 7.14). First came the four horsemen, then the seven angels with their tumpets, and finally the kingdom itself was established on earth, the kingdom of the-LORD-and-his-Christ (Rev. 11.15). One of the characteristics of Revelation is the pairing of heavenly and earthly figures,[15] and so this form 'the-LORD-and-his-Christ' indicates the divine being present in the human. This pairing is first found in Psalm 2.2 where the earthly powers conspire against the LORD-and-his-Christ. They have become One. So too in: 'the throne of God-and-the-Lamb shall be in it and *his* servants shall worship *him*' (Rev. 22.3, singular forms after an apparent plural).

This sequence is also found in the *Parables of Enoch*, where the Righteous One takes his blood to the throne and offers it. Then he is given the Name in the timeless state beyond the creation, that is, in the holy of

---

[14] Lev. 16.2 could imply a pre-Moses situation where the high priest had entered more frequently.
[15] See below, pp. 129–30.

holies, then wisdom is revealed to him and by him, and finally the judgement begins. In the *Parables*, the Righteous One is also called the Anointed One.[16] In the Enoch sequence, 'wisdom' takes the place of the sealed book in Revelation. There is no proof that the Christians knew this part of *1 Enoch*, but they certainly knew the temple sequence it describes. Paul's words in Philippians 2, thought to be an early hymn, have the same setting as the throne vision in Revelation, and assume the scene in *1 Enoch*, but Paul gives the additional information that the Righteous One was the Servant, as in Isaiah 53.11:

> Christ Jesus, who, though he was in the form of God, did not count equality with God a thing to be grasped, but emptied himself, taking the form of a servant, being born in the likeness of men. And being found in human form, he humbled himself and became obedient unto death, even death on a cross. Therefore God has highly exalted him and bestowed on him the name that is above every name, that at the name of Jesus every knee should bow in heaven and earth and under the earth, and every tongue confess that Jesus Christ is Lord, to the glory of God the Father. (Phil. 2.6–11)

This passage has the awkwardness of a translation. The significance of the last line should not be overlooked because it is so familiar: it means that all creation would acknowledge that Jesus the Anointed One was Yahweh, and would worship him. After the real, not symbolic, death, he was exalted and given the Name Yahweh, as happened to Solomon at his coronation, when everyone worshipped him. Just as the assembled people had recognized the anointed Solomon as the LORD, so too the whole creation would recognize the anointed Jesus as the LORD. The difference in the New Testament is that the events were not symbolic but real, and so the exalted Servant received the worship of all creation when he had received the Name.

'Servant' was an important title for Jesus in the early Jerusalem church. In the New Testament, the Greek word *pais* was used for the Hebrew *'ebhedh*, 'servant': 'Behold my servant whom I have chosen' (Matt. 12.18); and so when the same title occurs in other places, it probably has the same significance. In his temple sermon, Peter spoke of Jesus as the Servant, the Holy and Righteous One, and the Author of Life. God had raised up his Servant and then sent him to the people, and, if the order of events here is significant, the Servant was 'raised up' before he was sent out (Acts 3.26). The first Christians saw Psalm 2.1–2 fulfilled when Herod, a king, conspired with Pontius Pilate, a ruler, against the LORD and his anointed.

---

[16] A summary of *1 Enoch* 47—51.

Jesus was the holy and anointed Servant, through whose name signs and wonders were performed (Acts 4.25–30). The *Didache*, the earliest known Christian text outside the New Testament, used the title Servant in eucharistic prayers that do not mention the last supper.

> We give thanks to thee, our Father, for the holy vine of thy servant David, which thou hast made known to us through thy servant Jesus.
>
> We give thanks to thee, our Father, for the life and knowledge thou hast made known to us through thy servant Jesus ...
>
> Thanks be to thee, holy Father, for thy sacred Name which thou hast caused to dwell in our hearts, and for the knowledge and faith and immortality which thou hast revealed to us through thy servant Jesus ...[17]

It seems that Jesus the Servant had ritual meals with his followers before the last supper, that is, during his ministry as the Servant. The Servant in these early prayers, revealing life and knowledge, looks like Isaiah's Servant, the royal figure who was raised up and became wise, and whose knowledge made others righteous.

The scene and sequence of the exalted Servant is assumed in Hebrews, which opens with the summary: 'When he had made purification for sins, he sat down at the right hand of the majesty on high, having become as much superior to the angels as the Name he has obtained is more excellent than theirs' (Heb. 1.3b–4). A series of quotations follows, mostly drawn from the royal texts (Heb. 1.5–13):

- 'Thou art my Son, today I have begotten thee' (Ps. 2.7);
- 'I will be to him a father and he shall be to me a son' (2 Sam. 7.14);
- 'Let all God's angels worship him' (Deut. 32.43 Lxx);
- 'Thy throne, O God, is for ever and ever ... therefore God, thy God, has anointed thee ...' (Ps. 45.6–7);
- 'Sit at my right hand, till I make thy enemies a stool for thy feet' (Ps. 110.1).

This writer was interpreting the life and work of Jesus within the old royal cult, and s/he saw Jesus as a Melchi-Zedek priest (Heb. 7.1–25). Hebrews 9 adds detail: Christ appeared as the high priest, but unlike the ancient high priests, he did not enter the holy of holies that represented heaven carrying animal blood that represented his own life/blood. Jesus entered heaven itself, having offered his own life (Heb. 9.11–14). The time of substitutes had passed, and so Jesus or John saw the slain Lamb standing (that is, resurrected) and enthroned.

---

[17] *Didache* 9, 10.

## The king in the New Testament

This scene is also assumed in Peter's sermon in Solomon's porch (Acts 3.12–26). The incident is recorded as the next major event after Pentecost, and so could well have happened at the next great temple festival, the Day of Atonement. Peter used imagery from this festival: 'Repent therefore, and turn again, that your sins may be blotted out ...' (Acts 3.19), and he interpreted recent events in the light of the Day of Atonement. Just as the high priest used to emerge from the holy of holies with the blood that cleansed, consecrated and renewed the creation, so too the followers of Jesus were waiting for him to return, the Messiah who had to remain in heaven until the appointed time (Acts 3.19–21). Peter used titles from the royal cult to describe Jesus: 'His servant Jesus', 'the Holy One, the Righteous One'. This royal and temple imagery is what Luke thought appropriate to attribute to Peter in the very earliest days of the Jerusalem church; and he had the disciples ask Jesus if he was about to restore the kingdom to Israel, which meant far more than independence from Roman rule (Acts 1.6).

Paul, originally a persecutor of the Jerusalem church, opened his letter to the Romans with the words: '... the gospel concerning his Son, who was descended from David according to the flesh, and designated Son of God in power according to the Spirit of holiness by his resurrection from the dead ...' (Rom. 1.3–4). This looks like a formula that Paul was quoting, perhaps an early statement of belief; it also has the awkwardness of a translation. 'Spirit of holiness' is an over-literal rendering of an idiomatic Hebrew form 'spirit of holiness'. In the Hebrew Scriptures, the nearest equivalent (translating literally) is 'the spirit of his holiness' (Isa. 63.10, 11) which is equivalent to 'the spirit of Yahweh' (Isa. 63.14). In the New Testament, the usual form is *pneuma hagion*, 'Holy Spirit' (Matt. 1.18; Rom. 5.5), but here in Romans 1.4 there is the unusual *pneuma hagiōsunēs*, suggesting that the formula originated among the Hebrew-speaking Christians. When, we ask, was Jesus designated Son of God by the Holy Spirit? It was at his baptism, when, according to Peter, Jesus was *anointed* with the Holy Spirit and with power (Acts 10.38). Luke implied this too, when, immediately after his baptism, he had Jesus claim to be fulfilling Isaiah 61.1: 'the Spirit of the Lord is upon me, because he has *anointed* me ...' (Luke 4.18).

Jesus' anointing happened at his baptism, the moment he was declared to be the divine Son, just as in the royal ritual of the original temple. When the king had been anointed and declared to be the Son, he was also 'raised up', resurrected, and was no longer simply a mortal human being. He became a Man. In temple discourse, this was called his resurrection. So

## The background to John's Gospel

too, Jesus' own experience of resurrection happened in the Jordan, and the Easter event confirmed the earthly reality of what had already taken place. During his ministry, Jesus was already, to use Enoch's phrase, 'one of the glorious ones', and this is how he was seen by his disciples at the Transfiguration – outside time and matter, within the pre-created light of the holy of holies. The first Hebrew Christians understood and interpreted the events of Jesus' life within the ancient pattern of kingship, and warned against the non-Hebrew interpretations that were seeping into the Church. Resurrection was the moment when a human being was transformed into an angel, a Man, and this happened when s/he was granted the vision of God.

Thus when Philip, one of the first-called disciples (John 1.43), asked Jesus: 'Lord, show us the Father, and we shall be satisfied' (John 14.8), he was asking for this vision of God. Jesus replied: 'He who has seen me has seen the Father.' Jesus was the transforming presence, the vision of the LORD, and the moment of recognition was resurrection. Philip's 'we shall be satisfied' alludes to the fourth Servant song, which is best preserved in the great Isaiah scroll found at Qumran. This says: 'As the result of his suffering, his Servant will see light *and be satisfied*, and by his knowledge the Servant, his Righteous One, will make many righteous' (Isa. 53.11, my translation). The Servant would learn something as he saw the light of the glory, and what he learned would make him the Righteous One and enable him to make others righteous. Jesus understood 'seeing the glory' as resurrection, and according to Luke, explained this to his disciples on the road to Emmaus: the Easter event, the suffering of the Anointed One and his entering the glory, he said, had all been prophesied, and the only possible prophecy for these was Isaiah's fourth Servant song *in its Qumran form* (Luke 24.27). The gospel attributed to Philip, perhaps compiled by one of his disciples, shows how the exchange between Jesus and Philip was understood. The *Gospel of Philip*, found in Coptic at Nag Hammadi in 1945, is a deeply Hebraic text and enables us to touch, if not always to see and understand, the very earliest Christians. 'Philip' warned:

> Those who say that the Lord died first and rose up are in error, for he rose up first and died. If one does not first attain the resurrection, will he not die? As God lives, he would be [already dead].[18]

The resurrection was something that Jesus experienced before he was crucified, and other early texts show this happened at his baptism.

---

[18] *Gospel of Philip*, CG II.3.56.

The Christians linked baptism and resurrection in their own practices. Paul taught that the Christian was buried with Christ in baptism, and then resurrected: 'We were buried therefore with him by baptism into death ... For if we have been united with him in a death like his, we shall certainly be united with him in a resurrection like his' (Rom. 6.4–5). This could imply just a future resurrection, but elsewhere Paul showed that for a Christian, the resurrection had already taken place: 'If then you *have been raised* with Christ, seek the things that are above, where Christ is, seated at the right hand of God' (Col. 3.1). It would have been natural for Christians to re-enact the baptism of Jesus, and evidence from third-century Syria shows that at baptism the new Christian did relive the Jordan experience. The baptizing bishop was the one 'through whom the LORD in baptism, by the imposition of the hand of the bishop, bore witness to each one and uttered in his holy voice saying "You are my Son. I have this day begotten you."'[19] The new Christian was anointed and became a child of the light.

Justin explained baptism to a Roman enquirer in the mid-second century but did not describe the rite itself. He said that those who had been convinced of the truth of Christian teaching prayed and fasted and were then 'brought to the water and regenerated'. This was called illumination, because 'those who learn these things are illuminated in their understanding'.[20] The earliest evidence, then, is that at baptism new Christians were born again as children of light, and learned something that illuminated the mind. This is what temple tradition meant by resurrection.[21] John implied in his first letter that imparting knowledge at baptism had been practised from the beginning: 'You have been anointed by the Holy One and you know all things ... his anointing teaches you about everything and is true' (1 John 2.20, 27, my translation).

At his baptism/resurrection, Jesus saw the heavens opened. No Evangelist records what he saw, apart from the Spirit coming upon him like a dove. Origen,[22] however, the greatest biblical scholar in the early Church, had contacts with Jewish scholars when he was living and writing in Caesarea. He said that when Jesus saw the heavens open, he saw what Ezekiel saw. This means that at his baptism, Jesus saw the chariot throne

---

[19] *Didascalia Apostolorum* II.32, in R. H. Connolly, *Didascalia Apostolorum*, Oxford: Clarendon Press, 1929, p. 93.
[20] Justin, *Apology* 1.61, 65.
[21] For more detail, see my book *Temple Themes in Christian Worship*, London: T&T Clark, 2007, pp. 99–134.
[22] He died in 253 CE.

and the one enthroned there; he saw the kingdom of God. The vision of the chariot throne is important for recovering the neglected kingship elements in the New Testament.

Ezekiel came from a family of first-temple priests, and his visions described the throne of the LORD as he knew it, the chariot throne of the cherubim in the holy of holies. He saw it leaving the polluted temple (Ezek. 10—11), and when he was by the river Chebar he saw it arriving in Babylon (Ezek. 1). Origen noted that both Ezekiel and Jesus were by a river when they had their vision of the throne, and that both saw the Spirit.[23] The Hebrew of Ezekiel's visions is not easy to translate, but one important feature has been obscured in many modern translations. Ezekiel saw a *female* figure in his vision, 'the Living One'. In most instances, the words translated 'living creatures' (plural)[24] are in fact a feminine singular noun 'Living One' (Ezek. 1.20, 21, 22; 10.15, 17), and she was underneath the throne that carried the glorious human figure. The throne was formed from cherubim, and it is possible – one can say no more – that the throne was imagined as alive, a divine presence. Although this may seem curious, the Qumran *Songs of the Sabbath Sacrifice* do describe how the pillars and corners, the doors and gates of the temple praised the LORD, as though they were alive, and Peter described the Church as a temple of living stones (1 Pet. 2.5). A living throne is consistent with this.

Visions of the throne are rarely described in the Bible. Apart from Ezekiel, who gave the most detailed description, Isaiah, Daniel and Jesus/John saw the throne (Isa. 6; Dan. 7; and all through Revelation). There was, however, a tradition of temple mystics ascending in their visions to stand before the throne and to see the one enthroned. Much of the detailed evidence is later than the New Testament, but most would agree that this Jewish material has ancient, temple roots. The Book of Revelation is valuable evidence for the existence of such material at the end of the second-temple period, and also *for its importance in the formation of Christianity*. Further, anything concerned with the throne and what it represented – the secret knowledge – was forbidden to Jews for public discourse. The story of creation, that is, Genesis 1, could not be explained to two persons, nor the chariot even to one unless he was wise and already knew what it meant; and the four things that these texts represented – what is above, what is beneath, what was before time and

---

[23] Origen, *On Ezekiel*, Homily 1.
[24] Thus RSV, NEB, GNB.

what would come after – were also forbidden.[25] According to Clement of Alexandria, however, such matters were precisely the content of Christian 'knowledge' (often translated 'gnosis') which had been revealed by prophetic sayings about 'the present, the future and the past ... how they are, were, and shall be'. 'And the knowledge itself is that which has descended by transmission to a few, having been imparted unwritten by the apostles.'[26]

Suppose that Origen, himself originally from Alexandria and a pupil of Clement,[27] was correct, and that there had been an oral tradition that Jesus saw the throne at his baptism. What would this have implied? First, that any details would not have been discussed in public. Jesus did teach his inner circle of disciples in private 'the secret of the kingdom of God' (Mark 4.10–11), and these secrets would have been about the holy of holies, which was the place of the throne and so was the kingdom of God. Second, if Jesus saw at his baptism the throne and the Lamb as described in Revelation 4—5, perhaps his experiences in the Jordan and immediately afterwards in the desert were his call, like those of Isaiah and Enoch. Isaiah stood before the throne and was then sent out with a message and a warning for his people (Isa. 6); Enoch was swept up to heaven to stand before the throne, and he too was given a message and a warning for his people.[28] In each of these cases, it was probably not the people as a whole for whom the message was intended, but only those who had corrupted the temple. Enoch was given a message of warning for the fallen angels, long recognized as a way of describing the second-temple priesthood;[29] and Isaiah's experience, read in the light of the Enochic *Apocalypse of Weeks*, suggests that he too was sent to warn 'those who dwell in the temple', the priests who had lost their spiritual vision and abandoned the true teaching.[30]

The only prophecy attributed to Jesus was that the temple buildings he knew would be destroyed (Mark 13.1–2 and parallels) – a message of warning that was long remembered and cited as proof that Jesus had indeed been the Most Holy One. Athanasius,[31] for example, said that the

---

[25] Mishnah *Ḥagigah* 2.1.
[26] Clement, *Miscellanies* 6.7.
[27] Eusebius, *History* 6.6.
[28] *1 Enoch* 14—16.
[29] D. Suter, 'Fallen Angel, Fallen Priest: The Problem of Family Purity in *1 Enoch* 6—16', *Hebrew Union College Annual* 50 (1979), pp. 115–35.
[30] *1 Enoch* 93.8.
[31] He died in 373 CE.

destruction of the city and temple was proof that the prophecy in Daniel 9.24–27 had been fulfilled: the Most Holy One had appeared, and thus both vision and prophecy had been fulfilled and ceased.

> For it is a sign and an important proof of the coming of the Word of God, that Jerusalem no longer stands, nor is any prophet raised up nor vision revealed [to the Jews] ... But if there is neither king nor vision [among the Jews] but from that time forth all prophecy is sealed and the city and temple taken, why [do the Jews not recognize who Jesus was]?[32]

Jesus also retold Isaiah's parable of the vineyard (Isa. 5.1–7) for the chief priests, scribes and elders (Mark 11.27—12.12). These would have been educated men, knowing all too well what he was saying. Isaiah's parable was about the corrupted temple of his own time, and the whole passage is full of the temple wordplay of double meanings. The Targum knew that the tower in the vineyard was the temple: 'I built my sanctuary among them and gave them my altar to make atonement for their sins',[33] and the 'beloved' for whom the vineyard was built was probably the king.[34] Jesus described the temple authorities as only the 'tenants'. The words Isaiah used to describe the vineyard have other meanings: 'dig' sounds like 'strengthen' – as when the LORD *grasps* the Servant by the hand (Isa. 42.6); 'cleared of stones' sounds like 'wise' – as when the Servant was *made wise* (Isa. 52.13); the *hedge* that would be removed and devoured/burned sounds the same as the 'shrine/vestment' of the cherub that Ezekiel saw in Eden (Ezek. 28.13); 'prune' is the same word as 'making music to praise the LORD'; and 'hoed' sounds like 'make glorious'. Isaiah predicted that the temple of the Davidic kings would be desolate: no more shrines or music or glory. The Targum knew that this passage was about the destruction of the temple: 'I will break down their sanctuaries'; and Isaiah himself made clear that he was using wordplay, because his final comparison was spelled out: the LORD saw bloodshed, *miśpaḥ*, when he had expected justice, *mišpat*; the LORD heard a cry of despair, *ṣeʿaqâ*, when he had expected righteousness, *ṣedhaqâ* (Isa. 5.7). The owner of the vineyard, said Jesus, sent servants and finally his beloved son. 'Beloved', too, would have echoed the original parable: 'Let me sing for my beloved a love song concerning his vineyard' (Isa. 5.1). The tenants killed him. Jesus said that

---

[32] Athanasius, *On the Incarnation* 40.
[33] Targum of Isaiah 5.2.
[34] 'Beloved' and 'David' are similar words, and both may have been royal titles; see N. Wyatt, '"Jedidiah" and Cognate Forms as a Title of Royal Legitimization', *Biblica* 66 (1985), pp. 112–25.

the LORD, the owner of the vineyard, would come to destroy the present tenants and give the vineyard to others.[35]

If the initial impetus for Jesus' ministry had come from a throne vision, these warnings of the imminent destruction of the priesthood and the temple buildings would have been consistent with what is known elsewhere. The Book of Revelation is a sequence of visions about the destruction of the temple and the restoration of the throne and the Lamb/Servant. The harlot who burns is the faithless city (Rev. 17—18; cf. Isa. 1.21–26); and the final scene has the holy of holies of the first temple restored, with the tree of life, the throne and the divine king – 'God-and-the-Lamb – receiving the worship of his high priests, those who wore his Name on their foreheads (Rev. 22.1–5).

The brief sequence with which Mark opens his account of Jesus' public life supports the possibility of a throne vision experience and is very similar to the vision of the open heaven in Revelation 12. As Jesus came up from the water of the Jordan, he saw the heavens rent open, *schizō*, the verb used for the tearing of the temple veil at the crucifixion (Matt. 27.51; Mark 15.38; Luke 23.45; cf. 'God's temple in heaven was opened', Rev. 11.19), and the implication is that Jesus looked into heaven, which in the temple would have been beyond the veil. In the Book of Revelation, as in the first temple, this was the place of the cherub throne and also of the Woman clothed with the sun giving birth to her male child who was then taken up to the throne (Rev. 12.1–6). The child escaped from the ancient serpent who was waiting to destroy him. Jesus saw the Spirit coming upon him like a dove, and he heard a voice from heaven: 'You are my beloved son, with you I am well pleased' (Mark 1.10, my translation). The early Christians who used the *Gospel of the Hebrews* understood that this was the voice of Jesus' heavenly Mother.[36] The words at the baptism are a very free rendering of the Hebrew of the first Servant song (Isa. 42.1), not a quotation from the Septuagint which is very different here. In other words, this incident was 'thought' in Hebrew before Mark wrote it in Greek, and Jesus was identified, or identified himself, as the Servant. The Servant had also received the vision, according to the older Hebrew text of Isaiah 53.11: he had seen the light of the glory after his suffering, and he became the Righteous One. The Spirit then drove Jesus, *ekballō*, into the desert, whereas in Revelation 12.6 it was the woman herself who fled to

---

[35] For details, see my *The Hidden Tradition of the Kingdom of God*, London: SPCK, 2007, pp. 15–17.
[36] Jerome, *Commentary on Isaiah* 11.

the desert. The Spirit 'driving' Jesus implies a violent action; he was forcefully expelled, and then tempted by Satan for 40 days. Mark gives no detail – we find this in Matthew and Luke; he simply sums up the desert experience by saying that Jesus was with the beasts, *thēria*, and the angels ministered to, *diakonō*, him.

We have seen that this baptism–temptation sequence was 'thought' in Hebrew, and so the 'wild beasts' will originally have been the Hebrew *ḥayyôth*. This meant both (wild) animals such as Jesus might have encountered in the desert, but also the creatures of the cherub throne. Since the 'animals' in the account of Jesus' desert experiences are linked to angels serving him, it is more likely that these *thēria* were the creatures of the cherub throne than wild animals, and so being with the creatures and the angels meant a mystical experience of the throne. What happened during the 40 days? A distinct possibility is that Jesus received the throne vision in Revelation 4—5: the Lamb/Servant approached the throne, was given the scroll to open, and then the angels served before him (Rev. 4—5). If he had received the vision of the Woman clothed with the sun at his baptism, the temptations in the desert would have been the-devil-and-Satan's attempt to devour him. In the vision, the child escaped and was caught up to the heavenly throne (Rev. 12.1–6), and Satan and his host were driven from heaven by Michael and his angels. Thus in the enthronement vision 'the Lion of the tribe of Judah, the Root of David' had conquered and could open the book with seven seals and take his place on the throne (Rev. 5.5).

The fuller version of this story of the conflict with Satan and his fall is found in the *Life of Adam and Eve*, which was known in the time of Jesus and probably long before that, but was not included in the Old Testament. When Adam was created in heaven as the image and likeness of the LORD God, the archangel Michael ordered all the angels to worship the image of the LORD. The devil refused because, he said, Adam was younger than him and inferior. Adam should worship the devil. As punishment for his refusal to worship Adam, the devil and his angels were thrown from heaven, and vowed revenge.[37] The devil would try again to make Adam worship him, and this is why, when he tempted the new Adam in the desert, he offered Jesus all the kingdoms of the world if he would, at last, worship him.

In his vision of the chariot throne leaving the temple, Ezekiel saw Adam enthroned there, although this is not clear in the English

---

[37] *Life of Adam and Eve* 12—16.

translations. On the throne he saw a fiery form, the likeness of the glory of the LORD, and he described the figure as *Adam* (not 'a human form') (Ezek. 1.26). Adam was the original king, and since he had also been created as the high priest, Ezekiel saw the priest-king of the first temple on his throne. Ezekiel's vision and the story in the *Life of Adam and Eve* are also echoed in Psalm 2:

> Be wise now therefore, O ye kings: be instructed ye judges of the earth.
> Serve the LORD with fear, and rejoice with trembling.
> Kiss the Son, lest he be angry, and ye perish from the way, when his anger is kindled but a little ...
> (Ps. 2.10–12, AV, which is closer to the Hebrew)

This was Adam enthroned as king in Zion, here called the Son, as in Luke 3.38, which completes Jesus' genealogy with 'who was the son of Adam, who was the son of God'. The other rulers (perhaps here the earthly rulers as counterparts of the angels in heaven) are warned to serve the Son.

All these texts are the deep roots of the vision of the Woman clothed with the sun, to which we shall return, but it was necessary to introduce them here as they are also background for Matthew's and Luke's accounts of Jesus' time in the desert. The temptations that followed the baptism must have been Jesus' own account of what happened, since he was alone at the time, fasting for 40 days. He must have told the disciples of his struggle to come to terms with what he had heard at his baptism: 'You are my beloved son ...' (Mark 1.11 and parallels, my translation), and he experienced this as a struggle with Satan who asked him three times: '*If you are the Son of God ...*' The challenges must have been what was expected of the Son of God.

First, the Son was Yahweh, the name meaning 'He who causes to be', and so the starving Jesus should have been able to turn a stone into bread. The devil taunted: 'If you are the Son of God, command this stone to become bread' (Luke 4.3). This is echoed in Jesus's own saying: 'What man of you, if his son asks him for bread, will give him a stone?' (Matt. 7.9). The other two visions suggest that he was meditating on Psalm 2, the enthronement psalm which seems to presuppose the 'Adam enthroned' story even at that early date. A verse from this psalm became a key proof text for the early Christians, for example when the writer of Hebrews was demonstrating that Jesus was the Son enthroned on high. The sequence of royal texts in Hebrews 1.5–13 begins with Psalm 2.7: 'Thou art my Son, today I have begotten thee', and the earliest texts of Luke's Gospel give these as the words Jesus heard at his baptism.

Codex Bezae, now thought to be a very early version of Luke, gives Psalm 2.7 as the words at the baptism, and this is found in a number of other writers from the second century onwards. Bart Ehrman argued that this was the original reading, 'but orthodox scribes who could not abide its adoptionist overtones, "corrected" it into conformity with the parallel in Mark'.[38] Ehrman went on to show that Luke believed something actually happened to Jesus at his baptism: he was anointed and chosen. Luke's Peter said this when he was speaking to Cornelius: at the very start of his public ministry, he said, after the baptism of John, 'God anointed Jesus of Nazareth with the Holy Spirit and with power …' (Acts 10.38). Luke also set the rejection in Nazareth at the start of the ministry (Luke 4.16–30), whereas Mark set it later, after a period of public teaching and healing (Mark 6.1–6). One of Luke's reasons may have been to emphasize the passage Jesus chose to read in the synagogue: 'The Spirit of the LORD is upon me, because he has anointed me to preach good news …' (Luke 4.18, quoting Isa. 61.1, my translation).[39] This was immediately after the baptism and temptations, and so, like Peter's address to Cornelius, implied that the baptism was the anointing.

The Targum to the Psalms shows that Psalm 2.6–7 was understood in later Jewish circles as the *anointing* of the king, rather than his 'birth': 'I have anointed my king and installed him on Zion, the mountain of my sanctuary. I will tell of the decree of the LORD: he said to me "You are as dear to me as a son to a father, pure as though I had created you this day."'[40] Nobody can date this Targum, although 'a very tentative suggestion would be the fourth to sixth century CE'.[41] The word changes here reveal an agenda: 'Since Christians saw in the Psalms allusions to the divinity of Jesus, TgPss was concerned lest this verse be understood literally.'[42] In the Targum, the king was only *like* a son, but *created*, not begotten, by his anointing on the day he became king. Something similar happened in the Targum to Psalm 87: 'This one was born there', which occurs in verses 4, 5, 6 was deemed to refer to the kings, and the line became each time: 'This [king] was anointed there.'[43] Jewish tradition,

---

[38] B. D. Ehrman, *The Orthodox Corruption of Scripture*, Oxford: Oxford University Press, 1993, p. 62.
[39] Ehrman, *Orthodox Corruption*, pp. 62–7.
[40] Translation in D. M. Stec, *The Targum of Psalms*, Collegeville, MN: Liturgical Press, 2004.
[41] Stec, *Targum of Psalms*, p. 2.
[42] Stec, *Targum of Psalms*, p. 30.
[43] Stec, *Targum of Psalms*, p. 165.

then, was sensitive to the Christian use of Psalm 2.7, continuing to link it to anointing, but to 'creation' rather than birth.

Before returning to the temptations, let us trace further this thread of royal associations. Psalm 2.7 opens the sequence of proof texts in Hebrews 1, followed by the promise to David about his son: 'I will be to him a father and he shall be to me a son' (2 Sam. 7.14, my translation). This emphasized the human birth of the Davidic king. Then 'when he brings the firstborn into the world, he says, "Let all God's angels worship him."' This verse was part of the pre-Christian Hebrew text of Deuteronomy 32.43 – it was found at Qumran[44] and is in the Septuagint – but it is not in the post-Christian Hebrew text. Perhaps it was another case of sensitivity due to Christian claims based on the verse. The missing half-verse included the proof text: 'Let all God's angels worship him'. The writer of Hebrews says this described the moment when God brought the Firstborn into the world. In Deuteronomy, the truncated passage is the last verse of the *Song of Moses*, which describes how the LORD will come to punish the enemies of his people and heal – literally 'atone' – the soil of his people. Even the shortened verse shows that this was the LORD coming on the day of the LORD to judge and to heal; and the additional lines found at Qumran included a command to the *ᵉlohîm* to worship the LORD. For Hebrews, the LORD in this proof text was the Firstborn, and we are reminded again of that Adam story, when all the angels were commanded to worship Adam, who was the Firstborn and also the Image of the LORD.

Returning now to the temptations, the second and third suggest that Jesus was indeed meditating on Psalm 2 when he was in the desert, something that increases the likelihood that the words at the baptism were Psalm 2.7. Matthew 4 and Luke 4 record the same experiences, but in a different order. Matthew's second and Luke's third temptation was Jesus set on a pinnacle of the temple and tempted to cast himself down: 'If you are the Son of God, throw yourself down.' The devil's further taunt was Psalm 91.11–12, 'He will give his angels charge of you ... On their hands they will bear you up, lest you strike your foot against a stone.' In Psalm 2, this had been the king set on Zion, the holy hill, where the angels were commanded to serve him, and Jesus was being tempted to test this. Matthew's third and Luke's second temptation had Jesus taken to a very high mountain, where he could look down on all the kingdoms of the world. 'All these I will give you,' said the devil, 'if you will fall down and

---

[44] 4QDeut<sup>q</sup>.

worship me.' This is that Adam story again, but here the devil offers Jesus great worldly power if, at last, he will worship him. It alludes to Psalm 2.8, the LORD's promise to his Son: 'Ask of me, and I will make the nations your heritage, and the ends of the earth your possession.' Luke offers one small hint that these were the experiences of a temple mystic. When the devil took Jesus to the high mountain, he was shown 'all the kingdoms of the world *in a moment of time*' (Luke 4.5). The temple mystics had this same experience of seeing all time in one instant.

One example: Rabbi Ishmael the high priest, who lived early in the second century CE, ascended to heaven. Since he lived after the temple had been destroyed, he can never have served as a high priest, and so his traditional title must mean that he was from the high-priestly family and presumably knew the secret traditions of the temple. In heaven, he was met by Enoch, who had been transformed into the great angel Metatron, and he was shown round the world of the angels. What he saw is now recorded in *3 Enoch*, a collection of temple traditions from various periods, that focus on the chariot throne, the *merkavah*. At one point Metatron showed R. Ishmael the inner side of the temple veil – the side they would see when they were by the throne in heaven, i.e. in the holy of holies. On it were depicted 'all the generations of the world and all their deeds, whether done or to be done, till the last generation. I went and he showed them to me with his fingers, like a father teaching his son the letters of the Torah.'[45] He, like Jesus, saw all the history of the world in a moment of time.

There are other indications that Origen knew an authentic tradition about Jesus seeing the throne when the heavens were rent at his baptism. Several early texts hint at this when they mention a fire or a great light in the Jordan. Fire or light around a person was the sign of a throne experience, and the Spirit and the fire were expected to return in the time of the Messiah.[46] Stories were told about R. Joḥanan ben Zakkai, who lived in Galilee in the time of the first Christians. After the destruction of Jerusalem, he built up Jabneh to become the new centre of Jewish life and study; in other words, he was not from a fringe sect but represented mainstream teaching and belief. *He and his disciples studied the secret traditions of the throne chariot and the holy of holies*, and it was said that when one of his students, R. El'azar ben 'Arakh, began to expound the *ma'aseh*[47] of the

---

[45] *3 Enoch* 45.
[46] See above, p. 37.
[47] A technical term, perhaps 'the work'?

throne chariot, fire came down from heaven and an angel spoke from the fire, saying: 'Behold, behold, the *ma'aseh* of the chariot.' R. Joḥanan then kissed his student, and blessed the LORD for giving Abraham such a son.[48] A longer version of the story adds that he blessed the LORD because R. El'azar was able 'to expound the glory of our father in heaven'.[49] This is reminiscent of John's claim for Jesus: 'The only son, who is in the bosom of the Father, he has made him known' (John 1.18).[50]

Justin was born in Palestine at the end of the first century and brought up only 30 miles or so from where R. Joḥanan had his academy. He knew there had been a fire in the Jordan when Jesus went into the water.[51] So too the *Gospel of the Ebionites*, used by the Hebrew Christians, mentions a light appearing when Jesus was baptized, which may explain the saying in the *Gospel of Philip*: 'The father of everything united with the virgin [that is, the Spirit] who came down, and a fire shone for him on that day ...'[52] Now the Ebionites used only the Gospel of Matthew, and interestingly, there are two Old Latin texts of Matthew which also mention a light at the baptism. Each has different words, showing that there were at least two distinct channels of transmission of this story.[53] There was also Ephrem in mid-fourth-century Syria, who knew of the bright light in the Jordan.[54] Petersen concluded: 'In the case of the light at Jesus' baptism, the presence of the tradition in both eastern and western Christendom in the second century seems to point more towards rejection [of this detail] than ignorance.'[55] It would be possible to conclude that the temple and throne context for the baptism was gradually lost or rejected: the words 'I have begotten you' and the light in the Jordan dropped from the texts of Luke and Matthew respectively.

The Davidic kings used to ascend to heaven and sit on the throne, but Deuteronomy, as we have seen, rejected the idea of anyone going to heaven to bring down knowledge. The Servant was exalted, lifted up and

---

[48] Babylonian Talmud *Ḥagigah* 14b, my translation.
[49] Tosefta *Ḥagigah* 2.2, Jerusalem Talmud *Ḥagigah* 2.1. After the time of Joḥanan ben Zakkai, Judah and Akiba, the tradition of the *merkavah* was no longer clear.
[50] *Kolpos*, 'bosom', can also mean 'womb'.
[51] Justin, *Trypho* 88.
[52] *Gospel of Philip* 71; see above, p. 76.
[53] Matt. 3.15. Codex Vercellensis, fourth or fifth century, has: 'et cum baptizaretur, lumen ingens circumfulsit de aqua'; Codex Sangermanensis, seventh century, has: 'et cum baptizaretur Jesus, lumen magnum fulgebat de aqua'.
[54] Ephrem, *Commentary on the Diatessaron* IV.5.
[55] W. L. Petersen, *Tatian's Diatessaron. Its Creation, Dissemination, Significance and History in Scholarship*, Leiden: Brill, 1994, p. 20.

made wise; he saw the light of the glory, and an obscure (obscured?) passage in 1 Chronicles 17.17 seems to link the heavenly ascent to the royal house. David was praying after Nathan had promised that the LORD would make his descendants the kings in Jerusalem, and he thanked the LORD: '... thou hast ... spoken of thy servant's house for a great while to come, and hast shown me future generations ...'. Then the text is opaque. The parallel version is quite clear at this point and links the royal house to keeping the law: 'This is the law of man, O my Lord Yahweh' (2 Sam. 7.19b). The Septuagint is similar: 'This is the law of man, O LORD, my LORD.' The RSV omits the problem words in 1 Chronicles, but has the footnote: 'Heb. uncertain'; the Good News Bible has 'you, LORD God, are already treating me like a great man'; the Jerusalem Bible has 'You show me as it were a line of men, and it is Yahweh God who promises it.' The Septuagint, however, has 'you looked upon me as a vision of a human being and exalted me, LORD God'. Bearing in mind that the Greek title for Chronicles is *Paralipomena*, 'the things left out', it seems that the Hebrew here recorded one of the things that were left out of the Deuteronomist's account in 1 Samuel: that David would have a vision and be exalted. The Hebrew is opaque, but it has letters that can be read as 'you caused me to see', 'the Man' (the Adam) and 'ascent', which the Greek read as 'you exalted me'. The most problematic word is $k^e tôr$, which could be 'as an outline form'[56] or, read as *katur*, could mean 'crowned'. This now-opaque text must once have been similar to the royal psalm, which has the same motifs but uses different words:

> Of old thou didst speak in a *vision* to thy faithful one and say:
> 'I have set the *crown* upon one who is mighty,
> I have *exalted one* chosen from the people.
> I have found David my servant; with my holy oil I have anointed him ...' (Ps. 89.19)

Even though material about the royal ascent was suppressed by the Deuteronomists and their heirs, and much had been secret knowledge anyway, enough breaks the surface in the New Testament and in early Christian writings for us to be confident that this royal tradition was not lost and was fundamental to the teaching of Jesus.

The Transfiguration was the next stage of Jesus' baptism experience, revealing his glorious state to a small group of disciples. Again there was a voice from heaven, this time speaking to the disciples: 'This is my beloved

---

[56] The related verb is used in Isa. 44.13. This is the temple language of Ezekiel; see above, p. 103.

Son; listen to him' (Mark 9.7).[57] Jesus' prayer after the last supper was that all his disciples would join him and see the glorious state which he had been given 'before the foundation of the world' (John 17.24), and this was the final vision in Revelation, where his servants worshipped him in the light of the holy of holies (Rev. 22.1–5). This is yet another indication that the kingship visions in Revelation had been given to Jesus himself and explained later to John.

## The birth

There is a second vision of enthronement in Revelation: the vision of the Woman clothed with the sun whose newborn child was snatched up to the throne of God (Rev. 12.1–6). This is the centre of the Book of Revelation, both literally in terms of the extent of the text, and also as the key point of the drama in heaven. After the Servant/Lamb had been enthroned and taken the little book, he began to open the seals. When he opened the seventh and final seal, the seven angels began to sound their trumpets, one after another; and when the seventh angel sounded his trumpet, the kingdom of the LORD and his Christ began on earth (Rev. 11.15). Bearing in mind that there were no chapter divisions in the original text, the scene in heaven described immediately after the seventh angel's proclamation – the woman giving birth to her son – corresponded to the inauguration of the kingdom on earth, in other words, establishing the kingdom on earth and the birth of the child were aspects of the same event.

This was the ancient temple pattern. When the Davidic prince became king, he was born in the holy of holies and sat on the throne of the LORD, and so the woman giving birth was the temple context for the words of Isaiah, the Psalmist and the Chronicler: 'On earth as it is in heaven.' Origen, who knew about Jesus' throne vision at his baptism, also knew how events and characters in heaven could be simultaneously events and characters on earth. He explained how John the Baptist could have been the angel/messenger of the LORD and also a man on earth. Origen knew of a Jewish text that is now lost, the *Prayer of Joseph*, which described Jacob as both a man on earth and an angel in heaven, and he quoted this to make his point: 'I, Jacob, who am speaking to you, am also Israel, an angel of God and a ruling spirit.' In the same way, said Origen, John the Baptist

---

[57] Matt. 17.5 includes 'with whom I am well pleased'; Luke 9.35 includes 'my Son, my Chosen …'.

was (the embodiment of) the heavenly voice whom Isaiah had heard crying out 'In the wilderness prepare the way of the LORD' (Matt. 3.3; Isa. 40.3).[58] The idea of a heavenly being who was simultaneously human must have been familiar in the time of Jesus, and a later Jewish text also mentioned the heavenly and earthly identity of Jacob: the man who slept at Bethel was at the same time an image on the throne in heaven, and the angels came down to see him.[59]

The belief in a heavenly counterpart to human beings was indicated in the curious form of words found in Revelation: two names side by side that should perhaps be run together with hyphens to emphasize that they were one being, e.g. 'the kingdom of our-LORD-and-of-his-Christ'. The Davidic kings, once they had been anointed, became the LORD, and so 'our-LORD-and-his-Christ' meant the anointed king: the heavenly being – the LORD – identified with the human being – the anointed one. The still-human Servant/Lamb approached the throne and took the little book, but the seer did not record the precise moment when the Lamb became the divine being. By the end of the chapter, however, the elders and the living ones worshipped 'the-one-who-sits-on-the-throne-and-the-Lamb' (Rev. 5.13–14), and so the *theōsis* must have taken place. It is not unambiguously clear at this point that the one on the throne and the Lamb have become One – but by Revelation 22.3 there is no doubt: 'The throne of God-and-of-the Lamb shall be [there] and *his* servants worship *him*', two singular forms following the double identity. There are similar double forms at Revelation 7.10; 14.4; and 11.15, where 'the kingdom of our-LORD-and-of-his-Christ' is followed by 'and *he* shall reign for ever and ever'.

When the Woman clothed with the sun gave birth to her child, this was the Lady of the ancient temple giving birth to the LORD. She had been the Mother of the sons of God, whose Firstborn was the LORD, and the LORD in turn became the Immanuel, God with us. The still-human Davidic prince entered the holy of holies and there he was 'born' and enthroned. The enthronement vision in Revelation 4—5 described this moment when the human prince approached the throne; this was the human side of the ritual. The vision of the Woman clothed with the sun giving birth to her child was the other aspect of the process, the heavenly side; the birth of the heavenly LORD in eternity who would become the human king. This two-stage process of birth can be seen in Gabriel's words to Mary:

---

[58] Origen, *On John* 2.31.
[59] *Genesis Rabbah* LXVIII.12.

> [Jesus] will be great and will be called the Son of God Most High
> And the LORD God will give him the throne of David his father ...
> (Luke 1.32, my translation)

The first line was the birth of the LORD from the heavenly Lady; the second was the LORD becoming the human king.

Two ancient poems incorporated into the end of Deuteronomy describe the double process of becoming the king. Now known as the *Song of Moses* (Deut. 32.1–43) and the *Blessing of Moses* (Deut. 33.2–29), they show what Moses' lawgiving in Deuteronomy was intended to replace. Israel had originally received the divine law from the Davidic king, who had become the LORD, the son of the Lady. After the demise of divine kings and the increased influence of Deuteronomy and Moses, Israel received the heavenly law not from the king but from Moses. The new context of the poems and the editorial changes were the first steps in the process of turning Moses into the God and King of his people.[60] The two poems are now separated by a short passage in which the LORD tells Moses to ascend Mount Nebo and look out over the land that he would never enter. The poems could easily have been a single composition at one time, as they show a familiar sequence of events, and in the same order as the throne vision in Revelation 11–12.

In the first poem, the *Song*, the Most High divided the nations of the earth among his sons, and allocated Jacob to the LORD. He cared for his people after he had found them in a desert place. They rebelled against him and suffered for their folly, but he came to rescue them from their enemies and to heal (atone) their land. Two verses, verses 8 and 43, were significantly different in the Qumran text from the later Masoretic Hebrew text: in the Qumran text, verse 8 described how the Most High had sons, of whom the LORD was one; and verse 43 described how the LORD came forth on what is clearly the Day of Atonement, and the angels had to worship him as he came to punish his people's enemies and heal their land. Both verses were important for Christian claims, but their post-Christian Hebrew form no longer supported the Christian claims: verse 8 had shown that the LORD was the son of God Most High; and verse 43 had been used as a proof text in Hebrews 1.6. The longer form of verse 43 was the inspiration for Revelation's song in heaven as the kingdom was established:

> We give thanks to thee, LORD God Almighty, who art and who wast,
> That thou hast taken thy great power and begun to reign.

---

[60] See below, p. 133.

> The nations raged, but thy wrath came,
> And the time for the dead to be judged,
> For rewarding thy servants, the prophets and saints,
> And those who fear thy name both small and great,
> And for destroying the destroyers of the earth.'
>
> (Rev. 11.17–18, my translation)

The older poem had been:

> Praise him, heavens [peoples],
> *And worship him all *lohîm* [the same as Ps. 97.7c]
> For he avenges the blood of his sons [servants]
> Brings vengeance on his adversaries,
> *Requites those who hate him,
> And heals the soil of his people
> (Deut. 32.43, my translation)[61]

The current Hebrew lacks the lines marked *, and differs from the Qumran text at peoples and servants. In other words, the heavenly context – the heavens praising and the sons of God – was not in the shorter, later form of the text. The poem in Revelation was sung by the elders in heaven, and so corresponds to the first two lines of the longer text of Deuteronomy 32.43; the middle section of the poem in Revelation, the judgement, corresponds to the central section of Deuteronomy 32.43; and the 'destroying the destroyers of the earth' corresponds to 'healing the soil of his people'.

The second [part of the] poem, the *Blessing of Moses*, once described the LORD and the Lady coming in glory with the angels on the day the LORD became king.

> The LORD came from Sinai ...
> He came from the ten thousands of holy ones,
> With *flaming fire* at his right hand. (Deut. 33.2)

The key word has been edited into obscurity: the 'flaming fire' at the LORD's right hand, sometimes translated 'the fiery law',[62] has been achieved by dividing one Hebrew word – the name of the Lady – into two, and changing the Hebrew letter *r* into a *d*. These two letters are almost identical both in the old Hebrew script and also in the different script used in the second-temple period, so the letter change gives no indication of when this happened. The change of letter could have been a scribal

---

[61] 4QDeut<sup>q</sup>.
[62] The AV has 'a fiery law', following the Latin Vulgate.

error or a deliberate alteration. One of the new words created by dividing the letters into two words, however, was a Persian loan word, *dat* = law, suggesting that the change was made early in the second-temple period, when Jerusalem and Judah were ruled by the Persians. The present Hebrew text is *'šdt*, 'fiery law'; the original was probably *'šrth*, 'Ashratah', one of the names of the Lady, the Mother of the LORD, who appeared in Revelation crowned with stars because she was a queen, and clothed with the sun because in the temple she had been the Sun Lady.

The *Blessing of Moses*, before it was linked to Moses, described how the LORD became king, on the day he appeared in glory with a host of angels and with the Queen (his Mother) at his right hand. This is where she stood at the royal wedding, when the Psalmist addressed the king:

> Your divine throne endures for ever and ever ...
> At your right hand stands the queen in gold of Ophir ...
> (Ps. 45.6a, 9b)

The detail of the LORD becoming king is not clear in Deuteronomy 33.

> Moses commanded us a law, even the inheritance of the congregation of Jacob. And he was king in Jeshurun,[63] when the heads of the people and the tribes of Israel were gathered together.
> (Deut. 33.4–5, AV, which is closer to the Hebrew)

The present text says *Moses* became king, as indeed he did in later legend, but the word 'Messiah' looks very similar to 'Moses': *mšh*, Moses, and *mšyḥ*, Messiah. Had this poem originally described the LORD becoming the Davidic king, then it would have been the newly anointed one, the Messiah, who gave the law to the assembly, when the tribes were gathered together and he emerged in glory with his angels and his Mother. Recall that the enigmatic history of Israel preserved in *1 Enoch*, the *Apocalypse of Weeks*, described how the law was given with a vision of the holy and righteous ones, but neither Moses nor the exodus was mentioned.[64]

Revelation's scene in heaven that corresponds to establishing the kingdom on earth was a theophany: lightning, voices, thunder, earthquake (Rev. 11.19). The LORD coming to Sinai had been described in the same way: thunder, lightning, a thick cloud and the mountain shaking (Exod. 19.16, 19). The woman who appeared, then, was of comparable status to

---

[63] Jeshurun seems to be an old name for the people of Israel. The first part of both names is written *yšr*. It is also found at Deut. 32.15 and 33.26; and at Isa. 44.2. In all cases it is a name for the people, represented by their ancestor Jacob/Israel.

[64] *1 Enoch* 93.6.

the LORD. When the temple in heaven was opened, the ark was seen, or rather, seen again. The ark was one of the temple furnishings that had disappeared at the end of the first-temple period, and which people said would return in the time of the Messiah. The woman (re)appeared in heaven too – she was in the temple – and there she gave birth to her son. The red dragon, 'that ancient serpent, who is called the Devil and Satan' (Rev. 12.9) was waiting to destroy the child, but the child escaped, and the dragon was thrown from heaven, together with his angels. He vowed revenge. This is the story of Adam that Jesus relived during his time in the desert, and which he recalled when he said: 'I saw Satan fall like lightning from heaven' (Luke 10.18). The dragon in the vision went off to make war on the woman's other children (Rev. 12.17).

The birth stories in the Gospels were the earthly counterparts of the heavenly realities, and it is likely that they were written after the rest of the Gospels. Luke's nativity story does seem to be a distinct preface to the rest of his work, written when the story of Jesus' life was being told in the light of temple traditions about the ancient kings. The Gospel writers, or the people and communities whose reflections they recorded, saw more and more significance in the events, and told the stories in this light. Luke noted twice that Mary kept all these things and pondered them in her heart (Luke 2.19, 51). Eventually, the *Infancy Gospel of James* was written as a separate book, and this is the most detailed telling of the nativity story in terms of royal and temple symbolism.

Luke began his Gospel with the annunciation to Zechariah. He was a priest who saw Gabriel while he was serving in the temple and was told that his future son would be the herald of the LORD, 'the spirit and power of Elijah' (Luke 1.17). Then Gabriel spoke to Mary, first in terms of who her Child would be – the LORD, heavenly Son of God Most High who became the Davidic king – and then how he would be born:

> The Holy Spirit will come upon you,
> And the power of the Most High will overshadow you;
> Therefore the child to be born will be called holy, the Son of God.
> (Luke 1.35)

Again, it is the *Gospel of Philip* that has preserved the original meaning of these words: 'Some said "Mary conceived by the Holy Spirit". They are in error. They do not know what they are saying. When did a woman ever conceive by a woman?'[65] 'Spirit' in Hebrew is a feminine noun, and so the

---

[65] *Gospel of Philip*, CG II.3.55.

## The king in the New Testament

presence of the Spirit was a female presence. The word 'overshadowing', *episkiazō*, was the word used in the Septuagint for the cloud that overshadowed the tabernacle at Sinai, when the glory of the LORD came down and filled it (Exod. 40.35: RSV 'abode'), and it seems – one can say no more – to have been a mother-presence. There was that bitter wordplay in Isaiah 57.3, based on the fact that two words, both written *'nnh*, had very different meanings. The prophet called the corrupt priests of his time 'sons of a sorceress', *'on^enâ*, a thinly veiled comment on what must have been their real claim or title: 'sons of a cloud', *^anānâ*.

Gabriel's words imply that the Child would not be born by a supernatural version of normal conception, since he was answering Mary's question: 'How can this be since I have no husband?' The Child would be born by the temple process, the presence of that cloud which had filled the temple when it was consecrated, when the glory of the LORD came to fill the holy place (1 Kings 8.10–11) and which Ezekiel saw filling the temple when the glory of the LORD was departing (Ezek. 10.4). The overshadowing cloud also occurs in all three accounts of the Transfiguration, when a voice spoke from the cloud: 'You are my son' (Matt. 17.5; Mark 9.7; Luke 9.35, my translation). It is usually assumed nowadays that this was the voice of God, but the *Gospel of the Hebrews* remembered that the voice from the cloud was the Holy Spirit, and that Jesus called the Holy Spirit 'my Mother'.[66] Philo knew that the Logos, the second God, was 'the son of Wisdom his mother, through whom [fem.] the universe came into being',[67] and the great Isaiah scroll from Qumran described the Virgin who would bear Immanuel as 'the mother of the LORD'.[68] This would explain Elizabeth's formal greeting to Mary, and the word used to describe it: the RSV has 'she exclaimed', the AV 'she spake out with a loud voice'; but in the Septuagint, this verb was used to describe the Levites making loud music in a temple procession or service (1 Chron. 15.28; 16.42). There was a liturgical feel to it, which suits the formality of the greeting. The question is: was 'the mother of [my] LORD' an expression that Elizabeth knew in another context?

Luke's story of the Annunciation assumes the meeting of heaven and earth as in Origen's explanation of how John the Baptist could be both a man and an angel. Just as the heavenly mother gave birth to her Child in the holy of holies, so too Mary would give birth to that same Child. Luke

---

[66] *The Gospel According to the Hebrews*, in M. R. James, *The Apocryphal New Testament*, Oxford: Clarendon Press, (1924) 1980, p. 5.
[67] Philo, *On Flight*, 109.
[68] 1QIsa^a 7.11 has 'from the mother of the LORD', not, as in other texts, 'from the LORD'.

## The background to John's Gospel

therefore described the birth of Jesus in Bethlehem as the birth in the holy of holies, and he gave only four details. He was the Firstborn son (Luke 2.7). This was literally the case, but 'Firstborn' was also the title given to the Davidic king – 'I will make him the firstborn' (Ps. 89.27) – and the title which the writer of Hebrews gave to the LORD himself when he came into the world (Heb. 1.6). Since all Christians were one in Christ, the gathering in heaven was called the assembly of the Firstborn (Heb. 12.23).

Mary wrapped him in swaddling clothes – literally 'wrapped him around' – and this is mentioned twice, suggesting that the detail was important (Luke 2.7, 12). Clothing the newly 'born' high priest was an important part of the ritual; the garments symbolized his resurrected state. When Enoch stood before the heavenly throne and was transformed into an angel, he was taken from his earthly garments and dressed in robes of God's glory because he had become a part of the glory.[69] An early Christian text, the *Teaching of Silvanus*, has Wisdom invite her child to receive from her 'a high-priestly garment woven from every kind of wisdom'.[70] Here, Mary reverses the process and her child wears the garments of his human state, which he left behind again, symbolically, when the linen grave clothes were found on Easter morning.

Then Mary set the Child in a manger, wordplay on the similarity between the Hebrew words for manger, *'ēbûs*, and the ancient name for Jerusalem, *yᵉbûs*. This was not the king set on Zion (Ps. 2.6), but the king set in a manger, because there was no room for them in the inn, *kataluma*. This word too is an allusion to the place of the temple birth, since it sounds like the Hebrew *taᵃlumâ*, meaning 'hidden'. He was set in a manger in an inn because there was no room for them in the hidden place in Zion.

This is not reading too much into the text. When the *Infancy Gospel of James* was written, the temple features of the story were clearly spelled out, almost as if there had been a risk that they would be forgotten. In the *Infancy Gospel*, Mary had worked as as temple weaver, making a new veil.[71] This is perfectly possible: Herod was refurbishing the temple at that time, and a new veil would have been made. The veil of the temple was woven from four colours to represent the matter that hid the glory of God from human eyes. Philo and Josephus, both from high-priestly families, gave the same explanation: the white linen warp represented the earth; the

---

[69] *2 Enoch* 22.8–9.
[70] *The Teaching of Silvanus*, CG VII.4.89. This text was used by St Anthony, an important figure in early Egyptian monasticism, who died 356 CE.
[71] *Infancy Gospel* 10.

red, blue and purple wool for the weft represented fire, air and water respectively.[72] Exodus had prescribed how the veil should be woven, but did not explain the symbolism, presumably because this was secret knowledge (Exod. 26.31). The same fabric, interwoven with gold, was used for the outer vestment of the high priest, and again, no reason was given for this (Exod. 28.5–6). The writer of Hebrews knew this, however, and assumed that the readers did too. The veil represented the flesh of Christ, the vestment of matter which he wore in the world (Heb. 10.20).

Hebrews is full of temple symbolism, yet does not mention the fall of the temple in 70 CE. We could conclude that the temple was still standing when Hebrews was written, and if so, then the veil-as-matter symbolism was known in the first or, at the latest, the second generation. The significance of Mary working as a weaver while she was pregnant with her Child would have been noted, and so the birth stories were being told within a temple framework from the outset.

This is why Luke described the place of the nativity as the holy of holies. In the *Infancy Gospel*, Joseph settled Mary in a cave while he went to find a midwife, and when they returned, there was a bright cloud overshadowing the cave. As the cloud withdrew, a light appeared in the cave, and as the light faded, a child appeared in the cave with his mother.[73] With the years, detail accumulated. The *Arabic Infancy Gospel*, perhaps first compiled in Syriac in the fifth to sixth century, described the cave as a place of worship. The detail could have come from the Church of the Nativity as pilgrims remembered it, or it could have been a fusion of that and the older holy of holies tradition. When the child was born, 'the cave was filled with lights more beautiful than and more splendid than the light of the sun'. When the shepherds arrived, 'the cave was made like a temple of the upper world, since both heavenly and earthly voices glorified and magnified God on account of the birth of Christ'. A scene like this must have inspired the words of Isaiah, and we can never know if what he described existed only in his imagination, or was inspired by temple ritual: 'The people who walked in darkness have seen a great light ... For to us a child is born, to us a son is given' (Isa. 9.2, 6). This was the birth of the king in Jerusalem, presumably when the veil across the holy of holies opened to reveal the great light and the newly 'born' king as he emerged.

---

[72] Philo, *Questions on Exodus* II.85; Josephus, *War* 5.212–13.
[73] *Infancy Gospel* 19.

## The background to John's Gospel

Matthew began his Gospel with the royal genealogy of Jesus, and had the annunciation to Joseph set in the context of Isaiah's royal oracle. The Virgin who conceived and bore a son named Immanuel was not simply an unnamed female who was pregnant, whose expected child would still be a small boy when the power of Jerusalem's enemies was shattered (Isa. 7.10–17; Matt. 1.22–23). The Virgin was the heavenly Mother of the crown prince, and so Isaiah's oracle proclaimed the future of the Davidic house, the birth of the next king. Mary's Child was born in Bethlehem, the ancestral home of the family of David (1 Sam. 16.1), and then magi came asking, 'Where is he who has been born king of the Jews? For we have seen his star in the East, and have come *to worship* him' (Matt. 2.2). 'In the East' here means that the star was seen in the eastern sky at dawn, not that the magi were in the east when they saw it. The star was the sign of a great leader: 'a star ... out of Jacob; a sceptre ... out of Israel ...' (Num. 24.17). The Targums knew it was the sign of the Messiah: 'When a mighty king shall reign from the house of Jacob, and there shall grow up a Messiah and a mighty sceptre from Israel.'[74] In temple ritual, the king, newly born in the holy of holies, was named the Morning Star (Ps. 110.3), and in Revelation, Jesus or John saw the angel in the sunrise, bringing the seal of the living God with which to mark the faithful and protect them from the imminent judgement (Rev. 7.2–3).

The gifts brought by the magi were another royal sign, or rather, a sign from the original temple of the priest-kings in Jerusalem. There are various versions of the story about Adam bringing gold, frankincense and myrrh from Eden. As the Eden story was retold and incorporated into Genesis, it came to represent Adam the original high priest being driven from Eden, the original temple. Rejecting the tree of life symbolized losing the holy anointing oil, and the gifts brought from Eden were a reminder of the older ways. A Jewish text says Adam brought seeds from Eden so that he could continue to grow plants for perfume;[75] a third-century Christian text that included older Jewish material says that Adam brought gold, frankincense and myrrh from Eden to remind him of the temple and priesthood he had lost: gold was characteristic of the temple vessels, but also of the distinctive vestments of the high priests (Exod. 28.5); frankincense was the incense, and filling the hands (with incense) was the sign of high-priestly ordination (e.g. Exod. 28.41; 29.9, 33, 35);[76] myrrh

---

[74] Targum *Pseudo-Jonathan* Num. 24.17. Targum *Onkelos* is similar.
[75] *Apocalypse of Moses* 29.
[76] The AV translates 'fill the hands' as 'consecrate'; the RSV as 'ordain'.

was the myrrh oil used for anointing. All three occur together in the prescription for making Aaron and his sons the high priests: 'And you shall put [the garments for glory and beauty] upon Aaron your brother and his sons, and you shall anoint them and you shall fill their hands and make them holy and they shall serve me as priests' (Exod. 28.41, my literal translation). The gold, frankincense and myrrh that Adam brought from Eden were buried with him and then taken from the burial cave to be offered by the magi to the infant Jesus.[77] If this story was originally told in Hebrew – and it is generally agreed that Matthew collected the stories of a Hebrew-Christian community – then the magi would have been wise men, and 'from the east' might once have been 'from ancient times' since both are written in the same way in Hebrew.

What, then, might the Hebrew Christians, those who asked Jesus if he was about to restore the kingdom to Israel, have 'heard' as they listened to this story, or had in mind when they told it to Matthew? That the new Adam had been born, the new priest-king who would restore the ancient temple, its ways and its wisdom?

## The life and death

The baptism, Transfiguration and birth stories were shaped by allusions to the priest-kings. So too was the rest of the Gospel story: the life of Jesus, his death and his resurrection. Take Matthew as an example, since he shaped his narrative by the prophecies. The healing ministry fulfilled the prophecy of the Servant who took away the griefs and sorrows (which could also be translated 'sicknesses and pains') (Matt. 8.17; cf. Isa. 53.4). Matthew did not quote the Septuagint here, but gave his own translation of the Hebrew; he was thinking in Hebrew. So too with the later healing miracles, where he gave his own translation of another Servant passage (Matt. 12.15–21 quoting Isa. 42.1–4). Jesus calming the storm on Galilee and later walking on the sea during a storm (Matt. 8.23–27; 14.22–33) fulfilled the promise to the king, that he would have power over the sea and the rivers (Ps. 89.25). The blind men and the Canaanite woman called out to the Son of David (Matt. 9.27; 15.22; 20.30). Jesus was able to reveal the secrets of the kingdom (Matt. 13.11), and much of his teaching was about the kingdom, the world of the holy of holies. In Revelation, this was the golden city that came down from heaven. He taught his disciples to pray for the coming of the kingdom (Matt. 6.10). At Caesarea Philippi,

---

[77] Testament of Adam 3.6.

Peter recognized that Jesus was the Anointed One, the Son of the living God (Matt. 16.16), and Jesus saw himself at the centre of the throne vision in Revelation, 'the Son of Man sitting on his glorious throne' with his disciples around him (Matt. 19.28).

Holy Week is the story of the king coming to his city and his temple. Palm Sunday was, in effect, Jesus asking the people the question he had asked his disciples at Caesarea Philippi: 'Who do you say that I am?' He chose to ride into Jerusalem on a donkey and so he chose to act out Zechariah's prophecy:

> Rejoice greatly, O daughter of Zion!
> Shout aloud, O daughter of Jerusalem!
> Lo, your king comes to you;
> The Righteous and Victorious One,
> Humble and riding on an ass,
> On a colt, the foal of an ass.
> (Zech. 9.9, my literal translation)

Matthew noted that this was to fulfil the prophecy (Matt. 21.5). A crowd formed around Jesus, and the procession moved towards Jerusalem, spreading garments and leafy branches in the road.[78] Their response to Jesus' implied question was verses from Psalm 118, variously reported by Matthew, Mark and Luke.

> Save us [*Hosanna*], we beseech thee, O LORD!
> O LORD, we beseech thee, give us success!
> Blessed is he who enters in the name of the LORD!
> We bless you from the house of the LORD.
> The LORD is God, and he has given us light.
> Bind the festal procession with branches,
> Up to the horns of the altar.    (Ps. 118.25–27)

*This was a psalm for Tabernacles, and Palm Sunday was a Tabernacles procession, even though it happened just before Passover.* Hosanna, 'Save us!', is another form of the verb that gives the title Victorious One, and 'in the name of the LORD' could also be translated 'with the name of the LORD'. 'He has given us light' is a difficult text, which the Septuagint understood as 'he has shone forth for us' – the answer to the ancient high-priestly prayer: 'May the LORD make his face shine upon you' (Num. 6.25). The Gospel writers present Palm Sunday as the people's recognition of Jesus as the Davidic king. They expanded the psalm: 'Hosanna to the

---

[78] Luke does not mention the branches.

Son of David' (Matt. 21.9); 'Blessed is the kingdom of our father David that is coming' (Mark 11.9). Luke adds at this point a prophecy of the destruction of Jerusalem, 'because you did not know the time of your visitation' (Luke 19.44).

Then Jesus cleansed the temple – the role of the high priest – and the events of the next few days are presented as the king coming to his city. The order of events is clearest in Mark because Matthew and Luke have additional material from the collection of Jesus' teachings (known as Q) that many scholars detect as a source used by Matthew and Luke.

First, the Jewish leaders in the city – the chief priests, scribes and elders – challenged the King's authority, and in return, Jesus asked them about the authority of John the Baptist. The leaders dared not answer, because the people believed that John had been a prophet sent from heaven (Mark 11.27–33). At this point Matthew includes the parable of the two sons (Matt. 21.28–32), to show who were the real workers in the vineyard – those who heeded the preaching of John the Baptist. Then Jesus retold Isaiah's parable of the vineyard, which the leaders recognized was a warning, and they must have realized, after the acclamation on Palm Sunday and the cleansing of the temple, that Jesus was claiming to be the true heir to the temple (Mark 12.1–12). Finally, according to Matthew, Jesus told the parable of the wedding feast, inspired by the vision of the wedding of the Lamb and his Bride (Rev. 19.6–9; Matt. 22.1–14; Luke has it elsewhere, 14.16–24). The Bride was 'the daughter of Zion' who rejoiced when her king came to her;[79] she was both the Mother of the LORD and also the city of Jerusalem. Those invited to the marriage were too busy to attend, and so others enjoyed the feast.

Second, the King taught about his tribute money, and he said that the tribute due to God was distinct from the tribute due to Caesar. What bore the image of Caesar should be given to him, implying that those who were made in the image of God were to be given to him.

Third, the King was asked about the citizens of his kingdom, the resurrected, which in temple discourse meant those living the life of the holy of holies. There would be no marriage in heaven, Jesus taught,

---

[79] The Bride is one element of a complex of imagery linked to the Lady of the ancient temple. She was the Mother of the King but also his spouse because she was the mother of the next king too. She was the genius of the city, as can be seen from the the vision of 'Ezra', which was recorded shortly after the temple was destroyed in 70 CE. Ezra had seen a woman in mourning who had been transformed before his eyes into a great city, and the archangel Uriel had explained: 'This woman whom you saw, whom you now behold as an established city, is Zion' (2 Esd. 10.44).

## The background to John's Gospel

because all would be like the angels (Mark 12.18–27). Luke adds that the resurrected 'cannot die any more; because they are equal to angels and are sons of God, being sons of the resurrection' (Luke 20.36).

Fourth, the King gave his law, drawn from two passages in the Hebrew Scriptures (Mark 12.29–31):

> Hear, O Israel: The LORD our God is one LORD; and you shall love the LORD your God with all your heart, and with all your soul and with all your might.
> (Deut. 6.4–5)

> You shall love your neighbour as yourself. (Lev. 19.18)

The Gospel accounts add, 'love God with your mind', but this would be included within the original Hebrew idea of 'loving with your heart'.

Fifth, there was the question about the nature of the king. The Jewish teachers said he would be the son of David, but Jesus then asked how this could be, if David had written of the king: 'The LORD said to my Lord, sit at my right hand, till I put thy enemies under thy feet' (Ps. 110.1). Jesus said: 'David himself calls him Lord, so how is he his son? (Mark 12.37). The original Hebrew text has two different words for 'Lord': the first is *Yahweh*, the second *Adoni*, and so the line was 'Yahweh says to my Lord ...' But the point remains: the king, after his enthronement, was no longer just a son of David; he was also the son of the LORD, as is clear later in the same psalm, where the LORD says: 'I have begotten you' (Ps. 110.3).[80] The Hebrew text here is now pointed differently to give 'your youth', but the Septuagint read the Hebrew as 'I have begotten you'. The debate between Jesus and the Jewish teachers about the divine or human nature of the Messiah may have caused the change of pointing in this verse.

At this point there follows a warning against the Jewish teachers, who, according to Matthew, have shut the kingdom of heaven, neither entering themselves nor allowing others to enter (Matt. 23.13). Luke, elsewhere, puts it differently: 'Woe to you lawyers! For you have taken away the key of knowledge; you did not enter yourselves and you hindered those who were entering' (Luke 11.52). The Jewish teachers had prevented people from knowing about the kingdom, an echo of the scorn in Deuteronomy: that no heavenly knowledge was necessary if people had the law.

Then Jesus predicted the destruction of the temple, and there follow the parables about being prepared for the day of the LORD: the watchful householder, the faithful servant, the bridesmaids and their lamps, the talents, and finally, in Matthew, the prediction of the judgement (cf. Rev.

---
[80] See above, pp. 75–6, 87.

20.11–15). The Man, the King, would be enthroned with his angels, and decide who was worthy to enter his kingdom (Matt. 25.31–46).

Mark then describes how the King was anointed on the head by a woman in the house of a leper (Mark 14.3–9), anointed for death, in contrast to the temple ritual of anointing that gave life. Then Judas arranged to betray him. At the last supper Jesus took bread and wine (only!) from the Passover table, the great feast that celebrated the work of Moses, and he used them to renew the great covenant of the older priest-kings. He did not compare himself to the sacrificed lamb, despite Paul's words in 1 Corinthians 5.7: 'Christ our Passover lamb has been sacrificed' and John's noting that Jesus died at the time when the Passover lambs were being sacrificed in the temple (John 19.36). The clue to understanding why John noted the precise time of Jesus' death – when the Passover lambs were being sacrificed – is found in Matthew, the most Hebraic of the Gospels. He had Jesus distinguish which covenant he was renewing: 'blood of the covenant poured out for many for the putting away, *aphesis*, of sins' (Matt. 26.28). This was not the Sinai covenant, which had been an agreement between the LORD and his people that they would keep his laws and he would be their God (Exod. 24.4–8). There was nothing about the forgiveness of sins in the original Sinai story, although the Targum here expanded the Hebrew text to: 'Moses took half the blood and put it on the altar to make atonement for the people ... and said "This is the blood of the covenant"'.[81] Forgiveness was effected by atonement, and especially the Day of Atonement, when, in the first temple, *the priest-king had made a symbolic self-offering of his life/blood, which he poured out to remove the effects of sin and so heal the creation.* This was the role of the Servant in Isaiah's enigmatic poem that became so important for the Christians. He made himself a sin offering and poured out his soul to death (Isa. 53.10, 12), just as Jesus 'emptied himself, taking the form of a servant ... and became obedient unto death' (Phil. 2.7–8). Jesus, as we shall see, was replacing the dominant Passover festival that represented the ways of the pro-Moses second temple and restoring to prominence the ancient royal feast of Atonement-Tabernacles.

The symbolism of bread and wine is deeply rooted in the temple imagery of the Hebrew Scriptures and has many facets.[82] Here, the wine is the blood of the sin offering, of which the priests had to consume a token

---

[81] Targums *Pseudo-Jonathan* and *Onkelos*. There is no way of knowing if this understanding was ancient or a reaction to Christian claims.
[82] For detail, see my book *Temple Themes in Christian Worship*, pp. 167–220.

## The background to John's Gospel

amount on the Day of Atonement, along with the 'LORD's portion', some of the entrails of the sacrifice.[83] The bread was the most holy food of the high priests (later all the priests) which had to be consumed each Sabbath. 'Most holy' food would have imparted holiness, and so this was their spiritual food. Hence those words in the *Didache*, where the thanksgiving over the bread was for life and knowledge revealed through Jesus. Important for our quest is the fact that atonement blood and most holy bread had originally been the exclusive preserve of the high priests. This was a priest-king's supper, and reminiscent of Melchi-Zedek who had brought out bread and wine. Hebrews declared that Jesus made the true Day of Atonement sacrifice (Heb. 9.11–14) and that he was Melchi-Zedek (Heb. 7.11–17).

Jesus was taken captive in Gethsemane by agents of the chief priests and rulers (Mark 14.43), and was taken first to the high priest's council. Mark and Matthew report the accusation that Jesus claimed he would destroy the temple and rebuild it. This was something that 'the Lord of the sheep' was expected to do, according to Enoch,[84] and so it was a claim to being the LORD. Enoch saw a new temple brought by the Lord of the sheep, 'greater and loftier than the first, and set up in the place of the first ... the old one which he had taken away'. The high priest certainly knew this expectation, because his response to those claims was to ask Jesus if he was 'the Christ, the Son of the Blessed' (Mark 14.61).[85] Jesus replied, 'You will see the Son of Man seated at the right hand of Power and coming with the clouds of heaven.' Jesus claimed to be the Man who would be enthroned in heaven, and at this perceived blasphemy, the council said he deserved to die (Mark 14.64). He was taken to Pilate, who asked: 'Are you the King of the Jews?', and he then had this written as the accusation to be displayed on the cross. Jesus was mocked as the powerless 'Christ, the King of Israel' (Mark); 'the Son of God ... the King of Israel' (Matthew); 'the Christ of God, his Chosen One ... the King of the Jews' (Luke). These must all have been titles associated with the King: the Christ, the Son of God, the Chosen One.

Jesus was taken down from the cross and put into a new tomb, which the women found empty on the third day. The tomb itself came to be seen as another holy of holies, from which the resurrected King emerged.

---

[83] *Letter of Barnabas* 7, and also Mishnah *Menaḥoth* 11.5.
[84] *1 Enoch* 90.28–36.
[85] Matt. 26.63 has 'the Christ, the Son of God' and Luke 22.67 has 'the Christ', and later 'the Son of God'.

# Part 2

# TEMPLE THEOLOGY IN JOHN'S GOSPEL

# Introduction to Part 2

> *Now Jesus did many other signs in the presence of the disciples, which are not written in this book, but these are written that you may believe that Jesus is the Christ, the Son of God, and that believing you may have life in his name.*
> (John 20.30–31)

In other words, John's purpose in writing his Gospel was to show that Jesus was the anointed Davidic priest-king as described in Psalm 89:

> I have found David, my servant;
> With my holy oil I have *anointed him* ...
> He shall cry to me, 'Thou art *my Father*'...
> And I will make him the firstborn,
> The highest of the kings of the earth.
> (Ps. 89.20, 26, 27)

According to Psalm 110.4, the king was also a Melchi-Zedek priest: 'You are a priest for ever, after the order of Melchi-Zedek' (my translation).

The declaration at the end of John's Gospel shows how the Prologue should be read: it was about the royal rituals in the temple in which the human prince became the divine priest-king when he was anointed. The Davidic prince became the human presence of the LORD, Immanuel, although John did not use that title. John then chose examples from the life and teaching of Jesus to show the anointed priest-king at work among his people, some of whom recognized him, some of whom did not, and the Gospel concludes by reminding the reader what John had set out to achieve. It is important to look closely at the Prologue, since it is the framework within which the whole Gospel must be read.

Another framework of John's Gospel is the Book of Revelation, which, as I have argued elsewhere, was John's interpretation and compilation of visions that Jesus knew or received.[1] Both books describe the conflict of good and evil, light and darkness: Revelation does this by means of visions and images; John's Gospel by means of certain events and teachings in the

---
[1] See my book *The Revelation of Jesus Christ*, Edinburgh: T&T Clark, 2000.

## Temple Theology in John's Gospel

life of Jesus that had been prompted by the visions he knew. Both describe the divine judgement:

> In the Apocalypse, the thought is of an outward coming for the open judgement of men: in the Gospel of a judgement which is spiritual and self executing ... Of the two books, the Apocalypse is the earlier. It is less developed both in thought and style ... The crisis of the Fall of Jerusalem explains the relation of the Apocalypse to the Gospel. In the Apocalypse, that 'coming' of Christ was expected and painted in figures: in the Gospel, the 'coming' is interpreted.[2]

Embedded in Revelation are the visions that shaped Jesus' ministry and which can sometimes be seen in each of the New Testament Gospels.[3] It was John's vision of the *parousia* (Rev. 10.1–11) that prompted him to write his Gospel and to teach a new understanding of the Eucharist.[4]

Then there are the temple festivals, which are such a distinctive feature of John's Gospel. The synoptic Gospels mention only the Passover when Jesus died, but John mentions three Passovers (2.23; 6.4; 12.1), perhaps two Tabernacles (7.2 and possibly 5.1) and then Ḥanukkah (10.22). The symbolism of Tabernacles is prominent in Jesus' teaching as John presents it, and this is to be expected if, as we are suggesting, John knew that Jesus saw himself as the true Davidic priest-king. In Revelation there is the vision of the new heaven and the new earth, and a voice calls out from the throne: 'Behold, the tabernacle of God is with men. He will tabernacle with them and they shall be his people, and God himself will be with them' (Rev. 21.3, my translation). In the Prologue, John describes the Incarnation as the Logos making his *tabernacle* among us; he could have used a less colourful word such as 'lived' or 'came', but he chose 'tabernacle', and this in the context of the light coming into the darkness. The Logos came to his own people, as in the vision, to make all things new, but his own people did not receive him.

There are many indications in John's Gospel, as we shall see, that Jesus was replacing the spring Passover and Moses traditions with the older ways of the first temple represented by the autumn festivals of the Day of Atonement and Tabernacles, when all creation was renewed and the king was enthroned. Tabernacles meant different things to different people, and it is necessary to look briefly at this great variety of traditions in order

---

[2] B. F. Westcott, *The Gospel According to St John*, London: John Murray, 1903, pp. lxxxv–lxxxvii.
[3] See above, p. 111.
[4] See below, pp. 322–3.

*Introduction to Part 2*

to set John's presentation of Jesus (or even Jesus' presentation of himself) into its original context.

## The feast of Tabernacles

Tabernacles was the last of the three feasts in the month of Tishri: New Year, Day of Atonement, and then Tabernacles. It was celebrated at the autumn equinox, when the sun rose in the true east and shone through the eastern gate of the temple. An autumn festival was mentioned in all the old calendars, even before the temple was built, but it had various names: in Exodus it was the feast of Ingathering at the end/beginning of the year (Exod. 23.14–17; 34.18–23), and it must have been associated with judgement, because harvest images were used to describe the divine judgement: Amos saw a basket of summer fruit, *qayiṣ*, that prompted his oracle about the LORD's judgement, the end of Israel, *qēṣ*;[5] Isaiah compared judgement to the winepress (Isa. 63.3–6); the Baptist compared the judgement to the grain harvest and burning the chaff; and both images occur in Revelation (Rev. 14.14–20). In Leviticus there was the feast of Trumpets, the Day of Atonement and then the feast of Tabernacles (*sukkôth*, 'booths') (Lev. 23.4–43). In Deuteronomy it was only the feast of Tabernacles (Deut. 16.1–17). Leviticus says of Tabernacles, but of no other feast, that it was celebrated as the feast of the LORD (Lev. 23.41), presumably an echo of the older name found in Judges 21.19: 'the yearly feast of the LORD at Shiloh'; and implied by Elkanah's annual sacrifice to the LORD there (1 Sam. 1.3).

Solomon dedicated the temple at this time of the year, when the sun rose in the true east, although the feast itself is not named. The cloud of the glory of the LORD came to fill the temple (1 Kings 8.2, 10–11, 64–66). As soon as the first group returned from Babylon, Jeshua and Zerubbabel set up an altar in Jerusalem and kept the feast of Tabernacles (Ezra 3.1–6). Later, Ezra gave a public reading of the law at Tabernacles, before the people went to gather leafy branches to keep the festival (Neh. 8.1–18). Exodus and Deuteronomy describe a harvest festival, but Leviticus says that Tabernacles was to remind people of the time they had spent living in the wilderness (Lev. 23.37–44). It seems that the original harvest festivals in the spring and the autumn had coincided with a sun festival, but later became linked to events in the Moses tradition: the spring barley harvest festival commemorated the Passover/exodus, and the autumn grape-

---

[5] The two words sounded very similar.

gathering festival commemorated the time in the wilderness. Eventually, the wheat harvest festival of Weeks (Pentecost) was linked to Sinai and the Ten Commandments, since the Israelites reached Sinai on the third new moon after leaving Egypt (Exod. 19.1), but this link was only made after the destruction of the temple in 70 CE.

Tabernacles had originally marked the end of the autumn New Year festivals, but after the pro-Moses changes in the time of Josiah, New Year moved to the spring and Passover, and in the new calendar, Tabernacles was in the seventh month. It remained the greatest of the festivals. Josephus said it was the holiest and greatest of the Hebrew feasts,[6] but there had been a radical change in its meaning. The Mishnah records a prayer at Tabernacles, in which the people of the second temple formally reject the ways of their ancestors at Tabernacles:

> Our fathers when they were in this place turned with their backs towards the temple of the LORD and their face towards the east, and they worshipped the sun towards the east; but as for us, our eyes are turned towards the LORD.[7]

This implies that the original Tabernacles had included a sunrise ritual of light coming into darkness that had been rejected by the second-temple/pro-Moses group. Ezekiel described such a ritual, which he condemned as a pollution of the temple. He saw a group of men standing between the door of the temple and the great altar, facing east and 'worshipping the sun' while holding branches (Ezek. 8.16–18). The Book of the Twelve Prophets, however, ends with a prophecy of the LORD returning to his temple – a prominent theme in John's Gospel. Elijah would return first, to warn of the imminent day of judgement for the sons of Levi, and when he appeared, so too would the Sun of Righteousness. The true light would return with healing in *her* wings (Mal. 4.2, translating literally).[8]

A collection of oracles at the end of Zechariah shows that at Tabernacles the LORD was expected to return with his angels as king of the whole earth (Zech. 14.9). 'On that day' – the characteristic opening for such oracles – the LORD would stand on the Mount of Olives and then come to Jerusalem with his holy ones (Zech. 14.5); on that day (and here the text is now confused) everything would return to the pre-created state of the holy of holies, with neither day nor night (Zech. 14.6); on that day living waters would flow from Jerusalem (Zech. 14.8); on that day people from all nations would come to Jerusalem to worship the King, the LORD

---

[6] Josephus, *Antiquities* 8.101.
[7] Mishnah *Sukkah* 5.4.
[8] 'Sun', *šemeš*, can be a masculine or a feminine noun; here it is treated as a feminine noun.

## Introduction to Part 2

of Hosts, and to keep the feast of Tabernacles so that they would enjoy the blessing of rain (Zech. 14.16–17); and on that day there would be no more traders in the house of the LORD of Hosts (Zech. 14.21). This chapter of Zechariah echoes throughout the writings of John: Jesus coming from the Mount of Olives to Jerusalem (John 12.12–16), a state with neither day nor night (Rev. 21.22–26), living waters flowing from Jerusalem (John 7.37–38; Rev. 22.1); all nations coming to the King, the LORD (John 12.20–23; Rev. 7.9–17); and no traders in the house of the LORD (John 2.16, alluding to Zech. 14.21). The heavenly host around the throne were praising the One who is to come (Rev. 4.8).

Zechariah's hopes for the future were shaped by memories of the past, and were in sharp contrast to the reality of the second temple, from which not only 'foreigners' but even some worshippers of the LORD were excluded. The Third-Isaiah spoke for these people, as the policy of exclusion was enforced: foreigners and eunuchs who were excluded under the (new) laws of Deuteronomy would be welcomed into the house of prayer for all peoples (Isa. 56.3–8; cf. Mark 11.17, where this text is attributed to Jesus at the cleansing of the temple). The Third-Isaiah condemned the cult of the second temple as a mockery, since those who officiated were also excluding the ancient worshippers of the LORD (Isa. 66.1–6). Later disciples added their vision of all nations coming to the temple (Isa. 66.18–21). The very first oracle of Isaiah is a picture of the great ingathering of people, almost certainly a Tabernacles image, when all nations would come to learn the law of the LORD in Jerusalem, and he would judge them and establish peace on earth (Isa. 2.2–4).

Allusions to Tabernacles in the earlier prophets, however, are more difficult to identify, because the name 'Tabernacles' is not used. The later addition to the text at Isaiah 4.2–4 has Tabernacles motifs: the branch of the LORD (which also means the Messiah) and the fruit of the land would be glorious after the pollutions of Jerusalem had been judged and cleansed, a reference to the Day of Atonement six days before Tabernacles. Then there would be a cloud by day and a flaming fire by night as a tabernacle to provide shelter from both heat and storm. Whatever the date of this piece, the tabernacle here is the protecting divine presence in the form of a cloud. Isaiah 12 celebrates the protecting presence of the Holy One in Zion: 'With joy you will draw water from the wells of salvation' (Isa. 12.3). The Greek of Psalm 29 has a heading that is not in the Hebrew text: 'For the end of Tabernacles'. The psalm celebrates the glory of the LORD as he enters (the temple?) to be enthroned over the

## Temple Theology in John's Gospel

waters of chaos and worshipped by the angels. Psalm 118 may depict the same scene: the people call on the LORD:

> *Save us [Hosanna], we beseech thee, O LORD!*
> *O LORD, we beseech thee, give us prosperity!*
> Blessed is he who enters with the Name of the LORD
> We bless you from the house of the LORD
> The LORD is God
> And he has given us light.
> (Ps. 118.25–27a, my translation)

The words in italics were chanted by the priests with willow branches as they walked around the altar at Tabernacles.[9] The second half of verse 27, 'Bind the festal procession with branches, up to the horns of the altar', is an opaque text with no certain translation.[10]

The Mishnah describes the rituals for Tabernacles in the time of Jesus: how the branches of palm, myrtle and willow were cut and tied into bundles. People carried them in procession to the temple, while singing Psalm 118. The whole bundle was called a *lûlābh*, literally a 'palm', and when Jesus entered Jerusalem on Palm Sunday it must have looked like a Tabernacles procession. John says the crowd went out from Jerusalem to meet him with palms, crying out lines from Psalm 118, so they too must have thought it was a Tabernacles procession. John notes that the disciples did not at first understand what was happening (12.16), but the crowd from Jerusalem was also proclaiming the King of Israel (12.13), words not found in Psalm 118, but presumably known by the crowd to be its context. Tabernacles, as described in Zechariah's prophecies, was the time for the LORD the King to come to Jerusalem from the Mount of Olives. We shall return to this.[11]

Each day of the feast there were numerous sacrifices and a water libation when about a litre of water from Siloam was carried in a golden jug and poured into a vessel on the great altar, along with wine for the drink offering. Music accompanied the libations. Psalms 113–118 were sung, accompanied by flutes on every day but the Sabbath. The gift of rain was linked to Tabernacles; Zechariah said it was the reward for celebrating Tabernacles (Zech. 14.17). A text known as *Pseudo-Philo*,[12]

---

[9] Mishnah *Sukkah* 4.5.
[10] See below, pp. 348–9.
[11] See below, p. 347.
[12] Given this name because it was formerly thought to be a work of Philo, but is now thought to be the work of someone writing in Palestine and in Hebrew. It survives only in a Latin

which shows how the people of Palestine in the time of Jesus were telling the Bible stories from Adam to David, links Tabernacles to the autumn rains. When the feast of Tabernacles is celebrated, says the LORD,

> I will remember the whole earth with rain, and the measure of the seasons will be established, and I will fix the stars and command the clouds, and the winds will resound, and the lightning bolts will rush about and there will be a thunderstorm. And this will be an everlasting sign ...[13]

During each night of Tabernacles, four huge candelabra, each with four bowls, were lit in the Court of the Women, and men holding torches danced through the night to music from temple musicians. Perhaps this represented the 'light at evening time' that was promised by Zechariah (Zech. 14.7).

What did Tabernacles celebrate? For some, it would have been the time in the wilderness, as prescribed in Leviticus. For some it would have been the memory of the Davidic kings and the hope for their return as set out in the prophecies in Zechariah 14. Since the work of Mowinckel on the Psalms,[14] there has been a growing recognition of the importance of the Psalms for understanding the role of the Davidic kings, and especially of their enthronement ceremony at Tabernacles. Deuteronomy retains a trace of the older festival, ordering the Levitical priests and the elders to read out the law every seven years at the feast of Tabernacles, when all Israel assembled before the LORD in the temple (Deut. 31.9–11). The original festival is described in an old poem appended to Deuteronomy, now known as the *Blessing of Moses* (Deut. 33).[15] Here, the LORD comes to be made King and to give his law to the assembled tribes: he appears with his holy ones and with the Lady, rising/dawning from Seir, shining forth from Mount Paran. The imagery in the poem shows that the LORD came with the sunrise when he came as the King to give his law. This would explain why the former worshippers in the temple had faced the sun at Tabernacles, and why the priests of the second temple, who had abandoned these customs, deliberately turned to face the other way. Zechariah's prophecy of the LORD the King coming from the east with his

---

version, but scholars detect a Hebrew original underneath some passages where the Latin is awkward.

[13] *Pseudo-Philo* 13.7.

[14] Published during the 1920s; English translation S. Mowinckel, *The Psalms in Israel's Worship*, Oxford: Blackwell, 1962.

[15] See above, p. 30.

holy ones and the *Blessing of Moses* were inspired by the same temple ceremony. So too was the blessing given by the high priests:

> May the LORD bless you and keep you:
> May the LORD make his face/presence shine on you and be gracious to you:
> May the LORD lift up his face/presence on you and give you peace.
> (Num. 6.24–26, my translation)

For yet others in the time of Jesus, Tabernacles was the festival inaugurated by Abraham at Beer Sheba to celebrate the birth of Isaac, the father of a nation of priests and a holy people.[16] Abraham offered sacrifices and incense, and then cut branches of palm and willow to carry in procession round the altar seven times each day. This story is found in the *Book of Jubilees*, a longer version of a part of Genesis, small pieces of which have been found at Qumran. An assumption has developed among biblical scholars – maybe an unconscious assumption – that *Jubilees* is in some way inferior to Genesis, not least because it says that some of the Jewish festivals were not established by Moses but by Abraham and the patriarchs. The people who wrote and used *Jubilees* were saying, in effect, that these temple festivals were adopted by the pro-Moses group from the traditions of the pre-Moses group, that is, from the first temple.

Some would also have associated Tabernacles with Jacob's dreams at Bethel. According to *Jubilees*, Jacob had a second dream at Bethel. After the dream of the ladder (Gen. 28.10–22) and his time working for Laban, Jacob set out with his family on the first day of the seventh month to go to Bethel and offer the tithe he had promised to the LORD on his safe return. On the eve of Tabernacles, his son Levi had a dream there, and on the last night of the festival, Jacob had his second dream, that he should add an extra day to the feast of Tabernacles.[17] Levi dreamed that he had been appointed the priest of God Most High, and the details of this dream are found in the *Testament of Levi*: the heavens opened, and he saw God Most High on his throne, appointing him as his priest: 'Levi, to you I have given the blessing of priesthood until I shall come and dwell in the midst of Israel.'[18] Later Levi saw seven angels bringing him the vestments and insignia of priesthood, 'in order that I might serve as priest to the LORD God'.[19] But his priesthood was temporary, only until the LORD God

---

[16] *Jubilees* 16.19–31.
[17] *Jubilees* 32.1–2, 16–29.
[18] *Testament of Levi* 5.1–2.
[19] *Testament of Levi* 8.1–11.

himself returned to dwell with his people. This is a theme in *Jubilees* too. The LORD said that after a time of rebellion and apostasy, 'I shall gather them from the midst of the nations ... and I shall build my sanctuary in their midst, and I shall dwell with them.'[20] Moses had to write down all that was revealed to him on Sinai about the future of his people 'until I descend and dwell with them in all the ages of eternity'.[21] The *Temple Scroll*[22] mentions the covenant with Jacob at Bethel immediately after its prescriptions for Tabernacles. The text is broken, but seems to imply that the correct rules for the temple and the cult were given to Jacob at Bethel, that is, before they were given to Moses on Sinai, and that these should be observed until the LORD himself created a new sanctuary, 'according to the covenant which I made with Jacob at Bethel'.[23] The temporary covenant with Jacob at Bethel was associated with Tabernacles.

There is an obvious similarity between Jacob's vision at Bethel, when he saw the LORD beside him and the angels ascending and descending (Gen. 28.10–22), and Levi's vision at Bethel, when he saw the seven angels bringing him the tokens of high priesthood. The Egyptian-Jewish community said that when Jacob was at Bethel, '[Wisdom] showed him the kingdom of God and gave him knowledge of the holy ones/holy things' (Wisd. 10.10, my translation). The rabbis linked Jacob's dream at Bethel to Moses and Aaron ascending Sinai, but Rab Kappara, who taught in Caesarea at the end of the second century CE, said that his dream vision was about high priests going up and down a staircase.[24] Whatever underlies all these cultural memories, Tabernacles, outside the Moses traditions, was linked to the high priesthood and the kingdom of priests, and to the revelation of heavenly knowledge. When Jonathan was appointed high priest by the Syrian king Alexander in 152 BCE, he chose to put on the holy garments at Tabernacles (1 Macc. 10.21).

Tabernacles: The time in the wilderness? The enthronement of the Davidic king which was also his heavenly birth? The LORD shining forth with the Lady to give his law? The dreams at Bethel that established the temporary priesthood of Levi until the LORD himself returned? The glory coming to the newly consecrated temple? The gift of rain and establishing the seasons and weathers? Any or all of these could have been in the minds of the crowd who listened to Jesus teaching in the temple courts at

---

[20] *Jubilees* 1.15, 17.
[21] *Jubilees* 1.26.
[22] *Temple Scroll*, 11QT.29.
[23] J. Maier, *The Temple Scroll*, Sheffield: JSOT Press, 1985, pp. 32, 86.
[24] *Genesis Rabbah* LXVIII.12.

Tabernacles, and those who greeted him with palms when he entered Jerusalem.

There was another ritual with branches at Tabernacles, apart from the procession with palms. Priests went to gather willow branches which they set up around the great altar, bent over to form a covering.[25] There were detailed prescriptions for all these branches, both the *lûlābh*s and the willows: how and where they could be gathered, and their condition, but nothing of their meaning. None that was cut from a sacred tree, an Asherah, could be used, nor any from an apostate city,[26] *which implies that people not recognized by the temple Jews also celebrated Tabernacles.* A vision received by Hermas, a Christian prophet in Rome in the early second century CE, may preserve the meaning of the willow branches. He saw a huge willow tree that covered all who were called by the Name of the LORD, and he saw the angel of the LORD cut branches and give one to each person. Then the angel took the branches back and examined them: the people whose branches were green with buds or green with buds and fruit were allowed into the angel's tower which represented the temple or the church. He gave them crowns of palm and white robes. There were many conditions for the willow branches in Hermas' vision that made them unacceptable, corresponding to the many conditions that made the willow branches unacceptable for the Tabernacles ritual. Whatever the symbolism of the willow branches, it was an important part of Tabernacles, and even in Rome the Christians both knew and used that symbolism.[27]

The clearest examples of Tabernacles symbolism in the New Testament are in Revelation. A crowd was waiting for the angel of the sunrise to mark the faithful from all 12 tribes with the name of the LORD, 'to seal the servants of our God upon their foreheads' (Rev. 7.3, my translation). They then became the Tabernacles throng, clad in white robes and waving palms, who acclaimed the Lamb on the throne (Rev. 7.9–12). They had seen the LORD make his face shine upon them, and then they had been marked with the Name, thus receiving the blessing promised through the ancient high priests (Num. 6.24–27). Then there is the heavenly birth and enthronement of the King, where events of earth and heaven are set side by side: the seventh angel proclaims that 'the kingdom of the earth has become the kingdom of our-LORD-and-his-Anointed-One' (Rev. 11.15,

---

[25] Mishnah *Sukkah* 4.5.
[26] Mishnah *Sukkah* 3.1–3.
[27] *Shepherd of Hermas*, Similitude 8.2.

*Introduction to Part 2*

my translation); and the Woman clothed with the sun appears in heaven – the Sun of Righteousness with healing in her wings (Mal. 4.2) – giving birth to her Son who is taken up to the throne. As she appears, there are phenomena like those associated with Tabernacles: lightning, thunder, and earthquake and hail.

John emphasizes the temple feasts as he demonstrates that 'Jesus is the Anointed One, the Son of God' (20.31, my translation). This implies a particular interest in Tabernacles, since this was the festival of the LORD the King. The opening scenes – the Baptist and then Jesus calling his first disciples – may have been set in the season of Tabernacles, thus giving John's Gospel three Tabernacles and three Passovers. The events take place over four days (1.19, 29, 35, 43), and the titles used all derive from Day of Atonement and Tabernacles expectations: the Lamb of God who takes away the sin of the world was the focus of the Day of Atonement; and Son of God, Anointed One, King of Israel, Son of Man were titles for the Davidic priest-king whose return was expected at Tabernacles.[28]

## The shape of the Gospel

John's Gospel falls into distinct sections, but these do not correspond to the current chapter and verse divisions, which were not a part of the original text.

The greater Prologue introduces Jesus, the Messiah, the Son of God (1.1—2.11).

John makes his story of Jesus Christ begin outside the time and matter of the visible world (1.1-18). Matthew and Luke included a genealogy in their Gospels, rooting Jesus firmly in this world, but for John, the origin of the Christ was 'in the beginning', and his human life began when the Logos became flesh. John introduces the Baptist as the herald of the Incarnation, and does this by literally interweaving the story on earth with the glimpse of heaven. The Baptist – 'a man sent from God … to bear witness to the light' (1.6-8) – is introduced before John mentions the divine light coming into the world. The shape of John's story corresponds to his theme. Then he describes the light in the world – 'the Logos became flesh' (1.14, my translation) – and the Baptist bearing witness to the light (1.15).

Then John introduces 'the Jews', who are uneasy about the Baptist's work (1.19-28), before finally bringing Jesus into the scene. The Baptist

---
[28] See below, p. 347.

recognizes him (1.29–34), then he points out Jesus to two of his own disciples. Jesus goes to Galilee and more people recognize him. Finally, he goes to Cana and changes the water into wine. This is the first of Jesus' public signs; he reveals his glory, and his disciples believe in him.

The central part of the Gospel divides into two sections as John indicates in the Prologue: 'He came to his own home, and his own people did not receive him, but to all who did receive him, he gave power to become children of God' (1.11–12, my translation). First Jesus goes to his own people, who do not recognize and accept him, which is the theme of 2.12—10.42. Throughout this section, Jesus is teaching the Temple Theology of the ancient priest-kings, and John shows that 'the Jews', the disciples of Moses, have lost touch with their own roots. Then there is a linking passage, 11—12, and in the second section Jesus teaches his disciples privately, 13—17. This is often called 'The Farewell Discourse'. The final section describes the trial, death and resurrection of Jesus.

# John 1

## 1.1–18: The Prologue

The Gospel begins, as did both the theology and the rituals of the Davidic kingship, in the holy of holies. Luke implies this in his account of the nativity,[1] and the *Infancy Gospel of James* tells the story of Jesus' birth with clear allusions to the holy of holies, as we have seen.[2]

The mystery in the holy of holies is never explained in the Hebrew Scriptures, although there are places where it is assumed. The Qumran texts called it the *raz nihyeh*, the mystery of how things come to be. Life emerges from the holy of holies, described as the LORD sending forth his Spirit (Ps. 104.30, as in Gen. 1.2). The Qumran text of the previous verse is significantly different from the one used for the English translations. Instead of 'When you take away *their* breath/spirit, they die', it is 'When you take away *your* breath/spirit, they die',[3] implying that the Spirit was the life in all creation. Further, taking away their/your Spirit was the equivalent of the LORD hiding his face/presence:[4]

> When you hide your face/presence they are terrified
> When you take away their/your spirit they return to the dust.
> (Ps. 104.29, my translation)

The face/presence of the LORD brought life, and the presence, as we have seen, was sometimes described as the *memra*, the Logos.

This must be set alongside the blessing of the ancient high priests, that the LORD would cause his face/presence to shine on his people and so bring them both grace and peace (Num. 6.24–26). The high priests had to put the Name of the LORD on his people, to mark them with the X that both identified them and protected them. In the temple the people hoped to be blessed with the shining presence of the LORD, although nobody

---

[1] See above, pp. 136–7.
[2] See below, p. 174.
[3] 11QPs[a].; Ps. 104.29a is not in this text.
[4] 'Face' and 'presence' are the same word in Hebrew.

knows exactly how they understood this. They sang 'Hallelujah', which means 'Shine, LORD'. The face/presence of the LORD brought light, and this light was understood as illumination of the mind, the gift of perception and vision.[5]

Although there is no description of the mystery of the holy of holies in the Hebrew Scriptures, there are non-canonical texts that offer a glimpse. Enoch stood before the throne and described how he was anointed and transformed into an angel.[6] This was his experience of the mystery. The opening scene in the Book of Revelation was Jesus or John watching the mystery when the Lamb – a human figure – was seen in the holy of holies and deemed worthy to open the sealed book and to sit on the throne. Opening a sealed book is an obvious symbol for saying that he learns the secret things, and from this point, the Lamb is both divine and human: God-and-the-Lamb, one figure. He sits on the throne and *his* servants worship *him* (e.g. Rev. 22.3). Elsewhere he is called our-LORD-and-his-Christ, one figure (Rev. 11.15), whence the acclamation 'Jesus is LORD' (1 Cor. 12.3), or 'Jesus Christ is LORD' (Phil. 2.11, my translations). This means: 'Jesus the Anointed One is [has become] Yahweh', just as the Davidic priest-kings did when they were anointed and became themselves the meeting point of heaven and earth. They became Immanuel.

Matthew and Luke both include a genealogy for Jesus that traces his family back to David (Matt. 1.6; Luke 3.31); and the early creed quoted by Paul says that Jesus was 'descended from David according to the flesh' (Rom. 1.3). Both Matthew and Luke record the birth in Bethlehem (Matt. 2.1; Luke 2.4), the ancestral home of David (1 Sam. 16.1). Both record the earthly side of the story, what the Orthodox Church calls 'the nativity according to the flesh'.

John, however, tells the other side of the story, how the LORD came to earth and became flesh as this son of David. This was the moment described in the ancient *Blessing of Moses*, when 'the LORD became king', shining forth – that shining again – with a host of holy ones, angels (Deut. 33.2, 5). Luke records the angels singing at Bethlehem, announcing the birth of Christ the Lord in the city of David (Luke 2.11). The familiarity of those words in English should not be allowed to distract from what they actually mean: 'Christ the Lord' meant 'the anointed one, the LORD', the anointed Davidic prince who was the presence of the LORD in human form: 'The form of a servant, being born in the likeness of men' (Phil. 2.7–8).

---

[5] See above, p. 97.
[6] *2 Enoch* 22.

## John 1

There are other early Christian texts which tell the heavenly side of the story. The *Ascension of Isaiah*[7] is Jewish legendary material about Isaiah reworked and expanded by a Christian in perhaps the third generation. The prophecies of Isaiah often lie just beneath the surface of John's Gospel, confirming what Matthew makes clear by his quotations: Isaiah was a major influence on Jesus and the first Christians. 'Isaiah' in the *Ascension of Isaiah* was probably a pseudonym for James the leader of the Jerusalem church.[8] He ascended to the seventh heaven and then stood and watched as the LORD was told by God Most High that he had to descend to earth. 'Isaiah' watched as the LORD passed down through the ranks of angels and came to the lot allocated to him.[9] This refers to the ancient myth of the sons of God, to whom God Most High allocated the nations. The LORD, the Firstborn of those sons, received Jacob as his lot, and so he became the guardian angel of Israel/Jacob (Deut. 32.8–9). 'Isaiah' gave no details of the birth on earth; he saw Jesus' earthly life as a time of conflict with 'the adversary', and then he saw him return to heaven to sit beside the Great Glory. The *Epistle of the Apostles*,[10] thought to be a mid-second-century text, describes the Incarnation in a very similar way. Jesus told his disciples he had passed down through the heavens, robed in the wisdom and might of the Father (cf. 1 Cor. 1.24); he had taken the form of Gabriel and thus entered into the body of Mary.

The Prologue to Hebrews is in many ways similar to the Prologue to John's Gospel: both begin with a brief account of the Son before his Incarnation; he was the agent of creation, reflecting the glory, and sharing the divine nature. Both use images from the royal rituals in the temple. Hebrews describes the work of atonement and the Ascension, describing the death and resurrection of Jesus in terms of the Day of Atonement sacrifice and his ministry as the priesthood of Melchi-Zedek restored. John summarizes the 'heavenly' side of the nativity story, but without the details. The language may be Greek, but the setting of the Prologue is the Temple Theology of the Davidic priest-kings. It describes how the LORD, one of the sons of God in the invisible creation, emerged from the holy of holies into the world, just as the Davidic priest-kings had done.

---

[7] This text has survived, in whole or in part, in several languages: Ethiopic, Latin, Slavonic, Coptic. The original was most likely Hebrew, first translated into Greek.
[8] See my book *The Revelation of Jesus Christ*, Edinburgh: T&T Clark, 2000, pp. 192–4.
[9] *Ascension of Isaiah* 10—11.
[10] Ep. Ap. 13. The whole text survives in Ethiopic, and fragments in Coptic and Latin.

John's Prologue can be separated into an underlying poem and a commentary that was added later.[11] Some of this makes clear how John the Baptist related to Jesus: he himself was not the Messiah but only the forerunner, the one who identified Jesus as the Messiah (John 1.6–8, 15). The rest is clarification of three major points of Temple Theology (John 1.17–18):

- *How a Christian was born as a child of God.* It was not the process of physical birth, but the spiritual birth assumed in the LORD's words to David: 'I will be [Solomon's] father, and he shall be my son' (2 Sam. 7.14). The birth took place in the holy of holies, and was described in Psalm 110.3, the verse that is now unreadable.
- *The sharp contrast between the law of Moses and the way of the Messiah.* Grace and truth came through the Messiah, or perhaps we should say 'returned' through the Messiah. The LORD in Deuteronomy, which epitomized the law of Moses and how it was understood, was very different from the LORD in the Psalms. The latter was enthroned on righteousness and justice, attended by mercy, *ḥesedh*, and truth, *'emeth* (Ps. 89.14), whereas mercy and truth have little place in Deuteronomy. They are found only twice, describing the LORD (Deut. 7.9, 12), whereas mercy, *ḥesedh*, occurs 118 times in the Psalms, and truth, *'emeth*, occurs 34 times in the Psalms. The contrast here has been linked to Moses' request to see the glory of the LORD, and the LORD's reply: 'I will proclaim to you my Name Yahweh ... and I will be gracious to whom I will be gracious and show mercy to whom I will show mercy ...' (Exod. 33.19, my translation), and there may be such a link, but the episode in Exodus 33 does not concern the law, which is the focus in John 1.17. There is, however, an implicit contrast between *death* for anyone who sees the glory of the LORD (Exod. 33.20), and the light of the glory being the *life* of humankind (1.4). The law and the temple were very different worlds,[12] and when John was writing the Prologue, the law had for many people replaced the world of the original temple.
- *The older belief in the LORD as Israel's second God.* The Hebrew Scriptures record many theophanies, for example to Abraham at Mamre (Gen. 18.1) or to Isaiah in the temple (Isa. 6.5), but Abraham and Isaiah saw the LORD, the Son; not El Elyon, the Father. The presence of Jesus, the incarnate LORD, was also a theophany. There are two versions of the

---

[11] Survey in R. E. Brown, *The Gospel According to John I—XII*, Anchor Bible 29, London: Geoffrey Chapman, 1971, pp. 3–37.

[12] For detail, see my book *The Mother of the Lord*, vol. 1, London: T&T Clark, 2012, p. 174.

## John 1

text here: 'the only-begotten *Son* ... has made [God the Father] known' and 'the only-begotten *God* ... has made [God the Father] known'. The question is: which was John's original? Was 'God' introduced into the text in the light of fourth-century Christological controversies, or was 'Son' introduced when the Church was losing touch with its temple roots?[13] Given that Philo knew of the second God, the more difficult text – 'only-begotten *God*' – is likely to have been John's original. 'Only-begotten' is also a problem, since Paul describes Jesus as 'the Firstborn among many brethren' (Rom. 8.29, my translation), and says that 'all who are led by the Spirit of God are sons of God' (Rom. 8.14). Although there was a distinction between the Son and the sons, it was not a simple one. The titles for Jesus – 'Firstborn' and 'Only-begotten' – are contradictory if taken literally. 'Only-begotten', *monogenēs*, probably represented the Hebrew *yāḥîdh*, 'only', used to describe Isaac (Gen. 22.2, 12, 16), who was not in fact Abraham's only son as there was also Ishmael. The Septuagint translated the word as 'beloved', *agapētos*, but Hebrews chose *monogenēs* (Heb. 11.17). The familiar translations 'only begotten Son' (AV) or 'only Son' (RSV) should perhaps be 'beloved God'. 'He hath declared him' [AV] and 'He has made him known' [RSV] both add 'him' to the Greek text, which just says 'he showed the way'. The Greek verb *exēgeomai* has many meanings of which 'showing the way [to God]' is one and 'explaining the mysteries' is another. Both would be appropriate here.

Who could have needed such clarifications? Jesus making known the new life as a child of God and making known the mystery is the gift for which the eucharistic prayers in the *Didache* give thanks:

> We thank you, our Father, for the *life and knowledge* which you have made known to us through Jesus your servant.
> 
> We thank you, holy Father, for your holy name which you have made to tabernacle in our hearts, and for the *knowledge and faith and immortality* which you have made known to us through Jesus your servant.[14]

Eucharistic prayers without reference to the last supper fit well with John's Gospel which does not mention instituting the Eucharist at the last supper, but links the meal to the work of the Servant and to his teaching

---

[13] B. D. Ehrman, *The Orthodox Corruption of Scripture*, Oxford: Oxford University Press, 1993, pp. 78–82 is a good example of how scholarly/theological presuppositions determine the outcome of an enquiry into, in this case, the variants in a New Testament text.

[14] *Didache* 9, 10, my translation.

## Temple Theology in John's Gospel

about life and knowledge. It is possible that the poem in the Prologue to the Gospel and the eucharistic prayers in the *Didache* were all known to Jesus' disciples during his ministry, before the crucifixion. This possibility is strengthened by the fact that John's Gospel also shares with the *Didache* imagery of the vine and of reuniting the broken fragments, which in the *Didache* are fragments of bread.[15]

In this translation of the original poem, I have not used the familiar 'Word' but kept the original 'Logos', and the later explanatory comments are in italics.

A.
[1]In the beginning was the Logos
And the Logos was with God
And the Logos was God.
[2]He was in the beginning with God.

B.
[3]All things were made through him
And without him was not anything made that was made.
[4]In him was life
And the life was the light of men.
[5]The light shines in the darkness
And the darkness has not overcome it.
[6]*There was a man sent from God whose name was John.*
[7]*He came for testimony, to bear witness to the light, that all might believe through him.*
[8]*He was not the light, but came to bear witness to the light.*
[9]*The true light that enlightens every man was coming into the world.*

C.
[10]He was in the world
And the world was made through him
Yet the world knew him not.
[11]He came to his own home
And his own people received him not
[12]But to all who received him, who believed in his name,
He gave power to become children of God.
[13]*Who were born not of blood nor of the will of the flesh, nor of the will of man but of God.*

D.
[14]And the Logos became flesh and dwelt among us,

---

[15] See above, p. 53.

*John 1*

And we have beheld his glory,
The glory as of the only Son from the Father,
Full of grace and truth.
¹⁵*John bore witness to him and cried, 'This was he of whom I said, "He who comes after me ranks before me, for he was before me."'*

¹⁶*And from his fullness we have all received, grace upon grace.*
¹⁷*For the law was given through Moses; grace and truth came through Jesus Christ.*
¹⁸*No one has ever seen God. The only Son who is in the bosom of the Father, he has made him known.*

The poem has four sections:
The first part describes the 'beginning', the state represented in temple thought by the holy of holies.

> ¹In the beginning was the Logos
> And the Logos was with God
> And the Logos was God.
> ²He was in the beginning with God.

This was 'before' creation and 'beyond' the visible creation; it was the hidden present, the divine state in the midst; cf. 'the glory which I had with you before the world was made' (17.5). In Genesis 1.1, with which John's Prologue is often compared, 'the beginning' is the the pre-creation light from which darkness was separated before the material world was brought into being. In Isaiah 40.21 it was the state from which Isaiah had seen the future: 'Has it not been told you from the beginning?' It is not accurate to say that John's Prologue was modelled on the opening lines of Genesis; both Genesis and the Prologue presuppose the same temple world-view of the visible and invisible creation. The first three lines suggest a Hebrew pattern of thought even if they were not originally written in Hebrew: sentences beginning 'and' ... 'and' are normal Hebrew style. The difficult Greek is trying to express something alien to Greek thought.

The Logos is introduced without any explanation. John's readers must have known what was meant by the Logos, and so it is not likely to have been a complex construct from Greek philosophy. Rather, it would have been familiar to them from the language of their synagogues, and so the evidence of the *memra* in the Palestinian Targum is important. 'In the beginning was the Logos and the Logos was *pros* God.' This does not really mean 'with' God, which implies a distinction and separation not possible within the unity of the 'beginning'. It seems to represent the Hebrew $l^e$, in the sense of 'belonging to' or even 'as'. The Logos was $l^e$ God in the sense of representing, or functioning as, God, and yet was God. The Logos was the angel of the LORD, as we shall see, and the controversy over this angel – was he the LORD himself or only a messenger from the LORD? – is reflected in the translation of key texts in the second-temple period.[16] 'The Logos was God' is another aspect of the same problem of how to express the older ways which recognized El Elyon, then the LORD, his Son, and then the angel of the LORD who was the LORD in visible form. Thus 'the Logos became flesh ... and we beheld his glory' (v. 14). Translating literally, John says that the Logos was *pros* the God, and then that God (not 'the God') was the Logos. This could be no more than a nicety of Greek grammar, or it could be the theological distinction explained by Philo: 'the God' indicated the supreme God, whereas 'God' without 'the' indicated the Logos, God in a different sense.[17]

Origen used the same distinction, and set out a fundamental of Johannine theology:

> For [John] adds the article when the noun 'God' stands for the uncreated cause of the universe, but he omits it when the Logos is referred to as 'God' ... Many people who wish to be pious are troubled because they are afraid that they may proclaim two Gods ... We must say to them that at one time God, with the article, is very God ... On the other hand, everything besides the very God, which is made God by participation in his divinity, would more properly not be said to be 'the God' but 'God'. To be sure, his 'firstborn of every creature' [Col. 1.15] inasmuch as he was the first to be with God and has drawn divinity into himself, is more honoured than the other gods beside him, of whom God is God ... It was by his ministry that they became gods, for he drew from God that they might be deified ...[18]

This is another aspect of the mysteries of the temple: how the divine Unity existed as many; how the angels were all One. This can be illustrated by a description of Wisdom, the Mother of the angels,[19] as she was known in the time of John:

> Though she is but one, she can do all things,
> And while remaining in herself, she renews all things;
> In every generation she passes into holy souls
> And makes them friends of God, and prophets.
>
> (Wisd. 7.27)

---

[16] See below, p. 462.
[17] Philo, *On Dreams* I.229.
[18] Origen, *Commentary on John* 2.14–17.
[19] *Gospel of Philip*, CG II.3.63.

## John 1

The Divine emerged into the earthly priest-king when he was anointed and then sent out into the world as the Son. Jesus reminded the Jews of this when they accused him of blasphemy: 'Do you say of him whom the Father consecrated and sent into the world "You are blaspheming" because I said "I am the Son of God"?' (10.36). John's Jesus here speaks as the Logos of the Prologue who had come into the world as the Son. The Baptist had been the witness that he was the Son of God (1.34).

'Yahweh our angels is a Unity' is a literal rendering of the familiar 'the LORD our God is One' (Deut. 6.4), and here in the Prologue John puts into few words the highest level of the temple mystery, later expressed as 'I and the Father are One' (John 10.30, my translations). The mystery of the One and the Many is well expressed by Theodotus, a second-century teacher now labelled as a Gnostic, but whose teaching was deeply rooted in the world of the temple. These words sum up the meaning of John's Prologue:

> They say that our angels were put forth in unity and are One in that they came out from the One. Since we all existed in a state of separation, Jesus was baptized so that the undivided should be divided until he should unite us with the angels in the fullness. Thus we many having become One might be mingled in the One which was divided for our sakes.[20]

There are many examples of similar texts.[21] The 'fullness' here is the state of the holy of holies, filled with angels who were all aspects of the divine Unity, and through whom the divine was present in the visible world. As the name 'angel' implies, they were the messengers, and the Davidic king was the angel/messenger of Wisdom (LXX Isa. 9.6).

The Prologue opens by setting the story of Jesus within the temple mystery – how the Unity becomes many – and then shows how the human can become divine and return to the Unity. This, as we shall see, was the theme of Jesus' prayer in John 17.[22] 'He gave [them] power to become children of God', with the explanation 'who were born, not of blood nor of the will of the flesh nor of the will of man, but of God' (1.12b–13), meant returning to the angel state, and thus to the original Unity. This way of expressing the work of Christ is not unique to John; it is found also in the letter to Ephesus:

> For [God] has made known to us in all wisdom and insight the mystery of his will, according to his purpose which he set forth in Christ as a plan for

---

[20] Clement of Alexandria, *Excerpts from Theodotus* 36.
[21] See my book *The Great Angel. A Study of Israel's Second God*, London: SPCK, 1992, pp. 169–72.
[22] See below, pp. 489, 512–14.

the fullness of time, to unite all things in him, things in heaven and things on earth. (Eph. 1.9–10)

The second part of the poem describes the work of the Logos in making the visible world.

> ³All things were made through him
> And without him was not anything made that was made.
> ⁴In him was life
> And the life was the light of men.
> ⁵The light shines in the darkness
> And the darkness has not overcome it.

The Logos was Yahweh, a name now thought to mean 'He who causes to be'. The Enthroned One in Revelation 4, soon to be united with the Lamb, was not described in detail ('he ... appeared like jasper and carnelian', v. 3), but the heavenly host sang hymns to him as Yahweh, the One who causes to be. 'Who was and is and is to come' (Rev. 4.8b) is the Greek version of the Name as it appears in the Palestinian Targum, how the first Christians would have heard it in their synagogues. The LORD's revelation of his Name to Moses at the burning bush in the form *'ehyeh ᵃšer 'ehyeh* (Exod. 3.14), literally 'I cause to be what I cause to be', was explained in the Targum as: 'The one who said, and the world was there from the beginning, and is to say to it "Be there" and it will be there ...'[23] In Targum practice, the double verb in *'ehyeh ᵃšer 'ehyeh* had to be represented twice and so was said to mean the power of 'causing to be' both in the past and in the future. This is reflected in the second part of the heavenly hymn:

> Worthy art thou, our Lord and God,
> To receive glory and honour and power,
> For thou didst create all things,
> And by thy will they existed and were created.
> (Rev. 4.11)

In the Prologue this appears as 'All things were made through him, and without him was not anything made that was made.' This is why, in his sermon in Solomon's porch, Peter described Jesus as the Author of Life (Acts 3.15). Presumably this is how the earliest Jerusalem Christians described him. But the heavenly hymn in Revelation praised the One 'who was and is and comes', *erchomenos* (translating literally). The 'one who comes' was the hope and expectation fulfilled by the claim in John's

---

[23] Targum *Neofiti* Exod. 3.14.

## John 1

Prologue: 'He came to his own ... the Logos became flesh ... we beheld his glory.'

The Logos as Yahweh may seem surprising, but the Christians understood the LORD of the Hebrew Scriptures to be the second divine figure, distinct from El Elyon.[24] Philo described the Logos as this second figure *who could be seen*. Moses on Sinai saw the Logos.[25] The Logos for Philo was also the second source of life: '[The] God is the supreme source of life, and second the Logos of God ...'[26] The Logos did not mean 'Word' in any normal sense of that word. It was, as we have seen,[27] more likely to represent the Aramaic word *memra* that is found in the Palestinian Targums and is closely linked to the *'ehyeh ᵃšer 'ehyeh* form of the Name. It indicated the presence of the LORD, and so a study of the matter concluded: 'the Name of the *memra* is YHWH, given to men to use in worship: God's own Name is 'HYH'.[28] Thus the heavenly host in Revelation 4 used the expanded form of Yahweh, not of 'Ehyeh, since they were worshipping the LORD. When the LORD himself used his Name, it was the threefold form *'ehyeh ᵃšer 'ehyeh*, and this explains an otherwise curious passage in the *Gospel of Thomas*. Jesus took Thomas aside and told him three things. When Thomas returned, the other disciples asked him what Jesus had said, and Thomas replied: 'If I tell you one of the things which he told me, you will pick up stones and throw them at me.'[29] In other words, it would be blasphemy for Thomas to repeat the three things. Jesus had spoken the threefold Name, revealing his identity to Thomas.

In this presence ('in him') was the light of humankind, shining in darkness that has not *overcome* it. The verb here has at least two possible meanings, suggesting that the poem was employing the temple style of double meanings even in Greek since both meanings are appropriate. The verb *katalambanō* has a whole range of meanings: 'overcome' was the sense adopted by Origen and most of the early Greek tradition of interpretation – 'the darkness has not overcome the light'; and 'comprehend' was the sense adopted by Cyril of Alexandria and the Latin tradition of interpretation – 'the darkness has not comprehended

---

[24] See above, p. 67.
[25] See my book *The Great Angel*, n. 21 above, pp. 114–33.
[26] Philo, *Allegorical Interpretation* II.86.
[27] See above, p. 103.
[28] C. T. R. Hayward, 'The Holy Name of the God of Moses and the Prologue of St John's Gospel', *New Testament Studies* 25 (1978), pp. 16–32, p. 24.
[29] *Gospel of Thomas* 13.

the light'.³⁰ Either meaning makes sense, and perhaps both meanings were intended: *katalambanō* meaning 'overcome' occurs again in Jesus' final public words, 'Lest the darkness overcome you', and 'comprehend' is implied in: 'he who walks in the darkness does not know ...' (12.35).

The third part of the poem recounts what happened when the LORD did come into the material world; it is history and refers to the Incarnation of the LORD as Jesus and how his own people refused or failed to recognize him.

> ¹⁰He was in the world
> And the world was made through him
> Yet the world knew him not.
> ¹¹He came to his own home
> And his own people received him not
> ¹²But to all who received him, who believed in his name,
> He gave power to become children of God.

This is the major theme of the Gospel: the Jews did not accept him and did not recognize him because they had lost touch with those very temple traditions that would have enabled them to know who he was. Even though they are not mentioned in the nativity stories until the eighth century CE,³¹ the ox and the ass of Isaiah's oracle were soon used in Christian art as symbols of the Jews' failure to understand. Justin, in the mid-second century, said this had been prophesied by Isaiah:

> The ox knows its owner,
> And the ass its master's crib;
> But Israel does not know,
> My people does not understand.
> (Isa. 1.3)³²

The Logos came to his own, *ta idia*, a neuter plural noun, which means 'the things that belonged to him'. Here it probably means the entire cultural heritage of Israel, and especially of the temple. His own, *hoi idioi* – here a masculine plural noun meaning 'his own people' – did not accept him. The verb here can mean 'accept', but it also has the sense of receiving a tradition or an inheritance. In other words, the very cultural setting in which he should have been recognized and received had become the darkness that did not understand the light.

---

³⁰ See Brown, *Gospel According to John*, n. 11 above, p. 8.
³¹ In the *Gospel of Pseudo-Matthew*.
³² Justin, *Apology* 1.63.

## John 1

In contrast, to all those who did accept/understand him, the Logos gave the right/power, *exousia*, to become children of God. They were given the means to access what 'his own' had rejected. In the synoptic Gospels, this is expressed in the parable of the vineyard, where the current tenants of the vineyard/the temple reject the owner's Son and so lose their right to the vineyard (Mark 12.1–12 and parallels). 'He gave power to become' is not a good translation, since it implies a teaching that John does not attribute to Jesus. The Greek *exousia*, meaning 'power' or 'authority', is probably an attempt to convey the Hebrew idiom *nāthan*, meaning 'give', which can have the sense of 'create a status' or 'appoint to a position'. For example, the risen LORD promised the angel/bishop of the church in Thyatira: 'To him who conquers/is faithful ... I will *give* the Morning Star' (Rev. 2.26–28, my translation). This means 'I will make him a Morning Star'. 'Morning Star', as can be seen from the parallelism of the Hebrew poetry at Job 38.7, was another name for a son of God, an angel. The risen LORD therefore promised to the faithful angel/bishop of Thyatira that he would become a son of God, exactly how John summarized the teaching of Jesus: 'to all who received him ... *he gave power to become* children of God'.

In Revelation, this was the subject of the hymn to the newly enthroned Lamb in heaven:

> Worthy art thou to take the book [RSV 'scroll'] and to open its seals,
> For thou wast slain and by thy blood didst *ransom* men for God
> From every tribe and tongue and people and nation,
> And hast made them a kingdom and priests to our God
> And they shall reign on earth.     (Rev. 5.9–10, my translation)

The crux here is how to translate *ēgorasas*, 'ransom'. The word is literally 'bought in the market', which suggests that a Hebrew text has suffered in translation. The original was probably *qānâ*, which can mean 'buy' but also 'redeem' (as in Ps. 74.2, where *qānâ* is parallel to 'redeem'). In the old temple, however, the word meant 'beget': El Elyon was the 'begetter' of heaven and earth (Gen. 14.19); and the LORD was the 'begetter' of his people:

> Is not [the LORD] your father who begat you,
> Who made you and established you?
>     (Deut. 32.6, my translation)

The hymn says that by sacrificing himself, the Lamb has 'begotten' a royal priesthood. They appear later as the followers of the Lamb who have been 'begotten' from humankind as the firstborn of God-and-the-Lamb (Rev. 14.4).[33] These were the children of God, the assembly of the Firstborn (Heb. 12.23), the many brothers of the Firstborn (Rom. 8.29). Hence the explanation in the *Gospel of Philip*: 'The father makes a son, and the son has not the power to make a son. For he who has been begotten has not the power to beget but the son gets brothers for himself, not sons.'[34]

The explanation inserted in the Prologue poem contrasts heavenly birth and human birth, as does Jesus' meeting with Nicodemus (3.3–6): '[those] born not of bloods, nor from the will of the flesh, nor from the will of a human male, but from God' (1.13, translating literally). 'Bloods' probably indicates the two parents necessary for a human birth, and this verse emphasizes that the birth of the Son of God, or of the sons of God, is not a normal physical process.

The final part of the poem reflects on this temple birth, the Incarnation of the Logos, and so this is John's nativity story (my translation).

> [14] And the Logos became flesh and dwelt among us,
> And we have beheld his glory,
> The glory as of the only Son from the Father,
> Full of grace and truth.
> [16] And from his fullness we have all received, grace upon grace.

John does not describe the process of the mystery. He simply states: 'The Logos became flesh and dwelt [literally 'tabernacled'] among us'. This evokes the command to Moses at Sinai: 'Let them make me a sanctuary, that I may dwell in their midst' (Exod. 25.8), which in the Septuagint became '... that I may be seen in their midst'. The word 'dwelt' derives from *skēnē*, the tent or tabernacle, and does not necessarily imply a temporary dwelling. It alludes rather to how the LORD had been present in the tabernacle/temple and how he was expected to return. When Moses had completed the tabernacle, 'the cloud covered the *tent* of meeting, and the glory of the LORD filled the *tabernacle*' (Exod. 40.34). The Septuagint has *skēnē* each time. So too when Solomon consecrated the temple, 'a cloud filled the house of the LORD ... for the glory of the LORD filled the house of the LORD' (1 Kings 8.10, 11). After the temple had been destroyed in 586 BCE, Jeremiah took the *skēnē*, the ark and the incense altar and hid them in a cave. They would be restored, he said, only when God gathered again his scattered people: 'and the glory of the LORD and the cloud will appear ...' (2 Macc. 2.4–8). This text was written about

---

[33] Firstborn rather than firstfruits; see my book *The Revelation of Jesus Christ*, p. 244.
[34] *Gospel of Philip*, CG II.3.58.

## John 1

100–50 BCE and so the story was known in the time of Jesus. The LORD and his *skēnē* were linked to the glory and the cloud, and they would return. Ezekiel had seen the glory of the LORD and the bright cloud leaving the polluted temple (Ezek. 10.3–4; 11.22–23) and in a later vision he saw it return through the eastern gate (Ezek. 43.1–5). In Revelation, the LORD provides a *skēnē* over those who serve before his throne (Rev. 7.15, translating literally); and in the vision of the heavenly city 'behold the *skēnē* of God is with men and he shall *skēnē* with them ...' (Rev. 21.3, my translation). For John, the *skēnē* of the Logos is the LORD with his glory coming again to his holy place as a human being. It is the realization of the royal ritual when the king became the LORD and the LORD became the King.

'We have beheld his glory', said John, and this is likely to refer to the Transfiguration, which John does not mention elsewhere in his Gospel, but all the synoptic Gospels do, and they also describe the cloud overshadowing Jesus. Matthew, writing within a Hebrew-Christian community, says there was a *bright* cloud (Matt. 17.5). A voice from the cloud said, 'This is my beloved Son ... ', the same as at Jesus' baptism, when the heavens opened and the Spirit came like a dove (e.g. Matt. 3.16–17). On both occasions, it is usually assumed that the voice was the Father, but a Son also has a Mother, and this is how the Hebrew Christians told the story of the baptism. It was the Spirit, the Mother of Jesus, who spoke to her Son.[35] We suggest that this was also the case at the Transfiguration; the Spirit recognizing her Son.

Now 'sons of the cloud' had been a designation of the first-temple priests, as can be seen from the Third-Isaiah's wordplay when he condemned the corrupted priests of the second temple and called them the sons of a sorceress: 'sorceress' and 'cloud' were written in the same way but pronounced differently,[36] and here the prophet condemned the new priests and their new 'mother' (Isa. 57.3). The (bright) cloud appears often in the Hebrew Scriptures, and read without presuppositions, the text could be describing 'the glory' as something/someone distinct from the LORD. Ezekiel, for example, saw a great cloud with brightness round about, within which was the throne and the human figure. *All these* comprised 'the appearance of the likeness of the glory of the LORD', and the throne seems to have been a female figure (Ezek. 1.4, 28).[37] All four

---

[35] Jerome, *Commentary on Isaiah* 11, quoting the (now lost) *Gospel of the Hebrews*.
[36] See my book *Mother of the Lord*, pp. 196–7.
[37] See above, p. 118.

New Testament Gospels say the Baptist fulfilled one prophecy from the Second-Isaiah: 'A voice cries: "In the wilderness prepare the way of the LORD"', but the text continues: 'and the glory of the LORD shall be revealed' (Isa. 40.3, 5). The restoration of which the prophet spoke would turn darkness to light and lead the blind in a new way. It was compared to a woman with labour pains about to give birth (Isa. 42.14–17); and the great proclamation 'Behold your God', *ᵉlohîm*', was by a female figure: 'the herald of good tidings' is a feminine participle (Isa. 40.9). Further, there is wordplay here, because *mᵉbaśśeret*, 'female herald', has the same root as the word 'flesh', *bāśār*, and had there been a word for 'the female who incarnates' it would have been the same word as 'herald'. Later writers described the fiery pillar of cloud that led Israel across the wilderness as the throne of Wisdom (Wisd. 10.17; Ben Sira 24.4).

The cloud and the glory could have been the way that the Mother of the LORD was described, the one who made possible his appearance on earth and his return to heaven. She was the means of Incarnation, and this is how the Church understood the image. We cannot assume that the Church was wrong. The Bethlehem shepherds saw the glory of the LORD when the LORD, the Messiah, was born (Luke 2.8–12); a cloud took Jesus from human sight at the Ascension (Acts 1.9); angels said he would return with a cloud (Acts 1.11); and this is how he did return, the mighty angel wrapped in a cloud and wreathed in a rainbow (Rev. 10.1). The *Infancy Gospel of James* depicts the cave of the Nativity as the holy of holies: a bright cloud overshadowed the cave, the cloud then withdrew and there was a light in the cave; the light then diminished and the Child was seen with his Mother.[38] Joseph and the midwife who saw this sight could easily have said, 'The Logos became flesh and dwelt among us, and we saw his glory, the glory of the beloved Son from the Father, the glory that was full of grace and truth.' This is a literal translation of John 1.14, where 'full of grace and truth' could as well apply to the glory as to the Son.[39] In Revelation the Lady was seen again in the temple and she gave birth to her son who was the LORD's Anointed, the man who was the Incarnation of the LORD and would establish his kingdom on earth (Rev. 11.15—12.6).

The Prologue poem ends: 'And from his fullness we have all received, grace upon grace.' The fullness was the heavenly powers of the invisible

---

[38] *Infancy Gospel of James* 19.

[39] The RSV *changes the order* of the text so that the 'grace and truth' can apply only to the Logos. The Greek order is: the Logos became flesh and dwelt among us, and we saw his glory, the glory of the beloved of the Father, full of grace and truth.

## John 1

creation, and 'sevenfold' was a way of expressing totality or completeness – the sevenfold presence/fullness of the LORD:

- The anointed high priest was a sevenfold presence, as can be seen from the seven identical angels, all dressed in white linen and the golden sash of the high priest, who emerge from the holy of holies bringing the wrath (Rev. 15.1–8).
- Isaiah knew that the sevenfold Spirit would rest (again) on the Anointed One who was the new branch from the royal tree (Isa. 11.1-2), and the imagery in the Hebrew Scriptures shows that this new branch would spring from the stump of the felled tree (Isa. 6.13). The mother vine, said Ezekiel the priest, had been uprooted and taken to the wilderness, and there were no more strong stems to be rulers (Ezek. 19.10–14).
- The sevenfold fullness is also depicted in Revelation as seven horns and seven eyes of the enthroned Lamb (Rev. 5.6). John explains the seven eyes – they are the seven spirits or the sevenfold spirit that make the recipient the LORD (the meaning of 'Spirit of the LORD') – and the seven horns are the seven rays of light that indicate complete illumination: the sevenfold Spirit that Isaiah describes affects the mind and so the way that knowledge is held and used.

The Enochic *Apocalypse of Weeks*, as reconstructed from Qumran material,[40] predicts that at the end of the apostate generation who built the second temple (what the *Apocalypse* calls the seventh week), sevenfold wisdom and knowledge would be restored: 'The chosen from the elect plant of righteousness will be elected to serve as witnesses to righteousness; and sevenfold wisdom and knowledge will be given to them.'[41] The plant of righteousness was Abraham,[42] and those of his descendants who were chosen would become the witnesses and would receive the sevenfold knowledge: Christ first, and then those who followed him and also received the Spirit. Thus Paul quoted a hymn when he was writing to the Christians in Colossae: 'For in [Christ] all the fullness of God was pleased to dwell', and then, warning them about the deceits of false spirits, affirmed: 'For in [Christ] the whole fullness of deity dwells bodily' (Col. 1.19; 2.9). For the Christians at Ephesus, Paul prayed that they might be

---

[40] 4QEn$^g$.
[41] *1 Enoch* 93.10 reconstructed from 4QEn$^g$, translation in D. Olsen, *Enoch: A New Translation*, North Richland Hills: Bibal Press, 2004.
[42] *1 Enoch* 93.5.

filled with all the fullness of God (Eph. 3.19), to have knowledge and Christ's love that surpasses knowledge:

> That Christ may dwell in your hearts through faith; and that you, being rooted and grounded in love, may have power to comprehend with all the saints what is the breadth and length and height and depth, and to know the love of Christ which surpasses knowledge, that you may be filled with all the fullness of God. (Eph. 3.17–19)

The many gifts of the Spirit through Christ would enable Christians to become one, and to have the knowledge that the Son of God has, to become fully the Man, and so attain the fullness of Christ.

> And his gifts were ... for building up the body of Christ, until we all attain to the unity of the faith and of the knowledge of the Son of God, to mature manhood, to the measure of the stature of the fullness of Christ.
> (Eph. 4.11, 12–13)

This would be the gift to, and the sign of, the witnesses.

'Witnesses' was a key term for the Second-Isaiah and also for John's account of the Baptist, for he was the first witness:

> Bring forth the people who are blind, yet have eyes,
> Who are deaf, yet have ears ...
> Let them bring their witnesses to justify them,
> And let them hear and say, It is true.
> 'You are my *witnesses*,' says the LORD,
> 'And my servant whom I have chosen,
> That you may know and believe me
> And understand that I am He ...'   (Isa. 43.8, 9, 10)

The recurring theme in John's Gospel is the Jews' failure to recognize Jesus as the LORD, and he concludes his account of Jesus' ministry with a reflection on Isaiah's oracle of the blind eyes and hardened hearts, the ones who could not see and did not understand (12.37–43). The chosen ones from Abraham, however, would be witnesses who would 'know and believe me And understand that I am He'. The people who prayed the *Didache* prayers gave thanks for the life and knowledge made known through Jesus, the Servant.

Woven into the poem about the coming of the Logos is the role of the Baptist, presented as the sevenfold witness to the oracle of Isaiah:

> That you may know and believe me
> And understand that *I am He* ...
> (Isa. 43.10)

## John 1

This piece about the Baptist culminates with his recognition of the Son, the LORD – in other words, his understanding 'I am He' – and the word 'witness' occurs seven times.

> ⁶There was a man sent from God whose name was John.
> ⁷He came for *witness*, to bear *witness* to the light, that all might believe through him.
> ⁸He was not the light, but came to bear *witness* to the light.
> ⁹The true light that enlightens every man was coming into the world ...
> ¹⁵John bore *witness* to him, and cried, 'This was he of whom I said, "He who comes after me ranks before me, for he was before me."'

The story continues:

> ¹⁹And this is the *witness* of John ...
> ³²And John bore *witness*, 'I saw the Spirit descend as a dove from heaven, and it remained on him ...
> ³⁴And I have seen and have borne *witness* that this is the Son of God.'

The Prologue ends by contrasting the way of Moses and the way of the Anointed One: the law came through Moses, grace and truth through Jesus Christ. 'Grace and truth' most likely represents mercy, *ḥesedh*, and truth, *'emeth* (or *ᵉmûnâ* which is from the same root), which are often found together in the Psalms, linked to the LORD and the Davidic kings. 'Mercy and truth' accompany the LORD and protect the king.

- 'All the paths of the LORD are mercy, *ḥesedh*, and truth, *'emeth*' (Ps. 25.10);
- 'I have not concealed your mercy, *ḥesedh*, and truth, *'emeth*' (Ps. 40.10);
- 'May your mercy, *ḥesedh*, and truth, *'emeth*, always preserve me' (Ps. 40.11);
- 'God will send forth his mercy, *ḥesedh*, and truth, *'emeth*' (Ps. 57.3);
- 'Bid mercy, *ḥesedh*, and truth, *'emeth*, to watch over [the king]' (Ps. 61.7);
- '[As a sign of salvation] mercy, *ḥesedh*, and truth, *'emeth*, will meet together' (Ps. 85.10);
- 'A merciful and gracious God, slow to anger and great in mercy, *ḥesedh*, and truth, *'emeth*' (Ps. 86.15).[43]

The text which has most details about the LORD and the role of the king is Psalm 89, which has both *'emeth* and *ᵉmûnâ* paired with *ḥesedh*. The Psalmist sings of the mercy and truth that are firmly established and praised by the angels in heaven (Ps. 89.1, 2, 5); they go before the LORD (Ps. 89.14); the LORD promises that his mercy and truth will be with the

---

[43] My translations.

king, his mercy to protect him and his truth to establish the covenant, and his mercy and truth would never be removed or prove to be false (Ps. 89.24, 28, 33). But after the monarchy had ended and the city was destroyed by enemies, the Psalmist asked: 'Where are your original mercies [the plural of *ḥesedh*], which you swore to David in your *ᵉmûnâ*?' (Ps. 89.49, my translation). The mercy and truth that accompanied the LORD and protected the Davidic kings had gone. An oracle attached to the Book of Micah promises that the LORD will not be angry for ever, because he delights in *ḥesedh*, and will again show *'emeth* to Jacob and *ḥesedh* to Abraham (Mic. 7.18, 20). John proclaims that mercy, *ḥesedh*, and truth, *'emeth*, have returned with Jesus the Messiah.

The Prologue ends with a clear statement of first-temple belief. One of the points at issue between the teaching of the first temple and the teaching of the second was 'seeing God'. The older texts knew that people had seen the LORD: Isaiah saw the King, the LORD of Hosts (Isa. 6.5); Abraham built an altar where the LORD appeared to him (Gen. 12.7); Moses, the high priests and the 70 elders saw the God of Israel on Sinai (Exod. 24.9–10).[44] But the pro-Moses reformers denied that the LORD was seen (Deut. 4.12), and their heirs were responsible for rereading the old calendar texts that had originally exhorted all the people of Israel to go to the temple three times a year to see the face of the LORD. John reminds his readers of the second God – the LORD, the Son of God Most High – by saying that no one has ever seen God (meaning God Most High) but that the beloved/only-begotten God who is in the *kolpos* of the Father has revealed or led the way. Now *kolpos*, a 'hollow place', can mean many things: a bay, a fold in a garment, a lap, a bosom, and a womb. The only-begotten God in the womb of the Father, who revealed the mysteries/showed the way,[45] was the LORD who became the Davidic king in the temple mystery. Thus the Prologue ends as it began, in the holy of holies – the 'beginning' or 'the womb' – whence Immanuel came forth.

## 1.19–51: The Baptist and his disciples

All the New Testament Gospels say that the Baptist was the herald of Jesus. All quote the prophecy of Isaiah, that he was the voice crying in the wilderness, 'Make straight the way of the LORD.' All say that he baptized in the Jordan, that he baptized Jesus, and that he spoke of someone greater

---
[44] See above, p. 47.
[45] See above, p. 78.

than himself who would come after him whose sandals he was not worthy to carry or untie. The synoptic Gospels say that the coming one would baptize with the Holy Spirit. Matthew and Luke say he would also baptize with fire, and they describe the imminent judgement in language reminiscent of Matthew 13: the wheat would be gathered in, and the chaff/weeds would be burned.

Mark and Matthew describe the Baptist's way of life, clothed in rough garments and eating wild food. Mark also quotes the prophecy of Malachi: 'Behold I send my messenger/angel before your face, who will prepare your way' (Mal. 3.1; Mark 1.2, my translation).[46] Matthew attributes this to Jesus, who said the Baptist fulfilled Malachi's prophecy (Matt. 11.10), preparing the way for the messenger/angel of the covenant who would suddenly come to his temple, to judge and purify the sons of Levi. The Baptist himself was a hereditary priest, the only child of elderly parents: his father Zechariah served as a temple priest and his mother was from the high-priestly family, a daughter of Aaron (Luke 1.5). He had grown up in the wilderness (Luke 1.80). His elderly parents could have died when he was a child, and, since the son of a priest is unlikely to have grown up living rough in the wilderness, he could well have been brought up by the priestly Essene community living near Ein Gedi. They were a celibate group who survived by taking people into their community,[47] and the Baptist could have been one of them. Had he lived with the Essenes, he would have grown up with the learning of the time, including the expectation that Melchi-Zedek was about to return. This would explain his being linked to the prophecy from Malachi, that someone greater than a Levitical priest was coming to judge them.

Matthew and Luke give details of his preaching: he warned the people (Matthew says it was the Pharisees and Sadducees) to flee from the imminent wrath and he called them the children of the snake – 'You brood of vipers'. They claimed to be children of Abraham, and so, by implication, were expecting to be saved from the wrath. The same images occur in John's account of Jesus' debates with 'the Jews', as we shall see. Luke includes the Baptist's examples of repentance: generosity, honesty, peaceful behaviour and contentment (Luke 3.10–14).

Josephus also wrote about the Baptist and had some of the elements in the synoptic Gospels, namely, that he preached repentance and a return to piety and upright living. Herod Antipas, said Josephus, had gone to war

---
[46] Not the Greek of the Lxx but a different rendering of the Hebrew text.
[47] Pliny, *Natural History* V.15.

with his father-in-law Aretas, king of Arabia. Men from his brother Philip's territory had joined Aretas and betrayed him, and so his army was destroyed. Some Jews said this was divine punishment for killing the Baptist, a man who exhorted the Jews to return to moral living and piety towards God, washing their bodies to purify them once their souls had been cleansed by righteousness. Herod had been afraid of his influence and so imprisoned him in the fortress at Machaerus, where he had him executed. This, said some Jews, was why Herod's army had been destroyed.[48] Josephus did not mention the Baptist's relationship to Jesus nor his role as the herald of someone greater who was to come.

John's picture of the Baptist is unique. He begins his Gospel with the Logos 'in the beginning' and brings his story into the world by interweaving profound Temple Theology with the story of the Baptist who believed he had been 'sent' to baptize and to identify the expected One. John does not say who sent him. It could have been a leader or prophet among the desert community who were expecting Melchi-Zedek, the Messiah. One of the prophecies in the Qumran *Melchizedek* text seems to be Isaiah 61, but this has to be recovered from a very damaged fragment. The critical edition of this text finds traces of Isaiah 61 in lines 6, 18, 19 and 20.[49] The allusions probably indicate the whole of what is now chapter 61, that being the only way to identify a text before there were chapter and verse numbers. One anointed by the Spirit of the LORD would bring the day of judgement, build up ancient ruins (perhaps meaning restore the true temple), and restore the ousted priesthood: 'You shall be called priests of the LORD, men shall speak of you as the ministers of our God' (Isa. 61.6). The role of the Baptist could be seen as the Levitical priesthood recognizing and handing over to someone greater, who was before, yet would come after. In the context of Isaiah 61, the ousted priests would be the first-temple priests, and this is what the writer of Hebrews explained: Melchi-Zedek had replaced the family of Aaron.

The Baptist was baptizing in Bethany on the east side of the Jordan. John emphasized that it was the priests and Levites who came with anxious questions, sent by the Jews to ask the Baptist if he was the Messiah or Elijah or the prophet (vv. 19–21). They must have feared the judgement threatened for the sons of Levi: 'Like a refiner's fire ... he will purify the sons of Levi' (Mal. 3.2, 3). There must have been rumours, just

---

[48] Josephus, *Antiquities* 18.116.
[49] F. Garcia-Martinez, ed., *Qumran Cave 11. Discoveries in the Judaean Desert* XXIII, Oxford: Oxford University Press, 1998, pp. 230–1.

*John 1*

as there would be about Jesus. Some said that Jesus was the Baptist back from the dead, or Elijah, or one of the prophets (Mark 8.28). The Messiah was expected at any time, and Elijah would return 'before the great and terrible day of the LORD' (Mal. 4.5–6; Ben Sira 48.10). Melchi-Zedek was expected to appear during the first seven years of the final jubilee,[50] and presumably the Baptist would have known this. Since the final jubilee began in 17/19 CE, according to calculations based on Daniel's prophecy of the 490 years (Dan. 9.24–27), the priests and Levites who studied these matters asked the Baptist who he was.[51] People were expecting the promised 'most holy one' at any time (Dan. 9.24). There had been other Messiahs who had caused trouble (Acts 5.36–37). Some of the Baptist's own disciples thought he was the Messiah: 'Some of the disciples of John have separated themselves from the people and proclaimed their own master as the Christ.'[52] This was dangerous speculation: in the early years of Herod's reign temple priests had been studying the prophecies and could not believe that Herod was the Messiah who was due to appear. Herod was told of their discussions by an informer, and he had all the priests killed.[53]

The Baptist himself said he was neither the Messiah nor Elijah nor the prophet. He was the voice of one crying in the wilderness, 'Make straight the way of the LORD.'[54] This quotation from Isaiah, however, must be read in context, which the Baptist, the son of a priest, would have known. The voice in the Second-Isaiah announced that the glory of the LORD was about to be revealed and return to the temple. 'In the wilderness prepare the way of the LORD ... and the glory of the LORD shall be revealed' (Isa. 40.3–5). This links to the Prologue: 'We beheld his glory' and also the conclusion of the greater Prologue: 'He revealed his glory' (2.11). Ezekiel had seen the glory of the LORD leave the polluted temple of his own time and go to the exiles in Babylon (Ezek. 1; 10). In another vision he saw the

---

[50] *Melchizedek*, 11QMelch. See my book *The Great High Priest. The Temple Roots of Christian Liturgy*, London: T&T Clark, 2003, pp. 34–41.
[51] See below, p. 189.
[52] *Clementine Recognitions* 1.54, 60.
[53] This is in the Slavonic text of Josephus, *War* 1.364–70, but not in the Greek. It can be found in the Loeb edition as an Appendix after Book 7.
[54] There is no way of knowing from the original Hebrew whether the voice was in the wilderness or the way of the LORD was to be in the wilderness. In other words, whether we should read: 'A voice crying in the wilderness, "Prepare the way of the LORD"' or 'A voice crying, "In the wilderness prepare the way of the LORD"'. The great Isaiah scroll from Qumran gives no indication of how this verse was to be understood, but the *Community Rule*, 1QS VIII, understood that the way of the LORD had to be prepared in the wilderness. That is why the members of the community had gone to live there.

glory return to fill the restored temple (Ezek. 43.1–5). So too his younger contemporary the Second-Isaiah: he saw the glory of the LORD returning along the way prepared in the wilderness, the LORD coming as a shepherd with his flock (Isa. 40.11) as a sign that Jerusalem's time of trouble was ended (Isa. 40.1–2).

This trouble could have been the Roman occupation of the land – as implied by the Qumran *War Scroll* – but the visions in Revelation imply something very different: that the enemy was the harlot city and her corrupted temple. Her identity is encoded in Revelation – 'This calls for a mind with wisdom' (Rev. 17.9) – but the ten horns and the beast joined forces to attack the harlot. Since the beast was Nero, who was assassinated in 68 CE, and the ten horns were the ten heirs of Herod the Great, the original harlot city was not Rome.[55] When the prophecies of Isaiah were collected into one scroll and given their Preface, Jerusalem was condemned: 'The faithful city has become a harlot' (Isa. 1.21), and the people who became the Christians were inspired by the oracles of Isaiah. Nobody knows when this Preface to Isaiah was composed, but the era of the second temple was regarded by many as the time of apostasy and the age of wrath. Much blood had been shed in the city, and again this cannot be dated. The harlot was drunk with the blood of the holy ones and the martyrs of Jesus (Rev. 17.6). The heavens rejoiced when the harlot was destroyed (Rev. 19.1–4), and then the Lamb could come to his Bride (Rev. 19.6–8). She was described as the radiant holy city of Jerusalem, but built as a huge holy of holies (Rev. 21.9–21). She was the new temple.

The Pharisees asked why the Baptist was baptizing if he was neither the Messiah nor Elijah nor the prophet, and he replied that the Messiah had already come and, unknown to them, was living in their midst (v. 26). This was apparently a belief at the time, as can be seen from Trypho's words to Justin: 'But Christ – if he has indeed been born and exists anywhere – is unknown and does not even know himself, and has no power until Elijah comes to anoint him and make him manifest to all.'[56] John does not describe Jesus' baptism, but the day after his encounter with the Pharisees, and presumably still speaking to them, the Baptist saw Jesus approaching and pointed him out as 'the Lamb of God, who takes away the sin of the world' and 'the Son of God' (vv. 29, 34), because Jesus was the one on whom he had seen the Spirit descend at his baptism. If we try to align this account with the synoptic Gospels'

---

[55] For detail, see my book *The Revelation of Jesus Christ*, pp. 284–7.
[56] Justin, *Trypho* 8.

account, then Jesus would have been returning from his time in the desert after his baptism.

The Baptist must have been one of those to whom Jesus spoke of his *merkavah* experiences in the desert, because a short while later the Baptist would say of Jesus: 'He who comes from heaven is above all. He bears witness to what he has seen and heard, yet no one receives his testimony' (3.31b–32). If John was attributing accurately, then Jesus must have told the Baptist of his experiences in the desert, one of which was the vision of the enthroned Lamb (Rev. 5). There must have been a close relationship between Jesus and the Baptist, and after learning of the vision, the Baptist could identify Jesus as the Lamb of God who takes away the sins of the world. This is summarized in Hebrews as 'When he had made purification for sins he sat down at the right hand of the Majesty on high, having become as much superior to the angels as the Name he has obtained is more excellent than theirs' (Heb. 1.3b–4, my translation).

The Baptist told the Pharisees that he had not known the identity of the Messiah, but as with Simeon, it had been revealed to him that he would recognize the Messiah (Luke 2.26); he would be the one on whom he saw the Spirit coming down and remaining. 'The Spirit descending as a dove from heaven and remaining on him' (v. 32) could mean that the Baptist literally saw a dove hovering over Jesus as he was baptized and that he recognized the sign; or there could have been some other movement of the air, just as the Spirit is described in Genesis: 'fluttering over the face of the waters' (Gen. 1.2, translating literally). The Spirit *remained* on Jesus – something not mentioned in the synoptic Gospels, but found in the *Gospel of the Hebrews* that was used by Jerome in his commentary on Isaiah 11.2:

> It came to pass when the Lord was come up out of the water, the whole fount of the Holy Spirit descended and rested upon him, and said to him: 'My son, in all the prophets was I waiting for thee that thou shouldst come, and I might rest in thee. For thou art my rest, thou art my first-begotten son, that reignest for ever.'[57]

Jerome was saying that Isaiah's first-temple prophecy, a new branch from the royal tree, was fulfilled at the baptism of Jesus when the sevenfold Spirit came to him, rested on him, and declared him to be her Son. The Spirit was the Mother of the LORD in temple tradition. In the *Gospel of the Hebrews*, according to Jerome's commentary on Isaiah 11.9, Jesus also

---

[57] In M. R. James, *The Apocryphal New Testament*, Oxford: Clarendon Press (1924) 1980, p. 5.

## Temple Theology in John's Gospel

spoke of 'My Mother the Holy Spirit'. From the sign of the resting Spirit, the Baptist could proclaim that Jesus was both 'the Lamb of God who takes away the sin of the world' and also 'the Son of God'.

Despite arguments to the contrary,[58] there is a pattern in the titles that John introduced in this chapter, and they were all (except Rabbi) royal titles. The one who bore the sins of the world was the royal high priest in the first temple, where the Day of Atonement had been a major part of the New Year festival. The Second-Isaiah's fourth Servant song, reused by his later disciples, had originally been the First-Isaiah's reflection on the fate of Hezekiah, inspired by this atonement ritual.[59] The Servant of the LORD who suffered was called the Lamb not because the atonement offering was a lamb – it was usually two goats – but because temple discourse used wordplay, and both Servant and Lamb could be represented by the same Aramaic word *talyā'* – literally 'young one'. Temple tradition also represented heavenly beings as 'men' and mortals as animals, so that 'Lamb' would indicate the Servant in his human state. Arguments that *talyā'* is not found elsewhere meaning 'the Servant' have to ignore the evidence of the Johannine writings, and even doubters have to admit that 'there seem to be enough indications in the Gospel to connect the Lamb of God and the Suffering Servant'.[60] Both were royal titles, and so in Revelation the Lamb was enthroned (Rev. 5.6–10).

The Baptist knew of one who was to come, and presumably others did too. We have suggested that the visions of Revelation 4—5 were Jesus' experience in the desert, in which he saw the heavenly host around the throne and heard them praising the LORD, using the expanded form of the Name that is found in the Targums,[61] but adding that the LORD would come:

> Holy, Holy, Holy, is the Lord God Almighty,
> Who was and is and *is to come*. (Rev. 4.8b)

From this vision, Jesus learned that he was the coming one, that he was to bring the day of the LORD, whence the claim in John's Gospel that judgement had been committed to him (5.27). The Baptist was his Elijah, but the Baptist did not know he was Elijah until he learned of Jesus' desert experiences. John's account is historically accurate insofar as the Baptist denied being Elijah before he knew who Jesus was.

---

[58] E.g. Brown, *Gospel According to John*, n. 11 above, p. 61.
[59] See above, pp. 91–2.
[60] Brown, *Gospel According to John*, n. 11 above, p. 5.
[61] See above, p. 168.

## John 1

The following day, the Baptist told two of his own disciples that Jesus was the Lamb of God, and they followed him. This small incident shows that the core group of Jesus' disciples had first been followers of the Baptist, and this was the criterion for choosing a replacement for Judas: 'one of the men who have accompanied us during all the time that the Lord Jesus went in and out among us, beginning from the baptism of John until the day when he was taken up from us', whereas Mark implies that Jesus called his disciples after John had been arrested (Acts 1.21–22; cf. Mark 1.14–20). Jesus himself may have been a disciple of the Baptist. Dodd suggested that this was the most natural way to understand the words 'he who comes after me ...'. They meant 'one who follows me', in the sense of being a disciple, and the same words, *opisō mou elthein*, were used by Jesus: '[Let him] take up his cross and follow me' (Mark 8.34). Thus 'He who comes after me ranks before me, for he was before me' (vv. 15, 30) would mean 'One of my disciples is more important than I am ...' Dodd concluded:

> We are reaching back to a stage of tradition scarcely represented elsewhere in the gospels ... that Jesus was at one time regarded as a follower or adherent of John the Baptist. If, as the synoptic gospels report, he accepted baptism at his hands, how else should he be regarded?[62]

John reveals more titles as more disciples join the group: Jesus is recognized by Andrew as the Messiah. Nathanael is sceptical at first: 'Can anything good come out of Nazareth?' (1.46), but Jesus recognizes 'an Israelite indeed, in whom [there] is no guile'. The significance of his words is lost, beyond the allusion to Israel/Jacob, but this man did not deceive, unlike the original Jacob whose name has the same root as the word 'deceive'. Hence Esau's words: 'Is he not rightly named Jacob? For he has deceived me twice: he took away my birthright and now he has taken away my blessing' (Gen. 27.36, translating literally). Then Nathanael, who speaks the truth, recognizes Jesus as the Son of God, the King of Israel. Jesus picks up Nathanael's allusion to the original Jacob and his deception by alluding to Jacob's subsequent dream at Bethel: 'the angels of God ascending and descending' being an exact quotation from the Septuagint of Genesis 28.12b.[63] Jesus said the heavens would open and

---

[62] C. H. Dodd, *Historical Tradition in the Fourth Gospel*, Cambridge: Cambridge University Press, 1963, p. 275.

[63] Even though this is a direct quotation from the LXX, 'no Christian writer before Augustine seems to have noticed this'. See J. H. Bernard, *The Gospel According to St John*, vol. 2, ICC, Edinburgh: T&T Clark, 1928, p. 67.

## Temple Theology in John's Gospel

the angels ascend and descend not upon Jacob but upon the Son of Man (1.51), which just means 'the Man', and 'Man' in temple discourse meant an angel. In the context of the other titles here, it must have meant the human who had been transformed and then returned to earth.

This understanding of Jacob's dream is implied in the discussion of two scholars in Palestine, R. Hiyya and R. Yannai, some two centuries after the time of Jesus, but we cannot know how long the story had been told in this way. They linked Jacob's dream and a text in Isaiah – 'You ... Israel, in whom I will be glorified' (Isa. 49.3) – explaining that Isaiah meant 'You, Israel, are he whose image is engraved on high.' Thus the angels at Bethel 'ascended on high and saw his image, they descended to earth and saw him sleeping'.[64] Jacob existed both in heaven as the image on the throne, and on earth as the sleeping man. Origen, a contemporary of the two rabbis and also in Palestine, knew this idea, as we have seen.[65] In his *Commentary on John*, when he was explaining how the Baptist could be both the angel sent from heaven to prepare the way (Mal. 3.1) and also a human being, he quoted from the *Prayer of Joseph*.

> But if someone also accepts the apocryphal document in circulation among the Hebrews entitled *The Prayer of Joseph*, he will find this doctrine clearly stated outright and clearly there, namely that those who, from the beginning, possessed something superior to men, being much better than other souls, have descended to human nature from being angels. Jacob at least says: 'For I who speak to you am Jacob and Israel, an angel of God and a primal spirit ... I am Jacob ... he who was called Israel by God, a man who sees God, because I am the firstborn of every living being which is given life by God.'[66]

So too with Jesus. If he had already received the vision of the Lamb on the throne, he would have known that he too was like Jacob. The Servant/Lamb who takes away the sins of the world existed both in heaven and on earth, and the allusion to Jacob well describes the Logos from 'the beginning' who had become flesh.

The allusion is to the royal rites when the human prince returned to his people as the LORD, the one consecrated and sent forth as the Son (10.36). According to Psalm 110.3 he was born in the glory of the holy ones, and then emerged as Melchi-Zedek; this was the 'earthly' aspect of the

---

[64] *Genesis Rabbah* LXVIII.13.
[65] See above, p. 130.
[66] Origen, *Commentary on John* 2.31, tr. R. E. Heine, *Commentary on the Gospel According to John, Books 1–10*, Washington, DC: Catholic University of America Press, 1989, p. 145.

*John 1*

*theosis*.[67] The human figure became the heavenly figure, the Man. According to Deuteronomy 33.2–5, which described the heavenly aspect, the 'Incarnation' was when the LORD came in glory from Sinai with a host of angels and became the king.[68] The human becoming divine and the divine human, accompanied by the host of angels, is the scene in Revelation 5, where the human being, the Lamb, becomes the One on the throne. The process is not described, but the result is assumed in the use of singular forms of speech for 'the One-who-sits-on-the-throne-and-the-Lamb' (Rev. 5.13, my translation). This is why Jesus responds with the allusion to the host of angels when Nathanael recognizes him as the Son of God and King of Israel.

The sequence of events in the opening scenes of John's Gospel implies that Jesus had returned from his time in the wilderness when he had endured the temptations described in the synoptic Gospels and received the visions implied by John's saying, 'He bears witness to what he has seen and heard' (3.32). These included the vision of the Lamb being enthroned. Jesus' words to Nathanael about the vision at Bethel could also have implied the end of the priesthood given to Jacob and his son Levi until the LORD himself came to dwell with his people, as described in Deuteronomy 33 and Psalm 110. The next incident John records is the wedding at Cana, where Jesus first shows his glory and gives a sign that he is indeed the expected Melchi-Zedek.

---

[67] See p. 75.
[68] See p. 133.

# John 2

## 2.1–11: The miracle at Cana

On the third day[1] Jesus and his disciples were invited to a wedding in Cana, the home town of Nathanael (21.2). This miracle is only recorded in John's Gospel. Jesus' mother was there, and so presumably was John himself, the figure concealed in the story as the unnamed second disciple of the Baptist who became a follower of Jesus (1.37–40). The detail about the water pots being made of stone is not necessary to the story and may be an eyewitness recollection. This must have been an observant Jewish household, since stone jars did not become ritually unclean in the way that pottery or metal vessels did, and so were often used for storing food and drink.[2] Jesus' own disciples were accused of disregarding such purity rules and eating without the ritual handwashing (Mark 7.1–5). Jesus ordered the six stone vessels to be filled with water, and when the liquid was drawn out, it had become wine.

Turning water into wine was not a sign of the Messiah, although people hoped that the Messiah would bring abundant crops and so plenty of everything. Offering wine instead of water was the sign of Melchi-Zedek. Philo referred to this aspect of the Melchi-Zedek story in order to make another point – the divine intoxication offered by the Logos who was Melchi-Zedek.[3] This suggests he was drawing on something already known, and wine instead of water would have been recognized as the sign of Melchi-Zedek. This link on its own would not be strong enough to establish the case for the miracle at Cana being a Melchi-Zedek sign, but Melchi-Zedek was expected to appear (again) at exactly that time, as we have seen.[4]

---

[1] It may have been the third day after meeting the first disciples, but there is no way of knowing.
[2] Mishnah *Kelim* 10.1.
[3] Philo, *Allegorical Interpretation* III.82: 'But let Melchizedek instead of water [the customary hospitality gift] offer wine, and let him offer souls undiluted wine to drink, so that they become possessed by divine intoxication ...'
[4] See above, p. 181.

## John 2

The Qumran *Melchizedek* text is only a piece from the end of a work whose other contents we can only guess. It looks for the return of Melchi-Zedek in the first seven years of the tenth jubilee, and so calculates in terms of 490 years (10 x 49 years). This time scale fits with the prophecy in Daniel about events at the end of 70 weeks of years (70 x 7 = 490 years). In Daniel the words are enigmatic, but seem to prophesy the coming of the Righteous One of eternity and the anointing of the most holy one (Dan. 9.24, translating literally). In the Qumran text the expected figure is Melchi-Zedek. Later Jewish tradition said that the 490 years ended in 68 CE, and calculating the 490 years from the jubilee year for which Ezra returned to re-establish the city, 424 BCE, makes the end of the tenth jubilee fall in 66 CE. A discrepancy of two years is not significant, and so the tenth jubilee would have begun in 17 or 19 CE, during the ministry of the Baptist. Melchi-Zedek was expected to appear in the first seven years of the tenth jubilee, that is, between 17/19 CE and 24/26 CE.[5]

The Qumran *Melchizedek* text is woven around several passages from the Hebrew Scriptures, but the text is often broken. Allusions that have been identified are Psalm 82.1: Melchi-Zedek was to take his place in the divine council and judge the angels who had failed to uphold justice and who had abused their 'knowledge and understanding'; he was the one whom the messenger announced to Zion: 'Your God reigns' (Isa. 52.7); and he was the one 'anointed by the Spirit to bring good tidings to the poor ... and to proclaim the year of the LORD's favour' (Isa. 61.1–2). Melchi-Zedek seems to be divine, just as other late second-temple material implies.[6] Until this text was discovered, there was no means of knowing that all the Gospels begin by proclaiming Jesus as Melchi-Zedek.

- Mark says Jesus began his ministry by proclaiming, 'The time is fulfilled, and the kingdom of God is at hand' (Mark 1.15). What time? Presumably the 490 years, and then the kingdom would be established.
- Matthew has Jesus begin his preaching: 'Repent, for the kingdom of heaven is at hand' (Matt. 4.17).
- Luke has Jesus read a Melchi-Zedek text, Isaiah 61.1, in the synagogue at Nazareth and then declare: 'Today this scripture has been fulfilled in your hearing' (Luke 4.16–21).

---

[5] See my book *The Great High Priest. The Temple Roots of Christian Liturgy*, London: T&T Clark, 2003, pp. 34–41.
[6] See above, pp. 71–3.

Turning water into wine was how John introduced Jesus as Melchi-Zedek. 'This was the first of his signs ... and he revealed his glory; and his disciples believed in him' (2.11, my translation). Jesus was the new priest, Melchi-Zedek, replacing the house of Levi, and the Baptist had recognized him as 'the one who comes after me, who ranks before me, because he was before me' (1.15, 30, my paraphrase).

The sad decline of the priesthood is set out in the *Testament of Levi*,[7] especially chapters 14—18, which claim to be drawing on the writings of Enoch. There is a 'prophecy' of the history of the second-temple priesthood, stylized as seven jubilees, and in the last of them the priesthood beomes corrupt: 'idolaters, adulterers, money lovers, arrogant, lawless, voluptuaries, pederasts and those who practise bestiality'.[8] This list is very similar to those whom Revelation excludes from the heavenly temple/city (Rev. 22.15), and there are other similarities between the *Testaments* and some of the Qumran scrolls: the struggle between light and darkness, the two spirits and the two ways.[9] The *Testaments* show the longing for a new high priesthood, and whether they are predominantly early Christian or pre-Christian, they show the importance of the new high priesthood for the early Church.

> And after their punishment shall have come from the LORD, the priesthood shall fail.
> Then shall the LORD raise up a new priest.
> And to him all the words of the LORD shall be revealed ...
> And the glory of the Most High shall be uttered over him,
> And the spirit of understanding and sanctification shall rest upon him [in the water*] ...
> And he shall open the gates of Paradise,
> And shall remove the threatening sword against Adam.
> And he shall give to the saints to eat from the tree of life,
> And the spirit of holiness shall be upon him
> And Beliar shall be bound by him,
> And he shall give power to his children to tread upon the evil spirits.

---

[7] One of the *Testaments of the Twelve Patriarchs* (*T12P*). This type of literature – the last words of a famous person and particularly of the sons of Jacob – was popular during the later second-temple period. There are many references to the Messiah in *T12P*, and in some cases these may have been editorial additions by Christians who preserved the texts. The present form of the text is thought to be pre-Christian material edited by Christians in the second century CE.
[8] *Testament of Levi* 17.11.
[9] E.g. *Community Rule*, 1QS III–IV.

*John 2*

And the Lord shall rejoice in his children
And be well-pleased with his beloved ones for ever.[10]

The similarity to the picture of Jesus in the Gospels and in Revelation is clear, but this is all set out in the context of a priesthood to replace the sons of Levi.

## 2.13–25: Cleansing the temple

After a brief visit to Capernaum with his mother, his brothers and his disciples (2.12), Jesus went to Jerusalem as Passover was approaching. He went into the temple area, *hieron*, where he found the money changers and the usual market for sacrificial animals. He drove the traders out and found himself in conflict with 'the Jews'. The synoptic Gospels describe his critics not as 'the Jews' but as 'the chief priests and scribes' (Mark 11.18//Matt. 21.15; Luke 19.47), which fits with our earlier conclusion that 'the Jews' were only one group within the Hebrews. The chief priests and scribes were the authorities in the second temple and the custodians of the written traditions.[11]

In the synoptic Gospels, the cleansing of the temple happens on the day after Palm Sunday, whereas John sets it at the beginning of Jesus' public ministry in Jerusalem. All the Gospels agree that it happened just before Passover. This has caused problems over the precise timing of the incident. John is often said to have misplaced the incident as part of his theological scheme, but it could equally well be said that the synoptic Gospels had to place the incident at the end of Jesus' ministry as they do not record any earlier time spent in Jerusalem. The disturbance in the temple is not mentioned at Jesus' trial, which is strange if it had occurred only a few days earlier. On the other hand, there are hints in the synoptic Gospels that Jesus had already spent time in Jerusalem. The saying 'How often would I have gathered your children together ... and you would not' (Matt. 23.37; Luke 13.34), which Matthew places in Holy Week and Luke on the journey to Jerusalem, does imply that Jesus knew the city; and the number of people he knows in Jerusalem, for example the man whose guest room was used for the last supper and with whom he had arranged the sign of the water carrier (Luke 22.10), suggest this too. As Scott Holland observed: 'Obviously the Master finds himself at Jerusalem

---

[10] *Testament of Levi* 18.2, 7, 10–13. *This is thought to be a Christian addition.
[11] See below, pp. 228–9.

among a circle of devoted adherents, of whose origin the Synoptic Gospels have nothing to say. He has been here before.'[12]

The money changers converted pilgrims' money to pay the temple tax. This was 'half a shekel according to the shekel of the sanctuary' (Exod. 30.11–16), and was a second-temple addition to the law. Under Nehemiah's leadership the people agreed to keep certain rules – 'a firm covenant' – and to distinguish themselves from the peoples of the lands. One of the rules was to pay a third of a shekel each year for the upkeep of temple services and to buy the offerings (Neh. 9.38—10.10). The tax was therefore a characteristic of the second temple and marked the separation of the Jews from those we might call 'Hebrews', the long-established worshippers of the LORD. It had to be paid each year by 1 Nisan. Tables were set up in the temple five days before this, on 25 Adar, and so the temple at that time would have been crowded with people exchanging their money for temple shekels. The Mishnah links this payment to the building of the second temple and to the returned exiles refusing to allow the other worshippers of the LORD to contribute: 'You have nothing to do with us in building a house to our God; but we alone will build to the LORD, the God of Israel, as King Cyrus, the king of Persia has commanded us [Ezra 1.3]'.[13] It was in effect a membership fee and paid for atonement to be made (Exod. 30.15–16).

John presents the cleansing of the temple as the true way of making atonement, which was effected by sprinkling blood (Lev. 16.15–19), and he presents Jesus' action as the great high priest coming to reclaim his holy place. He made a whip of cords to drive out both the traders and the animals, a detail unique to John's Gospel, but linking Jesus' action to the great cleansing of the temple on the Day of Atonement. The high priest sprinkled the cleansing and consecrating blood 'as though he were wielding a whip'.[14] It would be interesting to know how many people knew the prescriptions for the high priest's actions, since they were performed inside the temple, but Jesus knew about them and so did John.

It would also be interesting to know how the people who saw Jesus' action understood Ezekiel's prescription for the Passover in the restored temple. Introducing the Passover as a temple festival had been the hallmark of the pro-Moses temple reformers: Hezekiah and Josiah both marked the completion of their temple purges by celebrating a great

---

[12] H. S. Holland, *The Fourth Gospel*, London: John Murray, 1923, p. 33.
[13] Mishnah *Shekalim* 1.3.
[14] Mishnah *Yoma* 5.3–4.

Passover in the temple (2 Chron. 30.1–27; 2 Kings 23.21–23). Ezekiel, however, from a family of first-temple priests, saw a very different Passover in his vision of the restored temple of the future. It would be like the autumn festival, with bull's blood put onto the corners of the altar, the doorposts of the temple and the doorposts of the inner court. Ezekiel's Passover was a ritual to cleanse the temple, the springtime equivalent of the Day of Atonement (Ezek. 45.18–25), and this is what Jesus did.

John tells of three Passovers in the ministry of Jesus: the first when he cleanses the temple and in effect restores Ezekiel's (first-temple) spring festival of cleansing; the second when he offers the bread from heaven to replace the manna of the exodus that sustained the people when they were wandering in the wilderness (6.30–34); and the third when John emphasizes that Jesus died like a Passover lamb (19.36), but perhaps, as we shall see,[15] to replace the Passover lamb. Restoring the true temple meant restoring the older calendar and feasts, and John's Gospel, with its emphasis on the temple feasts, suggests that this was a part of Jesus' mission. Whoever wrote the *Damascus Document* believed that in the age of wrath, Israel had gone astray concerning the hidden things, and these included the feasts.[16]

The second temple was the harlot and she was at the centre of Jerusalem's economy. The money changers and the pure animals for sacrifice were only a part of the temple marketing complex. When Jerusalem was destroyed in 70 CE, John was among those who fled during the amnesty and he looked back from Joppa at the burning city.[17] He saw the merchants and the sailors weeping that their trade was gone, and he listed their cargos destined for Jerusalem (Rev. 18.11–13).

> Alas, alas for the great city,
> That was clothed in fine linen, in purple and scarlet,
> Bedecked with gold, with jewels, and with pearls!
> In one hour all this wealth has been laid waste.
> (Rev. 18.16–17)

Ridding the temple of traders was one of the prophecies of the day of the LORD, and Jesus' words: 'You shall not make my Father's house a house of trade', are a paraphrase of Zechariah 14.21: 'There shall no longer be a trader in the house of the LORD of hosts on that day.' 'That day' was the time when the LORD would become king over all the earth. This whole

---

[15] See below, pp. 358–9, 562.
[16] *Damascus Document*, CD III.
[17] See my book *The Revelation of Jesus Christ*, Edinburgh: T&T Clark, 2000, pp. 292–8.

collection of prophecies in the last chapter of Zechariah is royal prophecy: all nations coming to Jerusalem to worship the king, the LORD of hosts at Tabernacles, and living waters – a symbol of Wisdom – flowing again from Jerusalem (Zech. 14.8–17).

In addition to the *Testament of Levi*, there are other prophecies from the early second-temple period that look forward to the cleansing of the temple and especially to the purging of the corrupt priesthood. There was Malachi's warning of the LORD coming suddenly in his temple, to purify the sons of Levi (Mal. 3.1–3). The synoptic Gospels give a different text and have Jesus quoting from Isaiah as he drives out the traders: 'Is it not written, "My house shall be called a house of prayer for all the nations"? But you have made it a den of robbers' (Mark 11.17//Matt. 21.13; Luke 19.46, quoting Isa. 56.7). The context in Isaiah is significant here too, and suggests that this is an accurate memory of Jesus' teaching. The quotation is from the Third-Isaiah – although the text would not have been divided in Jesus' time – where the prophet speaks out for those who have been excluded from the temple: 'Thus says the Lord [Yahweh], who gathers the outcasts of Israel, I will gather yet others to him besides those already gathered' (Isa. 56.8). John has Jesus say: 'I have other sheep, that are not of this fold; I must bring them also …' (10.16), suggesting that the words from Isaiah are an accurate memory of Jesus' teaching about the temple.

The Jews confronted Jesus and asked him for a sign as proof of his authority, and, in an allusion to the purpose of the temple tax, Jesus said: 'Destroy this temple and in three days I will raise it up.' At that time, the LORD, that is, the Messiah, was expected to appear to destroy the existing structure and restore the true temple. This is clear from the *Dream Visions*, in which Enoch saw the history of his people as an animal fable. The patriarchs associated with the priesthood of the first temple are described as bulls (Adam, Noah, Abraham)[18] but after the flood (which symbolizes the Babylonian destruction of the temple and monarchy) their offspring are asses, boars and sheep.[19] The history of the sheep is one of apostasy and disaster; they become blind sheep and fall into the hands of the shepherd angels. Eventually some of the lambs recover their sight, and the Lord of the sheep comes to punish both the shepherds and the blinded sheep. The details of the history are not clear, but there is no doubt about the destruction and rebuilding of the temple.

---

[18] See my book *The Hidden Tradition of the Kingdom of God*, London: SPCK, 2007, pp. 64–8.
[19] *1 Enoch* 85—89.

They folded up that old house and carried off all the pillars, and all the beams and ornaments of the house were at the same time folded up with it, and they carried it off and laid it in a place in the south of the land. And I saw until the Lord of the sheep brought a new house, greater and loftier than the first, and set it up in the place of the first which had been folded up: all its pillars were new, and all its ornaments were new and larger than those of the first, the old one which He had taken away, and all the sheep were within it.[20]

The eyes of the remaining sheep are opened, and they all become white bulls.[21] This implies that they return to the religion of the patriarchs and Melchi-Zedek. The text immediately before this section of *1 Enoch* is quoted in the *Letter of Barnabas* as proof that the Scriptures themselves had predicted the destruction of the city, the temple and the Jewish people. The new temple, said Barnabas, would not be the physical structure like the one that the Jews were planning to rebuild after its destruction by the Romans, but a spiritual temple.[22]

Some parts of the Hebrew Scriptures look forward to a new temple: there is Ezekiel's vision of the restored temple, with water flowing from it to transform the desert, to which the glory of the LORD returned (Ezek. 40—47); and there is the Melchi-Zedek prophecy in Isaiah 61, which continues with the restored people building up ancient ruins. At the time of this prophecy, the second temple was already rebuilt, and the Third-Isaiah spoke out against the corrupted temple leaders and their cult (Isa. 66.1-4). His prophecy that the one anointed with the Spirit would bring the year of the LORD's favour and rebuild the ancient ruins may be an early reference to the role of the Messiah replacing the second temple.

Jesus' claiming to destroy and rebuild the temple was widely known and reported. It was an accusation at Stephen's trial (Acts 6.14) just as it had been at the trial of Jesus. According to Mark and Matthew, the false witnesses reported that Jesus had said, 'I will destroy this temple that is made with hands, and in three days I will build another, not made with hands' (Mark 14.57-61; cf. Matt. 26.60-63), but the high priest's response shows that building a new temple was the expected role of the Messiah: 'Are you the Messiah, the son of the Blessed One?' The claim to replace the temple was a claim to being the Messiah and this in itself was a case of blasphemy. Jesus' prophecies against the temple are reported in the 'Little

---

[20] *1 Enoch* 90.28-29.
[21] *1 Enoch* 90.35, 38.
[22] *Letter of Barnabas* 16, quoting *1 Enoch* 89.56. *Barnabas* was known to Clement of Alexandria, and so must have been written between 70 CE and 200 CE. It treats *1 Enoch* as Scripture.

Apocalypse' (Mark 13//Matt. 24; Luke 21),[23] but not in John's Gospel because the synoptic apocalypses are summaries of Revelation 6—7. The claim to *rebuild* the temple, however, is only attributed to Jesus himself in John 2.19.

In the synoptic Gospels, 'rebuilding' the temple is *oikodomō*, 'build' (Matt. 26.61; Mark 14.58), but in John the word is *egeirō*, which means both 'erect a building' and also 'resurrect' (2.19). Such double meanings are an important part of John's style and theology, and are a legacy from temple discourse but transposed into Greek. The temple here is specifically the building, *vaos*, not the entire enclosure, *hieron*. The claim to rebuild – 'in three days I will resurrect it' – is then nuanced with the explanation: 'But he spoke of the temple of his body' (v. 21), an insight given to the disciples only after the resurrection. The Christian community came to describe themselves as both the body of Christ (1 Cor. 12.27) and as the temple in which God's Spirit dwells (1 Cor. 3.16). They were the new temple built of living stones, the place where spiritual sacrifices were offered (1 Pet. 2.5). Jesus said this to the Samaritan woman (4.23). The risen LORD in Revelation promised that the faithful Christian would be a pillar in the (new) temple, and Paul told the Christians in Ephesus that they were being built upon the foundation of the apostles and prophets into a holy temple in the Lord, Christ Jesus himself being the cornerstone (Eph. 2.20-21). The Qumran community also saw themselves as a living temple: the council of the community was a (living) holy of holies, their prayer was incense, and their 'perfection of way' was their freewill offering.[24] Fragments of their commentary on Isaiah 54.11–12 show that the community saw themselves as the prophesied new Jerusalem. They were its jewels: the 'foundations of sapphires' were the priests and the people who laid the foundations of the community; the pinnacles of agate were the 12 [chief priests]; and the gates of carbuncles were the leaders of the tribes.[25] So too in their hymns. The temple itself took part in the living liturgy: the pillars and corners of the holy of holies joined in the heavenly song, and the gates offered praise.[26]

---

[23] The claim also appears in the longer Slavonic text of Josephus, *War* 5 (after 195, in the Appendix to Book 7 in the Loeb edition), and so it may be an addition to the original text. Describing the inscriptions in the temple courts, he says there were three in Greek, Latin and Hebrew warning that foreigners should not pass beyond that point, and then (the extra material): 'one announcing that King Jesus did not reign (but was) crucified because he prophesied the destruction of the city and the devastation of the temple'.

[24] *Community Rule*, 1QS VIII, IX; 4Q174.

[25] *Commentary on Isaiah*, 4Q164.

[26] *Songs of the Sabbath Sacrifice*, 4Q403, 405.

## John 2

Having asked Jesus for a sign, the Jews did not understand the sign but offered a literal and incredulous response. In this they were unlike the high priest at Jesus' trial who took the claim seriously enough to declare it blasphemy. They said: 'It has taken forty-six years to build this temple, and will you raise it up in three days?' Forty-six years is remarkably precise dating, and since Herod began the rebuilding in 20/19 BCE,[27] this incident happened in 27/8 CE, the time when Melchi-Zedek was expected to return.

The cleansing of the temple must have made a great impact; John simply says that many believed in Jesus when they saw what he did at Passover in Jerusalem. One of them may have been a priest who witnessed the event, or who knew that Jesus had prophesied the destruction of the temple (Mark 13.1–2 and parallels). He was Rabbi Zadok who then fasted for 40 years to try to prevent the temple being destroyed.[28] Forty years may not be a precise number, but the link to Jesus' actions and words against the temple is the most likely reason for beginning his fast at that time.

---

[27] Josephus, *Antiquities* 15.380.
[28] Babylonian Talmud *Gittin* 56a.

# John 3

### 3.1–21: Meeting Nicodemus

One of those who had been in Jerusalem when Jesus drove the traders out of the temple at Passover was Nicodemus, a Pharisee and a ruler of the Jews. John mentions him in two other places: Nicodemus defended Jesus when he caused another tumult in the temple at Tabernacles, asking: 'Does our law judge a man without first giving him a hearing and learning what he does' (7.51); and he provided the spices for Jesus' burial (19.39). Some have speculated that he was the wealthy man who asked Jesus what he should do to inherit eternal life (Mark 10.17 and parallels); he was certainly wealthy if he could provide so much spice for Jesus' burial. As a Pharisee and a ruler, Nicodemus would have known the Hebrew Scriptures, and Jesus addressed him as *the* teacher of Israel, so perhaps John was using him as a representative of that group who did not understand even though they had studied the Scriptures (3.10; cf. 5.39–40, the Jews who searched the Scriptures but did not know what they meant). If the cleansing of the temple had been a conflict with the temple authorities, then this meeting with Nicodemus should be seen as a meeting of the two teachers of Israel.

Nicodemus came by night, perhaps because he feared being seen with Jesus, but perhaps because, as we shall see, he feared he would be given forbidden teaching. The 'night' was also symbolic and prompted Jesus' closing words about coming to the light and the contrast between light and darkness (vv. 19–21). Although the contrast of light and darkness was characteristic of John's writing, it was not unique to him. The Qumran community saw themselves as the sons of light. The Master of the community had to instruct all the sons of light, also called the children of righteousness, who were ruled by the Prince of Light and walked in the ways of light (cf. 1 John 1.7). There was also an Angel of Darkness who tried to lead the sons of light astray.[1] The sons of light were preparing for

---
[1] *Community Rule*, 1QS III.

the final battle against the sons of darkness, confident that the angels in heaven led by the Prince of Light would come down to fight among them.[2] There are similar scenes in Revelation, e.g the army of the Lamb (Rev. 14.1–5); and the army of the Word of God riding out from heaven on white horses (Rev. 19.11–16).

In reaction to Nicodemus saying 'Rabbi, we know that you are a teacher come from God; for no one can do these signs that you do, unless God is with him', Jesus says that only those born anew/from above can see the kingdom of God. This implies that Nicodemus was one of those 'outside' who would not be able to understand what he was teaching. To his 12 disciples Jesus had said:

> To you has been given the secret of the kingdom of God, but for those outside everything is in parables; so that they may indeed see but not perceive, and may indeed hear but not understand; lest they should turn again, and be forgiven. (Mark 4.11–12)

This was the judgement on those who had rejected Wisdom – to live with what they had chosen[3] – and this theme runs all through John's Gospel as does the very similar idea that the judgement on those who reject Jesus is to live with what they have chosen. The exchange with Nicodemus shows how a man learned in his own Jewish tradition did not understand what Jesus was teaching. Nicodemus was a Pharisee, and John depicts him as a generous and fair-minded man who wanted to learn from Jesus. Nevertheless, his own tradition prevented him from understanding.

This is the first example of the LORD coming to his own people, and their failure to understand when he spoke of being born as a child of God, here a child of the Spirit (v. 6), a reference back to John 1.12–13 but also forward to the Bride of whom the Baptist speaks later. This is also the first illustration of how far the Jewish teachers in the time of Jesus had lost touch with their own temple roots. It is sometimes asked if Nicodemus could have been expected to understand the enigmatic language about being born of the Spirit and seeing the kingdom – which means seeing the heavenly throne. The language is there in the temple traditions of the Hebrew Scriptures, but Nicodemus could have been a spiritual heir of the Deuteronomists who denied the vision of God and discouraged any interest in the secret things. In the Mishnah there is a ruling that may have existed in Jesus' time which forbad any interest in the 'secret things':

---

[2] *War Scroll*, 1QM XII, XIII.
[3] See above, p. 96.

'Whosoever gives his mind to four things, it were better for him if he had not come into the world: what is above, what is beneath, what was before time and what will be hereafter.'[4] This may have made Nicodemus uneasy about coming to Jesus.

Only those born from above can see the kingdom, said Jesus, and only those born of water and Spirit can enter the kingdom. This was drawn from Jesus' own experience at his baptism, when he had been born from above and so born again. The Greek word *anōthen* means 'from above' and 'again', and here it means both. At his baptism, Jesus had both seen and entered the kingdom; he had been taken up into a *merkavah* experience and he had heard the voice of the Spirit declaring him to be her divine Son. As with Enoch and the other mystics such as Isaiah who ascended to the throne, he was then sent back from heaven with a message for his people: Isaiah had to give warnings about the fate of his people and their land; Enoch was sent as a divine messenger to the fallen angels, and after learning the secrets of the calendar and reading the tablets of heaven, he was brought back to earth and told he would have one year to teach his children 'and bear witness to all of them'. Then he would be taken from them.[5] Jesus was another such teacher sent from God, but not in the way that Nicodemus had intended those words. In the desert Jesus had wrestled with what it meant to be a son of God.

Nicodemus did not understand this language of divine birth, and yet it had once been in the Hebrew Scriptures; the royal birth ritual was described in Psalm 110, but 'corrected' out of the Hebrew text as a blasphemy, and then rebranded and redefined by Deuteronomy. All the people were the sons of the LORD, because the LORD had chosen them, and they showed their status by observing the purity laws: they could eat only the permitted foods, and were forbidden certain external marks such as lacerations and shaving (Deut. 14.1–21). The name was the same, but the meaning was different. Just as the Deuteronomists changed the meaning of *dābhaq* from 'being united with' to 'obeying',[6] so too sonship was no longer being joined to the LORD but rather obeying him. Nicodemus did not understand the language of heavenly birth. Jesus then said to Nicodemus: 'the Spirit blows where it will, and you hear the voice of it . . . so it is with everyone who is born of the Spirit' (v. 8, my translation). The Greek word for spirit is *pneuma*, a neuter noun, but we assume the

---

[4] Mishnah *Ḥagigah* 2.1.
[5] *1 Enoch* 15.1; 81.1–6.
[6] See above, p. 47.

conversation between Jesus and Nicodemus was in Hebrew, and so 'Spirit' would have been *rûaḥ*, a feminine noun, and the birth image more natural. (This 'Spirit' must be distinguished from the 'Paraclete' of whom Jesus teaches in his farewell discourse.[7]) Baptism as rebirth to enter the kingdom (also described as resurrection) appears in another form in Matthew's Gospel. 'Unless you turn and become like children, you will never enter the kingdom of heaven' (Matt. 18.2) looks as though it was originally a saying about being born so as to enter the kingdom.[8]

Jesus then tells Nicodemus of his ascent experience: 'We bear witness to what we have seen, but you do not receive our testimony ... how can you believe if I tell you of heavenly things?' (v. 12). In the synoptic Gospels there are hints of Jesus' visionary experiences, and the Book of Revelation is a record of the visions and their interpretation.[9] Here in John's Gospel Jesus speaks of himself as the Son of Man, an idiom that just means 'a man', or, in this case 'the Man'. In the Septuagint, this was a title for the Messiah: Balaam's prophecy, 'a star shall come forth out of Jacob, and a sceptre shall rise out of Israel' (Num. 24.17), was translated in the Egyptian Jewish community as: 'a star will rise from Jacob, and a man shall rise up [the same word as 'be resurrected'] from Israel' (LXX Num. 24.17). In the Enoch tradition, people who had ascended and learned the heavenly knowledge were transformed into 'men': Noah, for example, was born a white bull, but after an archangel taught him 'a mystery' he became a Man; Moses was born a sheep, but after his ascent of Sinai he became a man.[10] In the language of the apocalypses, a man was an angel: Daniel saw the man Gabriel, who flew to him to bring wisdom and understanding (Dan. 9.20–22); and in Revelation 'a man, that is, an angel' measured the heavenly city (Rev. 21.17). In the temple the Man was the high priest or the sacral king. David thanked God that he had been granted the vision of the Man (the Adam, so a human rather than a male) on high, or perhaps the Eternal Man, the LORD God (1 Chron. 17.17).[11] The Man was the Melchi-Zedek figure, whom the first Christians knew had been raised up/resurrected to his high priesthood, in contrast with the Aaronite priests who inherited the role through the death of their predecessors (Heb. 7.11–17).

---

[7] See below, p. 410.

[8] Justin, *Apology* 1.61 explained that baptism was the process of rebirth and enlightenment; see above, p. 117.

[9] See above, p. 111.

[10] *1 Enoch* 89.1, 36; cf. Ben Sira 45.2: God made Moses equal in glory to the holy ones.

[11] Two possible translations of a line that is now hopelessly corrupted, possibly the work of the scribes who removed 'blasphemies'.

John's double meaning here is *hupsoō*, which can mean both 'to raise up', that is, to be raised on the cross; and 'to be exalted', that is, raised to the heavenly throne. These are also the meanings of the Hebrew verb *rûm*, which can be 'to lift up' (Gen. 7.17, the ark; Ezek. 10.16, the cherubs' wings); or 'to exalt' (Ps. 89.19, the Davidic king; Isa. 52.13, the Servant). The ambiguous 'lifting up' is found three times in John's Gospel: here, and at 8.28 and 12.32–34. Each time, it is *the Son of Man* who is lifted up. These three instances look very like the three predictions of the Passion and resurrection in the synoptic Gospels where it is also the Son of Man who suffers and rises (e.g. Mark 8.31; 9.31; 10.33–34). Mark says that the Son of Man has to suffer and then rise again – two verbs for the two aspects – and the details of the suffering were doubtless added after the event; but John combines the suffering and the raising up in this one word *hupsoō*. Much has been written about the Son of Man and about the synoptic predictions of the Passion and resurrection, wondering if they could have been genuine sayings of Jesus; but if the synoptic Gospels are read in the light of Jesus' mystical experiences and his knowledge that he would fulfil prophecies, then the basis of the sayings about the Son of Man and the Passion is found in the royal tradition of ascent. John's Gospel gives the key for understanding the synoptic sayings by using wordplay on the verb *hupsoō*, 'to exalt/to raise up', which is thus similar to the meanings for the Hebrew *rûm*.[12]

The thought then moves from heavenly birth and exaltation to the snake in the wilderness, and Jesus compares his own lifting up to the serpent lifted up in the wilderness which had saved the Israelites from snake bites (Num. 21.6–8). The bronze serpent was preserved and was a sacred object until Hezekiah destroyed it (2 Kings 18.4). We are not told where the serpent was set up, but people used to burn incense before it, presumably to protect them from evil. When the Israelites were smitten with snake bites in the desert, they were told: 'Look at the bronze serpent and live' (Num. 21.9). So too, the lifting up of Jesus would protect those who looked to him, and this lifting up would bring them eternal life.

The three themes of this chapter – heavenly birth, lifting up, and a snake bite – are all found in Revelation 12.13–17: the Woman in heaven gave birth to her son, the ancient serpent was ready to bite him, about to 'devour' him (Rev. 12.4), and the child escaped by being lifted up to the throne of God. The serpent went off to attack the Woman's other children, those who were keeping the commandments and bearing

---

[12] This is also the key wordplay in the account of Palm Sunday (Ps. 118.28); see below, p. 350.

## John 3

witness to Jesus, and presumably these were the snake bites that were an ever-present danger to Jesus' followers. Looking to the exalted Jesus would protect them. The mark of the ancient serpent was worn on the right hand and the forehead of his followers (Rev. 13.16), exactly where the observant pro-Moses group wore their phylacteries (Deut. 6.8).

'The Son of Man *must* be lifted up' (3.14, my translation) implies the fulfilment of prophecy or an existing expectation, and the man lifted up is Isaiah's suffering Servant. In the Qumran version of the text which Jesus expounded on the road to Emmaus (Luke 24.25–27), the Servant was lifted up, *anointed* and transfigured beyond the appearance of a human being. This story is proof that Jesus saw himself as the Servant. Isaiah's Servant was raised up and anointed before he suffered and then saw the light (of the glory). The result of his experience was knowledge by which others could be made righteous. Jesus also used Psalm 110 to show to his critics that the Messiah was more than just the human son of David; he was also the divine Son (Mark 12.35–37 and parallels). The fourth Servant song and Psalm 110 are the two most frequently quoted texts in the New Testament: both deal with exaltation and both were used by Jesus himself to demonstrate the role of the Messiah. We should expect at least a trace of them in John's report of Jesus' teaching on 'raising up'.

Another key proof text for the early Hebrew Christians was that Jesus was the Firstborn (of the sons of God), brought into the world to bring judgement on the enemies of his people and to heal their land (Deut. 32.43). Jesus does not quote this text himself, but one line is quoted at Hebrews 1.6: 'Let all God's angels worship him.'[13] This indicates that the whole prophecy applies to Jesus. The Masoretic Hebrew text used for English translations does not include this line, and so 'Let all God's angels worship him' is not found in a traditional English Old Testament. The longer Hebrew text found at Qumran, however, does have the line: the sons of God bowed before the Lord as he emerged to bring judgement, to punish the enemies of his people and to heal their land.[14] This was the theme of the angels' song at Bethlehem when the Lord came into the world: the angels praised his glory and said there would be peace on earth (Luke 2.14). Worship followed by judgement is taken up again at John 9.38: the man who had been blind worshipped Jesus, and Jesus immediately spoke of judgement.

---

[13] This was how they identified passages of text before there were chapter and verse numbers.
[14] The Lxx was also translated from this longer form of the text.

There is no complete account of the royal ascent in the Hebrew Scriptures, nor in the Greek, and so the rituals in the holy of holies and their meaning have to be reconstructed from what remains. The first Christians would have known far more than we do, but the pattern that can still be discerned is exaltation, anointing, becoming the Son, and then ruling/coming in judgement. This is the pattern implicit in how Jesus describes himself to Nicodemus: Jesus has been born from above (vv. 3–8; cf. 10.36), raised up and transformed into the Man (vv. 13–15), and then sent into the world to bring the judgement and heal the land (vv. 16–17). Jesus' unique interpretation was the nature of the judgement: God so loved the whole created order, *kosmos*, that he gave his beloved (the meaning of *monogenēs*, if not the literal translation)[15] Son, the LORD, to save (i.e. heal) not just the land but the whole *kosmos*. This is the substance of the heavenly acclamation in Revelation as the LORD-and-his-Anointed establish the kingdom on earth: judging the enemies and rewarding the servants, prophets and saints who fear the Name, and destroying the destroyers of the earth, that is, healing the land of the people (Rev. 11.17–18). In John's Gospel the criterion at the LORD's judgement is believing that Jesus is the LORD, that he has been given the Name. Those who did not believe this would in effect condemn themselves since they would live with the choice they had made.

It has been suggested that verses 15–19 are a summary of John's theology, and that the substance of these verses is repeated at 12.46–48.[16] Setting 12.46–48 alongside 3.15–19, the similarity is clear: the light coming into the world so that those who believe will not remain in darkness; Jesus did not come to condemn the world but to save it; but those who reject him and do not believe condemn themselves. These two summaries are set at the beginning and end of the first section of John's Gospel which shows how 'he came to his own and his own received him not'. The first summary is addressed to Nicodemus, the teacher of the Jews, and the second is Jesus' last words about the Jews. Then he hid from them because 'Though he had done so many signs before them, yet they did not believe in him' (12.37). John reflected that this fulfilled Isaiah's prophecy; those who rejected Wisdom were punished by having to live with what they had chosen: eyes that could not see and a heart/mind that could not understand (12.37–40, quoting Isa. 6.10).

---

[15] See above, p. 163.

[16] M.-E. Boismard, 'L'évolution du thème eschatologique dans les traditions Johanniques', *Revue Biblique* 68 (1961), cited by R. E. Brown, *The Gospel According to John I–XII*, Anchor Bible 29, London: Geoffrey Chapman, 1971, p. 147.

## John 3

Underlying Jesus' conversation with Nicodemus and the explanation of who he is are three royal texts: Psalm 110; Isaiah 52.13—53.12; and Deuteronomy 32.43, all of which would have been well known to those who studied the Hebrew Scriptures, *but all of which are different in the Masoretic Hebrew from which English Bibles are translated.*

- No text of Psalm 110 has been found at Qumran to show what the text was in the time of Jesus; this has to be reconstructed from the Greek.
- The Isaiah passage in the Qumran Isaiah scroll has a few more letters than the Masoretic Hebrew text, and so says that the Servant is 'anointed' rather than disfigured (Isa. 52.14) and that he sees the light (that is, the glory) after his suffering (Isa. 53.11).
- The Qumran text of Deuteronomy 32.43 has four more lines than the Masoretic Hebrew text, and these include the Christian proof text.

It would be possible to conclude from this evidence that texts which were important for Christian claims – and indeed for Jesus' own understanding of his role – were removed from the Hebrew text or significantly altered. They may have been removed after Jesus made his claims and in reaction to them, or they may have been royal and temple texts that had already been edited out of some copies of the Hebrew Scriptures during the second-temple period, the work of the 'restoring scribes'. If the latter, then Nicodemus could not have recognized and understood what Jesus was saying.

### 3.22–36: Last words from the Baptist

In the pattern for his Gospel, John has Jesus move out from the temple, then into the city, where Nicodemus comes to him, and then into the land of Judea. The Baptist was still baptizing, and so John knew that Jesus had been in Jerusalem and Judea before he moved north to Galilee. After the Baptist's disciples became involved with 'a Jew' in a dispute over purifying, they told him that Jesus was attracting many people. Whatever the significance of the dispute with 'the Jew' (some early copies of John's Gospel say 'the Jews'), it is now lost. The Baptist here reaffirms that he is only the forerunner of the Messiah (v. 28), the friend of the Bridegroom who makes preparations for the wedding. Jesus is the Bridegroom because he has the Bride. The complementary material in the Book of Revelation shows that the Bride is the new Jerusalem coming from heaven, having within her walls the throne of God and the tree of life. This is the city to replace the harlot and all that she had represented. The story of the Bride and the Logos who is both her son and her consort has to be explored to understand the significance of the Baptist's words.

The contrast between the bride and the harlot was prominent in the school of Isaiah; the two female figures represented the contrast between the ethos of the first temple and the ethos of the second. When the writings of several generations of the school of Isaiah were collected as one scroll and given a Preface, the compiler wrote: 'How the faithful city has become a harlot, she that was full of justice' (Isa. 1.21), and the image of the Lady – first the Bride, then the abandoned wife and then the restored wife – runs through the collection. She was also the heavenly Mother of the king: the Virgin who would bear a son to be called 'Immanuel' (Isa. 7.14); the unnamed Mother of the Davidic king to be called 'Wonderful Counsellor, Mighty God, Everlasting Father, Prince of Peace', or, as the Septuagint put it, 'the Angel of Great Counsel' (Isa. 9.6); and the root of Jesse from which the Branch would grow (again) and upon whom the sevenfold Spirit would rest (Isa. 11.1–2). The Lady is a complex figure, perhaps because this way of thinking is so strange to us: the heavenly mother of the royal house who was also the genius of the city. She had many names: Wisdom, the Spirit, the Queen of Heaven, and the characteristic of the second temple was that she was no longer there.

She represented and 'taught' a characteristic way of living, and her teachers had their own literary style based on observing the harmony of the creation. Their literary forms reflected this: pairs of meanings in their wordplay; pairs of parallels in their poetry and sayings; and the correspondence of heaven and earth in their visions and parables. She had been represented by the tree of life; by the oil extracted from the tree that anointed the kings and transformed them into sons of God; by the holy of holies where the kings were 'born'; by the throne on which they sat; and by the water of life that flowed from the throne to bring wisdom and righteousness to the land. This was the role of the king.

> [Wisdom] is more precious than jewels,
> And nothing you desire can compare with her.
> Long life is in her right hand;
> In her left are riches and honour.
> Her ways are ways of pleasantness and all her paths are peace.
> She is a tree of life to those who lay hold of her;
> Those who hold her fast are called happy. (Prov. 3.15–18)

The Davidic kings had been both son and spouse of the Lady: '[Wisdom] will meet him like a mother, and like the wife of his youth she will

## John 3

welcome him' (Ben Sira 15.2), and so Zechariah had told the city/daughter of Zion to rejoice because her king was coming to her (again) (Zech. 9.9). According to John, these were the words of the crowd who went out from Jerusalem on Palm Sunday (12.15), and Jesus' disciples did not at the time realize the significance of what they were hearing. In the Book of Revelation, the Lady is both the Mother and the Bride, and her presence pervades John's Gospel.

The Lady had been driven from the temple by the pro-Moses group and replaced by their law; Deuteronomy denied the relevance of her secrets (Deut. 29.29) and declared that the law was the new Wisdom (Deut. 4.6). Proverbs described her successor as the strange woman, the foreign woman (Prov. 2.16, translating literally), and young men were warned against her. The Lady herself called out to her foolish children and told them what they would bring upon themselves by rejecting her (Prov. 1.20-33). Isaiah realized the folly of abandoning her when he confessed that he was a man of unclean lips among a people of unclean lips. In other words, there was false teaching (Isa. 6.5). He had to warn what would happen, that the punishment would be to live with what they had chosen. They would lose the perception that the Lady gave to her children (Isa. 6.9-12). The result of that choice is the theme of John's Gospel: eyes and minds that can no longer see, and so the return of the Bride and her gifts was fundamental for John. Each time John mentions those lines in Isaiah about people who cannot see, he is alluding to the absent Lady. Enoch preserves a short poem about rejecting her. When she found no place to dwell on earth:

> Wisdom returned to her place
> And took her seat among the angels.
> Unrighteousness went forth from her chambers;
> Whom she sought not, she found,
> And dwelt with them,
> As rain in a desert land
> And dew on a thirsty land.[17]

Zechariah saw the foreign woman as Wickedness, returning from Babylon in a parody of Ezekiel's throne vision when he had seen the Lady leaving the temple.[18] The angel told Zechariah that the winged creatures were taking her back to Babylon, to build a temple for her (Zech. 5.11).[19]

---

[17] 1 Enoch 42.2-3.
[18] See my book *The Mother of the Lord*, vol. 1, London: T&T Clark, 2012, pp. 231-54.
[19] See my article 'The Evil in Zechariah', *Heythrop Journal* 19 (1978), pp. 12-27.

A Qumran text describes her as 'the beginning of all the ways of iniquity'.[20] The visions in Revelation describe the Lady's return: as the Bride of the Logos/the Lamb (Rev. 19); as the Mother of the King (Rev. 12.1–6); as the tree of life with its healing leaves (Rev. 22.2); and as the Spirit and the Bride who invites the thirsty to drink freely (Rev. 22.17).

In Isaiah, the Lady is as important as the Servant, but has received far less attention than the male figure.[21] The city has become a harlot, said the compiler of the scroll, and the daughter of Zion is left 'as a cottage in a vineyard, as a lodge in a garden of cucumbers' (Isa. 1.8 AV). She had formerly been set on the mount of Zion (Isa. 10.32) whence she had scorned the king of Assyria who tried to attack her (Isa. 37.22). Then she had been humiliated and abandoned (Lam. 2.1), but the prophet announced her restoration by asking her children:

> Where is your mother's bill of divorce? ...
> For your transgressions was your mother put away.
> (Isa. 50.1)

It was the actions of her children that had made the LORD abandon her. Then the LORD spoke to the the Lady herself:

> Put on your beautiful garments, O Jerusalem the holy city ...
> Loose the bonds from your neck, O captive daughter of Zion.
> (Isa. 52.1, 2)

> O afflicted one, storm-tossed, and not comforted,
> Behold, I will set your stones in antimony,
> And lay your foundations with sapphires.
> I will make your pinnacles of agate, your gates of carbuncles,
> And all your wall of precious stones. (Isa. 54.11–12)

Another voice spoke of the future:

> You shall no longer be termed Forsaken,
> And your land shall no more be termed Desolate ...
> As the bridegroom rejoices over the bride,
> So shall your God rejoice over you. (Isa. 62.4, 5)

A few descriptions of the Lady survive in the Wisdom of Solomon, a text from the Egyptian Jewish community, and from these it is clear that she and her city were one and the same.

---

[20] 4Q184.8.
[21] J. F. A. Sawyer, 'Daughter of Zion and Servant of the LORD in Isaiah. A Comparison', *Journal for the Study of the Old Testament* 44 (1989), pp. 89–107.

## John 3

- 'Honour Wisdom that you may reign for ever' (Wisd. 6.21); cf. '[His servants in the holy city] shall reign for ever and ever' (Rev. 22.5);
- 'Nothing defiled gains entrance into [Wisdom]' (Wisd. 7.25); cf. 'Nothing unclean shall enter [the city]' (Rev. 21.27);
- 'Wisdom is the reflection of eternal light' (Wisd. 7.26); cf. 'The Bride ... the holy city Jerusalem ... having the glory of God' (Rev. 21.9–11);
- 'Compared with the light she is found to be superior, for it is succeeded by the night' (Wisd. 7.29–30); cf. 'There shall be no night there ...' (Rev. 21.25);
- 'She reaches mightily from one end of the earth to the other' (Wisd. 8.1); cf. the huge extent of the heavenly city (Rev. 21.16);
- '[I, Solomon] desired to take her for my bride' (Wisd. 8.2); cf. 'The Bride, the wife of the Lamb' (Rev. 21.9).

The city as prophesied by Isaiah, and Wisdom as described by 'Solomon', can both be seen in Revelation's new Jerusalem, the bejewelled city coming down from heaven as the Bride of the Lamb (Rev. 21.9–10). She replaces the harlot who has been burned – the punishment for a harlot from a priestly family (Lev. 21.9). The harlot has shed the blood of the holy ones who have borne witness to Jesus (Rev. 17.1–6), and she is punished with the LORD's punishment on his enemies (Rev. 19.2; cf. Deut. 32.43b).

The Baptist emphasizes to his disciples that he is neither the Bridegroom nor the Messiah, but that the Bridegroom-and-Messiah is the one who has the Bride (3.28–29). The implication here is that the Bride is the focus: to be the Messiah one must have the Bride. These enigmatic lines reflect the visions in Revelation and the history of the rejected Lady. The Baptist is saying clearly that Jesus is the LORD, coming to restore the holy city to her former self; he is the King coming to the daughter of Zion (12.15, quoting Zech. 9.9), and Zechariah's oracle continues: 'He is the Righteous One [i.e. one who makes righteous] and the Victor' (Zech. 9.9, translating literally) The question is: how? The saying about the Bride and the Bridegroom is followed immediately by words from an unknown speaker (vv. 31–36), who could be the Baptist, Jesus, or John himself reflecting on the meeting with Nicodemus and the words of the Baptist. Whoever the speaker might have been, 'He who comes from heaven is above all; he bears witness to what he has seen and heard' implies that Jesus had seen or knew the vision of the Bride and her Bridegroom in Revelation. That vision, however, is about the Logos coming into the world. As the Bride prepares for her wedding, the Logos of God comes out from heaven with his army clad in white linen, prepared for battle with the beast, the kings of the earth and the false prophet (Rev. 19.11–21). He has to destroy the powers of darkness before he weds his Bride.[22]

In John's writings there are three descriptions of the Logos either in heaven or emerging from heaven: he is the warrior in Revelation 19, where he rides out wearing an outer garment dipped/sprinkled[23] in blood; he is the figure in the midst of the seven lamps in Revelation 1, where he wears the long white garment and golden sash of the high priest; and he is the Logos in the Prologue to the Gospel who became flesh and 'tabernacled' in the world. These are all descriptions of the LORD as the high priest. The two descriptions in Revelation are of the same figure: the warrior Logos has eyes like fire (Rev. 19.12), as does the high-priest figure in the first vision (Rev. 1.14): and he has a sharp sword coming from his mouth, to represent his teaching (Rev. 19.15), as does the high-priest figure in the first vision (Rev. 1.16). The warrior Logos wears the secret Name (the *'Ehyeh*) and has a garment that is bloodstained *before* he begins his battle, suggesting a warrior high priest who has made the atonement offering of sprinkled blood *before* going out to defeat his enemies. This is imagery from the Day of Atonement. The warrior is the oldest of John's pictures of the Logos, and he is like the figure in the Wisdom of Solomon, where the Logos is the LORD who brings destruction to the Egyptians at Passover (Exod. 12.23):

> Your all-powerful Logos leaped from heaven, from the royal throne,
> A stern warrior into the midst of the land to be destroyed,
> Bearing the sharp sword of your clear command,
> And standing filled everything with death
> And touched heaven while standing on the earth.
> (Wisd. 18.15–16, my translation)

Here too the sword is his teaching, as it was for the Servant (Isa. 49.2), and Jesus alludes to this: 'Do not think I have come to bring peace on earth; I have not come to bring peace, but a sword' (Matt. 10.34). In Revelation 19, the warrior Logos destroys the evil from the land; the bodies of the fallen are eaten by birds of prey; the beast and his false prophet are cast into the lake of fire; and the ancient serpent is bound for

---

[22] So too the LORD-and-his-Messiah establish the kingdom on earth by rewarding the servants and saints and destroying the destroyers of the earth as the Lady gives birth to her son in heaven (Rev. 11.15—12.6).

[23] There are two alternative versions in the ancient texts.

## John 3

a thousand years (Rev. 19.11—20.3). The text of Revelation, however, is disordered at this point, and the sequence resumes with the vision of the Bride coming from heaven once the land has been cleansed (Rev. 21.9).[24] This is the traditional judgement sequence: the LORD who can both kill and give life brings the lightning of his sword to take vengeance on his enemies, devouring the flesh and blood of the slain before healing his land (Deut. 32.39–43).

At the beginning of Revelation, John sees the Logos as the risen LORD in the midst of the seven lamps, which, in the Revelation temple, means he is in the holy of holies and near the throne and the seven torches of fire (Rev. 1.12; 4.5). It is not clear whether the LORD is sitting or standing. He gives oracles to John his prophet, to be passed on to the seven persecuted and weakening churches of Asia Minor, just as the LORD gave oracles to Isaiah as he stood before the throne. They were to hold fast to their faith despite the synagogues of Satan in Smyrna and Philadelphia 'who say that they are Jews and are not' (Rev. 2.9; 3.9); a false prophet named Balaam in Pergamum where Satan has his throne (Rev. 2.13–14) and a false prophetess in Thyatira named Jezebel (Rev. 2.20); teachers in Ephesus who claimed to be apostles (Rev. 2.2); and Nikolaitans active in Ephesus and Smyrna (Rev. 2.6, 15). The churches of Asia Minor received oracles in temple imagery, and so the Nikolaitans would have been the deceivers, since the Hebrew *nkl* means 'deceive', and so by implication they were disciples of Satan the Deceiver (Rev. 12.9; 20.2). A Qumran hymn describes their enemies as 'an assembly of deceit and a horde of Belial [Satan]',[25] and their Bible commentaries refer to the Liar or the Spouter of Lies.[26] It would seem that the divisions in Palestine between the Jews and the followers of Jesus, which are so prominent in John's Gospel, were present also in the communities in Asia Minor. Further, the churches who received these oracles were expecting the imminent return of the LORD: 'I will come to you soon' (Rev. 2.16); 'Hold fast what you have, until I come' (Rev. 2.25; 3.11); 'You will not know at what hour I will come upon you' (Rev. 3.3).

Contemporary with these letters is the *Assumption of Moses*[27] which describes the great high priest rising from his throne to establish his kingdom throughout the whole creation.

---

[24] One page of the original was dislocated and reversed. The original sequence after 20.3 was 21.9—22.5, then 20.4—21.8. Each of the sections has 2,429 letters. See my book *The Revelation of Jesus Christ*, Edinburgh, T&T Clark, 2000, p. 316.

[25] *Hymns*, 1QH X.

[26] *Commentary on Habakkuk*, 1QpHab X; *Micah*, 1Q14.

[27] Also known as the *Testament of Moses*, extant in Latin but thought to have a Semitic original.

> Then will be filled the hands[28] of the messenger/angel
> Who is appointed in the highest place,
> He will at once avenge them of their enemies.
> For the Heavenly One will rise from his royal throne,
> He will go forth from his holy habitation,
> With indignation and wrath on behalf of his sons.[29]

Since the *Assumption of Moses* is a reworking of Deuteronomy 31—34 with contemporary allusions, this description corresponds to Deuteronomy 32.43 and shows that, in the time of Jesus, the LORD coming to avenge his sons was imagined as the high priest leaving his throne in heaven/the holy of holies and emerging into the world/the *hêkhāl* of the temple. This could be how the early Christians envisaged the Logos/the risen LORD in Revelation 1.

The third description of the Logos emerging is in John's Prologue, which does not mention the appearance of the figure and has no obvious reference to the high priest. Philo's contemporary description of the Logos/high priest, however, shows that this is probably how the Logos of the Prologue was imagined: he comes from the Womb of his Mother. John's Logos brings the light that the darkness neither understands nor overcomes, and he becomes flesh, meaning that he is born from above. This is that birth from the Spirit that Jesus describes to Nicodemus, replying to his question 'Can a man enter a second time into his mother's womb and be born?' Philo explained:

> We say, then, that the high priest is not a man but a divine Logos ...
> His Father is God, who is also the Father of all things, and his Mother is Wisdom, through whom [feminine] all things came to birth. And because [the high priest] has been anointed with oil [which means that] his reason is illuminated with brilliant light, he is considered worthy to put on the garments. The greatest Logos of the One Who Is put on the creation as garments, that is, earth, water, air and fire, and all that comes from them.[30]

In the temple, the veil was woven from four colours to symbolize the four elements,[31] and so the veil represented matter. The Logos emerging came through the veil into the world, and the high priest's outer vestment was made from the same fabric as the veil (Exod. 26.32; cf. Exod. 28.5–6). In other words, as he emerged through the veil, the Logos/high priest

---

[28] The Hebrew idiom for 'make a high priest', i.e. fill the hands with incense.
[29] *Assumption of Moses* 10.2–3.
[30] Philo, *On Flight*, 108–10, my translation.
[31] Josephus, *War* 5.212–13.

became incarnate. Hence the writer of Hebrews could say 'the curtain, that is, his flesh' without any further explanation, and so, we must assume, 'the curtain, that is, his flesh' was understood by the users of this text.

The expected sequence was that the Logos/the Son brought the judgement, as depicted in Revelation 19, and the judgement passages in John's Gospel must be read in the light of that expectation *and how Jesus understood it*. Immediately after the Logos/Lamb has come into the world and been recognized, John describes *a wedding feast* at Cana, and Jesus' mother, not named, is there.

After the Baptist has spoken about the Bride and the Bridegroom, this section concludes with the words of the unknown speaker (vv. 31–36). There is a similar reflection at 12.44–50, but there the reflection is attributed to Jesus. Here, the words could be from Jesus, but if so, it is strange that John does not say so. The reflection sums up the teaching of the Nicodemus episode:

- the gift of the Spirit (vv. 5–8, 34);
- the one who comes down from heaven (v. 13) and is coming from above (v. 31);
- the contrast of earth and heaven (vv. 12, 31);
- testimony to what Jesus has seen in heaven, but people do not believe him (vv. 11, 32);
- the Father's love for the Son (vv. 16 (as we have translated *monogenēs*), 35);
- the one sent by God (vv. 17, 34);
- belief in the Son gives eternal life (vv. 15, 16, 36).

A natural break in the texts follows, marked now by the end of chapter 3. This chapter has set out the first part of the teaching that had been lost from the second temple.

# John 4

## 4.1–42: Jesus in Samaria

Jesus moves away from Judea into Samaria. The Pharisees had heard that he was making even more disciples than John, and so he decided to return to Galilee. The usual route for Galileans to take, according to Josephus, was through Samaria: 'It was the custom of the Galileans, when they came to the holy city at the festivals, to take their journeys through the country of the Samaritans ...'[1] This was the shortest route, again according to Josephus, who said the journey took three days.[2] Only John records this incident at Jacob's well. The synoptic Gospels suggest hostility from the Samaritans, since the people would not receive Jesus and his disciples because he was going to Jerusalem (Luke 9.51–54). This may explain Jesus' command to his disciples: 'Go nowhere among the Gentiles, and enter no town of the Samaritans, but go rather to the lost sheep of the house of Israel' (Matt. 10.5–7). Linking Gentiles and Samaritans may have been the particular view of Matthew's community, since John's account of Jesus and the Samaritan woman offers a very different picture.

The origin of the Samaritans is not known. The Deuteronomic historian, who had his own characteristic view of Israel's history and a low opinion of the Samaritans and their capital city, is responsible for the biblical account of their origins. Their great king Omri, who reigned for 40 years and married his son Ahab to the Phoenician princess Jezebel, was dismissed by the D historian as a man who did evil and died. He left his mark in history by buying a hill from Shemer for two talents and building a fortified city there. This was Samaria, named after the previous landowner (1 Kings 16.23–28). The Samaritans themselves, *šōmrōnîm*, said that their name derived from *šāmar*, 'keep' (the law), but the Jews regarded them as far from faithful observers of the law. As the woman observed to Jesus: 'The Jews do not share things with the Samaritans' (4.9,

---

[1] Josephus, *Antiquities* 20.118.
[2] Josephus, *Life* 52: 'It was absolutely necessary for those that go quickly [to Jerusalem] to pass through [Samaria] for on that road you may go in three days from Galilee to Jerusalem.'

## John 4

my literal translation). It was this failure to observe the strict purity laws that made it possible for a Samaritan to help the man who had been attacked and left for dead (Luke 10.30–37). The priest and the Levite were both going to the temple and had to be in a state of ritual purity, which prevented them from helping him. The feeling was mutual. A story was told of a rabbi in the mid-second century CE who was travelling to Jerusalem through Samaria.

> R. Jonathan was going up to worship in Jerusalem when he passed the Palatinus [Mount Gerizim] and was seen by a Samaritan, who asked him: 'Where are you going?' 'To worship in Jerusalem,' he replied. 'Would it not be better to pray at this holy mountain than at that dunghill?' he jeered.[3]

Jesus came to a spring[4] and sat by it (or perhaps 'on it') at about the sixth hour (v. 6). This is likely to have been noon, although some argue that it was in the evening. The spring was near Sychar, possibly a scribal error for Shechem, since the latter makes more sense. It was, says John, near the field that Jacob gave to his son Joseph, but there is no record of Jacob having a piece of land at Sychar. He did buy some land near Shechem (Gen. 33.18) which became the inheritance of Joseph's family after his bones had been brought from Egypt and buried there (Josh. 24.32). This could have been the field that Jacob gave to Joseph (v. 5), and it was at the foot of Mount Gerizim, the Samaritans' holy mountain where their temple had stood.

While Jesus was there, a woman came to draw water, and Jesus asked her for a drink. This was unusual for two reasons: the woman assumed that Jesus was a Jew, and as such would have avoided conversation with a woman. Rabbi Jose b. Joḥanan, a famous teacher about a century before the time of Jesus, had said: 'Talk not much with womankind ...' Other teachers had added: 'He that talks much with womankind brings evil upon himself ...'[5] and so a conversation with a stranger would have been unusual. Second, it was not normal for Jews to have dealings with Samaritans.

John then shows how Jesus saw their meeting on two levels. Each element of the story has a surface meaning and a hidden meaning. There is an implied contrast between the privileged Nicodemus, who had access to all the learning of his people and yet did not understand what Jesus was saying; and the unnamed Samaritan woman of whom we are told only

---
[3] *Genesis Rabbah* XXXII.10.
[4] The Greek here is *pēgē*, literally 'a spring', but in v. 11 the word is *phrear*, 'a well'.
[5] Mishnah *Aboth* 1.5.

that she had been married five times. It was the woman who realized what Jesus was saying and who he was, although John does present Nicodemus as a loyal defender of Jesus. The woman is often presented in commentaries as having a dubious past, but she may well have been a victim of her own society. She had had five husbands, and in a society where it was not easy for a woman to leave her husband – divorcing a spouse was usually a man's prerogative – this means she had been abandoned five times; or she had been widowed five times and married in succession to her brothers-in-law (Deut. 5.5–6; Mark 12.18–23 and parallels). In both cases the reason for the multiple marriages would have been that she was childless: bearing no child was grounds for divorce, since a man was obliged to father two children; and for the same reason, a childless widow had to marry a brother-in-law in order to give her first husband an heir. These were the Jewish customs, but something similar in Samaria would account for the woman's having five husbands, and then coming to the well alone at noon, to avoid the other women who would have seen her childless state as a punishment from God.

The woman also represented Samaria itself, rejected by the Jews as impure on the grounds that their land had been settled with foreigners after the destruction of Samaria in 723 BCE. The five husbands represented the gods of the five nations who were settled there: people from Babylon, Cuth and Hamath, and the Avvites and Sepharvites (2 Kings 17.29–30). This was still remembered in Jesus' time, and Josephus told their history thus: 'The Cutheans who removed into Samaria ... each of them, according to their nations, which were five, brought their own gods into Samaria, and by worshipping them, as was the custom of their own countries, they provoked Almighty God ...'[6] Both the D writer and Josephus were 'Jews', whom many other voices of the period regarded as apostate; what they say about the Samaritans is only the 'Jewish' point of view. There had been separate shrines in the north at Dan and at Bethel since the reign of Jeroboam in the tenth century BCE, following the northern people's rejection of Solomon's son Rehoboam as king, but people of the north – Shechem, Shiloh, Samaria – continued to worship in Jerusalem (Jer. 41.4–5). The remains of a temple built in the early fifth century BCE have been found on Mount Gerizim, the Samaritans' holy mountain. This was the temple built after their exclusion from the second temple in Jerusalem and it was only 30 miles/50 kilometres to the north. Nehemiah had later enforced the stricter post-exilic purity rules on the

---
[6] Josephus, *Antiquities* 9.288.

old priestly families, and those who did not accept them went to the north (Neh. 13.28). The Samaritans had offered to help 'the Jews' rebuild the Jerusalem temple, but their offer was refused. They appear in the Jewish account of the period as the 'adversaries', people who had only been worshipping the LORD since the king of Assyria brought their ancestors to the land (Ezra 4.1–3).

Accounts of the post-exilic period and events surrounding the building of the second temple are so fragmented and confused that nothing is certain except the bitterness and contempt that characterized the second-temple period. Ben Sira, a scholar living in Jerusalem about 180 BCE, wrote this:

> Two nations annoy/offend me, and the third is no nation:
> Those who live on the mountain of Samaria, and the Philistines,
> and the foolish people who live in Shechem.
> (Ben Sira 50.25–26, Greek text, my translation)

This may have been prompted by the Samaritans' reaction to the Hellenization imposed by the Syrian king Antiochus Epiphanes (175–164 BCE); he decreed that the temple in Jerusalem had to be renamed the temple of Olympian Zeus, and the temple on Gerizim had to become the temple of Zeus Xenios (Friend of Strangers), which apparently was a name already used by the people there (2 Macc. 6.1–2). Not long after this, in 129 BCE, the temple on Gerizim was destroyed by the Jewish high-priest-king John Hyrcanus. Josephus commented that 'the temple which was at Gerizim, which resembled the temple in Jerusalem' lay deserted after 200 years.[7] The Samaritan woman, then, brought to her meeting with Jesus the social memories of how her people had been rejected by the Jews who had built the second temple in Jerusalem, and how the Jewish priest-king had left the Gerizim temple in ruins some two centuries before her time.

The Samaritans acknowledged only the first five books of the Hebrew Scriptures, which could have been the essential scrolls that the banished priests brought from Jerusalem when the Gerizim temple was built. There are some significant differences between the Jewish texts and the Samaritan texts insofar as passages in the Jewish Old Testament appear in a different place in the Samaritan text. Since 'cutting and pasting' has long been proposed as the way some post-exilic Jewish scribes worked when preserving their sacred texts, it is no surprise to find that the Samaritans did something similar but with a different result. One

---
[7] Josephus, *Antiquities* 13.256.

expanded passage is the Ten Commandments in Exodus, where the first two become one commandment and the tenth is that the LORD had to be worshipped on Mount Gerizim. Exodus 20 is expanded with several passages that appear elsewhere in the Jewish text:

- with Deuteronomy 27.1–8, about setting up on the holy mountain plastered stones bearing the commandments, but naming the mountain Gerizim and not Ebal (Deut. 27.4);
- with Deuteronomy 5.28–29, about the LORD wishing that his people would always keep the commandments;
- with Deuteronomy 18.18–22, about the LORD sending a prophet like Moses to give his people guidance in the future.

Then the Jewish Exodus text resumes. Nobody knows when this Samaritan form of the text was made, but it may be relevant to understanding the thought of the woman of Samaria, who links a promised prophet to a ruling on the correct place to worship. John's account of the woman at the well may show that this form of Samaritan text was used in the time of Jesus.[8]

The first topic of Jesus' conversation with the woman was water; he asked for a drink and prompted the woman's astonished reply that Jews have no dealings with Samaritans. Jesus then spoke of the water he had to give – living waters which quenched every thirst – and the woman, though interested, did not understand. Living water was expected to flow out from the restored temple (Ezek. 47.1–2; Zech. 14.8), and this water was a sign that Wisdom was restored. The water flowed from fountains by the heavenly throne (Rev. 22.1–2), and these fountains were a symbol of Wisdom/the Spirit flowing forth. Enoch saw them in his vision of the throne: 'many fountains of wisdom, and all the thirsty drank of them, and were filled with wisdom'.[9] Those who drank from the fountain filled others with wisdom and understanding (Ben Sira 24.21–27, but omitting vv. 23–24 which are a later insertion). Living water (that is, flowing water) was a Johannine image and carried the second meaning 'water that gives life'. The-Spirit-and-the-Bride invited the thirsty to drink (Rev. 22.17). John had Jesus invite the thirsty to drink the Spirit from him, and he taught that rivers of living water would flow from the innermost part/mind of those who believed in him (John 7.37–39).[10]

---

[8] *Samaritan Documents*, tr. and ed. J. Bowman, Pittsburgh: Pickwick Press, 1977, pp. 16–27.
[9] *1 Enoch* 48.1.
[10] The scripture referred to is Ben Sira 24.21–22, 25–27.

## John 4

Jesus then instigated the conversation about the woman's husbands, including a reference to her current status – not married to her present partner – which may allude to the current situation with Zeus Xenios in Samaria. The woman concluded that he was a prophet and immediately asked him about the correct place of worship: Gerizim or Jerusalem. A prophet was expected to give such rulings. In 164 BCE, when the Jerusalem temple had been recaptured from the occupying Syrians and purified for worship again, the desecrated altar stones were put to one side 'until there should come a prophet to tell them what to do with them' (1 Macc. 4.46). The Samaritan woman hoped for a similar ruling from Jesus: an answer to the problem created by the building of the second temple and the exclusion of the other worshippers of the LORD.

Jesus told her that neither holy mountain would be the site of worship in the future, because the hour was coming when people would worship in spirit and in truth. The new temple would replace and transcend the older temples, presumably the future temple to be built by the Messiah. The woman seems to have made this link also, because she immediately spoke of the coming Messiah who would reveal all things. The problem here is Jesus' words in verse 22: 'You worship what you do not know; we worship what we know, for salvation, *sōtēria*, comes out from the Jews' (translating literally). Some people have suggested that this is a later insertion into the text – the easy solution – not least because this is a non-hostile reference to the Jews. Jesus was perhaps saying that the Samaritans knew less about the expected Messiah than the Jews because they only acknowledged the first five books of what became the Jewish Scriptures, and did not recognize the prophets and the Psalms, which were the source of so many messianic texts. These pointed to the Jerusalem temple as the cultural matrix from which the Messiah, and so 'salvation', would emerge.

The Samaritans expected a prophet like Moses to return (whom they called the Taheb) rather than an anointed Davidic king, and so when the woman spoke of the future Messiah, she may have had the Taheb in mind. A Samaritan prophet did appear a few years later, about 36 CE: 'A man ... bade them get together on Mount Gerizim ... and assured them that when they came there, he would show them the holy vessels that were hidden under that place, because Moses had put them there.'[11] An expectant crowd assembled to ascend Mount Gerizim, but Pilate suppressed the movement and killed the leaders.

---

[11] Josephus, *Antiquities* 18.85.

John resumes the narrative (v. 27). The disciples came with the food and were surprised to find Jesus talking to a woman. She then went away to tell her neighbours about the conversation, and they came out to meet Jesus. His disciples tried to persuade him to eat, but he said that he had other food – the task in hand that he had to complete, *teleioō*. He then looked at the arable land all round them and saw, in both senses of the words, that harvest time was near. The harvest was a frequent but positive image for the end time: the Baptist had spoken of the Coming One who would gather his wheat into his granary (Matt. 3.12//Luke 3.17); Jesus told the parable of the angel reapers who would gather the weeds to burn them and then gather the wheat into the barn, meaning that the righteous would be gathered into the kingdom of their Father where they would shine like the sun (Matt. 13.30, 41–43); and there was the vision of the Man with a golden crown who reaped the harvest of the earth (Rev. 14.14–16). Jesus told his disciples: 'I sent you to reap that for which you did not labour; others have laboured, and you have entered into their labour' (v. 38). Who were these 'others'? Perhaps the communities that prayed the *Didache* prayers, or even their predecessors, those who had been preparing the way of the Lord, or perhaps the disciples of the Baptist. These may not have been distinct groups.

Jesus stayed there two days, and many Samaritans believed that Jesus was the Saviour of the world.

## 4.43–54: Jesus returns to Galilee

Then Jesus resumed his journey northwards and reached Cana where the people of Galilee welcomed him. Here there is a problem in the text (vv. 44–45), which could be resolved by understanding the lines thus:

> Jesus himself had testified that a prophet had no honour in his own country, but when he came to Galilee, the Galileans welcomed him because they had seen all he had done in Jerusalem when they too had been there for the feast.

Jesus then gave his second sign. A royal official, *basilikos*, came from Capernaum to ask Jesus to save his dying son. Jesus assured him that his son would live, and as he returned home, his servants met him with the news that his son was recovering. The whole household became followers of Jesus. This is very similar to the story of Jesus healing the centurion's servant when he was in Capernaum (Matt. 8.5–13; Luke 7.1–10), and there have been ingenious suggestions as to how the stories relate to each other, and how and why they changed. There has also been speculation

## John 4

about the *basilikos*: was he perhaps Chuza, Herod's steward, the husband of Joanna who became a follower of Jesus (Luke 8.3); or perhaps Manaen, one of Herod's courtiers who became a leader of the church in Antioch (Acts 13.1)? Who can know?

The people of Galilee had seen the first two signs: Melchi-Zedek had offered them wine instead of water, and he had saved a child from death.

# John 5

### 5.1–9: Jesus heals at Bethesda

Whenever Jesus goes to Jerusalem in John's Gospel it is for a temple festival, and in the temple he debates with 'the Jews' about an element of the original Temple Theology that they are not aware of or are not able to understand.

- He visits Jerusalem at Passover, a feast of the Jews. He cleanses the temple and debates with the Jews about rebuilding the temple (2.13, 18–20).
- He visits Jerusalem for an unnamed feast of the Jews, but probably Tabernacles, enters the temple and debates with the Jews about the relationship of Father and Son (5.1, 14–47).
- [The next Passover is spent away from Jerusalem – feeding the 5,000 (6.1–15).]
- He visits Jerusalem for the Jews' feast of Tabernacles, enters the temple and debates with the Jews about the true children of Abraham (7.2—8.59).
- He is in the temple for the feast of Ḥanukkah, and debates with the Jews about the consecrated one who was sent into the world as the Son (10.22–39).
- He comes to Jerusalem for Passover and enters the city. John reflects that the Jews cannot understand what he has been teaching (12.1, 12–19, 37–43).

In his Gospel, John records only an outline of these debates and discourses, but there is sufficient detail given both in his Gospel and in the synoptics to see that Jesus lived and taught as a rabbi of his time. He had his own disciples, whom he taught privately (e.g. Mark 4.10), and who would have committed themselves to his characteristic teaching and interpretation of Scripture. They took his yoke upon them. 'Take my yoke upon you, and learn from me ... for my yoke is easy, and my burden is light' (Matt. 11.29, 30). The burden was the complicated system of rules that had grown up

## John 5

around the law of Moses: 'The scribes and the Pharisees ... bind heavy burdens, hard to bear, and lay them on men's shoulders ...' (Matt. 23.2–4; Luke 11.46). The Jerusalem church used the same language. Discussing how much of the law should be kept by Gentile Christians, Peter asked why they were trying to put a yoke on their necks which had been too much even for the Jews, and so the assembly decided to require only the minimum from Gentile converts: kosher meat and Jewish standards of chastity (Acts 15.10, 28). Paul emphasized this to the Galatian Christians who were being pressured to keep the law of Moses: 'Christ has set us free ... do not submit again to a yoke of slavery' (Gal. 5.1).

## Jesus the rabbi

Jesus taught in synagogues, in the temple, and in his own 'school' – perhaps this is what was meant by 'privately', since he denied that he had ever taught 'secretly'. At his trial, when the high priest asked Jesus about his teaching, he replied, 'I have spoken openly to the world; I have always taught in synagogues and in the temple, where all Jews come together; I have said nothing secretly' (18.20). There had long been houses of study where people could learn more of the Scriptures and the Jewish way of life. Ben Sira, teaching in Jerusalem in the early years of the second century BCE, invited people to his house of study:

> Draw near to me, you who lack learning,
> And live in my house of learning.
> Why do you say you are deprived,
> And that your souls are very thirsty? ...
> Put your neck under the yoke
> And let your soul receive teaching.
> (Ben Sira 51.23, 24, 26, my translation)

His grandson translated his teachings into Greek, 'so that those who love learning should make even greater progress in living according to the law' (Prologue to Ben Sira), and his younger contemporary in Palestine, Rabbi Jose ben Joezer, taught, 'Let your house be a meeting place for the wise; and sit in the dust at their feet and thirstily drink in their words.'[1] Jesus also described his teaching as quenching thirst (4.14; 7.37–38), and his 'school', according to early tradition, was a cave on the Mount of Olives. The Emperor Constantine's mother had a church built at the site, and a pilgrim in the late fourth century said that some processions in Holy

---
[1] Mishnah *Aboth* 1.4.

Week began at the 'church of the cave' where Jesus used to teach his disciples.² This appears in the synoptic Gospels as Jesus teaching 'privately' on the Mount of Olives (Matt. 24.3; Mark 13.3), and what follows in both accounts is a summary of the vision of the seven seals (Rev. 6.1–17), 'the revelation of Jesus Christ which God gave to him to show his servants what must soon take place' (Rev. 1.1).

Jesus taught in several synagogues: he taught in an unnamed synagogue where the Pharisees asked for his interpretation of the Sabbath law (Matt. 12.9) and he taught in synagogues at Capernaum and in all of Galilee (Mark 1.21, 39). John says that after feeding the 5,000 he taught in the synagogue at Capernaum (6.59), and here his words reflect the three-year synagogue lectionary and so the memory of an actual event:

> The lections for the second year of the cycle [for the period immediately after Passover] tell of the crossing of the Red Sea and the gift of manna; hence the two miracles [the walking on water and the feeding] are just those that would be most appropriate for Passover-time, and the theme of Jesus' sermon is precisely that which would drive home to the crowd assembled in the synagogue the lesson of the Old Testament passage[s] already read.³

This suggests that Jesus was trained in expounding Scripture. Luke describes another sermon in the synagogue at Nazareth, where Jesus interpreted Isaiah 61, concerning the one anointed by the Spirit to teach the good news, and claimed that he was the fulfilment of that prophecy (Luke 4.21). The people were angry and threw him out of the synagogue. Mark's version of the story says there was a mixed reaction: people were astonished that Jesus, whose family they knew, could teach so well:

> On the sabbath he began to teach in the synagogue; and many who heard him were astonished, saying, 'Where did this man get all this? What is the wisdom given to him? What mighty works are wrought by his hands!'
> (Mark 6.2)

John too knew Jesus' claim that the Scriptures spoke of him (5.39), and elsewhere it is clear that Jesus was aware of an older form of the Scriptures, presumably the form that pointed to him, the LORD in human form. The law of Moses, he said, was a later addition to God's original law, added because of 'your hardness of heart' (Mark 10.5); and further additions from the tradition of the elders 'make void the word of God' (Mark 7.13).

---

² The Eleona Church, now the Pater Noster Church, where Jesus taught his disciples the LORD's Prayer. The pilgrim was Egeria, *Egeria's Travels* 68, 71.

³ A. Guilding, *The Fourth Gospel and Jewish Worship*, Oxford: Clarendon Press, 1960, p. 61.

## John 5

These verses were taken up in the early second century by Ptolemy[4] in his *Letter to Flora*, and this is the earliest known source criticism of the Old Testament. The *Letter* was prompted by Christian concern for the status of the Old Testament in the Church, since it was obvious that the entire Old Testament was not relevant to Christianity. Ptolemy was a disciple of Valentinus. Their contemporary was Marcion, who had rejected the religion of the Old Testament because it was irrelevant to Christianity. Marcion was declared a heretic, but the roots of his argument can be seen in John's picture of Jesus who found himself in the older Scriptures. Ptolemy solved the problem of the Old Testament in the Church by saying that there were three strata within the text:

> The law is divided into three parts. For we have found in it legislation belonging to Moses himself, to the elders and to God himself. The analysis of the law as a whole, as we have divided it here, has made clear which part is genuine.[5]

In other words, the law of Moses and the tradition of the elders were later accretions to the law of God.

The examples in Mark about divorce, handwashing, denying support to parents, and food laws, may be examples of Jesus' criticism of the law of Moses and the tradition of the elders, but are not necessarily all that Jesus taught on the subject. There is an enigmatic *agraphon* attributed to him: 'Be approved bankers',[6] which seems to mean: 'Be able to detect forgeries'; and there is the equally enigmatic saying of Jesus: 'one jot or one tittle shall in no wise pass from the law ...' (Matt. 5.18, AV), which has added significance in the light of the differences between the Hebrew texts found at Qumran and those that became the Masoretic Jewish text. A single letter dropped from the text could completely alter its meaning.[7] Enoch also claimed that Scripture had been altered: 'Woe to you who write down lying and godless words ... Sinners will alter and pervert the words of righteousness in many ways.'[8] The Enoch tradition regarded the second-

---

[4] A follower of Valentinus, the brilliant Christian theologian in the early second century CE. Later detractors labelled his disciples as Gnostics, but they considered themselves Christian, and as late as 200 CE a follower of Valentinus could hold office in the church in Rome.

[5] Quoted in Epiphanius, *Panarion* 33.4.

[6] An *agraphon* (meaning 'not written') is a saying attributed to Jesus that is not written in the canonical Gospels. This *agraphon* is in Clement of Alexandria, *Miscellanies* 1.28.

[7] The Qumran Isaiah scroll at 52.14 has 'anointed' where the Masoretic has 'disfigured', a difference of one letter. The Qumran text is about the Messiah; the Masoretic is not.

[8] *1 Enoch* 98.14–99.2; 104.10–11.

temple Jews as an apostate generation, and so would have rejected all the work of Ezra and the men of the great synagogue.

John emphasized that Jesus taught in the temple, and for him, the temple is above all the symbolic setting for the meeting of the two ways: those of the first temple and those of the second. The other Gospels mention that Jesus taught in the temple during the days immediately before he died, but the setting does not have the significance that it does for John:

> And he was teaching daily in the temple. The chief priests and scribes and the principal men of the people sought to destroy him; but they did not find anything they could do, for all the people hung upon his words.
>
> (Luke 19.47)

There is a description of a Jewish temple teacher who lived a few years after Jesus – Rabbi Neḥunyah the mystic. He used to sit on a marble bench in the temple precincts, and his disciples sat around him as an inner and an outer group. He told them to write down what he taught them, and it is said that fire and torches were seen around him.[9] Some of his sayings survive in the Mishnah[10] and more elsewhere. We must imagine Jesus teaching like this, and what John records is his own recollection of the temple debates: 'This is the disciple who is bearing witness to these things, and who has written these things; and we know that his testimony is true' (21.24). The exchanges and discourses in John's Gospel should be read as the summary of what was said, but a faithful summary. The characteristics of Rabbinic debate are preserved, such as scrutinizing passages of Scripture, setting one text alongside another, and answering a question with a question.

Jesus had known of the temple teachers for many years. The only story known about his boyhood is his meeting with the temple teachers, 'listening to them and asking them questions' (Luke 2.46). As in the synagogues, so too in the temple the scribes and Pharisees tried to test Jesus' knowledge of the law. When he came to the temple early in the morning and 'all the people came to him, and he sat down and taught them' (8.2), the scribes and Pharisees brought to him a woman accused of adultery and asked how he would interpret the law: 'What do you say about her?' (8.5). His interpretation of the law was: 'Let him who is without sin among you be the first to throw a stone' (8.7). His disciples

---

[9] *Hekhalot Rabbati* 202–3, 228, Schäfer's numbering.
[10] Mishnah *Berakhoth* 4.2; *Aboth* 3.5.

## John 5

would later teach in the temple: Peter spoke in Solomon's porch, and as with John's brief reports of Jesus' teaching, so too Luke records only a summary of what he said. It is unlikely that Peter spoke only for the two minutes required to read the words of Acts 3.12–25. There are also stories about James, the leader of the Jerusalem church, teaching in the temple and debating with Sadducees, Pharisees and scribes. These are doubtless reconstructions of what people thought had happened, but this is how the early Church remembered the temple debates. Crowds gathered to hear James, and on one of these occasions he was attacked by Saul, an agent of the temple authorities, 'a Pharisee [and] persecutor of the church' (Phil. 3.5, 6). James and many of the Christians fled from the city the next day.[11]

Jesus was often called Rabbi, a title that was not given lightly. Like other leading rabbis, he had his own interpretations of Scripture and applying the law. This was his 'yoke'; his disciples accepted it, following both his teachings and his understanding of Scripture. Since he had supreme authority and he sent his disciples out to teach 'all that I have commanded you' (Matt. 28.18, 20), *the interpretations of Scripture elsewhere in the New Testament probably originated with Jesus himself.* Luke says that Jesus found himself in Moses and the prophets (Luke 24.25–27); John's Jesus said the Scriptures spoke of himself (5.39); the proof texts and illustrations in Hebrews could well go back to Jesus' understanding of himself and his role (e.g. Heb. 1.5–13; 8.8–12). John quoted Isaiah 6.10 when reflecting on Jesus' failure to communicate to his own people (12.40); and Luke quoted the same verse of Paul who had failed to convince the Jews in Rome (Acts 28.17–28).

There was a similar situation at Qumran as can be seen from the remains of their commentaries on Scripture. Everything was a mystery to be interpreted. Their leader, the Teacher of Righteousness (or perhaps that should be translated 'the True Teacher') spoke of all the things that would happen in their own time, and the meaning of 'the secrets of his servants the prophets', exactly as the mighty angel said to John (Rev. 10.7).[12] The Master had to instruct all the sons of light,[13] and the leaders of the community had to be learned in the *Book of Hagu.*[14] The Therapeuts in Egypt, as described by Philo, listened to their leader expounding Scripture after their communal evening meal. 'He discusses

---

[11] *Clementine Recognitions* 1.66.
[12] *Commentary on Habakkuk*, 1QpHab II, VII.
[13] *Community Rule*, 1QS III.
[14] One possible way to read the title of the book mentioned in the *Damascus Document*, CD X, XIII, and in the *Messianic Rule*, 1Sa I.

some question arising in the holy Scriptures ... to enable them to discern the inward and hidden through the outward and visible.'[15] What Cross imaginatively reconstructed as the scene at Qumran could well have applied to the Therapeuts and their study sessions, and even to Jesus and his disciples:

> Certain set forms of exposition and a traditional body of biblical exposition grew up, stemming from a pattern laid down in the early period. This was transmitted and supplemented, no doubt, in the regular study of scholars of the community, and particularly in the regular sessions of the sect mentioned in our sources, where Scripture was read and systematically expounded by those who had become the experts of the community. In a later era, the body of traditional exegesis was put into writing in the commentaries and related documents which have come into our hands.[16]

To be accepted as a rabbi implied considerable education and knowledge of the Scriptures, and we know nothing of this aspect of Jesus' life. There was a saying: 'At five years old, one is ready for Scripture, at ten for the Mishnah, at thirteen for the commandments [presumably *bar mitzvah*], at fifteen for the Talmud ...', and perhaps Jesus' childhood and youth were devoted to study rather than working in a carpenter's shop as popular imagination supposes. Nicodemus, himself a Pharisee and teacher of Israel, addressed Jesus as Rabbi, and acknowledged that he was a teacher sent from God (3.2). Peter addressed him as Rabbi (Mark 9.5; 11.21), as did Nathanael (1.49) and the disciples of the Baptist (1.38). Jesus' other disciples called him Rabbi (4.31; 9.2; 11.8); the people called him Rabbi (6.25), the blind man called him Rabbi (Mark 10.51); even Judas called him Rabbi (Matt. 26.25, 49). There are many other places where the equivalent Greek word *didaskalos*, 'teacher', is used. Jesus himself discouraged the use of the title and had no time for distinctive dress and expected public honours, nor for the subtleties of exegesis that destroyed the real meaning of the law (Matt. 23.1–36). He criticized some contemporary scholars: 'Woe to you, scribes and Pharisees, hypocrites' (Matt. 23.13, 14, 15, 16, 23, 25, 27, 29), and he knew teachers who were making the law a great burden and were 'blind guides' (Matt. 23.4, 16).

The rabbis thought of themselves as belonging to an unbroken chain of teaching transmitted for generations from a teacher to his pupil. In particular, they handed down the oral law which was all the material

---

[15] Philo, *Contemplative Life* 75, 78.
[16] F. M. Cross, *The Ancient Library of Qumran*, 3rd edn, Sheffield: Sheffield Academic Press, 1995, p. 91.

given to Moses on Sinai but not committed to writing. The oral law, they said, was entrusted to 'the men of the great synagogue' who returned from Babylon with Ezra. In other words, the oral law was the teaching of the second-temple period, and John presents Jesus as restoring first-temple teaching. The claim to a chain of tradition appears in their writings, each rabbi citing an earlier teacher as the authority for his own words. Thus in the Mishnah, which finally committed the oral law to writing about 200 CE, there is:

> Rabban Simeon ben Gamaliel says *in the name of* Rabbi Joshua: 'Since the day that the temple was destroyed, there has been no day without its curse, and the dew has not fallen in blessing, and the fruits have lost their savour.'[17]

There is a similar style in the *Midrash Rabbah*, which collected the interpretations of Scripture from many generations. Discussing the meaning of Genesis 3.16, one paragraph has the following:

> R. Judah b. R. Simon and R. Joḥanan *in the name of* R. Eleazar b. R. Simon said ... R. Ababa b. Kahana said *in* R. Biryi's name ... R. Joshua b. Nehemiah answered *in* R. Idi's name ... R. Levi said *in the name of* R. Ḥama b. R. Ḥanina ...'[18]

This way of establishing the meaning of Scripture should be contrasted with Jesus' sayings: 'But I say to you ...' and 'he whom God has sent utters the words of God' (John 3.34) or 'I have come in my Father's name, and you do not receive me ...' (5.43), 'His voice you have never heard' (5.37). Jesus was recognized as a rabbi with authority to give his own interpretation of the Scriptures: 'The crowds were astonished at his teaching, for he taught them as one who had authority, and not as their scribes' (Matt. 7.28–29). What he taught was not learned from his (earthly) teachers. Authority had been given to him, not by two other rabbis laying their hands upon him as was the custom, but by the witness of the Spirit and the Baptist (1.32–34), and by the witness of the Father and the Baptist (5.33, 37). Thus Jesus said that his teaching and actions came from the Father who had given him authority (5.19; 26–27, 30), and that Isaiah's prophecy about the restored Jerusalem was being fulfilled: 'All your sons shall be taught by the LORD' (Isa. 54.13, cited in John 6.45). Matthew shows in the Sermon on the Mount how Jesus expounded the Scriptures:

---

[17] Mishnah *Sotah* 9.12.
[18] *Genesis Rabbah* XX.6.

> Think not that I have come to abolish the law and the prophets; I have not come to abolish them but to fulfil them ... You have heard that it was said to the men of old ... *But I say to you* ... (Matt. 5.17, 21, 22)

This is what had prompted the response that he taught with authority and not like the scribes (Matt. 7.29).

The temple authorities challenged his right to teach in this way:

> And when he entered the temple, the chief priests and the elders of the people came up to him as he was teaching, and said, 'By what authority are you doing these things, and who gave you this authority?' Jesus answered them, 'I also will ask you a question; and if you tell me the answer, then I also will tell you by what authority I do these things.' (Matt. 21.23–24)

In the style of the rabbis, Jesus answered a question with a question, and then told a parable – here the parable of the two sons sent to work in the vineyard.

It is often suggested that the five blocks of teaching in Matthew's Gospel could represent the five books of the law; similarly, there are five blocks of teaching 'to the Jews' in John's Gospel, representing the points at which the teaching of the first temple differed from that of the second:

- chapter 3, about birth from heaven;
- chapter 5, about judgement and new life;
- chapter 6, about food from heaven;
- chapters 7—8, about the light and water of Tabernacles;
- chapter 10, about the Son of God consecrated and sent into the world.

\*\*\*\*\*

Pilgrimage to the temple was an ancient custom. The earliest calendars say that all men had to go to the temple for the three great feasts: Unleavened Bread which became Passover; Harvest which was called Weeks; and Ingathering which later became the great autumn festival of New Year, Day of Atonement and Tabernacles (Exod. 23.14–17). It became the custom, however, to read the ancient texts differently from the way they were written, to avoid the impression that pilgrims saw the face of the LORD.[19] Originally, as we have seen, that is what pilgrims went to the temple to see, but this became controversial. Seeing the face/ presence at the festivals had probably been the setting for the high-priestly blessing 'May the LORD make his face/presence shine upon you', but by the end of the second-temple period, it was forbidden to explain

---

[19] See above, pp. 98–9.

## John 5

these words.[20] The Qumran community understood this to mean illumination of the mind with the gift of life-giving wisdom and the knowledge of eternity,[21] and Jesus' debates with the Jews in the temple at the times of pilgrimage should be understood in this context. People saw the presence of the LORD and were illuminated with life-giving wisdom. This Christian emphasis may even have contributed to the different way of reading the Hebrew text and reticence about expounding the blessing. The culmination of the high priests' blessing was: 'So shall [the high priests] put my name upon the people of Israel, and I will bless them' (Num. 6.27). The Christians saw themselves as the new royal priesthood (1 Pet. 2.9; Rev. 22.3–5) and they marked the X on the foreheads of the baptized. This was the ancient sign for the Name of the LORD, and thus it completed the blessing of the high priests. The popular explanation of the name 'Israel' was 'the man who has seen God',[22] and the Christians claimed for themselves the status of Israel. 'We have beheld his glory' (1.14).

After his second sign in Galilee, Jesus returned to Judea for a feast of the Jews and healed a paralysed man at the pool of Bethesda, outside the city walls and near the Sheep Gate. There were five porticoes there, and it was a place where invalids came – weak, blind, lame, paralysed (literally 'dry/withered', *xēros*) – for healing. There used to be speculation about the pool: where it was and how much of the description was only symbolic, the five porticoes representing the five books of the law of Moses, for example. Archaeologists have now found the site of the pool, possibly the great reservoir dug by Simeon the high priest and described by Ben Sira as 'like the sea in circumference' (Ben Sira 50.3).[23] It was north of the 'Temple Mount' and had been developed from the 'upper pool' mentioned in Isaiah as the location of his Immanuel prophecy (Isa. 7.3, 10–14). In Jesus' time there were two pools, the upper acting as a reservoir for the lower which was shallow and had steps down into it. It could have been used as a pool for ritual immersion before entering the temple, perhaps for pilgrims. There were five porticoes: one along each side and one across the middle between the upper and lower pools. There were non-Jewish sites there too, one dedicated to the Greek god of good

---

[20] Mishnah *Megillah* 4.10.
[21] See above, p. 97.
[22] C. T. R. Hayward, *The Interpretation of the Name Israel in Ancient Judaism and Some Early Christian Writings*, Oxford: Oxford University Press, 2005.
[23] There is no agreement as to which Simeon this was: there was a high priest of that name who is said to have met Alexander the Great, and another about 200 BCE.

fortune[24] and another to Asclepius, god of healing. When Hadrian rebuilt Jerusalem, these pools became an Asclepeion. This would explain the many invalids who were waiting there. The name is a mystery; it may have derived from Bet-Eshda', the 'house of flowing'. A place of that name seems to occur in the Qumran *Copper Scroll*, where treasure was said to be hidden 'in the reservoir where you enter the small pool at Bet-Eshdatain', a longer form of the name, meaning 'the two flowings'. The name in the *Copper Scroll* is not certain, however, but it would be an appropriate name for the two pools and their flowing water.[25] It was known also (or perhaps later renamed by the Christians) as Bet Ḥesda', the house of healing.

Here it was that Jesus saw a man who had been 'weak' for 38 years. Jesus told him to get up, take his mat and walk. He did. This was the third sign.

Just as the five porticoes were thought symbolic, and they may have been symbolic in John's mind even though they actually existed, so too there has been speculation about the 38 years' illness of the 'weak' man, who was lying beside the abundant waters for ritual purification but was still 'weak'. First, Israel's time in the wilderness was reckoned as 38 years from their time in Kadesh until they reached the brook Zered (Deut. 2.14). The time was not reckoned from their leaving Egypt, but from the time when Miriam/Wisdom died at Kadesh and there was no more water for Israel, except what Moses drew from a rock (Num. 20.1–2). In other words, *the time in the desert was reckoned from the time they lost Wisdom*.[26] In terms of the history of Jerusalem, the event encoded into the Pentateuch as the loss of Miriam and her water occurred when Josiah purged the temple. Jeremiah, who witnessed Josiah's purges, commented on what was happening as people changed their source of water:

> Has a nation changed its gods, even though they are no gods?
> But my people have changed my[27] glory for that which does not profit.
> Be appalled, O heavens at this, be shocked, be utterly desolate,
> says the LORD,
> For my people have committed two evils:
> They have forsaken me, the fountain of living waters,
> And hewed out cisterns for themselves,
> Broken cisterns, that can hold no water.                (Jer. 2.11–13).

---

[24] Mishnah *Zabim* 1.5.
[25] 3Q15 XI, in *Discoveries in the Judaean Desert* III, ed. M. Baillet, J. T. Milik and R. de Vaux, Oxford: Clarendon Press, 1962, p. 271.
[26] There may have been wordplay on the original Hebrew telling of this story. 'Wither' as in Isa. 24.4, and 'be foolish, lack Wisdom', as in 2 Sam. 3.33, are both *nābhal* in Hebrew.
[27] This is a recognized 'correction of the scribes', and the text now has 'its glory'.

## John 5

Now a pool for ritual immersion such as the pool at Bet Ḥesda' was a *miqveh*, but this was a Hebrew word with two meanings: a 'gathering of water', or 'hope'. There are places where Jeremiah plays on this double meaning. These passages were his reaction to losing the first temple (and Wisdom), and they seem to be the background to the events in John 5.

> O LORD, the hope, *miqveh*, of Israel,
> All who forsake thee shall be put to shame,
> Those who turn away from thee
> Shall be written in the earth,
> For they have forsaken the LORD,
> The fountain of living water.
> Heal me, O LORD, and I shall be healed;
> Save me, and I shall be saved;
> For thou art my praise.     (Jer. 17.13–14)

What was Jeremiah saying here? That the LORD was the true *miqveh* of Israel in both senses? Even closer to the situation in John 5 is Jeremiah's other *miqveh* passage.

> Though our iniquities testify against us,
> Act, O LORD, for thy name's sake;
> For our backslidings are many,
> We have sinned against thee.
> O thou hope, *miqveh*, of Israel,
> Its saviour in time of trouble,
> Why shouldst thou be like a stranger in the land,
> Like a wayfarer who turns aside to tarry for a night? ...
> Yet thou, O LORD, art in the midst of us,
> And we are called by thy name;
> Leave us not.                (Jer. 14.7–9)

So far we have met three representative figures: Nicodemus the teacher of Israel who came out of the darkness to talk to Jesus and did not recognize the fundamentals of his own temple tradition; the Samaritan woman who wanted to know which was the true temple; and here, an unnamed man who was healed and immediately went into the temple, a man who had been dried up for 38 years and thought he needed access to the waters of purification. Even though we have been told nothing about the man's life, Jesus says to him, 'Sin no more, that nothing worse befall you' (v. 14). The dried-up man represented those who had been in the wilderness for 38 years.

## 5.9b–47: Debates with the Jews

The man was healed on the Sabbath, and the Jews rebuked him for carrying his mat, since carrying anything was forbidden on the Sabbath.[28] The man did not know who had healed him, but after Jesus had met him in the temple, he realized who he was. On his pilgrimage to the temple the withered man had seen the presence of the LORD, and it had healed him. He was then able to tell the Jews, but they did not recognize the presence of the LORD in the temple, since they were preoccupied with the matter of carrying a mat on the Sabbath. Instead, they accused the newly healed man of breaking the Sabbath. Nehemiah had strictly enforced the 'no carrying on the Sabbath' rule in the restored Jerusalem, even for foreign traders (Neh. 13.15–22). Jesus, however, responded to his critics with his own interpretation of the Sabbath rule: 'My Father is working still, and I am working' (v. 17), implying that he was still carrying out his Father's work of creation. The Jews took issue with both claims: working on the Sabbath and claiming equality with God who was his Father.[29] The summary of two discussions follows: the first about the Sabbath and the second about the relationship between Father and Son.

The Sabbath debate is not spelled out, but has to be reconstructed from other sources, namely two non-literal understandings of the Sabbath in early Christian texts that both use temple imagery. Hebrews interprets Psalm 95.7–11 to show that the people who rebelled in the wilderness under Moses never entered into the rest of the promised land. The rebellion which the psalm describes began after Moses had drawn water from the rock to replace the water given by Miriam (Exod. 17.7; Num. 20.13 – two versions of the same story). The writer of Hebrews, while admitting that there is an understanding of the Sabbath based on Genesis 2.2, argues that the Sabbath was also the promised future rest which the rebels in the wilderness never enjoyed.

> So we see that they were unable to enter [the Sabbath rest] because of disbelief ...
>
> For [the] good news came to us just as to them; but the message which they heard did not benefit them, because it did not meet with faith in the hearers ...

---

[28] Mishnah *Shabbath* 7.2.
[29] Philo wrote of both: on the seventh day the Creator, having brought to an end the formation of mortal things, begins the shaping of others more divine. For 'God never leaves off making ...' *Allegorical Interpretation* I.5.

## John 5

> Since therefore it remains for some to enter [the Sabbath rest], and those who formerly received the good news failed to enter because of disobedience ...
>
> So then, there remains a sabbath rest for the people of God; for whoever enters God's rest also ceases from his labours as God did from his.
>
> (Heb. 3.19; 4.2, 6, 9)

The people of Moses heard the good news but did not receive it, exactly as John says: 'He came to his own home and his own people did not receive him ...' (1.11, my translation). Those who did receive the good news were still working and waiting to enter the Sabbath rest.

The second text is the *Letter of Barnabas*, which uses temple imagery and supplements the argument in Hebrews. Beginning with the Genesis creation story, Barnabas explains that the six days are symbolic of 6,000 years and the seventh day is yet to come.

> Notice particularly, my children, the significance of 'he finished them in six days'. What that means is that he is going to bring the world to an end in six thousand years, since with him one day means a thousand years [quotes Ps. 90.4]. After that, 'he rested on the seventh day' indicates that when his Son returns, he will put an end to the years of the lawless one, pass sentence on the godless, transform the sun, moon and stars, and then, on the seventh day, enter into his true rest.[30]

Hebrews and *Barnabas*, the evidence of two witnesses, show that some people with temple roots viewed the days of creation as an outline of history and regarded the present age as the sixth day. It was the era of Adam who was created to be the image of God in creation. At the end of the sixth day, the Creator would be able to see his work completed and to say that everything was very good (Gen. 1.31). Thus Adam had to work with the Creator until the end of the sixth day. John recorded the words of Jesus on the afternoon of the sixth day of the week: 'It is accomplished' (19.30, translating literally); and his words in the temple after healing the withered man were: 'My Father is working still, and I am working' (v. 17).

Jesus then explains this role of the Son in creation: 'The Son can do nothing of his own accord, but only what he sees the Father doing; for whatever he sees, that the Son does likewise' (v. 19). This is the role of the Logos as John described it in the Prologue: 'All things were made through him, and without him was not anything made that was made' (1.3),[31] but we need to explore further the role of the Logos to understand what Jesus

---
[30] *Letter of Barnabas* 15.
[31] See above, p. 168.

is saying here. The Logos was the *memra*,[32] the presence of the LORD; but Philo, John's contemporary, shows that the Logos had many names and titles. This is not to say that John (or Jesus) was dependent on Philo, but that some Jewish discourse at that time was familiar with much of what appears in John's Gospel. The titles Philo used for the Logos are all drawn from the royal cult and show that the Logos was the great high priest.[33] Thus Philo said the Logos was: 'God's Firstborn [that is, the Son], the Logos, who is the oldest of the angels, as though an archangel having many names: Beginning and Name of God and Logos and Man after his image and the One Who Sees, Israel.'[34] John uses Son, Logos, Name and Man, and implies 'the One Who Sees' (3.32). Philo also described the Logos' role in the creation:

> For the world has come into being, and assuredly it has done so under the hand of some cause; and the Logos of Him who makes it is himself the seal by which each thing that exists received its shape.[35]

Paul taught this too: 'for in [his beloved Son] all things were created ... through him and for him' (Col. 1.16); and 'There is one God, the Father, from whom are all things and for whom we exist, and one Lord, Jesus Christ, through whom are all things and through whom we exist' (1 Cor. 8.6). Paul knew of two stages in the process of creation: the Father who created all, and the Lord who shaped the world. The Logos did not create on his own or independently. Discussing the Man who is named the Branch/the Dawn, Philo wrote:

> For that Man is the oldest son, whom the Father of all caused to rise up, and elsewhere named him the Firstborn. He was indeed the one begotten – imitating the ways of his Father, and looking to his archetypal patterns to shape [his] actions.[36]

Acting or creating according to heavenly archetypes sounds like Platonism, but in this context it is not. It is the older temple-wisdom that the law replaced in the pro-Moses era.[37] The temple world-view knew of an invisible world in which the patterns of all things were engraved, and these patterns were realized in the material world by angels. When Job was

---

[32] See above, p. 103.
[33] See my book *The Great Angel. A Study of Israel's Second God*, London: SPCK, 1992, pp. 114–33.
[34] Philo, *Tongues* 146.
[35] Philo, *Flight* 12.
[36] Philo, *Tongues* 62—63.
[37] See my book *The Mother of the Lord*, vol. 1, London: T&T Clark, 2011, pp. 290–300.

## John 5

claiming to understand the divine plan for the world, the LORD asked him from the whirlwind: 'Do you know the engraved things of heaven? Can you establish their correspondence on earth?' (Job 38.33, my translation). 'On earth as it is in heaven'. Hence the correspondence of the visions in Revelation and events on earth. The Logos shaped the world according to the heavenly engravings, and the secrets which a mystic was taught when he stood before the throne were these secrets of the divine plan for creation. Sometimes the ones who ascended learned the pattern of history as they stood outside time; sometimes they learned the pattern of creation: Enoch learned from the angel of peace (= completeness) all the hidden things, how the unity (the kingdom) was divided and became the visible world, and how the actions of human beings were judged.[38] Two rabbis living in Palestine had similar experiences: R. Nehunya, at the end of the first century CE, saw how the world was woven together to make everything whole, and R. Akiba, a generation later, saw the whole inhabited world.[39] It is experiences such as these that underlie the Baptist's words about Jesus: 'He who comes from heaven is above all. He bears witness to what he has seen and heard, yet no one receives his testimony' (3.31–32). Jesus claims that all he says and does is what he has learned and seen in heaven, and he is establishing this on earth. The equivalent of this teaching in the synoptic Gospels is found in the parables, in which Jesus compares everyday items and events to the kingdom of heaven, but warns that not everyone will understand (Mark 4.11–12). In Revelation it is the proclamation: 'The kingdom of the world has become the kingdom of our Lord-and-his-Anointed-One' (Rev. 11.15, my translation).

The second debate with the Jews was over the meaning of Sonship, and the accusation was that he 'called God his own Father, making himself equal to God' (v. 18). These are two distinct positions – God as Father and being equal to God – presumably the record of a complex debate. It had been the prerogative of the Davidic king to call the LORD his 'Father', and the king himself was the Servant of the LORD (Ps. 89.19–28). This meant that the king was the human presence of the LORD; the Image, but *not his equal*. He was Adam, the Man. The Deuteronomists said this was true of all the holy people; they were all sons of the LORD (Deut. 14.1). 'Making himself equal to God', however, implies the sins of pride and disobedience. Isaiah tells of someone with the royal title 'Morning Star', that is a

---

[38] *1 Enoch* 40.8; 41.1.
[39] *Hekhalot Rabbati* 201 and *Hekhalot Zutarti* 496, in P. Schäfer, *Synpose zur Hekhalot Literatur*, Tübingen: Mohr, 1981.

king, the son of the LORD,⁴⁰ who had tried to make himself equal to El Elyon, that is, equal to God Most High. He was thrown down from heaven because of his pride and even denied a decent tomb (Isa. 14.12–20). In its present context the proud ruler is the king of Babylon, but oracles were often reused. The original points to someone who was already 'the Morning Star', a Davidic king, but who claimed the position of El Elyon. This fusion of the LORD and El Elyon was proclaimed by the Second-Isaiah and was characteristic of second-temple Judaism.⁴¹ The oracle in Isaiah condemns the second-temple fusion, but the editor of the scroll has located it among the oracles against Babylon (Isa. 13—14), thus losing the original point of the oracle. Those such as the Christians who read the Scriptures in the old way would not have equated sonship and equality, but rather sonship and *servanthood*. Hence Justin's explanation to Trypho the Jew that the LORD who appeared in the Hebrew Scriptures was not God Most High but his Son and his Servant.

> If you had known who he is that is called at one time the Angel of Great Counsel [Isa. 9.6 LXX), and a Man by Ezekiel [Ezek. 1.26], and like the Son of Man by Daniel [Dan. 7.13] and a little child by Isaiah [Isa. 53.2 LXX] … you would not have blasphemed him who has already come.
>
> Then neither Abraham nor Isaac nor Jacob nor any other man ever saw the Father and ineffable LORD of all things whatever and of Christ himself; but they saw him who according to his will is both God his Son, and his angel from ministering to his will …⁴²

Note that Justin considered that Man, Son of Man, Angel of Great Counsel and the 'little child' (i.e. the Servant of Isaiah 53) were all titles for the second God, the Son of God Most High. The Adam in Genesis was already the Image and Likeness but was nevertheless tempted to disobedience by the snake and to become like *ᵉlohîm*. Thus he grasped at something he already had.⁴³

The original Adam, not just the figure found in Genesis 1—3, underlies the New Testament understanding of Jesus. A text quoted in Philippians, identified by some as a hymn, was more likely an early creed (Phil. 2.6–11).⁴⁴ It deals with the problem of equality and Jesus' relationship to God,

---

⁴⁰ See below, p. 405.
⁴¹ See above, p. 70. The Gnostics complained that the God of the Jews was arrogant and thought he was the only God.
⁴² Justin, *Trypho* 126, 127.
⁴³ The early Christian writers distinguished between Father and Son in the Old Testament; see my book *The Great Angel*, pp. 190–212.
⁴⁴ It may, of course, have been both.

and could even have been the official response to the Jewish accusation: 'He called God his own Father, making himself equal to God.' Were it possible to recover the Hebrew underlying the Greek, the original teaching about how Jesus related to God as Son and Servant would be clearer. The text seems to include the old priestly terms that Ezekiel used to describe the likeness and appearance of the LORD. Most English versions do not translate Ezekiel's words consistently, and so the pattern is lost.[45] 'Likeness', *d$^e$mûth*, is the invisible reality, and *mar'eh* is the 'appearance' as seen in a vision (Ezek. 1.26). In his vision, when Ezekiel saw the invisible reality of the LORD made visible, he saw Adam enthroned: '... the invisible reality of a throne ... and upon the invisible reality of the throne, the invisible reality as the appearance of Adam ... This was the appearance of the invisible reality of the glory of the LORD' (Ezek. 1.26, 28b, my literal translation). When the invisible reality becomes a physical reality, however, it is described as the *ṣelem*, 'image' (Gen. 1.26); Adam was created as the physical reality, the Image according to the invisible reality of *'elohîm*. In both Ezekiel 1.26–28 and Genesis 1.26 the visible states are Adam/a man: the word in Genesis is usually translated 'man' and in Ezekiel it is 'man' or 'human form'.

In the Greek of Philippians 2.6–11, *morphē*, 'form', corresponds to Ezekiel's *d$^e$mûth*, 'invisible reality'; *homoiōma*, 'likeness', corresponds to Ezekiel's *mar'eh*, 'visionary appearance' (as in Rev. 9.7, 'the appearances of the locusts ...'); and *schēma*, 'form', corresponds to *ṣelem*, 'image', as in Genesis 1.26.[46] Thus the early creed in Philippians 2.6–11 was probably:

> Christ Jesus, although he was in the beginning the invisible reality, *d$^e$mûth*, of God,
> Did not consider equality with God something to be snatched,
> But taking the invisible reality, *d$^e$mûth*, of a servant he poured himself out,
> He became the visionary appearance, *mar'eh*, of men[47]
> And was ready to be found[48] as a physical image, *ṣelem*, as Man,
> He humbled himself and was obedient to death, the death of the cross,
> Therefore God exalted him ...

---

[45] Since the AV translates the Hebrew terms consistently, it is the best translation to show how the words are used.

[46] See the note in J. H. Thayer, *A Greek–English Lexicon of the New Testament*, Edinburgh: T&T Clark, 1901, p. 418 on *morphē*, citing Lightfoot on this passage: *morphē* is that which is intrinsic and essential; *schēma* is the outward and accidental.

[47] The Hebrew idiom 'to be as' meaning 'to acquire a status', as in 'he became as prince, *l$^e$śar*' (1 Sam. 2.22).

[48] Assuming *māṣā'* as in Isa. 65.1: 'I was ready to be found ... I said, "Here I am, here I am."'

This is what John describes in the Prologue: 'In the beginning was the Logos ... The Logos became flesh ... We beheld the glory of the only Son from the Father ... No one has ever seen God. The only Son ... has made him known' (1.1, 14, 18, my translation). The creed in Philippians shows that the Son was the Servant: 'pouring himself out' and 'being obedient to death' were parallel terms, and both refer to the self-sacrifice of the Servant (Isa. 53.12) and not to shedding divine power before becoming incarnate (often described as *kenōsis*, 'emptying'). The theme throughout John's Gospel is the Servant – either as the Lamb of God in the greater Prologue or as the one who serves at the last supper: 'a servant is not greater than his master; nor is he who is sent greater than he who sent him' (13.16). The Jews' accusation – 'He calls God his own Father, making himself equal with God' – must be their (mis)understanding of Jesus' claim.

At the end of this exchange, Jesus raises the question of how to read the Hebrew Scriptures, and this is the key to understanding the first part of the debate: the problems have come about because the Jews do not read the Scriptures in the way that they should. 'If you believed Moses, you would believe me, for he wrote of me. But if you do not believe *his letters*, how will you believe *my words*?' (5.46–47, translating literally). The letters, *grammata*, of the Hebrew Scriptures are linked to the words of Jesus' teaching, and yet the Jews do not understand him on the question of Father and Son. This must be an allusion to the different versions of the Hebrew Scriptures in the time of Jesus, as testified by the Qumran texts and the 'restorations of the scribes'. These small changes to the written text were to remove what had come to be considered blasphemous, especially in writings attributed to Moses himself. This practice ceased around the beginning of the Christian era.[49] Jeremiah had complained of the practice: 'The false pen of the scribes has made [the law] into a lie' (Jer. 8.8); and Jesus knew of it, although these words are not usually understood in this way:

> Do not think that I have come to abolish the law and the prophets; I have come not to abolish them but to fulfil them. For truly I say to you, until heaven and earth pass away, not a single letter or part of a letter will pass away from the law until all is fulfilled. Whoever destroys one of the least of

---

[49] See S. Levin, *The Father of Joshua/Jesus*, New York: State University of New York Press, 1978, pp. 70–108. Mishnah *Mo'ed Katan* 3.4 says that such changes, even a letter in the master-scroll attributed to Ezra in the temple, cannot be made on the days at both ends of Passover and Tabernacles, the 'mid-festival' days.

## John 5

these commandments and teaches people thus shall be called the least in the kingdom of heaven, and whoever does and teaches them, he shall be called greatest in the kingdom of heaven. (Matt. 5.17–19, my translation)

Justin, in the early second century, accused the Jews of altering the Hebrew Scriptures to remove material that was important for Christian claims: 'They have deleted entire passages' from the Hebrew text that was used to make the pre-Christian Greek translation.[50] Until the Qumran texts were found, this was dismissed as Justin's pro-Christian propaganda, but the scrolls confirm that he was telling the truth.[51] Letters from Moses had been changed, and so the Jews did not understand Jesus. They accused him of blasphemy when he read the Scriptures in the older way (10.34–38).

Jesus said to the Jews: 'You search the Scriptures because you think that in them you have eternal life' (5.39, my translation; it could also be 'Search the Scriptures'). 'Searching' the Scriptures was a technical term: *dāraš*, 'search', giving the term *midhrāš*, which was the detailed exposition of Scripture. Jesus was quoting other rabbis when he said this. Hillel, who was teaching just before the time of Jesus, said: 'The more study of the law, the more life', and 'If a man has gained for himself the words of the law, he has gained for himself life in the world to come.'[52] Jesus said that the Hebrew Scriptures were in fact about himself, and that he was the source of the eternal life they sought. The early Christians understood the Hebrew Scriptures as accounts of the Son of God, and the theophanies as appearances of Christ. They found in the Hebrew Scriptures Father and Son: El Elyon, the Father; and Yahweh, the Firstborn of the sons of God, the guardian of Israel. This way of reading was not devised by the Christians following Jesus' example; it is how the Hebrew Scriptures were originally written, before monotheism was imposed in some circles by Josiah's purges and the work of the Deuteronomists. El and Yahweh then coalesced, and a new way of reading the Hebrew texts was introduced.[53] Jesus' discussion with the Jews at this point concerns the question of Father and Son, and the Son's role in bringing both life and judgement. There is important evidence from a Qumran text where some of the *letters* about Moses have been changed such that these actual older beliefs about the Father, the Son and the judgement have been obscured.

---

[50] Justin, *Trypho* 71.
[51] Not all the Hebrew Scriptures have been found at Qumran, and none of Justin's examples has been found. Plenty of other examples are known.
[52] Mishnah *Aboth* 2.7.
[53] See above, pp. 50–1.

Deuteronomy 32.1–43, the *Song of Moses*, is significantly different in the Qumran and Masoretic forms of the Hebrew text. The Qumran text has

> When the Most High gave to the nations their inheritance,
> When he separated the sons of men,
> He fixed the bounds of the peoples,
> According to the number of the *sons of God.**
> For the LORD's portion is his people,
> Jacob his allotted heritage.     (Deut. 32.8–9, my translation)

*The Masoretic text (MT) has 'sons of Israel'. This part of the *Song* originally described how the nations were allocated to their guardian angels/deities.

> Praise O heavens* his people
> And bow down to him all *elohîm*
> For he avenges the blood of his sons**
> And takes vengeance on his adversaries,
> *And requites those who hate him,*
> And atones/heals the soil of his land.***
>     (Deut. 32.43, my translation)[54]

*The MT has 'nations'. **The MT has 'servants'. ***The MT has 'people'. The lines in italics are not in the MT.

This part of the *Song* describes how the LORD comes to bring judgement, but the MT has no indication that when the LORD comes from heaven, he receives the adoration of the angels, before coming to save the (earthly) sons of God. The Masoretic form of the *Song of Moses* does not mention the sons of God, and so removes the possibility that Yahweh was a son of God. It also lacks the line that Christians used as a proof text fulfilled in Jesus: 'Let all God's angels worship him' (Heb. 1.6). Further, the *Song of Moses* was used at Qumran as a phylactery text.[55] Someone preparing the way of the LORD in the wilderness had a phylactery – and we cannot know how much of the *Song of Moses* was in it – which probably included the words about a nation with no counsel or understanding, no wisdom or discernment (Deut. 32.28–29), and even the hope that the LORD would come in judgement to avenge the blood of his sons and to heal the land. Here, then, is a text that was controversial and existed in two forms; was important for someone at Qumran; and

---

[54] Deut. 32.8 in 4QDeut$^j$; 32.43 in 4QDeut$^q$.
[55] Phylactery N, a fragment with vv. 14–20 and 32–33. *Discoveries in the Judaean Desert* VI, ed. R. de Vaux and J. T. Milik, Oxford: Clarendon Press, 1977.

## John 5

which concerned the Father and the Son, and how the Son came in judgement to destroy and to heal. This is the substance of Jesus' debate with the Jews after the healing at Bethesda. The *Song of Moses* says that this was the teaching of the days of old, of the fathers and the elders (Deut. 32.7), and in the light of the new theology that developed after the destruction of the first temple by Josiah and then the Babylonians, the Qumran text of the *Song of Moses* probably does represent the older belief.

The substance of Jesus' teaching in verses 19–30 is the first glimpse of the *raz nihyeh* in John's Gospel: how the Father and the Son relate to each other, how they are One, and how life comes forth through the Son.[56] Little remains of the *raz nihyeh* because the older wisdom texts have not survived in the Hebrew Scriptures, and the material from Qumran is fragmented. Amos described prophets standing in the divine council to learn the secrets of LORD's will (Amos 3.7); Jeremiah complained that the false prophets had not stood in the divine council and so had not spoken the truth (Jer. 23.21–22); but the Second-Isaiah was reminded that he had *seen* the fate of the wicked when he had stood 'in the beginning' (Isa. 40.21–24). Psalm 73 shows that this revelation was given in the holy of holies:

> I was envious of the arrogant,
> When I saw the prosperity of the wicked ...
> But when I thought how to understand this,
> It seemed to me a wearisome task,
> Until I went into the sanctuary of God;
> Then I perceived their end.
> (Ps. 73.3, 16, 17)

The Book of Revelation shows this in detail – symbolized by the sealed book that was opened for the Lamb to read – and proves that 'seeing' in the holy of holies was an important part of the early Christian world-view and went back to Jesus himself. When John said that Jesus bore witness to what he had seen and heard in heaven, he was describing him as an old-style temple seer. As the exilic or early second-temple writer of 1 Samuel explained: 'He who is now called a prophet was formerly called a seer' (1 Sam. 9.9).

They continued to 'see' at Qumran. These are lines about the *raz nihyeh* at Qumran, some of which are broken:

---

[56] See above, pp. 66–7.

- 'Gaze on the *raz nihyeh* and understand the birth time of salvation, and know who is to inherit glory and trouble ...'[57] The mystery was seen and gave knowledge.
- 'By day and night meditate on the *raz nihyeh* and study it always. Then you will know truth and iniquity; wisdom and foolishness you will ... all their ways together with their punishments ...' 'You, understanding one, gaze on the *raz nihyeh* and know the paths of everything that lives ...'[58] These broken lines show that the mystery concerned good and evil, the ways of 'things' and their outcome.
- Complete knowledge of the mystery enabled the teacher to pass on the divine wisdom to his community. The sevenfold light which shone from the teacher was the same as the seven horns [= beams of light] that shone from the enthroned Lamb as he took the little sealed book and prepared to open it (Rev. 5.6).

> These things I know because of understanding that comes from you,
> For you have opened my ears to wondrous mysteries ...
> Through me you have illumined the faces of many ...
> I shine forth with sevenfold light .... [ ]
> for you are an eternal light to me ...[59]

Jesus tells the Jews that he has seen the work of the Father and replicates it (5.19–20). Just as the Father is the source of life, so too the Son gives life (5.21, 26). This is implicit in the Name itself: Yahweh, the LORD, means 'He who causes to be', and so Peter described Jesus as the Author of Life (Acts 3.15). The Father raises the dead, and the Son gives life to whom he will (5.21, 28–29). This recalls the second of the 'Eighteen Benedictions'. In the time of Jesus Rabban Gamaliel taught: 'A man should pray the Eighteen every day',[60] and so those who heard Jesus say: '... the Son gives life to whom he will ... all those who are in the tombs will hear his voice and come forth ...' (5.21, 28–29) would have known these words and recognized that Jesus was claiming to be the LORD:

> Thou art mighty who bringest low the proud, mighty, he that judgeth the ruthless, that liveth for ever, that raiseth the dead, that maketh the wind to blow, that sendeth down the dew; that sustaineth the living, that quickeneth

---

[57] 4Q417.1.
[58] Reconstructed from 4Q417.2 and 4Q418.43.
[59] *Hymns*, 1QH XI.23, XII.28, XV.27, 28, my translation.
[60] Mishnah *Berakhoth* 4.3.

## John 5

the dead; in the twinkling of an eye Thou makest salvation to spring forth for us. Blessed art Thou, O LORD, who quickenest the dead.

The Father has given the task of judging to the Son (5.22, 27), because he is the Son of Man, the human who has become divine (5.27). Recognition of the Son is a key part of the judgement (5.24). These elements underlie Isaiah's fourth Servant song, where the Servant is anointed, recognized (too late?) by the kings, and makes many righteous.[61] They are also key elements in the *Song of Moses*, at the very places where the text exists in two different forms: first, where there is the Father and his Son the LORD; and second, where the LORD is acknowledged by the angels when he comes in judgement to punish enemies and to heal the land. Jesus seems to be referring to the two forms of this text when he says: 'If you believed Moses, you would believe me, for he wrote of me. But if you do not believe *his letters*, how will you believe *my words*?' (5.46-47, translating literally). If they no longer had Moses' letters, Jesus explained, then the Jews would not find the person and work of Jesus in the books of Moses.

Then Jesus appeals to the two witnesses required by Jewish law (Deut. 19.15), because no man could testify for himself: 'None may be believed when he testifies of himself.'[62] John the Baptist and the miracles, said Jesus, were the two witnesses supporting his claim to be the Son who brings judgement (5.30-35).

Finally, there is the question of the Hebrew Scriptures. There is Johannine irony – perhaps going back to Jesus himself? – in the near quotation from Deuteronomy at the very point where their new ways declared that the LORD was not seen, but only heard when the commandments were given: 'You heard the sound of words [when the commandments were given] but saw no form; there was only a voice' (Deut. 4.12). This text marks the point where belief in seeing the LORD was denied by the Deuteronomist disciples of Moses. It was this belief that prevented some people from recognizing who Jesus was, because they did not believe that the LORD could be seen. Jesus alludes to the claim by saying that not only had they never seen God; they had never *heard* God either. Jesus, however, was talking about El Elyon, the Father, who was never seen. The heirs of Deuteronomy had coalesced the Father and Son(s) of the older theology and so declared that the LORD was never seen, despite the many accounts of theophanies/visions in the Hebrew Scriptures. Because of their 'new' theology, said Jesus, the Jews do not

---

[61] See above, p. 81.
[62] Mishnah *Ketuboth* 2.9.

have the Father's Logos among them, because they do not believe the one who has been sent.

When did this debate occur? The meeting with the Samaritan woman in chapter 4 was during the summer months, if the sayings about harvest were prompted by what they saw around them. The events in chapter 6 were just before Passover (6.4). If John was following the calendar, then the healing at Bethesda happened either at Tabernacles in the autumn, or at Ḥanukkah in the winter. Invalids lying outside by the pool favours Tabernacles rather than midwinter, and Tabernacles was the feast associated with the appearance of the LORD, the King (Zech. 14, esp. vv. 9, 16, 17).

# John 6

### 6.1–21: Jesus feeds 5,000, and then appears on the water

A year had passed since the cleansing of the temple, and it was almost Passover time again. Jesus went across the Sea of Galilee, and there he fed about 5,000 people. In the evening, his disciples started to cross the sea again to Capernaum. When they had gone about three or four miles, and it was dark with a strong wind blowing, Jesus appeared to them. They took him into the boat and soon reached Capernaum. Only Luke says where the miracle happened: near Bethsaida (Luke 9.10), the home of Philip (1.44), which may explain why Jesus asked Philip about buying bread in the neighbourhood (6.5). The fact that Mark, Matthew and John all link the feeding miracle and Jesus appearing on the water suggests that this sequence was an authentic memory. John also says the fish were *opsaria*, pickled fish, not just fish, *ichthes*, suggesting that this was not simply a reworking of the synoptic material but an independent memory of the event; and the form of Jesus' synagogue sermon at Capernaum has the signs of being an authentic sermon of the time.

Since this miracle is recorded in all three synoptic Gospels, the differences between John's way of telling the story and the others could be significant. The details could indicate John's special purpose: to show how Jesus was restoring the first-temple ways. The synoptic Gospels all say that there were loaves, whereas John says barley, *krithinos*, loaves. Some have suggested that this is an allusion to the story of Elisha multiplying barley loaves (2 Kings 4.42–44), although this miracle happened near Jericho and not by the Sea of Galilee. It is more likely that the allusion was to the ancient pilgrimage feast of the barley harvest, which had been taken over and became the Passover when the Moses traditions came to prominence. Jesus had the crowd sit down, and according to the synoptic accounts, he looked up to heaven, blessed the bread and broke it, and then gave it to his disciples to distribute. John, however, says that Jesus gave thanks over the bread and then distributed it himself.[1] So too with the fish. When everyone had had sufficient, the fragments were gathered up in 12 baskets. Only John says that the crowd wanted to take Jesus and make him king. This may have been only a reaction to the feeding miracle. There is only one reference in the Hebrew Scriptures to the king distributing bread to a crowd – when David brought the ark to Jerusalem and gave everyone a loaf and portions of dried fruit[2] (1 Chron. 16.3). One wonders if the pilgrims had been fed when they came to the temple for the old-style harvest festivals, and that this was why they wanted to make Jesus their king.

That evening, the disciples set out in a boat to return to Capernaum, and John adds an observation with two meanings: 'It was now dark, and Jesus had not yet come to them' (6.17). What follows is a summary of his discourse about the presence, the ways in which the divine was present on earth: first in the man Jesus and then as the bread. The exposition is built around Hebrew wordplay. 'Bread', *lehem*, also means 'flesh' or 'fruit': it could be the flesh of a sacrifice, as in the Hebrew of Ben Sira 7.31c which has been read as the flesh, *lehem*, of sacrifices;[3] or it could be the fruit of a tree, as in Jeremiah 11.19: 'Let us destroy the tree with its fruit, *lehem*.' The fruit of the tree of life could have been 'the bread of the tree of life', which is the food that Jesus promised to his faithful followers (Rev. 2.7).

The discourse also assumes a knowledge of the roles and customs of the original high priests. Before the oil was hidden away, each had been marked on the forehead with X, the sign of the Name. This meant he 'was' the LORD on earth, the Man; and as a messenger/angel of the LORD he had to impart true knowledge and thus uphold the covenant (Mal. 2.4–9). In the early years of the second temple, Malachi condemned the priests for failing in these roles and he linked this to the offering of impure bread. Further, the high priest, 'the LORD', symbolically offered himself on the Day of Atonement to renew the eternal covenant with his own blood/life that was first offered in heaven and then brought out to restore the earth with life from heaven. This is what Peter taught in Solomon's porch (Acts 3.11–26). Those who shared the priestly role on the Day of Atonement did so by consuming a token piece of the sacrificed goat that represented the LORD.[4]

---

[1] The feeding of the 4,000 has Jesus giving thanks before breaking the bread (Mark 8.6–7), so this may be a distinction without a difference.
[2] One of the Hebrew words is uncertain.
[3] P. W. Skehan, *The Wisdom of Ben Sira*, Anchor Bible 39, New York/London: Doubleday, 1987, p. 204.
[4] See my book *Temple Themes in Christian Worship*, London: T&T Clark, 2007, pp. 185–90.

## John 6

Jesus' sermon in the synagogue at Capernaum does have the shape and style of synagogue preaching.[5] He begins with a quotation from the law of Moses – in this case 'He gave them bread from heaven to eat' (v. 31, paraphrasing Exod. 16.4) – and then introduces the theme: Moses did not give them bread from heaven; it was God who gave (and continues to give) the true bread from heaven (v. 32). Then the sermon touches on each element of the text: first 'bread' (vv. 35–40), then 'from heaven' (vv. 43–51), and then 'to eat' (vv. 53–58). It was customary to incorporate a verse from the prophets and then to finish by returning to the key verse and incorporating the gist of what has been said. Jesus does all this: in verse 45 he quotes from Isaiah 54.13, 'All your sons shall be taught by the LORD', a promise to the restored Lady and her Jerusalem. He finishes by saying that he himself is the true bread from heaven which lasts not for one day but to eternity: 'This is the bread which came down from heaven, not such as the fathers ate and died; he who eats this bread will live for ever' (v. 58). The bread of the Presence/his presence is superseding the manna that sustained the followers of Moses in the wilderness.

Further, there are allusions thoughout to the synagogue Scripture readings for the Passover season:[6] in the first year of the three-year lectionary cycle, the readings nearest to Passover would have been Genesis 2—3, in the second year Exodus 11—16, and in the third year Numbers 6—14. This discourse at Capernaum seems to have been a sermon in the second year, with its text from Exodus 16.4, but there are several allusions to the readings from Genesis in the previous year and to Adam and Eve eating from the forbidden tree. They rejected the tree of life, and so there was no tree of life in the second temple. Some of the oldest material in *1 Enoch* is a prophecy from the archangel Raguel who showed Enoch the fragrant tree that would be transplanted back to the temple after the judgement, to feed the righteous and holy ones, the chosen.[7] The Book of Revelation says that the tree of life was seen again in the temple, and Jesus promised that it would provide food for his faithful followers (Rev. 2.7; 22.1-2, 14). In the Enochic *Apocalypse of Weeks* the chosen witnesses to

---

[5] P. Borgen, *Bread from Heaven. An Exegetical Study of the Concept of Manna in the Gospel of John and the Writings of Philo*, Leiden: Brill, 1965.

[6] A. Guilding, *The Fourth Gospel and Jewish Worship. A Study of the Relationship of St John's Gospel to the Ancient Jewish Lectionary*, Oxford: Clarendon Press, 1960, pp. 60-8. 'The Johannine account of the feeding of the five thousand and the walking on the water is intimately related to the synagogue lectionary readings for Nisan ... The sermon preached by our Lord in the synagogue at Capernaum is based not merely on general Passover themes, but on specific lections – those that would fall to the last Sabbath in Nisan ...', pp. 67, 68.

[7] *1 Enoch* 24.4-5.

righteousness would receive sevenfold wisdom and knowledge at the end of the seventh 'week' which was the era of the apostates.[8] Allusions to the Eden story occur in Jesus' sermon: the fruit of the forbidden tree in Eden led to death (Gen. 2.17), in contrast to 'the bread which comes from heaven, that a man may eat and not die' (6.50, my translation); and the LORD drove from the garden the couple who ate the forbidden fruit, in contrast to the promise of Jesus: 'Him who comes to me I will not cast out' (v. 37). Since there is reason to believe that the forbidden tree in Eden represented the law of Moses,[9] this would be another contrast between the ways of the disciples of Moses and the ways of the older temple.

*****

A storm arose, and the disciples saw Jesus in the darkness as he walked towards them on the water. He said to them, 'It is I, *egō eimi*. Do not fear' (v. 20). Both Matthew and Mark have a similar saying: 'Take heart. It is I. Do not fear' (Matt. 14.27; Mark 6.50, my translations). The *egō eimi* is literally 'I am', and in the synoptic Gospels it may mean nothing more at this point than 'I am here'. In John's Gospel, however, the words have a special significance. They represent, as they do in the Greek Old Testament, the form of the divine Name that was used only by the LORD himself to indicate his presence. It was the Name revealed to Moses at the burning bush: *'ehyeh ªšer 'ehyeh*, meaning 'I am what I am', or 'I cause to be what I cause to be'. In the Greek translation, it became *egō eimi ho ōn*, 'I am the One who Is' (Exod. 3.14), and in John's Gospel, this is what *egō eimi* means. Thus, when Jesus was arrested in the garden, he said to the soldiers '*egō eimi*', and 'they drew back and fell to the ground' (18.6). John intended *egō eimi* to indicate the Name used only by the LORD himself and so to be a sign of his presence. In the Targums, this *'ehyeh* name became the enigmatic *memra*[10] that indicated 'the merciful presence of the LORD to create and sustain the world'. The use of *memra* was originally a sophisticated way to indicate the divine presence 'but at some point in the tradition, the context of *Memra* was lost; how or why we do not clearly know'. Hayward concluded: 'when He acts in, or by means of, his *memra*, God is there, actively present with men'.[11] There has been much discussion about the relevance of *memra* to the Prologue of John's

---

[8] *1 Enoch* 93.10.
[9] See my book *The Mother of the Lord*, vol. 1, London: T&T Clark, 2012, pp. 364–74.
[10] See above, p. 168.
[11] C. T. R. Hayward, 'The *Memra* of YHWH and the Development of Its Use in Targum Neofiti I', *Journal of Jewish Studies* 25 (1974), pp. 412–18, p. 418.

## John 6

Gospel, but it seems to be an important element all through the Gospel. Hayward again, comparing John 12.28 and 17.5, concluded: 'Jesus is God's Name come in flesh', so that 'the glorification of His Name and the glorification of Jesus are here equivalent'.[12] Hayward gives several striking illustrations of how *'ehyeh* in the Hebrew text, even when not obviously a name, was understood by Targum *Neofiti* as the *memra*. Thus:

> He said, 'But *I will be with you*, and this shall be the sign for you ...'
> (Exod. 3.12)

> He said, 'For *I will be there, my memra, with you*, and this shall be the sign ...' (*Neofiti* Exod. 3.12)[13]

It is possible that the *memra* represented the visible presence of the LORD, although not always in human form.[14] The memory that Jesus multiplied the loaves and then appeared to his disciples in a time of danger with the words '*egō eimi*' (also Matt. 14.27; Mark 6.50) shows that this was recognized as a *memra* theophany. It is John who links the bread to the theophany, the divine presence in the bread, and so the thought here moves to the bread of the presence in the temple.

The bread of the Presence, *leḥem pānîm*, had been a significant point of difference between the first and second temples. As with so many temple practices, nothing is said in the Old Testament of the meaning of this bread or the meaning of the Name. The 12 loaves were made of fine flour and set in the tabernacle/temple each Sabbath (Lev. 24.5–8); they were spread out on a golden table, together with wine and incense (Exod. 25.29–30), and the loaves were the only cereal offering taken inside the temple. They were not food for the LORD, such as other peoples offered to their gods:

> If I were hungry, I would not tell you;
> For the world and all that is in it is mine.
> Do I eat the flesh of bulls,
> Or drink the blood of goats?
> Offer to God a sacrifice of thanksgiving ...
> (Ps. 50.12–14)

---

[12] C. T. R. Hayward, 'The Holy Name of the God of Moses and the Prologue of St John's Gospel', *New Testament Studies* 25 (1978), pp. 16–32, p. 29.
[13] Hayward, 'Holy Name', p. 21.
[14] See my book *The Great Angel. A Study of Israel's Second God*, London: SPCK, 1992, pp. 114–33.

The bread of the Presence was food for the high priests, their most holy portion, to be eaten in a holy place (Lev. 24.9). 'Most holy' means 'imparting holiness', as can be seen from the instructions for anointing the tabernacle furnishings and the high priests: 'You shall consecrate them, that they may be most holy; whatever touches them will become holy' (Exod. 30.29). In the time of Jesus, people believed that the bread acquired this holiness while it was kept in the temple for seven days, as can be seen from the Mishnah's rules for placing the loaves on the tables:

> On the table of marble they laid the Bread of the Presence when it was brought in [to the temple], and on the table of gold they laid it when it was brought out, since what is holy must be raised and not brought down.[15]

The bread became the vehicle of the presence and was originally eaten only by the high priests. The Targums imply something similar.[16] The bread of the Presence was a 'memorial' offering, but since 'memorial' can also mean 'invocation' and is a technical priestly term, the bread of the Presence was bread to which the divine presence was invoked.[17] Paul had been taught that the bread at the last supper was a 'memorial' (1 Cor. 11.24), implying that it was like the bread of the Presence.[18]

The *leḥem pānîm* was described as an eternal covenant (Lev. 24.8), the most likely meaning of which is that it was a sign of the eternal covenant, consumed each Sabbath to mark the completion of the creation that was bound in place by the eternal covenant.[19] The bread imparted the knowledge and holiness needed to uphold the covenant, and it became the 'daily bread' of the LORD's Prayer. Jerome knew the Hebrew gospel in which 'daily' was *māḥār*, 'tomorrow', and since the tomorrow of the early Church was the Sabbath rest of the kingdom that the rebellious followers of Moses failed to reach (Heb. 3.7—4.13), the Christians were praying each day for the priests' *leḥem pānîm*.[20] But whose presence was this? There may be a clue in the Hebrew text itself, which says, literally: 'She will be for Aaron and his sons, and they shall eat [the Samaritan text here has 'eat her'] in a holy place, since for him it is most holy [the Samaritan text has 'she is most holy'] ...' (Lev. 24.9). With two exceptions,[21] 'bread' in Hebrew is a masculine noun, and this may be another exception. Or it

---

[15] Mishnah *Menaḥoth* 11.7.
[16] Targums *Neofiti* and *Onkelos* Lev. 24.7.
[17] See my book *Temple Themes*, n. 4 above, p. 210.
[18] See below, pp. 594–5.
[19] See above, pp. 42–3, 58.
[20] *Temple Themes*, n. 4 above, pp. 210–12.
[21] Gen. 49.20; 1 Sam. 10.4.

## John 6

could mean that with the bread the high priests took nourishment from a female figure who enabled them to uphold the eternal covenant. Ben Sira knew that 'wisdom will feed [the man who meditates on her] with the bread of understanding' (Ben Sira 15.3), that she offers to fill them with her fruits (Ben Sira 24.19, translating literally). She invited those without knowledge to eat her bread and drink her wine and thus walk in the way of insight (Prov. 9.4–6). Thus the saying in Deuteronomy, that people did not live on bread alone but by every word from the LORD, could well have been Moses' version of an older wisdom teaching that Jesus was restoring. The bread imparted the teaching.[22] Jesus, himself the messenger of Wisdom – the Angel of Great Counsel (LXX Isa. 9.6) – and the bread he was miraculously distributing were both the vehicles of Wisdom and her teaching. Wisdom had many children, including the Baptist and her other prophets and messengers, and many had been rejected (Luke 7.39; 11.49). Jesus too was rejected, and the Jews did not understand him (12.37–50).

Malachi, describing the second temple, implied that the bread was the means of theophany: 'With [polluted bread] from your hand, will he lift up his face/presence?' (Mal. 1.9, translating literally).[23] Malachi condemns the *leḥem* that is offered, which here must mean the bread offering since he contrasts it with the incense and pure cereal offering, *minḥâ*, of the future (Mal. 1.11). Enoch too, in his dream visions, saw the second-temple era as a time when blind sheep led by blind sheep put polluted bread on the table before the newly rebuilt tower.[24] Decoded, this means that the people who built the second temple lacked wisdom (their eyes were closed) because their temple bread was not pure. Malachi prophesied a time when there would be a pure cereal offering 'from the rising of the sun to its setting', and as early as the *Didache*, this was understood by Christians as a prophecy of the Eucharist.

> Break bread and offer the Eucharist ... for this is the offering of which the LORD has said, 'Everywhere and always bring me a sacrifice that is undefiled, for I am a great king, says the LORD, and my Name is the wonder of nations'.[25]

Jesus' first followers, when they prayed the *Didache* prayers, saw themselves as restoring the unpolluted bread of the Presence when they

---

[22] See below, p. 259.
[23] 'Polluted food' (RSV v. 7) is literally 'polluted bread'.
[24] *1 Enoch* 89.72–74.
[25] *Didache* 14, with a free rendering of Mal. 1.11, 14. It is also quoted by Justin, *Trypho* 41.

broke bread and gave thanks for the life and knowledge made known through Jesus.[26]

What words did Jesus use when he gave thanks over those five barley loaves, distributed them on the mountainside, and then had all the fragments collected? The situation is so like the prayers in the *Didache* that they must have been linked:

> As this bread, once dispersed over the hills, was brought together and became one loaf, so may thy Church be brought together from the ends of the earth into thy kingdom.
> Thanks be to thee holy Father, for thy sacred name which thou hast caused to dwell in our hearts, and for the knowledge and faith and immortality which thou hast revealed to us through thy servant Jesus.[27]

This is followed in the *Didache* by Malachi's prophecy of the pure cereal offering. The 'sacred name' was the *'Ehyeh*, and so this prayer over the bread was thanksgiving for the presence of the LORD in each heart, 'he ... abides in me, and I in him' (v. 56).

## 6.22–40: The bread of life: teaching the crowd

There is some confusion and consternation as to how Jesus managed to travel back to Capernaum, but when the crowd eventually catch up with him, he begins to teach in the synagogue about bread (v. 59). He suspects that their real interest was the free food, and immediately contrasts working for food that rots, and working for food that lasts until eternity. This is the gift of the Son of Man who bears the seal of God the Father. The title 'Son of Man' occurs three times in this discourse: here at verse 27, at verse 53 where the flesh and blood of the Son of Man give life, and at verse 62, where the Son of Man ascends to the place whence he came. The discourse is about the work of the heavenly Man who has been transformed from his mortal state, as were the high priests when they were anointed with the seal of the Name (Exod. 28.36).[28] Here Jesus refers to this temple ritual when he says: 'The Son of man ... on him has God the Father set his seal' (v. 27). What follows illustrates Jesus' reply to the devil when he was tempted to turn stones into bread: 'Man shall not live by bread alone but by every word that proceeds from the mouth of God.' The original saying in Deuteronomy referred to the manna (Deut. 8.3),

---

[26] *Didache* 9.
[27] *Didache* 9—10.
[28] See above, p. 87.

## John 6

but Jesus shows how another type of bread replaces the manna, and this too is teaching from the mouth of the LORD.

The first section of the teaching that follows compares the 'bread from heaven' that the LORD gave his people in the wilderness (Exod. 16.4), and the true bread from heaven which lasts until eternity. The manna had only lasted for one day and then 'bred worms and became foul'.[29] Philo spoke of manna as the heavenly food of the soul: 'The one who loves to see has been trained also to look clearly at the manna, the divine Logos, the heavenly and uncorrupted food of the soul.'[30] Here he implies that the Logos himself is the heavenly food, but later in the same treatise, when discussing the symbolism of sharing the Passover lamb with neighbours, he said something different: 'The heavenly food of the soul – wisdom – which [Moses] calls manna, the divine Logos distributes equally to all who make use of it ...'[31] Since John's account of the feeding miracle has Jesus distributing the food himself (v. 11), this may be an allusion to the ideas that Philo knew: the manna was Wisdom distributed by the Logos, but also that the Logos was distributing himself. The latter is consistent with the bread imagery found in the *Didache*, but the former is what Jesus taught in the synagogue in Capernaum. Jesus' teaching here may be an example of John's later reflection on events, or evidence that the ideas mentioned in Philo were widely known and familiar even to a crowd in Galilee.

'The bread of God is that which [or he who] comes down from heaven and gives life to the creation, *kosmos*' (v. 33, my translation) is not, however, Passover imagery: it is Day of Atonement imagery, when the bread/flesh of the great high priest gives new life to the world. Like the woman of Samaria who wanted the water of life (4.15), so too the crowd want this bread. Jesus then explains: 'I am the bread of life' (v. 35), and he describes his work as offering high-priestly *theōsis* to all. Just as Enoch had entered the holy of holies and stood before the LORD where he was anointed and became one of the angels,[32] so too all who recognize Jesus as the LORD incarnate will be transformed and raised up (6.40). Jesus prayed for this after the last supper: 'Father, I desire that they also, whom thou hast given me, may be with me where I am, to behold my glory which thou hast given me in thy love for me before the foundation of the world' (17.24). It was also the experience of the early Christian who sang:

---

[29] Exod. 16.14–27, but for the Sabbath it kept fresh for two days.
[30] Philo, *Heir* 79.
[31] Philo, *Heir* 191–3.
[32] *2 Enoch* 22.

I rested on the Spirit of the LORD: and She raised me on high: and made me stand on my feet in the height of the LORD, before His perfection and His glory, while I was praising Him by the composition of His songs. She brought me forth before the face of the LORD: and although a son of man, I was named the illuminated one, the son of God ...

He anointed me from His own perfection: and I became one of his neighbours; and my mouth was opened like cloud of dew: and my heart poured out as it were a gushing stream of righteousness.[33]

It was the experience of the unknown voice at Qumran who proclaimed: 'I am reckoned with the *ᵉlohîm* and my dwelling place is in the congregation of holiness ... and my glory is with the sons of the King.'[34] And it is the final scene in Revelation, where the servants of God-and-the-Lamb stand before the throne and worship him: 'They shall see his face, and his name shall be on their foreheads' (Rev. 22.3-4). The Name was the X with which they had been anointed at baptism, and this had given them all knowledge (1 John 2.20, 27). They were all high priests wearing the Name.

The sequence of feeding, and then the *'ehyeh* theophany, was followed by Jesus' second *egō eimi*: 'I am the bread of life' (v. 35), meaning that he was the restored bread of the Presence.[35] Originally given only to the high priests, Jesus gave the bread to all, and with it he gave the assurance of a place in the holy of holies: life in eternity, raised up/resurrected (v. 40).

## 6.41–59: The bread of life: teaching the Jews

The second half of the synagogue discourse was addressed to 'the Jews'; presumably the others in the synagogue were not Jews, but were nevertheless eager to listen to Jesus. These must have been the Hebrews, whose ancestors found themselves excluded from the second temple. A new word is introduced: 'flesh' (v. 51), in Hebrew *bāśār*[36] which also means 'good news'. This wordplay underlies Jesus' exchange with the Jews. 'Good news' was an important element in the exilic and post-exilic writings in Isaiah, as the prophet proclaimed the end of the exile and the return to Jerusalem. The words in italic are translations of *bāśār*.

> How beautiful upon the mountains
> Are the feet of *the man who brings good tidings*
> Who makes us hear about peace,

---

[33] *Odes of Solomon* 36.1–3, 5–7.
[34] *War Scroll*, 4Q491.11.
[35] The others are the light, the door, the shepherd, the resurrection and life, the way, truth and life, the vine.
[36] Hebrew *bśr* is the root, meaning both 'flesh' and 'good news'.

## John 6

> *Who brings us good tidings* of good,
> Who makes us hear of salvation,
> Who says to Zion 'Your God reigns'.
> (Isa. 52.7, my translation)

This prophecy occurs in the Qumran *Melchizedek* text, which identifies Melchi-Zedek as the man who brings good tidings and as the one anointed with the Spirit who was prophesied by Daniel (Dan. 9.24). Melchi-Zedek was also the Anointed One of Isaiah 61:

> The Spirit of the LORD God is upon me, because the LORD has anointed me
> He has sent me *to bring good tidings* to the poor/afflicted,
> To bind up those who are broken in heart/mind,
> To proclaim [jubilee] liberty to captives,
> And opening [eyes? prison?] to the bound.
> (Isa. 61.1, my translation)

The question raised by the *Melchizedek* text, and by all the other texts which put together a collection of prophecies, is this: was this the original understanding of the prophecies, or did the writer create a new meaning for them by creating a new context? In this instance, was Melchi-Zedek already known to be the character portrayed in the *Melchizedek* text, or was this figure created by the writer? This question also underlies all Christian use of prophecies.

The Second-Isaiah also spoke of a female figure bringing good tidings:

> Get up to a high mountain, Zion, *woman who brings good tidings*;
> Lift up your voice with strength, Jerusalem, *woman who brings good tidings*,
> Lift it up, fear not;
> Say to the cities of Judah, 'Behold your God'.
> (Isa. 40.9, my translation)

The 'woman who brings good tidings' is the participle formed from the word that also means 'flesh'. The Second-Isaiah's prophecy of good tidings describes the LORD coming like a shepherd to gather his flock and lead them home (Isa. 40.10–11), an image used by John's Jesus (10.1–18), but also by Micah who described the woman who gives birth to the great shepherd of Israel (Mic. 5.2–4). The prophecy of the woman 'who brings good news' is wordplay again, and could also mean 'who makes flesh', 'who gives birth to'. The great shepherd in the flesh is the good news: 'The Logos became flesh and dwelt among us' (1.14).

The Jews did not understand what Jesus meant by 'bread from heaven' just as Nicodemus had not understood birth from heaven (v. 42). Jesus explained that only those drawn by the Father can come to Jesus and understand him, and these people fulfil another part of the Second-Isaiah's prophecy for the restored Jerusalem. Assuring the stricken city that she would be built again in precious stones, the prophet said: 'All your sons shall be taught by the LORD, and your sons [your builders?[37]] will have great peace' (Isa. 54.13, my translation, quoted by Jesus in 6.45). If the context is implied with the quotation, then Jesus was saying that those who learned from him, the LORD, would be the children of the restored Jerusalem, and that those who did not learn from him would not be the children of the new Jerusalem. Those who believed Jesus would have eternal life and would be resurrected. He repeated: 'I am the bread of life', and contrasted the manna which sustained their ancestors in the wilderness, who all died, and the living bread from heaven that would lead to eternal life (vv. 48–50). This living bread was his flesh/his good news. The *Gospel of Thomas* begins in a similar way: 'These are the secret sayings which the living [resurrected] Jesus spoke ... whoever finds the interpretation of these sayings will not experience death.'

Double wordplay follows: 'I am the living *leḥem*, bread/flesh of sacrifice, that comes down from heaven; if anyone eats of this bread/flesh of sacrifice, he will live for ever; and the bread/flesh of sacrifice which I give for the life of the world is my *bāśār*, flesh/good news' (v. 51, my translation). *The sacrifice given for the life of the world was not the Passover.* It was the sacrifice offered on the Day of Atonement, a temple festival not even mentioned in the calendar of Deuteronomy, which has only Passover, Weeks and Tabernacles (Deut. 16.1–17). On the Day of Atonement the royal high priest, albeit using a substitute animal, offered his blood/life to cleanse the temple and thus to heal the creation that it represented and to restore the eternal covenant.[38] The Jubilee, the 'release', was proclaimed on the Day of Atonement (Lev. 25.8–12), and this was also the good news, the 'liberty' proclaimed by the Anointed One (Isa. 61.1) and by Melchi-Zedek,[39] which Jesus claimed to fulfil (Luke 4.21). The writer of Hebrews knew that the Day of Atonement sacrifice was the meaning of Jesus' death (Heb. 9.11–14), and Paul knew that this sacrifice was linked to a certain teaching: he exhorted Christians to offer

---

[37] A very similar word.
[38] See above, pp. 42–3.
[39] 11QMelch.

## John 6

themselves as living sacrifices, and to be transformed by the renewal of their minds (Rom. 12.1–2).

The Jews then debate among themselves the meaning of 'eating the flesh' (v. 52), and there follows a discourse about consuming the flesh and the blood of the Son of Man. Brown suggests that this may have been John's recollection of the institution of the Eucharist.[40] 'Flesh', *bāśār*, was the priestly word for the human body, and so 'This is my body' could have been 'This is my *bāśār*'. The holy anointing oil could not be poured on the body, *bāśār*, of ordinary men (Exod. 30.32; so too Lev. 6.10; 14.9; 15.13, 16; 16.4); the LORD would destroy Assyria, both soul and body, *bāśār* (Isa. 10.18); and, as though in a desert place, the soul thirsts and the body, *bāśār*, faints for God (Ps. 63.1). Ignatius, bishop of Antioch, knew 'flesh' rather than 'body' as the words of the Eucharist; he wrote of 'the bread of God, the flesh of Jesus Christ', of 'one common Eucharist, one flesh of our LORD Jesus Christ' and of 'the Eucharist, the flesh of our Saviour Jesus Christ'.[41] Whatever the origin, the word must be understood in the light of Jesus' own explanation which contrasts the 'flesh' that feeds[42] with the Wisdom that gives life: 'It is the spirit that gives life, the flesh is of no avail; the words that I have spoken to you are spirit and life' (v. 63). The Man's flesh/good news is his teaching, in accordance with the Wisdom tradition:

> Come, eat of my bread, and drink of the wine I have mixed.
> Leave the deceived ones and live, and walk straight in the way of insight. (Prov. 9.6, my literal translation)

Wisdom is the mother/the spouse who nourishes the one who seeks her:

> [Wisdom] will feed him with the bread of understanding,
> She will give him the water of wisdom to drink.
> (Ben Sira 15.3, my translation)

Wisdom feeds her bread/fruit to her children, and the bread of life is the fruit of the tree of life. The Man's blood is his life, in accordance with temple understanding: 'the life of the flesh is in the blood ... It is blood that makes atonement, by reason of the life' (Lev. 17.11).

The flesh and blood of the Son of Man are thus the knowledge and life of the Servant, for which the *Didache* prayer gives thanks: 'We give thanks

---

[40] R. E. Brown, *The Gospel According to John I—XII*, Anchor Bible 29, London: Geoffrey Chapman, 1971, pp. 287–9.
[41] Ignatius, *To the Romans* 7; *To the Philadelphians* 4; *To the Smyrnaeans* 7.
[42] Here 'flesh' has the ordinary sense of the word and links to the Passover lectionary for the previous year, the creation of Adam as a man of dust who was given life by the Spirit.

to thee, our Father, for the life and knowledge thou hast made known to us through thy Servant Jesus.'

In the same way as Jesus lives because he shares the life of his heavenly Father, so too his disciples who 'eat' him will live because of him (v. 57). The life and light of the Prologue are here the life and illumination/teaching which nourish Jesus' followers. The early Christians understood the bread as the vehicle of Wisdom: Clement of Rome wrote at the end of the first century: 'through him, the LORD permits us to taste the Wisdom of eternity';[43] and in mid-fourth-century Egypt, Bishop Serapion prayed at the Eucharist: 'Make us living men ... Give us Holy Spirit that we may be able to tell forth and enunciate thy unspeakable mysteries ...' 'Make us wise ... by the participation of the body and the blood.' The question that cannot be answered is: was this the original role of the bread of the Presence, eaten by the high priests each Sabbath to impart holiness? The Old Testament says nothing about the role of the *leḥem pānîm*, and yet the table on which it was set out was as holy as the ark, both being wrapped in three cloths, whereas the other furnishings were wrapped only in two (Lev. 4.5–15).

## 6.60–71: Some disciples leave Jesus

In Mark's Gospel (Mark 6.30—8.38) there is a long sequence that corresponds to this chapter in John's Gospel: the miracle of feeding 5,000, walking on the water, teaching about Jewish food traditions, healing a man who was deaf and unable to speak clearly, feeding 4,000, teaching about the leaven of the Pharisees and Herod, with the suggestion that there had been secret teaching: 'eyes that do not see, ears that do not hear' (Mark 8.17), healing a blind man, and finally Peter recognizing that Jesus was the Messiah and Jesus predicting his suffering. John has a similar sequence, but coalesces the two feeding miracles. *In both Gospels Jesus links the feeding miracle(s) to teaching against Jewish tradition*: in Mark it is the distortions of the Jewish law as interpreted by the Pharisees at that time (Mark 7.1–23) and then a warning against the leaven of the Pharisees (Mark 8.15); in John it is the whole discourse about the bread of life contrasted with the manna of the wilderness. Mark emphasized the nature of his sequence with the stories of the deaf man who could not speak clearly and the blind man.

---

[43] *1 Clement* 36.

## John 6

In John's Gospel, the final section of chapter 6 corresponds to Peter's confession at Caesarea Philippi and Jesus' first predictions of his suffering. Mark's account of Peter's confession has Jesus ask, 'Who do men say that I am?' and the disciples saying, 'John the Baptist, Elijah, or one of the prophets.' Then Jesus asked, 'But who do you say that I am?' and Peter replied, 'You are the Messiah' (Mark 8.27–29, my paraphrase). John used the same material in a different way: the crowd reacted to the feeding miracle by saying that Jesus was indeed the expected prophet (v. 14). Then when some people had left Jesus because of his teaching, he asked the Twelve – the first time the Twelve are mentioned by John – if they were also going to leave him. Peter replied, 'You are the Holy One of God', and that there was no one else with the words of eternal life (vv. 66–71). Peter would use the same title – 'the Holy and Righteous One' – in his temple sermon in Solomon's porch, and on that occasion Peter was presenting Jesus as the great high priest who had made the atonement offering and would return with new life (Acts 3.11–22, especially vv. 14–15, 19–22).

This was John's way of telling the story of Peter's confession, and several details are best explained if read in the light of Matthew's longer account of the same event. After Peter's confession, Jesus said to him, 'Blessed are you, Simon Bar-Jona! For flesh and blood has not revealed this to you, but my Father who is in heaven' (Matt. 16.17). John echoes this saying in: 'It is the spirit that gives life, the flesh is of no avail ... No one can come to me unless it is granted him by the Father' (vv. 63, 65), apparently contradicting the words of the preceding discourse about the value of the flesh, but in fact reproducing correctly Jesus' reaction to Peter's confession. In the synoptic sequence, Jesus then predicted that he would suffer: John said he predicted that he would be betrayed, and that one of the Twelve was a devil (vv. 70–71). In Matthew's account, Jesus recognized the words of Satan in the voice of Peter when he protested at the prediction of suffering (Matt. 16.22–23). Finally, Jesus asked how the faithful disciples would react if they saw the Son of Man ascending to the place he had come from (v. 62), which is most likely a reference to the Transfiguration. In the synoptic sequence, this follows immediately after Peter's confession and before the detailed predictions of Jesus' suffering.

As with the synoptic Gospels, the Transfiguration marked the beginning of the end of the ministry in Galilee. Jesus gave more teaching and then moved from the area, setting his face towards Jerusalem (Luke 9.51). John says that Jesus went about in Galilee because the Jews in Judea wanted to kill him. Then he went up to Jerusalem on his own.

# John 7

## 7.1–52: Jesus at the feast of Tabernacles

For six months, 'Jesus went about in Galilee' (v. 1), one of the very few indications of where Jesus spent his time. The incidents John chose to record fill only a few days of Jesus' three years in the public eye, and even if the stories in the synoptic Gospels are added, they account for only a few weeks. It would be interesting to know where Jesus lived for the rest of the time. Eusebius says that John wrote his Gospel when he had seen the other three and confirmed their accuracy 'but remarked that the narrative only lacked the story of what Christ had done first of all at the beginning of his mission'.[1] John says that Jesus began his ministry east of the Jordan where the Baptist was preaching, had several visits to the temple, and then returned to somewhere beyond the Jordan (10.40; 11.54).

Chapters 7—10 have Jesus back in Jerusalem, at first secretly (why?), then teaching openly and in debate with 'the Jews', and then hiding himself again (9.59). This section of John's Gospel has Jesus in Jerusalem for the feast of Tabernacles. John says nothing of Jesus observing the Day of Atonement, but it would have been possible to make the three-day journey from Galilee to Jerusalem between the Day of Atonement and the beginning of Tabernacles. Jesus' brothers went to Jerusalem without him (cf. Mark 6.3, which names the brothers), but he followed later, presumably with another group of pilgrims. Mark also mentions the secrecy of this journey to Jerusalem (Mark 9.30). Very little of the ceremonial and cultural context of Tabernacles is mentioned by John, but this would all have been known to the first users of the Gospel. In particular, there was the ancient link between Tabernacles and the-LORD-the-King coming to the temple.[2]

According to both 1 Kings and 1 Chronicles, Solomon dedicated the temple at 'the feast of the seventh month', although it is not named as Tabernacles (1 Kings 8.2; 2 Chron. 5.3), and this is when the glory of the

---
[1] Eusebius, *History of the Church* 3.24. This was what the early Church believed.
[2] See above, p. 150.

## John 7

LORD came to the temple. Josephus emphasized this: Solomon consecrated the temple at Tabernacles, 'a most holy and important feast, and the place was filled with incense which formed a cloud'. This was 'a visible image and glorious appearance of God's having descended into this temple and having gladly pitched his tabernacle there'.[3] The desert tabernacle that the temple represented gave the festival its name, and whatever the festival later celebrated, it had this important element in the first temple. John used this imagery in the Prologue: 'The Word [that is, the *memra*, the visible presence of the LORD], became flesh and tabernacled among us' (John 1.14, my translation). John 7—9 depicts the visible presence coming to the actual temple at Tabernacles, coming to his own who did not receive him. So too were Ezekiel's visions of the new temple on the Day of Atonement in 572 BCE, when the glory of the LORD returned to the temple (Ezek. 43.1–5). Since this was the season of Tabernacles, and Ezekiel was from a priestly family (Ezek. 1.3), it is likely that his memory of Tabernacles in the original temple prompted his vision of the glory of the LORD entering from the east.

The complex web of cultural memories linked to Tabernacles,[4] which for some did not emphasize the time of living in tabernacles in the wilderness, must be borne in mind when reading John's account of Jesus in the temple at Tabernacles. John was writing to show that Jesus was the Anointed One, the Son of God (20.31), and Tabernacles was the first-temple festival that marked the coming of the LORD, the Son of God Most High, to the temple in the person of the anointed king. This may have been the original context of Malachi 3.1: the messenger/angel of the covenant who would suddenly appear in the temple to purify the priests. John presents Jesus as the fulfilment of the older Tabernacles and its symbolism.

Jesus goes back to the temple a full year after the Sabbath healing of the man at Bethesda, and the debate was still raging (v. 23). To work on the Sabbath was a capital offence, according to the law of Moses (Exod. 31.15), and John makes the hostility clear. Jesus had not gone to Judea initially 'because the Judeans/Jews sought to kill him' (v. 1), and this atmosphere of fear and hostility pervades the narrative. No one spoke openly about Jesus in Jerusalem 'for fear of the Jews' (v. 13); 'Is not this the man whom they seek to kill?' (v. 25); 'they sought to arrest him' (vv. 30, 44). Many did believe, because they had seen the signs (v. 31), and

---

[3] Josephus, *Antiquities* 8.106.
[4] See above, pp. 149–57.

they became the Christian community in Jerusalem. A constant theme in John's Gospel is the return of the glory of the LORD (already at 1.14 and 2.11), and Isaiah had spoken of the signs of the glory: the blind see, the deaf hear, the lame walk, the dumb speak, and water comes to dry places (Isa. 35.5–6). Others expected the Messiah to revive the dead.[5] Thus far Jesus had restored the son of the official in Capernaum and the invalid man at Bethesda.

The narrative also has a full cast of characters, evoking the variety of people and opinions that would have been in Jerusalem for the feast. The chapter begins with Jesus' brothers urging him to return to Jerusalem and renew his contact with the disciples there (v. 3). People are looking for him and talking about him: the Jews (vv. 1, 11, 15, 35); the crowd (vv. 12, 31, 40–44, 49); the people of Jerusalem (v. 25); the Pharisees (vv. 32, 45, 48, 52); the chief priests (vv. 32, 45); and Nicodemus (v. 50). One year later, Peter would preach in the temple precincts and claim that Jesus had been the fulfilment of the Day of Atonement ritual. He urged repentance before the LORD returned from heaven (i.e. before the high priest emerged from the holy of holies) (Acts 3.19–21). There was a similar reaction from the Jewish authorities: high priests, rulers and Sadducees questioned Peter and John[6] about their teaching (Acts 4.1–8).

In the time of Ezra, the law was read in public at Tabernacles, but there is no mention of this in the Mishnah. Ezra records a vestige of the older lawgiving when the LORD came in glory (Deut. 33.4). Nevertheless, Jesus' first dispute with the Jews in the temple at Tabernacles is over the interpretation of the law of Moses (7.14–24). How did Jesus have such knowledge if he had never studied? Jesus says that his teaching is from God. Then he distances himself from the law of Moses: 'Did not Moses give *you* the law?', a reference to the newer way of reading Deuteronomy 33.4, when the Messiah had been changed into Moses.[7] The problem is still the healing on the Sabbath at Bethesda the previous year. They can circumcise a man on the Sabbath,[8] Jesus points out, but apparently it is not permitted to heal a man who cannot walk. Then there is a discussion with some people of Jerusalem: could Jesus be the Messiah? But nobody would know where the Messiah came from, and they knew, apparently, where Jesus came from. Jesus asks if they really know where he has come from. Some people then try to arrest him – the Pharisees and chief priests

---

[5] *Messianic Apocalypse*, 4Q521.
[6] Not John the Evangelist.
[7] See p. 133.
[8] Mishnah *Shabbath* 19.2.

## John 7

– but others begin to believe that he is the Messiah because of the signs (vv. 30–31). Jesus then speaks of where he is going, and the Pharisees and the Jews again misunderstand his words.

On the last day of the festival, the great day, Jesus makes a proclamation in the temple. Although the original festival had been extended from seven to eight days (Lev. 23.39), the great day was probably the seventh, when there was a longer and more elaborate procession carrying willow branches around the great altar.[9] There was also the procession bringing water from Siloam and the libation, and it is in this setting that Jesus proclaims: 'If anyone thirst, let him come to me and drink' (v. 37). There is then a problem with the Greek text, which can be read several ways:

- If anyone thirst, let him come; and let him drink who believes in me. As Scripture says, 'From within him shall flow rivers of living water';
- If anyone thirst, let him come to me and drink. He who believes in me, as Scripture says, 'From within him shall flow rivers of living water';
- If anyone thirst, let him come to me and drink, who believes in me. As Scripture says, 'From within him shall flow rivers of living water.'

There are two questions: who is the source of the living water: Jesus, or the one who believes in him? and what scripture is Jesus quoting?

Two other early Christian texts mention the living water:

First, the Spirit-and-the-Bride (that is, Wisdom, the Spirit who is the Bride[10]) summons people, and those who hear her summon in their turn.

> The Spirit-and-the-Bride say, 'Come.'
> And let him who hears say, 'Come.'
> And let him who is thirsty come,
> Let him who desires take the water of life without price.
> (Rev. 22.17)

The Spirit-and-the-Bride offer the water.

Second, Thomas' Jesus says to Thomas: 'Because you have drunk, you have become intoxicated from the bubbling spring which I have measured out.'[11] Here, Jesus offers the water, but he is not the source.

---

[9] Mishnah *Sukkah* 4.5.

[10] The verb is plural, but there is this problem of singular and plural elsewhere in Revelation where there is a pairing of two subjects. The one on the throne and the Lamb is followed by the *singular* (Rev. 22.3). In Rev. 6.17 the pair is followed by a plural, but several early texts have a singular here.

[11] *Gospel of Thomas* 13.

## Temple Theology in John's Gospel

The meaning of the first part of Jesus' saying must be determined by the scripture he is quoting, and most likely this is Ben Sira's great poem in praise of Wisdom (Ben Sira 24.1–34), but in its original form.[12] As in some other instances[13] a line has been inserted into an older text to make it refer to Moses and the law. The Wisdom poem exists in several forms, as can be seen from the additional verses implied by the numbering in some English translations,[14] and Ben Sira 24.23 detaches easily from the present text to give an entirely different meaning. Wisdom invites people to come, to eat and to drink (Ben Sira 24.19–21). There follows a sequence of verses beginning with a participle: he who obeys me (Ben Sira 24.22), he who fills (Ben Sira 24.25), he who makes full (Ben Sira 24.25), he who makes to shine (Ben Sira 24.27). What the present text attributes to the law of Moses was originally attributed to the disciple of Wisdom:

> He [not the law] fills men with wisdom, like the Pishon,
> and like the Tigris at the time of the firstfruits.
> He makes them full of understanding like the Euphrates,
> and like the Jordan at harvest time.
> *He makes instruction shine forth like light,*
> *like the Gihon at the time of vintage.*

Wisdom's disciple is the conduit for her teaching: he makes it shine like light and flow like the waters of her sacred spring at the autumn festival. From within him flow rivers of living water. Since Wisdom was also the-Spirit-and-the-Bride, John (or a later disciple) added the explanation of Jesus' words: 'This he said about the Spirit' (v. 39). This is very similar to some lines in a Qumran hymn:

> But you, O God, have put in my mouth [teaching] like early rain for all
> And a spring of living water that does not fail.
> When the heavens open, they do not cease but become a flowing river ...
> The hidden things bubble forth in secret.[15]

Jesus was described elsewhere as a child/disciple of Wisdom (the Spirit) (Matt. 11.19; Luke 7.35);[16] and in the Book of Revelation, Wisdom

---

[12] There have been many ingenious suggestions as to which text Jesus was quoting or whether it was just a collection of scriptural phrases. The Ben Sira poem is the simplest answer to the question.

[13] E.g. Deut. 33.4; see above, p. 133.

[14] The RSV gives vv. 18 and 24 as footnotes.

[15] *Hymns*, 1QH XVI.17, 18, 19, my translation.

[16] Also the *Gospel of the Hebrews*, where it is the Spirit who speaks to Jesus at his baptism and

## John 7

appears again in the temple as the Woman clothed with the sun whose son is taken up to the throne of God – an image from the first temple – but the Woman has other children whom the dragon attacks (Rev. 12.5, 17). The saying about living waters must be read in this context: just as Jesus is a conduit for the waters of the Spirit, so too those who drink the waters from him will become in turn children of Wisdom and a conduit for her teaching.

Water flowing out from the holy of holies was symbolism from the first temple, as can be seen in the Psalms:

> The children of men take refuge in the shadow of thy wings …
> Thou givest them drink from the river of thy delights.[17]
> For with thee is the fountain of life;
> And in thy light do we see light … (Ps. 36.7b–9)

Or 'There is a river whose streams make glad the city of God …' (Ps. 46.4).

The 'wings' are the cherub throne in the holy of holies, a place of light with a fountain of life. Amos associated justice and righteousness with flowing waters:

> Let justice roll down like waters,
> And righteousness like an ever-flowing stream.
> (Amos 5.24)

There could have been a source of water in the holy of holies to account for this all-pervasive imagery, possibly a conduit from the Gihon spring, whence came the waters of Siloam that were used at Tabernacles and which opened the eyes of the blind man (9.7).

When prophets described waters flowing (again) from the temple it meant that the glory of the LORD had returned (Ezek. 47.1–12; Zech. 14.8; also Rev. 22.1). Enoch knew that the source of the water was the holy of holies and described it springing up around the throne:

> In that place I saw the fountain of righteousness
> Which was inexhaustible:
> And around it were many fountains of wisdom;
> And all the thirsty drank of them
> And they were filled with wisdom.[18]

---

calls him 'my son'. Jerome, *On Isaiah* 11.2, in M. R. James, *The Apocryphal New Testament*, Oxford: Clarendon Press, (1924) 1980, p. 5.
[17] Literally 'your Edens'.
[18] *1 Enoch* 48.1.

So too the hymn at the end of the Qumran *Community Rule*:

> For from the spring of my knowledge comes my light,
> And my eyes have seen his wonderful works ...
> Knowledge hidden from a man,
> A skilful plan hidden from the sons of Adam.[19]

Jesus said, 'Blessed are those who hunger and thirst for righteousness, for they shall be satisfied' (Matt 5.6), another saying with the same temple context.

Joel, whose prophecy is not dated, shows one effect of the restored waters from the temple:

> In that day ... all the stream beds of Judah shall flow with water;
> And a fountain shall come forth from the house of the LORD
> And water the valley of Shittim.            (Joel 3.18)

Why Shittim? It was north-east of the Dead Sea on the other side of the Jordan, a good way from Jerusalem and so unlikely to be irrigated literally from Jerusalem. But the valley of Shittim was the place beyond the Jordan where Moses had taught the laws of Deuteronomy (Deut. 1.5) as Josephus knew,[20] and a prophecy that water from the temple would flow into the valley of Shittim looks like a reference to the law of Moses being irrigated by the older Wisdom.

Jesus' teaching prompted mixed reactions: some said he must be the Messiah, but they assumed that he came from Galilee, and so could not be the Messiah who was to come from Bethlehem (vv. 40–43); the temple officers were afraid to arrest him (vv. 45–46); the Pharisees, assuming that they were the ones to judge such matters, asked if any of *them* had believed Jesus' teaching (vv. 47–49); but Nicodemus, who was a Pharisee, reminded them that the law did not condemn a man without hearing him (vv. 50–51).

---

[19] My translation.
[20] Josephus, *Antiquities* 4.176, 'where the city of Abila now stands'.

# John 8

## 8.1–11: The woman accused of adultery

The story of the woman accused of adultery is not found in many early manuscripts of John's Gospel, but in others it is found in various places: after 7.36, and so immediately before Jesus proclaimed himself the conduit for Wisdom's teaching, or at the very end of the Gospel, after 21.25. It is also found sometimes after Luke 21.38. The story is included in the Codex Bezae, suggesting that it was significant for a community with Hebrew roots, and was also found in the (now lost) *Gospel of the Hebrews*.[1] It may be the same as the story about a woman 'falsely accused before the LORD of many sins' which Papias included in his book *The Sayings of the Lord Explained*, compiled in the early years of the second century CE. Papias claimed that he had heard it from the disciples of the original 12 Apostles, and also that he had learned from 'the elder John' who was still teaching at that time: 'Papias reproduces other stories communicated to him by word of mouth, together with some otherwise unknown parables and teachings of the Saviour …' Eusebius suspected, however, that he did not always fully understand what he was recording, 'misinterpreting the apostolic accounts and failing to grasp what they had said in mystic or symbolic language'.[2] This may be true of the story of the woman accused of adultery and brought to Jesus in the temple.

First, it is important to note that wherever the story has been inserted into the Gospel narratives, apart from as an Appendix to John's Gospel, *the story is set in the temple*. There is nothing in the story itself that demands a temple setting, and so the setting is probably the key to the meaning. Further, what was once mystical teaching may have become the report of an actual event, or, as often happens with John, an actual event was recognized as a sign of higher teaching.

The law prescribed that if a married woman committed adultery, both lovers had to be put to death (Deut. 22.22; Lev. 20.10), and the same

---
[1] Eusebius, *History of the Church* 3.39.
[2] Eusebius, *History* 3.39.

applied if the woman was only betrothed to be married. If a woman given in marriage was found not to be a virgin, then she was brought to the door of her father's house and the men of the city had to stone her to death (Deut. 22.21). If a woman's husband suspected her of adultery, then he took her to the temple where a priest subjected her to the 'ritual of the bitter water'. He put some water from the bronze sea into a new earthenware bowl, and then took some dust from beneath a special stone in the temple floor that was fitted with a ring to enable him to lift it. The dust had to be visible on the surface of the water. Then the priest wrote the curses on parchment with ink and washed them off into the water (Num. 5.19–22). The writing had to be such that it could be washed away, not permanent. The woman then had to drink the water, and if she suffered no ill effects, she was innocent.[3]

The story in John 8 is unusual in several ways: if the woman had been caught in the act of adultery, the law of stoning should have applied to her and to the man; but the man is not mentioned. If the woman was being brought to the temple for the test of bitter water, where was her husband or her betrothed that she had betrayed? Several details, however, do fit the situation in the time of Jesus. Jesus bends down and writes with his finger on the ground, presumably in the dust. Was this a reference to the impermanent writing of the curse and the dust of the bitter waters? There has been much speculation as to what Jesus wrote. The opening words of the curse perhaps? Or some words of Jeremiah which would have been apt in this context where Jesus has just proclaimed himself the conduit of the living waters:

> O LORD the hope/cleansing pool, *mikveh*, of Israel,
> All who forsake you shall be put to shame;
> *All who are apostates from me shall be written in the earth*,
> For they have forsaken the fountain of living water.[4]
> (Jer. 17.13, my literal translation)

The words in italics require only 14 Hebrew letters, and the scribes and Pharisees who brought the woman would have recognized the words and known their context. Further, the LORD as the cleansing pool for sinners would account for Jesus saying to the woman that he did not condemn her (v. 11).

The woman brought on her own suggests a woman who was not a virgin at her marriage, and 'caught in adultery' could mean that she was

---
[3] Mishnah *Sotah* 2.2.
[4] 'The LORD' is thought to be a later addition to the text.

visibly pregnant while betrothed to another man, as was the case with Jesus' own mother. The punishment for this was to be taken by the elders of the city to the door of her father's house and be stoned by the men of the city (Deut. 22.20–21). John says that the woman was brought by the elders – the scribes and the Pharisees – and it may be that she was brought to the temple because Jesus was there and they wanted to test him. It is also possible that a real event in the life of Jesus was being understood on a deeper level. The woman accused of adultery recalled the Lady of the first temple who was brought to 'the door of her Father's house'. She had been abused and betrayed by her lovers, and then punished for what they had done to her – brought to the door of the temple, and then burned (2 Kings 23.6). The rejection of the Lady and the destruction of her (first) temple, as recorded by contemporary writers, were due to her citizens being faithless and to the foreign rulers whom she had trusted failing to protect her.

> I called to my lovers but they deceived me;
> My priests and elders perished in the city ...
> For vast as the sea is your ruin; who can restore you?
> Your prophets have seen for you false and deceptive visions ...
> The LORD gave full vent to his wrath, he poured out his hot anger ...
> This was for the sins of her prophets and the iniquities of her priests ...
> (Lam. 1.19; 2.13–14; 4.11–13)

Jeremiah named the rulers for whom the Lady had betrayed the LORD, and they proved to be her killers: Egypt and Assyria (Jer. 2.36; 3.1; 4.31). Isaiah proclaimed that the LORD would return to his forsaken Lady, and she would be rebuilt in jewelled splendour (Isa. 54.4–17). Since a major theme in the Book of Revelation is the return of the Lady to the temple, this symbolic understanding of the incident is possible. The LORD returned to her, and she was restored as the jewelled city of Isaiah's prophecy (Isa. 54.11–13). The Lady Wisdom had been adulterated with alien teachings, but that was also true of the teachings attributed to Moses by the Pharisees and scribes. None could cast the first stone.

Trial by bitter water was abandoned not long after the time of Jesus when R. Joḥanan ben Zakkai taught: 'If you yourselves are above reproach, the water will put your wives to the test. Otherwise it will not put them to the test.'[5] There were so many men committing adultery, he said, that the words of Hosea had been fulfilled:

---

[5] H. Danby, *The Mishnah*, Oxford: Oxford University Press, (1933) 1989, p. 305n.

> I will not punish your daughters when they play the harlot,
> Nor your brides when they commit adultery;
> For the men themselves go aside with harlots ... (Hos. 4.14)

The stories of Jesus and R. Joḥanan – a much younger contemporary – are very similar, and it is possible that other Jewish teachers were influenced by this teaching of Jesus: 'Let him who is without sin among you be the first to throw a stone at her.' The custom was abolished.

## 8.12–20: Jesus as the light

During Tabernacles, the Court of Women was illuminated at night by four huge candelabra, each with four bowls for oil. They were so tall that young priests had to climb ladders to refill the bowls. Every house in Jerusalem reflected the light from the temple court. Every house in Jerusalem could probably hear the music too, as the Levites stood on the steps between the Court of Women and the Court of Israel and played harps, lyres, cymbals and trumpets all through the night. Men with burning torches used to dance all night.[6] The Mishnah does not say what the all-night illumination symbolized. The most likely explanation is that it enacted the prophecy in Zechariah which foresaw the LORD appearing with all his angels at Tabernacles and everything returning to Day One, which was the state of pre-created light before the visible creation was made. The text is damaged, but seems to be: 'On that day there shall be no light and the glorious ones [sun and moon?] shall grow small, and it shall be Day One ... no day and no night' (Zech. 14.6–7, translating literally). The great lights of heaven that were created on the fourth day would not be needed because the LORD would be the light (cf. Rev. 22.5).

Since Jesus' saying 'I am the light of the world' is only recorded by John – here and at 9.5 – the meaning should be established by comparing other Johannine texts. In the Prologue, John said that the true light was coming into the world, and that this light was life. It was also described as the glory of the Son of God, and as a state in which people could live (1 John 1.7). The image of the pillar of light at the exodus is not, therefore, likely to be the source. It should rather be sought in the holy of holies, the state of the pre-created light and the source of life. In the Hebrew Scriptures, seeing the LORD was described as seeing the light of his face/presence, and the effect of this was, literally, to see everything in a new light. Thus in the Psalms we read:

---

[6] Mishnah *Sukkah* 5.2–4.

## John 8

- 'The LORD is my light and my salvation' (Ps. 27.1);
- 'In thy light do we see light' (Ps. 36.9);
- 'Send out thy light and thy truth; let them lead me' (Ps. 43.3);
- 'That I may walk before God in the light of life' (Ps. 56.13);
- 'Blessed are the people ... who walk in the light of thy face/presence' (Ps. 89.15, my translation).

Isaiah described the servant of the LORD as the light for the nations (Isa. 42.6; 49.6), and the high priests invoked the light of the LORD's presence as a blessing (Num. 6.24–26). Among the spiritual heirs of temple tradition was R. Ishmael the high priest,[7] to whom many wise sayings are attributed. He described ascending to stand before the throne in the light of the presence, and how this changed his way of seeing and knowing.

> Ishmael/he said: When my ears heard this great mystery,
> The world was changed around me into a shining place
> And my heart was as if I/it had come to a new world,
> And every day it seemed to my soul
> As though I was standing before the throne of glory.[8]

The Qumran community also understood the light of the LORD's presence as illuminating the mind with life-giving wisdom and the knowledge of eternity, and they called themselves the 'sons of light', as did the Christians.[9] When Jesus says he is the light of the world, he is claiming to be the Incarnation of the LORD, the messenger of life-giving Wisdom, the one in whose presence the world is transformed.

The Pharisees dispute Jesus' claim to be the light on the grounds that a man cannot bear witness to himself. He replies that in *their* law, the testimony of at least two witnesses is required in a capital case (Deut. 19.15). Again, Jesus distances himself from the law of Moses; it was the law of the Jews (cf. 7.19). There are two witnesses to his claim, he says, himself and his Father. The Pharisees, thinking that this meant a human father, ask where he is, presumably so that they can question him. In his reply, Jesus contrasts the first- and second-temple understandings of God Most High and the LORD: in the first temple, people had understood God Most High as the Father, and then there was the LORD, his Firstborn, who was present in the Davidic king; in the second temple, God Most High

---

[7] He taught in Palestine in the early second century CE and so cannot literally have been a high priest. Presumably this was how high priests were remembered.

[8] *Merkavah Rabbah* 680, Schäfer's numbering; my translation of the gist of three almost parallel versions of the text.

[9] *Community Rule*, 1QS II, III. See also pp. 369–71.

and the LORD coalesced, and so any talk of Father and Son as 'two' witnesses would have had no meaning to 'the Jews'. Jesus would later claim the distinction of the two within the unity: 'I and the Father, we are one thing' (10.30, translating literally), and this should be understood in the context of the holy of holies which was a unity of the manifold heavenly powers. This contrast of first- and second-temple beliefs is the context for Jesus' words here: 'You know neither me [the LORD] nor my Father [God Most High]; if you knew me, you would know my Father also' (8.19). The teachers in the second temple are not able to understand what is before them because they – or rather their predecessors – have rejected the teaching that made any recognition possible. Despite this claim, which the Pharisees would have thought blasphemy, nobody arrests Jesus because 'his hour has not yet come' (v. 20).

## 8.21–30: Jesus speaks to the unbelieving Jews

John then reports, in his characteristic style, an exchange between Jesus and 'the Jews' based on the misunderstandings that are inevitable when the worlds of the first and the second temple meet each other. The key points are: Jesus says he is going away, the Jews will look for him, but they will die in their sins. The Jews think that 'going away' means suicide, going to his death where they could not follow, when in fact Jesus means going to eternal life. Jesus emphasizes that he and they are, literally, from different worlds: he from above, they from the material world. The Jews, he says, will (eventually) seek him, the traditional expression used for seeking the LORD:

- 'Those ... who seek the face/presence of the God of Jacob' (Ps. 24.6);
- 'Seek the LORD while he may be found' (Isa. 55.6);
- 'They seek me daily ... as if they were a nation that did righteousness' (Isa. 58.2);
- 'Seek the LORD and live' (Amos 5.4, 6).

Until they recognize who he is, they will not realize what is happening in their midst: '... unless you believe that I am he'. The LORD has come to the temple and they cannot see this. 'I am He' was the form of the Name used by the Second-Isaiah: 'I the LORD, the first; and with the last things, I am He' (Isa. 41.4, translating literally). The Greek understood this as: 'until the last things, I am'.

> An oracle of the LORD: You are my witnesses, my servants[10] whom I have chosen,
> So that you may know and believe me, and understand that I am He …
> From this day, I am He, and nobody can deliver from my hand …
> I, I am He, who blots out your transgressions for my own sake.
> (Isa. 43.10, 13, 25, my translation)

> I am He, I am the first, and I am the last. (Isa. 48.12)

Jesus saying 'I am He' is a claim that this is the expected appearance of the LORD to save his people, but only those who recognize him will be saved. This is the theme of Tabernacles: the LORD returning to become King and bring judgement.

The same titles appear in the Book of Revelation: 'Fear not, I am the first and the last, and the living one' (Rev. 1.17–18). The heavenly host sing praises to 'the one who was and is, and is to come' (Rev. 4.8). 'I am the Alpha and the Omega, the first and the last, the beginning and the end' (Rev. 22.13). The temple pattern is fulfilled in the Book of Revelation; the Servant, the royal high priest, offered himself as the atonement sacrifice and was then enthroned. His people were waiting for him to return from heaven/the holy of holies, to bring the judgement and the renewal of the creation. Those in Israel who recognized him would be marked with his Name, fulfilling the ancient blessing 'May the LORD make his face shine upon you', which preceded being marked with the Name. In Revelation, this was the shining presence of the angel of the sunrise who bore the seal of the living God and marked 144,000 drawn from every tribe of Israel, to protect them from the imminent judgement (Rev. 7.1–8). This vision describes all 12 tribes restored because it was set in the now-mythical time of David and Solomon, before the kingdom divided. They were marked with the seal of the Name.

Luke records Jesus' sorrow that Jerusalem did not recognize who he was. He wept over the city and said:

> Would that even today you knew the things that make for peace! But now they are hid from your eyes. For the days shall come upon you, when your enemies will cast up a bank about you and surround you … and dash you to the ground, you and your children within you, and they will not leave one stone upon another in you; because you did not know the time of your visitation. (Luke 19.41–44)

---

[10] Pointing the word as a plural.

## Temple Theology in John's Gospel

The visitation was the LORD appearing to bring the judgement, and the *Damascus Document* shows what the Qumran community understood by this.[11]

> The humble of the flock are those who watch for him. They shall be saved at the time of the visitation ... as it came to pass at the time of the former visitation, concerning which God spoke by the hand of Ezekiel saying: 'They shall put a mark on the foreheads of those who sigh and groan [Ezek. 9.4]. But the others were delivered up to the avenging sword ...

Those who recognized Jesus as the LORD and who accepted the Name (the baptismal X) on their foreheads would be kept safe during the coming judgement, when Jerusalem would be destroyed just as it had been in the time of Ezekiel. Jesus proclaimed from the beginning of his public ministry that he was bringing the judgement. He read Isaiah 61 in the synagogue at Nazareth and said it was being fulfilled, but the passage quoted in Luke 4.18–19 continues with the warning that the anointed messenger would bring the day of God's vengeance. The reference was to Deuteronomy 32.43, quoted also as a proof text in Hebrews 1.6: the LORD, the Firstborn, would come to avenge the blood of his sons; the angels would bow down to him; and he would heal the land of his people. Thus in Revelation, the visions show angels worshipping the one on the throne, the terrible punishment of enemies, the final salvation of those who bear the Name, and the creation of a new heaven and a new earth.

The Jews do not understand this and so ask Jesus who he is (8.25). What follows is not easy to translate. The gist is: 'I am what I have been telling you from the outset.' He repeats that he is the messenger bringing to earth what he has heard from the Father, but again, the Jews do not understand what he means. The opening lines of the Book of Revelation say the same thing but in greater detail:

> The revelation [given to] Jesus the Anointed One, which God gave to him to show his servants what must soon happen; and [Jesus] revealed and explained it by sending his angel to his servant John. John bore witness to the word of God and to the testimony of Jesus the Anointed One, and all that Jesus saw. (Rev. 1.1–2, my literal translation)

Jesus then predicts that when the heavenly Man is raised up they will recognize that he is the LORD: 'You will know that I am He' (8.28, my translation). This is another of John's double meanings: the raising up was

---

[11] The quotation is from CD VII, Ms B found in the Cairo Genizah. Some pieces of the *Damascus Document* were found in Cave 4, but not this actual passage.

both the crucifixion and the exaltation; and the allusion was to the Servant, who was anointed, according to the Qumran text, but disfigured according to the other (later?) version of the Hebrew (Isa. 52.14). Then the Servant was recognized, and made atonement for many peoples.[12] The other people discern what they have never been told, and understand what they have never even heard (Isa. 52.15). At this point many of the Jews are convinced and recognize who Jesus is.

## 8.31–59: The children of Abraham

The discourse that follows reads like another summary of long and wide-ranging exchanges, or even a series of exchanges, between Jesus and the Jews, each summary representing one of the many points at which Jesus and first-temple belief were set alongside 'the Jews' and second-temple belief, sketches of how and why 'the Jews' did not, and indeed from their point of view could not, understand what Jesus was teaching and claiming.

This short summary presupposes a knowledge of many beliefs that distinguished first-temple teachings from those of the second:

- *The older belief that the* LORD *who appeared to Abraham was the Son of El Elyon, and was the 'second God'.*
- *The question of Abraham's heirs.* Josiah had purged from his kingdom the religious practices of Abraham and the patriarchs,[13] and so the children of Abraham, in one sense, were those who preserved the ways of the first temple and were excluded from the second. On the other hand, the returning exiles were encouraged by the Second-Isaiah to see themselves as treading literally in the footsteps of Abraham as they returned from the land of the Chaldeans to settle in Canaan (Isa. 51.1–3).
- *The role of Adam.* The Genesis Eden story depicts the fallen Adam who listened to the snake, ate from the forbidden tree, and so lost his place in Eden and his direct contact with the LORD. Ezekiel, who gave the first-temple view of Adam, saw him seated on the heavenly throne as the divine Image, not struggling with the mortal state and a world of thorns and thistles.[14]

---

[12] 'Startle' (v. 15) is in fact the Hebrew for 'sprinkle', a reference to the sprinkling of the blood on the Day of Atonement.
[13] See above, pp. 69–70.
[14] See above, pp. 122–3.

- *The role of the snake, whose tempting tree in Eden represented the law of Moses.* The LORD had warned Adam: 'In the day that you eat [from the forbidden tree] you shall die' (Gen. 2.17), and so it was the law that brought death. This is such a startling idea that the texts which mention it are seen as problematic. There are difficult texts in the *Gospel of Philip* which seem to say this too. One is: 'There are two trees growing in Paradise. The one bears [ ] the other bears men. Adam [ ] from the tree which bore animals. He became an animal and brought forth animals.'[15] The very fragmented text that follows seems to say that if Adam had eaten from the other tree, he would have remained the Man, and all the angels would have worshipped him. The other text is: 'The law was the tree. It has power to give knowledge of good and evil. It neither removed him from evil nor did it set him in the good, but it created death for those who ate of it.'[16] Paul was wrestling with this idea too, when he tried to explain the relationship between the law – his former way of thinking – and the teachings of the Christians whom he had joined:

> Sin came into the world through one man and death through sin … Sin indeed was in the world before the law was given, but sin is not counted where there is no law. Yet death reigned from Adam to Moses, even over those whose sins were not like the transgression of Adam …
> (Rom. 5.12–14)

Neither the *Gospel of Philip* nor Paul is entirely clear, but it does seem that the law was described by the Christians as the forbidden tree, and this would explain why John the Baptist called the Pharisees and Sadducees the children of a snake and warned that the axe would soon fell every tree that did not bear good fruit (Matt. 3.7).

In addition, there was the political situation developing in Jesus' time. When their situation was obviously hopeless, Eleazar addressed the people besieged in Masada, for whom the idea of 'slavery' to the Romans or to anyone was unthinkable: 'Long ago, good men, we decided to be slaves/servants neither to the Romans nor to any but God, for he is the true and just ruler of men …'[17] And there is the old problem of translation: what terms did Jesus actually use in these debates with the

---

[15] *Gospel of Philip*, CG II.3.72.
[16] *Gospel of Philip* 74.
[17] Josephus, *War* 7.323.

## John 8

Jews, given that they are unlikely to have been in the Greek that now forms John's Gospel?

The first cluster of debates is summarized in verses 31–38. The text says that these words were addressed to the Jews who *believed* in Jesus, but the content of the exchanges shows that he was debating with unbelieving Jews. The text is a problem, and no suggested solution is convincing. Jesus says that those who are truly his disciples know the truth and the truth would set them free. The Jews reply that since they are the children of Abraham, they have never been slaves to anyone, implying a political understanding of freedom. Jesus deals first with this question of freedom and bondage, and says that anyone who commits a sin is a slave to sin (6.34), and the slave has fewer rights in the house (the temple) than does the son of the house. The Son of the house can set them free.

For Paul, this slavery was slavery to the law, as he explained in one of his earliest letters:

> When the time had fully come, God sent forth his Son, born of [a] woman, born under the law, to redeem those who were under the law, so that we might receive adoption as sons. And because you are sons, God has sent the Spirit of his Son into our hearts, crying 'Abba! Father!' So through God you are no longer a slave but a son, and if a son then [also] an heir. (Gal. 4.4–7)

Paul developed this further in Romans, trying to reconcile what must have been the teaching of his new faith with his own deep roots in second-temple Judaism that he found so hard to leave behind. The law itself was not sin, he insisted, implying that someone was saying that it was. In fact the law was holy and just and good, but it made people aware of sin, for sin deceived him through the commandment and so killed him (Rom. 7.7–12). This is one of the weakest parts of Paul's exposition, since he could not bring himself to accept what must have been a tenet of his new faith – that the law itself was sin and caused death. His conclusion was couched in the language of the conflict in Eden.[18]

Paul proclaimed the victory like this: 'The law of the Spirit of life in Christ Jesus has set me free from the law of sin and death' (Rom. 8.2). Now 'the Spirit of Life' is an unusual expression, but Ezekiel used it to describe the female figure whom he saw leaving the first temple. Although usually translated as a plural – 'living creatures' – most instances are

---

[18] Irenaeus knew this at the end of the second century CE. He spelled out the contrast between the Eden story and the New Testament story: Adam who sinned was contrasted with Christ who did not; Eve who listened to the snake was contrasted with Mary who listened to the voice of God. Irenaeus, *Demonstration* 32–33; *Against Heresies* V.21.

singular, 'the Living One/Life'. Ezekiel described 'the Spirit of Life' in the midst of the wheels, the circles of light (Ezek. 1.20; 10.17, translating literally), and this was the Lady leaving the first temple.[19] In other words, the way of the Spirit of Life, who was the Lady of the temple, had overcome the law which was the way of the serpent, just as Genesis foretold: there would be enmity and conflict between the seed of the woman and the seed of the snake, and the woman's seed would one day bruise the head of the snake, and the snake's seed would bruise her Son's heel (Gen. 3.15).

'Slave', *doulos*, is also used in Revelation where it is usually translated 'servant', as in 'servant of God' (Rev. 1.1–2). God gave Jesus the revelation 'to show his servants what must soon take place', and John his servant revealed them to others. The prophets were the servants of God (Rev. 10.7) who would be rewarded when the kingdom was established on earth (Rev. 11.18). In the final vision, the servants of the heavenly Servant – 'God-and-the-Lamb' – worship before his throne. The servants of God were in conflict with the followers of the beast who also wore the name of their god on their foreheads and had to worship his image (Rev. 13.13–17). This conflict underlies the debate in John 8, which introduces the devil into a debate about Abraham: 'If you were Abraham's children, you would do what Abraham did ... You are of your father the devil ...' (8.39, 44).

Jesus acknowledged that in a sense the Jews were the physical descendants, the seed, of Abraham. This was a sensitive issue at the time: the Second-Isaiah had reassured the exiles that they were not abandoned; they were the LORD's Servant Israel, the offspring of Abraham his friend (Isa. 41.8). In Genesis, compiled shortly after the time of the Second-Isaiah, the LORD promised Abraham numerous descendants who would be a blessing to all nations, after he had been willing to sacrifice Isaac (Gen. 22.15–18). The Jews affirmed this in the psalms of the second temple, where the everlasting covenant of the older temple – originally the covenant of creation – had become an eternal promise to give them the land:

> The covenant which he made with Abraham ...
> As an everlasting covenant,
> Saying, 'To you I will give the land of Canaan
> As your portion for an inheritance.'
> (Ps. 105.9–11)

---

[19] See my book *The Mother of the Lord*, vol. 1, London: T&T Clark, 2012, pp. 248–53.

## John 8

Being a child of Abraham was an important claim, as the Baptist's warning showed. When the Pharisees and Sadducees came to hear him, they were hoping to be safe from the expected day of judgement which proved to be the destruction of Jerusalem by the Romans. But they were children of the snake, said the Baptist, and their claim to be Abraham's children would not protect them. Only repentance would save them. 'You brood of vipers! Who warned you to flee from the wrath to come?' (Matt. 3.7–10).[20] According to John, Jesus described the Jews in the same way; they were the children of the devil (8.44). John emphasized this in his own teaching: 'He who commits sin is of the devil; for the devil has sinned from the beginning. The reason the Son of God appeared was to destroy the works of the devil' (1 John 3.8). The Jews retaliated that it was Jesus who was the son of the devil: 'You ... have a demon' (8.48).

The sonship was spiritual, not physical. The devil had appeared and sown evil seeds in the Man's field. His crop of good wheat became infested with weeds. At harvest time, the Man told his servants to gather the weeds and burn them, but to store the wheat in his barn. The wheat would then shine in the kingdom of God (Matt. 13.24–30, 36–43). The parable carried secret teaching: 'He who has ears, let him hear' (Matt. 13.43). In this detailed form, the parable is unique to Matthew, whose Gospel grew from a community of Hebrew Christians and therefore had details of particular interest for such people. Evil for them was the people in their midst who were the devil's seed. Those whom the evil ones converted were 'twice as much a child of hell' as those who had taught them (Matt. 23.15). The scribes and Pharisees, said Matthew's Jesus, have shut the kingdom of heaven and prevented people from entering (Matt. 23.13–15) – a reference to the ancient division marked by the emphases of the pro-Moses group. For the scribes, the Pharisees and the heirs of Deuteronomy, the secret things of heaven belonged to the LORD. They taught that his people had been given the law and that the law was all they needed; there was no place for teachers from heaven and their message (Deut. 29.29; 30.11–14). John knew this teaching about the weeds, but he knew it as Jesus' visions: a Man on a cloud, wearing a golden crown, who carried a sickle and reaped the harvest of the earth (Rev. 14.14–16); the song in heaven when the kingdom was established on earth, 'the time ...

---

[20] An early Christian text remembered that baptism and bearing the Name was thought by some to be protection against the impending destruction and war, *Clementine Recognitions* 1.39. This text was for centuries believed to be the work of Clement, bishop of Rome at the end of the first century, but is now thought to be later. Even with a later date, it shows how the earliest years of Christianity were remembered.

for destroying the destroyers of the earth' (Rev. 11.18); and the faithful standing in the kingdom, illuminated by the light of the LORD (Rev. 22.3–5). The scribes had accused Jesus of being an agent of the devil because he had power over demons (Mark 3.22), and Jesus replied that he was binding the Strong One – the literal meaning of 'Azazel', the leader of the fallen angels – so that he could plunder his house, meaning release his prisoners.[21] In Revelation, this was the vision of the angel from heaven who seized the ancient serpent, bound him, and sealed him in a pit (Rev. 20.1–3).

The Qumran *Melchizedek* text shows that this was the expected role of Melchi-Zedek: he would bring judgement on Belial and his spirits, releasing his own people from their power, and proclaiming to Zion the kingdom of God. He would fulfil Psalm 82.1: 'In the midst of the *ᵉlohîm* he holds judgement'; Isaiah 52.7: '... who proclaims salvation, who says to Zion "Your *ᵉlohîm reigns*"'; and he would bring comfort, a reference to Isaiah 61.2–3. This would be the great Jubilee, the final release. So too in the *Community Rule*, where the Master had to teach about the conflict between the children of light and the children of darkness. The Levites of the community had to recite all the rebellions and sins of Israel during the reign of Belial, and the priests interpreted their blessing – 'May the LORD make his face shine upon you' – as a prayer for life-giving wisdom and knowledge. God's Angel of Truth would teach the children of truth, and their rewards would be healing, great peace in a long life, fruitfulness, eternal joy, a crown of glory and a garment of majesty in unending light. They would be restored to the everlasting covenant and to all the glory of Adam.[22] The *Community Rule* describes the same conflict as John 8: the spiritual children of God (cf. 1.12–13) over against the children of the devil; the teacher who would show them the truth and set them free; and the heavenly multitudes in Revelation who were the redeemed in eternal light, clothed in their garments of glory.

Luke, who included several canticles in his nativity story, was a physician born in Antioch,[23] and gathered his material from Christian communities (Luke 1.1–2). The summaries of speeches in Acts are thought to be his own composition of something appropriate rather than eyewitness records, and so the canticles may be his too. On the other hand, they may have been composed by the early communities and

---

[21] See Isa. 1.31: when Zion was redeemed, the Strong One and his works would burn.
[22] *Community Rule*, 1QS II, III, IV.
[23] Eusebius, *History* 3.4.

simply incorporated by Luke. Either way, they reflect the situation *into which* Jesus was born, and they show that the Davidic kings and the promise to Abraham were linked in early Christian circles, or maybe in the 'Hebrew' communities where Christianity had its roots. Gabriel told Mary that her Child would be called the Son of God Most High, the first-temple title both for the LORD and for his image, the Davidic king (Luke 1.32–35); and Mary sang of the LORD who had remembered his promise to Abraham and had sent help to Israel (Luke 1.54–55). Zechariah sang when John the Baptist was born: the LORD had remembered his covenant with Abraham (the covenant to give his children the land, Gen. 15.18); he had visited and redeemed his people; he had raised up a Saviour from the house of David, who would deliver them from their enemies and from the power of those who hated them. His own newborn child would be the prophet preparing for the coming of the LORD. The Dawn (or the Branch) was coming (Luke 1.68–79).

The nativity canticles hoped for the restoration of the monarchy and the removal of the current rulers who were oppressing the children of Abraham: hoping that the proud would be scattered in the imagination of their hearts, the mighty put down from their thrones, and that they would be saved from their enemies and from the hands of those who hated them (Luke 1.51, 71). The enemies are usually assumed to be the Romans, but the hopes of those excluded centuries earlier by 'the Jews' when they established the second temple would have taken this form too. The same is true of the Beatitudes: the poor in spirit, those who mourn, the meek, those who hunger and thirst for righteousness, the merciful, the pure in heart, the peacemakers, those persecuted for the sake of righteousness could all have described the excluded Hebrews. The promised rewards also reflect their situation: they would have the kingdom of heaven, they would be comforted, be filled with righteousness after their thirst (for Wisdom?), they would find mercy, that is, *ḥesedh*, 'loving kindness', they would see God – a strong indication that these were first-temple aspirations – and they would be called sons of God, that is, angels. Above all, they would *inherit the land* (not the earth) (Matt. 5.3–12). The implied context of the Beatitudes strengthens the case that the nativity canticles expressed the hope of the Hebrews, and that the enemies who hated them were 'the Jews'.

All these echo the promises and prophecies of the Third-Isaiah who spoke for the excluded Hebrews in the early years of the second-temple period: priests would be restored to their rights and their land (Isa. 61.5–11); the chosen servants would eventually be blessed and given a new name in a new creation (Isa. 65.13–25); and the LORD would appear in the temple to bring judgement on his enemies, defined as *those who hate you and cast out their brothers* (Isa. 66.5-6). This was hoping for fulfilment of the ritual when the LORD, formerly represented by the Davidic king, would emerge from his temple dwelling as the angels bowed before him, to avenge the blood of his sons, to punish his enemies, and to heal the land of his people (Deut. 32.43). The Hebrew text here is damaged, but the longer (and original) form survived at Qumran. The lines missing from the shorter and later Hebrew text were a proof text for the Christians to show who Jesus was and what he came to do (Heb. 1.6). Healing the land and rescuing his people from their enemies was the hope expressed in the nativity canticles, and the oppressed people described themselves as the children of Abraham. Their enemies were 'the Jews'.

Jesus recognized that the Jews were the children of Abraham in one sense, but they did not have the family likeness in other respects because they were trying to kill *a man* who told them the truth he had heard from God (v. 40). This Greek word *anthrōpos*, without the article, was used in the Septuagint for Adam (e.g. LXX Ezek. 1.26; Hos. 6.7), but nowhere else in the New Testament for Jesus. It may be no more than the Semitic idiom for 'someone', but a reference to the unfallen Adam would fit this context better. Paul described Jesus as the unfallen Adam (1 Cor. 15.22, 45, 49), and Jesus himself, telling how he was tempted by Satan, implied that he was the Son of God who had not agreed to worship Satan, and so was the unfallen Adam.[24] He spoke as the image and likeness of God, whom he had seen, whereas the Jews did as they had *heard* from their father, an allusion to the statement in Deuteronomy that the LORD was not seen when the law was given and only a voice was heard (Deut. 4.12). 'The Man who has seen God' was the popular explanation of the name Israel,[25] and there may be an allusion to this too: Jesus spoke as the true Israel, despite the Jews' claim to be the children of Abraham.

Jesus argues that since the Jews are trying to kill the Adam sent from God, they are showing that their true father is the devil and that they are doing his will. The devil had vowed revenge after he refused to bow down to Adam and so he had been thrown from heaven.[26] By his lies in Eden, he had caused Adam to lose his angel state and to become mortal, subject to death. Adam had been warned that the fruit of the forbidden tree would bring death (Gen. 2.17) and so Jesus says: '[The devil] was a

---

[24] See above, pp. 125-6.
[25] *'îš*, 'man'; *rā'â*, 'sees'; *'ēl*, 'God'.
[26] See above, p. 122.

murderer from the beginning, and has nothing to do with the truth ... When he lies, he speaks according to his own nature, for he is a liar and the father of lies' (8.44). In Revelation, whose visions are the immediate background to John's Gospel, the devil was described as 'That ancient serpent, who is called the Devil and Satan, the deceiver of the whole world', and he was thrown from heaven (Rev. 12.9). The Jews' response to this accusation is to claim that God is their Father, and that it is Jesus who was born of fornication. Here, with characteristic irony, John also reveals that the claim of Jesus' virgin birth was known to 'the Jews' during the ministry. Jesus' response to the Jews' claim is that if they are children of God, they should recognize the one who came forth from God and they should understand what he is saying. 'The reason why you do not hear [the words of God] is that you are not of God' (8.47). This echoes the oracle to Isaiah, that those who spoke with unclean lips would hear and not understand, see and not perceive, fail to grasp with their minds, and so be unable to change their minds and be healed (Isa. 6.9-10).

Jesus even says that the Jews have never known God the Father whom they claim as their Father, an extraordinary accusation that echoes his words in 5.37, that the Jews did not read the Scriptures correctly. They had never known God the Father and so did not recognize his Son. Such an accusation again echoes the words of Jeremiah (cf. on 8.6-8) against the religious leaders of his own time who implemented Josiah's changes and were described as the 'blind' of Enoch's *Apocalypse of Weeks*. They precipitated the destruction of the first temple, because they had defiled the land and made it an abomination:

> The priests did not say 'Where is the LORD?'
> Those who handle the law did not know me;
> The shepherds transgressed against me;
> The prophets prophesied by Baal,
> And went after things that did not profit.
> (Jer. 2.8, my translation)

So too:

> How can you say, 'We are wise,
> And the law of the LORD is with us'?
> But, behold, the false pen of the scribes has made it into a lie.
> The wise men shall be put to shame,
> They shall be dismayed and taken;
> Lo, they have rejected the word of the LORD,
> And what wisdom is in them? (Jer. 8.8-9)

At the end of the section where John presents Jesus 'coming to his own' and being rejected, he has Jesus reflect on this theme of the Jews failing to understand because they had rejected wisdom (12.37–50). The theme of this whole section of John's Gospel is the fulfilment of Isaiah's warning that the punishment for abandoning Wisdom would be failure to understand.

The series of debates concludes with Jesus' claim to be the LORD. The devil brought death to Adam with his lies, Jesus is bringing life with his truth, and anyone who keeps his teaching will never die. Thus too Thomas' Jesus, who said: 'Whoever finds the interpretation of these sayings will not experience death.'[27] The Jews protest that Abraham and the prophets died, so who does Jesus think he is? Jesus replies: 'Your father Abraham rejoiced to see my day: he saw it and was glad' (8.56, AV). The Jews misunderstand again; Jesus could not possibly have been alive in the time of Abraham. But Jesus is claiming to be the LORD, the one who appeared to Abraham. This was how John understood Isaiah's vision; the prophet had seen the One who became incarnate in Jesus (Isa. 6.1–5; John 12.41). The Christians continued to read the Old Testament in the same way: Justin explained that the One who appeared to Abraham at Mamre was not God the Father, but that all the theophanies had been appearances of the Son, the Angel of his Father;[28] Irenaeus, the scourge of heretics, said that it was the Son of God in human form who had appeared to Abraham at Mamre;[29] Hippolytus said that the fiery man whom Daniel had seen (Dan. 10.4–9) was the Son, the LORD in human form;[30] Novatian said it was Christ who spoke to Hagar in the desert;[31] and for Eusebius, this was a major theme of his *Proof of the Gospel*.[32]

Jesus then says: 'Before Abraham was, I am' (v. 58), and the Jews react by stoning him. The temple complex was still being refurbished at that time, and there would have been loose stones lying around. Stoning was the punishment for blaspheming the Name, and so the Jews must have heard Jesus utter the Name, not the *yahweh* form but the *'ehyeh $^{a}$šer 'ehyeh* form, claiming to be the divine presence. Thomas' Jesus also claimed the Name:

---

[27] *Gospel of Thomas* 1.
[28] Justin, *Trypho* 56, 127.
[29] Irenaeus, *Demonstration* 44.
[30] Hippolytus, *On Daniel* 24.
[31] Novatian, *On the Trinity* 18.
[32] Set out in *Proof* I.5.

## John 8

Jesus said: 'I am not your Master. Because you have drunk, you have become intoxicated from the bubbling spring that I have measured out.' And [Jesus] took [Thomas] and withdrew and told him three things [three words?]. When Thomas returned to his companions, they asked him, 'What did he say to you?' Thomas said to them, 'If I tell you one of the things which he told me, you will pick up stones and throw them at me; a fire will come out of the stones and burn you up.'[33]

The same appears in the *Acts of Thomas*.[34]

[Thomas] began to say: 'Jesus, the hidden mystery that has been revealed to us, you are he who has shown us many mysteries; you are he who called me apart from my friends and spoke to me three words which set me on fire and I am not able to speak them to others ...'[35]

It is possible that the *Acts of Thomas* drew this saying from the Gospel, but the 'I am' sayings of John's Gospel do seem to be illuminated by this Thomas tradition that Jesus claimed the Name uniquely revealed at the burning bush (Exod. 3.14). The expanded form of the Name (as found in the Targums) was the version of the Sanctus known to the early Christians and recorded in Revelation 4.8.[36]

Jesus then hides himself and leaves the temple. He arrived in the temple privately (7.10) and he leaves in the same way.

---

[33] *Gospel of Thomas* 13.
[34] The *Acts of Thomas* is usually dated to the early years of the third century. It describes the missionary work of Thomas in India.
[35] *Acts of Thomas* 47.
[36] See above, p. 168.

# John 9

## 9.1–41: The waters of Siloam

Jesus heals a man blind from birth. The context implies that the man was waiting near the temple, possibly by the southern gate of the temple and so not far from the pool of Siloam. Jesus puts a clay of dust and spittle onto the man's eyes, and then tells him to wash it off in the pool of Siloam. The blind man can see. This happens on a Sabbath, and there is then a debate with the Pharisees about breaking the Sabbath law and the nature of blindness. In the synoptic Gospels, such a miracle was reported but not discussed. When Jesus healed the blind man/men near Jericho, the action of Jesus and the reaction of the healed man were reported (Matt. 20.29–34; Mark 10.46–52; Luke 18.35–43), but it was left to the reader or the preacher to work out the meaning of the miracle. John's style is different: he does not report everything he knows, but chooses a few signs and adds the ensuing debates to show 'that Jesus is the Christ, the Son of God, and that believing you may have life in his name' (20.31).

This miracle is usually reckoned as the sixth of the seven signs: changing water to wine, healing the boy in Capernaum, healing the man at Bethesda, feeding the 5,000, walking on the water, and here, opening eyes that had never been able to see. The seventh sign will be the raising of Lazarus. The Messiah was expected to perform miracles. A small fragment found at Qumran[1] gives a glimpse of that hope in the time of Jesus: the LORD would liberate captives, give sight to the blind and straighten the bent, a quotation from Psalm 146.7–8; he would heal the wounded, revive the dead and bring good news to the poor, the latter being a quotation from Isaiah 61.1. The work of the Messiah would be the work of the LORD because he was the LORD: he would call the righteous by name, and make the pious ($h^a sîdhîm$, those who practise $hesedh$, mercy) glorious on the throne of the eternal kingdom. This was the promise and the vision in Revelation: 'He who conquers, I will grant him to sit with me on my

---

[1] *Messianic Apocalypse*, 4Q521.

## John 9

throne, as I myself conquered and sat down with my Father on his throne' (Rev. 3.21); 'they shall be priests of God-and-Christ, and they shall reign with him a thousand years' (Rev. 20.6, my translation).

The miracle of the blind man and the miracle of the invalid man at Bethesda form a pair: both happen on a Sabbath, and both are by pools outside the city. There is no way of knowing if the pools were used by pilgrims for purification, but there have been important discoveries at both sites recently: Bethesda in 1964 and Siloam in 2005. It is possible that Bethesda to the north of the city and Siloam to the south were both huge purification pools. In both cases the circumstances of the healing were presented as symbolic: the man who had been an invalid for 38 years being symbolic of Israel's time in the wilderness, and here, the man who was born blind being symbolic of someone who had been born into the 'blindness' of those who had rejected Wisdom and the ways of the first temple. The Enochic *Apocalypse of Weeks* described the last years of the first temple thus:

> In the sixth week, all who live [in the temple] shall become blind,
> And the hearts/minds of all of them shall godlessly forsake Wisdom.
> In [the sixth week] a man shall ascend,
> And at its close the house of dominion shall be burned with fire,
> And the whole race of the chosen root shall be dispersed.

The previous section of this Apocalypse was quoted in the *Letter of Barnabas*, showing that it was known and used by the early Christians, and so almost certainly by Jesus.[2] Isaiah, the man who ascended, described the same events: he said that since Wisdom had been rejected by a people of unclean lips, the land would be devastated until the Lady returned. The people would live with what they had chosen: they would not be able to 'see', to 'hear' or to understand (Isa. 6.1–13). The contrast between first and second temples is here presented as restoring sight at the pool of Siloam, whose water came from the Lady's sacred Gihon spring.

In the time of Jesus, the area around Siloam was associated with the memory of Isaiah, according to the *Lives of the Prophets*, which is a collection of stories about the prophets compiled in Palestine about this time. It begins by explaining Isaiah's links to Siloam. He was martyred nearby in the time of Manasseh and was buried near the spring. People prayed at his tomb for the water to continue flowing. There were several

---

[2] *1 Enoch* 93.8.

tombs of the prophets in the area, some built or rebuilt recently by Herod, and Jesus spoke of them in his condemnation of the Jewish teachers: 'Woe to you! For you build the tombs of the prophets whom your fathers killed. So you are witnesses and consent to the deeds of your fathers; for they killed them and you build their tombs' (Luke 11.47–48). Jesus then described the prophets as the messengers of Wisdom whom the Jews had rejected, for whose blood they would be punished within a generation. Matthew added that these teachers were the children of the snake ('brood of vipers') and had Jesus lamenting over Jerusalem as he left the temple and walked towards the Mount of Olives, that is, through the area of the tombs:

> O Jerusalem, Jerusalem, killing the prophets and stoning those who are sent to you! How often would I have gathered your children together as a hen gathers her brood under her wings, and you would not. Behold, your house is forsaken [and desolate ...][3] (Matt. 23.37–38)

'Forsaken and desolate' echoes the prophecy of Isaiah to those who rejected Wisdom, and the promise to the city when it was rebuilt: 'You shall no longer be called "Forsaken", and your land shall no more be called "Desolate" ...' (Isa. 62.4, my translation, referring back to Isa. 6.11–12). Isaiah had presented the rejection of Wisdom as the rejection of the gentle waters of Siloam, and the Targum explained that the waters of Siloam meant the gentle rule of the Davidic kings. The prophet warned that rejecting the waters of Siloam meant that the land would be flooded by the river of the king of Assyria (Isa. 8.6–8). Rejecting the waters of Siloam meant rejecting Wisdom and the Davidic kings, the destruction of the temple and 'blindness', and rule by a foreign power.

The early Christians identified themselves closely with Isaiah. Matthew in particular shows frequently how Jesus fulfilled Isaiah's prophecies (e.g. Matt. 1.23; 2.23; 3.3, 17; 4.15; 5.4, 6, 35 and many more). This may have originated with Jesus himself, since Luke says that when he was in the synagogue at Nazareth, he claimed to be fulfilling Isaiah 61 (Luke 4.18–21). The Christians also expanded and preserved the *Ascension of Isaiah* – originally a collection of Jewish stories about Isaiah – and in the Christian version the prophet is a thinly veiled picture of James, the leader of the Jerusalem church.[4] The stories depict the same conflict as in John 8: the rulers in Jerusalem are the agents of Sammael Melkira, two names which

---

[3] Not found in some texts.

[4] Reconstructing from the *Clementine Recognitions* 1.66–70, Eusebius, *History of the Church* 2.23 and the *Ascension of Isaiah*, there is a clear parallel between the teachings attributed to

mean 'God of the Blind'[5] and 'King of Evil'. In the stories, Sammael is another name for Beliar/Belial. In the *Ascension*, the evil ruler in Jerusalem was named Manasseh, a man who had turned away from the LORD and from the words of Wisdom. In his reign, says the *Ascension*, Isaiah initially withdrew from Jerusalem to Bethlehem. There was corruption there too, and so he went to an (unnamed) mountain in a desert place where he lived with a community of prophets who believed in the ascension into heaven. 'Isaiah' later claimed that the disciples of Moses were false prophets, because they denied that anyone could see the LORD and still live. He, Isaiah, had seen the LORD and was still alive. The wicked ruler believed the words of Beliar, the agent of the disciples of Moses, and so Isaiah was killed.[6] James too was killed. Eusebius records that when the Jews had failed in their attempts to kill Paul because he claimed his rights as a Roman citizen, they turned against James, threw him from a temple parapet, and then stoned him.[7] The *Ascension* is an enigmatic text which says in effect that the Christians were the disciples of Isaiah and that their enemies were the disciples of Moses. John's Gospel could be read in that way too. The disciples of Moses were the enemies, and the original Isaiah's message of judgement on his people – that they would not see or understand (Isa. 6.9–10) – is the recurring theme of the Gospel.

The history of Jerusalem and the temple as told in Enoch's *Dream Visions* implies a similar situation and uses the same image of blindness. The story is told as an animal fable about the shepherd whose sheep become blind, and how the blind sheep became prey to wild animals. Not long after the temple was built, the sheep began to stray from their LORD:

> I saw that when they forsook the house of the LORD and his tower, they fell away entirely and their eyes were blinded … And I saw that [the LORD] forsook their house and their tower and gave them into the hand of lions, to tear and devour them, into the hand of all the wild beasts.

Then the LORD gave them over to the 70 shepherd angels, and finally the wild animals – foreign nations – devoured many of the sheep, burned the tower and demolished the house.[8] This was the destruction of the first temple.

---

James and the 'visions' of Isaiah in the *Ascension*. See my book *The Revelation of Jesus Christ*, Edinburgh: T&T Clark, 2000, pp. 192–5.

[5] *Hypostasis of the Archons*, CG II.4.87.
[6] *Ascension of Isaiah* 2.1–12.
[7] Eusebius, *History* 2.23.
[8] *1 Enoch* 89.51–67.

Who were the 70 shepherd angels who had care of Israel after the LORD had abandoned them? They were angels and not men because they all appeared together to receive the LORD's instructions about dealing with his sheep,[9] but then each in turn took charge of the same nation, so they were not the sons of God to whom were allotted the various peoples of the earth (Deut. 32.8). The shepherd angels each had charge of one period of time, and after 58 had held sway in turn, the lambs of the flock began to open their eyes.[10] There is Hebrew wordplay – shepherds, *ro'îm*, and guardians, *'ārîm* – but this would apply to both the angels of the nations and the angels of the eras. The 70 shepherds in some way replaced the LORD as the Shepherd, and *most likely they were the high priests*.

The sheep of Jerusalem lost their sight and were abandoned by their Shepherd long before the wild animals destroyed their temple. Enoch's *Dream Visions* imply that the sheep lost their sight when Jerusalem first became subject to a foreign ruler in the turbulent times of Isaiah, but this subjugation was punishment for losing their sight and not the cause of their blindness. Isaiah prophesied first in the reign of Uzziah, a powerful king who came into conflict with the priesthood, developed leprosy and was banished from the temple (2 Chron. 26.1–23). There are no details of this conflict, only that Uzziah wanted to burn incense in the temple and the priests would not allow it. In other words, Uzziah the Davidic king who was the LORD with his people (Immanuel, Isa. 8.8) was no longer allowed to be the high priest. Isaiah had lived through these events, and in his throne vision he saw the LORD as the King and recognized that he and his people had unclean lips – they had adopted wrong teaching. He was cleansed from this sin and told to give a warning to his people. The *Apocalypse of Weeks* has more information and says that at this time the priests lost their sight and abandoned Wisdom.[11] The wrong teaching must have been the result of abandoning Wisdom and the perception she gave.[12] The evidence of the two texts suggests that a different style of priesthood began, with no place for the Davidic/Melchi-Zedek priesthood, and the memory of this change and its implications prompted the writer of Hebrews to observe: 'For when there is a change in the priesthood, there is necessarily a change in the law as well' (Heb. 7.12). S/he was proclaiming Jesus as the restored Melchi-Zedek. With the rise of the

---

[9] *1 Enoch* 89.59.
[10] *1 Enoch* 90.5–6.
[11] *1 Enoch* 93.8.
[12] My book *The Mother of the Lord*, vol. 1, London: T&T Clark, 2012, pp. 87–108, has the details.

## John 9

Aaronite priesthood, Wisdom was rejected, together with the cult of the-Lord-and-King who was her Son. When Uzziah's grandson Ahaz was threatened by the kings of Israel and Syria (735–733 BCE), Isaiah gave him the sign of the Virgin's son to protect the city (Isa. 7.10–14), but Ahaz nevertheless paid tribute to the king of Assyria for protection and gave him silver and gold from the temple (2 Kings 16.5–9). Isaiah then gave his warning about rejecting the gentle waters of Siloam, the waters from the Virgin's spring, and the kingdom being flooded instead by the king of Assyria (Isa. 8.5–8).

The people offered themselves to a foreign ruler when they had abandoned Wisdom and, it seems, abandoned the royal priesthood. Enoch's 70 shepherd angels were the high priests who took charge of the temple when the Lord himself was no longer present in the Davidic king as the priest of God Most High.[13] The high-priest lists in the Hebrew Scriptures and elsewhere are far from complete, but there were 51 high priests in the second-temple period,[14] and the names of 11 can be recovered for the period from Uzziah to Jehozadak. If these 62 names that can be recovered were the 70 shepherds, and if Isaiah's throne vision marked the change in the temple and the loss of the Davidic high priesthood, this would explain why John emphasized this passage when reflecting on the Jews' rejection of Jesus (12.37–43). In John's scheme of presenting Jesus as the true Davidic king, he next (in chapter 10) has Jesus present himself as the Good Shepherd (angel) after sending a blind man to Siloam to have his eyes opened with water from the Virgin's spring.

When they first see the blind man, Jesus' disciples ask him why he is blind. Who has sinned? Neither the man nor his parents, says Jesus, implying that he rejected the Deuteronomists' view that the effect of sin and its punishment was inherited (e.g. 2 Kings 24.3–4, that Jerusalem was destroyed because of the sins of former kings). The man is blind, says Jesus, so that God can give him sight. He then 'anoints' the man's eyes. This was the symbolic opening of eyes that marked the return of Wisdom and the removal of blindness from those in the temple. It was light coming into darkness, and the clay that covered his eyes was the state of Adam when he was created from dust, before the Lord God made him a living being (Gen. 2.7). Just as the Lord God breathed life into Adam, so Wisdom gave sight to those whom she washed in the water that was 'sent'

---

[13] Melchi-Zedek was priest of God Most High (Gen. 14.18), and the Davidic king was a Melchi-Zedek priest (Ps. 110.4).

[14] J. C. VanderKam, *From Joshua to Caiaphas. High Priests after the Exile*, Minneapolis: Fortress Press, 2004, pp. 491–2.

from the spring. John emphasized that Siloam meant 'sent', and Ben Sira's poem about Wisdom depicts these waters as 'sent' by Wisdom, flowing out through her disciples to water her garden with teaching that shines like the dawn (Ben Sira 24.30–34). There was a similar sequence of events when Paul was baptized: Ananias was sent to the sightless Saul so that he could regain his sight and be filled with the Holy Spirit. 'Immediately something like scales fell from his eyes and he regained his sight. Then he rose and was baptized' (Acts 9.17–18). The Christians described baptism as their moment of illumination (Heb. 6.4; 10.32).[15]

When people notice that the blind man can see, they wonder if it is the same person or just someone like him. 'Some said, This is he: others said, He is like him: but he said, I am he' (9.9 AV). In these few words and their ambiguities, John introduces a major theme of the Gospel. The man saying 'I am he' is unlikely to be 'a purely secular use of the phrase'.[16] Once his eyes had been opened, the man claimed the Name. In temple terms, he had become one of the sons of God, an angel who bore the Name and so was a part of its presence. Paul, in language that is not easy to translate, described this as being 'conformed to the image of his Son, in order that he might be the first-born among many brethren' (Rom. 8.29). 'He is like him' (9.9) is another ambiguity, since those whose eyes were opened by anointing became the Image. The man saying 'I am he' points towards Jesus' high-priestly prayer in chapter 17, where he taught his disciples that they were one with him in the Name, sharing a unity such as he shared with the Father. 'Keep them in thy Name, which thou hast given me, that they may be one, even as we are one' (17.11, my translation).

John gives a glimpse of the consternation caused by the miracle and possibly by the use of the Name, which presumably sums up the general reaction to Jesus' miracles and claims. Some Pharisees consider this a matter of breaking the law since the man was healed on a Sabbath; others say that a sinner cannot do such things; the Jews say that the man cannot really have been blind; the formerly blind man says that Jesus is a prophet; and his parents do not want to get involved because they are afraid of the Jews. According to their law, a prophet or wonderworker who taught anything other than the ways of Deuteronomy had to be killed: 'That prophet or that dreamer of dreams shall be put to death, because he has

---

[15] Justin, *Apology* 1.61.
[16] R. E. Brown, *The Gospel According to John I—XII*, Anchor Bible 29, London: Geoffrey Chapman, 1971, p. 373.

## John 9

taught rebellion ... So you shall purge the evil from the midst of you' (Deut. 13.5).

The man's parents feared being cast out of the synagogue if they said that Jesus was the Messiah. John mentions this elsewhere too: many of the authorities believed in Jesus, but were afraid of the Pharisees (12.42). Luke knew that many of the priests became Christians (Acts 6.7). The persecution may be a detail from later years added to the story as it was told, at a time when Christians in Jerusalem were being driven out and killed by the Jews, but Jesus did warn that this would happen before the temple was destroyed, that they would be put on trial and their own families would kill them (16.2; also Mark 13.9-13 and parallels). In Revelation, the visions show these early persecutions: there were martyrs of the fifth seal (Rev. 6.9-10) who died before the 60s, since the additions to the vision of the sixth seal represented Nero's persecution in 65-6 CE (Rev. 7.13-14); and there is the dragon who pursued the Lady into the wilderness where she was kept safe, and who then went to attack her other children after her Son had been taken up to the throne of God (Rev. 12.17). These children were the *keepers* of the commandments of God, and in Hebrew that name would have been *nôṣrîm*. Paul was identified as a leader of the sect of the Nazorenes, *nazōraioi*, not Nazarenes (Acts 24.5).[17] Revelation described the great harlot, the corrupted second temple, and said she was 'drunk with the blood of the saints and the blood of the martyrs of Jesus' (Rev. 17.6).

The few stories that survive from the early Jerusalem church show that it was 'the Jews' who led the persecution: the high priests and the Sadducees had the apostles imprisoned and wanted to kill them (Acts 5.17-18, 33); Saul, with the authority of the high priest, organized the stoning of Stephen and the persecution that followed (Acts 8.1-3; 9.1-2); Herod killed James bar Zebedee, 'and when he saw that it pleased the Jews' he imprisoned Peter too (Acts 12.1-3). When Paul wrote to the church in Corinth (1 Cor. 12.3, sent about 55 CE), he contrasted those who cursed Jesus and those who declared 'Jesus is the LORD', that is, 'Jesus is Yahweh'. Presumably this curse was an early version of the so-called blessing which prayed that *nôṣrîm* and Minim[18] would be blotted from the book of the living. It is not known when 'the Jews' began to persecute

---

[17] Despite the customary translation.
[18] Almost certainly meaning Christians and heretics. Babylonian Talmud *Berakhoth* 28b says this was added to the Eighteen Benedictions after the council of Jamnia, about 90 CE. See also W. Horbury, 'The Benediction of the Minim and the Early Jewish-Christian Controversy', *Journal of Theological Studies* 33.1 (1982), pp. 19-61.

the followers of Jesus, but the disciples assembled behind closed doors on the evening of Easter Day 'for fear of the Jews' (20.19), and so it may well be that even during Jesus' ministry, the parents of the man whom Jesus healed had good reason to fear 'the Jews'.

When his parents refuse to discuss the matter, the Jews return to the man himself, who by that time regards himself as a disciple. They demand of him: 'Give God the praise' (v. 24), which was a solemn guarantee before an oath (cf. Josh. 7.19; 1 Esdr. 9.8) but here also used in irony: by telling how he had been healed, the man was giving glory to God. The man cannot agree with the Jews that Jesus is a sinner, but he can testify to the miracle. He asks if they *too* want to become disciples since they are so keen to hear the story again. Again there is the contrast: the man is a disciple of Jesus; the Jews are disciples of Moses (v. 28). They know that God has spoken to Moses, but – irony again – they do not know whence Jesus comes. The man becomes bold and asks the Jews how there can be any doubt that Jesus comes from God, if he has opened his eyes. 'They answered him, "... would you teach us?" [and] cast him out' (v. 34). It is not clear whether the man is simply driven away from the scene of the miracle, or if this is a formal exclusion from the synagogue.

Jesus finds the man again, having heard that he was 'cast out', which suggests a more formal process than simply being forced to leave a particular place. Jesus asks him, 'Do you believe in the Son of Man?' which could mean: 'Are you one of those who believe in the Man, the Messiah of the first temple?' or it could mean: 'Do you trust me?' The man's reply is equally ambiguous: 'Who is he, that I may believe in him?' This could mean that he has never heard of the Man, or that he has heard of him and wants to know who he (presently) is. Since the healed man worships Jesus when he reveals that he is the Man, it seems that the healed man knew about the Man, but not who he presently was. So too with the Baptist: he knew he would be shown the Son of God, but until he saw the sign, he did not know which person he was (1.33–34). The man's eyes are opened and he sees the presence of the LORD, the fulfilment of the high priests' blessing.

This is the only time in the Gospel when John says Jesus was worshipped, although Matthew often noted this reaction to Jesus: the magi came to worship the King of the Jews (Matt. 2.2); a leper worshipped him (Matt. 8.2); the men in the boat worshipped Jesus after he had calmed the storm (Matt. 14.33); the Canaanite woman worshipped Jesus (Matt. 15.25); and the disciples worshipped him when he met them in Galilee after the resurrection (Matt. 28.9). In each case the verb is *proskuneō*, which can

## John 9

mean no more than 'bow', but the same word was used to describe the worship of the-LORD-the-King at Solomon's enthronement (LXX 1 Chron. 29.20), and to describe the people's reception of the high priest when he emerged from the temple in his glorious vestments.[19] 'They fell to the ground upon their faces, to worship their LORD, the Almighty Most High' (Ben Sira 50.17). The text is not entirely clear, but it seems that the people worshipped the high priest, who for them 'was' the LORD, and if he was coming from the holy of holies – 'the house of the veil' – the occasion would have been the Day of Atonement. This is what a foreign visitor said he had seen in the temple, presumably looking down into the temple courts from the nearby citadel: 'The Jews fall to the ground and worship as the high priest explains to them the commandments ...' because the high priest was for them an angel of God.[20] Aristeas described the same scene when he visited Jerusalem.[21] The reaction of the formerly blind man should be understood in this context; he saw the presence of the LORD.

The man bows down/worships, and immediately Jesus speaks of bringing the judgement, *krima*, a sequence already used in the discourse with Nicodemus (3.16–21). The context in both instances is Deuteronomy 32.43, the LORD coming to complete the great atonement, and the angels bowing down to him (in the Greek, the verb is *proskuneō* again) as he emerges to bring judgement on those who have shed the blood of his servants and to heal the land of his people. This scene underlies Isaiah's prophecy of the Servant who would bring forth justice, *krisis*, to the nations, establish justice, *krisis*, in the land and open the eyes of the blind (Isa. 42.1, 4, 7). It also appears as the vision in Revelation 11.15–18, where the seventh angel blows the last trumpet and the elders in heaven worship, *proskuneō*, as the LORD God Almighty establishes his kingdom, rewards his servants, and judges the destroyers of the earth. It is not easy to distinguish between *krima* and *krisis* in John's Gospel, as both seem to represent the Hebrew *mišpat*. The word used here (9.39) is also used for the judgement of the great harlot (Rev. 17.1; 18.20) and for the power of judgement given to those seated on the thrones in heaven (Rev. 20.4). The language of the judgement is drawn from Deuteronomy 32.43: the harlot

---

[19] Ben Sira 50.5, my literal translation: 'When he came out from the house of the veil', which could mean that the high priest was coming from the holy of holies.

[20] Hecataeus, quoted in Diodorus of Sicily, XL.3.5–6. This famous passage describes the temple in about 300 BCE, and shows that the Jews did 'worship' a human being if he was the high priest, because the high priest was the LORD with his people.

[21] *Letter of Aristeas* 100: 'We climbed the neighbouring citadel and viewed [the temple courts] from there.'

is drunk with the blood of the saints and martyrs (Rev. 17.6) and God 'has avenged on her the blood of his servants' (Rev. 19.2).

The Pharisees would have considered themselves the people who brought *mišpat* to the land, because they were the custodians of the law and defined its correct interpretation. When Jesus claims: 'For judgement I came into this world, that those who do not see may see, and that those who see may become blind' they recognize themselves in this threat and ask: 'Are we also blind?' This must have been a major issue between Jesus and the Pharisees, as can be seen in the synoptic Gospels. Matthew in particular, writing for Christians with Jewish roots, has Jesus condemn the Pharisees' detailed interpretations of the law, especially in matters of ritual and purity. They transgressed the commandments for the sake of tradition and so were like blind men, a tree that the heavenly Father had not planted[22] (Matt. 15.3, 13). They were blind guides who had shut the kingdom of heaven and would not allow people to enter; they adorned the tombs of the prophets they had killed; they were the children of the snake[23] (Matt. 23.13, 16, 31, 33). The Pharisees are guilty, says Jesus, because they claim they can see.

All this, including the image of blindness, can be traced back not only to Enoch's *Apocalypse of Weeks*, but also to the Third-Isaiah, speaking for those whom 'the Jews' excluded from the second temple. The prophet described the leaders of the returned exiles as blind watchmen who lacked knowledge, and as shepherds without understanding who had turned to their own way (Isa. 56.10–11). He condemned the priesthood and those who had built the second temple. The sequence in Isaiah 66 sums up his message:

> What is the house which you would build for me?     (v. 1)

> He who slaughters an ox is like him who kills a man;
> He who sacrifices a lamb, like him who breaks a dog's neck ... (v. 3)

> Your brethren who hate you
> And cast you out for the sake of my Name
> Have said 'Let the LORD be glorified, that we may see your joy'
> But it is they who shall be put to shame.     (v. 5, my translation)

> As soon as Zion was in labour she brought forth her sons.     (v. 8)

> It shall be known that the hand of the LORD is with his servants,
> And his indignation is against his enemies.     (v. 14)

---

[22] The law is again described as the tree that the Father did not plant.
[23] The snake tempted Adam and Eve with the fruit of the tree that the Father did not plant.

## John 9

Those who offered the sacrifices were no better than murderers or pagan priests (v. 3); people were being cast out of the community by their brothers for the sake of the Name, and 'Let the Lord be glorified' is exactly what the Jews said to the man who had been blind, before they cast him out (v. 24). Zion, the Lady, was giving birth again to sons when the eyes of a blind man were anointed and opened, and there was a vision of the Woman clothed with the sun giving birth first to the king and then to her other children (Rev. 12.1–6, 17).

Ezekiel, the prophet of the exile, also condemned the shepherds who had failed to care for Israel. They had not tended the sick and the crippled; they had not rescued those who strayed. Presumably the evil shepherds were the same as the Third-Isaiah's blind watchmen without knowledge, and he too warned of the Lord's judgement. Ezekiel knew that the people had become sheep without a shepherd, and the shepherds had not searched for them (Ezek. 34.7). This became the teaching of Jesus: the lost sheep (Luke 15.4–7); and the sheep without a shepherd whom Jesus taught (Mark 6.34). Ezekiel prophesied that the Lord himself would come to search for his sheep and bring them home. He would bring them judgement, *mišpat*, judging between the sheep and the goats (Ezek. 34.4, 11–12, 16, 17, translating literally; cf. Jesus' parable, Matt. 25.31–46). Then the Lord would set up his servant David to be their ruler, and he would restore the covenant of peace that renewed the whole creation (Ezek. 34.23–31). In the *Dream Visions*, Enoch saw the Lord's judgement: first he cast the evil shepherds into the fiery abyss and then their followers, the blinded sheep. Finally, the temple was taken away, and the Lord of the sheep established a great new temple for all his sheep.[24] The sequence of ideas and images in this section of John's Gospel points to the ancient images of the day of judgement: seeing the Lord, worshipping him as he emerges to restore sight, to heal the land of his people and to restore the covenant of peace/the everlasting covenant, to bring judgement on the evil shepherds and to restore someone from the house of David to be his servant and his people's ruler. The same themes continue in chapter 10, after an artificial chapter division in the text introduced long after John's Gospel was written.

---

[24] *1 Enoch* 90.24–26, 28–29.

# John 10

## 10.1–6: The shepherd

After giving sight to the blind man, and still among the people in the days after Tabernacles (7.37 was the last day of the feast), John has Jesus say more about the shepherds. As with the earlier reports of Jesus' teaching, so too John gives here only the summary of what was said. The ideas are tightly packed and must represent a considerable body of teaching and discussion, in this case about Ezekiel's prophecies of the restored temple, the return of the Davidic kings, and the renewal of the covenant of peace/ the eternal covenant/the everlasting covenant. The entire section is a tapestry of temple texts, many drawn from the Psalms but also from the Enoch tradition where evil shepherds and blindness characterize the second-temple period.

In the first temple, the LORD had been the Shepherd of his people. 'The LORD is my shepherd' sang David (Ps. 23.1), and the people called on 'the Shepherd of Israel ... enthroned upon the cherubim' to save and restore them: 'Restore us, O God; let thy face/presence shine, that we may be saved' (Ps. 80.1–3, my translation). When Isaiah gave Ahaz the prophecy that the Virgin would bear a son and Jerusalem would be saved from her enemies (Isa. 7.10–16), his contemporary Micah prophesied that an unnamed woman was about to give birth to a son who would 'stand and feed his flock in the strength of the LORD, with the majesty of the Name of the LORD his God' (Mic. 5.3–4, my translation). Then his people would be safe. The Second-Isaiah described a mighty shepherd bringing his flock home from exile (Isa. 40.10–11). In the first temple and in the Isaiah tradition, the shepherd had been a heavenly king whose presence shone on his people and kept them safe. Jeremiah – or maybe a later disciple or editor – looked forward to a time when the LORD himself would return as the Great Shepherd to rescue the flock that the evil shepherds had scattered. The Davidic king would return:

## John 10

> Behold, the days are coming, says the LORD, when I will raise up for David a righteous Branch,[1] and he shall reign as king, and deal wisely, and shall execute justice and righteousness in the land. In his days Judah will be saved, and Israel will dwell securely. And this is the name by which he will be called: 'The LORD is our Righteousness' [or 'our Righteous One'].
>
> (Jer. 23.5–6)

Jeremiah 33.14–16 is almost identical. The Shepherd, the Righteous One, and the Branch were all titles for the LORD when he manifested himself in the Davidic king.

Jesus says that the sheep know the voice of their own shepherd when he calls them from the communal sheepfold, and they follow him (v. 3). This implies that the flock in Jerusalem was mixed, and the shepherd would call out those who belonged to him. Similar are the parable of the wheat and the weeds growing together until the harvest (Matt. 13.24–30), or the parable of the flock of sheep and goats being separated when the Son of Man comes in judgement (Matt. 25.31–46). Jesus knew there were weeds and goats among those listening to him. So too he spoke about sheep without a shepherd (Mark 6.34) and a lost sheep (Luke 15.4–5).

It is likely that many of the parables acquired new meanings as they were retold in the various communities, the Good Samaritan being an obvious example of a story that was originally about the priorities of the priests and Levites, but became a story about being a good neighbour. The Gospels themselves imply that there was more than one meaning to the parables, and so only those with the gifts of Wisdom would understand (Matt. 13.10–17), especially given the temple context of much of the teaching. Many people did not understand if Jesus used a proverb, *paroimia* (v. 6), just as they did not understand if he taught with a parable, *parabolē* (Mark 4.12). Both words translate the Hebrew *māšāl*,[2] the teaching form used by the wise in ancient Israel. Solomon was famed for 'songs and proverbs, *paroimiai*, and parables, *parabolai*, and interpretations' (Ben Sira 47.17). Enoch's three lengthy descriptions of the holy of holies and the judgement[3] are also called parables and defined as visions of wisdom.[4] The visions, parables and proverbs of Jesus were all in the style of one of Wisdom's teachers.

---

[1] 'Branch', *ṣemaḥ*, became in the Greek *anatolē*, which can mean either a shoot/branch, or the east/dawn/rising star.
[2] Proverbs 1.1, 6 has Hebrew *māšāl* in each case, but the Greek has *paroimia* in v. 1 and *parabolē* in v. 6.
[3] *1 Enoch* 37—71.
[4] *1 Enoch* 37.5.

## 10.7: The door of the sheep

Jesus then describes himself as the only door of the sheep, meaning the only access to the true flock and the true temple which was their home. This alludes to several psalms and also to Ezekiel's visions of the restored temple. There is Psalm 24, which first asks who is worthy to ascend the holy hill and enter the holy place, and then commands the gates and ancient doors (or doors of eternity) to open so that the LORD of Hosts, the King of Glory, can enter. There is no more detail, but the lines do suggest a procession into the temple, and the question and answer form of verses 7–10 suggests guardians of the gates and those asking for admission, perhaps a liturgy:

> 'Who is the King of Glory?'
> *The* LORD *strong and mighty,*
> *The* LORD *mighty in battle!* ...
> 'Who is this King of Glory?'
> *The* LORD *of Hosts,*
> *He is the King of Glory.*
>                         (Ps. 24.8, 10)

Psalm 68 depicts such a procession: 'My God, my King', going with singers and musicians into the holy place (Ps. 68.24–25).

> Open to me the gates of righteousness,
> That I may enter through them and give thanks to the LORD.
> This is the gate of the LORD;
> The righteous [ones] shall enter through it.   (Ps. 118.19–20)

'Righteousness' is written in the same way as Zadok, *ṣdq*, and Jesus may have understood the line as 'the gates of Zadok', the title given to the priest-kings[5] and also to Jesus, but translated in Acts 3 as 'the Righteous One' (Acts 3.14). 'The gates of Zadok' and 'the gate of the LORD' would then be parallel descriptions of a city entrance; a double gate of which one was the gate of the LORD, which the righteous people (also) entered in/with the Name of the LORD (Ps. 118.26), that is, *with* the Name (the person who bore it) or perhaps wearing the Name themselves. The righteous came through the gate of the LORD to find safety: 'Save us ... O LORD' (Ps. 118.25). This is the vision of Revelation 22.3–4, where the servants wearing the Name have all entered the temple/city to stand before the throne, and Psalm 118 is the key text for Palm Sunday in all the

---
[5] See above, p. 83.

## John 10

canonical Gospels. None of these psalms says which gate received the LORD of Hosts, the King of Glory, the God and King of his people.

Ezekiel's vision at New Year in 572 BCE, however, describes the glory of the LORD returning through the eastern gate. He saw the temple that would be restored in the future, and the glory returning to it (Ezek. 43.1–5). In his earlier vision he saw 'the appearance of the likeness of the glory of the LORD' on the chariot throne, leaving the temple and going to Babylon through the eastern gate (Ezek. 1.4–28; 10.1—11.22). He said he saw it return in the same way, and the earth shone. This was a sunrise vision on the tenth day of the first month (Ezek. 40.1), and whether he reckoned by the old calendar or the new, this was a vision at or near the equinox, in other words, at Passover or at the autumn festival.[6] His angel guide showed him the measurements of the true temple and said that the eastern outer gate of the temple, through which the LORD had returned, had to remain closed because the glory of the LORD had passed through it (Ezek. 44.1–2). Then the angel[7] told Ezekiel who would be allowed to enter the holy place and who would be excluded. The faithful sons of Zadok (wordplay on 'the righteous') would be allowed to serve in the restored temple and enter the holy place (Ezek. 44.15-16). The *Damascus Document* describes such a community, people who saw themselves as the faithful sons of Zadok, the remnant left when the LORD hid his face from his temple. Jerusalem was destroyed in 586 BCE, but the age of wrath which the *Damascus Document* describes had begun many years before this, as the Enochic histories show. It probably began when the priesthood changed in the time of Uzziah. According to the *Damascus Document*, there was a faithful remnant in those turbulent times who became custodians of 'the hidden things in which all Israel had gone astray'. They were promised eternal life and all the glory that Adam, the Man, had lost.[8]

The eastern gate was significant. The Mishnah has a whole tractate recording the plan and measurements of the temple, and it says there was one eastern gate to the temple area and a corresponding gate into the temple court itself, the Nicanor gate.[9] The outer gate, the Great Gate, was formed of two doors, and the southern door of the two was never opened because of Ezekiel's prophecy.[10] In the time of Jesus, nine of the ten temple gates were covered with silver and gold, but the tenth, the Nicanor

---

[6] See below, p. 542.
[7] Or possibly it was the LORD who spoke; the text is not clear.
[8] *Damascus Document*, CD I, III.
[9] Mishnah *Middoth* 1.3, 4.
[10] Mishnah *Middoth* 4.2; *Tamid* 3.7.

gate, was covered in Corinthian bronze which was far more expensive than gold or silver.[11] The effect must have been dazzling. The eastern side of the temple complex was set on an artificially constructed platform that towered over the Kidron valley, what Micah called 'the tower of the flock, the hill of the daughter of Zion' (Mic. 4.8). Josephus described it: 'Where the foundations were lowest, they built up from a depth of 300 cubits [about 150 metres]; at some spots this figure was exceeded.'[12] The temple that Jesus knew would have looked like a tower when approached from the east, its great inner gate covered in Corinthian bronze. The temple itself was covered on all sides with plates of gold, and 'the sun was no sooner up than it radiated so fiery a flash that persons straining to look at it were compelled to avert their eyes, as from the solar rays'.[13]

A curious Christian text,[14] which was condemned as a forgery and not known before the end of the fourth century, shows how this image of the golden gate was remembered. Paul was being taken round heaven by an angel guide, to see the place of the righteous:

> And he said to me: 'Follow me again, and I will take thee and show thee the places of the righteous'. And I followed the angel, and he took me up into the third heaven, and set me before the door of a gate; and I looked on it and saw, and the gate was of gold, and there were two pillars of gold full of golden letters; and the angel turned again to me and said: Blessed art thou if thou enterest by these gates, for it is not permitted to any to enter save only to those who have kept goodness and pureness of their bodies in all things [cf. Ps. 24.3].[15]

A golden gate in a tower would not normally be the way into a sheepfold, but imagery in *1 Enoch* links the temple, the tower and the flock: the tower was an image for the holy of holies, and those who deserted the tower were sheep who had lost their sight and fallen into the power of violent foreign rulers. This extract describes the first temple and the beginning of the age of wrath:

> A lofty and great tower was built on the house for the Lord of the sheep ... and the Lord of the sheep stood on that tower.
> I saw that when they forsook the house of the Lord and his tower, they fell away entirely and their eyes were blinded ...

---

[11] Josephus, *War* 5.201.
[12] Josephus, *War* 5.188.
[13] Josephus, *War* 5.222.
[14] *Apocalypse of Paul*, found in M. R. James, *The Apocryphal New Testament*, Oxford: Clarendon Press, (1924) 1980, pp. 525–55. His translation is based on the Latin text.
[15] James, *Apocryphal New Testament*, p. 535.

## John 10

And I saw that he forsook their house and their tower and gave them all into the hand of the lions, to tear and devour them, into the hand of all the wild beasts.[16]

The era of the 70 shepherds followed, and after the great judgement on the 70 shepherds and the blinded sheep who followed them, the angels took away their new temple (the second temple), and the Lord of the sheep brought a new and larger one in its place. All the sheep were gathered into the new temple, even those who had been destroyed and dispersed – the martyrs and the exiles – and their eyes were opened.[17]

Jesus claims to be the gate/door of the sheepfold which had been closed: 'I AM the gate/door.' He entered through the gate and so presumably was the prince, the shepherd of the sheep (v. 2; cf. Ezek. 44.1-2), and so the glory of the LORD returning. Those who came before him to lead the flock did not come through the gate, which was closed; they came in by another route and so were thieves and robbers. Those who come to join the flock through him, he says, will be safe and find pasture. Texts both Jewish and Christian confirm that the images of the gate/door and the conflict between the good and evil shepherds were about the high priests and access to the holy city, to the temple and to its teaching. This is the context for Luke's Jesus when he condemned the Pharisees: 'Woe to you lawyers! For you have taken away the key of knowledge; you did not enter yourselves, and you hindered those who were entering' (Luke 11.52). Clement of Alexandria would later use this image to distinguish true teachers from heretics: '[False teachers] neither themselves enter into the kingdom of heaven, nor permit those whom they have deluded to attain the truth. But not having the key that allows them to enter, but a false or counterfeit key ... they burst through the side door and dig secretly through the wall of the Church ...'[18]

Jesus was the door; he also held the key to the door, as John wrote to the church at Philadelphia: 'The words of the Holy One, the True One,[19] who has the key of David, who opens and no one shall shut, who shuts and no one opens.' The LORD had set before his followers an open door, and those who conquered would be given the LORD's own new Name (Rev. 3.7, 8, 13, my translation). The faithful, then, would have access to the holy of holies like the high priest, and they would also wear the Name.

---

[16] *1 Enoch* 89.50, 54, 56.
[17] *1 Enoch* 90.28-36.
[18] Clement, *Miscellanies* 7.17.
[19] Cf. Rev. 19.11, where this is one of the names of the Word who rides out from heaven.

## Temple Theology in John's Gospel

Ignatius of Antioch, writing to the same church about 100 CE, said that the door to the Father was their own high priest who had access to the holy of holies and was entrusted with the secret knowledge that this access represented. 'He is the doorway to the Father, and it is by him that Abraham, Isaac and Jacob and the prophets go in, no less than the Apostles and the whole Church, for all these have their part in God's unity.'[20] The unity was the state represented by the holy of holies, and the unity included the patriarchs and the prophets but not, apparently, Moses.

When the risen LORD described himself as the one 'who has the key of David, who opens and no one shall shut, who shuts and no one opens', he was quoting from Isaiah 22.22. This was originally a condemnation of Shebna, a corrupt palace official, warning that he would be removed and replaced by a true servant of the LORD.[21] In the Targum, however, the text was expanded and became a description of the Servant:

> I will put the key of the sanctuary and the government of the house of David into his hand; he shall open and there shall be none to shut; and he shall shut and there shall be none to open.

The new Servant, said the Targum – presumably with a contemporary relevance – would be the only way to enter the temple; he would be a faithful ruler in his father's house (the house of David), and the priests and Levites would be secure. Jesus may not have known these precise words in the Targum, but he could well have known that way of understanding the Shebna text and 'the key of David'.

Hermas, a Christian prophet in Rome and a contemporary of Ignatius of Antioch, saw a new tower being built, and the only way into it was through the Son of God. Even the stones for the tower had to enter through the gate, and only those with his Name could enter the kingdom.[22] These were the living stones of the spiritual house and holy priesthood (cf. 1 Pet. 2.5), and for Hermas all the Christians were collectively the high priest, and 'in Christ' they entered the holy of holies. This was the final vision in Revelation again: all the servants with the Name on their foreheads standing before the throne and seeing the face of the LORD.

When Jesus describes himself as the shepherd who enters by the door (vv. 7–9), he is combining the images used by the Second-Isaiah and

---

[20] Ignatius, *To the Philadelphians* 9.
[21] Was he perhaps involved in barring Uzziah from the temple, since he held the keys?
[22] *Shepherd of Hermas*, Similitude 9.12.

## John 10

Ezekiel to describe the LORD returning to the temple. The Second-Isaiah said: 'The glory of the LORD shall be revealed, and all flesh shall see it together ... Behold the Lord GOD comes with might ... like a shepherd ...' (Isa. 40.5, 10, 11). This followed immediately after the words used by the Baptist: 'Prepare the way of the LORD, make straight in the desert a highway for our God.' Ezekiel said: 'The glory of the LORD entered the temple by the gate facing east ...' – presumably from the highway in the desert (Ezek. 43.4), and presumably too the LORD returned as the Shepherd.

## 10.8–18: The evil shepherds

The other shepherds, Jesus says, did not enter through the door, and so were thieves and robbers (v. 8). This is not just a reference to the rapacious evil shepherds that the Third-Isaiah and Ezekiel had condemned five centuries earlier (Isa. 56.10–12; Ezek. 34.2–3). The Qumran community described their contemporaries in the same way: 'the last priests of Jerusalem who amass money and wealth by plundering the peoples', and 'the Wicked Priest who robbed the poor of their possessions'.[23] The *Psalms of Solomon* bewailed the sons of Jerusalem who defiled the sanctuary of the Lord.[24] The *Testament of Levi*,[25] citing Enoch texts that have not survived, has Levi predict that some of his descendants will become corrupt and bring a curse on their people. These corrupt priests would destroy the light of the law, plunder the offerings, deride the sacred things and live dissolute lives. As in Enoch's *Apocalypse of Weeks* which described an apostate generation in the seventh week, that is, in the second-temple era, the *Testament of Levi* 'predicted' priests who were 'idolaters, adulterers, money lovers, arrogant, lawless, voluptuaries, pederasts and those who practise bestiality'.[26] Then the LORD would raise up a new priest, whose star would rise in heaven like a king:

> The heavens shall be opened
> And from the temple of glory, sanctification shall come upon him
> With a fatherly voice as from Abraham to Isaac.

---

[23] *Commentary on Habakkuk*, 1QpHab IX, XII.
[24] *Psalms of Solomon* 2.3.
[25] One of the *Testaments of the Twelve Patriarchs*, a text with several similarities to the writings of John. There may be Christian additions to the text, or these may be yet more evidence of their similarity to the Christianity.
[26] *Testament of Levi* 17.11.

> And the glory of the Most High shall burst forth upon him
> And the spirit of understanding and sanctification shall rest upon him
> ...
> He shall open the gates of paradise;
> He shall remove the sword that has threatened since Adam,
> And he will grant to the saints to eat from the tree of life.[27]

The list of those excluded from the heavenly temple-city in Revelation must have had such priests in mind (Rev. 21.8; 22.15).

Josephus gave an eyewitness account of their rapacity in the time of Ishmael ben Fabi, high priest from 59 to 61 CE. The high priests and the leaders of Jerusalem were in open conflict with each other, he wrote, hurling stones as well as abuse, and the high priests used to send their servants to seize the tithes due to lesser priests so that they starved to death. The gangs went to the threshing floor and beat any who would not hand over the grain.[28] Josephus only mentions lesser priests who were robbed, but the New Testament says that the Christians were robbed. They considered themselves to be high priests 'in Christ', but were they recognized by others as priests? There is no way of knowing how literally their temple imagery was understood. James and John were both known as high priests (to whom?) and wore the insignia of a high priest;[29] Hebrews addressed the holy brethren who looked to Jesus as their high priest (Heb. 3.1), and who had suffered public abuse and robbery after they had 'been enlightened' (Heb. 10.32–34). James condemned the rich (the high priests?) who lived in luxury and yet did not pay their workers: 'Behold, the wages of the labourers who mowed your fields, which you kept back by fraud, cry out; and the cries of the harvesters have reached the ears of the Lord of hosts' (Jas. 5.4). And the Jews themselves looked back with bitterness on the evil high priests of the last years of Herod's temple.

> Woe is me because of the house of Boethus, because of their staves ...
> Woe is me because of the house of Hanin, woe because of their whisperings ...
> Woe is me because of the house of Kathros, because of their pens ...
> Woe is me because of the house of Ishmael ben Fabi, because of their fists; for they are high priests and their sons are [temple] treasurers and their sons-in-law are trustees and their servants beat the people with staves ...[30]

---

[27] *Testament of Levi* 18.6–7, 10–11.
[28] Josephus, *Antiquities* 20.179–81, 207.
[29] Eusebius, *History of the Church* 2.23; 3.31, and Epiphanius, *Panarion* 1.29.
[30] Babylonian Talmud *Pesaḥim* 57a.

The house of Boethus provided four high priests, the first of whom held office from 22 to 5 BCE, and the last from 41 to 42 CE; the house of Fabi provided three high priests, the first of whom held office from 30 to 22 BCE and the last from 59 to 61 CE. Jesus and the early Christians would have known ways of the evil shepherds who were literally thieves and robbers, but were also, as the Qumran community said, 'those who lead Ephraim astray through their false teaching, their lying tongue and their deceitful lips... Those who seek smooth things.'[31] Perhaps these were the high priests of the house of Kathros, condemned for their pens.

Jesus says twice, 'I am the good shepherd' (vv. 11, 14), first in contrast to the hired shepherds who have no real care for the sheep, and then contrasting the evil shepherds who came to steal and destroy and the good shepherd who comes to give life (v. 10).

First, the hired shepherds: these were the high priests who had held office since Herod became king in 37 BCE. He took it upon himself to appoint such high priests as would not threaten his position: 'Herod no longer appointed high priests from the family of the Hasmoneans, but appointed certain men that were not from eminent families but were only of priestly descent.'[32] He also kept their vestments in custody to ensure that they and their people did not plot against him, only releasing them seven days before a festival so that they could be ritually purified.[33] Later, when he wanted to marry the beautiful daughter of a priest, he made her father high priest and thus allied himself by marriage to the high priesthood: 'He removed Jesus son of Fabi from the high priesthood and appointed Simon to this office, and then married his daughter.'[34] After the death of Herod and the removal of his son Archelaus, the governor of Syria removed the high priest who had been appointed by popular acclaim and installed Ananas, who appears in the Gospel as Annas, the father-in-law of Caiaphas (18.13).[35] These were the thieves, robbers and hirelings who had no real concern for their flock, contrasted with whom Jesus was the Good Shepherd.

Second, Jesus contrasts those who exploit the flock and the Good Shepherd who has come to give them his life. The eternal covenant is not mentioned by name in this chapter, but it is the context for Jesus' words about laying down his life (vv. 11, 15, 17, 18). The eternal covenant was

---

[31] *Commentary on Nahum*, 4Q169.
[32] Josephus, *Antiquities* 20.248.
[33] Josephus, *Antiquities* 18.94.
[34] Josephus, *Antiquities* 15.319–22.
[35] Josephus, *Antiquities* 18.26.

fundamental to the world of the first temple, but had been replaced by the Moses covenant in the second temple. The eternal covenant was renewed and upheld by the Davidic priest-kings on the Day of Atonement by their symbolic self-sacrifice.[36] This was Jesus' 'laying down my life'. The ritual inspired Isaiah's fourth Servant song about the anointed one who made himself the 'āšām – now thought to mean the sacrifice that restored a broken covenant bond[37] – and poured out his soul/life to death. The temple ritual was enacted with two goats representing the LORD/the king and Azazel, where the one representing the LORD was sacrificed and the other was driven away bearing the sins. Isaiah's Servant song was prompted by the near-fatal illness and miraculous recovery of King Hezekiah, who survived the plague, and was understood by Isaiah to have borne the sins of his people and thus delivered Jerusalem from the Assyrian army.[38] From the beginning, the Christians held the fourth Servant song to be a prophecy of Jesus and they interpreted Jesus' death as the Day of Atonement sacrifice to renew the everlasting covenant and give his life to heal and restore the creation: 'But you denied the Holy One [Zadok] ... you killed the Author of life ... Repent ... that times of refreshing may come from the presence of the LORD' (Acts 3.14, 19, my translation). In contrast to Jesus' self-sacrifice, giving life to the flock, the robber shepherds exploited and killed their flock.

Two other clusters of Ezekiel's prophecy are echoed in Jesus' discourse about the shepherds. The first (Ezek. 34) condemns the selfish and greedy shepherds of Israel who have neglected the sheep and allowed the flock to be scattered. The LORD himself would come as the shepherd, heal his flock and restore them to their land. He would judge them and 'feed them with justice'. Then the Davidic king would be restored, together with the ways of the first temple.

> I will set over them one shepherd, my servant David, and he shall feed them: he shall feed them and be their shepherd. And I, the LORD, will be their God, and my servant David shall be prince among them; I the LORD have spoken. I will make with them a covenant of peace ...
> I will make them and the places round about my hill a blessing ...

---

[36] See above, pp. 69, 92.

[37] J. Milgrom, *Leviticus 1—16*, New York: Doubleday, 1991, p. 347.

[38] See my article 'Hezekiah's Boil', *Journal for the Study of the Old Testament* 95 (2001), pp. 31–42. The sins had been an early attempt to change the religion of his kingdom by destroying the altars and high places of the LORD and making everyone worship at the central temple (Isa. 36.7) – a forerunner of Josiah's purge that would establish the pro-Moses group in Jerusalem.

## John 10

They shall know that I, the LORD their God, am with them, and that they, the house of Israel, are my people, says the Lord GOD.

(Ezek. 34.23–25, 26, 30)[39]

The second (Ezek. 37) begins with the vision of dry bones being brought to life when the Spirit comes back to them, and then the oracle:

> Thus says the Lord GOD: Behold, I will open your graves, and raise you from your graves, O my people; and I will bring you home into the land of Israel. And you shall know that I am the LORD, when I open your graves, and raise you from your graves, O my people. And I will put my Spirit within you, and you shall live, and I will place you in your own land; then you shall know that I, the LORD, have spoken, and I have done it, says the LORD.
> 
> (Ezek. 37.12–14)

Then Ezekiel received the sign of the two sticks named Judah and Ephraim which became one again, and finally, the prophecy of the return of the Davidic king:

> My servant David shall be king over them; and they shall all have one shepherd ... I will make a covenant of peace with them; an everlasting covenant shall be with them ... My tabernacle shall be with them; and I will be their God and they shall be my people.
> 
> (Ezek. 37.24, 26, 27, my translation)

Whoever compiled the Ezekiel scroll must have thought these sequences appropriate: the return of the good shepherd; the restoration of the Davidic kings and their one kingdom; the ingathering and resurrection of the scattered people; and the restoration of the covenant of peace. And even if the original compilation had been random, this is the sequence that Jesus and his contemporaries knew. These were the hopes of the original community whence Christianity grew: 'the Son of [God] Most High ... the throne of his father David ... a horn of salvation for us in the house of his servant David ... that we should be saved from our enemies, and from the hand of all who hate us' (Luke 1.32, 69, 71).

Jesus also has other sheep in other folds, presumably the Hebrews of the Diaspora to whom the early Christians took the Gospel.[40] Under the Good Shepherd, there would again be one flock and one Shepherd (v. 16), as Ezekiel had prophesied when he looked for the people brought back to their own land, the return of the Davidic kings, the undivided kingdom

---

[39] The last line (v. 31) is opaque in the Hebrew, but seems to say that the flock is Adam.
[40] James wrote 'to the twelve tribes of the Dispersion' (Jas. 1.1); Peter wrote to 'the exiles of the Dispersion in [Asia Minor]' (1 Pet. 1.1).

and the restoration of the eternal covenant. Hence the vision of all 12 tribes receiving the seal (Rev. 7.1–8). The bond between the Shepherd and his flock is the same as the bond between Jesus and the Father (v. 15), the theme of unity that occurs again in the high-priestly prayer in John 17. The Good Shepherd knows his own sheep, and they recognize him. Presumably the sheep recognize Wisdom and her messenger: 'She is easily discerned by those who love her, and is found by those who seek her' (Wisd. 6.12).

These teachings cause division among the Jews (v. 19), as on previous occasions (7.43, 9.16). Some say that Jesus is possessed, others that a man possessed by a demon cannot open blind eyes.

## 10.22–39: Blasphemy at Ḥanukkah

The scene then moves to the winter festival of Ḥanukkah, and John does not say how much time has passed between the teaching that began at Tabernacles and this next debate with the Jews, who press Jesus to say clearly whether or not he is the Messiah. Jesus replies that they have been told already, through his works, but they do not belong to his flock and so cannot believe them. Yet again, John shows that the Jews, first exemplified by Nicodemus the teacher of Israel (3.10), have moved so far away from the teaching of the original temple that they cannot understand what Jesus is teaching and doing, and so cannot recognize who he is. 'My sheep hear my voice, and I know them, and they follow me; and I give them eternal life ...' (v. 27), echoing the words of the Prologue:

> To all who received him, who believed in his name, he gave power to become children of God; who were born, not of blood nor of the will of the flesh nor of the will of man, but of God.  (1.12–13)

Nobody can take them away from their Father, or from Jesus, because 'I and the Father are one thing' (v. 30, my translation). This is another foreshadowing of the high-priestly prayer; Jesus does not explain the nature of the unity, but only its effect.

The Jews again prepare to stone him (v. 31), with the loose stones lying around in the building site because the second temple was being refurbished and extended. This time the charge is blasphemy, as prescribed in the law of Moses: 'He who blasphemes the name of the LORD shall be put to death; all the congregation shall stone him ...' (Lev. 24.16). Jesus has been guilty of working on the Sabbath, which had to be punished by stoning (Num. 15.32–35); and some considered that he was

## John 10

leading the people astray and that the miracles were magic,[41] which was also punishable by stoning (Lev. 20.27; Deut. 13.1–5).

The blasphemy here is Jesus' claim to be divine: 'You, being a man, make yourself God' (v. 33), whereas the Christian claim was that he was God who became a man (Phil. 2.6–7). John's Jesus responds with an argument from Scripture. *This shows that his claim to be Son of God originated in his own discussion with the Jews and was not a later development in the Christian communities under the influence of Greek culture.* He cites as his proof text Psalm 82[42] and he emphasizes that he is quoting *'your* law' (v. 34), and so something that they accept as authoritative. The concept 'son of God', though considered blasphemous by the Jews, was nevertheless used by Hebrews, and had been a part of the older faith. A fragment from Qumran that describes how a kingdom will be established says: 'He will be proclaimed son of God; he will be called son of God Most High.'[43] There are no more details, but these same titles were used by Gabriel to tell Mary about her Child, who would restore the Davidic kingdom (Luke 1.32).

In Psalm 82 the ambiguity of the Hebrew *ᵉlohîm*, 'gods', makes translation impossible, but it also underlies Jesus' claim to be One with the Father.

> *ᵉlohîm* has taken his place [singular] in the assembly of El,
> In the midst of *ᵉlohîm*, he sits in judgement ...
> I have said, 'You are *ᵉlohîm*, and all of you sons of the Most High,
> But you shall die [plural] like Adam,
> They shall fall like one of the princes.
> (Ps. 82.1, 6, 7, my translation)

Here is the mystery of the One and the many within the divine, and the many are sons of the Most High. The psalm implies that these sons should have been doing the works of God: giving right judgements (from the Hebrew *špṭ*) for the poor and the orphan, justice (from the Hebrew *ṣdq*) for the destitute, and help to the weak and needy (Ps. 82.3–4). These were the foundation virtues of the Davidic kings (e.g. Isa. 11.33–35; Ps. 72.1–4), but the condemned *ᵉlohîm* had failed in their duties because they lacked knowledge and understanding and they walked without light. The rulers had lost sight of the old-covenant virtues because they had lost the

---
[41] The evidence for this is set out in M. Smith, *Jesus the Magician*, Wellingborough: Aquarian, 1985.
[42] It may not be coincidence that this was one of the Melchi-Zedek proof texts in 11QMelch.
[43] 4Q246.

benefits of Wisdom. This had been Isaiah's earliest condemnation of the new ways taking hold in Jerusalem, which he gave in the form of a parable. The LORD's vineyard had produced a harvest of bloodshed and cries of despair when the LORD had expected justice (from the Hebrew *špṭ*) and righteousness (from the Hebrew *ṣdq*) (Isa. 5.1-7).

In the synoptic Gospels, the events corresponding to this debate in the temple at Hannukah are Jesus' encounters with the chief priests, scribes and elders in the temple in the days immediately before his death (Matt. 21.23-46; Mark 11.27—12.44; Luke 19.47—21.4). As in John's account, the issue was Jesus' authority, and all three synoptic Gospels say that Jesus told his version of Isaiah's parable of the vineyard. He was the Son and heir, coming to the vineyard which had been let to *tenants* – the current high priests – while the owner was away. (The owner was the LORD, who had forsaken the house and tower of his sheep, and abandoned them to the wild beasts – the foreign rulers – and the shepherd angels.)[44] They had ignored the owner's other servants – the prophets – who came to gather the fruit, and so the son himself was sent. The tenants here correspond to the shepherd angels left in charge of the people, and the fate of the unjust tenants would be the fate of the shepherd angels: they would be destroyed and the vineyard given to others, just as the shepherd angels were judged and their temple destroyed before the LORD of the sheep set up his new temple.

> Those seventy shepherds were judged and found guilty, and they were cast into the fiery abyss ...
>
> [The angels] folded up that old house ... and carried it off and laid it in a place in the south of the land ...
>
> The LORD of the sheep brought a new house greater and loftier than the first, and set it up in the place of the first that had been folded up ...[45]

Here in the Hanukkah encounter, John implies that the *ᵉlohîm* were facing judgement, because they too were hearing the word of God. The allusion to the corrupt high priests is clear. Jesus is doing the works of God, and they prove to anyone with knowledge and understanding who he is (v. 38). The condemned *ᵉlohîm* in the psalm lacked both knowledge and understanding (Ps. 82.5) and so they would fall from their position and die. The failure of the temple authorities to recognize Jesus would be the judgement upon them, rejecting the light because they preferred

---

[44] 1 Enoch 89.56: 'And I saw that he forsook their house and their tower and gave them into the hands of the lions ...'
[45] 1 Enoch 90.25, 28, 29.

darkness (cf. John 3.19). After hearing the parable of the vineyard, '[the chief priests and scribes and the elders] perceived that he had told the parable against them ...' (Mark 12.12).

Ḥanukkah means 'dedication': the feast marked the rededication of the temple after the occupying and polluting Syrians had been driven out in 164 BCE (1 Macc. 4.36–59). 'Blameless priests' were appointed when the temple was repossessed, and new furnishings were made. The polluted stones of the old altar were set aside until a prophet should come and say what should be done with them, and it was in this context that Jesus, recognized by many as the promised Prophet (e.g. Matt. 21.11; Mark 8.28 and parallels; John 6.14; 7.40, 52) decreed the fate not just of the altar stones, but of the stones of the entire temple (Mark 13.2). It is in this Hanukkah context that Jesus proclaims himself the high priest, the one whom the Father consecrated/dedicated and sent into the world (v. 36). In temple tradition, the high priest was anointed and thus consecrated (Exod. 30.30).[46] The holy oil represented the perfumed oil from the tree of life, but this had been 'lost' in the time of Josiah – symbolic of rejecting Wisdom and her tree of life – and so in the second temple there were no correctly anointed high priests who had the gifts of Wisdom. Anointing, according to Psalm 110, had transformed the anointed one into a Son – 'I have begotten you' – who was given the title Melchi-Zedek. But the Hebrew text of Psalm 110 is at this point damaged beyond hope of translation, and this meaning has to be recovered from the Greek. The anointing that transformed a Davidic prince into the LORD's son, his human manifestation Melchi-Zedek, was a sensitive issue, and Jesus' claim may have led to the obscuring of the Hebrew text.

The issue was anointing and sonship. The Jews say to Jesus: 'If you are the [Messiah], tell us plainly' (v. 24), but they consider 'sonship' blasphemy. It was the nature of the Messiah that was the issue. Again, the synoptic Gospels all say that this was discussed in the temple in the last days before Jesus was killed, but they record the proof text of the debate as Psalm 110. Jesus asked the crowd in the temple how the scribes could teach that the Messiah is (only) the son of David, when Psalm 110 clearly says that the Messiah is the son of the LORD. David called the anointed king his Lord, and so he cannot have been simply his son (Matt. 22.41–46; Mark 12.3–37; Luke 20.41–44). The Evangelists cite only the opening lines of the psalm but this was the way of identifying a passage of Scripture

---

[46] In Exod. 28.41 there is the additional 'fill his hands' (with incense), sometimes translated 'ordain'.

before the texts were divided into numbered verses and chapters. The debate in the temple was about the meaning of the whole of Psalm 110, and it says (or rather, originally said) that the anointed one was the divine son, consecrated/born in the holy of holies and then sent out into the world as the human presence of the LORD with his people, his son. The old title remained even in the writings of the Deuteronomists, but its temple context is not given. When Nathan the prophet brought the word of the LORD to David, he said: 'I will be [your son's] father, and he shall be my son' (2 Sam. 7.14).

Of the synoptic Gospels, only Matthew says that Peter recognized the Messiah with the double title: 'You are the Christ, the Son of the living God', and Jesus said to him: 'Blessed are you, Simon Bar-Jona! For flesh and blood has not revealed this to you, but my Father who is in heaven' (Matt. 16.17). Recognizing the Son was a divine gift. Matthew's Gospel was for Christians with Hebrew roots, and so the double naming was an important distinction for them. Mark and Luke do not mention the title 'Son of God' (Mark 8.29; Luke 9.20). So too with the synoptic account of Jesus' trial. Mark had the high priest ask: 'Are you the Christ, the Son of the Blessed?' (Mark 14.61), and when Jesus replied 'I AM', the high priest condemned him for blasphemy. Jesus then identified himself as the figure of Daniel's vision, the Son of Man who went with clouds to be seated on the throne in heaven (Dan. 7.13–14). This vision of the Man ascending was inspired by Psalm 2,[47] and so in Daniel's account the context implied by the psalm is given. This is how people, including the high priests, would have pictured the words of the psalm. The Son of Man (or simply the Man) was the Davidic king going to be enthroned in heaven. All three synoptic Gospels agree that 'Messiah', 'Son of God' and '[Son of] Man' were the titles used at Jesus' trial before the high priest, and that these were rephrased for Pilate in terms he would understand. Pilate therefore asked Jesus, 'Are you the *King of the Jews*?' (Matt. 27.11; Mark 15.2; Luke 23.3). John does not mention the question of titles at Jesus' trial before Annas, but does have Pilate ask the same question: 'Are you the *King of the Jews*?' (18.33). In John's Gospel, the question of blasphemy is raised in the temple discourse at Ḥanukkah, when the Jews again try to arrest Jesus (10.39).

Jesus then goes back across the Jordan, to the place where John had been baptizing and where his own public ministry began (10.40–42). For John's Gospel, this completes the section: 'He came to his own, and his own received him not' (1.11, my translation).

---

[47] See A. Bentzen, *King and Messiah*, English translation London: Lutterworth, 1955.

# John 11

Chapter 11 begins the second half of John's Gospel. Not only is it almost the mid-point in the text; it is also the moment when Jesus returns to the place where his ministry began, 'across the Jordan ... the place where John at first baptized' (10.40). John has shown how 'He came to his own home, and his own people received him not' (1.11); now he shows how 'all who received him, who believed in his Name' (my translation), became children of God. Luke's Jesus defines the resurrected as 'equal to angels ... sons of God ... sons of the resurrection' (Luke 20.36), and here John weaves the same fundamental Christian imagery around the story of a man called back from his tomb. The children of God are the resurrected, and their resurrection happens not after they die, but when the LORD comes to them. Luke added no such teaching when Jesus raised the widow's son at Nain or Jairus' daughter (Luke 7.11–17; 8.40–56), but John addresses a pressing concern of the early Church.

## The return of the LORD

The first Christians looked for the literal return of the LORD, and they prayed, 'Come, LORD', *Maranatha* (1. Cor. 16.22; also Rev. 22.20 and *Didache* 10). As the years passed, they became increasingly anxious about the delay in Christ's return and the resurrection of their own dead into the kingdom.[1] Paul's letter to the Thessalonians (about 50 CE) sets out the earliest belief about the resurrection of the dead and the return of the LORD:

> Since we believe that Jesus died and rose again, even so, through Jesus, God will bring with him those who have fallen asleep ... We who are alive, who are left until the coming of the LORD, shall not precede those who have fallen asleep. For the LORD himself will descend from heaven with a cry of

---

[1] A. Guilding links the Lazarus story to this concern for the second coming and the resurrection of Christians, but on a different basis; see *The Fourth Gospel in Jewish Worship*, Oxford: Clarendon Press, 1960, pp. 143–53.

command, with the archangel's call, and with the sound of the trumpet of God. And the dead in Christ will rise first; then we who are alive, who are left, shall be caught up together with them in the clouds to meet the LORD in the air; and so we shall always be with the LORD.

(1 Thess. 4.14–17, my translation)

Paul wrote in the same way to the Christians in Corinth: 'We shall not all sleep, but we shall all be changed ... For the trumpet will sound, and the dead will be raised imperishable, and we shall be changed' (1 Cor. 15.51–52). In Revelation, Paul's expectation in 1 Thessalonians was the vision of the kingdom:

> Then I saw thrones, and seated on them those to whom judgement was committed. Also I saw the souls of those who had been beheaded for their testimony to Jesus ... They came to life, and reigned with Christ for a thousand years. (Rev. 20.4)

The first Christians believed that they would rise from the dead when Christ returned in judgement, and their earliest images were drawn from the *Song of Moses* (Deut. 32) and the *Blessing of Moses* (Deut. 33). This ancient poem is now divided into two parts, but was remembered as a single celebration of divine kingship as can be seen from the very similar pattern in the hymn in Revelation: when the LORD-and-his-Anointed established his kingdom on earth, it was the time of judgement and reward (Rev. 11.15–18), as the Lady gave birth to the king (Rev. 12.1–5). Enthronement and judgement had been linked in the earliest temple practice. When the LORD became king, he came in glory with his holy ones to bless the 12 tribes (Deut. 33), but he also came to bring judgement on his enemies and those who had harmed his people (Deut. 32). Paul's early letters to the Thessalonians show that this is what the first Christians were expecting: the LORD and his angels in flaming fire would come to bring judgement (2 Thess. 1.5–10), the Christian dead would be raised to life again, and those still living would be caught up to heaven and 'changed' (1 Thess. 4.13–18; 1 Cor. 15.51–53). 'Let all God's angels worship him' (Deut. 32.43; Heb. 1.6) was a proof text, and they knew that when the LORD came in shining splendour with his angels to establish his kingdom (Deut. 33.2–5), his people would be blessed: 'Happy are you, O Israel! Who is like you, a people saved by the LORD ...?' (Deut. 33.29).

The Christians called this the *parousia*, literally 'presence', of the LORD, which is often translated 'coming': 'at the coming, *parousia*, of our Lord Jesus with all his saints' (1 Thess. 3.13). At his *parousia*, those who belonged to Christ would be raised (1 Cor. 15.23). The disciples asked

Jesus: 'What will be the sign of your *parousia* and of the close of the age?' (Matt. 24.3); and he replied: 'As were the days of Noah, so will be the *parousia* of the Son of man …' (Matt. 24.37, 39). The preceding prophecies – false messiahs, wars, persecution – all described events before the *parousia* of the Son of Man, who would come like lightning shining from east to west (Matt. 24.27).[2] Some thought that the Roman assault on Jerusalem in 70 CE would bring the *parousia*, and so they shouted, 'The Son is coming!' as rocks were hurled into the besieged city. They reproached God for being so slow in punishing their enemies.[3] They were looking for the fulfilment of the *Song of Moses*:

> For I lift up my hand to heaven
> And swear as I live for ever,
> If I whet the lightning of my sword,
> And my hand takes hold on judgement,
> I will take vengeance on my adversaries,
> And will requite those who hate me.
> (Deut. 32.40–41, translating literally)

Josephus says there were many phenomena in the years preceding the destruction of the temple; one was a star shaped like a sword that hung over the city for a year,[4] which must have heightened expectations that this was the lightning (sword) of the *parousia* of the Son of Man (Matt. 24.27). Many scoffed at the Christian hope: 'Where is the promise of his coming, *parousia*? For ever since the fathers fell asleep, all things have continued as they were from the beginning of creation' (2 Pet. 3.4).

It was in response to this crisis that John received a vision of the *parousia*, which was incorporated into Revelation after the vision of the seven seals. When the Lamb/Servant opened the seventh seal, the seven angels began to sound their trumpets. The original sequence had been the last angel sounding his trumpet, John measuring the temple before its destruction,[5] and then the kingdom established on earth (Rev. 11.15–18). But John saw the LORD coming to earth before these events (Rev. 10.1–4), and he was given new teaching. The LORD spoke again through John his

---

[2] The parallel passages in Luke 21 have the 'day' of the Son of Man.
[3] Josephus, *War* 5.272; 6.4. 'When the stone was coming, they shouted in their native language, "The Son is coming."' In Hebrew, 'a stone', *'ebhen*, and 'the son', *habben*, sound similar, but Josephus was a native speaker of Hebrew and not likely to have made such a mistake.
[4] Josephus, *War* 6.289.
[5] This curious expression was associated with judgement. The psalm of Habakkuk describes the LORD coming from his temple to save his people: 'He stood and measured the earth; [he] looked and shook the nations' (Hab. 3.6).

prophet, as he had done when he dictated the seven letters (Rev. 2—3). In his vision of the *parousia*, John was given new teaching for the crisis in the Church caused by the delay in the LORD's return.

The early Christians were expecting the LORD to return in a cloud (Acts 1.9-11; Rev. 1.7), and this is what John saw: the mighty angel[6] coming from heaven wrapped in a cloud, with a rainbow over his head, his face like the sun and his legs like pillars of fire (Rev. 10.1). He had in his right hand a little book that was open. This was the figure whom Ezekiel saw enthroned, 'the appearance of the likeness of the glory of the LORD' (Ezek. 1.28), and he was the Man whom Daniel saw raising his hands to heaven and swearing by 'him who lives for ever' (Dan. 10.5-14; 12.6-7). The LORD swore by himself (e.g. Jer. 22.5), as did the fiery figure John saw coming from heaven.[7] He told John to keep secret the message of the seven thunders which he had heard (Rev. 10.4) and to eat the little book, in other words, to keep secret what he read there, just as he had commanded Ezekiel (Ezek. 3.1-3). The mystery of God announced to his servants the prophets was about to be fulfilled (Rev. 10.7), but there is no indication of which prophecy was about to be fulfilled. The text implies that the fulfilment was linked to teaching that could not be made public. 'Mystery' and its 'interpretation' is a style familiar from the Qumran commentaries on Scripture, which said that God would make known to the Teacher of Righteousness 'all the mysteries of the words of his servants the prophets'.[8] The commentaries applied ancient texts to contemporary events, and John's vision of the mighty angel suggests that he was learning a new way to understand some text or teaching that was already familiar. Origen (and so presumably other Christians too) knew that both Ezekiel and John had been given teaching that was not to be written down and thus made public: 'At the command of the Logos [Ezekiel] swallowed the book in order that its contents might not be written down, and so made known to unworthy persons. John is also recorded to have seen and done a similar thing ...'[9] The reason was not secrecy, but the danger of a text being misinterpreted; some things had to be taught only by a person who knew what they meant.

---

[6] Not 'another' but 'afterwards'. Hebrew *'ḥr* can be read *'aḥēr*, 'another', or *'aḥar*, 'afterwards'. The mighty angel was the LORD; see my book *The Revelation of Jesus Christ*, Edinburgh, T&T Clark, 2000, pp. 184-90.

[7] The early Christians knew that the fiery figure in Daniel was the LORD; see Hippolytus, *On Daniel* 24.

[8] *Commentary on Habakkuk*, 1QpHab VII.

[9] Origen, *Against Celsus* 6.6. Origen knew that the LORD who spoke to Ezekiel was the Logos.

## John 11

There is no context for the *agraphon* 'Keep my mysteries/secrets for me and the sons of my house',[10] but the synoptic Gospels hint that Jesus gave teaching in private to his disciples (e.g. Mark 4.11), and that this teaching was known to the early Christians as the LORD's mysteries.[11] John notes in his Gospel that the disciples did not always understand at the time what Jesus was teaching and doing: resurrection after three days and the temple of his body, for example (2.22); or his acts and the crowd's response on Palm Sunday (12.16). In his farewell teachings, Jesus told his disciples that after his death, the Spirit of truth, the Counsellor, *paraklētos*, would 'teach you all things, and bring to your remembrance all that I have said to you' (14.26). The Book of Revelation was the result of this angelic teaching that enabled John to interpret and set in order the visions of Jesus: 'The revelation of Jesus Christ, which God gave him to show to his servants what must soon take place; and he made it known by sending his angel to his servant John …' (Rev. 1.1). He could announce the fulfilment of his prophecies. Embedded within Revelation is the new/true understanding of the *parousia*, which was originally the prophecy of the Son of Man returning in clouds with great power and glory (Mark 13.26). This new interpretation was not to be written down and so made available to those who would not understand it.

Evidence for the existence of unwritten teaching is found in many early Christian writers,[12] but none says what it was. It breaks the surface in the writings of Irenaeus at the end of the second century when he wrote an outline of essential Christian teaching in the face of threats from what he perceived as Gnostic deviation:[13] the first major topic was the seven heavens, the various heavenly powers, and how cherubim and seraphim relate to the Word and to Wisdom, all of which were symbolized by the menorah. None of this is in the New Testament. Origen, his younger contemporary, revealed that hidden teaching was linked to the meaning of the temple furnishings, that neither baptism nor the Eucharist could be understood without this temple knowledge, 'entrusted to us by the High Priest and his sons'.[14] He was careful only to reveal such as could be done without sacrilege, since the Christians were called 'the chosen race, the royal priesthood' (1 Pet.

---

[10] See above, p. 84.
[11] *Odes of Solomon* 8.10; *Acts of John* 96.
[12] See above, pp. 16–17, and my book *The Great High Priest. The Temple Roots of Christian Liturgy*, London: T&T Clark, 2003, pp. 1–33.
[13] Irenaeus, *Demonstration of the Gospel* 3.
[14] Origen, *On Numbers*, Homily 5.

## Temple Theology in John's Gospel

2.9). Basil, writing a century later, had to reveal some of this unwritten teaching in order to justify what he was teaching about the Holy Spirit. He cited a list of unwritten teachings very similar to Origen's, but also mentioned the words of invocation, *epiklēsis*, at the Eucharist, which were not in the New Testament, but 'which we have received from the unwritten teaching'.[15] The liturgy attributed to Basil has these words of *epiklēsis*:

> We call on you, O Holy One of the Holy Ones, by the favour of your goodness, to send your all-holy Spirit upon us and upon these offerings set out and bless them, and consecrate them and show this bread to be the actual precious body of the LORD and our God and Saviour Jesus Christ, Amen. [And to consecrate and to show] that this cup is the actual precious blood of the LORD and our God and Saviour Jesus Christ, Amen.[16]

This was the *epiklēsis* that Basil said had come from the Apostles but was not written down. It concerned the bread and wine of the Eucharist being the actual body and blood of the LORD, in other words, the LORD himself present with his people.

The new understanding of the *parousia* that John received was that the LORD returned to his people in the bread and wine, and this became part of the unwritten teachings that Basil knew. Several early writers said it was the Logos that came to the bread and wine, but *logos* could mean either the Second Person or simply a prayer.[17] The process and the effect is set out clearly in Serapion's prayer:

> O God of truth, let thy Holy Word come upon, *epidēmēsato epi*, this bread, that the bread may become the body of the Word and upon this cup that the cup may become the blood of truth ... make us wise by the participation of the body and the blood.

In the Preface to the prayer, he prayed: 'We beseech thee make us living men [i.e. resurrected]. Give us a spirit of light, that we may know thee the true [God] and him whom thou didst send, Jesus Christ.'[18] The understanding of *epiklēsis* developed over the years as can be seen in the various forms of the prayers; there were three stages:

---

[15] Basil, *On the Holy Spirit* 66.
[16] My translation from the text in F. E. Brightman, *Liturgies Eastern and Western*. Vol. 1, *Eastern Liturgies*, Oxford, 1896, pp. 329–30. There are several versions of this text.
[17] Thus e.g. Irenaeus, *Against Heresies* V.2; Origen, *On Matthew* 11; Athanasius, *Sermon to the Baptized*, in Migne, *Patrologia Greco-Latina*, XXVI.1325.
[18] Mid-fourth-century Egypt. *Bishop Serapion's Prayer Book*, tr. J. Wordsworth, London: SPCK, 1910. Serapion here was quoting John 17.3.

## John 11

- *Christ* is requested to *come* and manifest his presence;
- the Father is requested that the *Son* or Spirit come upon the oblation;
- the Father is requested to *send* the Spirit to *make* the bread and wine the body and blood of Christ.[19]

Christ coming to the bread, the earliest understanding, was the new teaching given to John, or rather, the moment when he was enabled to understand the words at the last supper. Paul said he had taught the Christians in Corinth what he had learned from the LORD, that at the last supper Jesus told his disciples to break bread and drink from the cup 'in *remembrance* of me' (1 Cor. 11.23–25). Of the synoptic Gospels, only the later texts of Luke include 'in remembrance of me', and since Luke is likely to be dependent on Paul at this point, there is only the evidence of Paul, who was not present at the last supper, for *the translation of the words that Jesus actually used*, which are unlikely to have been Greek. The Hebrew/Aramaic would have been *'azkārâ/'adkarah*, which means both remembrance and invocation. Paul chose 'remembrance', *anamnēsis*, but the fiery angel enabled John to understand what Jesus had actually meant. The bread and wine were the means to invoke him, to summon his presence, and so the bread was literally the bread of the Presence, the *parousia*. Wisdom's Angel of Great Counsel had been present in the Davidic king (Isa. 9.6 LXX); he would also be present (again) in the bread. Thus those who ate the bread/the LORD would receive her gifts of light, life and wisdom, whence the prayer of Bishop Sarapion, that those who ate the bread would be resurrected, receive light and wisdom, and know the true God and Jesus Christ whom he sent.

This was the secret teaching that Basil and others knew. There can, by definition, be no written evidence for unwritten teaching, but something so fundamental as this understanding of the Eucharist must have come from a source that could not be questioned. The revelation of the LORD to John was that source, and so a later Gospel text could say that disciples had recognized Jesus in the breaking of the bread (Luke 24.35), and John incorporated this teaching into his account of the feeding miracle.

After the revelation, the LORD told John to go and prophesy *to* many peoples, nations, tongues and kings (Rev. 10.11). He had to pass on the new teaching 'to many', not 'about many'. The underlying Hebrew would have been 'prophesy *'al*', meaning 'prophesy to/upon' as in 'prophesy upon/to these bones' (Ezek. 37.4, AV/RSV). After his experience of the

---

[19] B. D. Spinks, 'The Consecratory Epiklesis in the Anaphora of St James', *Studia Liturgica* 11.2 (1976), pp. 18–39, p. 28.

*parousia*, John had to speak as a prophet to many people, prompted by teaching that he could not reveal. The context suggests that John's revelation about the *parousia* was received just before the fall of Jerusalem, and that his own experience of the *parousia* was receiving teaching that he ate. Since the expected *parousia* of the LORD was to be the moment of resurrection, and since John learned that the LORD had already returned, the Christians' future hope from that time on had to be understood as a present reality experienced when they received the bread and wine and met the LORD. This revelation prompted John to write his Gospel, and determined the way he wrote it. As he wrote in his first letter: 'We know that *we have passed out of death into life*, because we love the brethren' (1 John 3.14). The new revelation is illustrated in the raising of Lazarus, which should be read in the light of two related sayings from the *Gospel of Philip*:

> Those who say that the Lord died first and rose up are in error, for he rose up first and died. If one does not first attain the resurrection, will he not die? Those who say they will die first and then rise are in error. If they do not receive the resurrection while they live, when they die they will receive nothing.[20]

## 11.1–44: Raising Lazarus

The teaching at the raising of Lazarus is another pre-Passover discourse: Nicodemus, even though sympathetic to Jesus, did not understand what Jesus meant by being born again/born from above. Here, Jesus changes Martha's understanding of resurrection, and presumably the understanding of all the other early Christians. The presence of Jesus, his *parousia*, was the moment of resurrection, and this happened before physical death. In this respect, Lazarus represents all Christians:

> Jesus said to her, 'Your brother will rise again.' Martha said to him, 'I know that he will rise again in the resurrection at the last day.' Jesus said to her, 'I am the resurrection and the life; he who believes in me, though he die, yet shall he live, and whoever lives and believes in me shall never die ...'
> 
> (11.23–26).

Hence the first of the secret sayings of Thomas' Jesus: 'Whoever finds the interpretation of these sayings will not experience death.' Thomas and Philip are both prominent figures in John's Gospel.

---

[20] *Gospel of Philip*, CG II.3, 56, 73.

## John 11

The story of Lazarus echoes the words of the longer Prologue at the beginning of John's Gospel and indicates that the second part of the Gospel is parallel to the first but addressed to those who did receive the Logos and believe.

- The miracle at Cana had first shown his glory (2.11); here Lazarus' illness is to show the glory of God, and the believer will see the glory of God (vv. 4, 40).
- The miracle at Cana was just before Passover (2.13); here the raising of Lazarus was just before Passover (12.1).
- The light and life of human beings was not overcome by darkness (1.4–5); here those walking in the night stumble because they do not have the light within them (v. 10).
- The light was coming into the world (1.9); here the life is coming (v. 25).
- Those who receive and believe become children of God (1.12–13); here the resurrection comes (11.25).
- Jesus was recognized as Son of God (1.34, 49) and Messiah (1.41), the one who was to come (1.30); here Martha says, 'You are the [Messiah], the Son of God ... who is coming into the world' (v. 27).
- The Jews sent people from Jerusalem to observe and question Jesus (1.19–28); here the Jews come to mourn and to criticize – some believing but others plotting against him (vv. 31–37, 45–46).
- Jesus was recognized as the Lamb/Servant who takes away the sin of the world (1.29, 36); here Jesus fulfils the prophecy of the Servant and brings a prisoner from his darkness.

The story itself is simple: Jesus receives a message from his friends Martha and Mary in Bethany that their brother Lazarus is dangerously ill. Jesus waits for two days and then sets out for Bethany. Martha scolds Jesus for his delay; Mary reproves him more gently, although neither questions the fact that Jesus could have prevented Lazarus' death. They go to the tomb. Jesus tells those standing by to move the stone from the cave tomb, he prays, and then calls Lazarus out from his grave. Jesus tells 'them' – we are not told who they were, but Origen says they were the attendant angels – to remove Lazarus' grave wrappings, and shortly after this, Lazarus and his sisters have supper with Jesus in their home. The 'Jews' now divide into those who are sympathetic and even believers, who doubtless became the nucleus of the Jerusalem church (vv. 36, 45; also 12.9–11, 42); and the priests and Pharisees, who are alarmed by Jesus' popularity (vv. 37, 46–54, 57; also 12.10, 19).

None of the synoptic Gospels mentions this story, although it may have become the parable of the rich man and Lazarus just as the vision of the angel reapers (Rev. 14.14–16) became the parable of the wheat and the weeds with Jesus' explanation (Matt. 13.24–43; Mark 4.26–29). After his death, the rich man cried out from Hades to Abraham to send a warning to his brothers:

> But Abraham said, 'They have Moses and the prophets; let them hear them.' And [the rich man] said, 'No, father Abraham; but if some one goes to them from the dead, they will repent.' [Jesus] said to him, 'If they do not hear Moses and the prophets, neither will they be convinced if some one should rise from the dead.' (Luke 16.29–31)

This could easily have come from a disciple of John: a further discourse arising from the miracle, and from the condemnation of the rapacious high priests in chapter 10. The rich man is recognizable as one of the high priests, notorious in the time of Jesus for extortion and amassing wealth;[21] and the name Lazarus is an abbreviation of Eleazar, the ancestor of the Zadokite priests.[22] It was only the faithful Zadokites who would serve in the restored temple (Ezek. 44.15–16), and people who followed the *Damascus Document* claimed this prophecy for themselves: 'the sons of Zadok are the chosen ones of Israel, the men called by name who shall stand [i.e. be resurrected] at the end of days'. They were destined to live for ever, and 'all the glory of Adam shall be theirs'.[23] These were the true children of Abraham, the faithful priests from the first temple.

The home at Bethany is mentioned elsewhere: Jesus began his journey on Palm Sunday nearby (Mark 11.1; Luke 19.29); and returned there to stay the night (Matt. 21.17; Mark 11.11–12). He was anointed there, although Matthew and Mark say he was in the house of Simon the leper (Matt. 26.6; Mark 14.3); and it was from Bethany that he was taken from human sight into heaven (Luke 24.50). Here, at the beginning of the second part of John's Gospel, Jesus comes to his own and his own receive him, and John prepares the reader for the teaching Jesus would give (in private, at his table) to all who received him (1.12). This is presented as

---

[21] *Commentary on Habakkuk*, 1QpHab VII, IX, X.
[22] Two of Aaron's descendants were appointed by David: Zadok of the sons of Eleazar, and Ahimelech of the sons of Ithamar (1 Chron. 24.1–3), but David banished Ahimelech (1 Kings 2.35), leaving Zadok of the house of Eleazar as the priest in Jerusalem.
[23] *Damascus Document*, CD III—IV.

the discourse after the last supper, in the form of a farewell testimony that was a popular literary form at the time.[24]

The Prologue described how the Logos, who was the presence of the LORD, the *memra* and the *'ehyeh* *ᵃšer 'ehyeh* , the 'I cause to be what I cause to be', came into the world of time and matter, and how the Baptist proclaimed the incarnate Logos as the Lamb/Servant (John 1.29, 35).[25] He was the one on whom the Spirit rested (Isa. 61.1; John 1.33-34), symbolized in temple ritual by the anointed royal high priest emerging from the holy of holies. He was the chosen Servant anointed with the Spirit to bring forth right judgement, *mišpaṭ*, to the peoples (Isa. 42.1). Isaiah had known such a figure and explained Hezekiah's miraculous recovery from the plague in terms of the Servant who suffered and bore the sins of his people.[26] This poem, and the others about the Servant, were reused by the Second-Isaiah who set them in their present context, but originally they described the role of the royal high priest in Jerusalem. This is why the early Christians read the poems as prophecies fulfilled by Jesus.

The Servant would be a covenant to the people; he would be a light to the nations (Isa. 42.6) as John has described in 8.12; he would open blind eyes (Isa. 42.7a) as John has described in 9.7; and he would release the bound one from the closed place and those who dwell in darkness from the house of confinement (Isa. 42.7b, translating literally).[27] Here in the story of Lazarus, this role of the Servant is literally fulfilled: the one who came forth from the place of light and life calls Lazarus from the place of darkness and death where he has been bound – hence the emphasis on the wrappings that bound him in the tomb (11.44). The Servant 'was' Israel – meaning 'the one who has seen God' – in whom the LORD is glorified (Isa. 49.3; John 3.32; 17.4); he was to bring Israel (in the other sense of the word) back to the LORD (Isa. 49.5; John 10.16). The promise to the returning flock (Isa. 49.9b-11)[28] is quoted in the vision of ingathering in Revelation 7.16-17, where the enthroned Lamb/Servant is their Shepherd. The Servant in Isaiah was promised that his flock would return from the land of Syene (southern Egypt) and from the north and

---

[24] Thus for example, the *Testaments of the Twelve Patriarchs*; and Deuteronomy is the parting words of Moses.

[25] See above, p. 157.

[26] See my article 'Hezekiah's Boil', *Journal for the Study of the Old Testament* 95 (2001), pp. 31-42.

[27] See above, pp. 93-4.

[28] The image is of sheep being gathered in.

the west, that is, from Greece. The returning Greeks appear in the next chapter. The mouth of the Servant was like a sharp sword (Isa. 49.2) as depicted in Revelation 1.16; 2.12; and 19.15. He would speak with authority, and the LORD would show him to be correct (Isa. 50.8, from *ṣedeq*, 'righteous'). The final Servant poem described him as the sin-bearer who poured out his life, and as Zadok (the Righteous One) the Servant taught what he had learned from the LORD to restore many to righteousness (Isa. 53.10–11; 50.4). This is what John described in 3.34: 'He ... utters the words of God' and 6.45: 'They shall all be taught by God.'

The miracle happened at some time between Ḥanukkah and Passover, and, following John's three-year calendar for the ministry of Jesus and its correspondence to the three-year synagogue lectionary, the story of Lazarus would be set in the late winter, in the months of Tebet, Shebat and Adar, since Ḥanukkah fell early in Tebet. Guilding has shown some remarkable links between John's account of the raising of Lazarus and the synagogue readings set for Shebat in the third year of the lectionary cycle. From the law they would have been reading the last chapters of Deuteronomy – the very poems that shaped the early Christians' pictures of the *parousia* – and from the prophets from Joshua 24 onwards. A more detailed reconstruction allocates the readings thus:[29]

- The passage beginning at Deuteronomy 29.9 to the second Sabbath in Shebat; this reading includes 'the secret things belong to the LORD our God' (Deut. 29.29);
- The passage beginning at Deuteronomy 30.11 to the third Sabbath in Shebat; this reading includes 'Choose life, that you and your descendants may live, loving the LORD your God, obeying his voice, and cleaving to him ...' (Deut. 30.19–20);
- The passage beginning at Deuteronomy 32.1 to the fourth Sabbath in Shebat; this reading is the *Song of Moses*, which describes the LORD coming in judgement to save his people and includes 'See now that I, even I, am he, and there is no god beside me; I kill and I make alive ...' (Deut. 32.39);
- The passage beginning at Deuteronomy 33.1 to the first Sabbath in Adar, some five weeks before Passover; this reading is the *Blessing of Moses*, which describes the LORD coming in glory with all his holy ones (Deut. 33.2–3);

---

[29] Guilding, *Fourth Gospel*, n. 1 above, p. 150. I have developed her thesis to include Deut. 32 and 33.

## John 11

- Joshua 24 to the first or second Sabbath in Shebat; this reading describes the death of Joshua, the Hebrew form of the name Jesus, and the death of Eleazar, of which Lazarus is an abbreviation. Both were buried in Ephraim (Josh. 24.29, 30, 33).

There are echoes of these readings throughout the Lazarus story: resurrection before death was one of the secret things of the holy of holies; 'life' understood as loving the LORD, obeying his voice and 'cleaving' to him in the original sense of the word, namely, becoming one with him;[30] the 'coming' of the LORD in glory as the moment of resurrection; and the remarkable pairing of names: the death of Joshua and the death of Eleazar, both buried in Ephraim. Jesus retreated to 'a town called Ephraim' (11.54) which has never been identified. This may all be coincidence, but given John's precise dating of the miracle between Hanukkah and Passover, it is more likely that John was deliberately relating it to the synagogue themes for that time of year. Further, the men of the New Covenant described in the *Damascus Document* knew of a sealed book of the law which was not opened from the death of Eleazar and Joshua until the coming of Zadok.[31]

The story divides into three sections: the setting for the miracle (vv. 1–16); the mourning at Bethany (vv. 17–37); and the raising of Lazarus (vv. 38–44). It has no long discourse but only two dialogues: Jesus with his disciples because they misunderstand what Jesus means by 'Lazarus has fallen asleep' (vv. 7–16); and Jesus with Martha, who has to learn the real meaning of resurrection (vv. 21–27).

First, Jesus hears from Mary and Martha that their brother Lazarus is ill, but Jesus does not rush to him. He stays two days before setting out, saying that the illness will not to lead to Lazarus' death but to the glory of God. The chronology must be symbolic, and so discussions about why Jesus did not go immediately are not helpful. Jesus is living at that time on the eastern side of the Jordan, where John had baptized, and has to travel to Bethany near Jerusalem. When he arrives, Lazarus has already been dead for four days. Raising Lazarus, however, after two days evokes the words of Hosea:

> I will return again to my place,
> Until they acknowledge their guilt and seek my face,
> And in their distress they seek me saying,

---

[30] See above, p. 47.
[31] *Damascus Document*, CD V.1–4.

> 'Come, let us return to the LORD;
> For he has torn, and he will heal us;
> He has stricken and he will bind us up.
> After two days he will revive us;
> On the third day he will raise us up,
> And we shall live before his face.
> Let us know, let us press on to know the LORD;
> His going forth is sure as the dawn,
> He will come to us as the showers,
> As the spring rains that water the earth.'
> (Hos. 5.15—6.3, my translation)

This passage underlies the second of the Eighteen Benedictions, which would have been familiar to all those who came to console the sisters.

> You are mighty and cause those who take pride in their strength to fall, judging the violent, living for ever; you raise the dead, you make the spirit return, you send down the dew [of resurrection], you provide for the living, you give life to the dead, in the twinkling of an eye you make salvation spring up for us. Blessed are you, LORD, who cause the dead to live.

This is why 'many of the Jews ... who had come with Mary [to the tomb] and had seen what [Jesus] did, believed in him' (11.45). The physical miracle confirmed the spiritual reality of the LORD bringing new life, and so Jesus spoke plainly to his disciples: 'Lazarus is dead; and for your sake, I am glad that I was not there, so that you may believe' (11.14–15).

The second section (vv. 17–37), contrasts the two sisters; both knew that if Jesus had been there, Lazarus would not have died (vv. 21, 32). Mary weeps, but Martha speaks out and engages Jesus in an exchange about resurrection. There were many different beliefs about resurrection at that time: the Sadducees did not believe in resurrection (Matt. 22.23; Acts 23.8) whereas the Pharisees did (Acts 23.8); and the Samaritans believed they would be resurrected at the last day. But resurrection had many meanings, and so it may be that the Sadducees, for example, did not believe in one particular understanding of resurrection. It could mean an existence after death either as a resuscitated physical body, as a spiritual body, or as an immortal soul; or it could mean the transformed existence of a person who had mystically ascended to heaven and stood with the angels before the throne. There, like Enoch, s/he had become a Man or son of Man and then returned to earth to live as an angel. Someone living in the Qumran community at this time was giving thanks that the LORD had redeemed his soul from Sheol and raised him up to the everlasting height:

*John 11*

> An iniquitous spirit you have purified from great transgression
> that it may take its place with the host of the holy ones
> and enter into community with the congregation of the sons of heaven.[32]

The singer has not only been rescued from Sheol and raised up to heaven among the angels, but this had happened before his physical death.

## Deaths and resurrection

The existence of Sheol, the dark place of the dead, was an ancient belief. In the first-temple period, the dead went down below the earth: the LORD promised Abram that he would go to his fathers in peace (Gen. 15.15); Job knew he would go to a place of gloom and deep darkness from which he would not return (Job 10.21); Isaiah mocked a mighty king who died and went to Sheol where the shades greeted him and said, 'You ... have become weak ... like us' (Isa. 14.4–21). Enoch, however, knew of three (or four; the text is not clear) divisions in Sheol from which some of the dead did return: one was for the righteous dead, who had access to a spring of water and would be raised again to receive their reward on the day of judgement; one was for sinners who had lived in prosperity, died unpunished and were waiting in pain (and thirst; see Luke 16.24) until they were raised on the day of judgement; and one was for sinners who suffered in their lifetime and so did not suffer in Sheol but would not be raised again.[33] The problem is the date of *1 Enoch* 6—36: much of the content was known to Isaiah – although not this actual text – and he also has that detailed description of the mighty king in Sheol.[34] It may be that the belief in rising to face the judgement was as old as the Enoch tradition, or it may be that the preservers of 'Enoch' developed the idea of resurrection to judgement in the light of their own sufferings at the hands of 'the brethren who hated them and cast them out' (Isa. 66.5). People had formerly contacted the dead (1 Sam. 23.7), but Deuteronomy later forbad the practice (Deut. 18.11) and Josiah banned it (2 Kings 23.24). The influence of the Deuteronomists in editing and transmitting the Hebrew Scriptures may account for the sparse evidence for Sheol and the afterlife.

---

[32] 1QH XI.21, my translation.
[33] *1 Enoch* 22.1–14.
[34] See my section on Isaiah in J. D. G. Dunn and J. W. Rogerson, *Commentary on the Bible*, Grand Rapids, MI: Eerdmans, 2003.

In the first-temple period there had been another form of resurrection, when the royal high priests had been 'raised up'. Their experience in the holy of holies was remembered as a process of *theōsis*, becoming divine, and such a person was called a Man [or son of Man] in temple-influenced texts. The LORD then spoke through his human self, the resurrected one. Hence the last words of David:

> The oracle of David, the son of Jesse,
> The oracle of the man who was raised up,*
> The anointed of the God of Jacob ...
> The spirit of the LORD speaks within me
> And his word is upon my tongue.
> (2 Sam. 23.1–2, my translation)

*The text here is obscure(d); the Qumran Samaritan text and the Greek[35] both have 'whom the LORD raised up', but the Masoretic Hebrew is unreadable. The Greek verb here and in John's Gospel is *hupsoō* (LXX Ps. 88.20). Given the known interests of the 'restoring scribes', it is likely that the original referred to the resurrection of the Davidic king to become the LORD.

When the LORD became king (and the Davidic king became the LORD), he came in glory with his holy ones to assert his kingship, proclaim his laws, and bless the 12 tribes (Deut. 33.2–4). The resurrected one brought judgement on his enemies and restored the land of his people (Deut. 32.43). This ancient poem is now divided into two parts, but was originally a single celebration of divine kingship, as we have seen.[36] Paul's early letters to the Thessalonians show that this is what the first Christians were expecting: the LORD (the resurrected one) and his angels in flaming fire would come to bring judgement (2 Thess. 1.5–10); the Christian dead would be raised to life again; and those still living would be caught up to heaven and 'changed' (1 Thess. 4.13–18; 1 Cor. 15.51–53). Resurrection of the Christian dead has been added to the picture. The earlier Christian expectation was Jesus' parable of the sheep and the goats, which envisaged the LORD coming before any of his followers had died (Matt. 25.31–46). The (Son of) Man comes in glory with his angels and sits on his throne. Then Jesus describes the Man as the King, so to him they must have been equivalent terms: he judges those before him (there is no resurrection) and allows into his kingdom those who are 'blessed of my Father'. Matthew envisages this picture from the first temple as a future event, to

---

[35] 4QSam[a] and LXX.
[36] See above, p. 132.

happen before the fall of the temple and within the lifetime of the hearers, since this teaching answers the disciples' question: 'When will the temple be destroyed?' (Matt. 24.1–2). The myths and rituals of the ancient kings had been transformed during the second-temple period into the future hope, and so here the resurrected LORD and King comes *as the future judge*. He is not a resuscitated mortal facing the judgement. The Third-Isaiah had prophesied 'A voice from the temple! The voice of the LORD rendering recompense to his enemies' (Isa. 66.6); Malachi warned that a messenger would come, and then the LORD would appear in the temple, 'drawing near for judgement' (Mal. 3.5). This would be a future judgement on their enemies, but not after their death. The Deuteronomists, however, were hostile to the idea of sacral kingship and angel hosts,[37] and the potentially relevant verses of the ancient poems are now damaged (Deut. 32.8, 43; 33.2–3); other editors may have left no trace of their work, and so the cultural context of the second-temple prophesies of judgement is no longer clear.

In the second-temple period the idea of resurrection to face the day of judgement is better attested. It may have been in response to the injustices of life, the fact that faithful and observant Jews were persecuted simply for practising their faith, as happened in the early second century BCE. But injustice was nothing new; Job asked why the righteous suffered and was confident that when he had left his body he would see God (Job 19.25–26). This text, which could imply resurrection, is not easy to read. In the crisis of the early second century, Daniel's prophecies, set in and possibly derived from an exilic setting, were reused. He knew of both types of resurrection: images from the old royal cult, for example the Man being 'raised up' to be enthroned (Dan. 7.13–14), were deemed relevant to the current situation, and when Daniel said that many of those asleep in the dust would rise, either to everlasting life or to everlasting shame and contempt, he could have drawn this from what he knew of the first-temple heritage.[38]

> And those who are wise shall shine like the brightness of the firmament;
> And those who turn many to righteousness, like the stars for ever and ever. (Dan. 12.3)

---

[37] See above, p. 35.
[38] This could be implied by the description in *1 Enoch* 14. Too little is known about the sensitive subject of resurrection; absence of evidence is not evidence of absence, especially when it is certain that editors and correcting scribes were at work removing evidence of the older faith.

This was resurrection to a radiant state, perhaps what Paul would later call a 'spiritual body' (1 Cor. 15.42–44), but it was a future state. The idea of a bodily resurrection after death may have come into Hebrew thought through Ezekiel, who saw a valley of dry bones and watched them come alive again, but this was not a prophecy of individual resurrection; it promised hope for the whole people of Israel (Ezek. 37.1–14).

Resurrection was not necessarily linked to judgement in order to enter a final state known as 'the kingdom': in the first temple it had been transformation into the angel state, *theōsis*, but this was not for ordinary mortals and did not happen after death. It is what the singer at Qumran was describing: 'I am reckoned with the gods, *'elim*, and I dwell in the holy congregation ... my glory is with the sons of the king';[39] and it is what Deuteronomy forbad: 'The secret things belong to the LORD our God; but the things that are revealed belong to us and to our children for ever, that we may do all the words of this law' (Deut. 29.29). When the Davidic crown prince was 'born' as the divine son and became the priest like Melchi-Zedek, it was his resurrection. This is what Jesus tried to explain to Nicodemus: to see the kingdom or to enter the kingdom, one had to be born from heaven by water and Spirit. The first Christians understood that this was the difference between the Aaronite priests and the Melchi-Zedek priests: the former inherited the role through the death of their fathers – they *descended* as priests; whereas the latter *rose up* (the word for resurrection) to the priestly state 'by the power of an indestructible life' (Heb. 7.16).[40] The Aaronites were the high priests of the pro-Moses era, and the writer of Hebrews knew that temple-resurrection, being born from above, was characteristic of the first-temple priesthood. Daniel shows that transformation into the angel state became the reward for the righteous after death, when they would shine like stars (Dan. 12.2–3); the Qumran texts show it became the reward for the righteous *before* death, when they ascended, as had the ancient kings, stood before the heavenly throne, saw the LORD, and then became the LORD when they returned to earth.

John has already introduced the new understanding of resurrection after the miracle at Bethesda, when the man who had been lying weak for 38 years was empowered to get up and walk. This symbolized the dead receiving new life: the Father gives life and so does the Son (5.21); but the miracle was also linked to judgement: the Father judges no one, but gives

---

[39] 4Q491.11.
[40] See above, p. 107.

## John 11

this power to the Son (5.22). The powers of resurrection and judgement are both entrusted to the Man (5.26–27) and then, anticipating the Lazarus miracle as representing every Christian, Jesus says: 'The hour is coming when all who are in the tombs will hear his voice and come forth, those who have done good, to the resurrection of life, and those who have done evil, to the resurrection of judgement' (5.28–29).

Martha says she is expecting her brother to rise again on the last day, but Jesus responds: 'I am the resurrection and the life.' His presence, his *parousia*, is not in the future, but is the present moment when the dead are given life and the world is judged. The second benediction underlies his words: 'Blessed are you, LORD, who cause the dead to live.' Then Jesus' words have double meanings:

> He who believes in me, though he die, yet shall he live
> And whoever lives and believes in me shall never die.
> (11.25–26)

For the believer, physical death is followed by eternal Life, and having eternal Life means that there is no second death.

The second death was the final and total destruction of the whole person which followed the last judgement before the Father. The chronology of judgement is not set out clearly in the New Testament (e.g. 1 Cor. 15.20–28), and at the very point where a clear pattern might have been expected, the text is disordered (Rev. 20.1—22.5). It seems that two judgements were envisaged: the first when the LORD established his kingdom on earth, the Christian dead were raised, and the living were judged; the second at the end of the LORD's reign, when he returned all things to the Father, all the dead were raised, and the last judgement followed. This was the second death. Jesus promised the church at Smyrna that the faithful Christian would not be hurt by the second death (Rev. 2.11). At the beginning of this letter, Jesus described himself as 'The First and the Last, who died and came to life' (Rev. 2.8), and so his own triumph over physical death was the assurance that the faithful Christian would also triumph. The same assurance in almost the same words is found in the final throne vision in Revelation: the one who is the Beginning and the End gives the water of life to each faithful follower, who then becomes his son; to the others – the cowardly, the faithless, the polluted, the murderers, the fornicators, the sorcerers, the idolaters and the liars – he assigns the second death (Rev. 21.7–8). The sinners are barred from the new Jerusalem and from the tree of life (Rev. 22.14–15).

Matthew's Jesus taught a persecuted community: 'Do not fear those who kill the body but cannot kill the soul; rather fear him who can destroy both soul and body in Gehenna' and 'Every one who acknowledges me before men, I also will acknowledge before my Father who is in heaven ...' (Matt. 10.28, 32). Destruction of body and soul was the second death that followed judgement before the great white throne (Rev. 20.11–15); but the Christian should not fear, because those who had shared in the first resurrection would not be harmed by the second death (Rev. 20.6). John wrote, 'for we have an advocate with the Father, Jesus Christ *the Righteous One*' (1 John 2.1, my translation). Here again is the title of the Servant whose role had been to restore all things by his knowledge/teaching (Isa. 53.11). The second death is described as the lake of fire (Rev. 20.14; 21.8), and was the destiny of all who could not enter the kingdom.

Martha says she believes in the resurrection on the last day, and Jesus declares that the 'last day' and the new life has come: 'I am the resurrection and the life' (v. 25). Jesus uses the *'ehyeh* form of the Name, showing that he is the saving presence of the LORD. In the second-temple period there must have been some debate about the Presence, as can be seen in Isaiah 63.8b–9. The Hebrew text has two forms: 'and he became their Saviour. In all their affliction he was [the Qumran Isaiah scroll has 'was not'] afflicted, and the angel of his presence saved them',[41] but the LXX read the (Qumran) Hebrew differently as: 'he became a Saviour for them from all affliction. Not an envoy nor an angel, but the LORD himself saved them.' The Hebrew 'his presence' was translated 'the LORD himself', implying that the Hebrew 'angel of his presence' was being wrongly understood as a *substitute* for the LORD, rather than as the LORD himself. Challenged to say if she believed what Jesus was claiming, Martha replied: 'Yes, Lord. I believe that you are the Christ, the Son of God, he who is coming into the world.' This was the form of the Name sung in heaven: 'Who was and is' – the Targum's way of expressing the twofold *'ehyeh* *ʾašer 'ehyeh* of Exodus 3.14 – 'and is coming' (Rev. 4.8). Martha called her sister: 'The Teacher is here', *paresti*, the verbal form of *parousia*. The *'Ehyeh* had come. The sisters, Jesus and the watching Jews then went together to the tomb.

The detail in what follows resembles the Easter story: the stone sealing the cave, the dead man wrapped in cloths with a separate piece for his head (v. 44; cf. 20.6). Jesus asked for the door stone to be removed, and Martha raised the practical objection of the bad smell after four days.

---

[41] Thus the RSV; 'not' is in 1QIsa$^a$.

Jesus prayed, and then called Lazarus from his tomb. Practical considerations such as how he could walk if he was bound with grave wrappings are irrelevant. Lazarus was unbound from death and was free. The prophetic words spoken at Bethesda had been fulfilled: 'the hour is coming when all who are in the tombs will hear his voice and come forth ...' (5.28). 'All in the tombs' shows that the Lazarus miracle was a sign for all Christians and not just the raising of one individual. The *parousia* – resurrection, life and judgement – came with Jesus.

## 11.45–57: One Man should die

Then there is reaction to the miracle: many of the Jews who saw the miracle believe in Jesus; others go to the Pharisees, and a council is convened with the chief priests. Jesus and his signs are a threat to the fragile relationship with Rome, and as such are a threat to the temple and the nation. Caiaphas[42] reminds them of something they already know: that in the first temple, one man had symbolically died for the people. This was the self-offering of the royal high priest on the Day of Atonement, the supreme role of the Servant (Isa. 53.10–11). The Moses era had rejected this form of atonement, exemplified in the story of Moses speaking to the LORD after the sin of the golden calf. He offered himself – 'blot me ... out of thy book' – if the LORD would forgive the sins of his people, but the LORD rejected this form of atonement: 'Whoever has sinned against me, him will I blot out of my book' (Exod. 32.30–33). Caiaphas reminds the council of something that Jesus' followers believed insofar as they recognized him as the Servant of the LORD, 'the Lamb of God who takes away the sins of the world'. He was speaking as a prophet, but this was also John's irony: the leader of the Jews knew all too well what he was saying. John completes the reference to the Servant by adding that not only would Jesus die for the nation; he would also gather in the children scattered abroad: '[He] formed me from the womb to be his servant, to bring Jacob back to him, and that Israel might be gathered to him' (Isa. 49.5). Thus in order to avert any threat to the nation and the temple, the Jews plan to kill the one whose very role was to restore the nation. 'From that day on, they took counsel how to put him to death' (v. 53).

Jesus withdrew from their company and stayed with his disciples in the country near the wilderness, in an otherwise unknown town called

---

[42] Caiaphas was high priest 18–36/7 CE; 'high priest that year' means 'in that important year'.

Ephraim. This appears in the *Ascension of Isaiah* as the prophet withdrawing from Jerusalem, which was ruled by Satan, and going first to Bethlehem. Since there was corruption there too, he went to an (unnamed) mountain in a desert place where he lived with a community of prophets who believed in the ascension into heaven. 'Isaiah' later claimed that the disciples of Moses were false prophets, because they denied that anyone could see the LORD and still live. He, Isaiah, had seen the LORD and was still alive. This unnamed mountain place is a memory of Jesus' base on the eastern side of the Jordan, whence he came across into Jerusalem and Judea. The community of prophets were the community whence Jesus emerged, possibly those later called the Magharians whose books were kept in a cave.[43]

Many of the Jews at that time began their journey to Jerusalem, to purify themselves before Passover, and wondering if Jesus would come to the city. The chief priests and Pharisees were asking where Jesus was, so that they could arrest him, but, as Mark records, this would not have been practical during the feast: 'They said, "Not during the feast, lest there be a tumult of the people"' (Mark 14.2). Jerusalem would have been full of pilgrims: Josephus[44] says that when Cestius took a census (about 65 CE), on the basis of the number of Passover sacrifices, he estimated there were over two and a half million people in Jerusalem.

---

[43] See H. Wolfson, 'The Pre-Existent Angel of the Magharians and Al-Nahawandi', *Jewish Quarterly Review* 51 (1960–1), pp. 89–106; G. Quispel, 'The Origin of the Gnostic Demiurge', *Gnostic Studies I*, Istanbul: Nederlands Historisch-Archaeologisch Instituut in het Nabije Oosten, 1974, p. 213.

[44] Josephus, *War* 6.424–6.

# John 12

## 12.1–11: Jesus is anointed at Bethany

The third Passover of Jesus' ministry is approaching. John's description of the first and second Passovers – meeting Nicodemus, feeding the 5,000 – has shown that the three-year cycle of readings in the synagogue is reflected in John's narrative. The correspondence is too close to be coincidence, and so elements from the third-year Passover readings would be expected here also. In the lectionary cycle, the readings for the Passover season in the third year would have been Numbers 6—14, and these are echoed in John's account of Palm Sunday and Holy Week.

- Glorifying the Son of Man (v. 23) reflects the high priest's blessing (Num. 6.22–27).
- The voice from heaven (v. 28) reflects the LORD speaking to Moses (Num. 7.89).
- The crowd with palms reflects the crowd of the firstborn[1] in heaven (Heb. 12.23; Rev. 14.4), and this in turn is the Levites who were accepted as a substitute for the firstborn of all Israel (Num. 8.14–19).
- The anointing at Bethany by Mary reflects the story of Miriam's leprosy (Num. 12.1–15).
- The two sections about rejection (vv. 37–50) reflect the LORD's words to Moses: 'How long will this people despise me? And how long will they not believe in me, in spite of all the signs which I have wrought among them?' (Num. 14.11).

This section of Numbers also includes the command not to break any bone of the Passover lamb (Num. 9.12), which John quotes of the crucifixion (19.36), and the warning that the rebellious generation would not enter the promised land became the theme of Hebrews 3—4.

Six days before Passover, Jesus goes to Bethany for his evening meal. Lazarus, Martha and Mary are there, but John does not say that they ate

---

[1] First*born*, not first*fruits*; see my book *The Revelation of Jesus Christ*, Edinburgh: T&T Clark, 2000, pp. 244–5.

in their house. Mary anoints Jesus' feet with expensive perfume and Judas complains of the waste. The chief priests plan to kill Lazarus too. The next day a crowd comes out from Jerusalem to meet Jesus, carrying palm branches (v. 12). He finds a young donkey and sits on it. The crowd coming from Bethany with Jesus talk about the Lazarus miracle (v. 18), and the Pharisees realize they are powerless in the face of such popular acclaim. This is the story, but John has chosen the incidents and the details – the signs – to show 'that Jesus is the Messiah, the Son of God, and that believing you may have life through his name' (20.31). This must determine how the story is read.

John knew of many other signs done by Jesus, usually understood as the miracles, but 'signs' included far more than the miracles. A sign could take many forms:

- a future event – the LORD gave Ahaz the sign of the Virgin who would bear a son (Isa. 7.14);
- a distinctive mark – the faithful had to bind the words of the LORD on their hands and foreheads as a sign (Deut. 6.6–8);
- a natural phenomenon – Jesus warned the Pharisees that they could predict the weather by looking at the sky but they could not 'interpret the signs of the times' (Matt. 16.1–4);
- an unnatural phenomenon – Jesus turned water into wine (2.11).

The disciples asked Jesus for a sign, so they would know when the temple was to be destroyed (Mark 13.1–4), and Mark has Jesus give a summary of the signs of the seven seals in Revelation 5—11.[2] As John recorded the signs in Revelation, when the seven seals had been opened there was a sign in heaven: the Woman clothed with the sun giving birth to her Son (Rev. 12.1-6). John claimed that an angel had given him the gift of understanding these predictions (Rev. 1.1), and it seems that this gift also shaped his Gospel.

Chapter 12 is a sequence of signs that are not understood, and it ends with John reflecting on the words of Isaiah:

> He has blinded their eyes and hardened their heart,
> lest they should see with their eyes and perceive with their heart,
> and turn for me to heal them.   (12.40, quoting Isa. 6.9–10)

Jesus is anointed at Bethany, but Judas misunderstands and complains about the cost and the waste (vv. 4–5); Jesus rides into Jerusalem on a

---

[2] See my *Revelation of Jesus Christ*, pp. 152–7.

## John 12

donkey, but even the disciples do not understand this at first (v. 16); there is a voice from heaven, and some of the crowd say it is thunder (v. 29).

Mark has the anointing at Bethany during Holy Week, two days before Passover; it happens in the house of Simon the leper, and the woman who anoints Jesus' head is not named (Mark 14.3//Matt. 26.6-7). John tells the story differently: the event takes place *six* days before Passover, and Jesus enters Jerusalem the next day. Since the meal was a supper and days were reckoned from evening to evening, Jesus' entry into Jerusalem was also *six* days before Passover. There must have been a reason for this. The woman who anoints him is named Mary, and her sister Martha and brother Lazarus are also there. Nobody is named as the owner of the house, so it could have been Simon. The perfume is the same as in Mark, but Jesus is anointed on his feet, not his head. The house is filled with the perfume of the oil. The details John gives must be contributing to the picture of Jesus as the Messiah, the Son of God.

He is anointed, the sign of the Messiah, but why on his feet? Luke tells of a woman who anointed Jesus' feet in the house of Simon the Pharisee (Luke 7.36-38), and it has been suggested that John confused or conflated the stories known to Mark and Luke. John is too subtle and careful a writer for that, and so the question remains: why Jesus' feet as a sign that he is the Messiah, the Son of God? It was probably worship. For her hair to touch his feet, she must have been bending low before him, and this was the posture adopted before the LORD-and-king (1 Chron. 29.20); how the rulers of the earth were warned to honour him (Ps. 2.11-12, but this text is damaged); how the people received the high priest who was the LORD (Ben Sira 50.17); and how the disciples greeted the risen LORD (Matt. 28.9). It was the posture of worship, and pilgrims sang of it as they went up to Jerusalem:

> Let us go to his dwelling place;
> Let us worship at his footstool.
> (Ps. 132.7)

The names of the characters are also interesting: there may well have been a leper named Simon in Bethany who hosted a supper for Jesus and some disciples, along with Lazarus and his sisters, but these are also significant names.

- Lazarus/Eleazar was patriarch of the Zadokite priests (Num. 3.32; 1 Chron. 24.1-3), whose famous descendant had anointed Solomon before he built the temple (1 Kings 1.39), and whose faithful descendants were living at Qumran;

- Mary/Miriam was the name by which Wisdom was remembered;[3]
- Martha means 'the Lady',[4] and she served in the house, as did Wisdom in the temple (Ben Sira 24.10: 'I ministered before him');
- Simon was a leper, and to be stricken with leprosy was the traditional punishment for anyone who challenged the authority of Moses and his priests (Miriam in Num. 12.1, 9; Uzziah in 2 Chron. 26.16–21);
- they lived in Bethany, a name which means 'the house of affliction/poverty/humility'.

How is this scene a sign? Where was this Bethany, and what was the house there? Popular imagination has it as a village home on the Mount of Olives, but 'Bethany beyond the Jordan, where John was baptizing' (1.28) suggests at least two places of that name, and a 'house of affliction', beth $^a$nî, with anointing oil suggests that the Bethany where Jesus was anointed could have been a religious house, maybe a gathering place east of the Jordan for those who had left Jerusalem and chosen, like the Baptist, to live in the wilderness. Perhaps they were the people who had preserved the memory of the temple oil, which had been lost since the time of Josiah.

Mary pours out a quantity of liquid[5] nard, a costly perfume, and the house is filled with its fragrance. This is a sign of the divine presence. When consecrating the first temple at Tabernacles, as Josephus said, Solomon burned a huge quantity of incense, 'till the very air itself everywhere around was full of these perfumes ... an indication of the presence of God'.[6] Isaiah described the perfume of the branch from Jesse on whom the Spirit rested, and the Baptist recognized the sign of the resting Spirit when Jesus came to him to be baptized. 'His perfume shall be the fear of the LORD,' said the prophet (Isa. 11.3, my translation),[7] alluding to the perfumed anointing oil. This was the sacrament of the sevenfold gift when the Spirit/Wisdom poured herself out on her children (Prov. 1.23, translating literally). The Christians at Corinth knew this image because Paul wrote to them: '[God] through us spreads the perfume of Christ's knowledge ...' (2 Cor. 2.14, my translation). John tells how Martha served in the house, and how Mary anointed him in the presence of Eleazar. Judas says the perfume should be sold for the poor, but Jesus

---

[3] See above, p. 49.
[4] The feminine of *mar*, 'Lord'.
[5] *Pistikos* can mean either 'pure' or 'liquid', and pouring does imply a liquid.
[6] Josephus, *Antiquities* 8.101.
[7] Hebrew *rîaḥ* means 'perfume', and only occasionally 'delight'.

replies that there will always be the poor, but 'you do not always have me' (v. 8). Bearing in mind that the army of the sons of light at Qumran called themselves 'Thy Poor whom Thou hast redeemed',[8] and that the Hebrew Christians were known as the Ebionites, literally 'the poor', was Judas saying that the cost of the perfume would have been better used in the group's funds? This fits better with the character of Judas as depicted elsewhere – the keeper of the money (13.29).

The anointing oil in the temple conferred eternal life and was the sacrament of resurrection/*theōsis*; with John's characteristic irony, he has Jesus tell Mary to keep the rest of it for his death.

A crowd assembles at the house when they hear that Jesus and Lazarus are there, and the chief priests plan to kill Lazarus also, because his presence is convincing many Jews to believe in Jesus.

## 12.12–19: Jesus rides into Jerusalem

All four canonical Gospels describe how Jesus rode into Jerusalem on a donkey. The details differ: Luke says that garments were spread on the road but does not mention the branches; Matthew says there were two animals; Matthew and Mark mention the branches but do not say they were palms. Only John says the people carried branches of palm. The synoptic Gospels all mention the king or the kingdom, but only John mentions 'the King of Israel'; cf. 1.49: 'You are the Son of God. You are the King of Israel.' The synoptic Gospels say that Jesus sent two disciples to bring a colt, for which there was a password: 'The LORD has need of him.' Jesus had arranged to have a donkey. John does not mention this, saying only that Jesus found a young ass and sat on it (v. 14). John alone mentions that a crowd carrying palms *came out* from Jerusalem to meet Jesus (vv. 12–13). Had Jesus arranged this too?

Although the synoptic Gospels do not mention Jesus being in Jerusalem before he began his work in Galilee, they give many hints that he had been there. Eusebius' comment that John wrote to supplement the synoptic Gospels, and to record what Jesus did in Jerusalem before the Baptist was killed, implies that this period of his ministry was important. 'John deals with the early stages of Christ's career and the others cover the last period of his story.'[9] Holland asked the question:

---

[8] *War Scroll*, 1QM XI.
[9] Eusebius, *History of the Church* 3.24.

How is it that at Bethany, there is a house where he can always make his home, with those who passionately love him, and will stand by him in the day of peril? How is it that there is a man with a colt in a village near, who will yield it at once to his service at the word, 'The Lord hath need of him' (Mark 11.3)? How is it that a man, whose very name they fail to give, is so loyal in his faith, that in the very darkest hour he will keep an upper room ready for him at a moment's notice? Who is this with whom he can entrust himself to communicate, just when all the world is against him, by a pre-arranged code of signals? ... How did Joseph of Arimathea arrive at his faith?[10]

The time in Jerusalem that they do not record shows the synoptic Gospels to be secondary sources for the life of Jesus, and that John was closer both to the events and to the teaching than is often assumed.

Unlike the other Evangelists, John does not say that Jesus went to the temple when he reached Jerusalem. He has the cleansing of the temple at the start of the ministry, which is a more likely time for the event, as the disturbance is not mentioned at Jesus' trial.[11] The 'later' element in John's Gospel is his reflection on the events, and not his recording of the events. The palms, the King of Israel, and the people coming out from Jerusalem must be important for John's understanding of the story, and presumably he includes himself in the observation that the disciples did not at first understand what it meant (v. 16). But John wrote his Gospel after he had received his vision of the *parousia*, and so he was interpreting his memories of the life of Jesus in the light of that new revelation; the LORD had come, the judgement had happened.

Pilgrims carried palms at Tabernacles,[12] but some have questioned whether palms would be available in Jerusalem at Passover time. Pliny, however, writing in the late 70s CE, said that Judea was famous for its palm trees, and that the *caryota* variety was abundant, especially near Jericho.[13] Aristeas said that because of careful cultivation, Judea had fruit trees and palms beyond number.[14] Palm trees and palm branches were often depicted on Jewish coins, and for several years after the capture of Judea and the fall of Jerusalem, the Roman emperors issued commemorative coins, 'IUDAEA CAPTA', depicting a palm tree and two mourning figures. In the time of Jesus palm trees must have been so

---

[10] H. S. Holland, *The Fourth Gospel*, London: John Murray, 1923, pp. 32–3.
[11] See above, p. 191.
[12] See above, p. 152.
[13] Pliny, *Natural History* XIII.26, 44, 45.
[14] *Letter of Aristeas* 112. This letter cannot be dated with certainty.

## John 12

abundant that they were the symbol of Judea itself, and an episode in the life of Simon Maccabee shows that palm branches were available in the spring. They were carried in the triumphal procession when he re-entered the Jerusalem citadel five weeks after Passover in 141 BCE.[15] The more important question is: why were palms available in the city, apparently at short notice, before a temple festival that did not require them?

The palm branch was significant. For the crowd with their palms it could have been a sign of triumph, as it was for Simon Maccabee, or it could have been a sign of Tabernacles – as was the perfumed house – albeit at the wrong time of the year. Or it could have been the restoration of something condemned by Ezekiel and remembered each year at Tabernacles. As priests went to draw water from Siloam for the libation, they stopped at the eastern gate and formally rejected facing east, to pray towards the rising sun *as their fathers had done*. 'They turned their faces to the west and said, "Our eyes are turned towards the LORD."' The description of the custom Ezekiel condemned has been obscured by the correcting scribes, and so it is no longer clear what was done. This was what the correcting scribes intended. The text could have been: 'holding the branch to their face' (Ezek. 8.17), implying that a group of about 25 men was standing near the altar in the temple courtyard, looking towards the east through the aligned gates and worshipping the sun. They held branches in front of their faces, but this was one of the practices of the first temple that the scribes had to censor.

We have seen how several elements that were important for the Christians were obscured by the correcting scribes,[16] and people holding palm branches and facing east in the temple could have been one of them, since a sunrise ritual with palms is found in Revelation. In the vision, the angel[17] rises from the dawn and marks with the seal of the living God all those to be saved from the wrath (Rev. 7.1–3). This angel is also known as the Morning Star, an ancient title for the Davidic king that was claimed by Jesus (Ps. 110.3; Rev. 22.16: 'the Offspring of David, the bright Morning Star', my translation). The visions of Revelation were known to/given to Jesus himself as prophecies of what was soon to take place (Rev. 1.1), and if Jesus was making his own actions a sign, then the palms were a sign that the ways of the first temple had returned.

---

[15] 1 Macc. 13.51.
[16] See above, pp. 50–2.
[17] 'Afterwards', not 'another'; see below, p. 418.

## Temple Theology in John's Gospel

Zechariah the priest prophesied this role for Jesus: his son the Baptist would prepare the way for the LORD who would return:

> ... through the tender mercies of our God,
> By which the *anatolē* shall visit us from on high,
> To bring to the light those who are in darkness and in the shadow of death,
> And to guide our feet into the way of peace.
> (Luke 1.78–79, my translation)

The *anatolē* is the Greek translation of the Hebrew *ṣemaḥ*, which can mean either a branch or the rising of a heavenly body, or the east. In the English translations of the Hebrew Scriptures, *ṣemaḥ* is translated 'Branch', and so the link to Zechariah's words is lost. But Zechariah's prophecy of the *anatolē* would not have been uttered in Greek, and so his words alluded to Jeremiah's prophecies of the Branch, *ṣemaḥ*, the Righteous One, who would be the restored Davidic king and rescue his people (Jer. 23.5–6; 33.14–16).[18] They also evoked the prophet Zechariah's vision of the Branch, *ṣemaḥ*, who was the Servant of the LORD, and 'the Man whose name is the Branch ... who shall build the temple of the LORD' (Zech. 3.8; 6.12).

When 'the angel from the rising sun' (Rev. 7.2) is understood as the Morning Star, the vision is the expected Davidic king coming to his city from the east, bringing/wearing the Name with which to mark the people because he is the presence of the LORD.[19] This is like Ezekiel's vision of the Man in linen who, at the LORD's bidding, marked the foreheads of the faithful with the mark (literally a letter *tau*) of the LORD (Ezek. 9.4). In the time of Ezekiel this was written 'X', and was the sign of the Name.[20] The Baptist's father prophesied that the *anatolē* would 'visit', *episkeptō*, the people in darkness to bring them light, a reference to the royal birth oracle in Isaiah 9.2: 'the people who walked in darkness have seen a great light' and doubtless the meaning of a sunrise ceremony. John has this in the Prologue: 'the true light ... was coming into the world' (1.9). The light would 'visit' the people, as the *Damascus Document* predicted.

> The humble of the flock are those who watch for him. They shall be saved at the time of the Visitation, whereas the others shall be delivered up to the

---

[18] See above, p. 83.
[19] Cf. 'Where is he who is born King of the Jews, for we have seen the star in the *anatolē*' (Matt. 2.2, my translation).
[20] Ezek. 9.4 says literally: 'mark with a *tau*'.

sword when the Anointed of Aaron and Israel shall come, as it came to pass at the time of the former Visitation, concerning which God said by the hand of Ezekiel: They shall put a mark on the foreheads of those who sigh and groan [Ezek. 9.4].[21]

The Anointed One would bring both judgement and salvation – the theme that runs all through John's Gospel – but a passage unique to Luke associates this 'visitation'[22] with Jesus' entry into Jerusalem.

> And when he drew near and saw the city he wept over it, saying, 'Would that even today you knew the things that make for peace! But now they are hid from your eyes. For the days shall come upon you, when your enemies will cast up a bank about you and surround you, and hem you in on every side, and dash you to the ground, you and your children within you, and they will not leave one stone upon another in you; because you did not know the time of your visitation.' (Luke 19.41–44)

Jesus came to Jerusalem from the east, and people with palms came out of the city to meet him. Ezekiel had known such a scene, people holding branches and looking to the east. An oracle at the end of Zechariah said that when the LORD became king of the whole earth, he would come from the Mount of Olives with his holy ones. People from all nations would come to Jerusalem to worship the King and to keep the feast of Tabernacles, and on that day there would be no more traders in the house of the LORD (Zech. 14.4, 5, 9, 16, 21). John alluded to this prophecy when he had Jesus say as he cleansed the temple: 'You shall not make my Father's house a house of trade' (2.16). A procession coming from the Mount of Olives, escorting Jesus who had been anointed in Bethany after raising Lazarus from the dead, must have been planned as a visible sign that the prophecies were being fulfilled. The palms were prepared for the One who would gather in all nations to Jerusalem.

In Revelation, when the angel of the sunrise has appeared, a crowd of 144,000 (12,000 from each of the 12 tribes) receive the seal, that is, the Name he bears. Then the scene becomes 'a great multitude that no man could number', all wearing white and carrying palms (Rev. 7.9–12). They are worshipping God-and-the-Lamb (the Servant who had become the LORD), and he is seated on a throne. The same group appears in a later

---

[21] *Damascus Document*, CD VIII. There are variant texts here, and this passage has not been found among the fragments at Qumran. It is from manuscript B found in the Cairo Genizah. Translation from G. Vermes, *The Complete Dead Sea Scrolls in English*, Harmondsworth: Penguin, 1997, p. 133. See above, p. 26.

[22] The noun *episkopē*, from the verb *episkopō*, 'visit'.

vision, standing with the Lamb on Mount Zion (Rev. 14.1); they are probably the angel army (the hosts of the LORD of hosts) which rides out from heaven clad in white linen (Rev. 19.14), and in the final vision, they appear again.[23] No number is given here, but they are in the new Jerusalem, worshipping before the throne of God-and-the-Lamb, and his Name is on their foreheads (Rev. 22.1–5). John has Jesus pray after the last supper for the realization of this vision: 'Father, I desire that they also, whom thou hast given me, may be with me where I am, to behold my glory …' (17.24). Only in the first vision are the Name-wearers said to be clad in white garments as they stand before the throne, but it is likely that all the Name-wearers wore white. They are in the temple, wearing the holy garments of the priests. Ezekiel prescribed white linen garments for the faithful sons of Zadok who would be permitted to serve in the restored temple; they had to be worn only in the inner court, and then removed and stored within the temple lest they carry holiness beyond the sacred place (Ezek. 44.15–19).

The first Christians saw themselves as the new/restored priesthood. Peter explained that they had been given the interpretation of the prophecies, 'things into which angels long to look' (1 Pet. 1.12). 'You know that you were ransomed from the futile ways of your fathers', he wrote, and so 'like living stones, be yourselves built into a spiritual house, to be a holy priesthood … You are a chosen race, a royal priesthood, a holy nation, a people for his own possession …' (1 Pet. 1.18; 2.5, 9, my translation). This is a clear statement that the ways of the second temple have been rejected – 'the futile ways of your fathers' – and that the older royal priesthood is restored. Facing east to pray, as in the first temple, was one of the traditions about Christian worship passed down unwritten by the Apostles, according to Basil.[24]

All four New Testament Gospels say the people were calling out words from Psalm 118, one of the Hallel psalms sung at Tabernacles and Passover. Only John says it was the people from Jerusalem who sang this psalm. At Tabernacles, the pilgrims carrying palms sang the whole psalm, waving their palms during the first and last verses but also at the Hosanna,[25] but the priests used to carry willow branches and process around the altar each day saying [singing?], 'We beseech you, LORD, save us [= *hôšî'ânā*']! We beseech you, LORD, make us prosper' (Ps. 118.25, my

---

[23] There is a similar vision in the Christian additions to 2 Esdras: 2 Esdr. 2.42–48.
[24] See above, p. 322.
[25] Mishnah *Sukkah* 3.9.

## John 12

translation).²⁶ The Hebrew Scriptures say nothing of the reason for carrying the branches at Tabernacles; the huts of leafy branches are explained,²⁷ but the procession with branches could well have originated in a sunrise procession when the king came from the east into the temple. Solomon entered the city from the east after he had been anointed at the Gihon spring. He rode up the hill on the king's mule, and the city was in uproar from the rejoicing (1 Kings 1.44–45).

*Psalm 118 at this point has yet another unreadable text*, and it is important for understanding John's account of Palm Sunday that we explore this text closely, especially as he himself says that he did not understand at the time what was happening. Although the combination of palms and this psalm is sufficient in itself to identify Palm Sunday as a Tabernacles procession, the verse that seems to mention branches is far from clear. 'Bind the festal procession with branches, up to the horns of the altar' (Ps. 118.27b, RSV) is very different from 'Bind the sacrifice with cords, even unto the horns of the altar' (Ps. 118.27b, AV). Why should the Hebrew text have become opaque at this point? The Targum, which cannot be dated,²⁸ presents the psalm to be sung antiphonally: the architects/builders in dialogue with various others.

> ²⁴'This is the day the LORD has made', *said the builders/architects*;
> 'Let us rejoice and be glad in it', *said the sons of Jesse.*
> ²⁵'We beseech you, O LORD, redeem us now', *said the builders/architects*;
> 'We beseech you, O LORD, make us prosper now', *said Jesse and his wife.*
> ²⁶'Blessed is the one who comes in the name of the *Memra* of the LORD', *said the builders/architects*;
> 'We bless you from the house of the sanctuary of the LORD', *said David.*²⁹

This is a gate liturgy for entering the temple, as is clear from verses 19–20:

> Open to me the gates of righteousness,
> That I may enter through them
> And give thanks to the LORD.
> This is the gate of the LORD;
> The righteous shall enter through it.

---

²⁶ Mishnah *Sukkah* 4.5. On the seventh day of the festival they walked round the altar seven times.
²⁷ See above, p. 149.
²⁸ D. M. Stec, *The Targum of Psalms*, London: T&T Clark, 2004, p. 2: 'A tentative suggestion would be the fourth–sixth century CE.'
²⁹ Targum of Psalms 118.24–26.

The Targum here is a straightforward translation, but the significance of the characters involved and the identity of the 'builders' is not known.

Then there is that difficult verse:

> The LORD is God, and he has brought light to us.
> Bind the festal procession with branches, up to the horns of the altar [or]
> Bind the sacrifice with cords, even unto the horns of the altar.

The Targum here is: 'Bind the lamb/child/servant for the sacrifice of the festival with chains, until you offer it and sprinkle its blood on the horns of the altar ...'

The Targum may illuminate John's enigmatic comment: 'His disciples did not understand this at first; but when Jesus was glorified they remembered that this had been written of him, and *that they had done these things to him*' (v. 16, my translation). What had *they done to him*? The opening scene of Revelation is the Servant/Lamb standing/resurrected even though he had been sacrificed, *esphagmenon* (Rev. 5.6), and the Targum may preserve the cultural memory of the sacrifice of the Servant at Tabernacles.

The crowd called out, 'Save us! Blessed is he who comes in/with the Name of the LORD', which is an allusion to the royal high priest, and especially to his role on the Day of Atonement when he saved his people from the effects of their sins. The Name which the high priest wore was the visible sign that he was the presence of the LORD, and thus his 'Son'. The *Gospel of Philip* shows that the early Christians knew the significance of the person who wore the Name:

> One single Name is not uttered in the world, the Name which the Father gave to the Son, the Name above all things: the Name of the Father. For the Son would not become Father unless he wore the Name of the Father ... Those who have this Name know it, but they do not speak it. But those who do not have it do not know it.[30]

The Name empowered the one who bore it to make the great atonement: to remove the effects of sin; to drive out Azazel who was the source of sin; and to take into himself any iniquity, *ʿawon*, in the offerings and so make them acceptable (Exod. 28.38). The Name also protected him in the dangerous duty of dealing with sin, hence the commandment: 'You shall not wear the Name of the LORD lightly, for the LORD will not hold him guiltless [that is, untainted by the sin] who wears his Name lightly' (Exod.

---

[30] *Gospel of Philip*, CG II.3.54.

## John 12

20.7, translating literally). So too the wonder of Micah: 'Who is a God like you, carrying [away] iniquity, *ªwon*, and passing over transgression for the remnant of his inheritance?' (Mic. 7.18). This is why the crowd called out: 'Save us! Blessed is he who comes *with* the Name of the LORD.'

The Man was called the Righteous One, meaning the one who makes right, and the Victor/Saviour, meaning the one who has saved his people by overcoming their enemies. These titles were used by Zechariah to describe the king who would one day return to Zion. John implies that Jesus deliberately fulfilled the prophecy of Zechariah in response to Psalm 118 and the acclamation with palms. *He chose to ride into Jerusalem on a donkey.*[31] Zechariah wrote:

> Rejoice greatly, O Daughter of Zion!
> Shout aloud, O Daughter of Jerusalem!
> Behold, your king comes to you,
> He is a Righteous One and a Victor,
> Humble and riding on an ass ...
> (Zech. 9.9, my translation)

John does not quote the prophecy verbatim, but gives only the gist: 'Fear not, daughter of Zion; behold your king is coming, sitting on an ass's colt.' The original has the king riding rather than sitting on the animal, and calls on the Daughter of Zion to rejoice rather than 'fear not'. John omits the titles of the king, but they must surely be implied: 'Righteous One' [RSV 'triumphant'; AV 'just'], is *ṣaddîq*, which is also a title of the Servant, translated '*the Righteous One, my Servant*' (Isa. 53.11); 'Victor', *nôšā'*, is literally 'one who has been saved [from enemies]'; and *'ānî*, is 'afflicted/poor/humble'. John's understanding of Palm Sunday is expressed in these two texts: the disciples remembered that 'this had been written of him and had been done to him' (v. 16). 'Written of him' is an obvious reference to the prophecies in Zechariah and Psalm 118; and 'they had done these things to him' refers to how the text of Psalm 118 was understood before it was obscured because it was important for Christians. The Targum preserved the original meaning.

John says no more about Jesus entering the city, but many signs were remembered from that time, in particular the spontaneous opening of the doors of the temple. Josephus reported a series of omens 'before the revolt and the commotion that led to war', but gave no precise year. He did, however, remember the date:

---

[31] Presumably the equivalent of the king's mule that Solomon rode when he entered the city after being anointed at the Gihon.

> At the time when the people were assembling for the feast of unleavened bread, on the eighth of the month Xanthicus [= Nisan], at the ninth hour of the night, such a light shone round the altar and the sanctuary that it seemed like brilliant daylight; and this continued for half an hour. This seemed to the inexperienced to be a good [omen], but by the sacred scribes it was considered to concern what happened immediately afterwards. At the same feast, a cow, led by someone for sacrifice, gave birth to a lamb in the midst of the temple court, and the eastern gate of the inner court, made of brass and very thick..., was seen to open of its own accord at the sixth hour of the night. Again, it seemed to those with no real knowledge that this was a very good omen, that God had opened to them the gate of blessings ['good things']... The learned men, however, understood that the security of the temple was opening up of its own accord, and that the opening of the gate was a gift for enemies...[32]

The eighth of Nisan was six days before Passover, and John emphasizes that it was on the sixth day before Passover that Jesus was anointed in the evening and then entered Jerusalem the following day. By the Jewish way of reckoning the day from dusk to dusk, this was still the eighth of Nisan. Jesus therefore entered the city on the very date that Josephus says the phenomena occurred in the temple. *Josephus does not say in which year they occurred.* Did these phenomena prompt Jesus to come to the city, and does this explain John's emphasis on the *sixth* day before Passover? Mark says that it was late in the day before Jesus arrived at the temple (Mark 11.11), so he cannot have left Bethany early, and John says that the disciples did not at first understand what was happening (12.16), but the people who came out from the city had palms ready. Since it looks as though Jesus planned Palm Sunday as a sign, these phenomena could have prompted his action.

It is possible[33] that the phenomena Josephus described were interpreted by some on duty in the temple that night as fulfilment of the visions described in Revelation. Jesus did have sympathizers within the temple: Zechariah, the father of the Baptist, was a priest, and Simeon who saw the infant Jesus may not have been just a fictional or symbolic figure. A great number of the authorities believed in Jesus (12.42), a great number of priests soon became Christians (Acts 6.7), and we know that some priests were trying to calculate the time when the Messiah would come.[34] It has

---

[32] Josephus, *War* 6.289–94, my translation.
[33] Most biblical study is informed guesswork.
[34] The parts of Josephus that have only survived in Slavonic describe Annas the high priest and his fellow priests scrutinizing Daniel 9.24–27 to find out when the Messiah would come and

also been suggested that Luke wrote for the high priest Theophilus 'so that you may know the truth concerning the things of which you have been informed' (Luke 1.4).[35]

Josephus was from an eminent priestly family, the first family in the first of the 24 courses of priests.[36] He would have heard of the phenomena from his family, and so he could write about both sides of the debate that followed. From the little evidence available, it is possible that the reports of temple phenomena – the light, the doors and the cow giving birth – were a garbled version of curious happenings that prompted Jesus to enter Jerusalem, deliberately giving the sign that he was the prophesied King. One disciple, possibly John himself, was known to the high priest and his staff (18.15), and somebody must have arranged for people from Jerusalem to take out palms and welcome Jesus.

Josephus reveals that there were prophecies current in Jerusalem that his people – presumably the high priests – did not recognize as sacred texts and he speaks of them in a disparaging way. 'It is recorded in *their oracles* that the city and the temple would be captured when the temple became square'; and:

> ... there is found in *their* sacred writings, in an ambiguous oracle, that *at that time* one from their country would become ruler of the world. They understood this to mean that one of their own [would become king of the world], and many of the wise men were led into error over the interpretation, *krisis* [which can also mean 'judgement'].[37]

These enigmatic oracles also appear in Revelation, which was either incorporating them or was the source that Josephus knew. Someone was told to measure the temple, which would be trampled by the nations (Rev. 11.1–2), and the seventh angel proclaimed: 'the kingdom of the world has become the kingdom of our-LORD-and-his-Christ, and he shall reign for ever and ever' (Rev. 11.15). This repeats the gist of Psalm 2, but claims that it is actually happening, just as Josephus said: '*at that time* [someone] would become ruler of the world'. These prophecies have been preserved in Revelation, presumably because they were crucial for Christian claims

---

save them from Herod. See Appendix to Josephus, *Jewish War*, vol. 3, Loeb Classical Library, Cambridge, MA: Harvard University Press, (1928) 1997.

[35] Theophilus was high priest from 37 to 41 CE; his father Annas, two of his brothers Eleazar and Jonathan and his brother-in-law Caiaphas (John 18.13) had also been high priests. See R. H. Anderson, 'Theophilus. A Proposal', *Evangelical Quarterly* 69.3 (1997), pp. 195–215.

[36] Josephus, *Life* 1.

[37] Josephus, *War* 6.311–13.

which Josephus' high-priestly class did not accept. There were other prophecies that Josephus quoted whose source has not survived:

> Who does not know the records of the ancient prophets, and the oracle which threatens this suffering city and is about to happen? They foretold that when someone began to murder his own people, then the city would be taken.[38]

Although it is not in the current Hebrew Scriptures, Jesus knew this as a sign that the temple was about to be destroyed:

> And brother will deliver up brother to death, and the father his child, and the children will rise against parents and have them killed; and you will be hated by all for my Name's sake. But he who endures to the end will be saved. (Mark 13.12–13, my translation)

All the synoptic Gospels set Jesus' prophecies about the fall of the temple and the coming of the Man in the final days of Holy Week, when he sat on the Mount of Olives, looking across to the temple, and when he taught Peter, James, John and Andrew privately (Mark 13.3–4). The first prophecies are a summary of the first five seals in Revelation 6 (Mark 13.5–13). The persecution that Jesus' followers would suffer from their own people was the fifth seal (Mark 13.9–13; Rev. 6.9–11); and the sixth seal would bring the day of the LORD: cosmic upheaval (Mark 13.14–25; Rev. 6.12–17) and the return of the Man.[39] Jesus knew the prophecy of the expected woes and he believed that by becoming the Servant/Lamb he would inaugurate the woes that would lead to the destruction of the temple. He would also have known that to inaugurate the sequence it was necessary for the Servant/Lamb to be sacrificed and then, as the Lion of Judah and the Root of David, to take his place on the throne and open the sealed book (Rev. 5.1–5). The compiler of Revelation incorporated the fulfilment of the prophecies as they occurred: the third seal predicted a great famine, and the interpretation was probably the words of Agabus about the famine that occurred in the reign of Claudius (Acts 11.28; Rev. 6.6).[40] As he went to his death, Jesus reminded the women of Jerusalem of the sixth seal, when people would pray for the mountains to fall on them (Luke 23.27–31; Rev. 6.12–17). When the fifth seal was opened, probably with the death of James in 62 CE, people were looking for the LORD to

---

[38] Josephus, *War* 6.110, my translation.
[39] See my book, *The Revelation*, n. 1 above, pp. 152–7.
[40] Pliny noted that the highest Nile flood on record occurred in the reign of Claudius, and this caused famine, as the seed could not be sown on time, *Natural History* V.58; XVIII.167–8.

## John 12

return, and that is when John had his vision of the mighty angel giving him a new understanding of the mystery of God revealed to the prophets (Rev. 10.1–11).

Without revealing the year in which the portents happened, Josephus said that at one particular Passover the great eastern door of the temple opened itself at midnight, which would have fulfilled 'God's temple in heaven was opened' (Rev. 11.19). Then a brilliant light shone in the sanctuary three hours later that made the night seem like day, which fulfilled the portent of the Woman clothed with the sun (Rev. 12.1–2). The cow giving birth to a lamb in the temple also sounds like the Lady, who was depicted in the first temple as a cow. The true significance of the cow and calf has been obscured in the Hebrew Scriptures: the throne of Solomon was surmounted by a calf's head (1 Kings 10.19), and the graffiti found at Kuntilet 'Ajrud depict the LORD and his mother as two human-and-bovine figures.[41] Mary is described in ancient Christian worship as 'the perfect cow'.[42] The cow giving birth to the lamb in the temple is Revelation 12, where the Woman clothed with the sun gives birth to her Child, the Servant/Lamb who is then enthroned. This was the heavenly sign to accompany and announce the kingdom of the LORD-and-his-Messiah established on earth (Rev. 11.15–18), the theme of Palm Sunday when Jesus rode into Jerusalem, and the fulfilment of the ambiguous oracle about the ruler of the world. The crowd had wanted to make Jesus king at the previous Passover, but he withdrew from them (6.15). The vision in Revelation also includes the devil being driven from heaven as the Son of the Woman is enthroned in the temple.

Jewish sources preserve information about other ominous phenomena in the temple in the 40 years before it was destroyed, in other words, after the death of Jesus. There must have been a widespread belief that the temple no longer functioned after the time of Jesus.

'Our rabbis taught that during the last forty years before the destruction of the temple':

- 'The lot "for the LORD" did not come up in the right hand', meaning that the lot drawn on the Day of Atonement was never a good omen, since the lot for Azazel came in the right hand.
- 'Nor did the crimson-coloured wool become white', meaning that the sign that the sacrifice had been accepted was never given. 'A thread of crimson wool was tied to the door of the sanctuary, and when [the

---

[41] See my book *The Mother of the Lord*, vol. 1, London: T&T Clark, 2012, pp. 156–7.
[42] In the *Akathist Hymn*.

scapegoat] reached the wilderness, the thread turned white, for it is written "Though your sins be as scarlet, they shall be as white as snow."'[43]
- 'Nor did the westernmost light shine', meaning that the most significant light of the menorah did not burn all through the night.
- 'And the doors of the great hall of the temple [the Nicanor gate of the *hêkhāl*] would open by themselves until R. Joḥanan rebuked them.'[44]

For the Christians, these signs would have been confirmation that Jesus was the final atonement sacrifice, the true light and the door for the sheep. Hebrews explained that Jesus' death had been the reality which temple rituals and their substitutes had foreshadowed (Heb. 9.11–14), and the omens in the temple must have been understood in this light, even, it seems, by the rabbis:

> For since the law has but a shadow of the good things to come instead of the true form of these realities, it can never, by the same sacrifices which are continually offered year after year, make perfect those who draw near ... [Christ] offered for all time a single sacrifice for sins ... (Heb. 10.1, 12)

What was happening behind the scenes or is hidden beneath the present text we cannot know; John simply says that the crowd who had seen Jesus raise Lazarus from the dead had spoken about it, and another crowd went out from Jerusalem to see the man who had performed the miracle. They could have been the people who saw the earlier temple miracles: the invalid man at Bethesda who walked, and the blind man at Siloam who was able to see. But this was not a spontaneous demonstration; the crowd from Jerusalem had planned such a welcome, and had the palms prepared; and somebody must have started chanting words from Psalm 118. The Pharisees felt helpless in the face of Jesus' popularity.

## 12.20–26: The Greeks come to Jesus

Among the pilgrims coming to Jerusalem for Passover 'to worship at the feast' (v. 20) were some Greeks, who spoke to Philip – maybe he spoke Greek as he had a Greek name – and Philip involved Andrew, the other disciple with a Greek name. They both went and told Jesus that some Greeks, *Hellēnes*, wished to see him. Jesus recognized this apparently insignificant event as the sign he had been waiting for: 'The hour has

---

[43] Mishnah *Yoma* 6.8.
[44] Babylonian Talmud *Yoma* 39b.

## John 12

come for the Son of man to be glorified' (v. 23). The Greeks were coming to Jerusalem for Passover, so they were not Gentiles: they were Jews from the Diaspora.[45] The Jews had wondered if Jesus intended to go to the Diaspora of the Greeks, *Hellēnes*, and teach them (7.35); this is how John used the word *Hellēnes*. Thus another of the Servant's roles was fulfilled: he was a light to the nations; he opened blind eyes; he released those bound in darkness; and now he gathers Israel back to the LORD (Isa. 49.5; John 10.16). The Servant had to raise up the tribes of Jacob and to bring back those in Israel who had 'guarded [the faith]' (Isa. 49.6, my translation[46]). The Servant knew he did this 'So that [he] might be glorified in the eyes of the LORD' (Isa. 49.5, my translation). The flock would then be gathered in, said Isaiah, from Syene (southern Egypt) and from the north and the west, that is, from Ionia, Greece (Isa. 49.12).

Jesus recognizes the sign. The scattered flock has begun to come to him, and so 'the hour has come for the Son of man to be glorified'. All through the Gospel, John has had Jesus say that his time had not yet come, but the coming of the Greeks at Passover is the sign that his time has come. The wedding at Cana, just before the first Passover, was not the right time (2.4); at the second Tabernacles[47] the time had not fully come (7.6, 8), and nobody harmed him, because his time had not come (7.30); nobody arrested him during this Tabernacles, because his hour had not yet come (8.20). The 'time' was the moment when he knew he had to die, and John presents this as a deliberate plan:

> For this reason the Father loves me, because I lay down my life, that I may take it again. No one takes it from me, but I lay it down of my own accord. I have power to lay it down, and I have power to take it again; this charge I have received from my Father. (10.17–18)

The same recognition that he had to die is found in the synoptic Gospels: 'The Son of man must suffer many things, and be rejected by the elders and the chief priests and the scribes, and be killed, and after three days rise again' (Mark 8.31//Matt. 16.21; 9.22).[48]

When Jesus knows that Diaspora Jews have come to him, he knows the time has come for him to die (13.1). John implies that Jesus planned

---

[45] Some argue that these were Gentile Greeks, and not Hellenized Jews, but John used the word *Hellēnes* for Greek-speaking Jews. The Jews had wondered if Jesus intended to go to the Diaspora of the Greeks, *Hellēnes*, and teach them (7.35).
[46] Reading *nṣry*, 'preservers of', rather than *nṣyry*, 'preserved of'.
[47] The first is implied in chapter 5; see above, p. 227.
[48] Mark and Luke both have 'Son of Man' here; this was the Man, the divine king.

to die at a particular time, at a Passover when he arranged a Tabernacles procession to enter the city. Jesus was celebrating the great festival of the first temple at Passover, which was the great festival of the pro-Moses second temple. *He was replacing Passover with Atonement/Tabernacles.* This has been a theme running through John's Gospel: after the first Passover Jesus spoke with Nicodemus and tried to explain heavenly birth, the *theōsis* described in Psalms 2, 89 and 110, when the king became the divine Son; and just before the second Passover, Jesus fed the 5,000 and explained that the true bread from heaven was not the manna but the flesh and blood of the Man, a reference to the bread of the Presence and the Day of Atonement sacrifice.[49] Neither of these Passovers was the right 'time' for what Jesus had to do. The third Passover, however, is the appointed time, and the sign of the Greeks confirms this. Jesus comes to Jerusalem, and John reflects that the Jews – the people of Moses and the Passover – cannot understand what he has been teaching (12.37–43).

John emphasizes that the last supper is not a Passover meal, and he does not mention the Eucharist. The meal takes place on the day before the Passover lambs are sacrificed, and Jesus dies at exactly the time when the lambs for Passover are being killed in the temple. If the eve of Passover fell on the sixth day of the week, the eve of a Sabbath, then the regular temple sacrifices were offered earlier in the day so that the Passover lambs could be killed after the eighth hour.[50] John does not say when Jesus died, but Mark says it was at the ninth hour (Mark 15.33). Paul described Jesus as the Passover lamb (1 Cor. 5.7), but the other Christians, as we shall see,[51] understood Jesus' death as the Day of Atonement sacrifice and said that Jesus saw himself as the Day of Atonement sacrifice.[52] This was his final act of replacing Passover with Tabernacles, and explains why the first two Passovers of his ministry had not been the right time for him to die. John describes each of the three Passovers as 'the Passover of the Jews' (2.13; 11.55), or 'the Passover, the feast of the Jews' (6.4), which may indicate that John was writing for people who did not know about Jewish festivals.[53] But he may have been indicating the Jews' festival, to distinguish it from that of people who observed Passover by a different calendar and so at a different time. The

---

[49] See above, pp. 258–9.
[50] Mishnah *Pesaḥim* 5.1.
[51] See below, p. 556.
[52] See below, pp. 551–2.
[53] Also 7.2: 'the Jews' feast of Tabernacles'.

## John 12

enigmatic Qumran *Commentary on Habakkuk* mentions the Wicked Priest who pursued the Teacher of Righteousness when he was observing the Day of Atonement, and so the Wicked Priest must have observed the Day of Atonement at a different time.[54]

In the calendar used by the Jews in the second temple, Passover could fall on any day of the week; but in the old solar calendar used at Qumran, the year was exactly 52 weeks, and so the festivals fell each year on the same day of the week. The *Damascus Document* and *1 Enoch* were both clear that the second temple was using the wrong calendar, implying that their own solar calendar was correct.[55] In their solar calendar, *the Day of Atonement always fell on the sixth day of the week*[56] and Passover on the third. Jesus was waiting for the right time, when the eve of Passover in the new calendar, when the lambs were killed, *fell on the sixth day of the week*. Further, the festivals for the restored temple as envisaged by Ezekiel, and presumably based on the ways of the first temple, prescribed identical rituals for the festival he called Passover and for the festival of the seventh month that elsewhere is called the Day of Atonement and Tabernacles. Ezekiel's Passover does not mention Moses and the exodus (Ezek. 45.18–25). Presumably he knew the older style of Passover when a lamb was offered instead of the firstborn, before the feast was linked to the exodus from Egypt.

Jesus then describes his imminent death as sowing a seed. There are many parables in the synoptic Gospels about sowing seeds and how they grow: when the sower sows seed, the seed represents Jesus' teaching; when the wheat and the weeds grow together until the harvest, this represents good teaching/teachers corrupted by evil; when the tiny mustard seed grows secretly into a great plant, this represents awareness of the kingdom growing gradually (Matt. 13.1–32). Jesus comparing himself to a seed that will bear fruit after it has been buried in the ground is another use of this everyday image. Paul may have kept Jesus' meaning here when he used the image to explain the nature of resurrection: 'What is sown is perishable, what is raised is imperishable' (1 Cor. 15.42). Those who

---

[54] *Commentary on Habakkuk*, 1QpHab XI.
[55] CD III; *1 Enoch* 80.2–8; also my article 'The Temple Measurements and the Solar Calendar', in *Temple Scroll Studies*, ed. G. J. Brooke, Sheffield: Sheffield Academic Press, 1989, pp. 63–6, which shows that the eastern gates of the ideal temple prescribed in the *Temple Scroll* marked the position of the sunrise over the Mount of Olives at the equinoxes, and the north-eastern and south-eastern gates marked the solstices when viewed from the centre of the temple complex, probably a marked place on the temple roof.
[56] See J. Maier, *The Temple Scroll*, Sheffield: JSOT Press, 1985, p. 74.

follow Jesus must not love their physical life, because they will eventually die; but those who do not love their earthly life will be given eternal life. They will serve and follow Jesus and go where he is going (vv. 25–26). This is Jesus' prayer in 17.24, and also the vision of his servants before the throne in Revelation 22.1–5.

## 27–36a: The voice of the angel

The coming of the Greeks and the voice from heaven are the only events that John records in the first days of Holy Week. The synoptic Gospels have Jesus teaching in the temple at this time (Matt. 21.23; Mark 11.27; Luke 19.47) and then going to the Mount of Olives (Matt. 24.1; Mark 13.1–3; Luke 21.37–38). In the synoptic Gospels, Jesus debates with chief priests, scribes and elders (those John calls 'the Jews') (Matt. 21.23; Mark 11.27; Luke 20.1), and he *teaches about kingship*: his authority, the parables of the unworthy tenants of the vineyard and their fate, the tribute money and the image it bears, his belief about resurrection, and whether the Messiah is more than the son of David. Matthew also includes the parable of the wedding feast and the intended guests who would not come,[57] Jesus' condemnation of the Pharisees for their way of interpreting the law, and the parables of waiting: the wise and foolish bridesmaids waiting for the bridegroom to come; the servants entrusted with their master's money until he returned; and the Son of Man judging the sheep and the goats. In the synoptic Gospels, Jesus quotes from Psalm 110 to show that the Messiah is more than just the son of David, and from Psalm 118, the rejected stone that becomes the head of the corner. All the synoptic Gospels include in the last week a summary of the prophecies of the seven seals in Revelation.

John also has Jesus teaching about kingship, but in a different way. He does not say where the events of Holy Week took place, but the temple is the most likely location. Jesus had come into the city from Bethany and so through the eastern gate that led directly into the temple. He teaches about the restoration of the royal high priests of the first temple, but John records no more than allusions. Here, another of the prophecies that Josephus describes as *their* oracles may have been fulfilled. The *Testament of Levi* is a text of which nothing can be said with certainty: it is likely to be a late second-temple text, it was preserved only by the Christians, and they may have added to it. Similarities to John's Gospel have been

---

[57] The wedding feast of the Lamb (Rev. 19.9).

noticed,[58] and it draws on Enochic writings that are now lost.[59] One of Levi's prophecies concerns the new priest who will succeed the corrupt priests of the second-temple period, 'the seventh week'.[60]

> The heavens shall be opened,
> And from the temple of glory shall come upon him sanctification
> With the Father's voice as from Abraham to Isaac ...
> For he shall give the majesty of the Lord to his sons in truth for evermore,
> And there shall none succeed him from all generations for ever.[61]

A voice heard in the temple is a commonplace of temple texts: Samuel heard a voice (e.g. 1 Sam. 3.4); Amos heard a voice (Amos 9.1); Isaiah heard a voice (Isa. 6.8); Habakkuk stood in the holy of holies to wait for the LORD to speak to him (Hab. 2.2); Zechariah heard a voice (Luke 1.13). After condemning the second temple and its priests (in the synoptic Gospels, this became the parable of the tenants in the vineyard), the Third-Isaiah heard a voice from the temple:

> Hark, an uproar from the city!
> A voice from the temple!
> The voice of the LORD,
> Rendering recompense to his enemies.
> (Isa. 66.6)

Jesus told those standing by that the voice was for their sakes (v. 30), and so presumably a phenomenon they would recognize. Given the context – the calculations from the sacred calendar, the visions in the temple just before the Baptist was born, the Lazarus miracle, the procession with palms – hearing a 'voice' in the temple would have heightened expectations.

Jesus said he heard the voice of the Father, responding to his prayer as he contemplated death, and so Levi's prophecy of 'a fatherly voice as from Abraham to Isaac' would have been appropriate. Some of the crowd said it was the voice of an angel, but others blamed the weather. The synoptic Gospels set this event after the last supper, when Jesus prays in Gethsemane before being arrested (e.g. Mark 14.32–36), and Luke says an angel appeared to strengthen him (Luke 22.41–44). In Hebrews, Jesus'

---

[58] H. C. Kee, 'The Testaments of the Twelve Patriarchs', in *The Old Testament Pseudepigrapha*, vol. 1, ed. J. H. Charlesworth, London: Darton, Longman and Todd, 1983, p. 777.
[59] *Testament of Levi* 14.1.
[60] See above, pp. 51–2.
[61] *Testament of Levi* 18.6, 8.

prayers before he died are linked to his being Melchi-Zedek, a name said to mean 'king of righteousness' and 'king of peace' (Heb. 7.2). The sequence in Hebrews is the Servant, the Son, salvation for all who serve him, and Jesus being declared Melchi-Zedek (Heb. 5.7–10). This is how some Christians – maybe most Christians – understood Jesus' prayer before he died. The *Testament of Levi* also alluded to Melchi-Zedek, the priest for ever: 'And there shall be no successor for him from generation to generation for ever.'

The sequence of Incarnation, suffering, death and then exaltation as the LORD (that is, receiving the Name) was an established early Christian belief. In Philippians 2.5–7 Paul was quoting something his hearers recognized, perhaps an early statement of belief. Melchi-Zedek is not mentioned by name, but he is there, just as he is in the Prologue to Hebrews which alludes to Psalm 2: the Son, who reflects the glory of God and bears the very stamp of his nature,[62] made purification for sins and was then enthroned in heaven/on Zion (Heb. 1.1–4). In the psalm the-LORD-and-his-Anointed (one person) subdues the hostile powers; in Hebrews he makes purification for sins. Both describe atonement, which in the world of the temple meant restoring the covenant with his own blood in order to protect his people and punish their angelic and earthly enemies. On the Day of Atonement, the high priest with the Name sacrificed a bull and a goat as substitutes for himself, then offered their bloods representing his life to cleanse the creation, whose sin he absorbed. Then he transferred the sin to the Azazel goat, which was driven out.[63]

John uses 'Son of Man' and 'Name' as equivalents: the one who wears the Name is the Man,[64] and both indicate the human presence of the LORD. He has Jesus say: 'The hour has come for the Son of man to be glorified' (v. 23), and then 'Father, glorify thy Name' (v. 28, my translation). The Hebrew Scriptures often speak of 'the glory of the LORD' and 'the LORD being glorified', and this is how Jesus' use of 'Name' and 'Son of Man' should be understood. Jesus prayed that the Man/the One who bore the Name would be raised up and recognized as the presence of the glory. He was praying that the people in the temple would recognize in his presence the fulfilment of the old high-priestly blessing, the LORD making his face/presence shine on them to protect them and give them peace (Num. 6.22–27). As we have seen, this blessing had become

---

[62] Ambiguity, meaning that he bears both the sign of the Name, X, and that he is the Image.
[63] See above, p. 45.
[64] See above, p. 87.

controversial by the end of the second-temple period, and Targum *Neofiti* did not translate the blessing into Aramaic but left the text in Hebrew. The Qumran community and people, listening in their synagogues to what became Targum *Pseudo-Jonathan*, understood this to be the blessing of illumination of the mind, being able to understand.[65]

This is Targum *Pseudo-Jonathan*:

> May the LORD make the graciousness of his countenance shine upon you in the study of the Torah, and reveal to you obscure things and protect you. May the LORD show the graciousness of his countenance to you in your prayer and give you peace in all your space.

This is the Qumran *Community Rule*:

> May he bless you with all good, and keep you from all evil,
> May he illuminate your heart with the wisdom of life, and grant you knowledge of eternal things,
> May he show the presence of his mercy to you for eternal peace.[66]

The pro-Moses tradition of the second temple denied that the LORD could be seen, and even when the commandments were given, there was only a voice (Deut. 4.12). As a result, only one detailed description of the glory of the LORD, or rather, how the glory was envisaged in the first temple, has survived. Ezekiel saw the fiery Man/Adam on a sapphire throne, surrounded by a bright rainbow of light and all within a great bright cloud (Ezek. 1.1–28). Ezekiel saw the glory leave the polluted first temple and then, when the angel had shown him the restored temple, he saw the glory return in the same way, so presumably as the Man enthroned (Ezek. 40.1—43.5). Many voiced this hope when the second temple was built; for Haggai it was the only reason to rebuild the temple: '"Build the house ... that I may appear in my glory," says the LORD' (Hag. 1.8). His contemporary Zechariah, like Ezekiel, saw the angel with a measuring rod, and heard a message from the LORD: Jerusalem would again be prosperous and 'I will be the glory within her' (Zech. 2.1–5). Isaiah had a vision of the judgement and then the LORD reigning on Zion, 'and before his elders he showed forth his glory' (Isa. 24.23b, my translation); reigning implies a throne as in Ezekiel's vision, but Isaiah has no detail here. The Second-Isaiah spoke of the way of the LORD in the wilderness, and the glory of the LORD being revealed there (Isa. 40.5), presumably returning as in Ezekiel's vision; the Third-Isaiah prophesied the LORD returning to Jerusalem, like

---

[65] See above, p. 97.
[66] *Community Rule*, 1QS II.3–4, my translation.

the sunrise: 'Arise, shine; for your light has come, and the glory of the LORD has risen upon you' (Isa. 60.1) and 'I am coming to gather all nations and tongues; and they shall come and shall see my glory' (Isa. 66.18). Making the Man/the Name glorious meant causing him to shine out from the temple again, gathering people to experience the blessing of the high priests which was to see the shining presence of the LORD. 'Hallelujah', the summons to worship,[67] meant literally 'Shine, LORD'; and so the exhortation in Psalm 22 should perhaps be read: 'You who fear the LORD, make him shine ... glorify him ... stand in awe of him' (Ps. 22.23, my translation). This meaning for *Hallelujah* was known in the Church as late as the eighth century and said to be: 'Our God will come openly/visibly, *emphanōs*.'[68]

John, when setting out the meaning of the story he was about to tell, said that the incarnate Logos was the glory returning to the temple: 'The Logos became flesh and *tabernacled* among us' (1.14). Seeing the glory is a constant theme in his Gospel: 'We beheld his glory, the glory [seen as] the beloved Son of the Father' (1.14, my translation). Jesus showed his glory in the Melchi-Zedek miracle, and those who saw the glory believed (2.11). Jesus did not seek his own glory (8.50); he sought to show forth the glory of God so that people would recognize him as the Son who revealed the glory (11.4, 40). The voice from heaven reassured Jesus that he had indeed revealed the glory already, and would do so again (v. 28); and finally, Jesus knew that the time had come for him to be recognized as the one who was bringing the glory back to the temple.

When the voice has spoken from heaven, Jesus declares that the time has come for the world to be judged and the ruler of this world to be cast out (v. 31), a clear and unambiguous reference to the Day of Atonement when the leader of the fallen angels was driven out into the desert (Lev. 16.20–22).[69] This was the temple ritual; but in Revelation, it was the vision of Satan and his angels driven out of heaven, the kingdom of God-and-his-Christ established on earth, and the red dragon, the ancient serpent, the devil and Satan (Rev. 12.9), going to make war on the other children of the Woman (Rev. 12.7–10, 13, 17). Thus John wrote in his first letter: 'We know that we are of God, and the whole world is in the power of the evil one' (1 John 5.19). In Revelation the vision depicts what is happening on earth as it is in heaven:

---

[67] Apart from Ps. 135.3, it always occurs at the beginning or end of the psalm.
[68] Germanus of Constantinople, early eighth century, *On the Divine Liturgy* 29.
[69] See above, p. 45.

## John 12

- the kingdom of our-LORD-and-his-Christ is established on earth;
- there is thunder and lightning, voices, an earthquake and hail;
- the Woman appears, about to give birth to her son in the holy of holies;
- the red dragon stands ready to kill him;
- her child is immediately taken up to the throne of God, to rule with a rod of iron;
- Satan and his angels are driven out of heaven: 'the ruler of this world is cast out' (Rev. 11.19—12.5).

Jesus knew this vision; perhaps it was given to him during his 40 days in the desert, perhaps it was known among those with whom he grew up. The Woman's Child who ruled with a rod of iron is the Davidic king described in Psalm 2: he was the son of the LORD, set on Zion, the hill of his Holy One, and the rulers of the world who conspired against him were warned to serve him (my translation). Daniel's vision of the Man going up with clouds (Dan. 7.13-14) described the enthronement of the Man after he had been 'offered' before the Ancient of Days, and this too was inspired by Psalm 2.[70] All the details of this psalm were prophecy for Jesus and his disciples: Jesus wrestled with the words of Psalm 2 when he was in the desert, taunted by the question 'If you are the Son of God ...' (Matt. 4; Luke 4). He felt himself to be on a high place in the temple, and then on a high mountain looking out over the world, which was the kingdom of the devil. When the Jerusalem church praised God after Peter and John had been released by the Sanhedrin, they interpreted Psalm 2.1-3 as a prophecy of their situation: the kings of the earth and the rulers were Herod and Pilate who had plotted against the-LORD-and-his-Anointed, but without success (Acts 4.25-28).

Luke's account of the mission of the 70 shows that either the vision of the Woman and her Child overcoming the dragon shaped Jesus' ministry, or else that it shaped the way his disciples told the story. 'I saw Satan fall like lightning from heaven,' Jesus said, when the 70 returned from their mission proclaiming the kingdom of God (Luke 10.18). Establishing the kingdom on earth was the counterpart of Satan being driven from heaven, as in Revelation 11—12. Luke's Jesus had already spoken of Wisdom's other children (Luke 7.35), and he had already given authority to the 70 to tread on serpents and scorpions, and all the power of the enemy (Luke 10.19). The 70 were among the other offspring of the Woman, against whom the red dragon waged war (Rev. 12.17), and treading on serpents

---

[70] See above, p. 69.

was the obvious way to speak of defeating the angels of the ancient serpent. This image is rooted in the story of Eden, where the snake is cursed and warned that the offspring of the Woman will tread on his head (Gen. 3.14–15). Embedded in Luke' account of the 70 are words of Jesus that echo John's Gospel. He says to them: 'He who hears you hears me, and he who rejects you rejects me, and he who rejects me rejects him who sent me' (Luke 10.16).

Jesus predicts that he will be raised up from the earth and then draw all people to himself (12.32). This 'lifting up' and the wordplay – being raised up to heaven/resurrected and being raised up on the cross[71] – has been mentioned twice already: to Nicodemus (3.14–15); and to the Jews in the temple at Tabernacles (8.28). Each time, Jesus spoke of himself as the Son of Man but here he does not use the term. Instead, the crowd uses the term (v. 34), and asks who, that is, *what person at this moment*, is the Son of Man/the Man? The blind man whom Jesus healed had also asked this question (9.35–37). Raising up the Man must have been something the crowd recognized.

There is an enigmatic passage in *1 Enoch* that gives the context for the crowd's question. It has caused more debate than any other part of the book, because what seemed its obvious translation was not only unexpected but also unwelcome. After the third parable/vision, when Enoch has been raised up to heaven, entered the holy of holies and learned the secret knowledge, the Antecedent of Days speaks to him:

> You are the Son of Man who is born to righteousness,
> And righteousness has remained with you.
> The righteousness of the Antecedent of Days will not forsake you.[72]

The older translations and commentaries 'knew' the obvious meaning was a mistake, and so R. H. Charles assumed a lost passage that introduced the Son of Man as a heavenly figure coming with the Head of Days.[73] More recent work on *1 Enoch* has been able to use copies of the text only discovered in the 1970s, which have Enoch and the Son of Man as the same person.[74] Enoch the high priest becomes the Son of Man. 'Born to

---

[71] See above, p. 202.
[72] *1 Enoch* 71.14, tr. D. C. Olson, *Enoch. A New Translation*, North Richland Hills: Bibal Press, 2004.
[73] R. H. Charles, *The Book of Enoch*, Oxford: Clarendon Press, 1912, p. 144. 'Head of Days', 'Ancient of Days', 'Antecedent of Days' are various translations of the same name which means 'the one before time'.
[74] D. C. Olson, 'Enoch and the Son of Man in the Epilogue of the Parables', *Journal for the Study of the Pseudepigrapha* 18 (1998), pp. 27–38.

righteousness' surely reflects a Hebrew original 'born as the Righteous One/Zadok' since this would be the same Hebrew letters, *lṣdq*, and the setting for the Epilogue of the *Parables* can be seen as the king-making ritual in the ancient holy of holies. At that time, Enoch became the Righteous One, Zadok, the Man. The crowd ask Jesus about the current Man, something implied by John identifying Zechariah 9.9 as the prophecy fulfilled on Palm Sunday. This was the return of the King, the Righteous One, but the disciples did not at the time understand it. The two who walked to Emmaus had Jesus explain to them: 'Was it not necessary that the Christ should suffer these things and enter into his glory? And beginning with Moses and all the prophets, he interpreted to them in all the scriptures the things concerning himself' (Luke 24.26–27).

There is no text in the current Hebrew Scriptures that says the Messiah must suffer and enter his glory, but one Qumran version of Isaiah has small but significant differences, and that text does indeed tell of the Messiah who suffers and then enters his glory. *In other words, the text that Jesus used to explain who he was is no longer in the Hebrew Scriptures.*

The text is the fourth Servant song (Isa. 52.13—53.12), originally composed by Isaiah in the time of Hezekiah, and reused by a later disciple.[75] The song was prompted by the near-fatal illness of Hezekiah, interpreted first as a punishment for his sacrilege and then recognized as the suffering of the sin-bearer. It is a reflection on the role of the royal high priest. The song is the earliest evidence for the anointing, Transfiguration, exaltation, suffering and atonement implied in Philippians 2 and Hebrews 1.[76] Now the text of the song in the current Hebrew Scriptures mentions neither the anointing nor the light (of the glory) which the Servant sees, but in the great Isaiah scroll found at Qumran, the Servant is wise, resurrected, lifted up, made very high, anointed and transfigured beyond human semblance (Isa. 52.13–14, my translation). He is the sin-bearer who offers himself to restore the covenant,[77] and when he has seen the light (of the glory) his knowledge would enable him to restore many. The Righteous One would make others righteous (Isa. 53.11), but nobody believed what was said (Isa. 53.1). The Targum of Isaiah, which cannot be dated but is thought to include late second-temple material, was based on the Qumran version of the text. The

---

[75] Hence its present place in the scroll with the oracles of the Second-Isaiah; see my article 'Hezekiah's Boil', *Journal for the Study of the Old Testament* 95 (2001), pp. 31–42.
[76] See above, p. 113.
[77] He is the *'āšām*, the offering to restore the covenant (Isa. 53.10); see above, p. 92.

Targumist knew that the Servant was the Messiah who would prosper and be exalted (Tg. Isa. 52.13), and that he would not look like an ordinary man, that is, he would be transfigured (Tg. Isa. 53.2). He was to restore the temple that was polluted by transgression and lost because of iniquities (Tg. Isa. 53.5).

The crowd then respond to Jesus: 'We have heard from the law that the Christ remains for ever. How can you say that the Son of man must be lifted up?' (v. 34). For them the Christ and the Son of Man were synonymous. The Christ remaining for ever could refer to Melchi-Zedek: 'You are a priest for ever after the order of Melchizedek' (Ps. 110.4) and the crowd may even have known the previous verse of the psalm, before it became unreadable and while it still described the anointing and 'birth' of the Son.[78] They too believed, as did the Baptist, that the Coming One was among them, but unknown until revealed by a sign (1.29–34). 'Who is this Son of man [who is among us]?' (v. 34).

Jesus then speaks the last words of his public ministry (vv. 35–36), warning the crowd that the light is about to leave them. His words echo the Prologue:

- 'The Logos became flesh and dwelt among us' (1.14): 'The light is among you' (v. 35);
- 'The true light ... was coming into the world' (1.9): 'The light is among you for a little longer' (v. 35);
- 'The darkness ... has not overcome the light' (1.5): 'lest the darkness overcome you' (v. 35);[79]
- 'To those who believed in his Name ... he gave power to become children of God' (1.12): 'Believe in the light that you may become sons of light' (v. 36).[80]

Jesus' final exhortation is to become sons of light; those who choose to walk in darkness do not know where they are going – more irony, since not only can they not see, but they do not know where the way of darkness leads them. John uses the same image to describe Christians in his letters, which were almost certainly written before his Gospel. Christians walk in the light, as God is in the light; they have been anointed by the Holy One and know all things; they are children of God; they have passed from death to life because they love the community; they can

---

[78] See above, pp. 74–5.
[79] The same verb, *katalambanō*.
[80] My translations.

## John 12

distinguish between the spirit of truth and the spirit of error; they are 'in' (God's) Son, Jesus Christ (1 John 1.7; 2.20; 3.2, 14; 4.6; 5.20). Paul reminded the Christians in Thessalonika that they were all sons of light and sons of day (1 Thess. 5.5), and he reminded the Christians in Ephesus that they had been darkness but were now light in the LORD and should walk as children of light (Eph. 5.8). The *Didache* and the *Letter of Barnabas* contrast the way of light and the way of darkness. This is the beginning of the version in the *Letter of Barnabas*.

> Now there are two ways of teaching, and two who wield power: one of light, the other of darkness. Between those two ways is a very great difference, because the light-bearing angels of God stand over one way and the angels of Satan over the other. One of these two is the LORD from all eternity to all eternity, but the other stands supreme over this present age of iniquity.[81]

The early Church in Rome knew them as the 'angel of righteousness' and the 'angel of wickedness'.[82]

The sons of light also appear in some Qumran texts, but it is impossible to know if the Christian understanding of the sons of light was the same as in the Qumran texts. The community in the scrolls described themselves as the sons of light in conflict with the sons of darkness, which is similar to the Christian position. The *Community Rule* says that the Master shall instruct all the sons of light, who are also known as the 'children of righteousness'. They are ruled by the Prince of Light and walk in the way of light, but all the children of injustice are ruled by the Angel of Darkness and walk in the way of darkness. The God of Israel and his Angel of Truth would sustain all the sons of light.[83] Those born of truth spring from a fountain of light, but those born of injustice spring from a source of darkness. God has chosen them for an everlasting covenant, and all the glory of Adam shall be theirs.[84] The council of the community was three priests and 12 men, and they formed a living temple. They had withdrawn to the wilderness to prepare the way, and after two years with the group, any newcomer could learn the things hidden from Israel that their leader had discovered.[85]

Any of this could apply to the disciples of Jesus: the Jerusalem church was led by Peter, James and John, two of whom were remembered as high

---

[81] *Letter of Barnabas* 18.
[82] *Shepherd of Hermas*, Mandate 6.2.
[83] *Community Rule*, 1QS III.
[84] *Community Rule*, 1QS IV.
[85] *Community Rule*, 1QS VIII.

priests,[86] and there were the 12 Apostles. The Christians were a living temple (1 Pet. 2.5). John also gives the impression that Jesus and his disciples had a base east of the Jordan (1.28; 6.1; 10.40; 11.54; 12.1); Bethany is named, but there was also 'the country near the wilderness' where Jesus stayed (11.54). The disciples saw Jesus for the last time at Bethany, where he blessed them and parted from them (Luke 24.51).[87] Further, the disciples of Jesus are not given his most important teaching until they have been with him for two years: they were called before the first Passover of his ministry, did not understand what he meant when he spoke of building a new temple (2.21–22) and did not understand what he did on Palm Sunday (12.16) just before the third Passover of his ministry. It was only after two years that he could begin to teach them, and John presents this as the farewell discourse.

The sons of light also appear in the Qumran *War Scroll*, 'the attack of the sons of light on the company of the sons of darkness'. The army of the sons of light had to be ritually pure – no boys or women among them – because the holy angels would come to fight with them. The Prince of Light himself would fight with them, and the enemy would be led by Belial and his host. On the day appointed for the defeat of the Prince of Wickedness, God would send help to his chosen people, and would raise up the kingdom of Michael among the angels in heaven and the kingdom of Israel on earth.[88] Much of this, too, could describe the disciples of Jesus: ritual purity is not an obvious characteristic of the Christians, and Jesus did not separate himself from lepers or the woman who was bleeding, but the priestly army of the Lamb on Zion[89] had to be ritually pure (Rev. 14.4), and the morally impure were excluded from their new temple-city (Rev. 21.8; 22.15). The kingdom in heaven was established at the same time as the kingdom on earth, and the Logos of God would ride out of heaven with his army to defeat the army of the beast (Rev. 19.11–21).

The Qumran texts also show that the heavenly beings had several names: the texts in question are broken, but they seem to say that the Prince of Light was also Michael and Melchi-Zedek, and the Prince of Darkness was also Belial and Melchi-Resha' (Evil King). Melchi-Zedek would rescue his own people from the power of Belial on the final Day of Atonement at the end of the tenth jubilee, and it seems that his people

---

[86] Eusebius, *History* 2.23; 3.31.
[87] 'and was carried up into heaven' is not found in the earliest texts, e.g. the original wording of the Sinai Codex, the Codex Bezae and several Old Latin texts.
[88] *War Scroll*, 1QM I, VII, XIII, XVII.
[89] They wore the Name on their foreheads.

were the sons of light, although the text is broken at this point.[90] The community had rituals to curse Melchi-Resha'[91] and during the age of wrath, Belial was set free to attack Israel with his false teaching.[92] The early Christians presented the two opposing powers with similar imagery; Satan was a deceiver from the beginning, when he made the fruit of the forbidden tree in Eden seem like the fruit of the tree Adam was intended to eat. In Revelation, the red dragon and his beast are the evil counterparts of the LORD and his Christ: the beast rose from the water with blasphemous names on its heads, it had suffered a mortal wound but had recovered, and people worshipped both the dragon and the beast who exercised the authority of the dragon (Rev. 13.1–4). Paul warned the Corinthian Christians against false teaching, 'for even Satan disguises himself as an angel of light' (2 Cor. 11.14); and Ignatius of Antioch wrote to the Ephesians: 'Never let yourself be anointed with the foul-smelling oil of the doctrines of the prince of this world.'[93]

This was the world in which Jesus exhorted his followers to become sons of light, and having spoken, he went away and hid himself from them.

## 36b–50: Reflection on rejection

John now reflects on the story so far. He returns to the Servant who was initially rejected as a man being punished for blasphemy, then recognized as his people's sin-bearer.[94] Hezekiah, who inspired the original poem, had been a zealous purger of the temple: he had removed 'Asherah' from the temple, broken up the bronze serpent, and destroyed the pillars and high places (2 Kings 18.4). This had been perceived by some as weakening his kingdom's defences, and the invading Assyrians warned that the LORD would no longer protect them because Hezekiah had destroyed his altars (2 Kings 18.22). The king had committed sacrilege, and when he caught the plague Isaiah said he would die (2 Kings 20.1). Before the prophet had even left the palace, he received another oracle and returned to the penitent king, saying that he would survive the illness (2 Kings 20.4–5). The fourth Servant song is a reflection on these events, how the one who had been deemed a great sinner, worthy of death, was in fact the one who

---

[90] *Melchizedek*, 11QMelch.
[91] 4Q286.
[92] *Damascus Document*, CD IV.
[93] Ignatius, *To the Ephesians* 17.
[94] See my article 'Hezekiah's Boil', n. 75 above. There have been many analyses of the fourth song, due to the disordered state of the sources.

carried his people's sins. This was the role of the sacral king, and Isaiah understood Hezekiah's suffering in terms of the Day of Atonement. But this interpretation was not initially accepted: 'Who has believed what we have heard? To whom has *the arm* of the LORD been revealed?' (Isa. 53.1), but 'arm', $z^e r \hat{o} a^\prime$, can also mean 'strength' or 'child', and Isaiah is asking the question: to whom has the LORD's human presence been revealed? So too, Jesus was at first condemned as a blasphemer (10.36–38) and worthy of death, but others recognized him as the LORD.

The Jews could not understand what was happening because they had lost their powers of spiritual perception: their eyes could not see and their hearts (that is, their minds) could not perceive. This had been the situation in the time of Isaiah. There had been a great conflict in the time of Uzziah,[95] and in the year that he died Isaiah received his vision of the LORD enthroned (Isa. 6.1–13). He and his people had adopted false teaching – were 'a people of unclean lips' – and he was warned of the consequences: they would no longer be able to hear or to see or to understand. This was not a punishment but the consequence of the false teaching. Their sin must have been rejecting Wisdom, since she was the source of what they had lost. It was the same in the time of Jesus: many people could not understand what Jesus was teaching because they had rejected Wisdom. Isaiah 6.9–10 is quoted many times in the New Testament: the synoptic Gospels quote it to explain why people did not understand Jesus' parables (Matt. 13.14–15; Mark 4.11–12; Luke 8.10); and Luke's Paul quotes it to explain that he has taken Jesus' message to Gentiles, because the Jews could not understand (Acts 28.26–28). Isaiah asked how long his people would remain in this state, and the LORD said until the land was desolate and the people were scattered. What follows (Isa. 6.12b) can be read two ways: either 'And the forsaken places are many in the midst of the land', or 'And great is the Forsaken One in the midst of the land'.[96] Since a brief quotation from the Hebrew Scriptures was often a way of referring to the whole passage, John was most likely including the whole passage here. Jesus gave warning of the impending disaster, and Revelation does show the Woman returned to the temple, and her tree symbol restored to its place by the throne (Rev. 22.1–2).

Isaiah had seen the glory of the LORD, said John, the One whose glory they too had seen (v. 41; cf. 1.14).[97]

---

[95] See above, p. 292.
[96] See my book *The Mother of the Lord*, pp. 92–8.
[97] See above, p. 65.

## John 12

Many leaders of the Jews believed, but for fear of the Pharisees they did not admit this lest they be expelled from the synagogue.[98] Such an admission would have cost them their position in society, and so John observed: 'They loved the glory, *doxa*, of men more than the glory, *doxa*, of God' (v. 43, translating literally).

John then has Jesus reflect on who he is and what he has been trying to teach: that he is the King, the visible presence of the LORD and the one through whom the LORD speaks. 'I have not spoken on my own authority; the Father who sent me has himself given me commandment what to say and what to speak... What I say, therefore, I say as the Father has bidden me' (vv. 49, 50b). Since Jesus has just been acclaimed as the King of Israel (v. 13), his words should be compared with the last words of David. The name David means 'loved one', and is thought to have been a royal title rather than a name.[99] He was:

> David, my servant; with my holy oil I have anointed him...
> My *\*faithfulness and my steadfast love* shall be with him...
> My *\*steadfast love* I will keep for him for ever, and my covenant will *\*stand firm for him*...
> I will not remove from him my *\*steadfast love*, or be false to my *\*faithfulness*. (Ps. 89.20, 24, 28, 33)

*\*Steadfast love and faithfulness* became the 'grace and truth' that came with Jesus Christ, in contrast to the law that came through Moses (1.17).[100]

David's last words were:

> The oracle of David, the son of Jesse,
> The oracle of the man whom God raised up on high,
> The anointed of the God of Jacob,
> The delight of the songs/branches[101] of Israel:
> The spirit of the LORD speaks in me
> And his word is upon my tongue.
> The God of Israel has spoken
> The Rock of Israel has said to me,
> When the Righteous One rules over people,
> Ruling in the fear of God,

---

[98] See above, p. 295.
[99] No other person in the Hebrew Scriptures has this name, and versions of it are found in e.g. Isa. 5.1: 'my beloved, *my loved one*, my beloved'. See N. Wyatt, '"Jedidiah" and Cognate Forms as a Title of Royal Legitimization', *Biblica* 66 (1985), pp. 112–25.
[100] See above, p. 177.
[101] The word *zmrwt* can mean either.

> He appears as the sun, like the light of morning ...
> (2 Sam. 23.1–4, my translation)

The oracle continues with the promise of the everlasting covenant and the destruction of Belial, burning like thorns in a fire.

David's last words claim that he has been anointed and raised up, and that he speaks the words of the LORD. He is the Righteous One who comes to his people like the sunrise, and brings judgement on Belial. Compare David's last words with the last words of Jesus, rearranged to emphasize the themes:

- 'The spirit of the LORD speaks in me ...'
  - 'I have not spoken on my own authority; the Father who sent me has himself given me commandment what to say and what to speak ...' (v. 49);
  - 'What I say, therefore, I say as the Father has bidden me' (v. 50b);
  - 'He who believes in me, believes not in me but in him who sent me' (v. 44);
  - 'He who sees me sees him who sent me' (v. 45).
- 'When the Righteous One rules over people, ruling in the fear of God ...'
  - 'He who rejects me and does not receive my sayings has a judge; the word that I have spoken will be his judge on the last day' (v. 48);
  - 'If any one hears my sayings and does not keep them, I do not judge him; for I did not come to judge the world but to save the world' (v. 47).
- 'He appears as the sun, like the light of morning ...'
  - 'I have come as [a] light into the world, that whoever believes in me may not remain in darkness' (v. 46).

Jesus speaks the last words of the King, and concludes with: 'I know that his commandment is eternal life' (v. 50). This is the final challenge to the pro-Moses people, for whom the commandments were the bread of life, but they were only rules for daily living. Moses taught:

- 'All the commandment which I command you this day you shall be careful to do, that you may live and multiply ...' (Deut. 8.1), the commandments being rules for everyday living and multiplying in the land;
- 'Man does not live by bread alone, but ... by everything that proceeds out of the mouth of the LORD' (Deut. 8.3), the verse quoted by Jesus in the conflict with Satan (Matt. 4.4; Luke 4.4);

- 'Lay to heart all the words which I enjoin upon you this day, that you may command them to your children, that they may be careful to do all the words of this law. For it is no trifle for you, *but it is your life*, and thereby you shall live long in the land which you are going over the Jordan to possess' (Deut. 32.46–47).

The bread of Moses replaced the older food, just as the law replaced Wisdom (Deut. 4.6), but Moses' food was only rules for daily living: 'The secret things belong to the LORD our God; but the things that are revealed belong to us and to our children for ever, that we may do all the words of this law' (Deut. 29.29).

Thus it was that Peter affirmed his loyalty to Jesus. Having heard Jesus contrast the manna of the Moses tradition which only lasted a few hours and the true bread from heaven which led to eternal life, many had deserted him. Jesus then asked the Twelve, 'Do you also wish to go away?' Simon Peter answered him, 'Lord, to whom shall we go? You have the words of eternal life, and we have believed and have come to know that you are the Holy One of God' (6.67–69).

# John 13

### 13.1–20: Jesus washes the disciples' feet

Before the feast of Passover, Jesus has supper with his friends. During supper, Jesus takes off his outer garment, wraps a linen cloth round himself, washes the disciples' feet and dries them with the linen cloth. Peter protests and then has an exchange with Jesus about the significance of footwashing. John is the only Evangelist who mentions this incident and so it must have been another of the signs he chose to show that Jesus was the Christ, the Son of God. The footwashing shows that Jesus is the Servant/Lamb, just as the Baptist had said when pointing Jesus out to his disciples (1.36). Luke also said that Jesus spoke at the last supper about being a servant: 'I am among you as one who serves' (Luke 22.27).

This was not footwashing before a meal, such as a host or his servant would offer to guests when they arrived. Nor was it simply to make the guest's feet literally clean from the dust of the road, or even ritually clean from the pollution of wearing leather sandals. This would have happened before the meal. The footwashing was to show Jesus as the Servant and how he related to the One who sent him. Jesus describes himself as part of a hierarchy: no servant is greater than his Lord (and here the word means both LORD and Lord), and no apostle greater than the one who sends him (v. 16). Matthew has a longer version of this saying, albeit not at the last supper:

> A disciple is not above his teacher,
> Nor a servant above his master;
> It is enough for the disciple to be like his teacher,
> And the servant like his master.
> If they have called the master of the house Beelzebul,
> How much more will they malign those of his household.
> (Matt. 10.24–25)[1]

This implies that servants of their Master are a household of angels, just as the household of Beelzebul were the demons. Luke has a different

---

[1] The last two lines are an example of the *qal waḥômēr*, 'light and heavy', style of argument.

## John 13

nuance: 'A disciple is not above his teacher, but every one when he is fully taught will be like his teacher' (Luke 6.40).

The implication is that the possession of certain knowledge distinguished this community.

Jesus spoke enigmatically of knowing and doing 'these things' (v. 17), which may mean understanding and accepting the role of the servant in the sense of acting humbly; but it may mean knowing and doing what the Servant had to do. The disciples had to pass on his teachings, since those who received them would be receiving both the LORD and the One who sent him. The first Christians thought of themselves as servants, which meant much more than being humble workers. They took upon themselves the role of the high priest who made atonement, the Lamb of God who took away the sins of the world: they stood before the throne wearing the Name on their foreheads (Rev. 22.3–4); and the blood of their martyrs was poured out under the altar like the blood on the Day of Atonement (Rev. 6.9–11).

'Servant' was one of the earliest titles used for Jesus and it linked him to the royal temple tradition. The prayers of the *Didache* give thanks over the wine for 'the holy vine of your *servant* David, which you have made known to us through your *servant* Jesus'. The Servant revealed the holy vine of David, which explains why Jesus later spoke about being the true vine (15.1–11). Knowledge, faith and immortality were also revealed through 'your *servant* Jesus'.[2] The Servant taught a certain knowledge, just as in the original Servant song: 'By his knowledge shall my Servant, who makes righteous, make many righteous' (Isa. 53.11, my translation). 'Righteous' here means included again within the covenant bond, and this was effected by the high-priestly atonement, hence the Servant 'bore the iniquities'. Ezekiel described the LORD bringing those who had rebelled back into the bond (or it could be the 'number') of the covenant (Ezek. 20.37, translating literally).[3]

So too when the first Christians in Jerusalem spoke of Jesus as the Servant/Child.[4] God glorified his Servant (Acts 3.13) and having raised him up (the word for resurrection) sent him to the people of Israel (Acts

---

[2] *Didache* 9, 10.
[3] 'Into the bond of', *bmśrt*, looks very similar to 'into the number of', *bmśpr*. The latter would imply a certain number destined to be servants within the covenant, which explains the blood/souls of the martyrs/servants under the altar who were part of the great atonement, but whose 'number' was not yet complete (Rev. 6.11).
[4] The Greek *pais* means either 'servant' or 'child', and is the equivalent wordplay to Lamb/Servant in Hebrew/Aramaic.

3.26). Note that resurrection here occurs before the Servant is sent to Israel, and so presumably occurred at Jesus' baptism before the public ministry began. They recalled Psalm 2 – the kings and rulers had gathered together against the LORD's anointed – when Peter and John had been released after questioning by the Jewish authorities. They prayed for boldness to continue speaking, and they identified Jesus as the Servant King (Acts 4.25–27). Signs and wonders were happening through the name of God's holy Servant Jesus (Acts 4.30). The footwashing shows Jesus as the Servant.[5]

Jesus is enacting what is set out in Philippians 2.5–11. Exhorting the Philippians to Christian humility and service, Paul wrote: 'Have this mind among yourselves, which is yours in Christ Jesus …' and then quotes what seems to be a statement or hymn about the role of the Servant: though in the form of God himself, he submitted himself to death and was then exalted. Here at the last supper, Jesus lays down, *tithēmi*, his garments, the word John uses for Jesus laying down his life (10.11, 15, 17, 18), and then takes the garments again (v. 12), using the same word that John uses for Jesus taking back his life, *lambanō* (10.17, 18). As in Philippians, Jesus knows he has come from God and is going back to God (v. 3), that this is the hour when he will pass (literally 'interchange', *metalambanō*) from the world to the Father (v. 1). John used the same word in 1 John 3.14: 'We have passed from death to life …'

Jesus the Servant is also washing the feet of his new Levites. This is the third Passover of his ministry and so, according to John, two years since he called his disciples. It is also the third Passover of the synagogue lectionary cycle when the readings included Numbers 8—11[6] which tells of keeping Passover in the wilderness at the beginning of the second year since leaving Egypt (Num. 9.1–5). Before that Passover, however, the LORD told Moses to take Levites from among the people to attend Aaron and his sons serving in the tabernacle and join them in making atonement. Like the Passover lambs, they were offered as a substitute for the firstborn of Israel (Num. 8.17–19) and they were consecrated by being shaved and then washed (Num. 8.7).[7] The theme of establishing a new priesthood runs all through the farewell discourse. The community of the *Damascus Document* and the *Community Rule* regarded themselves as the faithful Levites described by Ezekiel who would serve in the restored

---

[5] But he does not regard the disciples as his servants (15.15); see below, pp. 441–2.
[6] A. Guilding, *The Fourth Gospel and Jewish Worship*, Oxford: Clarendon Press, 1960, pp. 34–5.
[7] The prescription in Ezek. 44.20 forbad shaving.

## John 13

temple (Ezek. 44.15–16).[8] Further, the *Rule* describes the council of the community as three priests and 12 men who were themselves a sweet smelling offering to atone for the land. 'When they have been established in uprightness of way *for two years* they shall separate themselves as holy in the midst of the council of the community, and every matter/word hidden from Israel but revealed to the man who seeks/interprets, shall not be hidden from these men ...'[9] These men saw themselves as a temple for Israel, a foundation of the holy of holies, the chosen ones, true witnesses to right judgement, *mišpāṭ*. After two years they received hidden teaching that had been revealed to the Interpreter. The *Rule* describes something that could easily have been like John's last supper which has footwashing for the new Levites and then the teaching. It may not be coincidence that Peter is the one who questions the nature of this footwashing and later teaches about the royal priesthood. Jesus knows, however, that Peter does not understand at the time what is happening: 'What I am doing you do not know now, but afterward you will understand' (v. 7). Peter would later teach the exiles of the Dispersion in what is now Turkey – presumably Christians with Hebrew roots – that they were the chosen race, the royal priesthood (1 Pet. 1.1; 2.9), showing that the early Church thought of themselves in the same way as did the community of the *Damascus Document* and the *Community Rule*.

The ritual washing of the high priest on the Day of Atonement shows that total immersion was a separate act from the additional washing of his hands and feet. The high priest had to immerse himself five times and sanctify his hands and feet ten times.[10] This distinction seems to underlie Jesus' words to Peter: 'He who has bathed does not need to wash, except for his feet ...' (v. 10). Presumably the disciples had already purified themselves for Passover, as did the other pilgrims who came from the country districts (11.55). This additional footwashing was a priestly requirement, to prepare for temple service. At the last supper, it was to change the status of the disciples; those whom Jesus did not wash 'had no inheritance with him' (v. 8), translating literally and assuming that the Greek *meros* represented the Hebrew *ḥēleq*, meaning 'inheritance/portion'. Luke included this teaching in his account of the last supper, but in another form: Jesus assigned to his disciples a kingdom, just as the Father had assigned a kingdom to him (Luke 22.28–30). Paul also spoke

---

[8] *Damascus Document*, CD IV; *Community Rule*, 1QS *passim*.
[9] *Community Rule*, 1QS VIII.10–13.
[10] Mishnah *Yoma* 3.3.

of Christians in these Johannine terms: being children of God and so 'fellow heirs with Christ, provided we suffer with him in order that we may also be glorified with him' (Rom. 8.16–17). The disciples were being incorporated into Jesus' high priesthood and into his Servanthood, and so he exhorted them also to wash each other's feet.

In the synoptic accounts of the last supper, Jesus transforms the Passover table into a high-priestly table (Melchi-Zedek's table?). He takes only the bread and the wine, but has no place in his new ritual for the lamb which was the central feature of a Passover table in Jerusalem. He then renews the everlasting covenant which was entrusted to the priests and upheld by atonement (Num. 25.10–13). In the synoptic Gospels the bread becomes the bread of the Presence and as such the most holy food of the high priests, their privilege. The wine becomes the covenant blood, which the disciples consume and thus become a part of the covenant/atonement sacrifice, their duty. John describes another element. With the footwashing, the new high priests are purified for their role as part of the restored high priesthood, and what follows in the farewell discourse is the teaching that was exclusive to the high priests, the secret things of God. A generation after John compiled his Gospel, Ignatius of Antioch wrote using the same imagery as John:

> The priests of old I admit were estimable men; but our own High Priest is greater, for he has been entrusted with the most holy things and to him alone are the secret things of God committed. He is the doorway to the Father, and it is by him that Abraham and Isaac and the prophets go in, no less than the apostles and the whole church; for all these have their part in God's unity.[11]

Not everyone whom he washed was clean; Jesus knew there was a traitor among them (vv. 10, 21, 27), and here there is an echo of the previous Passover. After Jesus' feeding the 5,000 and teaching about the true bread and drinking his blood (6.32, 56), John observed: 'Jesus knew from the first ... who it was that would betray him' (6.64). Jesus recognized that Judas' action would fulfil Psalm 41.9 (my translation): 'My close friend whom I trusted, who ate my bread, has lifted up his heel against me.' ('Lifted up his heel against me' is an idiom meaning 'deceived me greatly'.) Mark also links this psalm to the last supper (Mark 14.18–21), and the shorter (older) account in Luke 22.19 then 21 links betrayal to the

---

[11] Ignatius, *To the Philadelphians* 9.

bread. Jesus knew what was about to happen, and by telling his disciples he showed who he was: 'I am He' (v. 19, my translation).

The traditional sign of a true prophet from the LORD was that his words were fulfilled. Deuteronomy has clear guidance for identifying a genuine messenger from the LORD: if what he says does happen, that is the sign that he is a true prophet; if it does not happen, he is a false prophet and must be killed (Deut. 18.15–22). And even if his words did come true, he was a false prophet if he spoke anything rebellious against the LORD (Deut. 13.1–5). According to Jewish tradition, this is why Jesus was put to death,[12] but he had prophesied this too (e.g. Mark 9.31).

Jesus was the LORD and sent by the LORD, and those whom Jesus sent would also be the LORD. In Revelation, the risen LORD promised the faithful follower that he would write on him the Name of his God and his own new Name, just as the followers of the Lamb had on their foreheads his own Name and the Name of his Father (Rev. 3.12; 14.1).[13] He would appoint him as the Morning Star, a title he claimed for himself (Rev. 22.16).[14] In other words, the risen LORD in Revelation promises to his faithful followers the same power as he had received from his Father as well as the same status as the Morning Star.

## 13.21–30: The beloved disciple

The beloved disciple now introduces himself for the first time; he is the one who sits by Jesus at supper. John has Jesus give Judas a small piece (of bread) that he has dipped in the dish, and this is a sign to the beloved disciple that Judas is the traitor. Then Jesus tells Judas to go and do what he has to do, and the other disciples assume he has to buy food for the festival or give money to the poor. The synoptic Gospels do not say when Judas left the last supper, only that he had already made contact with the authorities to betray Jesus (Matt. 26.14–16; 20–29; Mark 14.10–11; 17–25; Luke 22.3–6; 14–38). In the synoptic Gospels Jesus knows he is to be betrayed and says this openly. The disciples ask, 'Is it I?' (Matt. 26.22; Mark 14.19), and all the synoptic Gospels say that the traitor is eating from the same dish or at the same table. Since they do not say when Judas

---

[12] Babylonian Talmud *Sanhedrin* 43a.
[13] Rev. 3.12 also mentions the Name of the new Jerusalem, which refers to another way of reading Ezek. 48.35: 'From that day, the name of the city, her name will be "The LORD"' (my translation).
[14] 'I will give him the Morning Star' is an over-literal translation of the underlying Hebrew, where 'give' can mean 'appoint or create'.

left, and John does not mention the bread and wine at the last supper, it is impossible to know if Judas consumed the bread and wine of the Eucharist.

The beloved disciple is an enigmatic figure but vital for understanding John's Gospel because he wrote it as an eyewitness of the events he recorded (19.35; 21.24). He reveals little about himself except this title and his close association with Peter, although he implies that he was younger than Peter: he had keener eyesight, since he was the first to recognize the LORD standing on the beach, and he ran faster than Peter to get to the tomb. When he was writing the final section of his Gospel, he already knew that Jesus' prophecy of Peter's death had been fulfilled (21.20–23) and that there were rumours that he himself would live until Jesus returned. These latter could have been prompted by half-heard stories of John's vision of the LORD returning (Rev. 10.1–11) which had given him the new understanding of the *parousia* and prompted him to write his Gospel. John also mentions 'another disciple' whom he does not name but who seems also to be the beloved disciple. Two of the Baptist's disciples were the first followers of Jesus (1.35–37), but only Andrew was named (1.40); the other one could have been the beloved disciple. Two unnamed disciples went fishing at night and caught nothing (21.2), but the beloved disciple is mentioned later in this account and it is likely that he was one of them. The unnamed disciple 'was known to the high priest' (18.15) and so was able to enter his house and to have Peter allowed in also. The beloved disciple stood at the cross with the women (19.26) and was the first man at the tomb on Easter morning. When Mary Magdalene told Peter and the beloved disciple what she had found, both men ran to see. The beloved disciple arrived first, but was more restrained; he looked into the tomb but did not go in. Peter arrived and did go in, and the beloved disciple then followed him (20.1–10). After the disciples had been fishing all night and caught nothing, a man they did not recognize called from the beach that they should cast their net on the other side of the boat. After the huge catch of fish, the beloved disciple recognized that it was the LORD; Peter jumped from the boat to go to Jesus, but again, the beloved disciple was more restrained.

There has been much speculation about the beloved disciple and who he was: John son of Zebedee, another John, Lazarus, Mary Magdalene, a symbol of the Gentile Christian, a symbol of any Christian. He was present at the last supper, but he does not say that only the Twelve were there. He just mentions 'the disciples' (v. 23), and so John the Evangelist does not have to be identified as one of the Twelve. Mark, who makes no claim to have been present at the last supper, says that the Twelve were there (Mark 14.17); Matthew, who may have been there (if Matthew the tax collector wrote the Gospel, Matt. 10.3), says the Twelve were there (Matt. 26.20); Luke, who was not there, implies that only the Twelve were there, since Jesus promised them 12 thrones in his kingdom (Luke 22.30). John the Evangelist, who was at the supper, does not say how many were there, and so the beloved disciple need not have been one of the Twelve.

It is possible that the beloved disciple was from the high-priestly family: he was known at the high priest's house (18.15); he knew the name of the slave whose ear was cut off when Jesus was arrested (18.10); he knew the words of Caiaphas to the council (11.47–53); and he knew that the group who took Jesus from the high priest's house to the Roman praetorium would not enter to avoid ritual defilement before Passover (18.28). Further, John did not enter Jesus' tomb until Peter had seen that it was empty, because a dead body was another source of defilement for a priest (Lev. 21.11). The Jews had sent priests and Levites to find out what the Baptist was doing (1.19), and the beloved disciple could have been among them. Polycrates, bishop of Ephesus about 190 CE, said that the John who leaned on the LORD's breast (at the last supper) was a priest wearing the *petalon*, the inscribed gold signet that only the high priest wore on his forehead.[15] Jesus entrusted his mother to the beloved disciple (19.26–27), which could have been more than simply a practical provision for her. As the mother of the Messiah, Mary herself would have had considerable status as the Lady restored, and John at this point became her next son, the custodian of her teaching. Had John been one of the high priest's family, he would have known of the phenomena in the temple – whether or not they occurred just before Jesus entered Jerusalem – and would have recognized their meaning.

The supper may have been a gathering like the one described in the *Community Rule*: three priests and 12 others, sharing their pure meal. Elsewhere the *Rule* describes a gathering of at least ten men of the council and a priest, at which the priest blesses the bread and the wine.[16] There was a period of probation before new members were allowed to join this community and the decision could well have been made by lot, *gôrāl*, or it may mean that the person joined the 'lot'/inheritance of the community.[17] The new member was not allowed to touch the pure food of the

---

[15] Quoted in Eusebius, *History of the Church* 3.31.
[16] *Community Rule*, 1QS VI.
[17] *Community Rule*, 1QS VI.16; cf. *War Scroll*, 1QM XIII.5, 12.

community until he had been with them for a year, and only after two years was he allowed to touch their drink.[18] The community shared property.[19] There are several similarities between this group and the way of life adopted by the Christians. This does not mean that the Christians were part of the Qumran community, but rather that when Jesus and his followers became a distinct group, they adopted similar ways. Lots were used to decide that Mattathias should become one of the Twelve after Judas had left them (Acts 1.23-26); the Jerusalem Christians shared their property (Acts 2.45); and the custom of admitting members by stages does correspond to John's scheme of three Passovers: at the first Passover Jesus called his disciples; one year later, he broke bread with them and taught about the true bread from heaven, which would correspond to the pure meal of the community to which new disciples were admitted after one year. One year later again, at the third Passover, the synoptic Gospels say that Jesus invited his disciples to drink from the covenant cup, which would also correspond to the practice of the Qumran community. John does not mention the bread and wine of the last supper, but has Jesus teach about the vine. The Qumran community were all bound by the covenant of loving kindness, *ḥesedh*,[20] based on truth, *'emeth*; righteousness, *ṣᵉdhāqâ*; and right judgement, *mišpāṭ*.[21] The exhortations of the Teacher of the Community echo Jesus' farewell discourse, and the word 'community', *yaḥad*, was either the word that Jesus used for the unity of himself, his Father and his disciples (17.21), or one very similar to it, *'eḥādh*, meaning 'united', a single unit.

The 'beloved' disciple may have been a title. If he was an eyewitness of the events he describes, he will have 'thought' in Hebrew even if he wrote in Greek,[22] and there are traces of a Hebrew style even in this account of the last supper.[23] 'Whom Jesus loved' recalls the Greek translation of Genesis 22, where Isaac is described as 'Isaac your *beloved son*, whom you love' (Gen. 22.2). The Hebrew is 'your *yāḥîdh*', meaning 'your only one', whence the English: 'your only son Isaac whom you love'. Since there was also Ishmael, Isaac was not literally Abraham's only son, and so 'your

---

[18] *Community Rule*, 1QS VI.16, 20.
[19] *Community Rule*, 1QS VI.24.
[20] *Community Rule*, 1QS I.8.
[21] *Community Rule*, 1QS I.5-8; VIII.2.
[22] John's Gospel, like Revelation, could have been translated into Greek. He was certainly recording speech that was not originally spoken in Greek.
[23] M. Wilcox, 'The Composition of John 13.21-30', in *Neotestamentica et Semitica. Studies in Honour of M. Black*, E. E. Ellis and M. Wilcox, ed. Edinburgh: T&T Clark, 1968, pp. 143-56.

*yāḥîdh*' was thought by the Greek translator to indicate a special status, in this case, Abraham's heir. In the case of the beloved disciple, the title would have meant that he was Jesus' heir, the authorized interpreter of his words and visions, as indeed he was.

Thus the Book of Revelation begins:

- 'The revelation of Jesus Christ, which God gave him to show to his servants what must soon take place', meaning: 'the visions that Jesus the Messiah received from God, to show his servants [his priests] what was about to happen';
- 'And he made it known by sending his angel to his servant John', meaning: 'Jesus sent his angel/messenger (the Paraclete[24]) to John to enable him to interpret the visions';
- 'Who bore witness to the word of God, and to the testimony of Jesus Christ, even to all that he saw', meaning: 'John bore witness to the Logos of God and to the testimony of Jesus the Messiah, to all that the Messiah saw'.

John knew the visions that shaped the teaching of Jesus, and his interpretation of those visions became the Book of Revelation. His later understanding of the visions and teaching of Jesus became his Gospel. John's earliest writings, however, were the seven letters to the churches of Asia (Minor) (Rev. 2—3), which he received in visions from the LORD, the Living One who died and was alive again (Rev. 1.18). He saw the LORD wearing the long robe and golden girdle of a high priest (Rev. 1.13) and standing in the midst of, or as the middle of, the seven golden lamps.[25] Since these lamps were set before the throne in heaven, what John saw was the great high priest risen from his throne and saying to his faithful: 'I am coming soon' (Rev. 3.11).

A text known at this time and possibly updated to include allusions to Herod the Great is the *Assumption of Moses*, and this gives details of how the expected high priest would appear. The text survives only in a damaged Latin translation, but it is important for understanding the writings of John. It takes the form of Moses' farewell speech to Joshua, and is in effect a rewriting of Deuteronomy 31—34. It shows how Deuteronomy 32.43 was imagined at the time. This became a key Christian proof text, as we have seen,[26] so crucial that it did not survive

---

[24] See below, pp. 456–90.
[25] This image corresponds to Jesus as the central stem of the vine/tree of life; see below, p. 424.
[26] See above, p. 131.

## Temple Theology in John's Gospel

after the work of the Jewish editors of the Hebrew text in the early Christian period. The mutilated verse, which describes the LORD coming in judgement, is quoted at Hebrews 1.6: 'Let all God's angels worship him.' The equivalent verse in the *Assumption of Moses* describes the angel high priest leaving his throne in heaven to judge the earth, and this is the figure John saw (Rev. 1.12–16).

> And then his kingdom shall appear throughout all His creation,
> And then Satan shall be no more,
> And sorrow shall depart with him.
> Then the hands of the angel shall be filled [with incense],[27]
> Who has been appointed chief,
> And he shall forthwith avenge them of their enemies.
> For the Heavenly One will arise from His royal throne,
> And he will go forth from His holy habitation[28]
> With indignation and wrath on account of his sons.[29]

In John's vision the risen LORD told him to send letters to the seven churches, warning them that he was about to emerge as the Judge.

John was the LORD's beloved, just as Jesus himself was declared at his baptism to be 'My Son, the beloved' (Mark 1.11). This was an allusion to the king (Ps. 2.7) and the Servant (Isa. 42.1), who was also called the Chosen One. 'The Beloved' is found throughout the Christian parts of the *Ascension of Isaiah* as a title for Jesus,[30] and this title and this role was passed on to John.

## The Passover discourse

From 13.31 to the end of chapter 16 is often called Jesus' farewell discourse, a popular Jewish literary genre at that time that took the form of a father's last words to his children. He usually gave advice for living a good life, and told them about the future. There is a *Testament of Job*, possibly composed in Egypt, a *Testament of Abraham*, a *Testament of Isaac* and a *Testament of Jacob*, all thought to come from Egypt, and the two latter have Christian additions. There is a *Testament of Moses*, now part of the *Assumption of Moses*, and there is a *Testament of Solomon* that could be an entirely Christian composition. Best known are the

---

[27] 'Fill the hands' is the Hebrew idiom for ordination, e.g. Exod. 32.29; Lev. 16.32.
[28] This line of text is damaged.
[29] *Assumption of Moses* 10.1–3.
[30] *Ascension of Isaiah* 1.4; 3.13, 17, 18; 4.3, 6, 9, 18, 21; 7.17, 23; 8.18, 25; 9.12.

## John 13

*Testaments of the Twelve Patriarchs*, the last words of each of the 12 sons of Jacob. Their origin has been much debated. It is likely that they were written by a Hellenized Jew, and acquired Christian additions which resembled Johannine thought.[31]

Earlier examples of this form are found in the Old Testament: Jacob gathered his sons together when he was approaching death, warned them of their failings, and gave them his blessing (Gen. 49.1-27). According to *Jubilees*, Abraham gave several testaments: he summoned all his children and grandchildren: Ishmael and his 12 children, Isaac and his two children, and the six children of Keturah, his last wife; and he gave them rules for living. Five years later he gave his farewell to Isaac, reminding him to keep God's commandments, especially those for offering sacrifice and dealing with blood, and warning him against the ways of foreigners. Many years later, when he was about to die, Abraham gave two blessings to Jacob, one warning him against the ways of foreigners and the other naming him as his heir.[32] The most extensive farewell in the Old Testament is Deuteronomy. The entire book is the words of Moses beyond the Jordan, before the people went over into Canaan, which Moses knew he would never enter (Deut. 1.1; 34.4). In Deuteronomy, Moses recalls the exodus from Egypt and the desert wandering, he sets out the commandments, and encourages the people for the task that lies ahead – entering the land of Canaan. *The themes, motifs and even the words of Deuteronomy shape Jesus' farewell discourse on the night before Passover, and so Jesus' teaching after the last supper is his Passover discourse, the moment when he leads his own chosen people on their exodus from Egypt.* In the later years of the second-temple period, Moses had taken over the roles of the ancient king;[33] here, Jesus reclaims them.

Luke reports the words of Moses and Elijah at the Transfiguration: 'They spoke of his exodus that he was to fulfil, *plēroō*, in Jerusalem' (Luke 9.31, translating literally), and an exodus from Jerusalem after persecution is implied in Revelation: 'Their dead bodies will lie in the street of the great city which is spiritually called Sodom and Egypt, where their LORD was crucified' (Rev. 11.8, my translation). John has already depicted Jesus as the great Shepherd of Israel, calling his own sheep and leading them out. When he has brought out all his own, he goes before them and the

---

[31] H. C. Kee in *The Old Testament Pseudepigrapha*, vol. 1, ed. J. H. Charlesworth, London: Darton, Longman and Todd, 1983, p. 777.
[32] *Jubilees* 20—22.
[33] See above, p. 31.

sheep follow him (10.3–4). The Baptist's father had sung of such a deliverance:

> Blessed be the LORD God of Israel,
> For he has visited and redeemed his people,
> And has raised up a horn of salvation for us
> In the house of his servant David,
> As he spoke by the mouth of his holy prophets from of old,
> That we should be saved from our enemies,
> And from the hand of all who hate us;
> To perform the mercy promised to our fathers
> And to remember his holy covenant,
> The oath which he swore to our father Abraham, to grant us
> That we, being delivered from the hand of our enemies,
> Might serve him without fear,
> In holiness and righteousness before him
> All the days of our life.     (Luke 1.68–75, my translation)

The promise to Abraham was the covenant described in Genesis 15, prophesying that his descendants would be slaves for 400 years in a land that was not theirs, that their oppressors would be judged and his people then brought out to possess a great land (Gen. 15.12–21). Zechariah's words are so familiar that their meaning can be overlooked; it is by no means certain that the enemies were the Romans, especially since Jesus spoke of the violent shepherds who were thieves and robbers – the high priests of the late second-temple period. The Saviour from the house of David could have been the LORD himself who said: 'I have seen the affliction of my people who are in Egypt, and have heard their cry because of their taskmasters; I know their sufferings, and I have come down to deliver them ...' The LORD then revealed himself as I AM (Exod. 3.7–8, 14). The I AM by which Jesus describes his own presence in John's Gospel is the Name linked specifically to the exodus.

Jesus was the new Joshua. The name is the same, despite the convention of distinguishing 'Joshua' from 'Jesus' when translating, and the sequence in Hebrews suggests that the pattern of the three Joshuas was part of early Christian teaching. It could have originated with Jesus, the Passover discourse being evidence of this, or it could have come from the circle into which he was born. It could even be the reason why he was named Joshua/Jesus. Moses had led the people in the wilderness years, but the one who led them into the new land was *Joshua/Jesus*, the first Joshua. When the exiles returned from Babylon, the one who led them back into the land and began to rebuild the temple was named Joshua/Jesus, the second Joshua (Ezra 3.2; Hag. 1.1-5; Zech. 6.11-12). In a vision, Zechariah saw him vested as high priest (but not anointed – there was no oil in the second temple) and given the right to enter the holy of holies if he walked in the ways of the LORD and guarded what was entrusted to him (Zech. 3.1-9). Jesus was the third Joshua.

The writer of Hebrews used the three Joshuas sequence: first s/he explained that the rebellious generation whom Moses led did not enter the promised land because of unbelief (Heb. 3.19). They did not enter the LORD's rest (Ps. 95.11), but the next generation were led in by Joshua. Then by word association, the argument turns to the story of creation and God resting on the seventh day, which, it is argued, must be still in the future if the rebels were told they would not enter.

> For if Joshua had given them rest, [God] would not speak later of another rest. So then, there remains a sabbath rest for the people of God; for whoever enters God's rest also ceases from his labours as God did from his.
>
> (Heb. 4.8-10)

The train of thought then moves immediately to the high priest, who enters the holy of holies (Heb. 4.14-16), described later as 'the new and living way which he opened for us through the curtain' (Heb. 10.20). Entering the holy of holies was the final rest for the people of God: the first Joshua led them into the land; the second entered the holy of holies; and the third led his people into the holy of holies. This was the final vision of Revelation (Rev. 22.3-4), certainly known to John and almost certainly known to Jesus because he speaks in the Passover discourse of leading his disciples there and then prays that this may be so (17.24).

The content of the Passover discourse was drawn largely from Moses' words in Deuteronomy, but its style resembles the supper discourse of the Therapeuts. It is sometimes said that the repetitions and doublets in the Passover discourse are a sign that it was compiled from various deposits of material preserved in the Johannine communities, but John was not such a writer. It is more likely that he was faithfully reproducing the style of the Therapeuts' discourse after a communal meal, which Philo described. The president, *proedros*, of the group, he said, spoke to them after their communal meal, discussing a question arising in the Scriptures, or answering one asked by someone else.

> He desires to behold more precisely, and having seen it, does not begrudge it to those who, even if they are not so perceptive as he, have at any rate just as great a desire to learn. He gives his teaching in a leisurely way, pausing and delaying with repetitions, engraving the thoughts in the souls, since the

interpretation of one who goes on at a breathless pace means that the mind of those further behind and unable to follow and keep up falls behind and fails to grasp what is said ...

The interpretations of the holy Scriptures are through hidden meanings in allegories. The whole law book seems to these people to be like a living being, the body being the spoken arrangement of the words, and the soul being the invisible meaning stored up in the words, in which the rational soul begins, by making connections, to see familar things, as though through a mirror of the words. [He sees the] extraordinary beauties of the thoughts, revealed and perceived, and the symbols unfolded and disclosed. Bringing unclothed into the light the things to be considered, those who are able, after a little reminding, perceive the invisible in the visible.[34]

Jesus spoke like this: interpreting Scripture by allusion to Moses' words of farewell in Deuteronomy; explaining the symbols, in this case, the mysterious vine of David which had been brought out of Egypt and then allowed to suffer at the hands of enemies (Ps. 68.8–18); bringing out the hidden meaning, repeating the ideas so that the hearers could grasp what was being said, answering the questions of those who did not fully understand, and helping them to recognize familiar ideas at a deeper level. At the end of the Passover discourse, the disciples said to Jesus: 'Now you are speaking plainly and not in parables' (16.29, my translation).

## 13.31–38: A new commandment

Deuteronomy begins with Moses explaining the words of the law to Israel (Deut. 1.1–5). Jesus' Passover discourse begins with:

> A new commandment I give you, that you love one another; even as I have loved you, that you also love one another. By this all men will know that you are my disciples, if you have love for one another. (vv. 34–35)

Moses had to teach the people to fear the LORD: 'Let them hear my words, so that they may learn to fear me ...' (Deut. 4.10). 'You shall keep the commandments of the LORD your God, by walking in his ways and fearing him' (Deut. 8.6). In contrast, John wrote: 'There is no fear in love, [for] perfect love casts out fear. For fear has to do with punishment, and he who fears is not perfected in love. We love, because he first loved us' (1 John 4.18–19). Fear, except for fear of the Jews, is not mentioned in John's Gospel; there was a different basis for the new covenant. Moses knew that he was about to die (Deut. 31.2); Jesus knew he was about to die (v. 36).

---

[34] Philo, *Contemplative Life* 75–76, 78, my translation.

## John 13

The only time Deuteronomy mentions the glory of the LORD is when the law was given: the people saw the fire and heard the voice, but they saw no form (Deut. 5.24; also 4.12–14); John emphasized that they had seen the glory of the Son in the flesh, that is, with a human form, contrasting the grace and truth brought through Jesus Christ and the law given through Moses (1.14, 17).

Here, at the beginning of the Passover discourse, Jesus says that the moment of theophany is near; the coming of the Greeks was a sign that his glorification was imminent (12.23, 28–29). Luke has Jesus explain to the disciples on the Emmaus road that the Messiah had to suffer to enter his glory, and so his death was the way into the glory (Luke 24.26). This, said Luke's Jesus, was the fulfilment of Scripture, although the present Hebrew text has nothing that suggests this. We have seen, however, that both the great Isaiah scroll from Qumran and the Targum say that the Servant who suffered was the Messiah who would see the light.[35] The glory and the Servant who suffered were a sensitive matter for the Jewish editors of the Hebrew text after the advent of Christianity. The complicated explanation in verses 31–32 is a summary of this belief. Underlying both this and the exhortation in Philippians 2.5–11 is the vision in Revelation 5, and it is this that Jesus says is to be fulfilled immediately (v. 32).

The vision in Revelation 5 draws on (or maybe was inspired by) the royal traditions that underlie Isaiah 24.23: the LORD of Hosts reigning in Jerusalem and being glorified before his elders. The vision shows someone from the royal house of David being enthroned. He is the Lamb/Servant, he is resurrected ('standing') after being sacrificed, and he shines with the sevenfold light (the seven horns) and the sevenfold spirit (the seven eyes). The glory is within him and shines through him, so he is united with the One seated on the throne (Rev. 4.2), and they are then worshipped as One (Rev. 5.13–14). 'Now is the Son of man glorified, and in him God is glorified; if God is glorified in him, God will also glorify him in himself, and glorify him at once' (vv. 31–32).

The king being One with the LORD is how the Chronicler described Solomon's coronation,[36] and being filled with the light that gave knowledge was the role of the Servant; after suffering, his soul would see light and be satisfied/filled with his knowledge (Isa. 53.11). Thus the (Son of) Man shines in glory, in him/through him God shines in glory,

---

[35] See above, p. 92. 1QIsa$^a$ 53.11 includes the word 'light' which is not in the MT.
[36] See above, p. 82.

and thus the priestly blessing is fulfilled: the LORD's face/presence shines and brings grace and peace. Isaiah prophesied the glory of the LORD returning to Jerusalem (Isa. 35.2, 10); he prophesied the glory of the LORD like sunrise over the city (Isa. 60.1); and he knew that the LORD would be glorified through his Servant (Isa. 49.3). The union of the LORD and the Davidic king, and the extension of that idea to include the union of the LORD and his disciples, is the major theme in the Passover discourse.

Jesus then gives his new commandment (vv. 34–35). When the LORD spoke at Sinai, he said the people of Israel would be his possession if they obeyed his voice and kept his commandments. In this language of Exodus that is taken up in Revelation 5.10, they would be a kingdom of priests and a holy nation (Exod. 19.5-6). Then Israel received the Ten Commandments, and Moses sealed the covenant with the blood of oxen (Exod. 24.4-8). The Christians were also chosen to be a kingdom of priests (1 Pet. 2.9): Jesus washed the feet of the new Levites, and choosing his disciples is another theme in the Passover discourse. The blood that established them, however, was not the blood of oxen but the blood of Jesus Christ (Rev. 1.5-6), the blood of the Lamb (Rev. 5.8-10); and what distinguished them from other people was keeping the new commandment to love. The synoptic Gospels describe the LORD establishing his covenant with his blood at the last supper; John does not mention the Eucharist, but has Jesus teach the commandment of his new covenant, that his disciples love one another. This was not universal love; it was love among the family of those who became children of God by believing in Jesus (1.12). Deuteronomy sets out the distinguishing marks of the sons of the LORD, those chosen to be his special possession: they have no tattoos or curious ways of cutting their hair, they eat only kosher meat and keep the other food laws, and they pay their tithes (Deut. 14.1-29). The distinguishing mark of the new chosen ones was love: they no longer live the life of this world but have passed into the life of heaven (1 John 3.13), and the distinguishing mark of this new life is love of the Christian family. The *Community Rule* called this 'the covenant of loving kindness, *ḥesedh*', within which the sons of light loved each other but shunned the sons of darkness.[37]

The covenant of the Christians was a bond of love, which should be understood as the Hebrew *ḥesedh*. Paul wrote of the bond of love, *agapē*, which binds everything together in perfect harmony (Col. 3.14), and of 'forbearing one another in love, *agapē*, eager to maintain the unity of the

---

[37] *Community Rule*, 1QS I.8, 10.

Spirit in the bond of peace' (Eph. 4.2–3). Hence the contrast that John set out in the Prologue, where ḥesedh and 'emeth, often translated 'mercy and truth' or 'grace and truth', were the characteristics of the older, pre-Mosaic covenant: 'The law was given through Moses; grace and truth came through Jesus Christ' (1.17).

Moses knew he was about to die when he spoke to Israel beyond the Jordan (Deut. 31.2), and Jesus too speaks of his departure (v. 33), as he has already spoken to the Jews (7.33–34; 8.21). Like the Jews, Peter does not at first understand what Jesus means, and asks why he cannot follow Jesus. Jesus predicts Peter's death – 'You shall follow afterwards' – and then predicts that Peter will deny him three times before the cock crows (vv. 36–38). This sequence – Jesus' departure and the disciples deserting – is repeated at 16.25–33 and so forms the beginning and the end of the discourse.

## Ḥesedh

John uses two Greek words for love: *agapaō* and *phileō*: he uses *agapaō* far more than *phileō*, but in his Gospel there seems to be no distinction in meaning. Thus 'the Father loves the Son', *agapaō* (3.35); and 'He who has my commandments and keeps them, he it is who loves me; and he who loves me will be loved by my Father, and I will love him and manifest myself to him' (14.21). All these are *agapaō*. John also has 'The Father loves the Son (5.20); and 'The Father himself loves you because you have loved me' (16.27). All these are *phileō*. 'The disciple whom Jesus loved' is *phileō* at 13.23, but is *agapaō* at 20.2. 'God so loved the world' (3.16) is *agapaō*, as are 3.19; 8.42; 10.17; 12.43; 13.1, 23, 34; 14.15, 21, 23, 24, 28, 31; 15.9, 12, 17; 17.23, 24, 26; 19.26; 21.7, 15, 16, 20. 'He who loves his life loses it' (12.25) is *phileō*, as are 11.3, 36; 15.19; 20.2; 21.15, 16, 17.

Some examples are not of theological importance, e.g. 'They loved the praise of men more than the praise of God' (12.43), but most examples are important for understanding John's presentation of Jesus' teaching. Both *agapaō* and *phileō* represent the many facets of the Hebrew root ḥsd. The verb ḥāsadh is rarely found, but ḥesedh (the noun) and ḥāsîdh (the adjective) occur frequently. The root meanings are goodness and kindness, faithfulness and mercy, and it is very close in meaning to wisdom, since both join together:

> [A good woman] opens her mouth with wisdom
> And the teaching of ḥesedh is on her tongue.   (Prov. 31.26)

In the Septuagint, Wisdom 'joins [the creation] in harmony', *harmozousa*, translating the otherwise unknown Hebrew word *'āmôn* (LXX Prov. 8.30).

The practice of *hesedh* was a religious duty, more important than sacrifices:

> He who refuses *hesedh* to his neighbour
> Forsakes the fear of Shaddai.
> (Job 6.14, my translation)

> I desire *hesedh* and not sacrifice,
> The knowledge of *ᵉlohîm* rather than burnt offerings.
> (Hos. 6.6)

The man of *hesedh* was a righteous man, *ṣaddîq*, a restorer of the covenant, as was the Servant (Isa. 53.11). 'Men of *hesedh* are taken away, and there is no discernment that the righteous man is taken away from evil' (Isa. 57.1b, my translation). LXX is 'Just men are taken away'.

The LORD also showed *hesedh* to his people:

- 'You guided with your *hesedh* the people whom you redeemed' (Exod. 15.13);
- 'The LORD your God will keep with you the covenant and the *hesedh* which he swore to your fathers to keep' (Deut. 7.12);
- 'Save me for the sake of your *hesedh*' (Ps. 6.4);
- 'You granted truth, *'emeth*, to Jacob and *hesedh* to Abraham, as you swore to our fathers, from the days of old' (Mic. 7.20; cf. 'to perform the *hesedh* promised to our fathers, and to remember his holy covenant' (Luke 1.72).[38]

The LORD's *hesedh* upheld the king:

> The king trusts in the LORD;
> And through the *hesedh* of Elyon he shall not be moved.
> (Ps. 21.7, my translation)

Psalm 89 shows that *hesedh* was fundamental in the bond between the LORD and the king who was his Son:

> I will sing of your *hesedh*, O LORD, for ever;
> With my mouth I will proclaim your faithfulness, *ᵉmûnâ*,
> to all generations.
> For your *hesedh* was established for ever,
> Your faithfulness, *ᵉmûnâ*, is firm as the heavens.
> (Ps. 89.1–2, my translation)

---

38 My translations.

The faithfulness of the LORD, *ᵉmûnâ*, was often linked to *ḥesed* and to righteousness, *ṣedheq*.

The ancient poem incorporated into the final section of Deuteronomy described the LORD, the son of Elyon, as:

> The Rock, his work is perfect, *tāmîm*,
> For all his ways are justice, *mišpaṭ*,
> A God of *ᵉmûnâ*, faithfulness, and without iniquity, *'āwel*,
> He is righteous, *ṣaddîq*, and upright, *yāšār*.
> (Deut. 32.4, my translation)

The throne of the LORD, that is, his royal power, was firmly founded, but it was the Davidic king who actually sat on the throne of the LORD (1 Chron. 29.23):

> Righteousness, *ṣedheq*, and justice, *mišpaṭ*, are the foundation of your throne,
> Steadfast love, *ḥesedh*, and faithfulness, *'emeth*, go before you.
> Blessed are the people who know the festal shout,
> They shall walk, O LORD, in the light of your face/presence.
> (Ps. 89.14–15, my translation)

When the king declared how he would rule, he began: 'I will sing, O LORD, of *ḥesedh* and justice, *mišpaṭ*' (Ps. 101.1; RSV: *'loyalty and justice'*), and then set out how he would establish them in his kingdom. He and his servants would walk in integrity, *tom*, and he would bar all those who practised evil, slander, pride and deception.

The LORD's faithfulness, *ᵉmûnâ*, and *ḥesedh* would be with the king (Ps. 89.24):

> For ever will I keep for him my *ḥesedh*,
> And my covenant will be firm [the verbal form of *ᵉmûnâ*] for him.
> (Ps. 89.28, my translation)

Even if the kings forsook the law of the LORD, he would not take from them his *ḥesedh* and his *ᵉmûnâ*; he would not break/profane his covenant nor alter what he had spoken (Ps. 89.33–34).

Reflecting on the situation after the temple was destroyed and the kings were no more, the Psalmist asked: 'Where are your former acts of *ḥesedh*, which you swore to David by your *ᵉmûnâ*'? (Ps. 89.49, my translation).

Covenant and *ḥesedh* were closely linked. The LORD would not neglect the *ḥesedh* promised in the covenant with the Davidic kings (2 Sam. 7.15), as was recalled by Solomon when he dedicated the temple: 'O LORD, the God of Israel... keeping covenant and showing *ḥesedh* to your servants...'

(1 Kings 8.23, my translation). Deuteronomy described the LORD as 'the faithful God who keeps covenant and *ḥesedh* with those who ... keep his commandments' (Deut. 7.9, 12). The LORD showed *ḥesedh* to those who loved him, *'āhēb*, and kept his commandments (Exod. 20.6; Deut. 5.10).

The covenant and *ḥesedh* were linked to the restoration of Jerusalem and the Lady who represented the city. The LORD would restore her with 'everlasting *ḥesedh*' (Isa. 54.8), and the Second-Isaiah declared:

> For the mountains may depart and the hills be removed,
> But my *ḥesedh* shall not depart from you,
> And my covenant of peace shall not be removed,
> Says the LORD, who has compassion on you. (Isa. 54.10)

The covenant of peace was the older, pre-Mosaic covenant that bound the whole creation,[39] and Psalm 33 shows that the fundamental principle of creation was *ḥesedh*:

> The word of the LORD is upright;
> And all his work is done in faithfulness,
> He loves righteousness and justice;
> The earth is full of the *ḥesedh* of the LORD. (Ps. 33.4–5)

The LORD watches over those who have hope in his *ḥesedh*: 'Let your *ḥesedh* be upon us, O LORD, even as we hope in you' (Ps. 33.18, 22, my translation).

The people who practised *ḥesedh* were the *ḥᵃsidhîm*, often mentioned in the Psalms, but the variety of translations obscures the fact that these are all the *ḥᵃsidhîm*. The AV translated consistently as 'saints' and the LXX as *hosios*. In each of the RSV translations below, the italics indicate the word *ḥāsîdh*:

- 'The LORD has set apart the *godly* [*man*] for himself' (Ps. 4.3);
- 'Sing praises to the LORD, O you his *saints* ...' (Ps. 30.4);
- 'Love, *'āhēb*, the LORD, all you his *saints*! The LORD preserves the faithful ...' (Ps. 31.23);
- 'The LORD loves justice; he will not abandon his *saints*' (Ps. 37.28, my translation);
- 'Gather to me my *faithful ones*, who made a covenant with me by sacrifice' (Ps. 50.5);
- 'I will proclaim your name for it is good, in the presence of your *godly ones*' (Ps. 52.9, my translation);

---

[39] See above, pp. 42–3.

- 'Of old thou didst speak in a vision to thy *ḥāsîdh* [AV holy one; RSV faithful one], and say: "I have set the [crown] upon one who is mighty, I have exalted one chosen from the people" (Ps. 89.19);
- 'Those who love the LORD hate evil; he preserves the souls of his *saints*' (Ps. 97.10, my translation);
- 'Let thy priests be clothed with righteousness, and let thy *saints* shout for joy ... Her priests I will clothe with salvation, and her *saints* will shout for joy ...' (Ps. 132.9, 16);
- 'Sing to the LORD a new song, his praise in the assembly of the faithful ... Let the *faithful* exult in glory ... This is glory for all his *faithful* ...' (Ps. 149.1b; 5, 9).

Love understood as *ḥesedh* restores the original nuances of John's words: goodness and kindness, faithfulness and mercy, the work of Wisdom joining all things together:

- 'God so loved the world that he gave his only Son, that whoever believes in him should not perish but have everlasting life' (3.16, my translation);
- 'The Father loves the Son, and has given all things into his hand' (3.35);
- 'You [the Jews who were persecuting Jesus] have not the love of God within you' (5.42);
- 'For this reason my Father loves me, because I lay down my life, that I may take it again' (10.17);
- 'Jesus loved Martha and her sister and Lazarus' (11.5);
- 'Jesus ... having loved his own who were in the world, he loved them to the end' (13.1).

We shall return to the role of *ḥesedh* later in the Passover discourse.

# John 14

The teacher of the Therapeuts, said Philo, used to discuss questions arising from the Scriptures, or questions which had been asked by someone else.[1] In the Passover discourse, Jesus does both: he takes the characteristic and familiar words and phrases of Deuteronomy and gives them new meaning, or perhaps restores an older meaning, and he receives questions from his disciples. These are some of the words of Deuteronomy that form the background to his teaching, and the italics show words of particular significance:

- 'Not with our fathers did the LORD make this *covenant*, but with us, who are all of us here alive this day' (Deut. 5.3);
- 'You shall walk in all *the way* that the LORD your God has commanded you, that you may *live*, and that it may go well with you, and that you may live long in the land which you shall possess' (Deut. 5.33);
- 'Be careful to do [*the commandments*] that it may go well with you, and that you may multiply greatly, as the LORD, the God of your fathers, has promised you, in a land flowing with milk and honey' (Deut. 6.3);
- 'Hear, O Israel, the LORD our God, the LORD is *one*; and you shall *love* the LORD your God with all your heart and with all your soul and with all your might. And these *words which I command* you this day shall be upon your heart' (Deut. 6.4–6, my translation);
- 'You are a people holy to the LORD your God; for the LORD your God has *chosen* you to be a people for his own possession, out of all the peoples that are on the face of the soil' (Deut. 7.6, translating literally);
- 'Because you hearken to these ordinances, and *keep and do them*, the LORD your God will keep with you the covenant and the *steadfast love* which he swore to your fathers to keep ...' (Deut. 7.12);
- 'So you shall *keep the commandments of the LORD your God, by walking in his ways* and by fearing him' (Deut. 8.6);
- 'You shall walk after the LORD your God and fear him, and *keep his*

---

[1] Philo, *Contemplative Life* 75.

*commandments and obey his voice*, and you shall serve him *and cleave to him*' (Deut. 13.4);
- 'You are the sons of the LORD your God' (Deut. 14.1);
- 'It is the LORD who *goes before you*; he will be with you, he will not fail you or forsake you; *do not fear or be dismayed*' (Deut. 31.8).

Jesus speaks as the third Joshua, but just as David was the LORD's anointed and the Spirit of the LORD spoke in him so that his words were not his own (2 Sam. 23.1–2), so too Jesus speaks as the LORD. The Deuteronomist made his own belief clear: 'The secret things belong to the LORD our God; but the things that are revealed belong to us and to our children for ever, that we may do all the words of this law' (Deut. 29.29). As a result, the words of Moses in Deuteronomy are concerned almost entirely with practical matters of everyday living; the secret things are dismissed as of no concern to the people listening to Moses. Jesus spoke as the LORD and taught the secrets. He told his followers to keep his secrets for the sons of his household, and they remembered that these were the teachings of the great high priest.[2]

There are several questions from the disciples: first from Peter who asks where Jesus is going, and Jesus tells him of the many places in his Father's house; then from Thomas who asks about the way, and Jesus says that he is the way; and finally from Philip who asks to see the Father, and Jesus says that whoever has seen him has seen the Father. Jesus asks them to trust him for the journey, because he goes ahead of them. Then Judas (not Iscariot, but the Jude who wrote the New Testament letter) asks a question (14.22), and finally some of the disciples question among themselves (16.17).

## 14.1–7: Courage for the journey

At the beginning of his own farewell discourse, Moses said to the people of Israel: 'Behold, the LORD your God has set the land before you ... do not fear or be dismayed' (Deut. 1.21; 31.6). He assured the people: 'The LORD your God ... goes before you' (Deut. 1.30; 31.3, 6–8) and he reminded them that the LORD had always gone before them, but they had not trusted him. '[He] went before you in the way to seek you out a place to pitch your tents ... to show you by what way you should go' (Deut. 1.33). He sent men ahead to explore the land and find the way to enter

---

[2] See above, p. 84.

(Deut. 1.22). So too Jesus told his disciples not to be afraid but to trust him; he was going ahead to prepare a place for them and would return to take them there (vv. 1–3; also 14.27–29). He spoke of the way he would go, but Thomas did not understand. Jesus said that he was the only way to the Father: 'I am the way, and the truth, and the life' (v. 6), which is very similar to the words of Wisdom in Ben Sira 24.[3] The first Joshua's journey was to lead the chosen people into the promised land; the second Joshua's journey was into the holy of holies; and now the third Joshua is to lead his chosen people into the holy of holies, to the Father.[4]

This fusion of the land and the temple is found in Exodus 15, which is the earliest account of the exodus. After the miraculous parting of the waters and the defeat of the Egyptians:

> Thou hast led in thy steadfast love, ḥesedh,
> The people whom thou hast redeemed,
> Thou hast guided them by thy strength to thy holy abode ...
> Thou wilt bring them in and plant them on thy own mountain,
> The place, O Lord, which thou hast made for thy abode,
> The sanctuary, O Lord, which thy hands have established.
> (Exod. 15.13, 17)

The story of the exodus, then, led naturally to the holy mountain and the holy of holies, and to the holy people being *planted there* (cf. Ps. 80.8–18). Jesus teaches his disciples about their own exodus, completing the journey remembered at Passover and entering the holy of holies where they become branches of the vine (re)planted in the holy place (15.1–5).[5]

This alludes to a hope of the time that is expressed in the Enoch literature. On his heavenly travels, Enoch saw a fragrant tree that would be brought back to the temple. In the oldest section of *1 Enoch*, whose roots lie in the traditions of the original temple priesthood, Enoch saw a great mountain like a throne, and a huge fragrant tree that never withered. The archangel Michael, who was Enoch's guide on this journey, explained that the mountain was the throne of God where he would sit when he came to earth:

---

[3] See below, p. 429.

[4] It is perhaps significant that Joshua was given his name – he had formerly been Hoshea son of Nun (Num. 13.8, 16) – when he had first gone into the land as one of the spies sent by Moses. He came back with some fruits of the land, especially a huge cluster of grapes (Num. 13.17–24).

[5] The *Gospel of Philip*, CG II.3.69, also describes the Christian journey into the holy of holies, through the areas of the temple that are increasingly holy, represented by the sacraments of baptism and Eucharist, and finally into the holy of holies that is the union.

## John 14

As for this fragrant tree, no flesh has authority to touch it until the Great Judgement, when he takes vengeance on all and brings everything to eternal consummation. Then it will be given to the righteous and holy. From its fruit, life will be given to the chosen; and it will be transplanted towards the north,[6] to a holy place beside the House of the LORD, the Eternal King.

> Then they shall rejoice with joy and be glad.
> And into the holy place shall they enter;
> And its fragrance shall be in their bones ...[7]

The fragrant tree is no particular tree – Wisdom compared herself to many trees: tall like a cedar, a cypress, a palm, an olive, a plane, spreading out her branches like a terebinth and bearing buds, blossoms and fruit like a vine (Ben Sira 24.13–17). The fragrant tree which Enoch saw was Wisdom's tree of life that had been dragged from the temple many times by those who purged the temple; it was the tree from which he said the chosen ones would eat again, just as Jesus promised his faithful disciples access again to the tree of life (Rev. 2.7; 22.14). Fragments of 20 copies of Enoch texts have been found at Qumran, showing that it was one of the most-copied texts. The Jesus of Revelation knew these Enoch traditions, and Jesus/John saw the tree restored ('transplanted') to the holy of holies, beside the throne (Rev. 22.1–3). Others at the time described the tree as a vine, as we shall see,[8] and in John's Gospel Jesus taught about the true vine (15.1–5). Those who prayed the *Didache* prayers gave thanks for the holy vine of David that had been made known to them (again?) through Jesus.[9]

The new exodus journey was also back into the state of light whence the Logos had come forth into the world (cf. 1 Pet. 2.9), and Thomas' question: 'LORD, we do not know where you are going; how can we know the way?' is echoed in the Gospel attributed to him:

> The disciples said to Jesus, 'Tell us how our end will be.' Jesus said, 'Have you discovered, then, the beginning, that you look for the end? For where the beginning is, there will the end be. Blessed is he who will take his place in the beginning; he will know the end and will not experience death.

Thomas' Jesus also spoke of the children of light who had come from the kingdom, which was also known as the bridal chamber and the holy of holies, and would find their way back:

---

[6] D. Olson, *Enoch. A New Translation*, North Richland Hills: Bibal Press, 2004, p. 61.
[7] *1 Enoch* 25.6.
[8] See below, p. 435.
[9] *Didache* 9.

## Temple Theology in John's Gospel

Jesus said, 'Blessed are the solitary and the elect, for you will find the Kingdom. For you are from it, and to it you will return.'

Jesus said, 'If they say to you, "Where did you come from?", say to them, "We came from the light, the place where the light came into being on its own accord ... We are its children, and we are the elect of the living Father."'

Jesus said, 'Many are standing at the door, but it is the solitary who will enter the bridal chamber [i.e. the holy of holies].'[10]

John's Jesus described his disciples as the elect/chosen ones (13.18; 15.16, 19), and the 'solitary' who appears in the *Gospel of Thomas*[11] may have been a translation of the Hebrew *yāḥîdh*, meaning 'the one' or 'the only one', but also the 'beloved'. This is the sense in Genesis 22.2, where Isaac is Abraham's *yāḥîdh*, his beloved son but not literally his only son. John was the beloved disciple in the same sense. The word is closely related to *yaḥadh*, the unity of which Jesus taught and for which he prayed in his high-priestly prayer (in chapter 17). The Qumran group were the *yaḥadh*, but this is usually translated 'community' and so the link to Jesus' teaching is not so obvious. It is possible that Jesus called his disciples the 'beloved', the 'members of the unity', and the 'chosen'.

Jesus is leading his followers to his Father's house, where there are many *rooms*. The word is *monē*, literally 'a stopping place', and here it recalls the places where the Israelites pitched their tents as they travelled to the promised land: '[He] went before you in the way to seek you out a place to pitch your tents ... to show you by what way you should go' (Deut. 1.33). 'My Father's house' is the temple (cf. Luke 2.49), and the many places where his followers would rest refers to Enoch's vision of the temple that the Messiah would build, 'greater and loftier' than the one it replaced and able to accommodate all the LORD's sheep.[12] When Enoch was caught up to stand before the throne in heaven, as was John (or Jesus) (Rev. 4.1–2), he saw 'the dwelling places of the holy and the resting places of the righteous'. They were among the angels, under the wings of the throne of the Chosen One, where they shone with fiery light.[13]

Jesus said: 'I am the way, the truth and the life' (v. 6), but how these three relate to each other is not clear. In his farewell, Moses warned the people to walk in all the way that the LORD had commanded them (Deut.

---

[10] *Gospel of Thomas* 18, 49, 50, 75.
[11] See also below, p. 511.
[12] *1 Enoch* 90.29.
[13] *1 Enoch* 39.1–7.

## John 14

5.33; 31.29), which implies following a set of rules for everyday living, 'doing the words of this law' and so living a good life.

> You shall walk in all the way which the LORD your God has commanded you, that you may live, and that it may go well with you, and that you might live long in the land which you shall possess. (Deut. 5.33)

But 'truth' and 'life' as Jesus uses those words are very different from the way they were used in Deuteronomy, which was almost exclusively concerned with the rules for everyday living. It warned against the secret things that belonged to the LORD (Deut. 29.29), thus distinguishing between the way of the law and another way – the secret things – of which traces can still be seen in the Old Testament. The world of Deuteronomy was very different from the world of the sacral kings and the older temple.

This is well illustrated by the change in meaning of *dābhaq*, which could mean 'cleave to', in the sense of 'being joined to', as when a man cleaves to his wife and they become one flesh (Gen. 2.24); or it could mean 'obey', as in:

> [Moses said] 'You who obeyed/held fast to, *dābhaq*, the LORD your God are all alive this day. Behold, I have taught you the statutes and ordinances, as the LORD my God commanded me, that you should do them in the land which you are entering to take possession of it. Keep them and do them; for that will be your wisdom and your understanding in the sight of the peoples ... (Deut. 4.4–6)

The distinction between the two meanings was long debated: did cleaving to the LORD mean simply doing works of piety, or was a mystical sense of union implied?[14] We shall return to this.[15] The latter meaning would explain Jesus' saying 'I am the way' rather than 'I teach you the way ...', and would be Jesus' allusion to, and contrast with, the ways of Moses.

The Psalmist had prayed:

> Make me know thy ways, O LORD,
> Teach me thy paths.
> Lead me in thy truth and teach me,
> For thou art the God of my salvation ...
> All the paths of the LORD are loving kindness, *ḥesedh*, and truth, *'emeth*,
> For those who keep, *nāṣar*, his covenant and his testimonies.
> (Ps. 25.4–5, 10, my translation; cf. 27.11)

> Teach my thy way, O LORD,
> That I may walk in thy truth ... (Ps. 86.11)

---

[14] See my book *The Mother of the Lord*, vol. 1, London: T&T Clark, 2012, pp. 172–6.
[15] See below, pp. 437–8.

Again, these tell of the ways of the LORD rather than of the LORD himself being the way, and yet the latter is what the Christians claimed. They saw Jesus himself as the living way (or maybe this should be understood as 'the way of life') into the holy of holies (Heb. 10.19–20), the only way to the Father. It was 'in him' – the older sense of 'cleaving' – that they were given the way *of* truth and life, which was also the way *to* truth and life. Jesus as the Way, and his disciples in union with him, may be the original meaning of 'the Way' in Acts, where it does not indicate just a lifestyle but the LORD present in his disciples. Some of the synagogue in Ephesus spoke ill of the Way (Acts 19.9), which could refer simply to the Christian teaching and way of living; but when Saul set out to arrest 'those of the Way' (Acts 9.2, translating literally), he heard a voice on the road to Damascus: 'Why are you persecuting *me*?' – when in fact Saul was persecuting the followers of Jesus. Jesus was the Way they were following.

The Way, the Truth and the Life, whatever the nuances, were summed up in knowing and seeing the Father (v. 7). This is similar to the gist of a fragmented Qumran text which exhorts the child/disciple to gaze on the mystery of becoming, *raz nihyeh*, the mystery of how things come to be. The child would then know the paths of all life and s/he would know truth and wisdom.[16] Jesus' 'Way' saying, and what immediately follows about seeing God, would then be equivalent to: 'No one has ever seen God; the only Son/God who is in the bosom of the Father, he has made him known' (1.18). Jesus is the presence of the LORD, the 'I AM' that was revealed to Moses when he was sent to bring the people out of Egypt (Exod. 3.16), and thus Jesus is the Way to see God.

## 14.8–14: Seeing God

Philip then intervenes: 'Lord, show us the Father, and we shall be satisfied' (v. 8), in response to Jesus' enigmatic 'If you had known me, you would have known my Father also; henceforth you know him and have seen him' (v. 7). Philip's request opens up a whole world of context for the teaching of John's Jesus, but first it is necessary to recall the hierarchy of sons in the temple world-view:[17]

God Most High was the Father of the angel sons of God, the firstborn of whom was Yahweh, usually rendered 'the LORD'. The human beings in

---

[16] Reconstructed 4Q417.2.i and 4Q418.43, in D. J. Harrington, *Wisdom Texts from Qumran*, London and New York: Routledge, 1996, pp. 52–3.
[17] See above, p. 10.

whom Yahweh was present were the sons of Yahweh, even though that title is not found in the Hebrew Scriptures. The LORD saying 'You are my son', however, *is* found (Ps. 2.7), where it was the LORD's promise to the king. The Davidic king was the son of the LORD. In his Passover discourse, Jesus speaks as this human son of Yahweh; and just as the Davidic king had spoken the words of the LORD (2 Sam. 23.1-2), so Jesus does not speak with his own authority but speaks as the LORD, who is a Son of God Most High. It was the LORD who had spoken at Sinai, but not through a human being: Moses was a messenger of the LORD, not his incarnation.[18] The present form of Exodus is an anthology of beliefs about Moses from many periods and sources, for example that he spoke with the LORD face to face (Exod. 33.11), even though such a possibility is denied in the very next section: 'You cannot see my face; for man shall not see me and live' (Exod. 33.20). Nowhere in canonical texts is Moses said to be the LORD's son, as was claimed for the Davidic kings. Here, the words of Jesus are the words of the LORD, the Son of God Most High. 'I am in the Father and the Father in me' (v. 11). Thus Jesus tells his disciples to keep *his* commandments (v. 15).

The words have been given to Jesus, and so too has the power signified by the name Yahweh [the LORD] which means 'He who causes to be'. Those who trust him and cleave to him will also receive the power, since they too will be part of the LORD.[19] When Matthew told of Jesus healing the centurion's servant, the centurion knew exactly how Jesus could draw on divine power: it was a hierarchy of obedience, like the army of which he was a part: 'I am a man under authority, with soldiers under me; and I say to one, "Go", and he goes, and to another, "Come", and he comes, and to my slave, "Do this", and he does it' (Matt. 8.9). Whatever the disciples asked would be done, because they were part of the LORD and kept his commandments. They were included within his Name, and so the Father would be glorified in the Son and in his body of disciples still on earth.

Moses reminded the people that when the commandments were given, they did not see the LORD: 'You heard the sound of words, but saw no form, $t^e m\hat{u}n\hat{a}$; there was only a voice' (Deut. 4.12), and this was repeated: 'Since you saw no form on the day that the LORD spoke to you ...' (Deut. 4.15). The people heard the voice which told them of the covenant on two pieces of stone, the statutes and ordinances of what they had to do. But

---

[18] Although Philo did describe Moses as God and King, thus making him the royal 'incarnation' of the LORD, giving him royal attributes, *Life of Moses* I.158.
[19] This is set out more fully in John chapter 17.

this was the later way of thinking; in earlier times, Isaiah *had* seen the LORD (Isa. 6.1–5) as indeed had the elders in the pre-Deuteronomic account of Sinai (Exod. 24.9–11). Seeing the LORD had been lost in the later pro-Moses ways of the Deuteronomists, and whether or not it was possible to see the LORD remained in dispute. The theme of John's Gospel is that the LORD was seen.

The *Ascension of Isaiah* shows that this was one of the major points at issue between the Jews and the first followers of Jesus, or perhaps, between the Jews and the community whence the followers of Jesus came. The *Ascension* is a composite work, set in the time of the First-Isaiah but in fact a thinly veiled description of the early Christian community and the circle whence it emerged. There is obvious hostility to 'the Jews', but this need not imply a date when the Christians had become a distinct community.[20] Knight found at least four instances of this hostility: Moses' denial that God could be seen; the list of Spirit-inspired writings that does not include the law of Moses; the predictions of the destruction of Jerusalem; and the emphasis that the Jews were responsible for the death of Jesus.[21] Only the fourth of these requires a Christian origin, but denying the vision of God was, as we have seen, characteristic of 'the Jews'.[22]

There is no agreement as to when the present form of the *Ascension* was compiled, but it could well have been a foundation text of the first Christian community, expanded during their early years. The Enochic *Apocalypse of Weeks* described how Isaiah had ascended in the sixth week, just before the temple was destroyed and after the people in the temple had lost their spiritual sight and had forsaken wisdom.[23] The biblical Book of Isaiah describes only the prophet's vision of the Glory and his commission to warn the people that they would be unable to see or perceive once they had rejected Wisdom. This became a key motif in John's Gospel (12.40), and the Jews' failure to understand is the subject of the first half of the Gospel. 'Seeing the LORD' was John's great proclamation (1.14; 1 John 1.1–3), and attributing a second vision to Isaiah would have made the *Ascension* similar to the visionary books attributed to Baruch or Ezra. These texts were prompted by the

---

[20] J. Knight, *Disciples of the Beloved One*, Sheffield: Sheffield Academic Press, 1996, p. 190, observed: 'previous research has all but ignored the anti-Jewish stance of the *Ascension of Isaiah*'.
[21] Knight, *Disciples*, pp. 190–6, citing *Ascension of Isaiah* 3.8–10; 4.21–22; 3.6, 10; 3.13; 11.19.
[22] See above, pp. 199–200.
[23] *1 Enoch* 93.8.

destruction of the temple in 70 CE, and a figure from the time of the first destruction was taken as a suitable pseudonym. But the Isaiah visions in both the canonical text and in the *Apocalypse of Weeks* were prompted by corruption in the temple, and so the new 'Isaiah' would have been someone opposed to the corruption of the temple – someone like Jesus and those in his circle.

The *Ascension of Isaiah* describes a vision in which 'Isaiah' saw the LORD: first how he ascended to see the Great Glory enthroned, and then how he saw, not a seraph sent forth to purify his lips, but the LORD sent forth to become incarnate as Jesus. Hezekiah, says the *Ascension*, met Isaiah and his son Josab who had come from Galilee (why Galilee, which has no place in the biblical Isaiah, apart from being a place of darkness, Isa. 9.1?) in the twentieth year of his reign [695 BCE]; this would have been six years after his near-fatal illness and some 47 years after Isaiah's biblical call vision. The *Ascension* records that Isaiah received another vision while he was in the king's presence and told the king what he had seen. He had been taken up through the seven heavens (whence the title of the book) in which he had seen the various ranks of angels. Then he had seen the Great Glory flanked by the LORD and the angel of the Holy Spirit. The Great Glory was the Father of the LORD who commanded him to descend to earth to be born from Mary. The angel of the Holy Spirit went to tell Joseph what was happening. Then Isaiah saw the life of Jesus, his death, resurrection and return to the seventh heaven where he resumed his place at the right hand of the Great Glory.[24]

After Hezekiah had died, says the *Ascension*, his son Manasseh became king and fell under the influence of Satan. Isaiah and his prophets then left Jerusalem because of the evil there, and the faithful went with them. They all lived for two years on a mountain in the desert. Their defining characteristic was that they believed in the Ascension into heaven, as opposed to the followers of Deuteronomy who did not (Deut. 30.11–13). They wore sackcloth and ate only the plants growing on the mountain, and they all lamented bitterly that Israel had gone astray. An enemy betrayed them and informed Manasseh in Jerusalem, saying that they were false prophets who spoke against the ways of Moses: Isaiah claimed that he had seen the LORD, but Moses had said that no man could see the LORD and live. 'Isaiah' himself had condemned Jerusalem and its rulers as Sodom and Gomorrah, which is exactly what the voice from heaven had said in Revelation: 'The great city that is spiritually called Sodom and

---

[24] *Ascension of Isaiah* 6—11.

Egypt, where their LORD was crucified' (Rev. 11.8, my translation). Manasseh had Isaiah arrested because he had received the vision and then spoken about it, and then the *Ascension* gives a longer account of the life of Jesus and the early community that had also been a part of the vision. Isaiah had seen how future leaders in the Church would themselves become corrupt and prophecy would decline. Nero would persecute the Church, and then the LORD would return and bring the great judgement. Nero is the Evil One incarnate, the counterpart of Jesus: 'He will act and speak like the beloved, and will say, "I am the LORD and before me there was no one."'[25] Because of his vision, Isaiah was killed with a saw.

The *Ascension of Isaiah* is a complex (one might even say muddled) text, usually thought to draw on various elements in the New Testament, but it is also possible that the various New Testament writers knew and alluded to the *Ascension* or an earlier form of it. There is no way of knowing if the writer of the *Ascension* collected interesting bits to make a patchwork or if the New Testament writers, and especially John, knew the *Ascension* and alluded to various parts of it. The latter does seem more likely.

- Peter knew that Jesus Christ had gone to heaven and was seated at the right hand of God with angels, authorities and powers subject to him (1 Pet. 3.22), as described in detail in the *Ascension*.[26]
- Paul knew that the rulers of this age, that is, the hostile angelic powers, did not understand who Jesus was or they would not have crucified him (1 Cor. 2.7–8), and because they did not know him, he was able to defeat them (Col. 2.15). This is not something Paul would have found in his studies of the Hebrew Scriptures, but according to the *Ascension*, this was how the Most High instructed the LORD before he came to earth:

> And I heard the voice of the Most High, the Father of my LORD, as he said to my LORD Christ who will be called Jesus: 'None of the angels of that world shall know that you are the LORD with me of the seven heavens and their angels ... And they shall not know that you are with me ... that you may judge and destroy the princes and the angels and the gods of that world, and the world which is ruled by them ... But in glory you shall ascend and sit at my right hand, and then the princes and the powers of that world will worship you.' This command I heard the Great Glory giving to my LORD.[27]

---

[25] *Asc. Isa.* 4.6.
[26] *Asc. Isa.* 11.23–33.
[27] *Asc. Isa.* 10.11–16.

## John 14

> And all the angels of the firmament saw him and worshipped. And there was much sorrow there as they said, 'How did our LORD descend upon us, and we did not notice the glory which was in him, which we [now] see was upon him from the sixth heaven? ... How did our LORD remain hidden from us as he descended and we did not notice?'[28]

The LORD returning with his angels or holy ones (1 Thess. 3.13; 2 Thess. 1.7), although found in the *Ascension*,[29] was probably drawn by Paul from Deuteronomy 33.2.

- John, our immediate concern, does present the LORD as a descending and ascending figure (3.13; 6.62), one who speaks of what he has seen in heaven (3.32); and the Baptist's words are so similar to the vision of the LORD being sent forth in the *Ascension* that there must have been a connection (3.31–35). So too in the summary of the vision:

> Through [Isaiah] there had been revealed the coming of the Beloved from the seventh heaven, and his transformation and his descent, and the form into which he must be transformed ... and his ascension to the seventh heaven from where he came.[30]

John's declaration in the Prologue – that the Word came forth from the beginning and became flesh (was transformed), that he came to his own and his own did not know him, that the world did not know him, and that the darkness did not overcome his light – could all have come from the *Ascension*, but the familiar words of John's Gospel are not usually read in that way. So too, the people of Jerusalem said they knew where Jesus came from, 'but when the Christ appears, no one will know where he comes from' (7.27), which is very similar to the *Ascension*'s 'They were all blinded concerning him. They all knew about him, but they did not know from where he was.'[31] Jesus' own prayer assumes a setting like that of the *Ascension*: 'Father, glorify thou me in thy own presence with the glory which I had with thee before the world was made' (17.5).

- The greatest similarities are to Revelation, John's other major composition. Both texts describe the angels worshipping in heaven, both see the LORD enthroned: the *Ascension* knows both the descent and the ascent, but Revelation describes only the ascent of the human – the Lamb – to be enthroned and thus become divine. Both texts see an

---

[28] *Asc. Isa.* 11.24, 26.
[29] *Asc. Isa.* 4.14.
[30] *Asc. Isa.* 3.13, 18.
[31] *Asc. Isa.* 11.13.

evil earthly ruler as the dark counterpart of the incarnate LORD: in the *Ascension*, Beliar (one name of the leader of the evil angels) would come to earth in the form of a wicked king who killed his own mother – Nero. He would claim to be the LORD, he would be treated like a god, and have his image set up in every city;[32] in Revelation, the beast from the sea received his authority from the dragon, and his number was 666, which, by the number encrypting known as *gematria*, represents the Hebrew equivalent of Neron Caesar (Rev. 13.17–18). This is not one text borrowing from another; it is two texts emerging from the same world and offering independent illustrations of their belief.

We shall return below to this question of evil powers.

Philip's request and Jesus' reply allude to Deuteronomy's version of the words of Moses, that the form of the LORD could not be seen (Deut. 4.12). Philip says, 'Lord, show us the Father and we shall be satisfied', an echo of the Servant who saw the light and was satisfied (Isa. 53.11) and of the Psalmist who suffered and then reflected:

> As for me, I shall behold your face/presence in righteousness,
> When I wake, I shall be satisfied with the vision of your form.
> (Ps. 17.15, my translation)[33]

Jesus replies to Philip: 'He who has seen me has seen the Father' (v. 9), because the form of the LORD was before Philip's eyes, and he had not fully realized this. Jesus was the ancient *Immanuel*, 'God with us', the royal son of the Virgin (Isa. 7.14).

## 14.15–31: The promise of the Paraclete

Jesus speaks next of the Paraclete, who also belongs in a Passover discourse because the Paraclete is the angel of the LORD. A comparison of their roles shows that this is the most likely identification. He does not appear with that name in Moses' farewell discourse, since Deuteronomy has no place for angels, and so here it is necessary to supplement that Passover story with other texts. As the people of Israel prepared to leave Sinai, the LORD said:

> Behold, I send an angel [my angel][34] before you, to guard you on the way and to bring you to the place which I have prepared. Give heed to him and

---

[32] *Asc. Isa.* 4.4–8.
[33] The LXX here has 'by the vision of your *glory*'.
[34] The Samaritan, Greek and Latin versions have 'my angel', as does v. 23.

## John 14

hearken to his voice, do not rebel against him, for he will not pardon your transgression; for my name is in him. (Exod. 23.20–21)

There is a similar command to Moses after the sin of the golden calf: 'But now go, lead the people to the place of which I have spoken to you; behold, my angel shall go before you' (Exod. 32.34); and also 'Depart, go up hence, you and the people whom you have brought up out of the land of Egypt ... and I will send an angel before you' (Exod. 33.1–2). The angel of God had guided them out of Egypt (Exod. 14.19; Num. 20.16). When Abraham sent his servant to find a wife for Isaac, he knew the LORD would send his angel before him on his quest (Gen. 24.7, 40); when Jacob blessed Joseph and his sons, he spoke of the God of Abraham and Isaac as 'the angel who has redeemed me' (Gen. 48.15–16). Isaiah knew of an angel who had always protected his people, and here the context is also the exodus:

> In all their affliction he was afflicted,[35] and the angel of his Presence saved them; in his love and in his pity he redeemed them, he lifted them up and carried them all the days of old. (Isa. 63.9, from the Hebrew)

The problems in this Isaiah text show that it was controversial: the first line of the Hebrew makes little sense, and the LXX has 'he became their Saviour from all affliction. Not an ambassador nor an angel but the LORD himself saved them through his love for them ...' This shows that when the LXX was translated, it was necessary to make clear that the angel of the Presence was the LORD himself. The older subtleties were no longer well known.

Sometimes the angel of the exodus was called 'the angel of the LORD' who acted to protect his people, such as Hagar in the desert (Gen. 16.7, 9, 10, 11); or he encamped around those who feared him and delivered them (Ps. 34.7); or led them as they conquered the land (Judg. 2.1, 4). He intervened when Isaac was about to be sacrificed (Gen. 22.10, 15) and when Balaam was preparing to curse Israel (Num. 22.21–35). He called Moses, Gideon and Samson to rescue his people (Exod. 3.2; Judg. 6.11–24; 13.3–20). He cursed those who did not help the LORD against his people's enemies (Judg. 5.23). In some cases – for example the stories of Moses and Gideon – it is not easy to distinguish between the angel of the LORD and the LORD himself; in others, the angel of the LORD is distinct from the LORD, for example the angel who came to destroy Jerusalem when David

---

[35] Or 'did not afflict'; the text here is not clear.

had conducted a census (2 Sam. 24.15-17) or the angel who vested Joshua the high priest (Zech. 3.1-10).

In Deuteronomy the guiding and protecting angel became the prophet who would succeed Moses.

> [The LORD said] 'I will raise up for them a prophet like you from among their brethren; and I will put my words in his mouth, and he shall speak to them all that I command him. And whoever will not give heed to my words which he shall speak in my name, I myself will require it of him.'
> (Deut. 18.18-19)

Childs commented: 'The tradition of the guiding angel is clearly pre-Deuteronomic, and indicates that an older tradition has been employed for the later homily.'[36] The angel of the LORD under any of his titles is found in neither the Deuteronomic nor the Priestly texts of the Pentateuch, which both represent the ways of the second temple. Other second-temple texts did remember the angel. The LORD spoke through Haggai as they entered the land a second time: 'As I promised when you came out of Egypt, my Spirit abides among you. Fear not' (Hag. 2.5, my translation); Ezra recalled his people's history when he prayed: 'You gave your good Spirit to instruct them, and you did not withhold manna from their mouth ...' (Neh. 9.20, my translation); and the people sang: 'Let thy good spirit lead me on a level path' (Ps. 143.10). Jesus' discourse for his new Passover promises the guiding and protecting angel of the older tradition for his people's new exodus.

Since an angel was also a spirit – 'He makes his angels spirits' (Ps. 104.4, my translation) – the angel of the LORD was also the Spirit of the LORD. The Spirit of the LORD could cause an ecstatic state, although this is not mentioned in every case. In the Hebrew Scriptures the Spirit of the LORD came on Saul when he met a group of prophets and he too began to prophesy, here meaning that he fell into an ecstatic state. He was later chosen as king (1 Sam. 10.6, 24). Then 'the Spirit of the LORD departed from Saul, and an evil spirit from the LORD tormented him' (1 Sam. 16.14). Saul was no longer the LORD's anointed. The Spirit of the LORD came upon men and women and made them judges and leaders: Othiel and Gideon were possessed by the Spirit of the LORD (Judg. 3.10; 6.34), but nothing is said of the Spirit leaving them. The Spirit of the LORD also gave the gift of prophecy (Num. 11.24-30); the Spirit of God came upon the prophet Oded and he prophesied to King Asa (2 Chron. 15.1); the

---

[36] B. S. Childs, *Exodus*, London: SCM Press, 1974, p. 487.

## John 14

Spirit of God came upon Jahaziel the Levite in the temple and he prophesied success in battle (2 Chron. 20.14). The Spirit of God *clothed itself* with Zechariah the son of Jehoiada the priest, who told the people that the Lord had forsaken them because they had forsaken him. The people stoned him to death (2 Chron. 24.20-22).

The Spirit of the Lord came mightily on David when he was anointed (1 Sam. 16.13) and so the Spirit of the Lord spoke through him (2 Sam. 23.2). The Spirit of the Lord God was upon the Third-Isaiah because the Lord had anointed him as his messenger to bring good news to the poor and afflicted (Isa. 61.1). Luke's Jesus claimed that he was fulfilling this prophecy (Luke 4.16-21); the Spirit of the Lord God was upon him. This is how John's Jesus describes the source of his teaching (14.10); it is not the words of the human Jesus but the words of his Father, in this case the Lord who was in him, perhaps *clothed* by him as was Zechariah the prophet. 'Clothing' the Spirit of the Lord had been symbolized by the vestment of the high priest, whose outer vestment was made of the same fabric as the temple veil and so represented matter.[37] Thus the high priest, with the Name on his forehead (bearing his X, his cross), was the presence of the Lord clothed in matter. The first Christians still knew that the temple veil symbolized the flesh of Jesus (Heb. 10.19-20).[38] A blessing for the sons of Zadok used at Qumran was that they would be as an angel of the Presence, the traditional role for the high priests.[39] Isaiah said that when the Spirit of the Lord rested on the Davidic king, his mind and perception were transformed (Isa. 11.2). The Spirit of the Lord was upon the Servant of the Lord (Isa. 42.1; 61.2), and the Lord would pour out his Spirit on the descendants of Jacob (Isa. 44.3). The 'Spirit of the Lord' meant both the Spirit from the Lord but also *the Spirit that transformed the recipient into the Lord*, the Son of God, and so Paul wrote: 'All who are led by the Spirit of God are sons of God' (Rom. 8.14).

Texts from the end of the second-temple period show the Lord/the angel of the Lord in conflict with an evil angel. This is not necessarily a sign that the two rival angels were a late addition to Hebrew tradition. The prose framework of Job apparently derives from an ancient tale set in the time of Abraham, and it depicts the Lord among the other sons of God, challenged by Satan to test the loyalty of his servant Job. The sons of

---

[37] Josephus, *War* 5.212-13; Philo, *Questions on Exodus* II.85; also my book *The Gate of Heaven*, London: SPCK, 1991, pp. 107-14.

[38] For detail, see my book *The Great High Priest. The Temple Roots of Christian Liturgy*, London: T&T Clark, 2003, pp. 210-12.

[39] 1QSb IV.25.

God stand against the LORD, *yāṣabh 'al*, exactly as the hostile kings stand against the LORD in Psalm 2.2. It is the same verb. In each case, the LORD and his servant Job triumph, or the LORD and his anointed king triumph, but they are challenged by hostile powers. In other words, the LORD is depicted even in the older ways as the guardian angel and guide of his people in the face of hostile spiritual powers. The leader of these powers was an angel who had rebelled and been thrown from heaven, and who then vowed revenge on Adam, who had caused his downfall.[40]

Evil spirits spoke through false prophets: the prophet Zedekiah gave a favourable prophecy to King Ahab, but Micaiah ben Imlah knew he had spoken the words of a lying spirit, in order to lead Ahab to disaster. The lying spirit, however, had been sent by the LORD, and was delivering the LORD's judgement (1 Kings 22.13–23), or testing the loyalty of his people (Deut. 13.1–3). The LORD *allowed* Satan to tempt Job (Job 2.6–8); an evil spirit from the LORD tormented King Saul (1 Sam. 16.14); the beast was permitted to rule for a certain period of time (Rev. 13.5). At some stage in the second-temple period, all prophecy was deemed the work of unclean spirits, because an isolated prophecy attached to Zechariah looked forward to a land with no prophets (Zech. 13.2–6).

The Qumran community knew of good and evil spirits, and these texts show how the conflict was described in the time of Jesus. Both the good spirit and the evil spirit were sent by God, and everyone had to choose which spirit to follow. These texts also show that the spirits had several names, and knowing about them was a core element in the teachings of the Qumran community. The good spirit was Melchi-Zedek, meaning the 'king of righteousness', who rescued his own people from the power of Belial and his spirits,[41] and his counterpart was Melchi-Resha', meaning the 'king of evil', whom the community cursed.[42] Other names for the good spirit were the Prince of Light, God's Angel of Truth, the spirit of truth, *'emeth*, the spirit of light. Other names for the evil spirit were the Angel of Darkness, the spirit of unrighteousness, *'awlâ*, the spirit of darkness.[43] Their titles and their attributes mirrored each other, as can be seen in the Book of Revelation, where the red dragon, also called the devil and Satan, the deceiver of the whole earth, together with his angels, fights against Michael and his angels. The dragon makes war on the other

---

[40] See above, p. 122.
[41] *Melchizedek*, 11QMelch II.5, 13.
[42] 4Q280.
[43] The description of the two spirits is in the *Community Rule*, 1QS III.13—IV.26.

## John 14

children of the Woman clothed with the sun (Rev. 12.1-17),[44] so presumably these children are Michael's angels on earth.

According to the *Community Rule*, the teacher[45] had to instruct the sons of light in the ways of the two spirits that affect human life: the spirit of truth and the spirit of unrighteousness. Those born of truth are called the sons of righteousness, they are led by the Prince of Light and come from the light; those born of unrighteousness are led by the Angel of Darkness and come from darkness. Each of the two spirits offers a distinctive lifestyle: those who walk in the spirit of the Angel of Truth have healing, peace, long life, fruitfulness, blessing, eternal joy, a crown of glory and a garment of majesty in eternal light; those who walk in the evil spirit have plagues from the destroying angels, and receive the punishment of divine wrath in the fires of darkness. A person could change from one way of life to the other. God could remove the spirit of unrighteousness by cleansing with the spirit of holiness, by pouring out the spirit of truth like waters of purification, and by immersing in the spirit of purification. After this baptism in the spirit, that person would have the knowledge to teach the sons of heaven, and they would enter the everlasting covenant and regain all the glory of Adam.

The *War Scroll* had a similar world-view – the struggle between the sons of light and the sons of darkness – but with some different names, and in the context of a real war rather than the struggle of everyday living and conflicting lifestyles. The sons of light were the exiles of the desert, drawn from Levi, Judah and Benjamin, that is, from the southern tribes and their priesthood, and they would fight against the army of Belial who were the sons of darkness.[46] The army of the sons of light had to be ritually pure, since they would be fighting alongside holy angels.[47] Belial, who is also mentioned in the *Community Rule*,[48] appears in the Hebrew Scriptures, but the word is translated in various other ways and not as a name: 'I will not set before my eyes anything that is *base*' (Ps. 101.3); 'The torrents of *perdition* assailed me' (Ps. 18.4); 'A *deadly* thing has fastened upon him' (Ps. 41.8); 'Never again shall the *wicked* come against you' (Nah. 1.15); and in Deuteronomy, it is 'sons of Belial' who tempt people to worship other gods (Deut. 13.13, my translation). The LXX translates Belial as *paranomos*, 'lawlessness', and the early Christians knew of a man

---

[44] See above, p. 365.
[45] The *maśkîl*, literally 'the one who gives insight/makes wise'.
[46] *War Scroll*, 1QM I.1-15.
[47] *War Scroll*, IQM VII.4-8.
[48] *Community Rule*, 1QS I.18, 24; II.5, 19; X.21.

of lawlessness, *anomia*, the son of destruction, who would appear before the return of the LORD (2 Thess. 2.3). Belial had his host, the angels of destruction/corruption, and the Prince of Light had his host which included the people of the Qumran community[49] and, in the New Testament, the host of the Lamb (Rev. 14.1–5).

The battle of the sons of light against the sons of darkness is described in Revelation 19. A warrior angel emerges from heaven with his host of angels, all riding white horses. Their leader is called Faithful, *'ōmen*, and True, *'emeth*, presumably the Angel of Truth. His other names are the Logos of God, King of Kings and LORD of Lords. The earthly part of the host gathers on Mount Zion, 144,000 wearing the Name on their foreheads, the ritually pure followers of God-and-the-Lamb (Rev. 14.1–5). Teaching about the Prince of Light and the Angel of Darkness appears in several early Christian texts: the *Letter of Barnabas*, the *Didache*, the *Shepherd of Hermas* and the *Ascension of Isaiah*.

> There are two ways of teaching, and two wielders of power; one of light and the other of darkness. Between those two ways is a vast difference, because over the one are posted the light-bearing angels of God, and over the other the angels of Satan; and one of these two is the LORD from all eternity to all eternity, while the other stands paramount over this present age of iniquity.[50]

> There are two Ways: a Way of Life and a Way of Death, and the difference between these two Ways is great.[51]

> There are two angels with man, one of righteousness and the other of wickedness... When the angel of righteousness comes into your heart, he at once speaks to you of righteousness, of purity, of reverence, of self control, of every righteous deed and of all virtue. When all these things come into your heart, know that the angel of righteousness is with you... Now see also the works of the angel of wickedness. First of all he is ill-tempered and bitter, and foolish, and his deeds are evil, casting down the servants of God. Whenever therefore he comes into your heart, know him from his works.[52]

There follows in each case a detailed description of the lifestyles of those on the Way of Light, which was the Way of Life ruled by the Angel of Righteousness; and those on the Way of Darkness which was the Way of Death ruled by the Angel of Wickedness.

---

[49] *War Scroll*, 1QM XIII.10–13.
[50] *Letter of Barnabas* 18.
[51] *Didache* 1.
[52] *Shepherd of Hermas*, Mandate 6.2.

## John 14

The *Ascension* tells the story of Isaiah and his community of prophets as a conflict between good and evil spirits, and, despite the familiar words which have often been domesticated to a different understanding, this is how John tells the story of Jesus too. The various translations of the text of the *Ascension* – a Hebrew original in some parts,[53] a Greek translation, then another into Ethiopic – means that some names have been distorted, but they can still be recognized. Isaiah predicted that Hezekiah's son Manasseh would have in his service an evil angel, Sammael Malki-Ra, and that he would serve Beliar rather than the Spirit who was speaking through Isaiah. Sammael was one of the three names for the proud Ruler who believed that he was the only God.[54] This proud Ruler is recognizable as the LORD described by the Deuteronomists, who recognized none but himself and whose followers had lost their (spiritual) sight. Elsewhere his name is said to mean 'the blind Ruler', or 'the Ruler of the blind', just as *1 Enoch* described the late first-temple priests as those who had lost their sight, and whose successors were an apostate generation.[55] Malki-Ra has the same form as Melchi-Zedek, and means 'the king of evil', the Melchi-Resha' of the Qumran texts.[56] Beliar is the same as Belial, and he would dwell within Manasseh.[57] Beliar/Sammael clung closely (? cleaved) to Manasseh and so the king served Satan.[58] Beliar acted through Malki-Ra and also through Manasseh;[59] in other words, this was the evil counterpart to the hierarchy the LORD, Melchi-Zedek and the Davidic king. It was an agent of Malki-Ra who betrayed Isaiah's community and accused them of being false prophets. Beliar the king of this world came to earth as Nero ('the man who killed his own mother') and acted in every way like the evil counterpart of the Beloved. When the LORD returned to earth, he would drag Beliar and his hosts into Gehenna. As he ascended through the heavens, Isaiah saw Sammael and his angels in the firmament that separated the earth from the seven heavens; they were in constant strife among themselves, 'fighting one another ... envying about trifles', and this was reflected on earth.[60] The angel who went with Isaiah told

---

[53] The wordplay in *Ascension of Isaiah* 2.1 only works in Hebrew: *mnšh* can be either the name Manasseh, or the Pi'el participle of the verb *nšh*, 'forget'.
[54] His other names were Yaltabaoth and Saklas, according to the *Apocryphon of John*, CG II.1.11.18.
[55] *Hypostasis of the Archons*, CG II.4.87.3; 94.25; *1 Enoch* 93.8–9.
[56] He also appears as Belkira, *Ascension of Isaiah* 2.5.
[57] *Ascension of Isaiah* 1.8–9; 5.1.
[58] *Asc. Isa.* 2.1–2.
[59] *Asc. Isa.* 5.15.
[60] *Asc. Isa.* 7.9; 10.30.

him that the LORD would come to earth to plunder the angel of death, to rise again and then take the righteous back to heaven with him. This is similar to the hope expressed in the Qumran *Melchizedek* text, that Melchi-Zedek would rescue his own people from the power of Belial and his spirits, and to Jesus' teaching: 'No one can enter a strong man's house and plunder his goods unless he first binds the strong man; then indeed he may plunder his house' (Mark 3.27//Matt. 12.29).[61]

The Spirit of the LORD and the Spirit of Belial each had his host and hierarchy, and each was known by several names. Each worked through human beings, and their characteristics were well known. The Angel of the LORD, the Spirit of the LORD, the Angel of the Presence, the Prince of Light, the Angel of Truth, the Angel of Righteousness, the LORD from all eternity, Melchi-Zedek – all these are titles for the presence of the LORD with and within human beings. The Paraclete was yet another of the names, and many possible meanings have been suggested – advocate, mediator, comforter, encourager – but none of these is satisfactory. Brown summarized thus:

> No one translation of *paraklētos* captures the complexity of the functions forensic and otherwise, that this figure has. The Paraclete is a witness in defence of Jesus, and a spokesman for him in the context of his trial by his enemies; the Paraclete is a consoler of the disciples for he takes Jesus' place among them; the Paraclete is a teacher and guide of the disciples and thus their helper.[62]

One problem may be '*another* Paraclete' (14.16). Unless Jesus delivered these teachings in Greek, which is unlikely, the word would have been *'aḥēr*, 'another', which is very easily confused with *'aḥar*, 'afterwards'. This happened when Revelation was put into Greek, resulting in a whole series of mighty angels when in some instances of 'another' it should be read as 'afterwards' (e.g. Rev. 7.2; 10.1; 18.1). This gives not several mighty angels, but several appearances one *after* another of one mighty angel, the Angel of the LORD, whom John called the Paraclete. The Sinai Syriac text was aware of this problem, and renders the verse 'He will give you Another, the Paraclete'.[63]

---

[61] The Strong One = Azazel, the leader of the fallen angels. The name is formed from *'zz*, 'to be strong'.
[62] R. E. Brown, *The Gospel According to John XIII–XXI*, Anchor Bible 29a, New Haven and London: Yale University Press, (1970) 2008, p. 1137.
[63] J. H. Bernard, *The Gospel According to St John*, vol. 2, Edinburgh: T&T Clark, 1928, p. 545.

The good and evil angels, by whatever name, speak in the heart; in other words, they influence the human mind. The Hebrew Scriptures also show the Spirit of the LORD speaking *within* a person, and so through that person. 'The Spirit of the LORD speaks *in me*,' said David (2 Sam. 23.2, translating literally), and the prophet Zechariah said that the angel spoke *in him* (Zech. 1.9, 19; 2.3) and then that the LORD spoke to the angel who was speaking in him (Zech. 1.14). Luke says Paul saw a great light on the road to Damascus (Acts 9.3–9). His contemporaries might well have described him meeting the Prince of Light. Paul himself says, 'He who had set me apart before I was born, and had called me through his grace, was pleased to reveal his Son *in me*, in order that I might preach him among the Gentiles' (Gal. 1.15–16, translating literally). The Son was revealed *in* Paul. Jesus told his disciples:

> I will pray the Father, and afterwards he will send you the Paraclete, to be with you for ever, even the Spirit of Truth, whom the world cannot receive because it neither sees him nor knows him; you will know him, *for he dwells with you and will be in you.* (John 14.16–17, my translation)

Compare 1.10–11, those who do not recognize or receive the Logos; and the words of Zechariah: 'The angel who spoke within me said to me ...' (Zech. 1.9). Hence Paul's words: 'All who are led by the Spirit of God are sons of God ... When we cry "Abba! Father!" it is the Spirit himself bearing witness with our spirit that we are children of God' (Rom. 8.14–16).

Like the teacher of the Therapeuts, who used to linger over his teaching with repetitions, in order to imprint it on the minds of his hearers, so too Jesus repeats important teachings. There are four sections dealing with the work of the Paraclete and his various names and roles, two before Jesus' teaching about the vine and two after. We shall return to this.[64]

## Ḥesedh in the teaching of Jesus

In the synoptic Gospels, the last supper was a covenant meal when Jesus took bread and wine from the Passover table and used them to re-establish or renew an older covenant.[65] John does not mention this ritual at the last supper, but Jesus' teaching in the Passover discourse is about the covenant of *ḥesedh*. According to their *Community Rule*, the Qumran community were in a covenant of *ḥesedh* to be joined together in the

---

[64] See below, pp. 456–90.
[65] See pp. 143, 512.

wisdom of God, and to walk before him in uprightness, cleaving, *dbq*, to all the works of good and doing truth, righteousness and justice. Each member was directed by spirits, or maybe by one spirit with several names:

- by the spirit of the counsel of truth about the ways of man, to purify him from all his iniquities so that he would see (things) in the light of life;
- by the spirit of holiness uniting him to (God's) truth and cleansing him from all the iniquities (of men);
- by the spirit of uprightness and humility to cleanse his iniquity.[66]

The titles of the spirits in the *Community Rule* are those of the Paraclete/Counsellor in the Passover discourse: the Counsellor, the Spirit of truth (14.16-17); the Counsellor, the Spirit of holiness (14.26); the Counsellor who will convict the world of sin, righteousness and judgement (16.7-8). We shall return to this.

Mutual *ḥesedh* is the distinguishing mark of Jesus' disciples, his new commandment that supersedes the law of Moses (13.34; 15.12, 17). He has chosen them from the world, and so *ḥesedh* comes to stand for everything that distinguishes them from 'the world': light, life, unity. At first Jesus speaks only of the *ḥesedh* that binds him and his disciples. 'If you love me, you will keep my commandments' (v. 15). 'Keeping my commandments' is synonymous with 'keeping my word': 'If anyone keeps my word, he will never see death' (8.51; also 14.23-24; 15.20; and 1 John 2.5). To those within this bond of *ḥesedh* the Father would send the Paraclete (v. 15). Jesus then extends the teaching: *ḥesedh* does not just bind him to his disciples; it also binds him to the Father, and his disciples, insofar as they are also bound to him, will be bound to the Father (v. 20). This is repeated several times: 'If a man loves me, he will keep my word, and my Father will love him, and we will come to him and make our home with him' (v. 23). 'If you keep my commandments [to have *ḥesedh*], you will be bound in my *ḥesedh* just as I have kept my Father's commandments and am bound by his *ḥesedh*' (15.10).

So too in John's letters, where it is clear that eternal life is not the reward for abiding in love; it is the present state or consequence or evidence of abiding in love:

- 'He who loves his brother abides in the light' (1 John 2.10);

---

[66] *Community Rule*, 1QS I, my translations.

- 'See what love the Father has given us, that we should be called children of God' (1 John 3.1);
- 'We know that we have passed out of death into life, because we love the brethren. He who does not love abides in death' (1 John 3.14);
- 'Beloved, let us love one another; for love is of God, and he who loves is born of God and knows God' (1 John 4.7);
- 'God is love, and he who abides in love abides in God' (1 John 4.16);
- 'I beg you ... not as though I were writing you a new commandment, but the one we have had from the beginning, that we love one another. And this is love, that we follow his commandments; this is the commandment, as you have heard from the beginning, that you follow love' (2 John 5–6).

This hierarchy – the LORD, the Spirit of the LORD and the human presence of the LORD – is bound by the covenant of *ḥesedh*, and is the counterpart of the hierarchy of evil that appears in the *Ascension of Isaiah* – Beliar, Malki-Ra, Manasseh – and also in Revelation: the dragon/Satan, who works through the beast from the sea and exercises his earthly authority through the beast from the earth who looks like a lamb (Rev. 12—13). The nature of their covenant is not mentioned, but is probably what underlies Paul's use of this combat image in Romans 8, where the Spirit-led children of God release creation, which has been 'subjected to folly, trifles, *mataiotēs* ... and will be set free from its bondage to corruption, *phthorē* . . .' (Rom. 8.20-21, my translation). This implies a covenant bond of *mataiotēs* (Hebrew *hbl*, *šw'*) and *phthorē* (Hebrew *šḥt*) that the sons of God had to destroy.

The new status of those within the covenant of *ḥesedh* is shown by wearing the Name; this covenant is a high-priestly bond. Long before he wrote his Gospel, John knew of the army of the Lamb on Zion who had the Name of the Lamb and the Name of his Father written on their foreheads (Rev. 14.1) They were the 144,000 who had been marked by the angel of the sunrise with the seal of the living God (Rev. 7.2), the X that was the ancient sign of the Name and also the mark of Christian baptism.[67] Jesus promised the faithful disciple in Philadelphia that he would write on him the name of his God and his own new name (Rev. 3.12).[68]

---

[67] See above, pp. 346-7.

[68] And also the name of the new Jerusalem, which Ezekiel said would be given the Name also (Ezek. 48.35). The Hebrew says, literally, 'The name of the city from that day, her name will be the LORD.'

Jesus teaches that those bound in the new covenant of *ḥesedh* should expect hostility from the world. Jesus has chosen his own out of the world (Church = *ekklēsia* = 'called out'], and the world only loves its own (15.18–19). John also says this in his first letter: 'Do not wonder, brethren, that the world hates you. We know that we have passed out of death into life because we love the brethren. He who does not love abides in death' (1 John 3.13–14).

In the vision of the Lady giving birth in the temple, her son escaped from the waiting dragon, who was angry, and made war on her other children instead (Rev. 12.17).

# John 15

## The vine

Only John records the image of Jesus as the true vine. It was recognized long ago that the image was inspired by the great golden vine that adorned the eastern gates of the temple.[1] Josephus described it:

> A golden vine with its branches hanging down from a great height, the largeness and fine workmanship of which was a surprising sight to the spectators, to see what vast materials there were and with what great skill the workmanship was done.[2]

Elsewhere he used the plural: 'Those golden vines from which hung grape clusters as tall as a man'.[3] The Mishnah says the vine was used to give offerings of gold to the temple: 'A golden vine stood over the entrance to the sanctuary, trained over posts; and whosoever gave a leaf or a berry or a cluster as a freewill offering, he brought it and [the priests] hung it thereon.' Danby adds: 'And when the temple treasury was in need, the treasurer took from the vine as much as was required.'[4] The golden vine, then, was the visible sign of the wealth of the temple.

There is no mention of a golden vine in Solomon's temple, even though the image of the vine or the vineyard was often used in the Hebrew Scriptures. But the 'choice vine', śōrēq (Isa. 5.2; Jer. 2.21), also means 'shining' (Ben Sira 50.7),[5] and maybe this prompted Herod's golden vine. It could have been one of his innovations, or perhaps there had been a choice/shining vine in the old temple, and Isaiah's poetic description of a choice vine on a hill by the holy of holies[6] was an allusion to something he knew. Herod had also set a huge golden eagle over the great gate of the

---

[1] B. F. Westcott, *The Gospel According to St John*, London: John Murray, 1881, p. 216.
[2] Josephus, *Antiquities* 15.395.
[3] Josephus, *War* 5.210; Tacitus, *History* V.5.
[4] Mishnah *Middoth* 3.8 in H. Danby, *The Mishnah*, Oxford: Oxford University Press, (1933) 1989, p. 595, n. 6.
[5] Also Gen. 49.11, śōrēqâ, which probably means 'her choice vine', a reference to the Lady.
[6] See n. 22 below.

temple, presumably to represent Rome, and when he was thought to be dying, two students let themselves down from the temple roof at midday and began to chop the eagle to pieces. Herod had them and their two teachers burned alive.[7] No similar protest is recorded about the vine, which suggests that it was a legitimate symbol for Jews, but why should Herod have placed it there?

The *Didache* prayer gave thanks for 'the holy vine of thy servant David, which thou hast made known to us through thy servant Jesus',[8] which suggests that for Christians, the vine was a symbol of the Davidic monarchy. Herod setting a huge golden vine in the temple could have been how he asserted his right to rule there: the eagle represented Rome and the vine represented the house of Herod claiming to be legitimate rulers in succession to the house of David. A contrast between Jesus as the true vine of David and the false vine of the impure temple of the Herodian kings would have needed no explanation. 'The vine, the true' (v. 1, translating literally) would then be a translation of the Hebrew wordplay: *hakkannâ*, 'the stem of the vine' (Ps. 80.16) and *hakkēn*, 'true/certain/honest'.

Both the eagle and the vine appear in Revelation. The visions of the seven trumpets describe the years of Roman rule in Palestine, the trumpets being the signal for holy war (Num. 31.6): the first trumpet was the arrival of Pompey in 63 BCE and the sixth was the ravaging of the land by Cestius in the autumn of 66 CE. The seventh was the fall of Jerusalem. Midway through this period, when the fourth trumpet sounded, an eagle was seen flying in the sky and warning of the woes yet to come (Rev. 8.13). The history of the seven trumpets is stylized, but the eagle at the time of the fourth trumpet appears at the point in the sequence when the golden eagle was torn from the temple.[9]

The golden vine was the vine of the land[10] which was reaped by the angel from heaven and trodden in the great winepress of the wrath of God (Rev. 14.17–20). The two harvest images in this chapter of Revelation were both part of Jesus' teaching. The grain harvest in the New Testament was a positive image, with the faithful being gathered into the LORD's store (Matt. 13.24–30, 37–42). The parable took various forms: removing the weeds at the time of harvest, or, in the Baptist's version, burning the chaff

---

[7] Josephus, *War* 1.648–53.
[8] *Didache* 9.
[9] For detail of the history of the seven trumpets, see my book *The Revelation of Jesus Christ*, Edinburgh: T&T Clark, 2000, pp. 171–9.
[10] 'Earth' and 'land' would have been the same word in the original Hebrew oracle, as is also true of Matt. 5.5, where the meek inherit the land.

when the grain was threshed (Matt. 3.12). The image of the vintage was always negative, possibly because grape juice looked like blood. Jesus told the parable of the tenants in the vineyard (Mark 12.1-9 and parallels), which was in turn based on Isaiah's parable of the vineyard that produced only bitter grapes and so was destroyed (Isa. 5.1-7). Isaiah described the day of vengeance and redemption as the LORD treading the winepress of his wrath (Isa. 63.1-6; cf. Lam. 1.15), and Joel used the same image:

> Put in the sickle, for the harvest is ripe.
> Go in, tread, for the wine press is full.
> The vats overflow, for their wickedness is great.
> (Joel 3.13)

This was the image used in Revelation 14.19.

The vine was a symbol of the royal house.[11] The Lady of the temple was the vine, the heavenly Mother of all the Davidic kings, and, as Ezekiel showed in his lament, the anointed kings were her 'branches' (Ezek. 19.10-14; cf. Isa. 11.1; Zech. 3.8; 6.12). The poem is not easy to translate, due to gender confusion and a mixture of singular and plural forms, but it is clear that the Mother was not one human woman, as the last kings of Judah had several mothers. She was the divine Lady, present in each of the royal mothers. Her central stem was the ruler, 'the strong rod, a sceptre to rule' (Ezek. 19.14).[12] Ezekiel's preceding poem described the Mother of the kings as a lioness with her cubs. She was the Mother of both Josiah's son Jehoahaz and his grandson Jehoiachin, but her two cubs were captured and taken away (Ezek. 19.2-9). The royal lion and the Davidic vine appear again in Revelation, where Jesus the Lamb/Servant is called the Lion of the tribe of Judah, the Root of David (Rev. 5.5), and the Root and Offspring of David, the bright Morning Star (Rev. 22.16).

The lioness and the vine appear together in a wall painting in the synagogue at Dura Europos in Syria, rediscovered in 1932. Since the synagogue was near the city walls, it was filled with sand to become part of the city's defences in 256 CE, not long after it had been completed. The western wall, which had been repainted at least twice, shows a spreading vine the size of a tree, with various other figures and symbols around it.[13]

---

[11] This may be why Aristobulus, the last of the Hasmonean kings, sent a golden vine to Pompey as a gift (bribe?), Josephus, *Antiquities* 14.34-36. It had no effect, and Pompey conquered Jerusalem in 63 BCE.

[12] See my book *The Mother of the Lord*, vol. 1, London: T&T Clark, 2012, pp. 359-60.

[13] See E. R. Goodenough, *Jewish Symbols in the Greco-Roman Period*, 11 vols, New York: Pantheon, 1953-65, vol. 9, pp. 78-9, figs 73-7.

The repainting long ago, and the deterioration after re-exposure to sun and air, mean that the figures are no longer clear, but they seem to be a man enthroned towards the top of the vine-tree; a lioness across the lower trunk; a table underneath the vine-tree to the left of the trunk, on which is a curved object, possibly one loaf of the bread of the Presence; a pair of ?horned animals browsing a tree to the right of the trunk; and two groups of people that seem to be, on the left, Jacob blessing his sons, and on the right, Jacob blessing his grandsons Ephraim and Manasseh (Gen. 49.2–27).[14] The king in the painting is the central stem of the vine-tree, as in Ezekiel's poem:

> She had strong branches to be the sceptres of rulers,
> She was exalted in height among the foliage,
> He was seen in his height among his many branches ...
> A fire has gone out from the stem of her branches and consumed her fruit,
> And she no longer has a strong rod, a sceptre to rule.
>
> (Ezek. 19.11, 14, my translation)

The symbols around the vine-tree are those of the Lady: the bread of the Presence, her lion, and the pair of animals browsing a tree that also appear on the Taanach cult stand and on pithos A found at Kuntillet 'Ajrud, both dating from the time of the first temple. The two animals feeding from the tree are thought to represent the two aspects of the king feeding from his Tree-mother.[15] On pithos A and in the wall painting there is a small figure of a harpist to the left of the picture. The vine-tree at Dura-Europos represented the Lady with the king as her central stem, enthroned within her branches.

The Lady also played a part in the original Blessing of Jacob that was depicted on the western wall of the synagogue. When Isaac blessed Jacob, he prayed for the blessing of El Shaddai, one of the ancient titles for the Lady that was later transferred to the LORD: 'May El Shaddai bless you and make you fruitful and multiply you, that you may become a company of peoples' (Gen. 28.3).[16] Jacob said that El Shaddai had appeared to him at

---

[14] This was recognized by J. Goldstein, 'The Central Composition of the West Wall of the Synagogue of Dura Europos', *Journal of Ancient Near Eastern Society* 16–17 (1984–5), pp. 99–142, pp. 99–110.

[15] The king was depicted as two identical figures, a custom known as gemination. The two animals fed from the tree of life, or, in the case of Ugarit, the two children were suckled by the goddess. For the archaeological evidence, see my book *Mother of the Lord*, pp. 154–63.

[16] *Mother of the Lord*, pp. 129, 133.

## John 15

Luz (Bethel) and had repeated the blessing (Gen. 48.3). Jacob then blessed his own sons, and to Judah he said:

> Judah is a lion's whelp ...
> The sceptre shall not depart from Judah,
> Nor the ruler's staff from between his feet/among his war banners,[17]
> Until he comes to ***;
> And to him shall be the obedience of the peoples.
> Binding his foal to the vine
> And his ass's colt to *the choice vine*,
> He washes his garments in wine
> And his vesture in the blood of grapes ... (Gen. 49.9–11)

Several words are uncertain in this passage. 'Choice vine' here is *śrqh*, which could be read as a feminine form of *śōrēq*, but this form is not found elsewhere, or it could be read as 'her choice vine'. Either way, it implies a feminine presence. And the word represented by *** is *šylh*, which makes no sense in this context. A small change, however, reveals 'to Siloam/Shiloaḥ', the water that flowed from the Lady's spring, the Gihon, and so the line was once 'until he comes to Shiloaḥ'. Following the rules of the correcting scribes, two letters were exchanged and one of them changed. It looks as though *šylh* was formerly *šlḥh*, since *y* (y) and *ḥ* (h) are similar in the Palaeo-Hebrew script. The line originally described the ruler from the tribe of Judah going to the Gihon spring just as Solomon had done when he rode on the king's mule to be anointed, and when all the people acclaimed him (1 Kings 1.33–40). 'Binding his foal to the vine' is at present opaque, but washing his robes in the blood of grapes looks like a lost ritual that is also mentioned in Revelation: 'Blessed are those who wash their robes, that they may have the right to the tree of life' (Rev. 22.14).

Jewish interpretation of this passage, compiled in Palestine in about the fifth century CE, showed that some understood the lines differently. R. Nehemiah[18] said that 'his foal' should be read as 'his city', since both 'foal' and 'city' are written *'yr* and so could be pronounced as either word. R. Nehemiah read: 'He binds to the vine his city, which alludes to "the city which I have chosen" [1 Kings 11.32].' The second half of the line – 'his ass's colt to the choice vine' – he read as: 'and strong sons will spring from him'.[19] Other interpretations said that the ass's colt referred to the

---

[17] For 'feet', the Samaritan text here has 'banners', in the sense of the warriors of his tribe, *dgl* rather than *rgl*.
[18] R. Nehemiah was a pupil of R. Akiba, and taught in the mid-second century CE.
[19] *Genesis Rabbah* XCVIII.9.

prophecy of the king who would come to the daughter of Zion, the Righteous One and Victor (Zech. 9.9), and that the vine was the one brought from Egypt (Ps. 80.8–11), the choice vine that the LORD planted which became a degenerate wild vine (Jer. 2.21).[20]

But the Hebrew text of Genesis 49.11 has '*her* foal/city', not 'his foal/city', even though it is the custom always to read 'his' at this point, and '*yr* could also mean 'guardian angel/protector'. If *śrqh* is read as 'her choice vine', the lines become:

> Binding *her* foal/city/guardian to the vine
> And his strong sons to *her* choice vine,
> He washes his garments in wine
> And his vesture in the blood of grapes ...

Perhaps the original was: 'Judah will bind her guardian to the vine, his strong sons to her choice vine'. That is speculation; but what is certain is that this is an important royal text that is no longer readable. Judah's descendant was the Davidic king, the LORD with his people, and as such he was the guardian and protector of his Mother and her city. This is found in the Hebrew Scriptures:

> Why do you cry aloud [daughter of Jerusalem],
> Is there no king in you?
> Has your counsellor perished,
> That pangs have seized you like a woman in travail?
> Writhe and groan, O daughter of Zion,
> Like a woman in travail;
> For now you shall go forth from the city
> And dwell in the open country;
> You shall go to Babylon.
> There you will be rescued,
> There the LORD will redeem you
> From the hand of your enemies. (Mic. 4.9–10)

Judah's blessing from Jacob, which is now opaque, could well have described the king espousing himself to the vine-Mother as her guardian or binding the city itself to the vine-Mother, and this was sensitive enough to attract the attention of the correcting scribes.

The *Testament of Judah*, when the patriarch prophesied that the spirit of blessing would be poured onto one of his descendants, described him as 'the Shoot of God Most High, the fountain of the life of all

---

[20] *Genesis Rabbah* XCIX.8.

## John 15

humanity',[21] and this image of the shoot, *nēṣer*, was also used of the young/expected Davidic king. He would be a shoot growing from the roots of Jesse (Isa. 11.1). A confused later text has the whole people as the shoot that the LORD would plant in the land (Isa. 60.21).[22] This same *nēṣer* was being nurtured by the Qumran community, although the meaning of the *Hymns* is not entirely clear. The men of the LORD's council, together with the angels of the Presence, would 'Raise up a *shoot* to be the branches of an eternal planting ... the spring of light shall become an everlasting fountain ...'. The community itself was Eden, where the trees and the fountain of life nurtured the *shoot* that would grow into an eternal planting: 'a shoot of holiness grows into a planting of truth, hidden and not considered, and because it is not known, its mystery is sealed'.[23] Powerful warrior spirits guarded the place and the fountain of life with its waters of holiness. It seems that in their Eden the community were nurturing and guarding the shoot (the person? the teaching?) that would grow and flourish, and the fountain of life. These are also the images of the restored temple in Revelation 22.1-5.

Wisdom described herself as a great vine in Ben Sira's poem, written, or perhaps only quoted by him, in about 180 BCE. There are several variations in the text at this point, which often omits verse 18:

> [16]Like a terebinth I spread out my branches,
> And my branches are glorious and graceful.
> [17]Like a vine I caused loveliness to bud,
> And my blossoms became glorious and abundant fruit.
> [18]I am the mother of beautiful love, of fear, of knowledge, and of holy hope;
> *Being eternal, I therefore am given to all my children, to those who are named by him.* (Ben Sira 24.16–18)

The verse numbering in the Latin is different, this section being verses 22–25, and the line in italics is replaced by: 'In me is every gift of the way and of truth, in me is every hope of life and virtue', very similar to Jesus' reply to Thomas in 14.6: 'I am the way, and the truth, and the life'.[24]

Ben Sira also described his own quest for Wisdom as though he had been contemplating a vine on the temple:

---

[21] *Testament of Judah* 24.4.
[22] 1QIsa^b lacks *nēṣer*, and the LXX understood the word as *noṣēr*, 'guardian'.
[23] *Hymns*, 1QH XIV.15, 17; XVI.10-11, my translation.
[24] R. E. Brown, *The Gospel According to John XIII—XXI*, Anchor Bible 29a, New Haven and London: Yale University Press, (1970) 2008, p. 630.

> I sought Wisdom openly in my prayer.
> *Before the temple I asked for her*,[25]
> And I will search for her to the last.
> From blossom to ripening grape,
> My heart delighted in her;
> My foot entered upon the *straight path*;
> From my youth I followed her steps.
> (Ben Sira 51.13–15)

And there is some regret in another of his reflections on Wisdom:

> I was the last on watch;
> I was like one who gleans after the grape-gatherers;
> By the blessing of the LORD I excelled,
> And like a grape-gatherer I filled my wine press.
> (Ben Sira 33.16, my translation)

This wise man from Jerusalem described the study of Wisdom as gathering grapes and he felt that the great days of Wisdom teaching were long past – he was a poor man gleaning after the main harvest (Lev. 19.10). He prayed before the temple for Wisdom, described again as the gathering of grapes, and thought immediately of the straight path, an allusion to Ashratah, that ancient name for the Lady which meant 'the one who keeps her disciple on the straight path' or 'the one who makes happy'.[26] Two younger contemporaries of Ben Sira were remembered as the last of the grape-gatherers: R. Jose b. Joezer and R. Jose b. Johanan were the first 'pair' to head the Sanhedrin (about 160 BCE), and after their death, 'There is no cluster to eat …'[27]

> Woe is me,
> For I have become as when the summer fruit is gathered,
> As when the vintage has been gleaned:
> *There is no cluster to eat*, no first-ripe fig which my soul desires.
> The godly man, *ḥāsîdh*, has perished from the land, and there is none upright among men. (Mic. 7.1–2)

These memories suggest that something was lost after the time of Ben Sira, R. Jose b. Joezer and R. Jose b. Johanan, and this may be why some people in the second century CE considered that the vine was evil. The clusters of the vine were no longer wise teaching to nourish the life of

---

[25] Thus the Greek; the Hebrew has 'she came to me in her beauty'.
[26] A sixth-century CE Syriac Ms, Codex Ambrosianus, names the author as Jesus Bar 'Asira, Jesus son of Asherah perhaps? An interesting name for a wise man.
[27] Mishnah *Sotah* 9.9.

*ḥesedh*, but had become money gathered for the upkeep of the temple. A fragment of text in minute letters was found at Qumran, the remains of a phylactery scroll, which contains words from the *Song of Moses*:

> Their vine comes from the vine of Sodom,
> And from the fields of Gomorrah;
> Their *grapes are grapes of poison*,
> *Their clusters are bitter*.
>     (Deut. 32.32, the italics being the words that are clear)[28]

Who was reading this text and of whom is not known; but the *Song of Moses* was being used to define enemies as people who produced poisonous grapes. By the time of R. Meir (his name means 'the illuminator'), a great teacher who flourished in the mid-second century CE, the vine had become the forbidden tree in Eden.[29] His contemporary, R. Judah ben Ilai, also taught this.[30] Both rabbis are cited many times in the Mishnah, showing that their teaching was highly regarded, and this hostility to what the vine had become may account for Jesus' claim to be the true vine stem and his disciples the branches who would (again) bear the good fruit/wise teaching that nourished the life of *ḥesedh*.

After the destruction of the temple in 70 CE, several texts were written (or rewritten), reflecting on the disaster, and they too used the image of a vine. The authors adopted pseudonyms from the time of the first destruction: Baruch, Jeremiah's scribe (Jer. 36.4), or Ezra, but the texts are thinly veiled descriptions of the late first century CE. 'Ezra' asked the LORD why, when he had chosen one vine from every tree in every forest, he had allowed this disaster to happen.[31] 'Baruch' went into the ruins of the holy of holies and received a vision of a great forest of wickedness alongside which there grew a vine with its peaceful fountain. Suddenly the fountain became a flood that swept away all the forest, including a great cedar. The vine then spoke to the cedar, which had been responsible for all the wickedness, and the cedar was burned. The LORD then explained the vision to Baruch: the forest of wickedness, where evil people hid themselves, was the four kingdoms which had oppressed the LORD's people, and when the forest was due for destruction, 'the dominion of my Anointed One, which is like the fountain and the vine, will be revealed'.[32]

---

[28] 4QphylN.
[29] Cited in Babylonian Talmud *Sanhedrin* 70a and *Genesis Rabbah*.
[30] *Genesis Rabbah* XV.7.
[31] 2 Esdras 5.23.
[32] *2 Baruch* 39.7.

The kingdom of the Messiah, then, was compared to two ancient symbols of Wisdom, and since John did not describe the tree of life that he saw in the holy of holies, it too could have been the vine from which came the river of the water of life (Rev. 22.1–2).

Two texts from the second century CE, now known only in their Christian form but both based on Hebrew material, show that the vine – perhaps the current Herodian vine – had become the forbidden tree. The *Apocalypse of Abraham*[33] is set within the story of Abraham's sacrifice (Gen. 15.1–21), and an angel took him up to heaven. There is good reason to believe that this angel was the LORD, who had just appeared to Abraham as Melchi-Zedek (Gen. 14.18–23). The angel was named Iaoel, that is, Yahwehel, and for the first Christians this would have meant 'the angel of the LORD'. The angel, dressed as a high priest, was the LORD whom John saw (Rev. 1.13). He took Abraham up to stand before the throne just as John was taken up to stand before the throne (Rev. 4.1–2). Abraham was told to look down and watch the story of his descendants unfolding beneath him. He saw the garden of Eden which was also the temple. Then he saw a huge man and woman, Adam and Eve, standing under a tree (?)[34] which had fruit like the fruit of a wild vine (c.f. Isaiah 5.2). Behind the tree was a creature like a great dragon, with hands and feet and six pairs of wings. He was enticing Adam and Eve with choice fruit from the wild vine. The voice from the fiery throne told Abraham that the dragon was Azazel, and that some of Abraham's descendants had been handed over to the dragon because they loved his ways; they worshipped him, and he was their Beloved.[35] The vine-tree from which Azazel fed some of Abraham's children was the wild vine that appears in the Genesis Eden story as the forbidden tree of the knowledge of good and evil. Abraham then saw the destruction of the temple and of the people of Azazel who had abandoned the LORD.[36] This echoes Jesus' accusation that the Jews were the children of the devil, the father of lies (John 8.44).

Another text from the same period is *3 Baruch*, which, like *2 Baruch*, was written as the reflections of Jeremiah's scribe Baruch after the destruction of Jerusalem in 586 BCE, but is in fact the reflections of a Hebrew Christian after the destruction in 70 CE. 'Baruch' was sitting by the Kidron when an angel of the LORD came to him and took him up through the heavens. In the second heaven he was shown the vine that

---

[33] Known only in Slavonic but thought to have a Hebrew original.
[34] The word is not clear.
[35] *Apocalypse of Abraham* 23.1–14; cf. the title 'Beloved' in *Ascension of Isaiah*.
[36] *Apocalypse of Abraham* 31.6–8.

## John 15

caused Adam to sin. The angel Sammael[37] had planted the vine, and so the LORD God had forbidden Adam to eat from it. One sprig of the vine survived Noah's flood, and an angel told him to plant it:

> Its bitterness will be changed into sweetness, and its curse will become a blessing. Its fruit will become the blood of God, and just as the race of men have been condemned through it, so through Jesus Christ Immanuel in it they will receive a calling and entrance to Paradise.[38]

The Christian reworking is clear, but the link of the vine and knowledge is also clear, bearing in mind the words of the *Didache* prayers that give thanks for 'the holy vine of thy servant David, which thou hast made known to us through thy servant Jesus' and for 'the life and knowledge made known through thy servant Jesus'.[39]

The image of the vine is at the centre of Jesus' Passover discourse, and in Psalm 80 the story of the exodus is told as the LORD transplanting a vine from Egypt to his holy hill.

> Thou didst bring a vine out of Egypt;
> Thou didst drive out the nations and plant it.
> Thou didst clear the ground for it;
> It took deep root and filled the land.
> (Ps. 80.8–9)

Here, the vine seems to be the people; but then the psalm continues with the stem as the king:

> Look down from heaven, and see;
> And visit this vine,
> The stock, *kannâ*, which thy right hand planted,
> [or 'make firm that which your right hand planted']
> [the vine] is burned with fire, it is cut down.
> They are destroyed with the rebuke of your presence.
> Let your hand be upon the man of your right hand,
> Upon the son of Adam whom you have strengthened for yourself.
> (Ps. 80.14–17, my translation)

The 'stock' could also be read 'her stock', *kannāh*, but the Greek has *katartisai autēn*, 'establish her', having read the Hebrew as a form of the verb *kûn*, 'establish/make firm'.

---

[37] Who appears also as the chief evil angel in *Ascension of Isaiah*.
[38] *3 Baruch* 4.15.
[39] *Didache* 9.

The same image of planting occurs in the *Song of Moses and Israel*, but without mentioning the vine:

> You will bring them in and plant them on the mountain of your inheritance,
> The place, O LORD, that you have made for your dwelling place,
> The sanctuary, O LORD, that your hands have established.
> (Exod. 15.17, my translation)[40]

The vine was an image with many facets: Israel itself was a luxuriant vine (Hos. 10.1), and yet the recurring theme was that the vine had failed to bear the expected fruit. Jeremiah compared the choice vine that had turned wild to a harlot, suggesting that the choice vine, *śōrēq*, represented a female figure (Jer. 2.20–21). Ezekiel warned the people of Jerusalem that the wood of the vine was useless and could only be burned (Ezek. 15.1–8). Isaiah had the LORD sing of the vineyard of his beloved, which was wordplay on the name David, or maybe the original form of the name.[41] In David's vineyard he planted a choice vine – the Hebrew word here is singular, *śōrēq*, but apparently a collective noun – and built a watchtower, understood to mean the holy of holies.[42] He looked for good grapes but found only wild grapes, meaning that the LORD had looked for justice and righteousness but found only bloodshed and cries of despair (Isa. 5.1–7). Here in Isaiah's parable the vineyard is the people of Israel and their temple, which are both destined for destruction.

But there is also the image of the stem of the vine, distinguished from the vine herself in Psalm 80.14–15 (my translation):

> Have regard for this vine, *gephen* [a feminine noun],
> And the stem, *kannâ* [or 'her stem'], which your right hand has planted,
> And on the son whom you have *made strong* for yourself.

This is royal imagery, found also in Psalm 89:

> My hand shall ever abide with [the anointed one],
> My arm also shall *strengthen him*. (Ps. 89.21, my translation)

Psalm 80 continues:

> Let your hand be upon the man of your right hand

---

[40] In *Pseudo-Philo* 12.8–10, the vine in danger is the theme of Moses' prayer after the apostasy of the golden calf.

[41] N. Wyatt, '"Jedidiah" and Cognate Forms as a Title of Royal Legitimization', *Biblica* 60 (1985), pp. 112–25.

[42] R. Yosi, early second century CE, said the tower in the vineyard was the holy of holies, Tosefta *Sukkah* 3.15.

## John 15

Upon the son of Adam whom you have *strengthened for yourself.*
(Ps. 80.17, my translation)

In both Genesis 49.11 and Psalm 80.14–17 the Hebrew text is not clear, and according to Justin, Psalm 96.10 was altered. The Jews, he said, had removed many words from the Hebrew Scriptures that were important for the Christians, and 'The LORD reigns' was originally 'The LORD reigns *from the tree*.'[43] This verse has not been found at Qumran, so there is no way of checking if there had been such a text, but Barnabas seems to have known it: 'The royal realm of Jesus is founded on a tree, and they who hope in him shall have eternal life.'[44]

The stem of the vine was the Davidic king, as in Ezekiel's lament for the uprooted vine/Lady, and in Isaiah's opaque words about the tree that had been cut down but kept the holy seed in her stump (Isa. 6.13). The king reigning from the tree is implied by the Dura-Europos painting, and the image survived also in Christian art. The great apse mosaic in San Clemente in Rome[45] shows the tree of life whose main stem is Jesus on the cross, and the tree is a great vine.

### 15.1–27: 'Abide in me'

When Jesus said: 'I am the vine, the true one', those who heard him would have known what he meant. Thomas' Jesus spoke of the false vine: 'A grapevine has been planted outside of the Father, but being unsound it will be pulled up by its roots and destroyed.'[46] The image of the vine, its branches and its fruit was widely used: 'You will know them by their fruits,' Jesus said of the false prophets: 'Are grapes gathered from thorns, or figs from thistles? ... Every tree that does not bear good fruit is cut down and thrown into the fire. Thus you will know them by their fruits' (Matt. 7.16, 19–20). 'Thorns and thistles' may have become proverbial, but originally they were the plants that grew outside Eden, the punishment for Adam when he had eaten from the forbidden tree (Gen. 3.17–19). Paul would extend the imagery and write of the fruit of the Spirit, another name for the Lady (Gal. 5.22–23), and of the branches of a wild olive that would be grafted into the tree to replace those branches broken off because they did not believe (Rom. 11.16–21). Justin

---

[43] Justin, *Trypho* 73.
[44] *Letter of Barnabas* 8.
[45] Made in the early twelfth century.
[46] *Gospel of Thomas* 40.

would use the image of the vine and its branches in a completely different way: the vine was the people of God and Jesus Christ; the branches broken off were the martyrs; but new branches would grow in their place.[47]

In the Passover discourse, Jesus took up Isaiah's image of the choice vine which the LORD planted on the fertile hill, but which proved to be a wild vine. This is the centre of the discourse, if its extent is reckoned from 13.31 to 16.33. The synoptic Gospels also have a parable about a vineyard as the first of Jesus' teachings after he had entered the city on Palm Sunday (Mark 12.1–12//Matt. 21.28–32; Luke 20.9–17), where it was Jesus' answer to the chief priests, scribes and elders when they asked him by whose authority he was teaching in the temple. Jesus' vineyard parable was built around Isaiah's (Isa. 5.1–7), and the temple authorities, described as 'the tenants' of the vineyard, 'perceived that he had told the parable against them' (Mark 12.12). He warned that the owner of the vineyard would come and destroy them and give the vineyard to others.

The vineyard parable was told in public in the temple, a few days before Jesus was arrested and killed. The future of the vineyard and its tenants – those who should have been preparing good grapes for the harvest – was the key issue in the final days of Jesus' conflict with 'the Jews': the authority to teach and the content of that teaching, the fate of those who had already come from 'the owner' and been rejected or killed, and the fate of the Son himself. Speculation about how much of this detail came from Jesus himself is not relevant: if it came from the early Christian communities and not from Jesus himself, it is evidence that this was how they remembered and still understood the teaching of Jesus about the temple and its vine during his last days in Jerusalem. At the centre of the Passover discourse, John sets Jesus' teaching about the vine as given to his inner group of disciples.

Wordplay had been characteristic of temple discourse, and Matthew preserves an example of Christian wordplay on this theme of the stem of the vine. Jesus lived in Nazareth, he said, to fulfil the prophecy that he would be called a Nazorene (Matt. 2.23), but the prophecy was that the Messiah would be called the *nēṣer*, the branch from the root of Jesse. Isaiah used the word elsewhere: of the proud king of Babylon who would be uprooted like an abhorred *branch* (Isa. 14.19, my translation); and of the future Jerusalem, when the glory of the LORD returned to his people, and the forsaken Lady was restored. The people would no longer need the light of the sun and the moon:

---

[47] Justin, *Trypho* 110.

## John 15

> Your [fem.] people shall all of them be righteous ones [*ṣaddîqîm*, like the Servant, Isa. 53.11],
> For ever they shall possess the land,
> The shoot, *nēṣer*, of his planting [or 'of the LORD's planting'[48]],
> The work of his hands
> That he might be glorified. (Isa. 60.21, my translation)

Here it seems that the shoot is the people of the Lady, but there are several variants in the text at this point, and it may be that Isaiah's prophecy of future prosperity answers the prayer of Psalm 80.14–19: that the LORD would have regard for the vine and the vine stem that he had planted, and once again would let his presence shine on his people.[49]

Jesus is the true vine and his Father is the vinedresser, but translating literally, 'vinedresser' is 'the one who works the soil'. Then there is wordplay: 'Every branch in me that does not bear fruit, he takes it [away], *airei*; and every one that bears fruit he cleanses, *kathairei*, it so that it may bear more fruit' (v. 2, translating literally). But the disciples are already 'made clean by the word which I have spoken to you' (v. 2). Isaiah's vineyard parable was also conspicuous for its complex wordplay;[50] when the LORD abandoned his vineyard, he would let it become a wasteland, no longer *pruned* nor *hoed* and growing only briers and thorns (Isa. 5.2). It is the hoeing and the pruning that are restored in Jesus' image of the vine: the one who works the soil and removes the unfruitful branches. The Hebrew word that Isaiah used for 'prune' is written in the same way as the word for 'make sacred music', *zmr*; and 'hoe', *'dr*, is very similar to *'dr*, 'majestic, glorious'. Isaiah's parable about David's vineyard and the choice vine that the LORD planted there was in fact about the temple and the one the LORD had planted there, but the bitter fruit of the vine meant that the vineyard would not be pruned/there would be no more sacred music in the temple; and the vineyard would not be hoed/the temple would no longer be glorious. In Jesus' new parable of the vineyard it is hoed again and it is pruned again. The LORD is restoring his vineyard, his glorious temple and the worship there, and his choice vine.

The keyword in verses 4–10 is *menein*, 'remain/continue/abide'. It occurs ten times in verses 4–10, and represents the Hebrew *dābhaq* which means 'cling to, hold fast, be joined to'. The word could be understood

---

[48] 1QIsa[a]. This text has problems; see n. 22 above.
[49] The wordplay on 'Nazareth' could also be that Jesus was the *nôṣēr*, the 'guardian', or the *nāṣûr*, the 'one who had been kept secret', as in 2 Esdras 13.25–26.
[50] For detail, see my book *The Hidden Tradition of the Kingdom of God*, London: SPCK, 2007, pp. 16–17.

literally, as in 'My bones cleave to my flesh' (Ps. 102.5); or it could mean the close bond of love between two people: 'Ruth clung to her' (Ruth 1.14), or '[A man] cleaves to his wife, and they become one flesh' (Gen. 2.25). In Deuteronomy, the word implied obedience, as in 'You shall fear the LORD your God; you shall serve him and cleave to him, and by his name you shall swear' (Deut. 10.20; 11.22 and 13.4 are similar). Before they crossed over into the land, Moses reminded the people that they had survived because they had held fast to the LORD and kept the commandments which were their new wisdom.

> You who held fast, *dābhaq*, to the LORD your God are all alive this day. Behold, I have taught you statutes and ordinances, as the LORD my God commanded me, that you should do them in the land which you are entering to take possession of it. Keep them and do them; for that will be your wisdom and your understanding in the sight of the peoples, who, when they hear all these statutes, will say, 'Surely this great nation is a wise and understanding people.' (Deut. 4.4–6)

Despite the emphases of the pro-Moses group, 'cleaving to the LORD' was remembered as far more than keeping the commandments which became their new wisdom. The original Wisdom had held all things together in harmony (*harmozousa*, LXX Prov. 8.30),[51] and this became the basis of Paul's 'the unity of the Spirit in the bond of peace' (Eph. 4.3).

The meaning of *dābhaq* was being debated in the early second century CE, and the teaching of Jesus in the Passover discourse must have been a factor in this – maybe as a contribution to the debate, or maybe as the catalyst for the (renewed) interest. R. Akiba and R. Ishmael were disputing the true meaning of Deuteronomy 4.4 – 'cleaving to the LORD' – and R. Akiba said that it meant literally cleaving, that is, being joined to the LORD, whereas R. Ishmael taught that it meant performing pious deeds.[52] Another contemporary, R. Eliezar, who knew the mystical tradition of the temple and the *merkavâ*,[53] taught that 'the holy Spirit will surely dwell on the one who cleaves to the Shekinah'. On this saying Moshe Idel commented:

> This text presupposes the possibility of cleaving to the Shekinah; from the context, it is not clear whether this entity is identical with God or is to be understood as a manifestation of him. Even if the latter alternative is the

---

[51] Maybe that is why the harpist appeared alongside the pictures of the Lady/her tree on the pithos at Kuntillet 'Ajrud and on the synagogue wall at Dura-Europos.
[52] Babylonian Talmud *Sanhedrin* 64a.
[53] Babylonian Talmud *Ḥagigah* 14b.

more congenial interpretation, assuming a certain independence of the Shekinah from God, it is nevertheless considered to be a divine entity, *cleaving to which was negated in other rabbinic texts.*[54]

The Shekinah, a feminine noun, was the glorious divine presence and another name for the Lady. Some people believed that it was possible to be joined to the Shekinah, and that the Holy Spirit rested on them.

Jesus taught his disciples that he was the stem of the vine and they were its branches; they were bound together (v. 4), and as his branches, they would bear the fruit. There follows a text pattern like branches, a clear chiasmus (vv. 7–17), with the centre point at verse 11: 'These things I have spoken to you, that my joy may be in you, and that your joy may be full.'[55]

### The vine and its branches

'If you abide in me, and *my words abide in you*, **ask for whatever you will, and it shall be done for you**' (v. 7).

'By this my Father is glorified, that you *bear much fruit*, and so prove to be <u>my disciples</u>' (v. 8).

'As *the Father has loved me, so have I loved you*; abide in my love' (v. 9).

'<u>If you keep my commandments, you will abide in my love</u>, just as I have kept my Father's commandments and abide in his love' (v. 10).

'<u>This I command you</u>, to love one another' (v. 17).

'You did not choose me but <u>I chose you</u> and appointed you that you should go and *bear fruit and that your fruit should abide*; **so that whatever you ask the Father in my name, he may give it to you**' (v. 16).

'No longer do I call you servants, for the servant does not know what his master is doing; *but I have called you friends, for all that I have heard from my Father I have made known to you*' (v. 15).

'<u>You are my friends if you do what I command you</u>' (v. 14).

'Greater love has no man than this, that a man lay down his life for his friends' (v. 13).

'<u>This is my commandment, that you love one another …</u>' (v. 12).

'These things I have spoken to you, that my joy may be in you, and that your joy may be full' (v. 11).

'Joy', *chara*, translates the Hebrew *śāśôn*, which means 'joy/gladness', but both the nominal and verbal forms connote the return of the LORD to

---

[54] M. Idel, *Kabbalah. New Perspectives*, New Haven and London: Yale University Press, 1988, p. 39, my emphases.
[55] Brown, *Gospel According to John XIII—XXI*, p. 667.

Jerusalem, or the return of the people to the LORD. There are many examples in Isaiah, and in the texts below, *śāśôn* in its various forms is indicated by italics.

> The LORD God is my strength and my song,
> And he has become my salvation.
> With *joy* you will draw water from the wells of salvation. (Isa. 12.2–3)

> The wilderness and the dry land shall *be glad* ...
> They shall see the glory of the LORD,
> The majesty of our God. (Isa. 35.1, 2)

> The ransomed of the LORD shall return,
> And come to Zion with singing ...
> They shall obtain *joy* and gladness,
> And sorrow and sighing shall flee away. (Isa. 35.10; 51.11)

> For the LORD will comfort Zion;
> He will comfort all her waste places,
> And will make her wilderness like Eden,
> Her desert like the garden of the LORD;
> *Joy* and gladness will be found in her,
> Thanksgiving and the voice of song. (Isa. 51.3)

> *Be glad* and *rejoice* for ever in that which I create;
> For behold, I create Jerusalem a rejoicing, and her people a *joy*.
> I will rejoice in Jerusalem, and be *glad* in my people ... (Isa. 65.18–19)

> Rejoice with Jerusalem, and be glad for her,
> All you who love her;
> *Rejoice* with her in joy ... (Isa. 66.10)

So too the *gladness* in Isaiah 61, the passage Jesus expounded in the synagogue at Nazareth (Luke 4.16–21). When the Anointed One proclaimed the day of the LORD's favour, those who mourned in Zion would receive 'the oil of *gladness* instead of mourning' (Isa. 61.3) and ousted priests would be recognized and restored (Isa. 61.5–7).[56] The Anointed One who spoke in Isaiah 61 and in the synagogue at Nazareth said that the LORD had clothed him with garments, *bᵉghādhîm*, of salvation and a robe, *meʿîl*, of righteousness (Isa. 61.10), the latter being a priestly word for the high priest's outer vestment edged with pomegranates and golden bells (Exod. 28.31 and many other examples in Exodus; Lev. 8.7). Both words can be used of ordinary garments, but given the

---

[56] The oil of gladness also occurs in Ps. 45.6–7: the king was anointed with oil of *gladness* and seated on the throne of God.

## John 15

context here of a restored priesthood, they probably indicate vestments.[57] The Anointed One *rejoices* with *rejoicing* like a bridegroom as he is clothed. This passage, for which Jesus claimed fulfilment at the start of his ministry, is about restoring an anointed high priest and his priests, and the high priest would be the Bridegroom (cf. John 3.29), presumably to the Lady and her city (cf. Rev. 19.6-10).

The passage in the Hebrew Scriptures that is closest to Jesus' words in verse 11 is Psalm 51.6-12. This is my translation.

> Behold, you delight in truth, *'emeth*, \*\*\*,[58] you have taught me wisdom in the secret place,
> Purify me with hyssop and I shall be clean, cleanse me and I shall be whiter than snow.
> Make me satisfied/full[59] with *gladness* and joy, let the person/power you have crushed rejoice,
> Hide your face from my sins, and wipe away all my iniquities.
> Create in me a purified heart, O God, and make new a steadfast spirit within me.
> Do not send me from your presence, and do not take your holy Spirit from me.
> Restore to me the *gladness* of your salvation, and support me with a willing spirit.

Jesus' disciples were already clean (13.10; 15.3), and now he teaches them the wisdom of secret places which concerns the vine stem and its branches. This satisfies them and fills them with joy. The Psalmist then asks to remain in the presence of the LORD and to keep the holy Spirit, just as Jesus assures his disciples that after his departure, the Spirit will come to them and be with them.

The secrets of the vine are 'abiding/being bound' and 'love': 'abide in love' – the love of Jesus and the love of the Father – occurs three times in verses 9–10. 'Love' here is *ḥesedh*, the characteristic of the older, pre-Mosaic form of the covenant, which was bound by love and not by obedience. No longer, says Jesus the LORD, do I call you servants (v. 15). One of the curious facts about the vocabulary of Deuteronomy is that the qualities characteristic of the rule of the anointed king are not found. John's observation: 'The law was given through Moses; grace, *ḥesedh*, and truth, *'emeth*, came [again] through Jesus Christ' (1.17), is what underlies

---

[57] Both words also have another meaning: *māʿal* and *bāghadh* usually mean 'act treacherously'.
[58] The meaning of this word is not known.
[59] The Hebrew text has 'make me hear', from *šmʿ*, but the the Syriac translator read it as *śbʿ*, 'to be satisfied/filled'. The words would have looked very similar.

the teaching about the vine. The throne of the Davidic king had been founded upon righteousness, *ṣedheq*, justice, *mišpāṭ*, grace, *ḥesedh*, and truth, *'emeth* (Ps. 89.14), but only one of these, justice, *mišpaṭ*, understood in the plural as 'rules', appears with any frequency in Deuteronomy. If the ancient poems (the *Song of Moses* and the *Blessing of Moses*) are excluded, 'righteousness' was used for the processes of law,[60] 'truth/faithfulness' was used negatively – 'You did not believe' – and *ḥesedh* only in the title 'the *faithful* God who keeps the covenant and *ḥesedh* with those who love him and keep his commandments' (Deut. 7.9). In contrast, *ḥesedh* occurs 118 times in the Psalms, and truth, *'emeth*, 34 times.[61] The ethos of the pro-Moses tradition was very different from that of the sacral kings which Jesus restored.

## The friends of the LORD

Having washed his disciples' feet and given the example of humble service, Jesus makes a very different statement: 'No longer do I call you servants' (v. 15). Instead, he would call them his friends. But when had Jesus called the disciples his servants? The reference here is to the LORD as depicted in the Hebrew Scriptures and his worshippers who were his servants. In Deuteronomy, the prescribed relationship was fearing and serving:

- 'You shall *fear* the LORD your God; you shall *serve* him, and swear by his name' (Deut. 6.13);
- 'What does the LORD your God require of you, but to *fear* the LORD your God, to walk in all his ways, to love him, to *serve* the LORD your God with all your heart and with all your soul, and to keep the commandments and statutes of the LORD, which I command you this day for your good?' (Deut. 10.12–13);
- 'You shall *fear* the LORD your God; you shall *serve* him and cleave to him, and by his name you shall swear' (Deut. 10.20);
- 'You shall walk after the LORD your God and *fear* him, and keep his commandments and obey his voice, and you shall *serve* him and cleave to him' (Deut. 13.4).

Here there is a new relationship: keeping the LORD's commandments is a sign that the disciples are his friends. He has taught them all that he has learned from his Father (v. 15). They, as branches from his stem, would

---

[60] Once in the context of kindness, Deut. 24.13.
[61] See my book *Mother of the Lord*, pp. 17–42.

bear the fruit of what he had taught them and would have access to the same power. This is similar to Jesus' saying at 6.56: 'He who eats my flesh and drinks my blood abides in me, and I in him.'

In this context of unity, the Hebrew word that became *philos* in John's Greek (15.14) was probably *ḥābhēr*, 'companion', which had significant associations. The root means 'to be joined', and *ḥebher*, meaning an 'association' or 'community', was written in the same way. The Qumran community called themselves a *ḥebher*,[62] companions who formed a unity. A similar word is used in the fourth of Isaiah's poems about the suffering Servant. This was the prophet's reflection on the role of the royal high priest as realized in the life and near-death of Hezekiah (Isa. 52.13—53.12).[63] The poem is full of the wordplay that characterizes temple discourse.

> He was wounded for our transgressions,
> He was bruised for our iniquities;
> Upon him was the chastisement that made us whole,
> And with his stripes we are healed.    (Isa. 53.5)

- 'He was wounded', *ḥll*, can also mean 'he was profaned', as in 'I will vindicate the holiness of my great name, which has been *profaned* among the nations, and which you have *profaned* among them' (Ezek. 36.23). The Servant was *profaned* by our transgressions, *pᵉšāʿîm*. Micah, a contemporary of Isaiah,[64] spoke against the sacrifice implied by the Servant poem, saying that the LORD required justice and love:

> Shall I give my firstborn for my transgression ...?
> He has showed you, O man, what is good:
> And what does the LORD require of you
> But to do justice, *mišpāṭ*, and to love kindness, *ḥesedh*,
> And to walk humbly with your God?    (Mic. 6.7, 8)

- He was crushed by our 'iniquities', which literally means 'distortions'.
- The 'chastisement', *mûsār*, can also mean 'bond', and 'whole', *šālôm*, usually means 'peace', so the line also means: 'The bond of our peace was his task/role'.
- 'His stripes', *ḥbrtw*, is one way of reading this word; another is 'his joining together', and so the line also means: 'By his joining together we are healed'.

---

[62] 11QPsᵃ XVII.1.
[63] See my article 'Hezekiah's Boil', *Journal for the Study of the Old Testament* 95 (2001), pp. 31–42.
[64] 'Hezekiah's Boil', pp. 31–42, where I show that the poem was written by Isaiah in response to Hezekiah's sickness.

Thus another way to read this description of the Servant's role is:

> He was profaned by our transgressions,
> He was crushed by our iniquities,
> The bond of our peace was his task/role,
> By his joining together we are healed.

This role of the Servant – upholding the bond of *šālôm*, healing by joining together – is found elsewhere in the Servant poems:

> I have given you *as a covenant to the people*,
> A light to the nations,
> To open the eyes that are blind ...
>                                        (Isa. 42.6–7)

> I have kept you and given you
> *As a covenant to the people*,
> To establish the land,
> To apportion the desolate heritages.
>                                        (Isa. 49.8)

These themes are taken up in Isaiah 61, the passage Jesus read in the synagogue at Nazareth at the start of his public ministry in Galilee (Luke 4.18–19), so they were remembered as a key part of his proclamation about himself. 'As a covenant to the people, *lbryt 'm*', however, is a curious phrase, but by moving one letter, *bryt 'lm*, or even adding one letter, *lbryt 'lm*, it becomes 'as the eternal covenant', which was also known as the covenant of peace. The binding and healing that the Servant effected by his sacrifice was the restoration of the covenant of peace, which was the ancient covenant of the high priesthood (Num. 25.10–12). Matthew also makes this clear in his account of the last supper, where Jesus (re)news with his own blood the covenant for the putting away, *aphesis*, of sins, which was the high-priestly act on the Day of Atonement.[65] John implies in the Passover discourse the same theme as Matthew makes explicit.

Jesus then explains that as his friends, they must expect the same treatment as he has received. He has been persecuted, and they will be persecuted. They will be driven from their synagogues and even killed (16.1–2).[66] They too take on the role of the suffering servants who renew

---

[65] See my article 'Atonement. The Rite of Healing', *Scottish Journal of Theology* 49.1 (1996), pp. 1–20, reprinted in my book *The Great High Priest. The Temple Roots of Christian Liturgy*, London: T&T Clark, 2003, pp. 42–55.

[66] See above, pp. 295, 373.

## John 15

the covenant by their blood. In the Book of Revelation, this is represented in the vision of the fifth seal, when the souls of those who had been slain for the Word of God were seen under the altar of the temple. In temple discourse, blood was the soul/life: 'The life of the flesh is in the blood; and I have given it for you upon the altar to make atonement for your souls; for it is the blood that makes atonement, by reason of the life' (Lev. 17.11). The vision of the fifth seal was the Day of Atonement. After he had sprinkled the blood to cleanse and consecrate the temple, the high priest poured the remainder at the base of the altar in the temple court, and it flowed underneath.[67] This was the vision: the souls of the martyrs who had themselves been part of the atonement, waiting until their *number* should be complete. What this means is not clear, but it occurs also in Enoch's vision of the Day of Atonement, where the Righteous One takes his blood to the throne and the number of the righteous is complete[68] (Rev. 6.9–11).

Jesus has chosen his disciples out of the world (v. 19), and so the world will hate them. The Good Shepherd has called his sheep and led them out (10.3). This too echoes Moses' exhortation:

> The LORD your God has chosen you to be a people for his own possession, out of all the peoples that are on the face of the earth ... Know therefore that the LORD your God is God, the faithful God who keeps covenant and *hesedh* with those who love him and keep his commandments ...
> 
> (Deut. 7.6, 9; also 12)

The Church, *ekklēsia*, means literally 'those called out'. Thus there is a conflict with the world and its powers (cf. 1 John 3.11–18), which initially takes the form of a conflict with the second-temple Jews, from whom Jesus has called his own flock. They have heard his words (v. 22), they have seen his works (v. 24), and so they are responsible for their own rejection of Jesus and the Father who sent him. This too echoes Moses' words in Deuteronomy:

- 'Has any *ᵉlohîm* tried to go and take a nation for himself from the midst of another nation, by trials, by signs, by wonders ...?' (Deut. 4.34, my translation);
- 'The LORD gave great and terrible signs and wonders, against Egypt, against Pharaoh and against all his household, before our eyes, and he brought us out from there ...' (Deut. 6.22–23, my translation);

---

[67] Mishnah *Yoma* 5.6.
[68] *1 Enoch* 47.1–4.

- '[You shall remember] the great trials which your eyes saw, the signs, the wonders, the mighty hand, and the outstretched arm, by which the LORD your God brought you out ...' (Deut. 7.19).

Jesus appoints his disciples as witnesses to who he is (v. 27), recalling the purpose of John's Gospel: 'that you may believe that Jesus is the Christ, the Son of God ...' (20.31). This too echoes the words of Isaiah:

> Bring forth the people who are blind, yet have eyes,
> Who are deaf, yet have ears! ...
> 'You are my witnesses,' says the LORD,
> 'And my servant whom I have chosen,
> That you may know and believe me
> And understand that I am He.' (Isa. 43.8, 10)

# John 16

The Passover discourse is now divided into chapters, but John did not write with these divisions. Chapter 15 moves seamlessly into 16, the warning of persecution. 'The hour is coming when whoever kills you will think he is offering service to God' (v. 2). Saul of Tarsus was one who thought in this way: 'I persecuted the church of God violently and tried to destroy it; and I advanced in Judaism beyond many of my own age among my people, so extremely zealous was I for the traditions of my fathers' (Gal. 1.13-14). One wonders if Saul the student 'brought up in [Jerusalem] at the feet of Gamaliel' (Acts 22.3) was among the Jews who had listened to Jesus in the temple. And one wonders whether the careful words of his master Gamaliel eventually made an impression upon him: 'Keep away from these [Christians] and let them alone ... You might even be found opposing God!' (Acts 5.38-39). Before his conversion on the road to Damascus, though, Saul had been a zealous persecutor and presumably not the only one. It was such men that Jesus had in mind when he warned his disciples of what lay ahead.

## Persecution

The prediction of persecution is also found in the synoptic Gospels, mainly towards the end of Jesus' ministry, but there is one warning that all three Gospels set earlier: 'If any man would come after me, let him deny himself and take up his cross and follow me' (Mark 8.34//Matt. 10.38; Luke 14.27). Some have wondered whether Jesus really did predict his crucifixion so early in his ministry, and there is no doubt that this is how the saying came to be understood, but other meanings are possible and even more likely. When Ezekiel saw the angel scribe marking the faithful who would be spared when Jerusalem was destroyed, he saw him put a cross, X, on their foreheads (Ezek. 9.4).[1] This was also seen in the vision of Revelation 7. Taking up the cross, then, could have meant taking

---

[1] Literally a letter *tau*, which in Ezekiel's time was written 'X'.

the mark of the Name, identifying oneself as a faithful follower of the LORD. Taking up the cross also had a priestly meaning: when he was anointed, the high priest was marked on his forehead with a cross, and this was known as taking up or bearing the Name.[2] 'Let him take up', *aratō*, is the verb *airō* that the LXX frequently uses to translate *nāśā'*, the verb for the high priest wearing the Name: 'You shall not *take up* the name of the LORD your God in vain' (Exod. 20.7, translating literally). Jesus warns that those who take the Name as the faithful/the new priests will face persecution, but prays that they too will be kept safe: 'While I was with them I kept them in [by? – both would have been the Hebrew $b^e$] thy Name, which thou hast given me. I have guarded them and none is lost but the son of perdition ...' (17.12, my translation). The Name here does imply protection, and Jesus concluded his discourse with both warning and encouragement: 'In the world you will have tribulation; but be of good cheer, I have *conquered* the world' (16.33, my translation). The verb is *nikaō*.

John's reconstruction of the Passover discourse was written long after he had received the visions of the letters to the seven churches, which also concern persecution and conquest (using the same verb *nikaō*), and they use temple imagery. These visions of the risen LORD talking to John are described as the Spirit speaking to the churches (e.g. Rev. 2.7) and they were the future teaching from the Paraclete that Jesus promised in the discourse (John 16.12-13). John received them in a temple setting from the LORD, who was dressed as a high priest and standing with the seven-branched lamp (Rev. 1.12-19), and the leaders of the churches to whom they were sent were the restored royal priesthood. Those who kept the faith and conquered would receive their rewards: access again to the tree of life and its fruit (Rev. 2.7); the crown of life (Rev. 2.10-11); the hidden manna and the white stone with a new name (Rev. 2.17); the status of the Davidic king as in Psalm 2, and the name 'Morning Star' (Rev. 2.26-28);[3] a white garment and their names in the book of life (Rev. 3.5); the Name written upon them as pillars of the new temple (Rev. 3.12); and a position sharing the throne in heaven (Rev. 3.21).[4] Their enemies were teachers of falsehood, and they had various names: the Nicolaitans (Rev. 2.6, 15); false Jews who are the synagogue of Satan and agents of the devil (Rev.

---

[2] See below, p. 507.

[3] 'I will give him the Morning Star' is a Hebraism meaning 'I will appoint him the Morning Star'.

[4] For detail, see my book *The Revelation of Jesus Christ*, Edinburgh: T&T Clark, 2000, pp. 96-110.

## John 16

2.9–10; 3.9); those who followed the teaching of Balaam (Rev. 2.14); those who followed the teaching of Jezebel the false prophetess and the deep things of Satan (Rev. 2.20–24). The Nicolaitans were the deceivers (from the Hebrew *nākhal*, 'deceive'), the name the Qumran community also gave to their enemies in Jerusalem; there was a Spouter of Lies;[5] there were 'teachers of lies and seers of falsehood';[6] and a Scoffer.[7] In the first throne vision, the Servant/Lamb who had conquered was enthroned and deemed worthy to open the sealed book. He was the Lion of Judah and the Root of David, the royal high priest (Rev. 5.1–7; cf. 3.21). The Lamb, who was the LORD of Lords and King of kings, together with his followers who were called and chosen and faithful, would conquer the harlot city and her allies and agents (Rev. 17.13–14). The LORD of Lords and King of kings was also the Logos who would ride from heaven with his angel army; from his mouth would come a sharp sword – the symbol of his teaching – and with this he would bring judgement (Rev. 19.11–16). All this imagery was known to John before he wrote his Gospel, and it must lie beneath the surface of the Passover discourse as he recorded it.

Even this image of the warrior Logos bringing the judgement was linked to Passover. 'At midnight the LORD smote all the firstborn of Egypt' (Exod. 12.29) was described somewhat curiously in the Wisdom of Solomon as the Logos coming from heaven with his sword to destroy their firstborn, so that they would recognize that the people of Israel were the Son of God.

> When their firstborn were destroyed,
> They acknowledged thy people to be God's Son.
> For while gentle silence enveloped all things,
> And night in its swift course was now half gone,
> Thy all-powerful Logos leaped from heaven, from the royal throne,
> Into the midst of the land that was doomed,
> A stern warrior, carrying the sharp sword of thy authentic command,
> And stood and filled all things with death,
> And touched heaven while standing on the earth.
> (Wisd. 18.13b–16, my translation)

Since John records that 'the great city ... where their Lord was crucified' was known cryptically as 'Egypt' (Rev. 11.8), the Logos overcoming the world at Passover and setting his people free from their own Egypt also

---

[5] *Commentary on Habakkuk*, 1QpHab X.9.
[6] *Hymns*, 1QH XII.9.
[7] *Damascus Document*, CD VIII.10.

underlies the Passover discourse. 'Be of good cheer, I have overcome the world' (v. 33).

Conflict with the world was a matter of right belief that led to right teaching and right living. Both as the great high priest in the temple and as the Logos who rode out with his angel army, the LORD held in his mouth a sharp sword to symbolize this teaching (Rev. 1.16; 19.15). John used the same image in his letters: the Logos (and his teaching) was dwelling *in* his faithful ones and enabling them to conquer, recalling: 'Abide in me, and I in you' (15.4). Young people had conquered the world because the Logos of God was abiding in them and they had conquered the Evil One (and his teaching) (1 John 2.13–14); 'little children' had recognized and conquered the spirits of the antichrist because 'he who is in you is greater than he who is in the world' (1 John 4.4); whatever was born of God conquered the world (1 John 5.4). This conquest included overcoming Satan's power to prevent belief. There is additional material in one ancient version of Mark's Gospel in which the disciples excuse themselves for not having believed the first reports of the resurrection. They were living in the age of Satan, they said, who did not allow such belief. Jesus told them that Satan's power was ended.

> The disciples excused themselves saying, 'This age of lawlessness and unbelief is under Satan, who does not allow what lies under the unclean spirits to understand the truth and power of God. Therefore reveal now your power to restore, *dikaiosunē*.' They spoke to Christ, and Christ replied that the limits of the years of the power of Satan had been reached but other terrible things were drawing near those sinners for whom [he] was handed over to death that they might inherit the spiritual and incorruptible glory of *dikaiosunē* in heaven.[8]

So too in the letters of Ignatius, where he described the Incarnation as a secret hidden from Satan, the appearance of a new star in the heavens.

> Every magic art and spell was loosed, evil failure to perceive vanished, the old kingdom was destroyed, ruined by God appearing as man to renew eternal life. Then what God had prepared began to happen and after that all things were in tumult because he devised the end of death.[9]

The vivid images of Revelation were the framework of early Christian life and belief.

---

[8] After Mark 16.14 in the fourth-century Codex Freerianus.
[9] Ignatius, *To the Ephesians* 19, my translation.

## John 16

Towards the end of his ministry, when they had glimpsed the glory in the Transfiguration, Jesus warned his disciples of his own suffering that was inseparable from the glory. Mark introduces the topic of his suffering immediately after the Transfiguration (Mark 9.2-8, then the suffering of Jesus at Mark 9.12-13, 31; 10.33-34; // Matt. 17.1-8, then the suffering at 17.22-23; 20.17-19; and Luke 9.28-36, then the suffering at 9.44; 18.31-33). The Beatitudes were Jesus' warnings for those who listened to him: those persecuted for the sake of righteousness would possess the kingdom of heaven; those reviled and falsely accused because of Jesus would have their reward in heaven (Matt. 5.10-12). The condition of the faithful, their promised rewards and the figurative language all show that the persecuted were the dispossessed of the first temple, who kept the older ways and longed to regain their former state and status. They were poor (in spirit), they were in mourning, meek, hungry and thirsty for righteousness; they were people of *ḥesedh*, they were pure in heart and they were makers of *šālôm*. Their rewards would be the kingdom of heaven, comfort, inheriting the land (not the earth: in Hebrew the word would have been *'ereṣ* which can mean either), satisfaction (like Isaiah's Suffering Servant who saw the light and was satisfied), they would receive *ḥesedh*, they would see God and be called the sons of God. They were the spiritual (and maybe the actual) heirs of those described by the Third-Isaiah in the section that Jesus read at Nazareth and said was fulfilled by his presence (Luke 4.21). The Third-Isaiah proclaimed good news to the poor (Isa. 61.1, sometimes translated 'afflicted'), and promised that they would (again?) be called priests of the LORD; they would possess their land and have everlasting joy.

> For I the LORD love justice,
> I hate robbery and injustice,
> I will faithfully give them their reward
> And I will make an everlasting covenant with them.
> (Isa. 61.8, my translation)

These were the poor of the Beatitudes who would see God and be called sons of God, the people with whom Jesus renewed the everlasting covenant and who regarded themselves as the ancient priesthood restored. These were the people he invited to take up their cross (again), their mark of priesthood.

Jesus gave more detail of the imminent persecution in his prediction of events that would precede the destruction of the temple: 'This generation will not pass away before all these things take place' (Mark 13.30). He described war, earthquakes and famines, but also the persecution of his disciples: delivered up to councils, beaten in synagogues, standing before governors and kings to bear testimony before them. Their own families would betray them, but they were not to be afraid: 'Do not be anxious beforehand what you are to say; but say whatever is given you in that hour, for it is not you who speak, but the Holy Spirit' (Mark 13.9–13). This is what John described in his letter as the Logos within them and in his Gospel as the Paraclete, the Spirit of truth within them (14.17). Matthew has a similar account of Jesus' predictions, but with some differences: there is no mention of being given what to say, but during the persecution, many would stumble and their love would grow cold because lawlessness increased (Matt. 24.12). Luke says the persecuted would be given 'a mouth and Wisdom which none of your adversaries will be able to withstand or contradict' (Luke 21.15, my translation).

Both Mark and Matthew agree that this time of persecution was the beginning of the birthpangs (Mark 13.8; Matt. 24.8), and John too has this image: 'When the woman is in travail she has sorrow, because her hour has come; but when she is delivered of the child, she no longer remembers the anguish, for joy that a child has been born into the world' (16.21). As with the Virgin prophecy in Isaiah 7, so too here, the female figure is *the* woman, not *a* woman as usually translated. *The* woman is the Lady giving birth to her son, an allusion to the vision in Revelation 12, where the birth of her child and his being lifted up to the throne is the moment when Satan the deceiver and his horde are thrown from heaven (cf. John 12.31–32: 'Now shall the ruler of this world be cast out; and I, when I am lifted up from the earth, will draw all men to myself'). The ongoing struggle with Satan in which the Paraclete will assist them is the dragon making war on the Lady's other children who bear testimony to Jesus (Rev. 12.17).

## Jesus goes away and returns

One of the factors that prompted John to write his Gospel was the delay of the *parousia*.[10] Here Jesus speaks of his departure and return. As long as he was still with his disciples, he did not speak of persecution, presumably because the hostility was directed to him (16.4b). Once he had been taken up to heaven, as in Revelation 12, the dragon would turn his anger on them.

---

[10] See above, p. 317.

Jesus says he is going to him who sent him (v. 5), just as he had said to the Jews in the temple (7.33) when they did not understand what he meant nor where he was going. 'Going', *hupagō*, has the sense of withdrawing and even of withdrawing secretly. John uses the same word in verse 10, 'I withdraw to the Father and you will see me no more'; and in verse 17, 'A little while and you will not see me, and again a little while, and you will see me ... because I withdraw to the Father.' Jesus' departure is like one scene in a drama, and he will not be visible for a short time. The verb *hupagō* is also used at 8.14, 21; 13.3, 33, 36; 14.4, 5, 28.

This is where John gives the new understanding of Jesus' departure, something revealed to him in his own vision of the *parousia* when the mighty angel, wrapped in a cloud and wreathed with a rainbow, showed him the little book that had been opened (Rev. 10.1–2). During his ministry, Jesus had said to the Jews (7.33), to the crowd (12.35) and to his disciples (13.33) that he would be with them only for a little while. Then in the Passover discourse he said that in a little while the world would see him, *theōrō*, no more; he would not leave his disciples desolate (literally 'orphans') but would come to them, and they would see him, *theōrō*, even though the world would not (14.18–19). This suggests a different manner of being present, a way not visible to all. The same is true of verse 16, but here John uses two different verbs: 'In a little while you will no longer see me, *theōrō*, and again a little while and you will see me, *optomai*.' The change of verb may be no more than a matter of style, but on the other hand, it may have been to emphasize a different way of seeing. Luke also implies this in Peter's summary of the life of Jesus: 'God raised him on the third day and made him visible, not to all the people but to the witnesses who had been prepared, *procheirizō*, beforehand ...' (Acts 10.40, my translation). So too in the longer ending of Mark: 'After this he appeared in another form, *en hetera morphē*, to two of them ...' (Mark 16.12).

The emphasis is on the 'little while', and on the disciples not at first understanding what Jesus meant about going to the Father in a little while and then, in a little while, returning. 'Little while' appears seven times: twice in verse 16, twice in verse 17, once in verse 18, twice in verse 19. In a little while Jesus would be going to the Father, and then in a little while, they would see him again, the two periods of time being similar. This was not the *parousia* after a long interval, but the LORD returning to his disciples after a little while, comparable to the time between the discourse and his death. John describes a few of the resurrection appearances, but his main emphasis is on the coming of the Paraclete, the implication being that *this is how Jesus will return and remain with his disciples.* This identification of Jesus as the Paraclete (and also as the angel of the LORD) was known to the disciples of Valentinus in the second century CE. Theodotus, according to Clement of Alexandria, said that Jesus was the Paraclete, but that the followers of Valentinus did not realize (no longer realized?) the true identity of the Paraclete: 'They do not know that the Paraclete, who now works continuously in the Church, is of the same substance and power as he who worked continuously according to the Old Testament.'[11] Theodotus based much of his teaching on the writings of John and he may well have preserved their original meaning.

There follows an extended allusion to Isaiah 66.1–14, which tells of Zion in childbirth, bringing forth her sons after the prophet's devastating condemnation of the second temple and the ways of its priests. Those whom Enoch called an apostate generation,[12] Isaiah described as the people who had driven out their brothers. They were the enemies of the LORD who would be put to shame (Isa. 66.5–6). Zion would give birth to more children:

> *You shall see, and your heart shall rejoice* ...
> And it shall be known that the hand of the LORD is with his servants,
> And his indignation is against his enemies.  (Isa. 66.14)

Jesus speaks of the woman bringing her man child into the world. Her birth pains are the disciples' sorrow; and then he says to her new children who were his disciples (v. 22): 'I will see you again and your hearts will rejoice and no one shall take your joy from you.' This could imply that he would see them but they would not see him, or at any rate, not in the familiar form.

As a final warning, Jesus said that his disciples would be scattered and that he would be left alone – and yet not alone because the Father was with him. 'You ... will leave me alone; yet I am not alone, for the Father is with me' (v. 32). 'Alone', *monos*, may mean no more than 'alone', as it doubtless does in the second instance; but the first suggests that the original was Hebrew wordplay on *yāḥîdh*, which meant the (only) one but also in the sense of the beloved, and as one who was part of a unity. This is the sense in which it was used in the *Gospel of Thomas*,[13] and here it could well have evoked the idea of being the beloved about to die (Isaac

---

[11] Clement of Alexandria, *Excerpts from Theodotus* 23, 24, in R. P. Casey, *The Excerpta ex Theodoto of Clement of Alexandria*, London: Christophers, 1934.
[12] *1 Enoch* 93.9.
[13] See below, p. 511.

## John 16

was Abraham's *yāḥîd*, Gen. 22.2) and also the unity with the Father: 'I and the Father are one thing' (10.30, my translation).

Jesus predicted that his disciples would be scattered (v. 32). Mark, followed by Matthew, also gave this as Jesus' final warning at the end of the last supper, but unlike John, they say that Jesus was quoting a prophecy:

> And when they had sung a hymn, they went out to the Mount of Olives. And Jesus said to them, 'You will all fall away; for it is written, "I will strike the shepherd and the sheep will be scattered."'
> (Mark 14.26–27; also Matt. 26.31, quoting Zech. 13.7)

Jesus was the Shepherd and his disciples would be scattered. Justin alluded to this,[14] as did Barnabas; he had a different understanding of the prophecy, but very close to the 'feel' of the original Hebrew which goes on to warn of judgement against the land. Barnabas has 'When they smite their own shepherd, then the sheep of the flock shall perish.'[15] This is not the LXX, and so must be Barnabas' own paraphrase and understanding, his own Targum, so to speak, of the Hebrew, which is:

> Awake, O sword, against my shepherd,
> Against the man who stands next to me, says the LORD of Hosts.
> Strike the shepherd and scatter the flock,
> And I shall turn my hand upon the little ones.
> And it shall be in all the land, says the LORD,
> That the double portion in it shall be cut off and die,
> And the third shall be left there.
> And I will bring the third part through the fire
> And I shall refine them as a refiner does silver,
> And test them like gold.
> This part shall call on my name
> And I will answer them.
> And I will say, 'It is my people'
> And this part will say, 'The LORD is my God.'
> (Zech. 13.7–9, my translation)

Smiting the shepherd and scattering the flock was a prophecy of destruction for two thirds of the people. Only one third would survive, and in a different and purified form. For Barnabas, the Jews had killed their own shepherd and that is why most of them had been scattered. Luke also shows that Jesus linked his own death to the destruction of

---

[14] Justin, *Trypho* 53.
[15] *Letter of Barnabas* 5.12.

Jerusalem: when he looked out over Jerusalem, he said that the city and its people would perish 'because you did not know the time of your visitation' (Luke 19.44).

## The Paraclete

The Paraclete is only mentioned in John's Gospel (14.15–17, 26; 15.26–27; 16.7–14), where he has many roles, but the name itself means 'one who is summoned/called'. The word is the passive participle of *parakalō*, 'call', 'encourage', but it came to be understood by Christian interpreters as an active participle, *parakalōn*, 'the encourager', 'the comforter'. The word is not found in the LXX. Westcott warned:

> [This interpretation, using the active participle] conveys a partial truth, but by an inaccurate method ... But this secondary application of the term cannot be used to confirm an original meaning which is at fatal variance with the form of the word, and also against undoubted use elsewhere. It may also be added that *parakalein* is not found in the writings of St John, though it is common in the other parts of the New Testament.[16]

The Hebrew equivalent of the original form would have come from *zākar*, which means 'invoke' but also 'remember', and so in the passive form 'the one invoked' or 'the one remembered'. Sometimes it is not clear which is the appropriate translation: 'The LORD ... this is my name for ever, and thus I am to be remembered/invoked throughout all generations' (Exod. 3.15, literally 'this in my remembrance/invocation ...'). In this example, either translation would make sense, but before the ark, where the Levites were appointed to praise, thank and remember/invoke, *lᵉhazkîr*, the LORD with their music (1 Chron. 16.4), 'invoke' would be the more likely meaning, since the LORD met with Moses over the ark and appeared there to the high priest (Exod. 25.22; Lev. 16.2). Two psalms (38 and 70) have the title *lᵉhazkîr*, translated as 'memorial offering', but 'to invoke' would be a more appropriate translation since the LORD is asked to come:

> Do not forsake me, O LORD,
> O my God, be not far from me!
> Make haste to help me,
> O LORD of my salvation.
>         (Ps. 38.21–22, my translation)

---

[16] B. F. Westcott, *The Gospel According to St John*, London: John Murray, 1903, p. 212.

## John 16

> Be pleased, O God, to deliver me!
> O LORD, make haste to help me ...
> I am poor and needy;
> Hasten to me, O God!
> Thou art my help and my deliverer;
> O LORD, do not tarry!  (Ps. 70.1, 5)

The Psalmist called on the LORD to come, and so the LORD was the one who was called, in other words, the Paraclete. The correspondence between the roles of the Paraclete and the nuances of *zākhar* is striking.

There are many examples of how *zākhar* was used; the italics in the extracts below represent a form of *zākhar* in the Hebrew.

There was a court office 'the recorder', literally 'the one who causes to remember', e.g. Jehoshaphat (1 Chron. 18.15) and Asaph (Isa. 36.3). Some angels also had this role, for example the 'watchers' on the walls of Jerusalem:

> You who *cause* the LORD *to remember*, take no rest,
> And give him no rest until he establishes Jerusalem.
> (Isa. 62.6, my translation)

The LORD says:

> *Cause me to remember*, let us argue together;
> Set forth your case that you may be proved right.
> (Isa. 43.26)

There was the context of recollection:

> I will call to mind the works of the LORD,
> I will surely *remember* your wonders of old ...
> (Ps. 77.11)

> I will *recount* the deeds of loving kindness of the LORD.
> (Isa. 63.7)

There was the context of help in time of need:

> The LORD answer you in the day of trouble!
> The name of the God of Jacob protect you!
> May he send you help from the sanctuary,
> And give you support from Zion ...
> Some *boast/call* on chariot and horses,
> We *boast/call* on the name of the LORD our God.
> Give victory, O LORD, let the King answer us when we call.
> (Ps. 20.1, 2, 7, 8)

457

There was the context of blessing:

> In every place where I cause my name *to be remembered/invoked*, I will come to you and bless you. (Exod. 20.24)

And, since we are considering the Passover discourse, there was the context of the exodus and the angel of the Presence:

> I will *recount* the deeds of loving kindness of the LORD.
> In all their affliction he was afflicted,
> and the angel of his presence saved them.
> He who put in the midst of them his holy Spirit,
> who caused his glorious arm to go at the right hand of Moses.
> (Isa. 63.7, 9, 11)[17]

If this was the origin of the name, we should expect the Paraclete to cause to remember and to come to help, and this is exactly how John describes him.

Invoking the LORD was one of the roles of the Levites, and their style of worship was adopted by the Christians: praising and thanking the LORD with music and being filled with the Spirit (Eph. 5.19). They too called on the Name of the LORD (Rom. 10.12; 1 Cor. 1.2); and they prayed 'Come, LORD', *Marana tha* (1 Cor. 16.22), to which the LORD responded: 'I am coming soon' (Rev. 22.20). They also thought of themselves as the holy priesthood (1 Pet. 2.5). The heavenly host in the first throne vision in Revelation sang praises to the one who comes: 'Holy, holy, holy is the LORD God Almighty, who was and is and *comes*' (Rev. 4.8, translating literally). 'Is to come' is the translator's assumption; the word is a present participle, 'the one who comes', as in the acclamation on Palm Sunday: 'Blessed is he who comes with/in the Name of the LORD' (John 12.13). The first Christians knew the LORD as the one who comes, just as he came to his ancient temple. 'Paraclete' would be the Greek equivalent of 'the one invoked'.

In the Passover discourse John has preserved an element of Jesus' teaching similar to something found later in the Merkavah and Kabbalah texts which preserve ancient temple tradition.[18] Early Judaism linked keeping the commandments to the indwelling of the divine presence, which had once been in paradise but left due to human sin. The Presence, that is, the angel of the Presence, was brought down to earth again by

---

[17] All the above extracts are my own translations.
[18] This paragraph is drawn from M. Idel, *Kabbalah. New Perspectives*, New Haven and London: Yale University Press, 1988, ch. 7: 'Ancient Jewish Theurgy'.

## John 16

good deeds, beginning with Abraham and culminating in the construction of Solomon's temple.

> This manifest correlation between human acts and the divine presence must be understood as the result of a theurgical conception of the commandments, whose performance is seen as having substantial bearing on the Divinity; the commandments not only draw it downwards, but also facilitate its indwelling.[19]

So too Jesus said: 'If you love me, you will keep my commandments, and I will pray the Father and then he will give you the Paraclete ...' (14.15–16, my translation), and: 'Where two or three are gathered in my name, there am I in the midst of them' (Matt. 18.20).

Peter wrote: 'Be yourselves built into a spiritual house, to be a holy priesthood ...' (1 Pet. 2.5).

The Christians who kept the LORD's commandments enabled the LORD to come to them and dwell in them. The Christians prayed *Marana tha*, and the Kabbalists had prayers and rituals to bring the angel of the Presence so that he could reveal the mysteries of heaven and earth and the secrets of wisdom, and he was accompanied by the Shekinah or the throne of glory. These revelations took place in a temple setting, and Idel concluded, on the basis of the later Kabbalistic texts: 'We can seriously consider the possibility that the Temple service was conceived as inducing the presence of the Shekinah in the Holy of Holies ...'[20] One might add 'and inducing the angel of the Presence'. In other words, they called on the divine presence, and even without the title, this was the Paraclete. John's Book of Revelation is a much earlier text within the same temple tradition, and he describes the Shekinah as the Bride appearing in clothes of fine linen that were the righteous deeds of the saints; she was proof that the commandments had been kept, and so the Logos rode forth to bring the judgement with the sword (of true revelation) in his mouth (Rev. 19.7–8, 13–14).

The Paraclete is a unique glimpse of the first Christians' way of thinking within the world view of the first temple, and searching for the Paraclete means entering again the world of the ancient angels, where heaven and earth were not always distinct, where one being had many names and many forms, and where the 'Jewish' sources show signs of unease and even hostility towards angels.

---

[19] Idel, *Kabbalah*, p. 167.
[20] Idel, *Kabbalah*, p. 168.

## Temple Theology in John's Gospel

Since we are considering *The King of the Jews*, we begin with the Davidic kings. The Spirit of the LORD, that is, *the Spirit that transformed the human into the LORD*, spoke within the king (2 Sam. 23.2; Ps. 2.7) and rested upon him to make him wise (Isa. 11.2). He received the Spirit of the LORD when he was anointed and enthroned and became the LORD. He had wisdom like the angel of God (2 Sam. 14.20). In other words, the Paraclete was within him (cf. John 14.17). This appears in Revelation as the Lamb/Servant who had seven eyes and seven rays of light (meaning the human figure who had the sevenfold Spirit and the sevenfold light) enthroned and then becoming (One with) the LORD (Rev. 5.6, 13).[21] The Davidic king was 'God with us' in human form (Isa. 7.14).

The presence of the LORD was also described as an angel who was seen in a vision, or whose presence was perceived:

- as the angel of the Presence (Isa. 63.9), see below;
- as the angel of the LORD who met Hagar in the desert (Gen. 16.7–14), and whom she named *El Ro'i*, 'God who sees'. Philo, John's contemporary, says she met the Logos, and this must be borne in mind when considering the meaning of 'Logos'.[22] The LORD opened Balaam's eyes and he saw the angel of the LORD as an armed man standing in his way (Num. 22.31). Philo says he too met the Logos.[23] Zechariah saw the angel of the LORD as he opposed Satan and ordered the vesting of Joshua (Zech. 3.1–5). In these examples the angel is not easy to distinguish from the LORD himself, and there are many such examples;[24]
- as the *memra*, the I AM, originally a way of describing the divine presence whose significance was almost lost.[25] A comparison of the *memra* of the Targums, especially the Palestinian Targums, and the Logos of Philo shows that, whatever the date of the various Targums, they reproduced faithfully what Philo knew. In other words, the Targumists show that people in the synagogues where the Targums originated had more or less the same way of thinking as Philo. Here are some examples of how Philo and the Targum describe the angel of Exodus:[26]

---

[21] See above, p. 244.
[22] *Cherubim* 3.
[23] *Cherubim* 35.
[24] This was the subject of my book *The Great Angel. A Study of Israel's Second God*, London: SPCK, 1992.
[25] See above, p. 100.
[26] For more detail, see my book *The Great Angel*, n. 24 above, pp. 134–61.

## John 16

- Philo: 'He has the divine Logos as his leader, since there is an oracle which says "Behold, I send my angel before your face, to guard you in the way ..."'
- Targum: 'The Shekinah of the *Memra* of the LORD will go before you.'[27]
- Philo: 'Of necessity was the Logos appointed as judge and mediator, who is called "angel".'
- Targum: 'Woe to them that are alive at the time when the *Memra* of the LORD shall be revealed to give the good reward to the righteous and to take vengeance on the wicked ...'

'His *Memra* will be among you for vengeance.'

'I let myself be entreated through my *Memra* by them that enquired not from before me.'[28]

In John's Greek the Presence was described in the Prologue as the Logos and here in the Passover discourse as the Paraclete, showing that the Paraclete was yet another name for the Spirit or angel of the LORD. The Spirit of the LORD (that is, the Spirit that made Jesus the LORD), spoke in Jesus the King of the Jews and would return to his disciples as the Paraclete. They too would become children of God: 'To all who received [the Logos], who believed in his name, he gave power to become children of God' (1.12). Paul said: 'All who are led by the Spirit of God are sons of God ... heirs of God and fellow heirs with Christ, provided we suffer with him in order that we may also be glorified with him' (Rom. 8.14, 17). Thus Jesus said:

> I will pray the Father and he will give you another[29] Paraclete, to be with you for ever ... I will not leave you desolate; I will come to you. (14.16, 18)

> It is to your advantage that I go away, for if I do not go away, the Paraclete will not come to you; but if I go, I will send him to you.
> (16.7, my translations)

The promise of the Paraclete alongside Jesus' own promise to return to his disciples must indicate that he was the Paraclete.

---

[27] Philo, *Migration of Abraham* 174; Targum *Pseudo-Jonathan* Deut. 31.6.
[28] Philo, *Questions on Exodus* II.13; Tg. *Ps-Jon.* Num. 24.23; Targum of Isaiah 8.14; 65.1.
[29] 'Another' should perhaps be 'afterwards', as in Rev. 7.2; 8.3; 10.1, 18.1, where each marks the beginning of a new scene. The mighty angel comes again, rather than 'another' mighty angel comes. This is because the Hebrew *'aḥar*, 'afterwards', is almost the same as *'aḥēr*, 'another'. 'Afterwards' makes better sense and removes a great difficulty, which may have been there from the beginning as the disciples recalled Jesus' original words. Or 'another' may mean the LORD in another form.

The presence of the LORD was also described as the angel with the Name who accompanied Moses during the desert wanderings:

> Behold, I send an angel before you, to guard you on the way and to bring you to the place which I have prepared. Give heed to him and hearken to his voice, do not rebel against him, for he will not pardon your transgression; for my name is in him. (Exod. 23.20–21)

> And [the LORD] said [to Moses], 'My presence will go with you, and I will give you rest.' (Exod. 33.14)

'Manifesting thy Name' is how Jesus described his own ministry, thus identifying himself as the angel of the Presence (17.6). In Isaiah 63.9 – a Passover context – the Presence is described as the angel of the Presence travelling with Moses in the desert, but the LXX emphasized that it was the LORD himself who accompanied Moses: 'It was no envoy nor angel but the LORD himself who saved them because he loved them ...' (LXX Isa. 63.9). The angel of the Presence was a way of speaking of the LORD, but when the LXX was translated there must have been a danger that the angel of the Presence would be understood as a distinct and lesser being and so the emphasis was necessary. So too in Ecclesiastes, where 'before the face of the angel' became in the LXX 'before the face of God' (Eccles. 5.6, but 5.5 in Heb. and Gr.). This angel was the Presence of the LORD on earth. *Jubilees*, however, does imply a distinction between the LORD and his angel: when Abraham was about to sacrifice Isaac, the LORD told the angel of the Presence to speak to him.[30] In the Genesis account the angel and the LORD are not distinct: the angel of the LORD called to Abraham and said, 'You have not withheld your son ... *from me*' (Gen. 22.12).

The angel of the Presence was a multiform presence. He revealed to Moses on Sinai all the history of his people and told him to write it down,[31] but the angel then spoke of himself in the plural. 'We appeared to Abraham at the oak of Mamre [Gen. 18] and we talked with him and we caused him to know that a son would be given to him by Sarah his wife.'[32] Now the Hebrew word for presence, which also means 'face' and 'appearance', has a plural form, *pânîm*. The LORD, though One, was thought to be a manifold presence, and so the angel of the Presence spoke of himself in the plural. This can also be seen in the way Josephus told the story of the LORD appearing to Abraham, apparently as three men (Gen.

---

[30] *Jubilees* 18.9.
[31] *Jubilees* 2.1.
[32] *Jubilees* 16.1.

18.1–2). In the biblical text, the LORD/the three men spoke in both singular and plural forms: 'They said to him ... The LORD said ...' (Gen. 18.9, 10). Then two of the men went towards Sodom and Abraham remained before the LORD (Gen. 18.22). Josephus does not mention the LORD, but says only that Abraham was visited by three angels: one to tell him about the birth of Isaac, and the other two to overthrow Sodom.[33] This means that an educated Jew in the time of Jesus could describe the presence of the LORD as three angels, and the Babylonian Talmud shows that this was the traditional way to understand the story. The three men were named as the archangels: 'Who were the three men? – Michael, Gabriel, and Raphael. Michael came to bring the tidings to Sarah [of Isaac's birth]; Raphael to heal Abraham; and Gabriel to overturn Sodom.'[34] Christians read this story as an appearance of the Son of God and two angels, thus implying that the Jews named as Michael the One whom the Christians named as the LORD. Constantine had a great church built at Mamre, to mark the place where 'the Son of God appeared to Abraham with two angels ... He who for the salvation of mankind was born of a Virgin, there manifested himself to a godly man.'[35] There can be no doubt who the Christians thought had appeared to Abraham at Mamre.

The angel(s) of the Presence(s) could thus take several forms simultaneously, and as such were sometimes called the archangels. Malachi described the priests as angels of the LORD of Hosts (Mal. 2.7), and the name Malachi itself means 'my angel'. These were all angels of the LORD, presumably because the Spirit of the LORD worked through them. So too in the Qumran blessing for the Zadokite priests, which prays for them the role of the archangel Uriel: 'May you be as an Angel of the Presence ... May he make you holy among his people [ ] light [ ] the world with knowledge and enlighten the face of the congregation [ ]'.[36] They were to enlighten their people, and the archangel Uriel means 'light of God'.

---

[33] Josephus, *Antiquities* 1.198.
[34] Babylonian Talmud *Baba Metzia* 86b, but reported differently in *Genesis Rabbah* L.2, where Michael brings the news to Abraham, Gabriel destroys Sodom, and Raphael rescues Lot.
[35] Sozomen, *History* 2.4, written in the fifth century CE. The appearance of the Son of God to Abraham was known to Justin, *Trypho* 56, 126, and to Irenaeus, *Demonstration* 44, both writing in the second. For early Christian belief about the Angel, see my book *The Great Angel*, n. 24 above, pp. 191–3.
[36] 1QSb IV.

Sometimes the presence was fourfold. Enoch saw the archangels as four presences around the LORD of Spirits, and heard them singing praises. They were named Michael, Raphael, Gabriel and Phanuel.[37] Elsewhere in *1 Enoch* Phanuel was named Uriel,[38] and although tradition said that the names of the angels came back with the Jews from Babylon,[39] Isaiah knew of the fourfold presence of the LORD as the four throne names of the newly born king:

- Wonderful Counsellor = Uriel, the light of God;
- Mighty God = Gabriel, the strength of God;
- Father of Booty[40] = Michael, the warrior;
- Prince of Peace = Raphael, the healing of God (Isa. 9.6).

The translator of the LXX knew that these four could be summed up as one title: Angel of Great Counsel (Isa. 9.6). Thus the fourfold presence of the One LORD in the king was known in the first temple. The fourfold LORD became a title in Merkavah texts. Among the many names for the LORD is the curious *Tootrousea Yahweh* found in the *Hekhalot Rabbati* and attributed to R. Neḥunyah, who taught in the early second century CE: 'R. Ishmael said: Thus said R. Neḥunyah ben Hakkanah: *Tootrousea Yahweh*, LORD of Israel, dwells in seven palaces, in the innermost room thereof …'[41] The title clearly derived from the Greek *tetra*, 'four', and *ousia*, meaning 'being' or 'essence', 'the LORD in four beings', and just as 'Paraclete' was transliterated into Hebrew as *prqlyṭ*,[42] this too originated in a Greek-speaking community but was adopted into Hebrew as *ṭwṭrwsyʾy*. This implies that the titles indicating the fourfold Presence and the One who was summoned were preserved in the Diaspora, beyond the reach of second-temple Jerusalem and what Enoch called its apostate generation.[43] It was the Diaspora community too, with their LXX, who emphasized that the angel of the Presence was the LORD himself and not another being (LXX Isa. 63.9), but it was the second-temple scribes who had Solomon deny that the LORD could dwell on earth. As he dedicated the temple, he said: 'But will God indeed dwell on the earth? Behold, heaven and the highest heaven

---

[37] *1 Enoch* 40.1–9.
[38] *1 Enoch* 9.1.
[39] *Genesis Rabbah* XLVIII.9.
[40] The Hebrew *ʾabiʿad* can mean 'father of eternity', 'father of booty', or 'father of the throne'.
[41] *Hekhalot Rabbati* 206.
[42] Mishnah *Aboth* 4.11.
[43] *1 Enoch* 93.9.

cannot contain thee; how much less this house which I have built!' (1 Kings 8.27).

Sometimes the primary plurality was a group of seven archangels, as also shown in *1 Enoch*.[44] In the Book of Tobit, Raphael explained that he was 'one of the seven holy angels who present the prayers of the saints and enter into the presence of the glory of the Holy One' (Tobit 12.15; cf. Rev. 8.3–4); and in Revelation, a sevenfold high-priestly angel – seven angels all dressed as the high priest – emerged from the temple to pour the wrath of God onto the land (Rev. 15.5–8). Since Isaiah knew that the Davidic king was endowed with the sevenfold Spirit (Isa. 11.2), the co-existence of the four and the seven was ancient, but how they related to each other is not known. Suffice it to say that the Shema‛ itself recognizes plurality within the One LORD: 'Hear, O Israel, the LORD our *ᵉlohîm* [plural] is One LORD' (Deut. 6.4, my translation), and this belief underlies Jesus' high-priestly prayer with which the Passover discourse concludes.

The angel of the Presence appears in the Merkavah texts that have the same temple setting as early Christian texts.[45] The angel of the Presence set crowns on the heads of the angels around the throne,[46] as did the Son of God (in the Christian Preface of 2 Esdras) when he greeted his faithful followers who had 'put off mortal clothing' and were praising the LORD on Mount Zion.

> In their midst was a young man of great stature, taller than any of the others, and on the head of each of them he placed a crown, but he was more exalted than they. And I [Ezra] was held spellbound. Then I asked an angel, 'Who are these, my lord?' He answered and said to me, 'These are they who have put off mortal clothing and put on the immortal, and they have confessed the name of God; now they are being crowned and receive palms.' Then I said to the angel, 'Who is that young man who places crowns on them and puts palms in their hands?' He answered and said to me, 'He is the Son of God whom they confessed in the world.' (2 Esdras 2.43–47)

So too the risen LORD's promise to his faithful followers: 'Be faithful unto death and I will give you the crown of life' (Rev. 2.10).

The angel of the Presence gave wisdom to those who prayed. R. Ishmael, who taught in the early second century CE, was a major figure in some Merkavah texts and was known as the high priest even though he

---

[44] *1 Enoch* 20.1–8.
[45] In this paragraph I draw on P. Schäfer, *The Hidden and Manifest God*, Albany: State University of New York Press, 1992.
[46] *Hekhalot Rabbati* 170.

lived after the temple had been destroyed. This is because the Merkavah mystics saw themselves as heirs to the high-priestly temple traditions as did the Christians. It was said that after much fasting and prayer, the angel of the Presence came with 70 angels to R. Ishmael and caused wisdom to dwell in his heart.[47] In *3 Enoch*, R. Ishmael ascended to the seventh palace, the innermost, where Metatron was sent by the Holy One to help him pass the terrifying angels who guarded the purity of heaven. Then he taught him to sing before the throne, and the heavenly beings joined with him in praise. Metatron told Ishmael that he had formerly been Enoch, but had been taken up to heaven and made the ruler of all the angels except those who bore the name Yahweh. Enoch/Metatron had been given a throne, a glorious robe and a crown, and then the Holy One named him 'the lesser Yahweh ... because my name is in him'. He was the angel of the exodus, and the first of his 70 names was Yahoel Yah.[48]

The angel Yahoel also appears in the *Apocalypse of Abraham*. He was sent from heaven in human form to strengthen and bless Abraham, and to be with him and his descendants.[49] He was dressed as a royal high priest, with turban and golden sceptre, and he guided Abraham up to stand before the throne. The *Apocalypse* is a fuller version of the story in Genesis 15, but there the one who appeared was the Lord Yahweh (in English versions 'Lord GOD'). Presumably the Lord Yahweh could also be described as the high-priestly angel Yahoel. Further, this meeting with the high-priestly angel happened immediately after Abram – not yet Abraham – had met Melchi-Zedek, the priest of El Elyon (Gen. 14.18),[50] so there is a strong possibility that the Lord Yahweh, remembered as the heavenly high priest in the *Apocalypse*, was also Melchi-Zedek. Problems with the Melchi-Zedek texts, as we have seen,[51] show that he was another aspect of the 'angel' problem, and the Christians identified Jesus as a Melchi-Zedek (Heb. 7.11–17). Jesus identified himself as fulfilling the prophecy of Isaiah 61: 'The Spirit of the Lord GOD is upon me' (Isa. 61.1; Luke 4.21), and the Lord GOD is the name of the One who appeared to Abram in Genesis 15. This name became Yahwehel in the *Apocalypse of Abraham*, but Yahwehel was Metatron the angel high priest, and in all likelihood he was also Melchi-Zedek.

---

[47] *Ma'asseh Merkavah* 565.
[48] *3 Enoch* 48D 1.
[49] *Apocalypse of Abraham* 10.3–4, 16; 11.3.
[50] See above, pp. 70–3.
[51] See above, p. 71.

## John 16

The identification of Metatron, who had been the human Enoch, as the angel of the Presence became a point of dispute between Jews and Christians, reflecting the same disagreement as is implicit in the Lxx translation of Isaiah 63.9: was the angel of the Presence only a messenger or was he the LORD? Here, the question is: should the angel of the Presence be worshipped, implying that the Christians did worship the angel of the Presence.[52]

> Once a Min [a Christian] said to R. Idith: 'It is written, And unto Moses He said, Come up to the LORD [Exod. 24.1]. But surely it should have stated, Come up unto me!'
>
> 'It was Metatron [who spoke]', he replied, 'whose name is similar to that of his Master, for it is written, For my name is in him' [Exod. 23.21].
>
> 'But if so [said the Min], we should worship him!'
>
> R. Idith replied, 'The same passage says: Do not rebel against/exchange him' [Exod. 23.21].*
>
> 'But if so [said the Min] why is it stated: He will not pardon your transgression?'**
>
> He answered: 'By our troth we would not accept him even as a messenger, for it is written, And he said unto him, If Thy Presence go not with me ... [Exod. 33.15].'[53]

*Playing on the two meanings of the Hebrew verb *mrh*: 'to rebel' or 'to exchange'. 'Do not rebel against him' and 'Do not exchange him for another'; that is, treat him as the LORD.

**One who forgives transgression cannot be just an angel; cf. Luke 5.21: 'Who can forgive sins but God only?'

The name Metatron is a mystery. Various meanings have been proposed, such as the Latin *metator*, the officer who prepares the way; or the Greek *metaturannos*, the one who is next to the ruler. Eusebius shows that the Christians understood the name as 'throne sharer', the one 'in the midst of the throne'. When expounding Psalm 45.6–7, 'Thy throne, O God, is for ever and ever ... Wherefore God, thy God hath anointed thee ...' he wrote:

> The Anointer, being the supreme God, is far above the Anointed, he being God in a different sense ... Therefore in these words you have it clearly stated that God was anointed and became the Christ ... And this is he who

---

[52] Cf. the report of the Gentile Hecataeus, who had seen the high priest in the temple about 300 BCE. 'The high priest ... is an angel to them of God's commandments.' When he speaks to them, the Jews 'immediately fall to the ground and worship, *proskunein*, the high priest as he explains the commandments to them'. Quoted in Diodorus of Sicily, XL.3.5–6.

[53] Babylonian Talmud *Sanhedrin* 38b.

was beloved of the Father and his Offspring and the eternal priest and the being called the Sharer of the Father's throne.[54]

The heavenly LORD promised the same to the faithful of Laodicea: 'He who conquers, I will grant him to sit with me on my throne, as I myself conquered and sat down with my Father on his throne' (Rev. 3.21). And the Lamb/Servant took his place in the midst of the throne and in the midst of the four living creatures and the elders (Rev. 5.6). We shall return to the picture of the LORD in Revelation. Suffice it here to note that Metatron is yet another title, along with Paraclete and *Toutrousea*, that originated in a Greek-speaking (i.e. Diaspora) community and was then transliterated into Hebrew. Further, as we have noted above, most of the texts on which we depend for our knowledge of early Judaism were collected and transmitted through channels which believed that the angel of the Presence, under his many names and titles, was a heresy – Christianity.[55]

This accounts for an entirely incongruous addition to *3 Enoch*. After extolling the glories of Metatron in heaven, the text suddenly describes how he had to stand up from his throne and receive 60 lashes of fire. The arch-heretic Elisha ben Abuyah (known as Aḥer, 'the other one', to avoid saying his name) ascended to see the chariot throne and concluded that there were two enthroned in heaven. He said: 'There are indeed two powers in heaven,' and for this he was banished, and Metatron, who had caused this blasphemous mistake, was punished and demoted.[56] Despite this, the Metatron texts survived, including the account of his coronation. The Holy One placed on his head a glorious crown bearing the letters by which the world was created, in other words, the crown of the high priest who wore the Name.[57] Metatron had just been given the name 'The lesser Yahweh', and so it was the sight of his new Name that caused all the powers of heaven to tremble and to fall prostrate before him.[58] This is why the heavenly LORD promised that he would write on (the forehead of) his faithful follower 'the name of my God ... my own new name' (Rev. 3.12),[59] and this is the scene in Philippians 2, where Jesus is the Metatron figure, and so the angel of the Presence:

---

[54] Eusebius, *Proof of the Gospel* IV.15.
[55] I explored the whole question of the Great Angel in my book *The Great Angel*, n. 24 above.
[56] *3 Enoch* 16, with a similar account in Babylonian Talmud Ḥagigah 15a.
[57] They may have been the 22 letters of the Hebrew alphabet by which it was believed that the world was created, but letters on a crown does suggest the four letters of the Name.
[58] *3 Enoch* 14.
[59] 'The name of the city of my God' is the other way to read Ezek. 48.35: 'The name of the city from that day, the LORD shall be its name' (my translation).

*John 16*

God has highly exalted him and bestowed on him the Name that is above every name, that at the Name [given to] Jesus, every knee should bow, in heaven and on earth and under the earth, and every tongue confess that Jesus Christ is Yahweh, to the glory of God the Father.

(Phil. 2.9–11, my translation)

The other enthronement scene in the New Testament is Revelation 4—5, where the heavenly host praise the one 'who was and is', represented by the title *memra*, the Presence,[60] and the one 'who comes', the Paraclete (Rev. 4.8). The visions then describe the future but imminent coming of the LORD. Before this, the Preface of the book presents Jesus as the high priest in heaven sending letters to his churches. This is the departed LORD, not yet returned. Each of the seven letters begins with a different aspect of the One dressed as a high priest *who calls himself the Spirit speaking to the churches*, and so these are the earliest Christian picture of the Paraclete. He is:

- the One who holds the seven stars in his right hand, who is amidst the seven golden lampstands (Rev. 2.1);
- the First and the Last who died and came to life (Rev. 2.8);
- the One who has the sharp two-edged sword (Rev. 2.12); cf. Rev. 19.15, the sharp sword in the mouth of the Logos;
- the Son of God, who has eyes like a flame of fire and whose feet are like burnished bronze (Rev. 2.18); cf. Rev. 10.1, the mighty angel with a face like fire and legs like pillars of fire;
- he who has the seven spirits of God and the seven stars (Rev. 3.1);
- the Holy One, the True One, who has the key of David, who opens and no one shall shut, who shuts and no one opens (Rev. 3.7);
- the Amon, the faithful and true witness, the beginning of God's creation (Rev. 3.14).[61]

The heavenly high priest was the Davidic king who had received the promises of Psalm 2 (Rev. 2.27) and would soon return (Rev. 2.16; 2.25; 3.11) to bring judgement (Rev. 2.5, 16, 20–23; 3.3, 9). John saw the heavenly LORD about to emerge and fulfil the words of Deuteronomy 32.43. The longer and older form of this verse has been found at Qumran, and Hebrews 1.6 shows it was used as a proof text by the first Christians:

> Heavens rejoice with him,
> *ᵉlohîm* worship/bow down to him

---

[60] See above, p. 101.
[61] Amon, not Amen; see my book *The Revelation of Jesus Christ*, p. 112.

> For he will avenge the blood of his sons,
> Take vengeance on his enemies,
> He will give those who hate him their reward,
> And will atone the soil of his people.
> (Deut. 32.43, translating literally)[62]

These images, titles and expectations from the temple – about angels, spirits and the Davidic king – were first-generation Christian discourse and so known to John before he wrote his Gospel. They should be used to illuminate his writings, and although the title Paraclete is unique to him, the associated ideas are not. Luke's Peter used the title Holy One when he spoke in the temple court: 'You denied the Holy and Righteous One ...' (Acts 3.14), and he went on to explain, in the imagery of the high priest departing on the Day of Atonement (leaving the scene for a while?), that the Righteous One (Melchi-Zedek?) was the anointed one who would emerge again from the presence of the LORD to bring renewal. This is also the setting for Hebrews 1.1–4, the Son who has made atonement and is now enthroned on high. While he was still in the heavenly temple, Jesus the high priest gave John the seven letters, each of which ended: 'He who has an ear, let him hear what the Spirit says to the churches' (Rev. 2.7, 11, 17, 29; 3.6, 13, 22). In other words, the heavenly high priest, who was the Spirit speaking to the churches, was the LORD: 'I am the first and the last' (Rev. 1.17; 2.8; 22.13), a title first found in Isaiah: 'I am He, I am the first, and I am the last' (Isa. 48.12b; also 44.6). Thus John, like Peter and the writer of Hebrews, knew the LORD as the heavenly high priest and the Righteous One, but John also calls him the Spirit and the Paraclete.

The Paraclete is the one who appears in the writings of Paul as the Spirit who is the LORD: 'the LORD is the Spirit, and where the Spirit of the LORD is, there is freedom ... for this comes from the LORD who is the Spirit' (2 Cor. 3.17–18, my translation). In Galatians, Paul described him as the Spirit of his Son: 'God has sent the Spirit of his Son into our hearts ...' (Gal. 4.6). The Paraclete as helper in time of trouble is 'the Spirit of Jesus Christ' (Phil. 1.19). In Acts, the angel/Spirit of the LORD appears frequently in the stories of the early community: an angel of the LORD released Peter from prison and sent him to speak in the temple (Acts 5.19–21); an angel of the LORD told Philip to go towards the Gaza road, where he met the man from Ethiopia, and after he had baptized him, the Spirit of the LORD took Philip away (Acts 9.26, 39); an angel of God appeared to Cornelius; Peter heard the voice of the LORD during his rooftop vision,

---

[62] 4QDeut<sup>q</sup>.

and then was told by the Spirit to go meet Cornelius' servants (Acts 10.3, 12–15, 19); Agabus prophesied by the Spirit (Acts 11.28); an angel of the LORD released Peter from prison at Passover (Acts 12.6–11); an angel of God came to Paul (in a dream?) and assured him that he would reach Rome safely (Acts 27.23). There are also many references to the Holy Spirit, which raises the question implicit in John's usage: was there originally a distinction between the Holy Spirit and the Spirit/Spirit of Jesus/Spirit of his Son? The problem is well illustrated by the visions that determined the course of Paul's second missionary journey, since we cannot know whether or not these names are synonyms: the Holy Spirit forbad them to go into Asia, the Spirit of Jesus did not allow them into Bithynia, and then a man of Macedonia appeared to Paul in a night vision and asked him to go to Macedonia. Paul understood this as a call from God (Acts 16.6–10).

This variety, one might say confusion, in early descriptions of the Spirit, must have been known to John, whose own usage is precise. He is the only New Testament writer to use the (technical?) terms Logos and Paraclete, which he distinguished from the Holy Spirit in all but one case (14.26). The LORD/the angel of the LORD/the Spirit of the LORD/the Spirit of Jesus continued with the Christian community, and so they did not believe that the LORD had left them and would return only with the *parousia*. John represents accurately what must have been Jesus' teaching about his future presence with them as the Paraclete: coming from the Father at Jesus' request, remaining with the disciples and teaching them, bearing witness against the world and showing that the world was wrong in its judgement. As Westcott observed of 16.7: 'The departure of Christ was in itself a necessary condition for the coming of the Spirit to men. The withdrawal of his limited bodily Presence necessarily prepared the way for the recognition of the universal Presence.'[63] But the Christians also expected the LORD Jesus to be revealed from heaven 'with his mighty angels in flaming fire, inflicting vengeance on those who do not know God and upon those who do not obey the gospel of our LORD Jesus' (2 Thess. 1.7–8). It was the delay in this return from heaven that caused the problems which John addressed in his Gospel.

John at first understood the promise of the Paraclete in terms of revealing to him the meaning and the future fulfilment of Jesus' visions:

---

[63] Westcott, *Gospel According to St John*, n. 16 above, p. 227. 'Spirit' here is in fact the word 'Paraclete'.

> The Spirit of truth ... will reveal to you, *anaggellō*, the things that are coming ... He will glorify me, for he will take from what is mine and reveal it to you. All that the Father has is mine, therefore I said that he takes from mine and reveals it to you. (16.13–15, my translation)

What Jesus received from the Father was 'The revelation of Jesus Christ which God gave to him to show to his servants what must soon take place'. The promised work of the Spirit of truth in revealing the meaning and the fulfilment of the visions is what was meant by 'He made it known by sending his angel to his servant John' (Rev. 1.1). This is the Paraclete by another name: the angel of the LORD. But the Paraclete had another role, causing to remember, and so 'the Paraclete, the Holy Spirit ... will teach you all things, and bring to your remembrance all that *I have said* to you' (14.26). He would reveal the meaning of Jesus' teaching after Jesus had left them and 'been glorified' (2.22 and especially 12.16).[64] 'Causing to remember' was an ancient role of the angel who came to his people.

John's Gospel must be understood in the light of the Book of Revelation, where the Great Angel is distinct from the Lady. Both return to their people: the Lady gives birth to her son, the king (Rev. 12); and she also appears as the Bride when her warrior spouse, the Logos, rides out from heaven to fight against the forces of evil (Rev. 19). These are visions of the spiritual world, and so both the Lady and the Logos would be described as spirits. In waiting for fulfilment of the visions, John would have been looking for a corresponding earthly reality. This was temple tradition. Ezekiel had received a vision of the chariot throne of the LORD leaving the polluted temple, which corresponded to the purge in the time of Josiah when the actual throne was removed from the temple.[65] John received a new revelation about the fulfilment of the visions, and learned that *they had already been fulfilled in the lifetime of Jesus*: the Lady had already given birth to her son; the Logos had already come forth to fight against the forces of evil, the Light in conflict with the darkness (1.5). 'Walk while you have the light, lest the darkness overtake you; he who walks in the darkness does not know where he goes' (12.35).[66]

Reading John's Gospel in this way – the Holy Spirit as the presence of the Lady, the Paraclete as the presence of her Son the LORD – aligns the

---

[64] This is the only place in John's writings where the Paraclete is identified as the Holy Spirit, and although there is good authority for reading the text as it is, there is also a suspicion that 'Holy' may have been added at an early stage. In all other instances, the Paraclete is the [angel of the] LORD.

[65] See above, p. 36.

[66] See above, pp. 370, 449.

## John 16

Gospel with Revelation and reveals a sophistication in the early Christian world-view that was later lost. Thus Jesus told Nicodemus about being born of water and the Spirit, and the resulting gift of spiritual sight (3.3–9), an allusion to baptism, but the birth/baptism image is not used of the Paraclete (1.33; 6.63). Birth, sight and living water were gifts of the Lady to her children. She was the Spirit-and-the Bride (Rev. 22.17). Running all through the Gospel is the contrast between those who have her gift of sight and those who do not, and John concludes his account of Jesus' public ministry with a reflection on Isaiah's warning about loss of sight and perception (12.40).

The visions of Jesus underlie all the writings of John, and the Gospel, as we have seen, was prompted by his own vision of the *parousia* when the mighty angel came from heaven with an open book in his hand, but not, apparently, to bring the expected judgement. Instead, John had to speak new words of prophecy *to* many peoples, nations, tongues and kings (Rev. 10.11).[67] Within the sequence of visions that marked the unfolding of events between the time of Jesus and the fall of Jerusalem, the mighty angel appeared to John just before the destruction of the temple. This was the original expectation: 'Then they will see the Son of man coming in clouds with great power and glory' (Mark 13.26) which in the vision was '[a] mighty angel ... wrapped in a cloud, with a rainbow over his head, and his face was like the sun' (Rev. 10.1). This revelation prompted John to write his Gospel and determined the way he wrote it, namely to show the new understanding that the *parousia* had been the return of the LORD to his disciples, and that the judgement had already occurred. The Son of Man had appeared, but as 'the Man' whom Pilate brought out to show to the Jews as their king (19.5, 14). Jewish tradition remembered that the fate of Jerusalem, the judgement upon it, was sealed some 40 years before the city fell:

> Our Rabbis taught: During the last forty years before the destruction of the Temple the lot ['For the LORD', Lev. 16.8] did not come up in the right hand; nor did the crimson-coloured strap become white;* nor did the westernmost light shine; and the doors of the Hekal would open by themselves, until R. Johanan b. Zakkai rebuked them, saying: Hekal, Hekal, why wilt thou be the alarmer thyself? I know about thee that thou wilt be destroyed, for Zechariah ben Ido has already prophesied concerning thee: Open thy doors, O Lebanon, that the fire may devour thy cedars.[68]

---

[67] See above, p. 323.
[68] Babylonian Talmud *Yoma* 39b.

*A crimson thread was tied to the door of the sanctuary, and when the scapegoat carrying the sins reached the wilderness (that is, when the sins had been successfully carried away), the thread turned white.[69]

The coming of the Logos into the world and his work would continue in the coming of the Paraclete and his work through the disciples. The climax of the original sequence of visions had been all the new priests, marked with the Name and standing in the holy of holies, beholding the Face/Presence (Rev. 22.3-4). Jesus had prayed for this: 'Father, I desire that they also, whom thou hast given me, may be with me where I am, to behold my glory which thou hast given me in thy love for me before the foundation of the world' (17.24). In the new understanding, John emphasized that the disciples were already beholding the Face/Presence even though they had not realized this (14.8-9). Jesus' soliloquy (12.44-50) reflects on his role as the incarnate Logos: 'He who sees me sees him who sent me' (12.45). As the incarnate Logos he has already come and continues to come 'to be with you for ever' (14.16). The *parousia* is no longer the LORD returning at some time in the future, and so the prayer *Marana tha*, 'Come, LORD' became *Maran atha*, 'The LORD has come.'

The Paraclete would come to the disciples and dwell in them: 'You know [the Spirit of truth], for he dwells with you, and will be in you' (14.17). In the Gospel, the coming of the Paraclete corresponds to the Logos coming into the world from his original state with God (1.14), and to Jesus' reflection: 'He who ... sent me ... I have come' (12.45, 46). The way the Paraclete comes confirms that he is the LORD who had been incarnate in Jesus, and who would come back once Jesus had departed:

- 'When the Paraclete comes, whom I shall send to you from the Father ...' (15.26);
- 'If I do not go away, the Paraclete will not come to you; but if I go, I will send him to you ... When the Spirit of truth comes ...' (16.7, 13).

The Paraclete comes from the Father:

- 'The Father ... will give you [afterwards/another] Paraclete, to be with you for ever' (14.16);
- 'The Paraclete ... whom the Father will send in my name* ...' (14.26);
- 'The Paraclete ... whom I shall send to you from the Father ...' (15.26).

*Possibly 'with the Name', just as Jesus was acclaimed on Palm Sunday as the one who came with the Name. At the time, John observes, the

---

[69] Mishnah *Yoma* 6.8.

## John 16

disciples did not understand this, 'but when Jesus was glorified, then they remembered that this had been written of him and had been done to him' (12.16). The Name was with him, as with the angel of the exodus, and the Paraclete who would be sent was also the angel with the Name. So too Iaoel (the Greek version of Yahwehel) was sent to Abraham by the LORD: 'Go, Iaoel of the same name, through the mediation of my ineffable name';[70] and this is also how 'Isaiah' described the LORD coming from heaven: 'And I heard the voice of the Most High, the Father of my LORD, as he said to my LORD Christ who will be called Jesus, "Go out and descend through all the heavens..."' After his Incarnation and birth from Mary, 'the adversary envied him and roused the children of Israel, who did not know who he was, against him.' When Jesus had returned to heaven, he sat at the right hand of the great Glory, and the angel of the Holy Spirit sat on the left.[71] This is a very early description of the Trinity as the Father and two angels whom he sends to earth,[72] very different from the later Christianity of the creeds, but very similar to John's world of the returning Paraclete, who is distinguished from the Holy Spirit.

The Paraclete will remain with the disciples and in them (14.17), just as the Spirit of the LORD was promised to Joshua (Jesus) the high priest and those who were rebuilding the temple in Jerusalem after the exile: 'My spirit dwells in the midst of you [pl.], says the LORD; fear not' (Hag. 2.5, my translation). The Paraclete *in* the disciples would be equivalent to the claim of David: 'The Spirit of the LORD speaks *by me*, his word is upon my tongue' (2 Sam. 23.2); and the claim of Zechariah: 'The angel who spoke *within me* said to me...' (Zech 1.9, translating literally). Jesus begged the Jews to recognize from his works who he was, 'that you may know and understand that the Father is in me and I am in the Father' (10.38). The incarnate Logos remained in those who ate his flesh and drank his blood (6.56), and the Truth was within Christians for ever (2 John 2). The Qumran community had a similar belief: the God of Israel and his Angel of Truth would succour all the sons of light.[73]

The Paraclete will teach the disciples all things (14.26), just as the angel of the LORD gave wisdom to those who called on him. After being anointed by the Holy One, the disciples would know all things and the

---

[70] *Apocalypse of Abraham* 10.3.
[71] *Ascension of Isaiah* 10.7, 19; 11.33.
[72] The angel of the Spirit came to Joseph when he was anxious about Mary being pregnant, *Asc. Isa.* 11.4.
[73] *Community Rule*, 1QS III.24.

truth (1 John 2.20-21, 26-27). The Paraclete is the Spirit of Truth who will come:

- 'I will pray the Father, and he will give you ... the Spirit of truth, whom the world cannot receive, because it neither sees him nor knows him' (14.17);
- 'When the Paraclete comes ... even the Spirit of truth, who proceeds from the Father, he will bear witness to me' (15.26);
- 'When the Spirit of truth comes, he will guide you into all the truth ...' (16.13).

In Jesus' visions, it was the Logos who was called Faithful and True, and he rode out from heaven as King of kings and LORD of Lords (Rev. 19.11, 13, 16). In the Gospel, the incarnate Logos brought grace and truth into the world (1.17), Jesus said that he was the way, the truth and the life (14.6), and he reflected: 'I have come as light into the world' (12.46).

The Paraclete will speak only what he hears and not on his own authority (16.13): so too the incarnate Logos bears witness to what he has seen and heard, and speaks the words of God because of the Spirit he has been given:

- 'He bears witness to what he has seen and heard, yet no one receives his testimony ... For he whom God has sent utters the words of God, for it is not by measure that he gives the Spirit ...' (3.32, 34);
- The incarnate Logos gives teaching from the One who sent him (7.16-17);
- The Paraclete will be recognized by the disciples (14.17): so too the incarnate Logos was recognized by the disciples and the Baptist (1.29-51);
- The Paraclete will be neither recognized nor received by the world (14.17): so too the Logos was neither recognized nor received by the world (1.10-11; 5.43; 7.7);
- The Paraclete will bear witness to Jesus (15.26): the Baptist, the Father and the Scriptures bore witness to Jesus (5.33, 37, 39); the works Jesus did showed who he was (10.37-39). The other children of the Lady were 'those who keep the commandments of God and bear testimony to Jesus' (Rev. 12.17).

The Paraclete will judge the world.

> When [the Paraclete] comes, he will convince the world concerning sin and righteousness and judgement: concerning sin, because they do not believe in me; concerning righteousness, because I go to the Father, and you will see

## John 16

me no more; concerning judgement, because the ruler of this world is judged. (16.8–11)

The day of the LORD was expected, when he would come with his angels to bring the judgement. The Logos would ride from heaven with his army, the forces of evil would be defeated, the beast and his prophet would be thrown into the lake of fire, and an angel from heaven would bind Satan for a thousand years (Rev. 19.13, 19; 20.1–3). The Son of Man would come with his angels and sit on his throne, separating the sheep from the goats, and sending sinners into the eternal fire prepared for the devil and his angels (Matt. 25.31–46). In this parable, the criterion at the judgement would be: did you recognize the LORD – but in the needs of the needy? John brought the judgement forward into the present time, and explained that the moment of judgement was not in the future when a person stood before the heavenly throne but whenever a person stood before Jesus and *recognized who he was*.

> For God sent the Son into the world, not to condemn the world, but that the world might be saved by him. He who believes in him is not condemned; he who does not believe is condemned already, because he has not believed in the name of the only [beloved?][74] Son of God. (3.17–18)

The Paraclete would convince, *elegchō*, the world about sin, righteousness and judgement. The verb here has the sense 'show where it is wrong' as in 'If your brother sins against you, go and *tell him his fault* ...' (Matt. 18.15). The Paraclete would show the world how it had been wrong about sin, and the real sin was not believing in Jesus. Sin, *hamartia*, here represents the Hebrew *ḥēṭ'*, and both have the significant connotation 'missing the mark', failing to find the right way or the correct meaning. Thus Wisdom said: '*He who misses me* does wrong to his soul' (Prov. 8.36, translating literally). There is an exactly similar sentence in Jesus' debate with the Jews about sonship: 'Which of you convicts, *elegchō*, me of sin, *hamartia*?' (8.46). The meaning here is: 'Which of you can show that I am wrong?' Those who are of God, says Jesus, can hear the words of God, and the reason that the Jews cannot 'hear' what he is saying is because they are not 'of God' (8.47). Thus when the time of judgement comes, the Paraclete will show the world that their 'sin' had been failing to recognize and believe in Jesus.

The Paraclete would show the world how it had been wrong about righteousness, because Jesus was going to the Father and his disciples

---

[74] See above, p. 163.

would see him no more. This sequence of thought suggests that Jesus actually said 'Righteous One', *ṣaddîq*, rather than 'righteousness', *ṣedheq*. The world had been wrong about the Righteous One, just as Peter accused the men of Israel of denying the Holy and Righteous One who would return from heaven (Acts 3.14, 21). The Paraclete and the disciples would be witnesses to Jesus and would show that he was the Righteous One because he had gone to the Father. Jesus himself had demonstrated this from Scripture (Luke 24.25–27), and John's Jesus emphasized that he was going back to the Father. Jesus said to the Jews: 'I shall be with you a little longer, and then I [shall] go to him who sent me …' (7.33). To his disciples he said:

- 'He who believes in me will also do the works that I do; and greater works than these will he do, because I go to the Father' (14.12);
- 'I go to the Father' (14.28; cf. 13.1; 16.28; 17.5; 20.17).

The Righteous One was Isaiah's Servant (Isa. 53.11) who bore the sin, *ḥēṭ'*, of many (Isa. 53.12). The Servant would be lifted up and glorified (Isa. 52.13), which in the LXX became the verbs *hupsoō* and *doxazō*, both of which John uses of Jesus' crucifixion, resurrection and Ascension:

- 'The Son of man [must] be lifted up' (3.14);
- 'When you have lifted up the Son of man, then you will know that I am he …' (8.28);
- 'How can you say that the Son of man must be lifted up?' (12.34);
- 'The hour has come for the Son of man to be glorified' (12.23);
- 'Now is the Son of man glorified' (13.31).

The Servant would be wise, *śākhal*, which in the LXX became *sunoida*, 'understand', 'share knowledge' (Isa. 53.11, often 'prosper' in English versions, which is a less common meaning), and by his knowledge he would make many righteous (Isa. 53.11). The world would be proved wrong about the Righteous One, kings would be dumbfounded; 'that which has not been told them they shall see, and that which they have not heard they shall understand' (Isa. 52.15). Then follows the text that John uses to explain why Jesus failed to make the Jews understand:

> LORD, who has believed our report,
> And to whom has the arm of the LORD been revealed?
> (Isa. 53.1; John 12.38)

## John 16

Isaiah does not say that the Righteous One went to the Father, although this is implied in the longer Qumran version of the text[75] and in the LXX 'he shall see the light' (Isa. 53.11).

The detail that provides the context for Jesus' brief statement – 'When [the Paraclete] comes, he will convince the world concerning sin and righteousness and judgement' – is in the second of the *Parables of Enoch*,[76] which also describes the fate of those who did not recognize the Chosen One. There has been much debate over the date of the *Parables* and whether or not they are relevant to the early Christian writings.[77] Nothing from them has been found at Qumran, but even if the nature of the relationship cannot be determined – influence, dependence or a common tradition – their relevance to the early Christian world-view is beyond doubt. The key figure is a king (presumably the Davidic king), who is Isaiah's Servant and Daniel's Man. These three were also used of Jesus, and it is unlikely that two entirely unrelated traditions came to the same conclusion about the use of images from the Hebrew Scriptures. It is evidence of an anachronistic mindset to ask if, for example, Matthew had access to a copy of the *Parables* as he wrote his Gospel, so that he could incorporate imagery of the Man judging the sheep and the goats. The world of the *Parables* was the world of the first Christians, and Jesus' warnings about the Paraclete as judge are exactly those of Enoch's *Parables*: 'concerning sin, because they do not believe in me; concerning the Righteous One, because I go to the Father and you will see me no more; concerning judgement because the ruler of this world is judged' (vv. 9–11).

The second *Parable*, now much confused through interpolations, first warns those who deny the Name of the LORD of Spirits (the LORD of Hosts).[78] The Name is the central figure, the Chosen One who is enthroned. He is the Son of Man who will judge the rulers that do not acknowledge the source of their powers,[79] whence Jesus' words to Pilate: 'You would have no power over me unless it had been given you from above …' (19.11). The rulers 'persecute the houses of his congregation, and the faithful who depend on the Name of the LORD of Spirits'.[80] The

---

[75] 1QIsaᵃ.

[76] *1 Enoch* 45—57.

[77] There is a good summary in D. Olson, *Enoch. A New Translation*, North Richland Hills: Bibal Press, 2004, pp. 11-12.

[78] *1 Enoch* 45.1.

[79] *1 Enoch* 46.5.

[80] *1 Enoch* 46.8.

scene is the time of judgement on the Day of Atonement, when the blood of the Righteous One has been offered.[81] In his first letter, John wrote: 'We have a Paraclete with the Father, Jesus Christ the Righteous One, and he is the atonement offering, *hilasmos*, for our sins ...'[82] (1 John 2.1–2, my translation). The link between the 'Counsellor/Comforter' of the English versions of John's Gospel, and the 'Advocate' is lost through translation, but the Paraclete who goes to the Father offering his blood on the Day of Atonement confirms that John's Paraclete is the great high priest. Then Enoch sees how the Son of Man, presumably the Righteous One, is given the Name, in a place where fountains of wisdom and righteousness flow for the thirsty (cf. Rev. 22.1, 17).[83] The wisdom of the LORD of Spirits reveals his identity to the holy and righteous ones, but those who do not recognize him are punished 'for they have denied the LORD of Spirits and his Messiah'.[84] Then the Chosen One sits on the throne of the LORD of Spirits,[85] and Azazel and all his hosts are judged, thrown into a 'deep valley burning with fire' (cf. the lake of fire, Rev. 19.20).[86]

The Paraclete would show the world it had been wrong about judgement, because the ruler of this world would be judged. He would be cast out at the moment when Jesus was lifted up from the earth, a phrase that could mean crucifixion – 'He said this to show by what death he was to die' – but 'from the earth' could imply resurrection and Ascension (12.31–33). 'The ruler of this world is coming', said Jesus, 'but he has no power over me' (14.30). The Paraclete would then glorify Jesus (16.14), showing the disciples that he was the risen LORD, and so it was through the Paraclete that John was able to say: 'We have beheld his glory, glory as of the only Son from the Father' (1.14).

---

[81] *1 Enoch* 46.1–4.
[82] As in LXX Num. 5.8, where *hilasmos* renders *kippur*.
[83] *1 Enoch* 48.1–2.
[84] *1 Enoch* 48.10.
[85] *1 Enoch* 51.3.
[86] *1 Enoch* 53—56; the quotation is *1 Enoch* 54.1.

# John 17

The Passover discourse now comes to an end, and as in the last words of Moses that are now the Book of Deuteronomy, here too there is a formal conclusion. Jesus' prayer, often called his high-priestly prayer, combines themes and phrases from the *Didache* and from several parts of the Hebrew Scriptures: from the Shema', from the high priests' blessing, and from the two ancient poems that are the conclusion of Moses' last words: the *Song of Moses* and the *Blessing of Moses*.

These two poems (Deut. 32 and 33) are now separated by a short narrative about Moses' telling the people to keep 'this law' which would be their life, and the LORD telling Moses to go up Mount Nebo and prepare to die. The second part of the poem originally described how the LORD became king in Israel and gave his law, when he appeared in shining splendour with his holy ones and blessed the 12 tribes assembled before him. The present text has been modified to include Moses (Deut. 33.4), but that whole line could be an addition. A very minor change to the existing text, however, would give 'Anointed One': *mšyḥ*, rather than 'Moses', *mšh*, and this would better fit the overall context. The poem would then describe a scene known elsewhere: the-LORD-and-his-Anointed-One (the double identity as in Ps. 2.2 and Rev. 21.2, where it is God-and-the-Lamb) appearing to become king and to give the law.

These two poems were originally one poem, and the final verse of the 'first' poem, that is, the verse before the description of the LORD-and-the-Anointed coming as king, became an important Christian proof text: 'When he brings the Firstborn into the world, he says, "*Let all God's angels worship him*"' (Heb. 1.6, quoting Deut. 32.43). So important were the words in italics (and others in Deut. 32.43) that they did not survive in the post-Christian Hebrew text, as we shall see. They are in the LXX and have been found at Qumran,[1] but until the Qumran text was found, the longer LXX text was assumed to be a Christian fabrication. It was not. The

---

[1] 4QDeut<sup>q</sup>.

words of the *Song of Moses* were used by the early Church to show who Jesus was, and like so many other Christian proof texts, they did not survive the bitter parting of the Scriptures in the late first century CE. Further, a fragment of Deuteronomy 32, written in minute letters for a phylactery, has been found at Qumran. No other example has been found of this text used for a phylactery, and Milik suggested that the original had been only verses 1–33.[2] One example, however, shows that it was so used, and therefore had some special significance. It is not surprising to find that it was also important for Christians.

The scene described in the *Blessing of Moses* (Deut. 33) is the scene in Revelation 7, where the angel appears in the sunrise to the assembled people of Israel and marks 12,000 from each tribe with the seal of the living God. They later appear as the 144,000 followers of the Lamb who wear the Name (Rev. 14.1). The 144,000 have been redeemed and they stand spotless before the throne as the firstborn, not the *firstfruits* as the Greek text says. The word used here, *aparchē*, is found in the LXX for a whole range of temple offerings, and elsewhere in the New Testament it does mean 'firstfruits' (e.g. 1 Cor. 15.20, 23; Jas. 1.18); but if Revelation had a Hebrew original, as is likely, the written form of 'firstfruits' would have been identical to the written form of 'firstborn',[3] although the words were pronounced differently. Since the 'firstfruits' were not redeemed but the 'firstborn' were, those redeemed from humankind to follow the Lamb must have been the firstborn. This is confirmed by 'the assembly of the firstborn' on Mount Zion (Heb. 12.22–23).

Redemption was a Passover theme and also a priestly theme. As a memorial of their redemption from Egypt when the firstborn of Egypt died in the tenth plague, all firstborn males, both animal and human, were consecrated to the LORD: firstborn animals were sacrificed, but each firstborn son was redeemed by the payment of five silver shekels (Num. 18.16)[4] and by appointing a Levite in his place (Num. 3.40–45). Thus the redeemed with the Lamb were a priestly group and they bore on their foreheads the Name of the Lamb and of his Father (Rev. 14.1). This too had been a part of the vision of the assembled tribes, because the angel who came with the sunrise bore the seal of the living God to mark the foreheads of the 144,000 to protect them from the imminent judgement (Rev. 7.2–4). These prescriptions for observing Passover and

---

[2] In *Discoveries in the Judaean Desert* VI, ed. R. de Vaux and J. T. Milik, Oxford: Clarendon Press, 1977, p. 72.

[3] Thus the construct plural for both is written *bkwry*.

[4] Mishnah *Bekhoroth* 8.7.

sacrificing the firstborn (Exod. 12.43—13.16) were also phylactery texts.[5]

In Deuteronomy 33, the LORD dawns on his people with his angels, he becomes King, and then gives the law and blesses the 12 tribes. In the Sinai story, which was inserted into the Moses saga when the Pentateuch was compiled,[6] the LORD came to Sinai with thunder and lightning, thick cloud and the sound of a trumpet (Exod. 19.16), or with a cloud of glory like a devouring fire (Exod. 24.16-17). Then he spoke to Moses, gave the law, and promised that the people of Israel would be 'a kingdom of priests and a holy nation' (Exod. 19.6), like the 144,000 who were marked with the Name and redeemed to be a kingdom of priests to reign on earth (Rev. 5.10). The whole Sinai section in Exodus is a complex collection of earlier material, giving to Moses the role that had formerly been the king's,[7] but other detail about the lawgiving survived in folk memories and in texts that were not included in the Hebrew Scriptures. There is no mention in the exodus accounts, for example, of the LORD with *a host of angels* coming to Sinai when he gave the law, but the early Christians knew that the law had been given by angels (Acts 7.53; Gal. 3.19; Heb. 2.2) as did Josephus.[8] The Enochic *Apocalypse of Weeks* also knew that the law had been given with 'visions of the holy ones', but Moses is not mentioned here nor any figure who could have been Moses.[9] Deuteronomy 33 (and 32) has its roots in the temple rituals of the Davidic monarchy, when the LORD-and-his-Anointed appeared from the temple with a host of angels (that is, angel priests) to give the law, the judgement and the blessing. Images from the older cult, such as people gathering round him, the Morning Star and the rainbow in the cloud (cf. Rev. 10.1; 22.16), still appear in Ben Sira's poem about Simon the high priest emerging from the temple to give the blessing:

> How glorious was he when the people gathered round him,
> As he came out of the house of the veil,
> Like the morning star among the clouds,
> Like the moon when it is full,
> Like the sun shining on the temple of the Most High,
> And like the rainbow gleaming in glorious clouds.
> (Ben Sira 50.5-7, my translation)

---

[5] See my book *The Revelation of Jesus Christ*, Edinburgh: T&T Clark, 2000, pp. 243-7.
[6] See above, pp. 31, 49-50.
[7] See above, pp. 31, 49.
[8] Josephus, *Antiquities* 15.136.
[9] *1 Enoch* 93.6.

## Temple Theology in John's Gospel

In Revelation 7, the angel appears from the dawn and then puts the Name on the foreheads of the 12,000 from each tribe. The link between Revelation 7 and Deuteronomy 33 is the high priest's blessing, now assigned to Aaron and his sons, but before them, surely, to the older high priests. The LORD appears and shines on his people, to protect them and give them grace and peace:

> May the LORD bless you and keep you:
> May the LORD make his face/presence shine on you and be gracious to you;
> May the LORD lift up his face/presence on you and give you peace.
> So they shall put my Name upon the people of Israel and I will bless them. (Num. 6.24–27, my translation)

Here, marking with the Name is how the blessing is given as the face/presence of the LORD dawns on his people. This blessing, however, had become a sensitive issue by the end of the second-temple period. There is a ruling in the Mishnah: 'The blessing of the priests ... is read out but not interpreted', with a variant reading 'is neither read out nor interpreted';[10] one early Targum in the Palestinian tradition did not translate these verses into Aramaic but left them in Hebrew;[11] another interpreted the blessing as a prayer for the LORD to illuminate the mind, to 'shine upon you in the study of the law and reveal to you obscure things and protect you'.[12] The Qumran *Community Rule* had a similar understanding. The priests had to bless 'all the men of the lot of God who walk in integrity perfection, *tammîm*, in all his ways':

> May he bless you with all good and keep you from all evil,
> May he illuminate your heart with the wisdom, *śēkhel*, of life,
> May he graciously favour you with the knowledge, *da'ath*, of eternity [pl.].
> May he lift up the face/presence of his love, *ḥesedh*, upon you and give you the peace of eternity [pl.].[13]

The shining presence of the LORD, then, imparted security, wisdom, knowledge and peace, and those who saw it were given the Name, yet despite this being the blessing given by the high priests, it became forbidden teaching. Since John presents this as an important teaching of Jesus, as we shall see below, Christian claims about the blessing may have

---

[10] Mishnah *Megillah* 4.10.
[11] Targum *Neofiti* Numbers.
[12] Targum *Pseudo-Jonathan* Numbers.
[13] *Community Rule*, 1QS II.1–3, translating literally.

## John 17

been a factor in the sensitivity about its meaning. The LORD appearing in his glory to bring grace and peace was a theme in John's Prologue, as we have seen.[14]

The visions in Revelation were almost certainly known to Jesus, and certainly known to John, which means that when he wrote his Gospel, he knew of the angel who marked some people with the Name that kept them safe. How, then, might the community depicted in the visions (and indeed whoever wore that phylactery at Qumran) have understood the words of Deuteronomy 32, and especially the lines about the LORD coming to bring judgement? Some examples have been found at Qumran which show that they interpreted Scripture by treating the texts as a 'mystery' that the teacher could interpret to show how they referred to contemporary events and characters. Thus 'Write down the vision and make it plain upon the tablets, that he who reads may read it speedily' (Hab. 2.2, my translation) referred to 'the Teacher of Righteousness to whom God made known all the mysteries of the words of his servants the prophets'.[15] 'Those who wait for the LORD shall possess the land' (Ps. 37.9b) meant 'the congregation of the Chosen ones who do the will of the LORD'.[16] The Christians also used this form of interpretation, because the mighty angel who came in a cloud to speak to John told him that the prophecies were about to be fulfilled: 'In the days of the trumpet call to be sounded by the seventh angel, the mystery of God, as he announced to his servants the prophets, would be fulfilled' (Rev. 10.7, my translation).

The earliest Christians understood that Deuteronomy 33.2 and the longer form of Deuteronomy 32.43 were prophecies of the second coming of Jesus as the LORD: 'When the LORD Jesus is revealed from heaven with his mighty angels and flaming fire, inflicting vengeance upon those who do not know God and upon those who do not obey the gospel of our LORD Jesus' (2 Thess. 1.7–8, my translation). Presumably they also expected the rest of the poem to be fulfilled in their own time. How might they have understood the following lines, and why were they worn in that Qumran phylactery?[17]

> I will proclaim the Name of the LORD...
> Ascribe greatness to our God.

---

[14] See above, p. 177.
[15] *Commentary on Habakkuk*, 1QpHab VII.
[16] 4Q171.5.
[17] There can be no proof, of course, but then there is very little in biblical study that can be proved.

> The 'Rock' [invisible God],[18] his work is perfect, *tāmîm*,
> For all his ways are justice, *mišpāṭ*,
> A God of faithfulness and without iniquity,
> The Just One, *ṣaddîq*, and Upright, *yāšār*, is he [or 'is the LORD']
>                                         (Deut. 32.3-4, my translation)

The next line is not easy to read. The LXX has 'They have sinned, they are disgraced and not his children, they are a crooked and perverted generation.' Various emendations are proposed for the Hebrew, to give:

> They have dealt corruptly with him,
> They are not his sons because of their defects,
> They are a twisted and crooked generation.
> Is this how you repay the LORD,
> You foolish/sacrilegious/withering* people who are not wise?
>                                         (Deut. 32.5-6a, my translation)

*The word *nābhāl* can mean any of these.

Irrespective of the original text and context of these lines, their gist is clear, and one can imagine how they would have been interpreted by the Qumran community and by the Christians.

The next section of Deuteronomy 32 also exists in various forms: the Qumran text[19] and the LXX both say that God Most High divided the nations of the world according to the number of the sons of God/angels of God, whereas the post-Christian Hebrew has 'according to the number of the sons of Israel': 'The LORD's portion is his people, Jacob his allotted heritage' (Deut. 32.9). The vital information missing from the later Hebrew text is that the LORD was one of the sons of God Most High, the one to whom Israel was allocated. This is how the Christians understood the relationship between God Most High and the LORD, and this distinction is essential for understanding the New Testament and especially John's Gospel, where Jesus the LORD claims those allocated to him by his Father (17.6).

Because his people had rejected him, the LORD turned his face/presence away from them (Deut. 32.19-22). Historically, this was the period from the mid-eighth century BCE, when the LORD turned from his faithless

---

[18] The word *ṣûr*, often translated 'Rock', was not understood that way by the LXX or by the writer of the Qumran *Songs of the Sabbath Sacrifice*. Both understood it to mean the invisible heavenly 'form'. See my book *The Great High Priest. The Temple Roots of Christian Liturgy*, London: T&T Clark, 2003, pp. 183-4.

[19] 4QDeut[j].

## John 17

people as they fell away and lost their spiritual sight.[20] The Qumran community called it 'the age of wrath', when the LORD hid his face from Israel and from his sanctuary and 'delivered them up to the sword'.[21] These themes are found in Isaiah 6 and in the Enochic *Apocalypse of Weeks*:[22] the rejection of Wisdom that led to loss of perception and so to disaster:

> They are a people, *gôy*, destroyed in respect of wise counsels
> And there is no discernment among them.
> They are *not* wise and do *not* know these things,
> They do not discern what their end will be.
> (Deut. 32.28–29, my translation)

Yet again, the Hebrew text shows signs of having been changed: what the LXX and the Samaritan text read as 'not', *lo'*, the later Hebrew has as *lû*, 'would that': 'Would that they were wise and knew ...' rather than 'They are *not* wise and do *not* know these things.'

Next there are the lines about the poisonous vine, some of which survive in that Qumran phylactery text:[23]

> Their vine comes from the vine of Sodom,
> And from the fields of Gomorrah;
> Their grapes are grapes of poison,
> Their clusters are bitter;
> Their wine is the poison of serpents,
> And the cruel venom of asps.
> (Deut. 32.32–33)

Jesus spoke of being the true/honest vine, and the community of the *Damascus Document* identified their enemies as those who walked in the ways of the wicked, whose 'wine is the poison of serpents, and the cruel venom of asps'.[24]

The final part of the poem (or perhaps, of the first half of the poem) describes the LORD bringing judgement:

> For *I lift up my hand to heaven*
> And say, '*As I live for ever,*
> If I whet the lightning of my sword,
> And my hand takes hold on judgement,

---

[20] *1 Enoch* 89.54–56.
[21] *Damascus Document*, CD I.
[22] *1 Enoch* 93.8.
[23] 4QphylN.
[24] *Damascus Document*, CD VIII.9.

> I will take vengeance on my adversaries,
> And requite them that hate me.'
> (Deut. 32.40–41, my translation)

The words in italics appear in Revelation 10.5–6 as the words that identify the mighty angel who brought the little book from heaven and announced that the mysteries of God would soon be fulfilled. After this the original sequence of Revelation resumes: the seventh angel sounds his trumpet, and the kingdom of the-LORD-and-his-Anointed is established on earth, a direct reference to Deuteronomy 33.4–5, where the LORD becomes king, and the Anointed (not Moses) gives the law.

The *Song of Moses* ends with the proof text quoted in Hebrews 1.6, but it was much reduced in the post-Christian Hebrew text, which is:

> Praise his people, you <u>nations,</u>
> For he avenges the blood of <u>his servants,</u>
> And takes vengeance on his enemies,
> And atones his soil, his people.
> (Deut. 32.43, my translation)

This is the longer (and older) Qumran Hebrew:[25]

> Heavens rejoice with him,
> \*All *'lohim* bow down to/worship him.
> Because he will avenge the blood of his sons,
> He will take vengeance on his adversaries,
> He will repay all those who hate him,
> And will purify [atone, *kipper*] the land/soil of his people.

\*The same words appear in Psalm 97.7, which celebrates the LORD becoming king, destroying his enemies and dawning for the righteous.

And this is the LXX; the words in italics do not appear in the Hebrew texts.

> Heavens, rejoice with him,
> And let all the sons of God worship him,
> *Nations, rejoice with his people,*
> *All you angels of God, confirm/strengthen him,*
> For he will avenge the blood of his sons
> And take vengeance on his enemies and repay them,
> And he will repay those who hate him,
> And the LORD will cleanse the land of his people.

---

[25] 4QDeut<sup>q</sup>.

## John 17

The quotation in Hebrews does not follow any of these precisely. It has 'Let all the angels of God worship him' for the LXX 'Let all the sons of God worship him' or the Qumran text 'Let all the *ᵉlohîm* worship him', but the gist is the same. It is the heavenly beings – angels of God, sons of God or *ᵉlohîm* – who are missing from the later Hebrew text.

The first Christians believed that the LORD would come in judgement in the near future, within their own lifetime (e.g. 1 Cor. 15.51–52). The Book of Revelation recorded visions of what they believed would soon take place (Rev. 1.1). The revelation to John in Revelation 10 was that some of the visions had already been fulfilled in the life of Jesus. The Firstborn had already come into the world, the disciples had already beheld his glory giving grace and peace, the royal high priest had already come to his people and had already brought the judgement on those who hated him and shed the blood of his sons, he had already brought resurrection and life, and he had already made the great atonement for the land of his people. This is why John is the only Gospel writer who describes Jesus pouring out his own blood as he died (19.34), the act of the high priest making atonement.[26]

The last words of Jesus, then, have much in common with the last words of Moses and with the high-priestly blessing. The third text that underlies John 17 is the Shemaʻ: 'Hear, Israel, the LORD our *ᵉlohîm*, the LORD is *'eḥādh*' (Deut. 6.4), where *ᵉlohîm* is plural, though by convention translated as a singular, 'God', and *'eḥādh* is a word with many meanings. It can be be simply 'one', as in 'Have you only one blessing …?' (Gen. 27.38); or it can imply the union of several parts, as when the curtains for the tabernacle were joined with clasps 'that the tabernacle may be one' (Exod. 26.6); or when the man and woman were joined together 'as one flesh' (Gen. 2.24); or 'Let all the waters be gathered into one place' (Gen. 1.9). The plural form *ᵉlohîm* does imply the latter meaning for *'eḥādh*: 'The LORD our *ᵉlohîm*, the LORD is a Unity.' This would explain why Josephus described the LORD as three angels when he told the story of Abraham at Mamre.[27] It would also explain the controversy over the meaning of *dābhaq*, 'cleave to', in the early second century CE, where the teaching of Jesus may have been a catalyst for the (renewed) interest. R. Akiba taught that *dābhaq* meant literally cleaving, that is, being literally joined to the LORD, whereas R. Ishmael taught that it meant performing pious deeds.[28]

---

[26] But see below, p. 557, on 19.34 and this appearing in early texts of Matthew.
[27] See above, pp. 462–3.
[28] See above, p. 438. Babylonian Talmud *Sanhedrin* 64a.

This could also be the source of Theodotus' teaching about angels and unity, which was preserved by Clement of Alexandria. Theodotus himself was a follower of Valentinus, who was born in Egypt and educated in Alexandria and who then became a brilliant Christian teacher in Rome in the mid-second century CE. His ideas were later condemned as Gnosticism, but in mid-second-century Rome they must have been acceptable because Valentinus had hopes of being chosen as bishop. This is what Theodotus wrote:

> Now they say that our angels were put forth in unity, and are one, in that they came out from One. Now since we existed in separation, Jesus was baptized that the undivided should be divided until he should unite us with them in the Pleroma [fullness], that we the many, having become one, might all be mingled into the One which was divided for our sakes.[29]

He also described Jesus as the Face (that is Presence) of the Father, thus fulfilling the high-priestly blessing,[30] and, as we have seen, he knew that Jesus himself was the Paraclete.

Other 'Gnostic' texts found in Egypt preserved memories of this Unity: 'The Saviour was a bodily image of the Unitary One.'[31] The Unitary One, the divine being, united the many into himself, as had been said to the Colossians:

> He is the image of the invisible God, the Firstborn of all creation; for in him all things were created, in heaven and on earth, visible and invisible, whether thrones or dominions or principalities or authorities – all things were created through him and for him. He is before all things, and in him all things hold together ...
>
> For in him all the fullness of God was pleased to dwell, and through him to reconcile to himself all things, whether on earth or in heaven, making peace by the blood of his cross.
>
> (Col. 1.15–17, 19–20, my translation; cf. John 1.3)

Since these lines are widely thought to be a quotation from an early hymn, the role of the Second Person as the Unitary One must have been part of the original teaching or even of the teaching whence Christianity grew. To identify the ideas in Colossians as evidence of an early heresy assumes that the earliest Christian teaching, and indeed the teaching of Jesus himself, *cannot* have included 'Gnostic' elements. The same certainty

---

[29] Clement of Alexandria, *Excerpts from Theodotus* 36, in R. P. Casey, *The Excerpta ex Theodoto of Clement of Alexandria*, London: Christophers, 1934.
[30] Clement of Alexandria, *Excerpts* 12.
[31] *Tripartite Tractate*, CG I.5.116.

about the nature of Jesus' authentic teaching also identifies a tendency towards Gnosticism in John's Gospel, even though the words of Jesus' prayer after the last supper show that this 'Gnosticism' was firmly rooted in temple discourse.

Quispel's question, posed many years ago, remains: 'It seems to me that the real issue is this: most Gnostics were against the Jewish God who created the world and gave the Law. Is it possible that this doctrine is of Jewish origin?'[32] The answer to his question lies in the distinction we are making between the teaching of the first temple and the teaching of the second: the former was the basis for the teaching of Jesus and the latter for the teaching of those who were called Jews. The most likely roots of Gnosticism lie in the rejection of the new understanding of Yahweh that followed the great changes at the end of the first-Temple period; those who rejected 'the Jewish God who created the world and gave the Law' would have been the old believers who preserved the world of God Most High and his Sons, the Firstborn of whom was the LORD, and of the Lady Wisdom who gave her children sight.

Significant among the 'Gnostic' texts found in Egypt is *Eugnostos the Blessed One* – the teaching for 'those who are his'; and a parallel Christian version, the *Wisdom of Jesus* – the teaching for the disciples assembled on a mountain in Galilee after Jesus' resurrection. The latter is an expansion of *Eugnostos*, as can be seen from the final words of *Eugnostos*:

> Now all these things that I have just said to you [sing.] I have said in the way that you can accept, until the one who does not need to be taught is revealed among you, and he will say all these things to you joyously and in pure knowledge.[33]

The twin texts explain the nature of the unity and plurality of the heavenly world, and so their subject matter corresponds to that of Jesus' prayer after the last supper. The additional material in the *Wisdom of Jesus* includes interjections from Thomas, Mariamne, Matthew and Bartholomew, and may be in conscious imitation of the Passover discourse, but the redaction was made by someone who did not know Palestine, since the Mount of Olives was said to be in Galilee.

*Eugnostos* says that the supreme divine being was the Father of the Universe, also called the First Father, and that the Father of the Universe had a multitude of Sons who were at rest in his ineffable joy and

---

[32] G. Quispel, 'The Origin of the Gnostic Demiurge', *Gnostic Studies I*, Istanbul: Nederlands Historisch-Archaeologisch Instituut in het Nabije Oosten, 1974, p. 213.
[33] *Eugnostos*, CG III.3.90.

## Temple Theology in John's Gospel

unchanging glory. The text is complex, and it is not always clear which titles belong to which characters.[34] The First Father had no name or human form and was unknowable. All the heavenly powers ('aeons') came from him and were embraced in him, and the process of creation was described as 'appearing' from the hidden. Thus the visible world could be a means of knowing the invisible: 'the belief in those things that are not revealed was found in what is revealed'.[35] The 'form' of the First Father was revealed as a great male–female power, brother and sister: he was the 'begotten' (and named in the Christian version as Christ) and she was the 'Sophia, the begetter'. The male–female power had a male–female child, the Son of Man, who in turn had a male–female child, the Saviour. The kingdom of the Son of Man was full of light and joy, and the Christian version adds that Jesus came to reveal this. The heavenly world was a hierarchy of gods, Lords, archangels and angels, each of whom was included within the Unity in the same way as units of time were all within time itself. This is a reconstruction of a broken part of *Eugnostos*:

- Our Aeon came to be as the type of Immortal Man.
- Time came to be as the type of First Begetter his son.
- The year came to be as the type of Saviour.
- The 12 months came to be as the type of the 12 powers.
- The 360 days of the year[36] came to be as the 360 powers who appeared from Saviour.
- Their hours and moments came to be as the type of angels who came from them, who are without number.[37]

Comparing aeons to units of time was appropriate, since 'aeon' means 'eternity' and was used to translate the Hebrew *'ōlām*, which means 'eternal' or 'hidden'. The aeons were the unseen forces of the eternal state, and the later Gnostic systems set out complex hierarchies to explain how these invisible divine processes related to each other and were all derived from the One and remained part of it. Basilides, an older contemporary of Valentinus in Alexandria, explained these forces in terms of 'sonship', *huiotes*, thus revealing their origin. They were the cultural descendants of the ancient sons of God, as Irenaeus recognized when he related them to

---

[34] Compare D. M. Parrott's very different translations in *The Nag Hammadi Library*, ed. J. M. Robinson, San Francisco: Harper and Row, 1977, and in the same volume revised and published by HarperCollins, 1990.
[35] *Eugnostos*, CG III.3.74.
[36] Since Egypt reckoned the year as 360 days, this probably indicates an Egyptian writer.
[37] *Eugnostos* III.3.83.

## John 17

the 'angels of God', who are found in the Lxx of Deuteronomy 32.8 but have disappeared from the Hebrew text:

> Those angels who occupy the lowest heaven, namely that which is visible to us, formed all the things which are in the world, and made allocations among themselves of the earth and of those nations which are upon it. The chief of them is he who is thought to be the God of the Jews; and inasmuch as he desired to render the other nations subject to his own people, that is, the Jews, all the other angel princes resisted and opposed him. Wherefore all other nations were at enmity with his nation. But the Father without birth and without name, perceiving that they would be destroyed, sent his own first-begotten Nous (he it is who is called Christ) to bestow deliverance on those who believe in him, from the power of those who made the world.[38]

The Christian conclusion of the *Wisdom of Jesus*, which has no counterpart in *Eugnostos*, has Jesus showing his disciples how he has revealed all these things to them. The disciples are children of Sophia, the Mother of the Universe, the consort, brought into existence without her male – in other words, they were children of a virgin birth. Jesus said: 'Behold, I have revealed to you the Name of the Perfect One, the whole will of the Mother of the holy angels, so that the masculine may be completed here...'[39] Other Christian texts expressed this differently: Luke knew of the children of Wisdom (Luke 7.35), and John of the children of the Woman who had fled to the wilderness (Rev. 12.14, 17).

This complex and enigmatic text should be read in the light of Paul's description: 'Christ the Power of God and the Wisdom of God' (1 Cor. 1.24), which shows that in Christ both a male and a female divine being were incarnate, and in the light of statements such as:

> For he has made known to us in all wisdom and insight the mystery of his will, according to his purpose which he set forth in Christ, as a plan for the fullness of time, to unite all things in him, things in heaven and things on earth. (Eph. 1.9–10)

Elements identified as (and therefore dismissed as) 'Gnostic' were part of the earliest Christian teaching, and so there is no reason why the system set out in *Eugnostos* could not have been at the very least close to what Jesus was teaching. Why else would a 'Christian' version have been produced, showing how Jesus fitted into this system? There is nothing polemical in either text, and neither includes the more colourful elements

---

[38] Irenaeus, *Against Heresies* I.24.4.
[39] *Wisdom of Jesus*, CG III.4.118.

of later Gnostic material. Speculation about the origin of the texts is just that: speculation. To say that they were, for example, missionary texts to attract Egyptian Gnostics implies that Gnosticism had nothing to do with Hebrew temple tradition.

The texts could have come from the community in which Jesus and his teachings had their roots, among those old believers who still recognized the ancient God of Jerusalem, El Elyon, who was the begetter, *qōnēh*, of heaven and earth (Gen. 14.19, translating literally), and his Sons, the firstborn of whom was Yahweh the God of Israel. Since the title 'LORD of Hosts' literally means 'He who caused the hosts of heaven to exist', and John knew that this was how the Name was understood in the heavenly hymns (Rev. 4.8, 11), the Gnostic emanations/sonships were not alien to Hebrew tradition. The Adam figure described by *Eugnostos* was the male-female image and likeness of the Firstborn, whom the old believers knew as a figure of light who lost his glory when he was driven from the Eden temple. The Christian version would then be demonstrating that Jesus had fulfilled the expectations. The origin of *Eugnostos*' Man who was revealed in divinity and kingship and 'created from himself gods and angels and archangels, myriads without number for his retinue'[40] is clear. *Eugnostos* and the related *Wisdom of Jesus* were both explanations of the 'secret things of the LORD' which the Deuteronomists did not deny, but said were not necessary since the law was all the revelation that was needed (Deut. 29.29). The secret things concerned the unseen world of the heavenly powers, the person and work of the King who became one of them, and the mystery of his origin in the holy of holies. They explained how things came to be, and in Jesus' prayer, how he caused his disciples to be the new *ᵉlohîm* that were the LORD.

The 'Platonic' and 'Pythagorean' elements in these 'Gnostic' texts could also have come from the old temple.[41] The hierarchy of emanations is very similar to Ezekiel's careful distinction between the various elements of his throne visions: he knew that he was seeing the *mar'ēh*, appearance, of things that also had a *dᵉmûth*, an invisible form. The final stage of the process of revelation and creation was the material world. Ezekiel's vision was the realm of the LORD enthroned upon a fourfold Living One, and she encompassed the spirits of all life.[42] Ezekiel saw strange life-forms – beings with four heads, for example – just as the later Gnostic texts would

---

[40] *Eugnostos* III.3.77–78: *Wisdom of Jesus*, CG III.4.102.
[41] See my book *The Great High Priest*, n. 18 above, pp. 262–93.
[42] See my book *The Mother of the Lord*, vol. 1, London: T&T Clark, 2012, pp. 290–301.

describe monstrous beings in heaven. He was seeing what the Qumran Wisdom texts would call 'the mystery of becoming', *raz nihyeh*, the mystery of how creation emerged from the invisible and unknowable source of life and became the material world. The person in the community who sought wisdom was told: 'Son, gaze on the mystery of becoming and know the paths of everything that lives ...'[43] They believed that the states existed simultaneously and were the stages by which the creative power of the Father materialized, and this was the hierarchy of emanations that *Eugnostos* described. This is the world view presupposed by Jesus' prayer after the last supper, as he establishes the hierarchy of the new creation.

## Jesus' prayer

The prayer forms a liturgical end to the last supper, like the hymn in Mark 14.26//Matthew 26.30. There are many similarities to the opening of the Passover discourse, as noted by Brown:[44]

- the hour has come (13.1; 17.1);
- the Son of Man glorified by God, and God glorified in the Son (13.31–32; 17.1, 4–5);
- 'completion': 'He loved them to the *telos* [end or completion]' (13.1); and 'I have ended/completed the work which you gave me' (17.4);
- his own who were in the world (13.1), and the disciples who were in the world (17.11, 15);
- all things in the hands of Jesus (13.3); and all power given to Jesus (17.2);
- Judas (13.2, 27; 17.12);
- the Scripture about the betrayer fulfilled (13.18; 17.12).

Jesus' words would not have been in Greek, and so we should look for Semitisms underlying the present text; and there are echoes of the *Didache*, suggesting that the prayer after supper may have been an elaboration of something already familiar to the disciples:

- 'As this broken [bread] ... was gathered and became one, so may your assembly be brought together from the ends of the earth into your kingdom';[45] cf. 'That they may be one' (17.11, 21);

---

[43] 4Q418.43.19.
[44] R. E. Brown, *The Gospel According to John XIII—XXI*, Anchor Bible 29a, New Haven and London, Yale University Press, (1970) 2008, p. 745.
[45] *Didache* 9.

- 'From the four winds gather what you have consecrated into your kingdom which you have prepared for it';[46] cf. 'Father, I desire that they also, whom you have given me, may be with me where I am, to behold my glory which you have given in your love for me, before the foundation of the world' (John 17.24, my translation).

This is the vision of gathering into the kingdom: the four angels restraining the four winds until the faithful have been marked with the Name (Rev. 7.1-8), and the final vision of the consecrated servants, marked with the Name, standing in the presence of the Lamb who is enthroned in the light of divine glory (Rev. 22.3-5).

The prayer divides into three parts of similar length:

- verses 1–8, when Jesus prays for himself and speaks of his own role and situation;
- verses 9–19, when Jesus prays for his immediate disciples, those whom later texts would call 'the sons of his house';[47]
- verses 20–26, when Jesus prays for those who will become his followers as a result of the disciples' work.

These three correspond to the three parts of the high priest's prayer on the Day of Atonement, when he first made an offering and prayed for himself and his house (Lev. 16.11) and then an offering and prayer for all the people (Lev. 16.15). In the time of Jesus this had become a prayer for the high priest and his house, and for the children of Aaron, the LORD's holy people.[48]

## Part 1 (vv. 1–8)

Jesus prays that he may return to the glory he shared with the Father before the world was made (v. 5). This gives the setting for his words. He prays as the One who was 'in the beginning with God; all things were made through him, and without him was not anything made that was made' (1.2–3), and now he is about to return to his former state. This is the temple world-view: Jesus speaks as the man who had become the LORD with his people, the high-priest king of the first temple. He had been consecrated and sent into the world (10.36), and now he prepares to return whence he came, to the state represented by the holy of holies. As

---

[46] *Didache* 10.
[47] 'My mystery is for me and the sons of my house' is an *agraphon* found in Clement of Alexandria, *Miscellanies* 5.10 and in *Clementine Homilies* 19.20.
[48] Mishnah *Yoma* 4.2.

## John 17

the LORD, the Son of God Most High (Deut. 32.8–9), he has received those allotted to him and given them eternal life (v. 2). This was implicit in the Name he had been given at his consecration: Yahweh – 'the one who causes to be', and echoes the Prologue: 'To all who received him, who believed in his Name, he gave power to become children of God' (1.12, my translation).

Temple discourse described the process of emerging from the divine as 'birth' – fathers and sons – and the later Gnostic systems of emanation were an elaborate development of this. Using the anachronism of Christian terminology which is simpler and clearer than the Gnostic terms but in essentials the same, the First Person was the Father of the Second Person (and of the other sons of God), and the person who was the Incarnation of the Second Person was called his son. The term 'son of Yahweh' is not found in the Hebrew Scriptures, but Yahweh does say to the king: 'You are my son' (e.g. Ps. 2.7). Eusebius was aware of this when he explained that Psalm 45.7 – 'Therefore God, your God, has anointed you' – described the ritual in heaven when the Second Person was anointed and became the Christ.

> The Anointer, being the supreme God, is far above the Anointed, he being God in a different sense, and this would be clear to anyone who knew Hebrew ...
>
> Therefore in these words you have it clearly stated that God was anointed and became the Christ.
>
> And this is he who was the beloved of the Father and his offspring and the eternal priest and the being called the Sharer of the Father's throne ...[49]

We have seen that the Sharer of the throne, Metatron, was the name given to the human Enoch *after he had been transformed into an angel with the Name*, and this change was effected by anointing the man Enoch in the holy of holies.[50] Thus it was the Second Person who became incarnate in Jesus, since Incarnation was the reciprocal of *theōsis*. Jesus was the Son of the Second Person, while the One incarnate in him was also the Son of the First Person. There is ambiguity in temple discourse as to whether 'Father' refers to the First Person or the Second Person, since each was Father to the rank below, but the heavenly state was undivided, and so this distinction has to be used only for the sake of describing the process with the language that we have.

---

[49] Eusebius, *Proof of the Gospel* IV.15.
[50] See above, p. 75.

'Giving the Name' was the ritual of birth/anointing that transformed the human being into the Second Person. It took place in the holy of holies, which represented Day One, and so was outside time and in the state before the material world was created. *1 Enoch* gives more detail of what the ritual represented: the second parable,[51] as we have seen, was the setting for Jesus' prophecy of the work of the Paraclete concerning sin, righteousness and judgement. The same parable says that the Son of Man was given the Name in a place where fountains of wisdom and righteousness flow for the thirsty (cf. Rev. 22.1, 17),[52] and that the Name was given 'before the sun and the heavenly signs were created, before the stars of heaven were made'.[53] In other words, it was given in the holy of holies before the material world was created. Then the wisdom of the LORD of Spirits revealed the identity of the Anointed One to the holy and righteous ones, just as Jesus says in his prayer: 'I have revealed/manifested your Name to the men whom you gave me out of the world' (v. 6, my translation). So too in John's Prologue: recognizing that Jesus bore the Name enabled other people to be transformed into heavenly beings, by receiving eternal life as children of God. In his vision, Enoch saw that those who did not recognize the LORD-of-Spirits-and-his-Anointed-One would be punished, which is also implied in John's Prologue: 'his own' did not receive him, and the darkness did not comprehend him (1.5, 11). In Revelation 7, receiving the Name was protection from the imminent judgement.

The Name meant the identity, the actual Presence. It was what the Targums called the *memra*,[54] and some early texts have preserved illustrations of what this meant. In the *Gospel of Philip*,[55] attributed to a disciple prominent in John's Gospel, there is this:

> One single Name is not uttered in the world, the Name which the Father gave to the Son, the Name above all things: the Name of the Father. For the Son would not become Father unless he wears the Name of the Father. Those who have this Name know it, but they do not speak it. But those who do not have it do not know it.[56]

---

[51] *1 Enoch* 45—57.
[52] *1 Enoch* 48.1–2.
[53] *1 Enoch* 48.3.
[54] See above, p. 101.
[55] The gospels found at Nag Hammadi are not necessarily Gnostic. Everything that does not precisely resemble the synoptic Gospels is not necessarily a late or Gnostic text.
[56] *Gospel of Philip*, CG II.3.53.

## John 17

The Name here must be the *'ehyeh*, the form that indicated the Presence, whereas 'Yahweh' was the form by which the LORD was invoked, and therefore, by definition, the form used when he was not present. In the *Gospel of Thomas*, another disciple prominent in John's Gospel, there is an enigmatic text about the Name. The synoptic Gospels describe Peter's recognition of who Jesus was (Mark 8.27–29//Matt. 16.13–20//Luke 9.18–21), but the *Gospel of Thomas*, reporting what must have been the same event, says that Jesus asked his disciples to describe him:

> Simon Peter said to him, 'You are like a righteous angel.'
> Matthew said to him, 'You are like a wise philosopher.'
> Thomas said to him, 'Master, my mouth is wholly incapable of saying whom you are like ...'
> And [Jesus] took him and withdrew and told him three things. When Thomas returned to his companions, they asked him, 'What did Jesus say to you?' Thomas said to them, 'If I tell you one of the things which he told me, you will pick up stones and throw them at me ...'[57]

Telling Thomas three things suggests that this has been translated from a Hebrew original, in which *dābhār* can mean 'thing' or 'word'. Jesus revealed his identity to Thomas as three words, which would have been Jesus claiming the three-word form of the Name that was revealed to Moses: *'ehyeh ªšer 'ehyeh* (Exod. 3.14), the form that revealed the Presence and was called the *memra*. To repeat just one of these words, *'ehyeh*, would have been a blasphemy, and so Thomas said that the disciples would stone him.

The fullest and earliest evidence for the meaning of the Name is found in the *Gospel of Truth*,[58] usually attributed to Valentinus. This work has no reference to the elaborate Gnostic myth as known in later texts, and is in fact a mid-second-century Christian mystical text that often alludes to the writings of John. As such, it is a uniquely valuable witness as to how the Name was understood. Further, its opening words are very similar to John's definition of eternal life – 'Eternal life [is] that they know thee the only true God, and Jesus Christ whom thou hast sent' (v. 3).[59] The opening words of the *Gospel of Truth* are: 'The gospel of truth is a joy for those who have received from the Father of truth the gift of knowing him, through the power of the Word that came forth from the

---

[57] *Gospel of Thomas* 34, 35.
[58] When found at Nag Hammadi, this text had no title, but it begins with 'The gospel of truth is a joy ...' and this was adopted as its title.
[59] Some have thought this verse to be an explanatory insertion added by a later writer.

## Temple Theology in John's Gospel

fullness ...'[60] Both these are similar to the thanksgiving over the bread in the *Didache*: 'We give thanks to thee our Father, for the life and knowledge made known to us through thy servant Jesus'; and to the post-Communion thanksgiving: 'We give thanks to thee, holy Father, for thy sacred Name which thou hast caused to dwell in our hearts, and for the knowledge and faith and immortality which thou hast revealed to us through thy servant Jesus.'[61]

The envoy in the *Gospel of Truth* was called the Saviour, because he saved those who had lost knowledge of the Father, a state which had brought them anguish and fear. Error (which here must mean second-temple Judaism) prevailed in the place of knowledge, and 'out of oblivion he enlightened them, he showed a way, and the way is truth which he taught them'.[62] Error persecuted the envoy, and he was nailed to a tree, thus becoming the fruit that did not destroy when it was eaten. Those who did eat became glad in their discovery:

> For he discovered them in himself, and they discovered him in themselves, the incomprehensible, inconceivable one, the Father, the Perfect One, the one who made the all, while the all is within him and the all has need of him, since he retained their perfection within himself which he did not give to the all ...[63]

Jesus went to those who considered themselves wise and they tested him, but he confounded them because they were foolish and so they hated him.

> After all these, there came the little children also, those to whom the knowledge of the Father belongs. *Having been strengthened, they learned about the manifestations of the Father.** They knew; they were known. They were glorified; they glorified.[64]

*This is the translation by G. W. Macrae; R. Grant, however, translated the words in italics as: 'When they became strong, they were taught aspects of the Father's face.' The similarities to John's Gospel are clear, for example Philip's request: 'Lord, show us the Father ...' (14.8).[65]

The complex exposition in the *Gospel of Truth* describes the state of second-temple Judaism as those who had lost knowledge of the Father

---

[60] *Gospel of Truth*, CG I.3.16.
[61] *Didache* 9, 10.
[62] *Gospel of Truth* 18.
[63] *Gospel of Truth* 19.
[64] *Gospel of Truth* 19.
[65] G. W. Macrae in *The Nag Hammadi Library*, ed. J. M. Robinson, New York: Harper and Row, 1977; R. M. Grant in *Gnosticism*, New York: Harper and Bros, 1961.

## John 17

(God Most High) and of the heavenly powers. The lost teaching that Jesus restored was 'the living book of the living', and this was the sealed book that Jesus was able to open because of his death: 'For this reason the merciful one, the faithful one, Jesus, was patient in accepting sufferings until he took the book, since he knows that his death is life for many.'[66] The Son revealed the lost Father, and in so doing he abolished the material world, because he restored both knowledge of and access to the heavenly realm. Hebrews called this the Sabbath rest at the end of the journey through the wilderness (a Passover theme), to which our high priest has opened the way (Heb. 4.14–16). The purpose of receiving knowledge is to know about the hidden Father, 'from whom the beginning came forth, to whom all will return who have come forth from him. And they have appeared for the glory and joy of his Name.'[67] Hence the words of Philip: 'LORD, show us the Father and we shall be satisfied' (14.8), alluding to Isaiah's fourth Servant song:

> Although you make his soul an offering for sin, and he will see his offspring, and he will prolong his days, and the will of the LORD will triumph in his hand. Out of his suffering his soul will see light and find satisfaction. And through his knowledge his servant, the righteous one, will make many righteous and he will bear their iniquities.   (Isa. 53.10–11, as in 1QIsa$^a$)

Here, the *Gospel of Truth* shows most clearly the temple myth whence it emerged. When Adam ate from the forbidden tree, he was driven from Eden and began to live in the world of dust and death. This is the state that the *Gospel of Truth* calls 'the deficiency':

> For the place where there is envy and strife is a deficiency, but the place of Unity is perfection. Since the deficiency came into being because the Father was not known, therefore when the Father is known, from that moment on the deficiency will no longer exist. As with the ignorance of a person, when he comes to have knowledge, his ignorance vanishes of itself, as the darkness vanishes when light appears, so also the deficiency vanishes in the perfection.[68]

In the Book of Revelation, the risen LORD promises to his faithful follower that he will return to paradise and eat again from the tree of life (Rev. 2.7); and when the Lamb has been sacrificed he is deemed worthy to open the

---

[66] *Gospel of Truth* 20.
[67] *Gospel of Truth* 38.
[68] *Gospel of Truth* 24–25.

sealed book (Rev. 5.1–7). Christ anointed those who wanted to return with the oil that was the mercy of the Father.[69]

The *Gospel of Truth* then explains the Name and thus illuminates Jesus' words: 'I have manifested thy Name to the men whom thou gavest me out of the world …' (17.6). The Name is the Presence, the *'ehyeh*, as can be seen by reading Name/Presence in this section of the *Gospel of Truth*:

> Now the Name/Presence of the Father is the Son. It is the [Father] who first gave a Name/Presence to the one who came forth from him, who was himself, and he begot him as a Son …
>
> His is the Name/Presence; his is the Son. It is possible for him to be seen, but the Name/Presence is invisible because it alone is the mystery of the invisible, which comes to ears that are completely filled with it … For indeed the Father's Name/Presence is not spoken, but is apparent through a Son.[70]

Jesus says that he manifested the Name/Presence to those who were chosen (v. 6); cf. 'No one has ever seen God; the only Son, who is in the bosom of the Father, he has made him known' (1.18); and, to the Jews after the healing at Bethesda, 'I have come in my Father's Name/as my Father's Presence, and you do not receive me' (5.43, my translation). Manifesting the Name is another Passover theme, since the LORD revealed his *'ehyeh ªšer 'ehyeh* Name to Moses before he led the people out of Egypt (Exod. 3.14); and the *Song of Moses* opens with 'I will proclaim the Name of the LORD' (Deut. 32.3). Jesus has caused the Name to be visible/known, *phaneroun*, to those who were allotted to him (17.6). This was the work he was sent to do (v. 4); cf. 5.36: 'the works which the Father has granted me to accomplish, these very works which I am doing, bear me witness that the Father has sent me'.

## Part 2 (vv. 9–19)

Jesus then prays for those whom the Father has allocated to him (v. 9). Like the Melchi-Zedek of the Qumran *Melchizedek* text, certain people are his *naḥªlâ*, inheritance, and his *gôrāl*, lot,[71] and to them he has shown the glory (v. 4; cf. the Melchi-Zedek miracle at Cana, 2.11, where Jesus showed his glory[72]); he has revealed the Name/Presence (v. 6); and he has given them the words of heavenly teaching (v. 8). This too resembles

---

[69] *Gospel of Truth* 36, with echoes of *Life of Adam and Eve* 32—39, where Seth returns to the gate of paradise to try to obtain some of the oil of mercy for his dying father Adam.
[70] *Gospel of Truth* 38.
[71] *Melchizedek*, 11QMelch.
[72] See above, pp. 188–91.

## John 17

Melchi-Zedek: a broken part of the Qumran text could be read: 'whose teachers have been hidden and kept secret ...'. Melchi-Zedek would bring judgement on Belial and his hosts, quoting Psalm 82.2; he would be the one announced to Zion as God and King (Isa. 52.7); and he would make atonement for all the sons of light who were his own 'lot'.[73] Since the public ministry of Jesus coincided with the date when Melchi-Zedek was expected to return,[74] and Hebrews presented Jesus as Melchi-Zedek, these Melchi-Zedek themes must be borne in mind.

Jesus does not pray for the world, *kosmos*, which in John's way of speaking represents the darkness that rejected the incarnate Logos. The Logos had made the *kosmos*, he came into the *kosmos*, and yet it did not know him (1.10); God so loved the *kosmos* that he gave his only begotten Son so that those who believed in him would not perish (along with the rest of the *kosmos*) but have everlasting life (3.16); the Son came to save the *kosmos*, but unbelievers condemned themselves (3.17–18); and so the work of Jesus and his followers was a battle against the *kosmos* that was under the power of the Evil One (1 John 5.19). Faith in Jesus – that he is the Son of God – overcomes the *kosmos* (1 John 5.4–5). By the work of the Paraclete, the *kosmos* would continue to be proved wrong in its rejection of Jesus (16.7–11).

Jesus already knew that the moment had come for the ruler (*archōn* – a word used by the Gnostics to describe the invisible powers) of this *kosmos* to be cast out when he himself was lifted up from the earth to draw all people to himself (12.31). This is the vision in Revelation 12, where the Son of the Woman clothed with the sun is threatened by the great red dragon at the moment of his birth, but he is snatched away and taken up to the throne in heaven. The dragon and his angels are cast to earth where they continue their attacks on the Woman's other children (Rev. 12.1–6, 17). Thus Jesus knew that the ruler, *archōn*, of this *kosmos* (the dragon) was coming to attack him, but that he had no real power (14.30) because he had already been judged (16.11). He knew that he was returning to the Father, as in the vision of the Woman's child being taken up to the throne, and that the red dragon would continue his war against the other children of the Woman, namely his disciples who would keep the commandments of God and the testimony, *marturia*, of Jesus (Rev.

---

[73] The readings as proposed in *Qumran Cave 11. Discoveries in the Judaean Desert* XXIII, ed. F. Garcia-Martinez, Oxford: Oxford University Press, 1998, p. 229. There are other suggested reconstructions of the damaged or missing pieces of the text which would add to the picture of Melchi-Zedek, but they cannot be used as certain evidence and so are not used here.

[74] See my book *The Great High Priest*, n. 18 above, pp. 34–41.

12.17). There are many allusions in Revelation to the sufferings of the early Christian community: the blood of the martyrs under the altar (Rev. 6.9–11); the great harlot – the evil counterpart of the Lady – who was drunk with the blood of the saints and those who had borne witness to Jesus (Rev. 17.6); the rejoicing of the multitude in heaven as the prophecy of Deuteronomy 32.43 was fulfilled, the blood of the LORD's servants was avenged, and Jerusalem was burned (Rev. 19.2). The original conflict was between Jesus and the Jews, and the vivid images of conflict with the ruler of this *kosmos* describe the struggle of the early Christians against the Jewish authorities of the time, those who had lost knowledge of the Father and of the Firstborn incarnate in the Davidic king.

The ruler of this *kosmos* is the Evil One (v. 15), and Jesus prays that his disciples will be kept safe from him. So too in the LORD's Prayer: 'Do not bring us to temptation [by the Evil One], but deliver us from the Evil One' (Matt. 6.12, translating literally; also *Didache* 8); in the assurance: 'The LORD is faithful; he will strengthen you and guard you from the Evil One' (2 Thess. 3.3, my translation); and in the confidence: 'Young men, you are strong, and the Logos of God remains in you, and you have conquered the Evil One' (1 John 2.14, my translation). All the letters to the seven churches, which John had received in visions from the risen LORD, end with promises to those who conquer, presumably conquer the Evil One (Rev. 2.7, 11, 17, 26; 3.5, 12, 21). This was the conflict depicted in the Qumran texts, between the Prince of Light and his sons of light, and the Angel of Evil and his sons of darkness. The evil angel was also Melchi-Resha' (King of Evil), the counterpart of Melchi-Zedek,[75] and the logic of the system leads us to suppose that since Melchi-Zedek the great high priest had a human counterpart, so too Melchi-Resha' had a human counterpart in the person of the Wicked Priest(s), another character in the Qumran texts.

Only one of Jesus' disciples has been lost, 'the son of perdition/destruction', *apōleia*. 'Son of' is a Semitism, and so the original description of Judas was probably *ben šaḥath*, literally 'son of the Pit', or 'son of destruction'. This would have been wordplay on its opposite, *ben šaḥar*, 'son of Dawn', a title found in the *Damascus Document*.[76] Jesus had the title 'the Bright Morning Star' (Rev. 22.16), presumably the Greek version of this title, which Jesus also promised to his follower who conquered (Rev. 2.28, where 'give' is a Hebraism meaning 'appoint as'). The 'son of

---

[75] See above, p. 8.
[76] *Damascus Document*, CD XIII.14.

## John 17

perdition/destruction' also appears in 2 Thessalonians as the 'man of lawlessness' who would appear before the *parousia* (2 Thess. 2.1–4). This was part of the early Church's expectation. The coming of the lawless one(s) would be the activity of Satan, accompanied by signs and wonders, for the deception of those destined to perish because they did not believe. On his return, the LORD Jesus would destroy the son of perdition (2 Thess. 2.9–12). This is a relatively early text, when the *parousia* was expected to happen in the near future. The language suggests that the man of lawlessness was akin to the beast from the land in Revelation, who was also described as an agent of Satan the deceiver, working great signs to deceive the people of the land (Rev. 13.11–19), a false prophet who would be destroyed by the Logos and his host when they rode out from heaven (Rev. 19.19–20). Luke depicts Judas as an agent of Satan (Luke 22.3–6), working with the chief priests whom the Qumran texts depicted as the embodiment of evil (Melchi-Resha'/the Wicked Priest), and there are two accounts of how Judas died shortly after betraying Jesus (Matt. 27.3–10; Acts 1.18–20). Since John shows throughout his Gospel how future expectations had already been fulfilled in the life of Jesus, here too he says that the son of perdition has already appeared in the person of Judas, and that he died when the LORD returned, meaning when the LORD returned at Easter. No date is given for Judas' death, but his place in the Twelve had been filled before Pentecost (Acts 1.15–26).

The loss of Judas was to fulfil the Scripture (v. 12), and the question is: what Scripture did John have in mind? Matthew cites Zechariah 11.12–13, where the Hebrew is: 'So they weighed out for my price 30 pieces of silver ... And I took the 30 pieces of silver and cast them to the potter in the house of the LORD.'[77] This would explain why the money was used to buy the potter's field (Matt. 27.7). Acts, however, cites the first lines of two passages from the Psalms:

> *May their camp be a desolation,*
> *Let no one dwell in their tents.*
> For they persecute him whom you have smitten,
> And they add to the pain of those you have wounded.
> Add iniquity to their iniquity,
> And do not let them come into your righteousness.
> Let them be blotted from the book of the living
> And not be inscribed with the righteous ones.
> (Ps. 69.25–28, translating literally)

---

[77] Several translations emend 'potter' to 'treasury', a similar word.

And then there is an appeal for judgement on one who has spoken lies and hatred:

> May his days be few,
> May another seize his goods [or his position],
> May his children be fatherless,
> And his wife a widow.     (Ps. 109.8–9)

There is another possibility for the fulfilled Scripture: that Jesus was alluding to the opening chapter of Isaiah, which prophesies the redemption of Zion and the destruction of sinners.

> Zion shall be redeemed by justice, *mišpāṭ*,
> And her penitent ones by righteousness, *ṣ<sup>e</sup>dhāqâ*.
> But rebels and sinners shall be destroyed together,
> And those who forsake the LORD shall be consumed ...
> And *the strong one* shall become like tow, and his work like a spark,
> And both of them shall burn together, with none to quench them.
>     (Isa. 1.27, 28, 31, my translation)

The Strong One was Azazel, whose name means 'Strong God', the leader of the rebel angels, who was destined for destruction by fire. In Revelation 12 the leader of the rebel angels is called Satan. Judas was his agent, the one who forsook the LORD.

Jesus prays that his disciples will be protected and held in unity by the Name:

> Holy Father,[78] keep them in thy Name, which thou hast given me, that they may be one, even as we are one. While I was with them, I kept them in thy Name, which thou hast given me; I have guarded them, and none of them is lost but the son of perdition ...
>     (vv. 11–12, my translation)

First, there is the question of the underlying Hebrew: 'in thy Name' translates *b<sup>e</sup>šimkā*, which can also mean 'by thy Name', as in 'Save me, O God, *by thy Name* ... (Ps. 54.1); or 'with the Name' as in 'Blessed is he who comes in/*with the Name* of the LORD' (Ps. 118.26, my translation). In a context of protection, the meaning would be 'Keep them safe by thy Name', evoking the vision of Revelation 7 where the angel from the dawn marked the faithful to protect them from the imminent judgement. The Name had always been worn as a protection: Ezekiel saw the angel scribe put a sign on the foreheads of the faithful, to protect them from the

---

[78] Also used as a form of address in *Didache* 10.

## John 17

imminent destruction of Jerusalem. It was, translating literally, the letter *tau*, which in Ezekiel's time was written 'X'. This had been the mark put on the forehead of the high priest when he was anointed,[79] and when he bore the Name, it protected him in his dangerous duty of dealing with evil: 'The LORD will not keep him pure from iniquity if he wears his Name lightly' (Exod. 20.7, translating literally).

Texts from the late second-temple period and from the early Christian era still knew that the Name was worn as a protection from evil:

> For God's mark is on the righteous for salvation.[80]

> [Aaron] conquered the wrath ... by ... thy majesty on the diadem upon his head ... (Wisd. 18.22, 24)[81]

> The humble of the flock are those who watch for him ... They shall be saved at the time of the visitation ... as it came to pass in the time of the former visitation, concerning which God said by the hand of Ezekiel: 'They shall put a mark on the foreheads of those who sigh and groan ...'[82]

> The LORD sealed upon the face of Cain the mark of the great and honourable Name, that anyone who might find him should not kill him when he saw it upon him.[83]

> Everyone who is baptized in his Name shall be kept unhurt from the destruction of war which impends over the unbelieving nation and the place itself; but those who do not believe shall be made exiles from their place and kingdom ...[84]

This must have been the original meaning of 'While I was with them, I kept them *by* thy Name, which thou hast given me; I have guarded them ...', and John must have known Jesus as the angel from the dawn who brought protection for his own people.

Jesus was the face/presence of the LORD who shone on his people, fulfilling the high-priestly blessing and putting the Name of the LORD upon them: he had kept them safe and he had illuminated their minds with his teaching – 'I have given them thy word' (v. 14). Thus too the *Didache*:

---

[79] Babylonian Talmud *Horayoth* 12a.
[80] *Psalms of Solomon* 15.6.
[81] A rewriting of the story in Num. 16.41–48, where the 'majesty on the diadem' refers to the Name written on a gold tablet that was tied to his turban (Exod. 28.36).
[82] *Damascus Document*, CD Ms B VII.
[83] Targum *Pseudo-Jonathan* Gen. 4.15.
[84] *Clementine Homilies* 1.39, attributed to Peter instructing Clement, but whatever its origin, it is evidence for how the protection given by the Name was remembered.

Thanks be to thee, Holy Father, for thy sacred Name which thou hast caused to tabernacle in our hearts/minds, and for the knowledge and faith and immortality which thou hast revealed to us through thy servant Jesus.[85]

This distinguished them from the people condemned in the *Song of Moses*:

> They are a nation void of counsel,
> And there is no understanding in them.
> If they were wise, they would understand this,
> They would discern their latter end. (Deut. 32.28–29)

Finally, Jesus the great high priest would give them his peace (20.19–23).

Jesus had consecrated himself (v. 19), which seems to contradict 10.36: 'him whom the Father consecrated and sent into the world ...'; but this is another Semitism whose nuance has not survived translation. 'I consecrate myself' is a rendering of the Niph'al of the Hebrew verb *qādaš*, 'to set apart/consecrate', which could mean 'I consecrate myself' but more usually 'I will show my holiness' as in 'I will show myself holy, *'eqqādhēš*, among those who are near me, and before all the people I will be glorified' (Lev. 10.3). This usage is found several times in Ezekiel, most often when he is describing the future glory of the restored people.

> I will *manifest my holiness* among you in the sight of the nations. And you shall know that I am the LORD... (Ezek. 20.41–42)

> They shall know that I am the LORD
> When I execute judgements in her [Sidon],
> And *manifest my holiness* in her... (Ezek. 28.22, also v. 25)

> The nations will know that I am the LORD... when through you I *manifest my holiness* before their eyes... (Ezek. 36.23, my translation; also 38.16)

> When I have brought them back from the peoples and gathered them from their enemies' lands, and through them have *manifested my holiness* in the sight of many nations, then they shall know that I am the LORD their God... (Ezek. 39.27–28, my translation)

What Jesus says to his disciples is: 'For their sake I have manifested my holiness, that they also may be consecrated in truth.' This is the consecration of the new high priests who have been in the presence of the Most Holy One and themselves become angel priests. They have become holy ones, the retinue of the LORD as he shines forth (Deut. 33.2–3). They no longer live the life of the *kosmos* because they have been transformed.

---

[85] *Didache* 10.

## John 17

Such was the experience of the early Christian who sang the *Odes of Solomon*:

> [The Spirit] brought me forth before the face of the Lord: and although a son of man, I was raised the illuminated one, the son of God.
> He anointed me from His own perfection, and I became one of His neighbours ...[86]

It was also the experience of Enoch when he ascended to stand before the throne: he was anointed and clothed in garments of glory, and he saw that he had become like one of the glorious ones.[87]

John's report of the last supper is set in the holy of holies, and recalls the description of the elders who ascended Sinai, saw the God of Israel, and then ate and drank (Exod. 24.10, 11). Sinai did absorb many of the traditions from the holy of holies,[88] and perhaps there had once been a meal before the LORD in the temple. The words have never been satisfactorily explained.

Jesus prays for his disciples: 'Consecrate them in the truth. Your Logos is truth', which appears also in *Didache* 10: 'The Church you have consecrated' (Greek *hagiazō*). Jesus does for his disciples what the Father has done for him: consecrates them as high priests and sons of God, before sending them out into the world (10.36): 'As thou didst send me into the world, so I have sent them into the world' (v. 18). It is possible that 'I have sent them' originally meant 'I send them', implying a future mission; Hebrew would not distinguish between the two. John does not mention that the disciples were sent out during Jesus' ministry (Matt. 10.5; Mark 6.7; Luke 9.2).

The holy anointing oil in the temple had been the sacrament of the Spirit; those who received it became most holy ones, able to communicate holiness to others (Exod. 30.26–30), and so the disciples are sent out: the Christians sent by the Christ. They had received the gifts of the oil (Isa. 11.2), as John wrote in his first letter: 'You have been anointed by the Holy One and you know all things'[89] (1 John 2.20, my translation). They would live in future in another state, and the *kosmos* would hate them (v. 14). John explained the implication of this too: 'Do not wonder, brethren, that the *kosmos* hates you. We know that we have passed out of death into life, because we love the brethren. He who does not love abides in

---

[86] *Odes of Solomon* 36.3, 5.
[87] *2 Enoch* 22.8–10.
[88] See above, p. 31.
[89] Or 'you all know'.

death ... (1 John 3.13-14). This was the covenant of *hesedh*: 'A new commandment I give to you, that you love one another ...' (13.34).

## Part 3 (vv. 20-26)

Jesus now prays for all those who will in the future hear his disciples and join them, 'those who believe in me through their *word*' (v. 20). Since Jesus now prays for unity, this should perhaps be written 'through their Word', since each disciple in turn becomes the Logos, 'I in them and thou in me, that they may become perfectly one ...' (vv. 21, 23). This wider Christian community is seen in Revelation immediately after the vision of the angel from the dawn. In addition to those drawn from the 12 tribes, a great multitude stands before the Lamb on the throne and joins the heavenly worship, 'a great multitude which no man could number' (Rev. 7.9). They are the martyrs and those who have endured the great tribulation/oppression, *thlipsis*, which translates the Hebrew *ṣārâ* (e.g. Pss. 22.11; 25.17; Isa. 8.22). Now *ṣārâ* can also be used of labour pains (e.g. Jer. 4.31), and since John's Jesus used this same image to warn his disciples of what lay ahead: 'anguish' (16.21) and 'tribulation' (16.33), this tribulation should be understood as the birth pains of the Lady's new family (Isa. 66.7-9). Matthew's Jesus warned there would be 'tribulation' (Matt. 24.9), and the Christians were scattered due to 'tribulation' after the death of Stephen (Acts 11.19). Paul exhorted the Christians in Rome to be patient in 'tribulation' (Rom. 12.12).

The great multitude serve in the temple before the throne. They are seen again in the final vision, where the servants of God-and-the-Lamb stand before the throne and worship. They see his face, and his Name is on their foreheads. In other words, the climax of Revelation is the fulfilment of the high-priestly blessing. The servants of God-and-the-Lamb all serve as high priests in the holy of holies and 'reign for ever and ever' in the light of the LORD God (Rev. 22.4-5). Jesus, about to return to the glory which he had shared with his Father before the creation (17.5), prays for the fulfilment of the final vision in Revelation. He prays that all those who have been allotted to him might see him in this state of glory (17.24). The holy of holies represented Day One, the light before creation and the state of unity before the process of separation that produced the material world. When Jesus prays that his disciples would see him in his glory, he is also praying for their unity. Thomas' Jesus taught his disciples that they were returning to the place of light whence they had come (cf. John 16.28), since they were the 'solitary' and the chosen ones, the sons of

## John 17

the pre-created light, just as James described the Father as 'the Father of lights' (Jas. 1.17):

> If they [the angel doorkeepers] say to you, 'Where do you come from?', say to them 'We came from the light, the place where the light came into being of itself [ ] It shows itself in their image. If they say to you, 'Who are you?' say 'We are the sons, and we are the chosen ones of the living Father.'[90]

When John's Jesus described his disciples as the elect/chosen ones (13.18; 15.16, 19), he may have used the word that appears in the *Gospel of Thomas* as 'solitary' one. This may have been a translation of the Hebrew *yāḥîdh*, meaning 'the one' or 'the only one', but also the 'beloved', as is the case in Genesis 22.2.[91] The word is closely related to *yaḥadh*, the unity for which Jesus prays. The Qumran group called themselves a *yaḥadh*, but this is usually translated 'community', and so the link to Jesus' teaching is not so obvious. Jesus called his disciples the beloved, the members of the unity, and the chosen.

In Jesus' prayer, the unity is linked to the Name that protects them: 'Keep them in/by thy Name, which thou hast given me, that they may be one even as we are one' (v. 11, my translation). The context of this saying is the eternal covenant/covenant of peace that was renewed on the Day of Atonement and sealed with the Name. The high priest used to call out the Name – a verbal seal – when he had completed the act of atonement/recreation.[92] Thus the Prayer of Manasseh described the creation as 'sealed with thy terrible and glorious Name';[93] and Isaac in *Jubilees* had his sons swear an oath 'by the glorious and honoured and great and splendid and amazing and mighty Name that created heaven and earth and everything together'.[94] The Name was the secret of the great oath/bond that secured the creation, as can be seen in a fragment of poetry preserved in *1 Enoch*. The text is disturbed, and the context is no longer clear, but the rebel angels are trying to learn the hidden Name in order to have power over the creation, because it is the Name that secures the creation:

> And these are the secrets of this oath ...
> And through it the earth was founded upon the water,

---

[90] *Gospel of Thomas* 50.
[91] See above, p. 163.
[92] Mishnah *Yoma* 3.8; 6.2.
[93] Doubtless written because such a prayer is mentioned in 2 Chron. 33.10–13. It is found in some copies of the LXX, e.g the Codex Alexandrinus.
[94] *Jubilees* 36.7.

> And through that oath the sea was created ...
> And through that oath are the depths made fast ...
> And through that oath the sun and moon complete their course ...
> And through that oath the stars complete their course ...
> And this oath is mighty over them,
> And through it their paths are preserved,
> And their course is not destroyed.[95]

*1 Enoch* is an Ethiopic text which gives the secret Name as *Akae*. This looks like a corrupted version of *'ehyeh*.[96] The Name that calls everything into being was known to the worshippers in heaven:

> Worthy are thou, our LORD and God,
> To receive glory and honour and power,
> For thou didst create all things,
> And by thy will they existed and were created.
> (Rev. 4.11, my translation)

This was the Name that Jesus made known to his disciples (v. 26), and which was promised to the faithful disciple in Pergamum who conquered: 'To him who conquers ... I will give ... a white stone, with a new name written on the stone which no one knows except him who receives it' (Rev. 2.17). A name on a white stone suggests the lot[97] on the Day of Atonement that bore the name 'the LORD' and which indicated that the recipient represented the LORD who would be sacrificed. The LORD also promised his Name to the faithful disciple in Philadelphia (Rev. 3.12), the Name he shared with his Father and with the new Jerusalem,[98] and this was probably the mysterious carved stone set before/upon Joshua (Jesus) the new high priest, so that the LORD could remove iniquity from the land (Zech. 3.9).

Removing iniquity renewed the eternal covenant/covenant of peace and thus restored the unity. This had been the ancient role of the high priest, and Matthew, writing for a community of Hebrew Christians, made clear that this was the covenant that Jesus renewed at the last supper, the covenant for the putting away, *aphesis*, of sins (Matt. 26.28). Ezekiel knew that the original Adam figure who was set in Eden was full of wisdom, but he was driven out because he had abused his wisdom. He was the

---

[95] *1 Enoch* 69.16, 17, 18, 19, 20, 21, 25.
[96] C. T. R. Hayward, *Divine Name and Presence. The Memra*, Totowa, NJ; Allenheld, Osmun, 1981, pp. 126–8.
[97] The word 'lot' *gôrāl*, probably meant 'stone' as it does in Arabic; cf. Greek *psēphos*, 'pebble/vote'.
[98] See above, p. 381.

## John 17

Anointed One, described as the seal of the pattern/plan of creation (Ezek. 28.12–19).[99] In other words, the Adam high priest was the seal of the eternal covenant. Isaiah's Servant who made atonement was also the covenant: 'I have given you as *a covenant to the people* …' (Isa. 42.6; also 49.8, translating literally). The original was probably 'I have appointed you as the eternal covenant'.[100] The Servant's role was to be the covenant bond and to join all things together (Isa. 53.5),[101] which is how the early Christians described Jesus:

> For he has made known to us in all wisdom and insight the mystery of his will, according to his purpose which he set forth in Christ, as a plan for the fullness of time, to unite all things in him, things in heaven and things on earth. (Eph. 1.9–10)

So too Colossians 1.15–20, where the Firstborn of all creation holds all things together and makes peace by the blood of his cross, restores the covenant of peace.

Since the prayer ends with 'I made known to them thy Name' (v. 26, my translation), this suggests that teaching about the Name as the means of protection and the means to unity was the most important aspect of Jesus' work, the key to everything he taught and did. Hence the words in the *Didache*:

> We give thanks to thee, holy Father, for thy sacred Name which thou hast caused to dwell in our hearts [that is, minds], and for the knowledge and faith and immortality which thou hast revealed to us through thy servant Jesus.[102]

So too Wisdom 15.3: 'For to know thee is complete righteousness, and to know thy power is the root of immortality.'

There is a repeated pattern in verses 21–23 that links unity to proof of divine origin. Jesus prays that his disciples may be one so that the *kosmos* might know he had come from God.

A. So that they may all be one thing, *hen*,
B. just as you, Father, are in me and I in you
C. so that they also may be in us
D. so that the *kosmos* might believe that you sent me (v. 21).

---

[99] See my book *Mother of the Lord*, n. 42 above, pp. 346–8. Ezekiel's oracle was originally about Zion, not Tyre.
[100] See above, p. 327.
[101] The other way to read that verse; see above, p. 92.
[102] *Didache* 10.

A. So that they might be one thing, *hen*,
B. just as we are one thing, *hen*, I in them and you in me,
C. so that they might be brought to completion/perfection in one thing, *hen*,
D. so that the *kosmos* might know that you sent me (vv. 22b–23).

'One thing' represents the Hebrew *'eḥādh*, and so this is the Shemaʿ: the LORD is One, and so all his *ᵉlohîm* are also one. Jesus is the firstborn of many brothers (Rom. 8.29), all of whom have become children of God (John 1.12), all of them the other children of the Woman clothed with the sun (Rev. 12.17). The presence of the LORD at that time was described as several angels, for example, by Josephus in his account of the three who appeared to Abraham at Mamre.[103] The Christians were the LORD's new holy ones, and although the customary translation is 'saints' (e.g. 2 Cor. 1.1), the word is *hagios*, 'holy', which translates the Hebrew *qādhôš*, and indicated his holy ones who shone forth with the LORD when he became King (Deut. 33.2). It was also the holy ones whose house in the temple (shrine?) Josiah destroyed (2 Kings 23.7). Sometimes there is a longer description of the Christians:

> The church [*ekklēsia* = 'called out'] of God which is at Corinth, those who are made holy in the LORD Jesus, called holy ones, together with all those who call upon the Name of our LORD Jesus Christ in every place ...
> (1 Cor. 1.2, translating literally)

The Christians were the new sons of God (Rom. 8.14, 19) and together in unity they were the LORD, the fulfilment of the Shemaʿ. This is why their unity proved their divine origin.

The LORD has given his new commandment, and his disciples have eaten a meal in his presence. The exodus episode that links the last supper to the events that follow is the vision of the God of Israel on Sinai. This must have been part of the pre-Deuteronomic stratum of temple tradition, because the elders on Sinai saw, *rā'â*, the God of Israel, and under his feet there was a pavement of sapphire stone. They saw God in a vision, *ḥāzâ*, and ate and drank before him. The Septuagint here is different, perhaps because it had a different text, but the Greek is of more immediate relevance to the scene at the last supper. 'And not one of those chosen out of Israel was out of harmony, and they were seen/they appeared in a vision in the place of God, and they ate and drank' (LXX Exod. 24.11). The disciples are the new leaders chosen out of Israel, they are united to show that they have come from God, and they have eaten in

---

[103] See above, pp. 462–3.

## John 17

the presence of the LORD. Nobody knows what holy of holies ritual this represented, bearing in mind that the holy of holies 'became' the summit of Sinai in the Moses saga.[104] There are echoes of it, though, in Psalm 23, where the LORD, the Shepherd, prepares a table for the one he anoints.

'Seeing the LORD' was the vision that Deuteronomy denied was possible (Deut. 4.12) and was the reason given in the *Ascension of Isaiah* for the persecution of the followers of the prophet from Galilee who spoke against Moses and claimed that he had seen God.[105] When Ezekiel had a similar vision, he described a firmament over their (the living creatures') heads, with a throne upon it like a sapphire stone,[106] and Adam (or a human being) seated on the throne. *John would see this vision replicated in the events of Jesus' trial.* He had already seen it in the vision of the mighty angel returning, wrapped in a cloud and with a rainbow round his head (Rev. 10.1; cf. Ezek. 1.26–28). The angel had in his hand a little open book, and John was told to eat the book and then prophesy (Rev. 10.8–11). Ezekiel too had been given an open scroll written on both back and front, and he too had been told to eat it and then speak to the rebellious people of Israel (Ezek. 2.8—3.11). Origen linked these two scenes: he explained to Celsus that eating a scroll or book meant receiving secret teaching such as Jesus gave to his disciples in their private retreats.[107] The Passover discourse is a summary of that teaching, and Jesus, whom John had seen as the mighty angel wrapped in a cloud and wreathed with a rainbow, goes forth to meet the rebellious house of Israel.

---

[104] See above, p. 31.
[105] *Ascension of Isaiah* 3.7–10; 6.1.
[106] It is possible that the sapphire stone originally described the firmament.
[107] Origen, *Against Celsus* 6.6.

# John 18—19

John now begins to tell the story of Jesus' physical death and resurrection. Since Jesus has already spoken of what he has seen and heard in heaven (3.31–33), his 'raising up' in the temple sense must have been at the beginning of his public ministry. This was the *merkavah* ascent implied by the synoptic accounts of his baptism when the heavens opened. Matthew and Luke record Jesus' own description of his experience in the desert immediately afterwards, when he wrestled with the implication of his status as Son of God, showing that he was aware of this status before he began his public ministry, and this claim became a key element in John's Gospel (e.g. 1.34, the witness of the Baptist; 10.36, Jesus' dispute with the Jews in the temple; 19.7, the Jews' accusation against Jesus to Pilate).

John's declared purpose in writing his Gospel was to show that Jesus was the Christ, the Son of God (20.31). This was already formulated in what seems to be an early creed quoted by Paul in his greeting to the church in Rome:

> Paul, a servant of Jesus Christ, called to be an apostle, set apart for the gospel of God, which he promised beforehand through his prophets in the holy scriptures, the gospel concerning his Son, who was descended from David according to the flesh, and designated *Son of God* in power according to the Spirit of holiness by his resurrection from the dead, *Jesus Christ* our LORD...
> (Rom. 1.1–4, my translation)

This is clumsy Greek. 'Spirit of holiness', *pneuma hagiōsunēs*, rather than 'holy Spirit', *pneuma hagion*, suggests that this was Paul's own literal rendering of the Hebrew *rûaḥ qodheš* (Ps. 51.11; Isa. 63.10, 11), where in each case the Septuagint translates as *to pneuma to hagion*. Now the only time that the Gospels record the holy Spirit speaking to Jesus and declaring him to be the Son was his baptism. The synoptic Gospels describe the voice from the open heavens: 'You are [or 'This is'] my beloved Son ...' (Mark 1.11; Matt. 3.17; Luke 3.22); and the Baptist knew that the one on whom he saw the Spirit rest was the Son of God (1.34).

The underlying Hebrew of this creed seems to derive from Psalm 110.3, which describes the heavenly 'birth' of the Davidic king as he becomes Melchi-Zedek.[1] The Hebrew text is now damaged, but it has 'I have begotten you', translated thus by the Septuagint, but now pointed in the Hebrew as 'your youth'. It also has the words 'on the day of your birth', but these are usually translated 'on the day of your power', since *ḥûl* can mean 'writhe in birth' or 'be strong'. In context, 'the day of your birth' is more likely. According to this psalm, the origin of Melchi-Zedek was his birth by means of the holy oil ('the dew'), when the Davidic king was 'begotten' as the son of the LORD, that is, as his human manifestation. Paul's 'creed' would have had the preposition $b^e$ three times, but each with a slightly different meaning:

- 'designated Son of God *in* power' should be understood as 'designated Son of God *by* his birth';
- '*according to* the Spirit of holiness' should be read as '*by* the Spirit of holiness';
- '*by* his resurrection from the dead' should be read as 'at the time of' or 'when' as in 'These are the generations of the heavens and the earth *when* they were created' (Gen. 2.4).

Thus the early creed based on Psalm 110.3 was:

> ... his Son, who was descended from David according to the flesh, and designated Son of God by his birth by the Spirit of holiness at the time of his resurrection from the dead, Jesus, the Anointed One, our LORD.

The first Christians knew that Jesus experienced his own resurrection at his baptism, when he heard the voice declare that he was the Son of God. Thus he, and presumably his inner circle of disciples, knew him as the resurrected LORD before he died.

In the New Testament, only Luke says that the time from Easter to Ascension was 40 days (Acts 1.3); but he was not one of the original disciples. Outside the New Testament, the period of post-resurrection teaching was remembered as much longer: 550 days in the *Apocryphon of James*;[2] 545 days in the *Ascension of Isaiah*;[3] and Irenaeus said the followers of Valentinus taught that Jesus stayed on earth for 18 months after his resurrection, during which time knowledge descended into him from above: 'He instructed a few of his disciples, whom he knew to be

---

[1] See above, pp. 74–8.
[2] *Apocryphon of James*, CG I.2.2.
[3] *Ascension of Isaiah* 9.16.

capable of understanding such great mysteries, in these things, and then was received up into heaven.'[4] There is a consistency in this tradition of 18 months/550 days that may not be due to one error copying another. There could have been a recollection that Jesus did teach his disciples after his resurrection, but that his resurrection was at the beginning of his ministry. The post-resurrection period was the time between his baptism and his death, when he was teaching his disciples.

The *Gospel of Philip*, which is attributed to a prominent figure in John's Gospel, states not only that Jesus' resurrection preceded his death, but that it was linked to baptism:

> Those who say that the Lord died first and rose up are in error, for he rose up first and died. If one does not first attain the resurrection, will he not die? As God lives, he would be dead [already].[5]

> Those who say they will die first and then rise are in error. If they do not first receive the resurrection while they live, when they die they will receive nothing. So also when speaking about baptism they say: 'Baptism is a great thing, because if people receive it they will live'.[6]

Several early Christian texts show that Jesus' baptism was regarded as his death, and his rising from the waters was his resurrection, prompting J. H. Bernard to write in the Introduction to his edition of the *Odes of Solomon* that there was a 'curious and remarkable connection' in early Christian thought between the baptism of Christ and his descent into Hades.[7]

This is what Paul was saying, when he explained that Christians were baptized into the resurrected life:

> Do you not know that all of us who have been baptized into Christ Jesus were baptized into his death? We were buried therefore with him by baptism into death, so that as Christ was raised from the dead by the glory of the Father, we too might walk in newness of life. (Rom. 6.3–4)

> If then you have been raised with Christ, seek the things that are above, where Christ is, seated at the right hand of God ... For you have died, and your life is hid with Christ in God. (Col. 3.1, 3)

---

[4] Irenaeus, *Against Heresies* I.3.14.
[5] *Gospel of Philip*, CG II.3.56.
[6] *Gospel of Philip* 73.
[7] J. H. Bernard, *The Odes of Solomon*, Cambridge: Cambridge University Press, 1912, p. 32. There are many examples in other writers; see my book *The Risen Lord. The Jesus of History as the Christ of Faith*, Edinburgh: T&T Clark, 1996, pp. 35–41.

So too John himself: 'We know that we passed out of death into life, because we love the brethren' (1 John 3.14).

John knew that from the start of his ministry Jesus spoke of what he had learned in heaven (3.12, 31–32), and Luke also knew of his vision: 'I saw Satan fall like lightning from heaven' (Luke 10.18). The disciples saw the risen LORD at the Transfiguration, and even though John does not include this in his Gospel, he does emphasize seeing the glory of the Son (1.14). His account of the physical death and resurrection of Jesus reflects this belief: that these events were the earthly counterpart of the heavenly realities. Just as his heavenly birth from the Virgin had its earthly counterpart in Jesus' physical birth (Rev. 12.1–5; John 8.41), so too his heavenly ascent and enthronement was part of his earthly life. Jesus knew what was about to happen.

John does not include many of the details that are in the synoptic accounts: the prayer in the garden, Judas' kiss, the disciples' desertion, the night-time trial by the Sanhedrin and the false witnesses, the council just after dawn, Simon of Cyrene, the reproaches of those who watched, the darkness, and the tearing of the temple veil. He does include several details that are unique to his account, which must have been necessary for him to show that Jesus was the Christ, the Son of God, as he understood that role: the place of his arrest as a garden in the valley of the Kidron, the 'I am' sayings at the arrest; the encounter with Annas; Pilate's first meeting with the Jews and then asking Jesus if he was the King of the Jews; 'Behold the Man'; the additional words in the title on the cross 'Jesus of Nazareth ...'; 'Behold your son ... Behold your mother'; 'I thirst' and 'It is finished'; not breaking Jesus' bones but piercing his side, and the flow of blood and water; and Nicodemus bringing the spices.

## 18.1–12: Jesus is arrested

Jesus now 'goes forth' from the place of new priesthood, a holy of holies, where those chosen out of Israel had eaten and drunk in the presence of the LORD. He goes with his disciples across the bridge over the steep valley of the Kidron, only mentioned by John, to the darkness of a garden, again, only mentioned by John (v. 1). When Cyril of Alexandria wrote a commentary on the Gospel of John in the early fifth century, he saw parallels between the garden where Jesus was found by Judas and the garden of Eden, both being places of conflict with Satan. Eden does not, however, explain why John chose to mention the Kidron and the 'garden/orchard', *kēpos*. The Kidron runs between Jerusalem and the Mount of

Olives, and so the synoptics say that Jesus went to the Mount of Olives. He had crossed the valley that was later identified as the Valley of Jehoshaphat, which means 'Valley of the LORD's judgement'. The great judgement described by Joel would take place there, and the early Christians used these prophecies of Joel, presumably building on Jesus' own interpretation.[8]

Joel prophesied a time when the LORD would be in the midst of Israel, and his people never again put to shame (Joel 2.27). There would be portents in the heavens; the sun darkened and the moon turned to blood (Joel 2.31). Jesus said these would precede the revealing of the Son of Man (Mark 13.24–25), a passage that summarizes his vision of the great day of wrath (Rev. 6.12–17). Joel prophesied that the LORD would gather the nations and judge them, because they had scattered his people and sold them as slaves and had looted the treasure of his temple (Joel 3.1–8). Joel reversed the vision of Isaiah and said, 'Beat your ploughshares into swords' (Joel 3.10); cf. 'I have not come to bring peace, but a sword' (Matt. 10.34). He called on the LORD to bring down his warriors for the day of judgement and to harvest the grapes into the winepress of wickedness. This is the vision in Revelation 14 where the army of the Lamb is seen on Mount Zion, and the harvest of the land begins: first the corn is reaped, which Jesus' parables show is to be gathered into the barn (Matt. 13.30; cf. John 4.35); then the grapes of the evil vine are crushed outside the city. Then, said Joel, 'You shall know that I am the LORD your God' (Joel 3.17). A fountain would come from the house of the LORD to water the valley of Shittim,[9] and the LORD would avenge the blood of his people, fulfilling Deuteronomy 32.43. This was the context of the prophecy fulfilled at Pentecost (Joel 2.28–29; cf. Acts 2.16–21) and of Paul's assurance that all who called on the Name of the LORD would be saved (Joel 2.33; Rom. 10.13). The day of judgement in the Valley of Jehoshaphat was a key expectation for the early Christians, but after his vision of the mighty angel with the opened book, John knew that these prophecies had already been fulfilled. The nations had been judged, and the ruler of this world had been cast out. The story of the next few hours is the story of the LORD's judgement, indicated by 'He went forth across the Kidron valley'.

Jesus and his disciples enter a garden, which Judas knew because Jesus often went there with his disciples (v. 2). According to early tradition, it was the site of the cave where he used to teach, 'privately', on the Mount

---

[8] See above, p. 227.
[9] See above, p. 268.

of Olives (Matt. 24.3; Mark 13.3).[10] Matthew and Mark name the place Gethsemane, the 'place of the oil press', presumably the press outside the city that became the press of the wrath of God in the vision of the last judgement. Judas comes with Roman soldiers (literally a third of a cohort, *speira*, 200 men), and servants, *hupēretai*, of the high priests and the Pharisees. Only John mentions the Roman soldiers, who would have come from many parts of the empire, an eyewitness detail of symbolic significance: the nations gathering for the judgement. John thus implies that Pilate was involved from the beginning, maybe because the Jews had already determined to kill Jesus after the raising of Lazarus (11.53), but he had hidden himself (11.54).

Only John mentions the torches and lanterns; there would have been a full Passover moon, but this could be another eyewitness detail: a cloudy night. John says the people came with weapons, *hoploi*, whereas the synoptics say that they came with swords and clubs. John has already recorded the moment when Jesus' soul was troubled and he heard an angel from heaven (12.27-29); the synoptics set this prayer in Gethsemane, and the disciples fall asleep while Jesus prays. Nor does John have Judas identify Jesus with a kiss; Jesus comes out himself – either from the group of disciples or perhaps from the garden. He asks them twice: 'Whom do you seek?' (vv. 4, 7).

The whole scene is symbolic; John knew what actually happened – the crowd coming by night to seek the LORD – but he also saw the heavenly drama unfolding: 'Jesus, knowing all that was coming upon him, came out and said to them "Whom do you seek?"' (v. 4, my translation). The forces of darkness had come against the Light, and Judas was leading them: he had left the supper table to betray Jesus and gone into the night (13.30). Judas is the agent of the Satan, just as in the *Ascension of Isaiah*, Belkira was the agent of Beliar and had Isaiah arrested and killed.[11]

'Seeking the LORD' had been at the heart of temple worship:

- 'Thy face, LORD, do I seek, *bāqaš* ... Hide not thy face from me' (Ps. 27.8, 9);
- 'You who seek, *bāqaš*, the LORD ...' (Isa. 51.1);
- 'The generation of those who seek him, *dāraš*, who seek, *bāqaš*, the face of the God of Jacob' (Ps. 24.6);
- 'I sought, *dāraš*, the LORD ...' (Ps. 34.4);

---

[10] See above, p. 224.
[11] *Ascension of Isaiah* 3.1-12.

- 'Blessed are those ... who seek, *dāraš*, him with their whole heart ... (Ps. 119.2);
- 'Seek, *dāraš*, the LORD while he may be found ...' (Isa. 55.6).

Closest to the scene of the arrest are the words of the LORD in the Third-Isaiah, and this is John's irony. These words were quoted by Justin as a prophecy of Jesus' trial:[12]

> I was ready to be sought, *dāraš*, by those who did not ask for me;
> I was ready to be found by those who did not seek me, *bāqaš*.
> I said, 'Here am I, here am I', to a nation that did not call on my name.
> I spread out my hands all the day to a rebellious people,
> Who walk in a way that is not good, following their own devices ...
> (Isa. 65.1–2)

Jesus responds three times: 'I am he' (vv. 5, 6, 8). The *egō eimi* could have been no more than Jesus identifying himself, but in this context – bearing in mind that Jesus would not have said these words in Greek – he could have uttered three times the Name revealed to Moses at the burning bush, *'ehyeh*. When they heard the Name, the crowd drew back and fell to the ground. Perhaps they were astonished that Jesus handed himself over so easily – who can know what prompted this detail? It has been suggested that Psalms 27.2; 35.4; and 56.9 could have shaped the incident,[13] but it does replicate exactly the description of what happened on the Day of Atonement when the Name was uttered in the temple: 'When the priests and the people who stood in the temple court heard the spoken Name come forth from the mouth of the high priest, they used to kneel and bow themselves and fall down on their faces ...'[14] John, with his high-priestly connections, would have known this.

The crowd ask for Jesus the *Nazorean* (vv. 5, 7; 19.19), not 'of Nazareth' as it is usually translated. For John, this title was an aspect of divine kingship, and he alone says that 'the Nazorean' was displayed on the cross (19.19). Nazorean derived from the Hebrew *nṣr*, meaning 'watch, guard', and described the LORD watching over his people: Isaiah sang of the LORD who *guarded* his vineyard day and night (Isa. 27.3), who *kept* the one who trusted him (Isa. 26.3), who *kept* his Servant (Isa. 42.6; 49.8); who *preserved* the faithful (Ps. 31.23); whose *ḥesedh* and faithfulness *preserved* his people and their king (Ps. 40.11; 61.7). His Servant restored the

---

[12] Justin, *Apology* 1.35.
[13] For detail, see R. E. Brown, *The Gospel According to John XIII–XXI*, Anchor Bible 29a, New Haven and London: Yale University Press, (1970) 2008, pp. 810–11.
[14] Mishnah *Yoma* 6.2.

*preserved* of Israel (Isa. 49.6). They in turn *kept* the commandments (Pss. 25.10; 78.7; 105.45; 119 *passim*). The followers of Jesus were called the Nazorenes (Acts 24.5), and *nôṣrîm* became the Hebrew term for Christians. They were the other children of the Woman clothed with the sun, 'who *keep* the commandments of God and bear testimony to Jesus', and the dragon, having failed to destroy the One who was taken up to the throne in heaven, made war on them instead (Rev. 12.17). While he is still with his disciples, Jesus guards them (17.12), and so he tells the crowd to let his disciples go free (v. 8).

Peter draws his sword and cuts off the right ear of Malchus, the high priest's servant. The synoptic Gospels all report this and they all say '*the* servant', perhaps implying a special status, but only John gives the names of Peter and Malchus. John even knows about Malchus' family (v. 26). Luke also knew that the servant's right ear was cut off and that Jesus healed him (Luke 22.51), which would explain why Peter was not arrested. The servant of the high priest also featured in the resurrection story in the *Gospel of the Hebrews*, quoted by Jerome: 'Now the LORD, when he had given the linen cloth to the servant of the priest, went unto James and appeared to him ...'[15] This implies that the guard at the tomb, requested by the high priests, comprised not only Roman soldiers but also members of the high priests' household (Matt. 27.62–66). So too in the *Gospel of Peter*: Petronius the centurion and his soldiers went with the elders and scribes to watch the tomb.[16] As he is being arrested, Jesus tells Peter to put away his sword, because he has to drink the cup that the Father has given him (v. 11). The synoptic Gospels have the same image, but they show Jesus accepting the 'cup' only after he has prayed that it might pass from him (Mark 14.36//Matt. 26.39; Luke 22.42).

Jesus is then bound and taken away, evoking the judgement against Jerusalem given by Isaiah, but obscured in the current Hebrew text. The Greek has '"Let us bind the Righteous One, for he is inconvenient to us"; but they will eat the fruit of their deeds' (Isa. 3.10). The Hebrew now reads: 'Say to the righteous that it shall be well with him; for they shall eat the fruit of their doings' (Isa. 3.10, AV), suggesting that '*srw*, 'bind', was read as/changed to '*mrw*. Barnabas said that this prophecy was fulfilled in the Passion of Jesus.[17]

---

[15] Jerome, *On Illustrious Men* 2.
[16] *Gospel of Peter* 8.
[17] *Letter of Barnabas* 6.

## 18.13–27: Jesus is questioned by the leaders of the Jews

Jesus is taken first to Annas, the father-in-law of Caiaphas. John is the only one who records this, another indication that he had links to the high priests. Even though Annas no longer held the office of high priest, he was still bound by most of the rules of the office[18] and clearly retained his influence. He had been appointed by the Romans in 6 CE but was deposed in 15 CE; his five sons and son-in-law became high priests, something which Josephus said had never happened before.[19] Annas is the first to question Jesus, and he asks about his disciples and his teaching (v. 19). Jesus replies that he has always spoken openly, in places where all Jews assemble: synagogue and temple. Nothing he had said was secret teaching even though the Jews had not always understood him. They had said: 'How long will you keep us in suspense? If you are the Christ, tell us plainly'; to which Jesus had replied: 'I told you, and you do not believe ... because you do not belong to my sheep' (10.24, 25–26). Jesus asks Annas to question those who had heard him teaching, as was his right under the law. If two witnesses agreed in their accusation (cf. Mark 14.59, the testimony of the witnesses did not agree), evidence had to be heard in favour of acquitting the accused.[20] One of the servants standing by strikes him for speaking to the high priest without proper respect. Jesus is then led to the house of Caiaphas, but John does not record what happened there.

Mark, followed by Matthew, mentions a trial at night before the Sanhedrin and the high priest (Matthew names him as Caiaphas), where witnesses say they heard him threaten to destroy the temple and build another (Mark has 'not made with hands'). The high priest recognizes that rebuilding the temple is the role of the Messiah and so asks Jesus if he is indeed the Messiah, the Son of the Blessed One/the Son of God.[21] According to Mark, Jesus replies 'I am', *egō eimi*; the high priest declares this a blasphemy worthy of death and so there is no need of further witnesses. The chief priests, elders and scribes begin to abuse Jesus – spitting on him, blindfolding him, striking him and asking him to prophesy. Then, with further blows, the guards take him away. When morning comes, the whole Sanhedrin confers and sends Jesus to Pilate

---

[18] Mishnah *Horayoth* 3.4.
[19] Josephus, *Antiquities* 20.198.
[20] Mishnah *Sanhedrin* 5.4.
[21] This is described in *1 Enoch*, and also in the Targum of Isaiah 53.5: '[The anointed servant] will build the sanctuary that was polluted by our transgressions and given up because of our iniquities.'

(Mark 15.1). Matthew's account is broadly similar, with the whole Sanhedrin meeting when it is morning to confer and have Jesus put to death (Matt. 27.1). Luke has different details: Jesus was brought to the (unnamed) high priest's house (Luke 22.54), but no trial is reported there. Jesus was beaten and blindfolded, reviled and told to prophesy. Then when it was day, the elders, chief priests and scribes assembled and led Jesus to the Sanhedrin, where there was no testimony against him about destroying the temple, but just the demand: 'If you are the Christ, tell us', followed by 'Are you the Son of God?' (Luke 22.67, 70).

If one of John's reasons for writing was to supplement the synoptic Gospels by recording the earlier part of Jesus' public ministry, before the Baptist was put in prison,[22] another must have been to record his work in Jerusalem before the final Passover when he was crucified. The synoptic writers knew the various charges brought against Jesus by the authorities ('the Jews') in Jerusalem, but knowing of only one visit to the city, they set all the charges within the one time that they knew Jesus had been confronted by the authorities and questioned about his claims and his teaching. John knows that these charges were made against Jesus on his earlier visits to Jerusalem. The claim to destroy the temple and build it in three days had been made on Jesus' Passover visit to Jerusalem when he drove out the traders (2.19). The later interpretation of the saying reflects John's understanding that the prophecies had been fulfilled in the life of Jesus (2.21-22). The claim to be Son of God had been made when Jesus was in the temple at Ḥanukkah, a few months before his death (10.31-39). The reaction to the 'blasphemy' was the same as the synoptists record at the trial: the Jews wanted to kill him – by stoning (10.31) – and they tried to arrest him (10.39). There had been earlier incidents: when Jesus said, 'My Father is working still, and I am working', and the Jews tried to kill him because he called God his Father 'making himself equal with God' (5.17-18); and when Jesus claimed to be the 'I AM' who had known Abraham, and the Jews in the temple began to stone him (8.58-59). This explains why John gives no detail of the Sanhedrin trial before Caiaphas: it has been summarized by Annas' question: 'What have you been teaching?' And the decision had already been taken after the raising of Lazarus: '[The Jews] took counsel how to put him to death' (11.53). This must have been the full Sanhedrin of 71 men and not a lesser court, since a false prophet or a high priest could only be tried by the full council.[23]

---

[22] Eusebius, *History of the Church* 3.24.
[23] Mishnah *Sanhedrin* 1.5.

Lazarus was raised at some time between Ḥanukkah and Passover; no date is given, but Origen records what must have been a Jewish account of Jesus' death: *Jesus was condemned some time before Passover but escaped and hid himself.* John says that after raising Lazarus and knowing of the Jews' resolve to kill him, 'Jesus therefore no longer went about openly among the Jews' (11.54). It would be interesting to know who told Jesus of Caiaphas' prophecy and the resolution of the Jews to kill him. John? (11.45–53). Origen's Jew says this:

> How should we deem him to be a God, who ... after we had convicted him, and condemned him as deserving of punishment, was found attempting to conceal himself, and endeavouring to escape in a most disgraceful manner, and who was betrayed by those whom he called disciples?[24]

The Mishnah says that a herald had to go before a convicted person on his way to execution, declaring his crime so that even at that stage, evidence could be heard in his favour. The Babylonian Talmud comments on this passage, in a section that has been removed from many editions:

> AND A HERALD PRECEDES HIM: ... It was taught: On the eve of Passover, Yeshu was hanged. For forty days before the execution took place, a herald went forth and cried, 'He is going forth to be stoned because he practised sorcery and enticed Israel to apostasy. Any one who can say anything in his favour, let him come forward and plead on his behalf.' But since nothing was brought forward in his favour, he was hanged[25] on the eve of Passover.
>
> Ulla retorted: 'Do you suppose that he was one for whom a defence could be made? Was he not an enticer, concerning whom Scripture says, 'Neither shalt thou spare, neither shalt thou conceal him' [Deut. 13.9]?[26]

'Forty days before the execution' implies that Jesus was condemned after the raising of Lazarus; as John says, 'They took counsel how to put him to death', and so Jesus went away to stay with some disciples who lived on the edge of the wilderness (11.53–54). The charges the Jews brought against Jesus were practising sorcery, presumably raising the dead, and teaching apostasy, presumably the reason for Annas' question: 'What have you been teaching?' According to Jewish sources, the action against Jesus was instigated entirely by the Jews and carried out by them.

---

[24] Origen, *Against Celsus* 2.9.
[25] 'Hanging', according to Mishnah *Sanhedrin* 6.4, was a punishment reserved by the Jews for blasphemy and idolatry. The body had to be removed and buried on the day of execution, and not left on the wood overnight (Deut. 21.22–23).
[26] Babylonian Talmud *Sanhedrin* 43a.

Caiaphas realized that it was Jesus' signs – his miracles – that made him popular, and that if too many people turned to him, the Romans would come and destroy both the temple and the nation (11.48). Jewish tradition remembered that they had executed Jesus. The Celsus whom Origen opposed said, 'Jesus was punished by the Jews for his crimes';[27] and Horbury observed: '*Many passages from Jewish texts would, if found in Christian sources, certainly be ascribed to anti-Jewish sentiment.*'[28]

Interwoven with the account of Jesus being questioned is the story of Peter being questioned (vv. 15–18, 25–27). Peter followed Jesus, as did 'another disciple' whom the high priest knew. Peter was not allowed into the courtyard, *aulē*, of the high priest's residence, but the other disciple asked for him to be let in. Only John has this detail, because the 'other disciple' was John. Peter stood warming himself with the servants and soldiers who had a charcoal fire (v. 18). Mark and Luke mention Peter warming himself at the fire (Mark 14.54, 67; Luke 22.55), all four Gospels mention Peter's three denials that he knew Jesus, and all four Gospels mention the cock crowing after Peter's third denial. Why should the people in the high priest's courtyard have wanted to know if Peter was a disciple? Perhaps they expected him to speak in Jesus' favour, as he was required to do if a person had been accused. It was immediately after Jesus' request to Annas to ask those who had heard him (v. 21) that people in the courtyard, and even the man related to Malchus, asked Peter if he was a disciple (vv. 25–26). They must have expected him to speak. Then a cock crowed (v. 27). Jesus had predicted that Peter would deny him three times before the cock crowed (13.38; cf. Matt. 26.75; Mark 14.72; Luke 22.61). It must have been a distant cock outside the city, because it was forbidden to keep poultry within Jerusalem.[29]

## 18.28–40; 19.1–16: The trial before Pilate

### Verses 28–32

John's main emphasis is on the Roman trial. Early in the morning 'they' – presumably members of the Sanhedrin – led Jesus from the house of Caiaphas to the Praetorium (v. 28). The events that John does not record may have been the meeting of the Sanhedrin described by Mark and

---

[27] Origen, *Against Celsus* 2.5.
[28] W. Horbury, 'The Trial of Jesus in Jewish Tradition', in *The Trial of Jesus*, ed. E. Bammel, London: SCM Press, 1970, pp. 103–21, p. 115.
[29] Mishnah *Baba Kamma* 7.7. Fowls eat dead creeping things, which would make unclean any place in the holy city where they went.

Matthew, but the location of neither the Sanhedrin chamber nor the Praetorium is known for certain. The Sanhedrin had met for many years within the temple precinct, in the 'Hall of Hewn Stone' that was half within the temple and half outside,[30] but about this time it moved to a building in the marketplace.[31] Jesus' trial could have taken place in the original stone chamber, or at the new site. Some have speculated that Jesus' trial was the last to be held in the ancient chamber. Christian tradition has for centuries held that the Praetorium in Jerusalem was in the Antonia fortress, but Philo, who lived at the time, said that Pontius Pilate caused a furore when he set up some gold shields in the palace of Herod, inscribed in honour of the emperor Tiberius.[32] This suggests that his Jerusalem residence was within Herod's palace. When Gessius Florus the last procurator (64–6 CE] was in Jerusalem he stayed at the palace. He had come to judge the men who had insulted him after he took 17 talents from the temple treasury, and set up a raised judgement seat, *bēma*, in front of the building. 'The chief priests, the nobles and the most eminent citizens then presented themselves before the *bēma*' to put their case.[33] This is exactly what John describes as the setting for the trial of Jesus: a *bēma* on a stone pavement outside the Praetorium (19.13).

The Jews did not enter the Praetorium, to maintain their ritual purity for eating Passover, and presumably, since there were priests in the group, the purity required for serving in the temple that afternoon at the time of the Passover sacrifices.[34] Many have commented that John here illustrates the Jews' concern for ritual purity but not for a human life. These Passover precautions are a clear indication that for John, the last supper was not a Passover meal, which agrees with the account in the Talmud, that Jesus was hanged on the eve of Passover.

The ritual impurity could have been what Peter feared before he went to visit Cornelius, the Roman centurion. There must have been a major change in the thinking of the first Christians, prompted by Peter's vision

---

[30] Mishnah *Middoth* 5.4.
[31] Babylonian Talmud *Abodah Zarah* 8b.
[32] Philo, *Embassy to Gaius* 299, written in 39 CE.
[33] Josephus, *War* 2.301. During another riot, Florus led his soldiers out of the palace, which implies that he was based there, *War* 2.328.
[34] C. K. Barrett warns against taking these Passover comments as proof that John was an eyewitness. The Jews could have removed any impurity by a bath at the end of the day, he said, before eating Passover after sunset, when the next day began, *The Gospel According to St John*, London: SPCK, (1955) 1970, p. 445. It is rash to assume that we know more about Jewish customs at the time than John did, given that our main source of information is the Mishnah, compiled around 200 CE.

at Joppa, when it was revealed to him that he should no longer consider the house of a Gentile unclean.[35] Thus when he entered the centurion's house, he said: 'You yourselves know how unlawful it is for a Jew to associate with or to visit any one of another nation ...' (Acts 10.28). In addition, there would have been the Passover requirement to have no leaven or leaven product in the house, and Pilate's residence would certainly have had some of the forbidden substances: perhaps not Babylonian porridge or Egyptian barley beer, but almost certainly a kneading trough for making bread and writer's paste.[36]

## Verses 33–38a

Pontius Pilate, who was procurator of Judea from 26 to 36 CE, came out to meet the Jews. Only John mentions this. Perhaps Pilate recalled the trouble that had been caused by setting up the gold shields in Herod's palace, when the people had reminded him that the emperor Tiberius did not want their laws or customs to be destroyed. They threatened to write to the emperor with a list of Pilate's misdeeds, and Philo's account of the episode gives an insight into both Pilate's character and his strained relationship with the Jews. When they had begged him to remove the gold shields, 'and not to make any alteration in their national customs which had hitherto been preserved without any interruption, without being in the least degree changed by any king or emperor ...', he refused. He was, said Philo, 'a man of very inflexible disposition, and very merciless as well as obstinate'. The Jews begged him not to cause a sedition because 'the honour of the emperor is not identical with dishonour to the ancient laws ... Tiberius is not desirous that any of our laws or customs be destroyed.' They threatened to write to the emperor with an account of his behaviour:

> and he feared lest they might in reality go on an embassy to the emperor, and might impeach him with respect to other details of his government, in respect of his corruption, and his acts of insolence, and his rapine, and his habit of insulting people, and his cruelty, and his continual murders of people untried and uncondemned, and his never ending and gratuitous and most grievous inhumanity.[37]

Philo had first-hand knowledge of the situation; although he came from an aristocratic family in Alexandria, he had strong links to the highest

---

[35] Mishnah *Oholoth* 18.7. Establishing cleanness and uncleanness was a complex matter, involving drains and menstruating women.
[36] Mishnah *Pesaḥim* 3.1.
[37] Philo, *Embassy* 301, 302.

levels of society in Judea. When he was writing this, his nephew was about to marry the princess Berenice, great-granddaughter of Herod the Great. Pontius Pilate, then, thought it expedient to come out of his residence to meet the Jews, to respect their customs and tell them to try the prisoner according to their own laws.

Pilate asks the Jews what accusation they are making; he assumes it is a matter of Jewish law, and John presents the scene as a terse exchange (vv. 30, 31).

> 'If this man were not an evildoer, we would not have handed him over ...'
> 'Take him yourselves and judge him by your own law ...'
> 'It is not lawful for us to put any man to death.'

There are problems: the Jews do not bring a specific charge against Jesus, although, by saying it is not lawful for them to order execution, they imply that he has committed a capital offence. They were, however, prepared to stone the woman who was brought to Jesus in the temple accused of adultery (8.5), and the Sanhedrin would soon find Stephen guilty of speaking blasphemous words against Moses and God and condemn him to death by stoning (Acts 6.11–12; 7.58). The Sanhedrin did have the power, at some periods, to pass a sentence of death – the permitted methods of execution are listed[38] – but John regards the Roman sentence as fulfilling the prophecy that Jesus would be lifted up (v. 32).

Pilate went out to the Jews, and now he comes in to question Jesus. John presents the trial before Pilate as two simultaneous scenes of action: first he goes out to enquire what charge the Jews bring against Jesus; second he goes out to offer to release a prisoner; third he goes out and presents Jesus: 'Behold the Man'; and finally he says to the Jews, 'Behold your King', and hands Jesus over to them. Separating these scenes before the crowd are three when Pilate talks privately with Jesus within the Praetorium.

Pilate's first question to Jesus is 'Are you the King of the Jews?' This has not been mentioned so far, and Pilate is the first to use the term in the trial. Luke has the Jews accuse Jesus of being 'Christ, a king' when they bring him to Pilate (Luke 23.2), but this is their explanation of the trial that has already taken place. This dealt with the blasphemous claim to be the Messiah/the Son of God and the imminent appearance of the Son of Man. Matthew and Mark also have the claim to destroy and rebuild the temple, but no explanation of the charge 'King of the Jews' when Jesus is

---

[38] Mishnah *Sanhedrin* 7.1.

brought to Pilate. The trial before Pilate in all the synoptic Gospels deals with the claim to be King of the Jews. This must have been how the Jews explained to Pilate the significance of the claim to be the Messiah, the Son of God. John, however, does not mention here the titles Messiah, Son of God, Son of Man, but they all appear in the opening scene of his Gospel as the Baptist and then Jesus' future disciples recognize who Jesus is. In the synoptic Gospels, Jesus' only words to Pilate are his enigmatic 'You have said so' in response to his question: 'Are you the King of the Jews?' (Mark 15.2//Matt. 27.11; Luke 23.3), but in John's Gospel, there is an exchange about kingship.

Jesus asked Pilate how he knew about the 'King of the Jews'. Jesus had rejected the claim 12 months previously, after he had fed the 5,000, and the people had wanted to make him king (6.15). There must have been informers: the Jews had sent priests and Levites to watch the Baptist and to ask if he claimed to be the Messiah (1.19–20); and at Hanukkah the previous year the Jews in the temple pressed Jesus to give them a plain answer: was he the Messiah? (10.24). Presumably it was not only the Jews who wanted to know who Jesus was. Caiaphas knew that a popular movement supporting him would bring the wrath of Rome, and so Jesus had to be killed to protect the temple and the people (11.48). Nor could Pilate have been unaware of the triumphal entry into the city only six days earlier, when the crowd had proclaimed Jesus the King of Israel (12.13). But Jesus wanted to know if someone had told Pilate about the King of the Jews. Pilate implies that the chief priests have explained this charge to him (v. 35), and he asks Jesus what he has done to deserve the accusation.

Pilate does not understand Jewish ways: 'Am I a Jew?' (v. 35); and Jesus explains that his kingship is not of this *kosmos*; he has been born and come into the *kosmos* (v. 37). This gives one of the contexts for the scene. It is the Davidic king born in heaven/the holy of holies and then emerging into the world. The other is the relationship between Roman, earthly power, and the kingdom that was proclaimed by the Christians. Practical questions such as 'Was there anyone present to record the exchanges between Jesus and Pilate?' are secondary and perhaps naive. This is a literary reconstruction of Jesus' teaching, set in an appropriate context, as are the temple discourses. It represents what Jesus taught about earthly and heavenly power, and loyalties to them, exemplified in the synoptics by the question about paying tribute to Caesar: 'Render to Caesar the things that are Caesar's and to God the things that are God's' (Mark 12.17 and parallels). It was the Jews who asked Jesus this question, not the Romans. The Roman question was 'Are you a king?'

## Temple Theology in John's Gospel

John was prompted to write his Gospel after the revelation that the *parousia* had already happened, that the LORD had already come to his people. The war against Rome that led to the destruction of Jerusalem had been instigated by people who believed that the powers of darkness were the Romans, the Kittim of the Qumran *War Scroll*, against whom the sons of light would fight, together with the army of angels from heaven.[39] For John (and for Jesus) the powers of darkness were the second-temple Jews. John depicts the Romans as agents of the Jews, helping them to achieve their aim. Pilate is depicted as the man he was: not willing to risk his position and the favour of Tiberius for the sake of Jewish custom and practice; and as the representative of Roman power who could not find Jesus guilty of any crime.

The context in which John was writing made this a pressing issue. Vespasian (emperor from 69 to 79 CE) had begun the war against the Jews, and his son Titus (emperor from 79 to 81 CE) completed the campaign and destroyed Jerusalem. Hegesippus, writing in the mid-second century, said that after the destruction of Jerusalem, Vespasian issued an order 'that no member of the royal house should be left among the Jews, and that all descendants of David should be ferreted out'.[40] This resulted in further persecution of the Jews, and it would have been imperative for the Christians, whose founder had been proclaimed as the Lion of Judah, the Root and Offspring of David, the heaven-sent divine King of the Jews (Rev. 5.5; 22.16; John 12.13), to make their position clear and show what Jesus had taught. Searching out the family of David continued into the reign of Vespasian's younger son Domitian (emperor 81–96 CE), who ordered the execution of all the royal line. The grandsons of Jude, a member of Jesus' extended family (Mark 6.3), were brought before Domitian, but when he saw that they were peasant farmers, he dismissed them and stopped his persecution of the Church. They explained to him that the kingdom of which they spoke was 'not of this world or anywhere on earth, but angelic and in heaven'. They still believed in the future second coming, though, and said that the kingdom would be established on earth when Christ came in glory on the day of judgement.[41]

Jesus explains to Pilate that his kingship is not of this world. His servants will not engage in earthly warfare to save him from the Jews (v. 36). These servants were the heavenly host, since he knew that he was the

---

[39] *War Scroll*, 1QM II, XII.
[40] Eusebius, *History* 3.12.
[41] Eusebius, *History* 3.19–20.

Lord of Hosts, and Matthew shows this in his account of the arrest where he has Jesus say to the unnamed disciple with a sword: 'Do you think that I cannot appeal to my Father, and he will at once send me more than twelve legions of angels?' (Matt. 26.53). In Revelation, these are the 144,000 with the Lamb on Zion (Rev. 14.1) who ride out with him from heaven to defeat the beast (who was the agent of the red dragon) and his false prophet (Rev. 19.11–21).

The Jews persecuted the Christians for many years, even if the punishments were carried out by others, and the words of John's Jesus reflect this.[42] Justin's words to the Jew Trypho, written after the second Jewish war against Rome (132–5 CE) show the bitterness, and this is but one of many examples in his writings:

> Accordingly, these things [the devastation after the war] have happened to you in fairness and justice, for you have slain the Righteous One, and His prophets before Him; and now you reject those who hope in Him, and in Him who sent Him … cursing in your synagogues those that believe in Christ. For you have not the power to lay hands upon us, on account of those who now have the mastery. But as often as you could, you did so … For other nations have not inflicted on us and on Christ this wrong to such an extent as you have, who in very deed are the authors of the wicked prejudice against the Righteous One, and us who hold by Him … You selected and sent out from Jerusalem chosen men through all the land to tell that the godless heresy of the Christians had sprung up, and to publish those things which all they who knew us not speak against us.[43]

Jesus makes clear to Pilate what Pilate already knows, that his own nation and their high priests have handed him over (v. 35). Pilate repeats the question about kingship, but this time does not say king *of the Jews* (v. 37).

Jesus then speaks as the Shepherd King whose sheep know his voice. He has come to testify to the truth, and this is the reason for his coming into the world. Elsewhere in John's Gospel, the testimony of Jesus Christ is what *he saw and heard in heaven* (3.31–32; cf. Rev. 1.2), which must have been 'the truth' that he taught. Elsewhere too, Jesus told the Jews that the truth would make them free and that the Son would make them free (8.32, 36). The truth and the Son were synonymous. Jesus linked 'the truth' to what he had 'seen with [the] Father' (8.38); and the Jews had tried to kill him because he taught the truth he had heard from God. This

---

[42] See above, pp. 447–52.
[43] Justin, *Trypho* 16, 17.

exchange was also about his origin, his Sonship (8.39–42). He said then what he later said to Pilate: 'He who is of God hears the words of God ...' (8.47). During his first meeting with Pilate, Jesus tells him what he said to the Jews in the temple, when they first tried to stone him (8.59). Pilate then asks what this truth is. According to John's Gospel, it was the truth of Jesus as the Son, as well as the temple teaching in which the idea of such Sonship originated, and this is why John has Pilate use the Son's royal titles as he presents Jesus to the Jews: 'the Man' (19.5) and 'the King' (19.15).

The first Christians who read John's Gospel would have known the answer to Pilate's question: 'What is truth?' It was the ways of the old temple, Father and sons, the Mother, the vision given by her anointing oil, the Unity and Life of the holy of holies. A further glimpse of this understanding of truth is found in the *Gospel of Truth*, a writing usually attributed to Valentinus, who was a Christian teacher in Rome and a contemporary of Justin. Marcellus of Ancyra (died 374 CE), said Valentinus was the first to formulate the idea of the Trinity in his book *On the Three Natures*,[44] and so his thinking has a significant place in the history of Christianity. According to (his?) *Gospel of Truth*, Jesus came to reveal the truth which was *the lost knowledge of the Father*, in other words, the lost teachings of the first temple. The Saviour came to redeem those who were ignorant of the Father. The gospel is 'the proclamation of hope, being discovery for those who search for him'. It was not knowing the Father that had caused all the ignorance and confusion in second-temple Judaism:[45]

> Ignorance of the Father brought about anguish and terror. And the anguish grew solid like a fog so that no one was able to see. For this reason error became powerful; it fashioned its own matter foolishly, not having known the truth.
>
> For this reason, despise error. Being thus without any root, it fell into a fog regarding the Father, while it was involved in preparing works and oblivions and terror in order that by these it might entice those of the middle [life on earth] and capture them.[46]

This enigmatic talk about ignorance of the Father, error, not being able to see, and not knowing the truth could have been just an amalgam drawn from contemporary philosophical discourse, but what follows shows that

---

[44] Quoted in B. Layton, *The Gnostic Scriptures*, London: SCM Press, 1987, p. 233.
[45] See above, p. 500.
[46] *Gospel of Truth*, CG I.3.17, tr. G. W. MacRae, in *The Nag Hammadi Library in English*, ed. J. M. Robinson, San Francisco: Harper and Row, 1977.

this was how Valentinus described the people of the second temple, those whom *1 Enoch* called the sheep who could not see and the apostate generation.[47]

> This is the gospel of the one who is searched for, which was revealed to those who are perfect through the mercies of the Father, the hidden mystery, Jesus the Christ. Through it he enlightened those who were in darkness. Out of oblivion he enlightened them, he showed a way, and the way is the truth which he taught them. For this reason, error grew angry at him, persecuted him and was distressed at him (and) was brought to naught. He was nailed to a tree ...[48]

> He went into the midst of the schools, he spoke the word as a teacher. There came the wise men – in their own estimation – putting him to the test. But he confounded them because they were foolish. They hated him because they were not really wise.[49]

But Pilate would not have known that this was what the followers of Jesus meant by the truth.

## Verses 38b–40

Pilate goes out again to the Jews and says that Jesus has committed no crime. Mindful of the need to respect Jewish customs, he suggests releasing at Passover the prisoner Jesus, the King of the Jews, but the crowd want Bar-Abbas the robber. Mark and Matthew seem to imply that this was Roman custom (Mark 15.6–8; Matt. 27.15), but whatever its origin, this is the only evidence for such a custom. It was seen as significant and therefore mentioned, because the random choice between two people, one of whom was released and the other killed, was an obvious allusion to the Day of Atonement. The ancient ritual had two goats: one representing Azazel, who was driven out into the desert, symbolic of banishing the Evil One; and the other representing the LORD, who was sacrificed and whose blood/life was used to purify and renew the temple/creation. I suggested some years ago that the original understanding of the death of Jesus was not the Passover lamb but the goat offered on the Day of Atonement,[50] and others have explored, independently, some aspects of this.[51]

---

[47] *1 Enoch* 89.74; 93.9.
[48] *Gospel of Truth* 18.
[49] *Gospel of Truth* 19.
[50] See my book *The Revelation of Jesus Christ*, Edinburgh: T&T Clark, pp. 373–88.
[51] E.g. J. K. Berenson Maclean, 'Barabbas, the Scapegoat Ritual, and the Development of the

The Barabbas question is likely to remain unanswered as there is insufficient evidence to reach any conclusion. The problem is that Bar-Abbas means 'son of the father' and so is very similar to the title given to Jesus. A few texts of Matthew 27.16, 17 even name Barabbas as 'Jesus Barabbas', making the two names exactly similar. It is not impossible that the robber had this name, but an addition to the text could have been made to emphasize the allusion to the two goats on the Day of Atonement. The Mishnah says the two goats had to be identical 'in appearance, in size and in value, and bought at the same time'.[52] Not long after Jesus' death, and quite likely around the Day of Atonement in the same year, Peter was speaking in the temple and comparing the death of Jesus to the high priest who had taken blood into the holy of holies and would return to bring renewal (Acts 3.19-21). The writer of Hebrews developed this understanding of the death of Jesus in great detail (Heb. 9.11-14), as did Barnabas, who was a Levite (Acts 4.36) and so was well acquainted with temple practice. He was the first named among the prophets and teachers in the church at Antioch, and was sent on a missionary journey, accompanied by Saul (Acts 13.1-2).[53] We shall return to the evidence in the *Letter of Barnabas*.

## 19.1-3

The people ask for Bar-Abbas to be released, and so Jesus is condemned. Pilate goes back into the Praetorium and there he has Jesus scourged. The soldiers plait a crown of thorns for Jesus and dress him in a purple cloak, *himation*, before striking him and mocking him: 'Hail, King of the Jews.' Matthew says the cloak, *chlamys*, was red (Matt. 27.28), perhaps thinking it had been one of the soldier's cloaks, but Luke knew that Pilate had sent Jesus to Herod when he learned that he was from Galilee, and Herod had dressed him in a magnificent garment before sending him back to Pilate (Luke 23.6-11). This could account for a purple robe.

The abuse of Jesus recalls the suffering of the Servant:

> I gave my back to the smiters,
> And my cheeks to those who pulled out the beard;
> I hid not my face from shame and spitting. (Isa. 50.6)

---

Passion Narrative', *Harvard Theological Review* 100 (2007), pp. 309-34; D. S. Ben Ezra, 'Fasting with Jews, Thinking with Scapegoats ...', in *The Day of Atonement*, ed. T. Hieke and T. Niklas, Leiden: Brill, 2011, pp. 165-87.

[52] Mishnah *Yoma* 6.1.

[53] This is usually called *Paul's* first missionary journey, although Barnabas is named first.

## John 18—19

The *Gospel of Peter*, which expanded the account of the mockery, took additional detail from this text in Isaiah, showing that the Christians did understand the abuse of Jesus as the suffering of the Servant. The *Gospel of Peter* also says that it was the Jews who abused Jesus, even though John makes clear it was the soldiers in the Praetorium.

> Let us hail the Son of God, now that we have authority over him. And they put on him a purple robe, and made him sit upon the seat of judgement, saying, 'Give righteous judgement, thou King of Israel.' And one of them brought a crown of thorns and set it upon the LORD's head, and others stood and spat in his eyes and others struck his cheeks. And others pricked him with a reed, and some of them scourged him saying, 'With this honour let us honour [or at this price let us value] the son of God.'[54]

The scene is one of John's ironies, the mockery of Jesus being a recognizable parody of the enthronement scene in Revelation 5. The crown of thorns represents the seven horns (that is, the seven rays of light) that encircle the head of the one on the throne; and the mockery of the soldiers – 'Hail, King of the Jews' – corresponds to the words of the elder, 'the Lion of the tribe of Judah, the Root of David', that is, the King of the Jews (Rev. 5.5-6). The enthronement itself was found by some readers in verse 13: 'Pilate brought Jesus out and *sat down* on the judgement seat …' The primary meaning of the verb *kathizō* is 'seat someone', not 'seat oneself', and so the line was read: 'Pilate brought Jesus out and *seated him* on the judgement seat …' This explains why the *Gospel of Peter* describes the Jews making Jesus sit on the seat of judgement, and why Justin wrote: 'As the prophet said, they tormented him and set him on the judgement seat, and said "Judge us".'[55]

## Verses 4–7

Pilate brings Jesus out dressed as a king and says: 'Behold the Man', which John's irony saw as an allusion to the royal ritual of the temple where the human emerged from the holy of holies as the transformed Man, the LORD. 'The Man' was a title for the Messiah (e.g. Zech. 6.12), but the Jews greet their King with the demand that he be crucified. Pilate finds Jesus innocent. The Jews say Jesus must die because he has made himself Son of God – more irony, since the temple ritual had been a symbolic self-offering of the Son.

---

[54] *Gospel of Peter* 6–9.
[55] Justin, *Apology* 1.35, alluding to Isa. 58.2.

In early Christian discourse 'Man' meant an angel, as can be seen from the explanation inserted into Revelation 21.17: 'He also measured ... by a man's measure, that is, an angel's'; or by the description of the figures seen at Jesus' tomb: 'Men in shining clothes' were later described as angels (Luke 24.4, 23). Justin,[56] like Josephus, knew that the three men who appeared to Abraham at Mamre were three angels,[57] and he knew that the titles Angel of Great Counsel, Man and Son of Man were synonymous.[58] Hermas, his older contemporary in Rome, described how the tower (the temple) was rebuilt under the supervision of a glorious Man who was the Son of God.[59] The Enoch tradition knew that a human being was transformed into a 'Man' after he had learned angelic knowledge. In the *Dream Visions*, which are told as an animal fable, Noah the bull became a Man after one of the archangels 'had instructed him in a secret', and Moses, born a sheep, became a Man after he had been on Sinai.[60] In temple discourse, a 'Man' was an angel: Ezekiel saw a man, *'îš*, clothed in linen, who marked the faithful before the destruction of Jerusalem (Ezek. 9.2); Daniel saw the man, *'îš*, Gabriel (Dan. 9.21) and then a man, *'îš*, clothed in linen (Dan. 10.5), whom Hippolytus, in the early third century CE, identified as the LORD.[61] The memory of the Messiah as the Man survived among the descendants of those who had fled from Jerusalem to Egypt after the destruction of the first temple. The Septuagint, their Greek translation of the Hebrew Scriptures, emphasized that the Messiah was the Man even when this word did not appear in the Hebrew original. The LORD would send to his people in Egypt a Man who would save them (LXX Isa. 19.20); and the messianic prophecy 'a star shall come forth out of Jacob, and a sceptre shall rise out of Israel' (Num. 24.17) became 'a star shall rise from Jacob, and a Man shall rise up [the word for resurrection] from Israel' (LXX Num. 23.17b). Zechariah has the original title in the Hebrew: 'Behold, [the] Man whose name is Branch, *ṣemaḥ* ... he shall build the temple of the LORD' (Zech. 6.12).[62] Closely linked to this were the traditions about Adam, the divine image and first human being, the original royal high priest.[63]

---

[56] Justin, *Trypho* 56.
[57] Josephus, *Antiquities* 1.196.
[58] Justin, *Trypho* 126.
[59] *Shepherd of Hermas*, Similitude 9.7, 12.
[60] *1 Enoch* 89.1, 36.
[61] Hippolytus, *Commentary on Daniel* 24.
[62] See W. Horbury, *Jewish Messianism and the Cult of Christ*, London: SCM Press, 1998, esp. pp. 36–59.
[63] See above, p. 65.

## John 18—19

Pilate brings out 'the Man', and yet again, John has the Jews fail to recognize what is being shown to them and said to them, only this time the speaker is not Jesus but the Roman procurator. Jesus had been scourged, and so presumably his tunic was stained with blood, and John specifically says that he was wearing the crown of thorns and the purple robe (v. 5). The corresponding scene in Revelation is the Word of God riding out from heaven (Rev. 19.11–16). He is called the Faithful and True One, he wears many crowns, he has a secret Name which no one knows but himself, and his robe is sprinkled with blood. The armies of heaven – his angel servants – appear with him, the Davidic king, who is about to rule with a rod of iron (Ps. 2.9). He is King of kings and Lord of Lords, and Pilate says: 'Behold the Man.'

The Jews give their reason for wanting Jesus crucified, which John records with yet more irony: 'We have a law, and by that law he ought to die, because he has made himself God's Son' (v. 7, my translation). The charge refers to the incident recorded in chapter 10, where the Jews did not object to Jesus claiming to be the Messiah – 'If you are the [Messiah], tell us plainly' (10.24) – but to his claiming that this meant being the divine Son. The nature of the Messiah was the issue, and it was one of John's aims in writing his Gospel to show that Jesus was the Messiah *and* the Son of God (20.31). John's record of the exchanges in the temple was a summary of many debates with the Jews. In the synoptics, this was summed up in the debate about the meaning of Psalm 110.1: 'David himself calls him Lord; so how is he [just] his son?' (Mark 12.37).[64] Psalm 110 says (or rather, originally said, because the Hebrew text is no longer readable at this point) that the anointed one was the divine Son, consecrated/born in the holy of holies and then sent out into the world as the human presence of the Lord with his people, his son: 'Today I have begotten you' (Lxx Ps. 109.3 = 110.3 in the English versions). The king was the 'I am'. This was the truth for which Jesus was born and came into the world (18.37). According to the Mishnah, 'The blasphemer is not culpable unless he pronounces the Name itself', and when this is heard, the judges have to stand and tear their garments.[65] Thus Mark says that after Jesus said 'I am', the high priest tore his garments and said, '"Why do we still need witnesses? You have heard his blasphemy. What is your decision?" And they all condemned him as deserving death' (Mark 14.62–64). Mark must have understood 'I AM' as the Name.

---

[64] See above, p. 124.
[65] Mishnah *Sanhedrin* 7.5, the current understanding of the blasphemy law in Lev. 24.11–16.

## Verses 8–11

Pilate has heard the accusation that Jesus claimed to be King of the Jews – a straightforward political claim that he must have thought he understood, a simple case of nationalism and treason. There was similar consternation in Thessalonica when some of the Christian community were dragged before the city authorities and accused of 'acting against the decrees of Caesar, saying that there is another king, Jesus' (Acts 17.7). Now – and this is the first time John mentions it – Pilate hears the term 'Son of God', and *he is more afraid* (v. 8). This case involved more than balancing his good standing with the emperor and the demands of the Jews; this involved divine powers, and any Roman would have hesitated before executing the son of a god. Pilate takes this title seriously and asks Jesus, 'Where are you from?' The people of Jerusalem had already answered this question for themselves: Jesus could not be the Messiah because they knew where he came from, and no one would know where the Messiah came from (7.25–27). Pilate is not so certain, but reminds Jesus of his power to release and to execute. Jesus reminds Pilate that his power has been given to him from above – another of John's ambiguities, because Pilate's power comes not only from the Roman emperor, but also from God.

In Revelation, the attitude to Rome was the same, but expressed rather differently and with the warning: 'If any one has an ear, let him hear' (Rev. 13.9). The Roman emperor when Revelation was compiled was the wounded beast from the sea (Nero), who received his authority from the red dragon, and so people worshipped the beast as the agent of the dragon (his Messiah, so to speak). But the beast was actually *allowed* to exercise its authority (by God), it was *allowed* to make war on the saints, and the whole world worshipped it – the whole world except those written in the Lamb's book of life (Rev. 13.1–9). Paul's letter to Rome was a public document and so gave a more diplomatic policy statement: 'There is no authority except from God', and so good law-abiding citizens had nothing to fear (Rom. 13.1–7). This was written before the beast from the sea began his persecution of the Christians in which Paul and Peter, and many others, were martyred. It was in this context that John wrote his account of Jesus before Pilate, emphasizing that those who handed Jesus over to Pilate were the greater sinners (v. 11).

## Verses 12–16

Pilate is still afraid: he wants to release Jesus, but the Jews remind him of the need to keep the emperor's favour. They emphasize the political

## John 18—19

nature of Jesus' claim: 'Everyone who makes himself a king sets himself against Caesar' (v. 12). Pilate brings Jesus out of the Praetorium for the fourth time:

- 'Take him yourselves and judge him by your own law' (18.31);
- 'Will you have me release for you the King of the Jews?' (18.39);
- 'Behold the Man' (19.5);
- 'Behold your King' (19.14).

Pilate sits (or seats Jesus) on the judgement seat on the place called Lithostrōtos, meaning 'a place paved with stone', an area known as Gabbatha, which Josephus says meant 'hill',[66] or perhaps 'raised place'.[67] John has given this information for a reason: it adds nothing to the story, but shows how he understood it. A seat on a raised pavement of stone echoes the descriptions of the LORD enthroned on a pavement of sapphire stone, seen by the elders of Israel (Exod. 24.9.10) and by Ezekiel (Ezek. 1.26).

John, and all the synoptics, use the same word for Pilate's next action: *paradidōmi*, here translated 'handed him over' (RSV) but in the synoptics 'delivered him' (Mark 15.15//Matt. 27.26; Luke 23.25).[68] John used the same word of Judas, he *betrayed* him (18.2), and later uses the same word to describe Jesus 'handing over' the Spirit (v. 30). This will have been intentional: Jesus was handed over so that he could hand over the Spirit; cf. 'If I do not go away, the Paraclete will not come to you; but if I go, I will send him to you' (16.7). Pilate hands Jesus over – but to whom? The last people mentioned are the chief priests, and so the natural meaning of the sentence is 'He handed Jesus over to the chief priests to be crucified' (v. 16). The memories of the Jerusalem church, recorded by Luke, agree: it was the 'men of Israel' or 'the Jews' who killed Jesus (Acts 2.36; 3.15; 10.39, all speeches by Peter). John also notes the time when Jesus was handed over to the Jews: the sixth hour, and so the beginning of the 'evening' part of the day. Mark says that Jesus was put onto the cross at the third hour, 9 a.m. (Mark 15.25), and there is no way to reconcile these two statements,[69] although the length of the trial proceedings make John's time the more likely. John also repeats that it was the eve of Passover (v. 14), making the death of Jesus coincide with the death of the Passover lambs.

---

[66] Josephus, *War* 5.51: 'a village named Gabath Saul, which means "Saul's hill"'.
[67] See Barrett, *Gospel According to St John*, n. 34 above, p. 453.
[68] Paul uses the same verb for Jesus handing over himself (Gal. 2.20; Eph. 5.2).
[69] One theory is scribal error: both Hebrew and Greek use letters for numbers: in Hebrew 3 is ג and 6 is ו. In Greek, 3 is Γ and 6 is ς. They could have been confused.

But the reason for this being Jesus' 'hour' (cf. 2.4; 7.30; 8.20; 12.23) was that the eve of Passover, according to the calendar of the second temple, fell that year on a Friday.[70] In the second temple, Passover was the feast of the spring equinox, and the Day of Atonement and Tabernacles was the feast of the autumn equinox. In Ezekiel's vision for the restored temple, however, he saw both the spring and autumn equinox festivals as similar: both were days of atonement to purify the temple. On the first day of the first month and on the seventh day, the priest had to atone the temple with the blood of a young bull, to purge away the result of any inadvertent sin. On the fourteenth day it was the feast of Passover with unleavened bread, when the prince had to provide a young bull as a sin offering for himself and his people, and for the seven days after that he had to provide daily offerings of animals and grain (Ezek. 45.18–25). This is very different from the Passover prescribed in Exodus 12.1–20, although Ezekiel's festival may be what Passover became after Josiah had made it a temple pilgrimage. *But Ezekiel's Passover is identical with his prescription for the autumn festival – the Day of Atonement and Tabernacles* (Ezek. 45.25) – and it is like the Pentateuch's prescription for the duration of Tabernacles: a festival of seven (or eight) days[71] beginning on the fifteenth day of the seventh month (Lev. 23.33–36). If Jesus was restoring the ways of the first temple, his 'Passover' would have been a day of atonement, and in the old solar calendar still used by the Qumran community, the Day of Atonement always fell on a Friday. The *Damascus Document* describes people who were keeping to the old ways, holding fast to the commandments of God, preserving the hidden things in which all Israel had gone astray, which included the calendar: the Sabbaths and glorious feasts;[72] and Enoch also knew that sinners had changed the calendar such that the stars did not appear at their appointed times.[73]

A Sabbath Passover such as John describes, with the lambs sacrificed on the Friday afternoon, makes it possible to establish the date of the crucifixion. This was Robinson's conclusion, taking into account both John's Gospel and the synoptics:

> Within the time limits available (AD 27–34), only three years in fact present themselves: 27 when [Nisan 14] was on a Thursday, 30 when it was on a Friday and 33 when it would have been on a Friday unless, as is probable

---

[70] See below, p. 556.
[71] See above, p. 265.
[72] *Damascus Document*, CD III.
[73] *1 Enoch* 80.2.

that year, an extra month had been intercalated, when it would have fallen on a Saturday ...

The Synoptic gospels say that Passover fell on a Thursday, in which case Jesus would have died in 27 ...

Of the other two [dates] 30 is widely accepted as the more likely ...

We may provisionally accept 30 as the date of the last Passover.[74]

Passover remembered the exodus when the LORD brought his people out of Egypt, and Jesus, as we have seen, saw his work as the exodus for those who had been allotted to him, his new people.[75] But Passover also remembered the plagues and especially the death of the firstborn of Egypt. The firstborn of Israel had been saved, protected by the blood of the Passover lambs that was marked on their doorposts (Exod. 12.21-27). The Christians recognized Jesus as the Firstborn: this had been a title of the Davidic king, $b^e kh\hat{o}r$ (Ps. 89.27), showing that he was the human presence of the LORD; and this passed into Christian discourse. Texts describing the LORD were used of Jesus as the Firstborn: 'When he brings the firstborn into the world, he says "Let all God's angels worship him"' (Heb. 1.6); and Paul, explaining that all who are led by the Spirit of God are sons of God, said that Jesus was the firstborn among many brethren (Rom. 8.29). Here, on the eve of Passover and celebrating the survival of their own firstborn, the Jews prepare to kill the Firstborn of the LORD, who, in the first temple, had been their King.

Pilate presents Jesus to the Jews as their king: 'Behold your King' (v. 14), but the chief priests respond: 'We have no king but Caesar.' This is the ultimate irony and betrayal. The mystics of the old temple tradition had always seen the LORD enthroned as King – Enoch, Isaiah, Ezekiel, Daniel – and even the Deuteronomists, who opposed the idea of monarchy, did so because the LORD was the King (1 Sam. 8.7) and not any human ruler. Enoch described foreign rulers – the lions, tigers, wolves and hyenas – as punishment for forsaking the LORD as King,[76] and here *the chief priests* declare: 'We have no king but Caesar' (v. 15).

## 19.17–30: The death

John did not write to give an orderly account of events, as Luke did (Luke 1.1-4). He wrote 'that you may believe that Jesus is the Christ, the Son of

---

[74] J. A. T. Robinson, *The Priority of John*, ed. J. F. Coakley, London: SCM Press, 1985, pp. 153-4.
[75] See above, p. 400.
[76] *1 Enoch* 89.55.

God, and that believing you may have life in his name' (20.31). John chose only such details of the crucifixion as served this purpose, and so much of what is found in the synoptics was not included by John. He did not include these details found in all three synoptics:

- Simon of Cyrene (Matt. 27.32; Mark 15.21; Luke 23.26);
- the mockery at the cross (Matt. 27.39–43; Mark 15.29–32; Luke 23.35–37);
- the darkness at noon (Matt. 27.45; Mark 15.33; Luke 23.44);
- Jesus' final loud cry (Matt. 27.50; Mark 15.37; Luke 23.46);
- tearing the temple veil (Matt. 27.51; Mark 15.38; Luke 23.45);
- the centurion's reaction (Matt. 27.54; Mark 15.39; Luke 23.47);
- the women watching the burial (Matt. 27.61; Mark 15.47; Luke 23.55).

He did not include the cry of dereliction understood as a cry to Elijah (Matt. 27.46–47; Mark 15.34–35); nor Mark's report of Pilate's investigation to see if Jesus was dead (Mark 15.44); nor Matthew's description of the earthquake and opened tombs (Matt. 27.51–53); nor several of Luke's details: the weeping women as Jesus went to his death (Luke 23.27–31), Jesus' prayer that his executioners might be forgiven (Luke 23.34), the good thief (Luke 23.40–43), Jesus' prayer: 'Into your hands I commend my Spirit' (Luke 23.46), and the penitent reaction of the crowd going home (Luke 23.48).

## Verses 17–22

Jesus carried his own cross, meaning the horizontal beam, as the vertical would have been left in place at the site of execution (v. 17). This apparently contradicts the accounts of Simon of Cyrene carrying the cross, but the synoptic Gospels say that Simon was compelled to help Jesus after he had begun his journey. John notes that Jesus carried his own cross at the beginning of his journey to Golgotha, and carrying the wood that would bring his death was probably an allusion to Isaac carrying the wood that would be used for his death (Gen. 22.6). Melito, bishop of Sardis (died 180 CE), compared Isaac and Jesus in this way,[77] and the image passed into Christian usage.[78] The earliest comparison of Jesus and Isaac was made by Barnabas the Levite, who did not mention the wood, but said that Isaac *was* sacrificed. He linked this sacrifice to the Day of

---

[77] Melito, *Catena on Genesis* and *On the Pasch*, frag. 9.
[78] E.g. Irenaeus, *Against Heresies* IV.5; Origen, *On Genesis*, Homily 8. John Chrysostom, *On John*, Homily 85 on John 19.16–18.

## John 18—19

Atonement:[79] 'In time to come [the LORD] would be sacrificing the vessel of his spirit for our sins – whereby the type created in Isaac, when he was sacrificed on the altar, would find its fulfilment.'[80]

There are two other early examples that could be saying that Isaac was sacrificed:

> By faith Abraham, when he was tested, offered up Isaac, and he who had received the promises was ready to offer up his only son, of whom it was said, 'Through Isaac shall your descendants be named.' He considered that God was able to raise men even from the dead; hence, figuratively speaking, he did receive him back. (Heb. 11.17–19)

> Was not Abraham our father justified by works, when he offered his son Isaac upon the altar? (Jas. 2.21)

John has already used language associated with Isaac to describe the death of Jesus – 'He gave his only Son ...'[81] – and so another allusion here is possible.[82] But linking Isaac to Jesus as a figure for atonement may have been a Christian innovation: as Kessler observed, 'Neither Philo nor Josephus interpret the Akedah [Binding of Isaac] in terms of atonement.'[83]

Jesus was taken to Golgotha, a Hebrew name meaning 'skull'.[84] He was taken outside the city walls, even though Melito says that Jesus died in the midst of the city.[85] Hebrews, which set out in detail how the death of Jesus was the Day of Atonement sacrifice (Heb. 9.11–14), related this sacrifice to Jesus dying outside the city:

> For the bodies of those animals whose blood is brought into the sanctuary by the high priest as a sacrifice for sin are burned outside the camp. So Jesus

---

[79] The Palestinian Targum implies that Isaac was sacrificed and then brought to life. The angels took him into the heavenly school of Shem, and there he remained for three years.

[80] *Letter of Barnabas* 7.

[81] See above, p. 163.

[82] The relationship between the binding of Isaac and the crucifixion, and whether Jewish interpretation influenced Christian or vice versa, is much debated. See G. Vermes, *Scripture and Tradition in Judaism*, Leiden: Brill, 1961, pp. 193-227; P. R. Davies, 'Passover and the Dating of the Akedah', *Journal of Jewish Studies* 30 (1979), pp. 59-67; C. T. R. Hayward, 'The Present State of Research into the Targumic Account of the Sacrifice of Isaac', *Journal of Jewish Studies* 32 (1981), pp. 127-50; 'The Sacrifice of Isaac and Jewish Polemic against Christianity', *Catholic Biblical Quarterly* 52 (1990), pp. 292-306; E. Kessler, *Bound by the Bible. Jews, Christians and the Sacrifice of Isaac*, Cambridge: Cambridge University Press, 2004.

[83] Kessler, *Bound by the Bible*, p. 139.

[84] *Calvaria* is the Latin for 'skull'.

[85] Melito, *On the Pasch* 72, 94. Melito had travelled to 'the east' to see the land of the Bible, Eusebius, *History* 4.26, and would have seen the enlarged Jerusalem, renamed Aelia Capitolina, where Golgotha was within the enlarged city walls.

also suffered outside the gate in order to sanctify the people through his own blood. (Heb. 13.11–12)

The animals referred to are the bull and the goat offered on the Day of Atonement:

> And the bull for the sin offering and the goat for the sin offering, whose blood was brought in to make atonement in the holy place, shall be carried forth outside the camp; their skin and their flesh and their dung shall be burned with fire. (Lev. 16.27)

Jesus was crucified between two thieves, and the phrase translated 'one on either side', *enteuthen kai enteuthen*, was used in the Greek Old Testament as a literal translation of the Hebrew *mizzeh ûmizzeh* (LXX Num. 22.24). This suggests a writer (or translator) whose Greek was coloured with Hebrew. The two thieves are often said to be the fulfilment of Isaiah 53.12: 'He was numbered with the transgressors', but two figures on either side of the body of Jesus occur elsewhere in John's story: the two angels at the head and at the foot of the place where Jesus' body had been (20.12). Since John has been using 'raised up' as wordplay to mean both the crucifixion and the exaltation of Jesus (3.14; 8.28; 12.32, 34, always in conjunction with 'Son of Man/Man'), we should expect enthronement symbolism in the account of the crucifixion, especially in the light of 'When you have lifted up the Son of man, then you will know that I am he' (8.28). The two thieves evoke the two cherubim of the ark or throne. The LORD said to Moses: 'From above the place of atonement, *kapporet*, from between the two cherubim that are upon the ark of testimony, I will speak with you ...' (Exod. 25.22, my translation; cf. Lev. 16.2). In the temple, Isaiah saw the LORD 'high and lifted up' on his throne amidst the seraphim (Isa. 6.1–2), and the Greek of Habakkuk 3.2, now almost unreadable in the Hebrew, is 'You will be recognized in the midst of two creatures, you will be known when the years draw near, you will be shown forth when the right time comes.'

The exalted king is named; Pilate has a title written for the cross in Hebrew, Latin and Greek: 'Jesus of Nazareth, the King of the Jews.' That is the usual translation. But the synoptic writers do not include 'of Nazareth': Matthew has 'This is Jesus the King of the Jews' (Matt. 27.37); Mark has 'The King of the Jews' (Mark 15.26); and Luke has 'This is the King of the Jews' (Luke 23.38). Nor do they say that the title was written in three languages. According to John, the title says: 'Jesus the *Nazōraios*', which is not the word used elsewhere for Jesus as a man of Nazareth. Mark has *Nazarēnos* (Mark 1.24; 14.67). Matthew explained that Jesus

## John 18—19

was called *Nazōrean* to fulfil a prophecy that he would come from Nazareth (Matt. 2.23), but no such prophecy is now known, and *Nazōrean* from 'Nazareth' seems a rather strained etymology. *Nazōrean* is the form used in John's Gospel (18.5, 7; 19.19) and all through Acts (2.22; 3.6; 4.10; 6.14; 22.8; 26.90, and Paul was described as a member of the sect of the Nazoreans, Acts 24.5). The question is: should this be translated 'from Nazareth' or 'the Nazorean'? The latter seems more likely, as there was another word meaning 'man of Nazareth', *Nazarēnos*. Jesus and his disciples were 'the preserved' and 'the preservers', those whom the LORD had chosen and those who kept the commandments, perhaps meaning the original commandments. In fact, they were like the group described in the *Damascus Document* who saw themselves as keeping the commandments and knowing the hidden things in which all Israel had gone astray, 'the testimonies of his righteousness, and the ways of his truth' as well as the correct calendar.[86] John says: 'Jesus the preserver of the old ways, the king of the Jews' was written on the cross, and he was an eyewitness (vv. 26, 35). The chief priests objected to what Pilate had written, but he would not alter it (v. 22).

The soldiers then share out Jesus' garments, as all the synoptics also record. Only John cites Psalm 22.18 as a prophecy fulfilled. It has been suggested that the parallelism of the psalm – 'They parted my garments ... they cast lots for my clothing', has influenced the way John recorded the incident, and this may be the case. John did, however, distinguish between the *himatia*, the clothes, which all the synoptics mention, and the *chitōn*, the tunic, which they do not. The clothes were divided into four parts, so presumably there were four garments since part of a garment is no use. The *chitōn*, however, was not divided, and since this is John's characteristic detail, there must be significance in this particular garment. He gives two details: 'The tunic was without seam, *arraphos*, woven from top to bottom, *ek tōn anōthen di'holou*' (v. 23). It used to be said with confidence: 'The idea of a high priestly robe does not enter here.'[87] But it does.

A robe without seam suggests the high priest's garment, which Josephus described thus:

[Over his other garments] the high priest puts on a vestment of blue colour. This is also a long robe, reaching to his feet [in our language called a $m^{e'}il$],

---

[86] *Damascus Document*, CD III.
[87] J. H. Bernard, *The Gospel According to St John*, vol. 2, ICC, Edinburgh: T&T Clark, 1928, p. 630.

and is tied around with a girdle, embroidered, as the others are [with flowers of scarlet and purple and blue], with a mixture of gold interwoven ...

Now this robe was not composed of two pieces, nor was it sewed together along the shoulders and the side, but was one long robe, so woven as to have an aperture for the neck; not an oblique one, but parted all along the breast and the back. A border was also sewed to it, lest the aperture should look too indecently: it was also parted where the hands were to come out.[88]

This was Josephus' version of the prescription in Exodus 28.31–35:

You shall make the robe, $m^{e'}il$, of the ephod all of blue. It shall have in it an opening for the head, with a woven binding around the opening, like the opening in a garment, that it may not be torn.

A woven binding round the neck would have meant a second piece in the garment, and so the woven binding is more likely to have been a special reinforced selvedge on the single piece of fabric. This would have secured the vertical slit front and back that was the opening for the head, to prevent tearing, which was forbidden for a high priest's garment. There were no side seams, but the garment was secured by the girdle interwoven with gold. The garment could have been made of wool or linen. Jesus' seamless garment was probably made like this, and when John mentions that it was not torn, the link to the high priest is clear. 'The priest who is chief among his brethren, upon whose head the anointing oil is poured, and who has been consecrated to wear the garments, shall not let the hair of his head hang loose, nor rend his clothes ...' (Lev. 21.10).

Jesus said he had been consecrated (as high priest) and sent into the world (10.36).[89]

'Woven from top to bottom' makes no sense: one piece of cloth used for a single garment would not have a top and a bottom. The problem word is *anōthen*, again, which John has already used with a double meaning: 'born again/born from above' (3.3). 'Woven throughout out of the [plural] *anōthen*' is the literal translation, and could be describing the type of fibres from which it was woven. Reused wool, perhaps? The first name used by the Christians was 'the poor' (cf. 12.5), and this may have had a literal as well as a spiritual meaning. We should expect a woollen

---

[88] Josephus, *Antiquities* 3.159–61.
[89] Did the first Christians wear distinctive priestly clothing? Eusebius said that John wore the *petalon* of the high priest, the gold seal bearing the Name that was tied to the forehead, *History* 3.31; and he also said that James, the first bishop of the Jerusalem church, wore priestly robes of linen and used to enter the temple to pray for the forgiveness of his people's sins, *History* 2.23. Epiphanius, *Panarion* 1.29, says that James also wore the *petalon*.

*John 18—19*

garment at that time of year; it had been cold the previous night (18.18). The other meaning – 'from above' – is easier to determine: an early Christian text described Wisdom clothing her children in a garment from above:

> Wisdom summons you in her goodness, saying: 'Come to me, all of you, O foolish ones, that you may receive a gift, the understanding which is good and excellent. I am giving you a high-priestly garment which is woven from every wisdom …
> 
> Clothe yourself with wisdom like a robe, put knowledge upon you like a crown, and be seated upon the throne of perception.'[90]

Luke incorporates this too in his telling of the birth story: Mary, the Wisdom figure, brings forth her Firstborn, wraps him around (translating Luke 2.7 literally), and sets him in *'ēbûs*, a manger, echoing *y<sup>e</sup>bûs*, Jebus, the old name for Jerusalem. Jesus being wrapped around by his Mother was the way the story was told. Here, John describes Jesus stripped of his tunic, and a seamless garment woven of every wisdom is what he saw in the old but untorn garment for which the soldiers cast lots.

There were women standing by the cross. The eyewitness says they were standing by the cross (v. 25), whereas the synoptics say that the women looked on from afar (Matt. 27.55; Mark 15.40; Luke 23.49). Nor is it clear which women were there: Luke gives no names, John mentions four women, but the synoptics only three:

- Mary Magdalene, who is not given any further identification, presumably because she was well known, is named by John, Matthew and Mark;
- Mary the wife of Clopas is named by John, and she seems to be the woman that Matthew and Mark name as Mary the mother of James and Joseph;
- The sister of Jesus' mother is mentioned by John but not named, and she seems to be the woman whom Mark calls Salome and Matthew calls the mother of the sons of Zebedee;
- The mother of Jesus is mentioned only by John, but not named, neither here nor at the wedding in Cana (2.1).

This must have been deliberate ambiguity, implying that it was not only Jesus' physical mother who was there. The *Gospel of the Hebrews*, now lost apart from quotations in some early writers, shows that the Spirit (as distinct from the Paraclete) was described as Jesus' Mother. Origen

---

[90] *Teaching of Silvanus*, CG VII.4.89.

## Temple Theology in John's Gospel

quoted from it: 'Even now did my mother the holy Spirit take me by one of my hairs and carried me away unto the great mountain Thabor ...' Jerome quoted the same lines several times, and implied that it was Jesus' Mother who spoke at his baptism when he quoted another passage from the *Gospel of the Hebrews*:

> When the LORD was come up out of the water, the whole fount of the holy spirit descended and rested upon him, and said to him: 'My son, in all the prophets I was waiting for thee, that thou shouldest come and that I might rest in thee. For thou art my rest, thou art my first-begotten son, that reignest for ever.'[91]

Jesus spoke from the cross to his mother and the beloved disciple, entrusting them to each other. When he wrote these words, John had already written about the Woman clothed with the sun and her other children, and about the angel of the LORD (the Paraclete) teaching him the meaning of the visions (Rev. 12.17; 1.1–2). None of Mary's stepchildren is mentioned, the children of Joseph who are named elsewhere (Mark 6.3; Matt. 13.55). There seems to have been some tension between them (7.5), because Jesus' family were embarrassed by his behaviour (Mark 3.21), and Jesus said that his true family were those who did the will of God (Mark 3.31–35; Matt. 12.46–50; Luke 8.19–21). This may be why Jesus entrusted his mother to John rather than to the other men whom she had brought up. Mary, the women from Galilee and 'his brothers' were, however, praying together with the disciples in the days before Pentecost (Acts 1.14). Mary then passes into Christian history and devotion: some say she went to Ephesus with John and died there; others that she remained in Jerusalem and died there. Shortly after John wrote his Gospel, though, she was being described in terms of Wisdom, the Lady of the first temple, the Mother of the LORD, and so more than just a human woman. The *Infancy Gospel of James* clearly described the cave of the nativity as the holy of holies and the birth of Jesus as a birth in the holy of holies; and Luke seems to have used the same imagery, describing the birth of the firstborn who was wrapped around by his mother.[92] The earliest known prayer to Mary was in use in Egypt in the mid-third century, and is still in use:

> Beneath your compassion,
> We take refuge, O Mother of God:
> Do not despise our petitions in time of trouble:

---

[91] Origen, *On John* 2.12; *On Jeremiah*, Homily 15; Jerome, *On Isaiah* 9. All these in M. R. James, *The Apocryphal New Testament*, Oxford: Clarendon Press, (1924) 1980, pp. 2–5.

[92] See my book *Christmas. The Original Story*, London: SPCK, 2008, pp. 74–8.

*John 18—19*

> But rescue us from dangers,
> Only pure, only blessed one.[93]

John does not mention the three hours of darkness while Jesus was on the cross (Mark 15.33; Matt. 27.45; Luke 23.44), nor the wine and myrrh/gall that he refused to drink (Mark 15.23; Matt. 27.34). The detail was authentic, as the practice is recorded in the Talmud:

> Again, what of R. Ḥiyya b. Ashi's dictum in Ḥisda's name: When one is led out to execution, he is given a goblet of wine containing a grain of frankincense, in order to benumb his senses, for it is written, Give strong drink unto him that is ready to perish, and wine unto the bitter in soul. And it has also been taught: The noble women in Jerusalem used to donate and bring it.[94]

This was not recorded by John, presumably because it was not part of his demonstration that Jesus was the Christ, the Son of God.

John now brings his two great books together. When he received his vision of the *parousia*, and saw the mighty angel coming from heaven, he learned that the visions of the future had been fulfilled in the life of Jesus himself: the judgement would not be a future event, rather it had been the presence of the LORD in Jesus and his people's response to him; eternal life was not a future state but the transformed state that began when one met and recognized the LORD; and the kingdom was not a political system to be established before too long – 'Lord, will you at this time restore the kingdom to Israel?' (Acts 1.6) – it was the unity of the kingdom as a living reality among Jesus' disciples. The Woman clothed with the sun had given birth to her Son; the prince of this world had been cast out. Hence the rest of John's purpose in writing his Gospel: 'These things are written that you may believe that Jesus is the Christ, the Son of God, and *that believing you may have life in his name.*'

The mighty angel of the *parousia* had proclaimed that the mystery of God as announced by the prophets was about to be fulfilled (Rev. 10.7); and the new message from the open book was that it had been fulfilled. Fulfilment is the recurring theme of Revelation, all the words in italics being forms of *teleō*: the two prophets *fulfilled* their testimony in Jerusalem (Rev. 11.7); the wrath of God *was ended* with the seven plagues (Rev. 15.1); the ten horns and the beast would destroy the harlot until the words of God *were fulfilled* (Rev. 17.17); the ancient serpent was bound in

---

[93] Translation from the Greek text.
[94] Babylonian Talmud *Sanhedrin* 43a.

a pit until the thousand years *were ended* and the dead came to life (Rev. 20.3, 5, 7). Very similar in form and meaning is *teleioō*, which John had Jesus use in the Passover discourse – 'I *accomplished* the work' 'that they may *become perfected* in one [thing]' (17.4, 23, my translation); and which he used in the same way in his first letter: 'Whoever keeps the commandments of God, in him love for God *is perfected*' (1 John 2.5, my translation); 'If we love one another, God abides in us and his love *is perfected* in us' (1 John 4.12, also 17, 18).

When Jesus speaks from the cross, he knows that all is now finished/fulfilled/accomplished/completed – the verb is *teleō* with all its many meanings, and that Scripture must be fulfilled – the verb is *teleioō*. Jesus calls out 'I thirst' and a sponge of vinegar (sour wine) is offered to him on hyssop.[95] Then he calls out 'It is finished' – the verb is *teleō*, and so any of the meanings is appropriate. And finally he hands over or hands on his spirit (v. 30).

Why should drinking vinegar fulfil Scripture? Some have seen here the fulfilment of Psalm 69.21: 'They gave me poison for food, and for my thirst they gave me vinegar to drink', which in the Septuagint became 'They gave me gall as my food and for my thirst they gave me vinegar to drink.' Matthew says the wine that Jesus refused was mixed with gall (Matt. 27.4). Mark says myrrh (Mark 15.23), and so the vinegar and gall of Psalm 69 could refer to the two liquids Jesus was offered. But John does not mention the wine that Jesus refused, and the *Letter of Barnabas* the Levite shows that the vinegar was understood by the Hebrew Christians in a very different way. A section of the letter deals specifically with the vinegar, which is mentioned in all the synoptics (Mark 15.36; Matt. 27.48; Luke 23.36). It had been prefigured, he said, by the temple priesthood. This is where he mentions the sacrifice of Isaac as prefiguring the crucifixion:

> In time to come he would be sacrificing the vessel of his Spirit for our sins – whereby the type created in Isaac, when he was sacrificed on the altar would find its fulfilment. And what does it say in the prophet? 'Let them eat of the goat which is sacrificed for their sins at the fast, and (note this carefully) let all the priests, but nobody else, eat of its inward parts, unwashed and with vinegar.' Why was this? When I am about to offer my body for the sins of this new people of mine, you will be giving me gall and vinegar to drink.[96]

---

[95] This cannot have been common hyssop, which is a shrubby plant. Mark and Matthew say a reed was used, and one mediaeval scribe, who must have sensed the difficulty, changed the text from *hyssōpos* to *hyssos*, 'javelin'.

[96] *Letter of Barnabas* 7.

The quotation is not from any known text, which shows that Barnabas and the early Church had more books of Scripture than we have today. Given the importance of the verse for the Church, it is easy to see why it 'disappeared' in the process of finalizing the Hebrew canon after the disaster of 70 CE.

Barnabas the Levite knew that parts of the sin offering on the Day of Atonement were mixed with vinegar and eaten raw by the priests. The ruling in the Mishnah is like that of Leviticus: the LORD's portion of the sacrificed animal – the entrails with the fat – should be burned on the altar of sacrifice (Lev. 4.8–10),[97] and the remainder of the carcase burned outside the city. There was, however, a different custom among the priests of the Egyptian Jewish community, the spiritual descendants of the first-temple refugees. They used to eat the portion raw if the Day of Atonement fell on a Friday and so, since the end of the day was the start of the Sabbath, they could not cook it.[98] The Pentateuch is not consistent about the regulations: perhaps they were from different periods, or represented two sides of a debate. Numbers 29.11, for example, says that of the two goats offered, one was a sin offering and one the atonement offering. But Barnabas describes the custom he knew, the one that led all the New Testament Gospel writers to say that Jesus drank vinegar just before he died. He was, said Barnabas, preparing himself as the Day of Atonement sacrifice that would be eaten with vinegar by his priests. This was the atonement sacrifice that established the covenant 'for this new people of mine'.[99]

Having drunk the vinegar, Jesus said: 'It is finished/accomplished/completed/perfected', and the scripture had been fulfilled. What scripture? The broken Qumran *Melchizedek* was based entirely upon the fulfilment of Scripture, and told of captives whose teachers had been kept hidden and secret. It looked for the appearance of Melchi-Zedek to bring God's judgement, to make the great atonement, to rescue his own people from the power of Belial, and to fulfil Daniel's prophecy of the anointed one.[100] Since the remains of the *Melchizedek* text resemble what John

---

[97] Mishnah *Menaḥoth* 6.7.
[98] The text says they were Babylonian priests, but the explanation in the Babylonian Talmud *Menaḥot* 100a is that 'Babylonians' was a term of abuse for the priests of Alexandria.
[99] Early Christian writers continued to link the death of Jesus to the Day of Atonement, both in liturgy and in their writings; see my book *The Great High Priest. The Temple Roots of Christian Liturgy*, London: T&T Clark, 2003, pp. 56-102.
[100] As reconstructed and translated in *Qumran Cave 11. Discoveries in the Judaean Desert* XXIII, ed. F. Garcia-Martinez, Oxford: Oxford University Press, 1998, pp. 223-8.

presents in his Gospel, the scripture fulfilled by drinking the vinegar was probably Gabriel's words to Daniel about the future of his people:

> Seventy weeks of years are decreed concerning your people and your holy city:
> *To finish* the transgression,
> *To seal/put an end* to sin,
> To atone iniquity,
> To bring eternal righteousness,
> *To seal/fulfil* vision and prophecy,
> To anoint a most holy one/place. (Dan. 9.24, my translation)

There are problems with the words in italics: 'to finish' requires that the Hebrew *kl'*, 'imprison', be read as *klh*, 'complete/fulfil/finish'; and *lhtm*, 'to complete', is easily confused with *lhtm*, 'to seal'.[101] The Hebrew text now has *lhtm* in both places: 'to seal sin' and 'to seal vision and prophecy'. There are, however, two Greek translations of Daniel which show how and when these lines changed: the Septuagint has 'to complete/put an end to sin' and 'to understand the vision'; but Theodotion, a late second-century CE Jewish translator, has 'to seal sins' and 'to seal vision and prophet'. This suggests that the Hebrew text had *htm*, 'seal', in the time of Theodotion, but *htm*, 'to complete/fulfil' in the pre-Christian version. Putting an end to sin and fulfilling vision and prophecy must have been sensitive issues in the post-Christian period and the text of Daniel was changed. The verb *tam*, 'to complete or fulfil', was taken from the text.[102]

Gabriel's words to Daniel were the scripture that Jesus fulfilled when he drank the vinegar, and his cry 'It is finished/completed', *tetelestai*, corresponds to the Hebrew verb *tam*. The cry could have been the emphatic *tāmôm tam*, 'It is truly completed'. This Hebrew root in its various forms was a key theme for the early Christians, since its meanings embraced much of what John sets out as the teaching of Jesus. In the Hebrew Scriptures the verb was used for Solomon *completing* the temple (1 Kings 6.22) and for the Psalmist *being blameless* (Ps. 19.13); the noun was used for *uprightness* of heart (Ps. 78.72), *uprightness* of way (Prov. 13.6), walking in *integrity* (Prov. 2.7); and the adjective described Job the *blameless man* (Job 1.8). It also meant 'finished': 'When the blossom *is over*, and the flower becomes a ripening grape' (Isa. 18.5). In Gabriel's words to Daniel, the word was used in two senses: to put an end to sin but also to make it whole/heal; and to fulfil the vision and prophecy.

---

[101] Hiph'il infinitive construct of *tm*, Qal infinitive construct of *htm*.
[102] This was the first word to be deciphered with certainty on the Jordan codices.

There is a long history of attempts to reconstruct Daniel 9.24–27 and to make sense of the passage.[103] The first question has to be why these lines are now unreadable. They predict events after 70 weeks of years, that is, after the ten jubilees implied in the *Melchizedek* text. Jesus began his public ministry by showing his glory as Melchi-Zedek,[104] and here he completes his role as Melchi-Zedek, offering the final atonement sacrifice. 'Eternal righteousness', *ṣdq 'lmym*, probably conceals Melchi-Zedek who was the Righteous King for eternity: *mlky ṣdq l'wlm* (Ps. 110.4), and anointing the most holy one/place was understood by Hippolytus (died 236 CE) to mean anointing the Son of God.[105] The Syriac and the Vulgate also understood 'the most holy' to mean the Messiah and not the holy place. The Firstborn coming into the world to make atonement was one of the proof texts listed at the beginning of Hebrews (Heb. 1.6), and here too, the Hebrew text in question survives only in the Qumran Hebrew and in the Septuagint. It is not found in the post-Christian Hebrew text.[106]

Jesus drank the vinegar and so fulfilled the prophecy and the vision, most likely Daniel's vision of the Son of Man going to heaven with clouds:

> And behold, with the clouds of heaven
> There came one like a son of man,
> And he came to the Ancient of Days
> And *was presented before him.*
> And to him was given dominion
> And glory and kingdom,
> That all peoples, nations and languages
> Should serve him;
> His dominion is an everlasting dominion,
> Which shall not pass away,
> And his kingdom one
> That shall not be destroyed.   (Dan. 7.13–14)

This was the raising up of the crucifixion. 'Was presented' before him, literally 'brought near', *haqrᵉbûhî*, must in the temple context of the vision mean that he was offered as a sacrifice, represented by the blood of the goat. The one who has been offered is then enthroned. In the *Parables of Enoch*, which are set in the holy of holies, the prayers of the righteous ones on earth ascend before the LORD of Spirits together with the blood of

---

[103] 'The dismal swamp of Old Testament criticism', J. A. Montgomery, *The Book of Daniel*, ICC, Edinburgh: T&T Clark, 1927, p. 400.
[104] See above, pp. 188–91.
[105] *Commentary on Daniel* 17.
[106] See above, p. 488.

the Righteous One. The holy ones in heaven pray and give thanks with one voice, and bless the LORD of Spirits.[107] All on earth worship him, and then the judgement begins for all those who have not acknowledged the LORD of spirits and his Anointed One (cf. 16.8–11).[108] This is the scene in Revelation 5, where the Lion of Judah, the Root of David, the Servant/ Lamb who is resurrected even though he has been sacrificed, takes his place on the throne, and all creation worships him. This is the scene in Philippians 2, where the Servant who has died on the cross is exalted, and every tongue in all creation acknowledges that Jesus the Messiah is the LORD (Phil. 2.6–11). This is the scene in Hebrews 1, where God's Son, having made the atonement sacrifice, sits enthroned on high (Heb. 1.1–4). And this is what Peter spoke about in the temple, most likely around the time of the Day of Atonement:

> You denied the Holy and Righteous One, and asked for a murderer to be granted to you, and you killed the Author of life, whom God raised from the dead …
>
> What God foretold by the mouth of all the prophets, that his Christ should suffer, he thus fulfilled. Repent therefore, and turn again, that your sins may be blotted out, that times of refreshing may come from the presence of the LORD, and that he may send the Christ appointed for you, Jesus, whom heaven must receive until the time for establishing all that God spoke by the mouth of his holy prophets from of old.
>
> (Acts 3.14–15, 18–21, my translation)

Paul said: 'Christ, our paschal lamb, has been sacrificed' (1 Cor. 5.7), but the rest of the New Testament understood the death of Jesus as the atonement sacrifice made by the royal high priest. Peter's talk in the temple represents the belief in the early years of the Church, when the LORD was expected to return in the future and complete the atonement work of the great high priest.

The Day of Atonement always fell on a Friday in the old solar calendar. The high priest renewed the covenant of creation (and thus renewed the creation) on the day when the Creator finished his work and 'saw everything that he had made, and behold it was very good' (Gen. 1.31). This is how Ben Sira described the Day of Atonement in the time of Simon son of Onias (just before 200 BCE): he came out of the house of the veil (the holy of holies), put on again his robe of glory and then poured out a libation of wine – 'the blood of the grape' – at the foot of the great

---

[107] 1 Enoch 47.1–2.
[108] 1 Enoch 48.5–10.

altar in the courtyard. There was music throughout the temple, until the *kosmos* of the LORD was completed, *sunteleō*, and his liturgy was completed, made perfect, *teleioō* (Ben Sira 50.5, 15, 18–19). Here Ben Sira shows that the ritual on the Day of Atonement was the rite of recreation, and when it was completed, the creation was restored. The Septuagint account of creation ends with similar words: the completion (from *sunteleō*) of the *kosmos* (LXX Gen. 2.1); so too the Septuagint account of Moses erecting the desert tabernacle, which ends with Moses completing, *sunteleō*, the work (LXX Exod. 40.33).[109] Jesus explained to Nicodemus that the Son of God would be lifted up 'not to condemn the *kosmos*, but that the *kosmos* might be saved through him' (3.17). All these senses of completion and fulfilment are caught up in the last cry '*tetelestai*'. Barnabas explained: 'When we were granted remission of our sins, and came to put our hopes in his Name, we were made new men, created all over again from the beginning ...'[110]

## 19.31–42: The burial

John emphasizes again that this was the day before Passover, and then describes the final moments before Jesus' body was taken from the cross. The Jews were concerned that the bodies should not remain on the crosses during the night, because according to their law, the dead person had to be buried on the day of death. Leaving a body on a cross overnight defiled the land (Deut. 21.22–23). Josephus observed: 'The Jews are so careful about funeral rites that even malefactors who have been sentenced to crucifixion are taken down and buried before sunset.'[111] Only John describes how the soldiers came to break Jesus' legs but found that he was already dead; and only John and some early texts of Matthew describe the spear wound to his side from which came blood and water.[112] Both these actions had a special significance for John, because he saw in each the fulfilment of Scripture.

All the synoptic Gospels say that Jesus died at the ninth hour (Mark 15.34–37; Matt. 27.45–50; Luke 23.44–46); John does not say when Jesus died, only that he was handed over to the chief priests at noon on the eve

---

[109] The Hebrew in each case is *kālâ*.
[110] *Letter of Barnabas* 16.
[111] Josephus, *War* 4.317.
[112] Two fourth-century Mss, the Sinai Codex and the Vatican Codex, and the fifth-century Ephraemi Rescriptus in Paris have after Matt. 27.49: 'and another took a spear and pierced his side and there came out water and blood'. This happens just *before* Jesus dies.

of Passover (vv. 14–16). At whatever time he died, it would have coincided with the sacrifice of the Passover lambs in the temple. There were special regulations if the eve of Passover fell on the eve of Sabbath: the daily offering was sacrificed earlier than usual, at half past noon, and offered one hour later. Then at about 2 p.m., the killing of the Passover lambs began. There were so many lambs to be killed that the people were admitted to the temple court in three groups, one after the other, while the Levites were continuously singing the Hallel psalms (Pss. 113—118) until all the lambs had been killed. The people watching at the cross would have heard the repeated blasts of the shofar, marking the deliverance of Israel from Egypt, and perhaps even the sound of the psalms, the last of which had been sung by the crowd as Jesus entered Jerusalem only six days before his death (12.13-16): 'Blessed is he who comes with the Name of the LORD' (Ps. 118.26, my translation); but also 'The stone which the builders rejected has become the headstone of the corner' (Ps. 118.22, my translation). John said of the Palm Sunday acclamation: 'His disciples did not understand this at first; but when Jesus was glorified [i.e. crucified] then they remembered that this had been written of him and had been done to him.' Perhaps the disciples by the cross – John and the women – could hear the psalms. The synoptic Gospels, but not John, say that there was darkness from noon for three hours – an eclipse of the sun perhaps; and that during the darkness, the veil of the temple was torn from top to bottom. Presumably this omen was reported by the priests who became Christians (Acts 6.7). Matthew reported an earthquake (Mark 15.33-38; Matt. 27.45-53; Luke 23.44-45); and it would have been an aftershock that moved the stone away from Jesus' tomb.

This was the moment, said the writer of Hebrews, when the holy of holies was opened to all. Hebrews is the book that explains more clearly than any other in the New Testament how the death of Jesus was the atonement sacrifice (Heb. 9.11-14). It does not speak of the temple in the past tense, and seems to have been written when the temple was still standing.

> The whole theme of Hebrews is the final supersession by Christ of the levitical system, its priesthood and its sacrifices. The destruction of the sanctuary which physically brought this system to an end must surely, if it had occurred, left its mark somewhere.[113]

---

[113] J. A. T. Robinson, *Redating the New Testament*, London: SCM Press, 1976, p. 200.

## John 18—19

Hebrews, then, could represent the interpretations of a first- or second-generation Christian. The veil of the temple was the flesh of Jesus, s/he wrote, without an explanation of the imagery used, so this must have been common knowledge. Josephus and Philo, both men from high-priestly families, knew that the veil was woven from four colours to represent the four elements from which the world was made. It therefore represented matter,[114] and so for the Christians, the flesh in which the LORD was clothed at his Incarnation. When the flesh was torn at his death, so was the veil. This opened up the way for the people of the great high priest to enter the holy of holies (Heb. 10.19–22), and to function as the new high priests with his Name on their foreheads, standing in his presence (Rev. 22.4; John 17.24). On the Day of Atonement the cleansing and renewing blood came from the holy of holies; Ezekiel and Joel had told of water flowing from the house of the LORD (Ezek. 47.1–12; Joel 3.18); and Zechariah had prophesied a fountain opened to cleanse the house of David and the people of Jerusalem (Zech. 13.1).

John does not mention the tearing of the temple veil, but he does record the piercing of Jesus' side, which for the writer of Hebrews would have been two aspects of the same event. When the way had been opened through the torn veil/flesh: 'Let us draw near with a true heart in full assurance of faith, with our hearts sprinkled clean from an evil conscience and our bodies washed with pure water' (Heb. 10.22). These were the three conditions for entering the holy of holies through the torn veil:

- *A true heart in full assurance of faith.* In the temple context of this text, we can assume the Hebrew meaning for 'heart', which was 'mind'. The mind of a person with full assurance of faith had been taught by the Paraclete, who Jesus said would come when he had departed from his disciples and 'teach you all things and bring to your remembrance all that I have said to you ... Let not your minds be troubled, neither let them be afraid' (14.26–27, my translation); 'When the Spirit of truth comes, he will guide you into all truth' (16.13).
- *A heart sprinkled clean from an evil conscience.* In the temple context of this text, sprinkling clean is an image from the Day of Atonement, when blood was sprinkled to cleanse and to consecrate and thus to remove iniquity (Lev. 16.19). Here the sprinkling is to remove the effect of evil knowledge (rather than 'conscience').
- *A body washed with pure water.* In the temple context of this text, this

---
[114] Philo, *Questions on Exodus* II.85; Josephus, *Antiquities* 3.183.

is the high priest washing himself before putting on the linen garments to serve in the holy of holies on the Day of Atonement (Lev. 16.4).[115]

What Hebrews describes are: the Paraclete, that is, the Spirit of the LORD returned to his disciples; the blood of the sacrificed goat; and the pure water. These were the three gifts of the LORD to his disciples as he died and opened the veil: he handed on/handed over, *paradidōmi*, his Spirit; and he poured out blood and water from his side. The Qumran *Rule* warned that those who did not fully accept the teachings of the community could not be considered perfect/blameless/completed, *tāmîm*, and could not be purified by atonements nor cleansed with purifying waters.[116] John emphasizes that he was an eyewitness and saw this (v. 35), and he alluded to it in his first letter (1 John 5.6–8). John was speaking the 'truth' (v. 35), meaning that the event was to be understood on a spiritual level, and the Spirit, the water and the blood were the witnesses.

The LORD had made the soul of his Servant the *'āšām*, the offering to restore the covenant: 'It was the will of the LORD to bruise him and *to pierce him*', according to the Qumran text of Isaiah 53.10.[117] He poured out his soul, *nepheš*, to death (Isa. 53.12), and this was ritualized as pouring out his blood, since 'the *nepheš* of the flesh is in the blood, and I have established it for you to atone your own souls, *nepheš*, on the altar, for the blood atones by means of the soul, *nepheš*' (Lev. 17.11, translating literally). The early hymn sang of Christ Jesus who, in the form of a Servant, emptied himself by death on a cross (Phil. 2.5–8). The atonement blood that was *sprinkled* (Heb. 10.22) was the blood sprinkled, *nāzâ*, on the Day of Atonement to cleanse and consecrate (Lev. 16.19), and also the blood sprinkled by the Servant on many nations, so that they would be able to see and understand (Isa. 52.15).[118]

The soldier piercing the side of Jesus fulfilled the prophecy in Zechariah 12.10: 'They shall look on whom they have pierced' (19.37, translating literally):

> [The LORD says] ... when [the house of David and the people of Jerusalem] look on me whom they have pierced, they shall mourn over him, like the mourning over the beloved/only son, *yāḥîdh*, and they shall grieve over him,

---

[115] Mishnah *Yoma* 3.3–6 prescribes the elaborate multiple immersions and washing required for the high priest on the Day of Atonement.
[116] *Community Rule*, 1QS III.4.
[117] 1QIsa[a]. The MT has 'made him sick'.
[118] Thus the AV, which is the correct translation; NEB, JB, RSV, NRSV, GNB translate differently because they did not understand the context of the passage, and so they have obscured the meaning from all their readers.

like the bitter grief over the firstborn, $b^e kh\hat{o}r$.

(Zech. 12.10, translating literally)

It is possible that the prophecy originally recalled the suspicious death of King Josiah, killed at the battle of Carchemish by an arrow that could have come from his own archers (2 Chron. 35.23). There was great mourning. In its present context, however, it is part of the collection of prophecies appended to Zechariah that describe the day of the LORD: all nations would come against Jerusalem and Judah but the LORD would destroy them; they would look on the LORD whom they had pierced, and there would be great mourning; and a fountain would be opened to cleanse the house of David and the people of Jerusalem, those who had pierced the LORD. The Hebrew text actually says *that the LORD was pierced*, and describes the person pierced as the beloved son and the firstborn, the latter being a title for the Davidic king (Ps. 89.27). The one pierced was the king who was the LORD with his people, and so John's use of this prophecy was apt.

John has already used the prophecy at the beginning of Revelation, to describe the LORD and his future return; it may have been part of the original community's collection of fulfilled prophecies.[119] His words there have the same themes as his Gospel:

- *To him who loves us*, the main theme of his Gospel;
- *and has freed us from our sins by his blood*, the atonement theme throughout his Gospel;
- *and made us a kingdom, priests to his God and Father*, the theme of the Passover discourse, where the people who have been allotted to Jesus and keep his commandment to love become the new royal priesthood (cf. Exod. 19.5–6);
- *to him be glory and dominion for ever and ever* (Rev. 1.5–6).

And then: 'Behold, he is coming with clouds, and every eye will see him, everyone who pierced him; and all the tribes of the earth will wail on account of him' (Rev. 1.7).

Barnabas alluded to John's account of the Passion in terms of the Day of Atonement: John depicted the scene fulfilled: 'Behold the Man' (v. 5); but Barnabas describes the scene still in the future:

They shall see him on that Day, clad to the ankles in his red woollen robe, and will say: 'Is this not he whom we once crucified, and mocked and

---

[119] Justin used it, *Apology* 1.52.

pierced and spat upon? Yes, this is the man who told us that he was the son of God.' But how will he resemble the goat? The point of there being two similar goats, both of them fair and alike, is that when they see him coming on the Day, they are going to be struck with the manifest parallel between him and the goat. In this ordinance, then, you see typified the future sufferings of Jesus.[120]

But for John, the return of the pierced one had already happened. On the evening of the day of resurrection, Jesus came to his disciples 'and he showed them his hands and his side' (20.21). For doubting Thomas, the sign of the piercing was proof that Jesus was 'My LORD and my God' (20.28).

The other prophecy John quotes is ambiguous, as we should expect at this moment when the Passover sacrifice of the Moses tradition becomes again the atonement sacrifice of the royal priesthood of the first temple. 'Not a bone of him shall be broken.' This could refer to the prescription for the Passover sacrifice: 'You shall not break a bone of it' (Exod. 12.46; Num. 9.12). But the passive form that John quotes is from Psalm 34 and concerns the sufferings of the Righteous One.

> Many are the afflictions of the Righteous One;
> But the LORD delivers him out of them all.
> He keeps all his bones;
> *Not one of them is broken.*
> Evil shall slay the wicked,
> And those who hate the Righteous One
> Shall bear their own sins. (Ps. 34.19–21, my translation)

Those who hate the Righteous One have no one to bear their sins as the *'āšām* sacrifice – this was the role of the Servant (Isa. 53.10) – and so they bear their own sins, *ye'$s^e$mû*, the related verb.

Joseph of Arimathea, a secret disciple for fear of the Jews (v. 38), asks Pilate for Jesus' body. Nicodemus brings a huge quantity of myrrh (used for embalming) and aloes (probably bitter aloes, as this was also used for embalming). The body of Jesus is wrapped in linen and spices – only John mentions that the spices were used on the Friday. Spices were the sign of a royal burial (Jer. 34.5), and Josephus says that when Herod the Great was buried, 500 servants were needed to carry all the spices.[121] Very little is known of the burial rites of the Davidic kings, but they were buried in their garden (2 Kings 21.18, 26). The body of Jesus is placed in a new

---

[120] *Letter of Barnabas* 7.
[121] Josephus, *Antiquities* 17.199.

tomb in a garden nearby, but only John says the garden was near the place of crucifixion (v. 41).

For John the tomb is the place of resurrection and so carries the symbolism of the holy of holies. When Aaron entered the holy of holies to make atonement, he was dressed in linen and carried the blood of a goat and a bull (Lev. 16.4, 14–16). When Jesus the great high priest, also wearing linen, made the atonement offering, 'Neither by the blood of goats and calves, but by his own blood he entered in once into the holy place, having obtained eternal redemption for us' (Heb. 9.12, AV).

# John 20

This chapter is the final section of John's original Gospel and balances the opening section. Both have temple settings: in the Prologue, the Logos emerges from the beginning – the holy of holies – into the world. In him is life. The Logos becomes flesh and tabernacles among us. Various people recognize him and acclaim him: the Son of God, the Lamb of God, the Teacher, the Messiah, the King of Israel. On the third day he manifests his glory at Cana. In the resurrection scene, also on the third day, the LORD emerges from his tomb, which is the place of resurrection and so the holy of holies. He comes first into the world but then goes to heaven. In him is life. The LORD has left behind the flesh – the linen grave clothes – and returns to the Father. Various people recognize and acclaim him: the Teacher, the LORD, 'my LORD and my God'. Again, he manifests his glory, and the disciples see the LORD.

As John unfolds the Gospel, he shows how the disciples came to realize what Jesus had been teaching them through his words and his signs; but he also shows how the expectations of the *parousia* had already been fulfilled. When he received further teaching from the risen LORD in the early 50s and sent it to the churches of Asia Minor, he was still expecting to see the pierced one return with clouds, the One who is and who was and is coming (Rev. 1.7, 8). 'Behold I am coming soon' (Rev. 2.16; 3.11; 22.7, 12, 20). When he wrote his Gospel, he knew that the pierced one had already returned. John has Jesus showing his wounds to his disciples, as does Luke (Luke 24.39), and when John compiled the present form of Revelation, Jesus' promises of an imminent return were put into the Appendix of the book.

John was also aware of the expectations cherished by the Qumran community, and doubtless by others too, that they would be restored to Adam's original state:[1] 'God has chosen them for an eternal covenant, and all the glory of Adam shall be theirs.'[2] '[Those who hold to the older ways]

---

[1] For detail of the Adam figure at the end of the second-temple period, see my book *Creation. A Biblical Vision for the Environment*, London: T&T Clark, 2010, pp. 193–236.
[2] *Community Rule*, 1QS IV.

## John 20

are destined to live for ever, and all the glory of Adam shall be theirs.' These people were the faithful priests, the sons of Zadok who did not go astray.[3] He would have known that there was far more to the Adam figure than is found in the Hebrew Genesis: that he had been the first high priest, a glorious figure who wore garments of light, but lost them when he listened to the snake; that he had originally been clothed in glory and righteousness, and when he was resurrected, he would once more have access to the tree of life.[4]

John would also have known that the tomb was found empty on the day after the Sabbath of Passover, Nisan 16, when the first sheaf of barley, the 'ōmer, was offered in the temple. This was the firstfruits of the new harvest:

> When you come into the land which I shall give you and reap its harvest, you shall bring the sheaf of the firstfruits of your harvest to the priest; and he shall wave the sheaf before the LORD, that you may find acceptance; on the morrow after the sabbath the priest shall wave it. (Lev. 23.10–11)

Towards the end of the Sabbath, servants of the Sanhedrin went to a field near Jerusalem and tied the token bundles of barley to mark them. A crowd gathered to watch, and at sunset the token quantity of barley[5] was reaped and brought to the temple, threshed and then lightly roasted before being ground. A tithe of this flour was mixed with oil and frankincense to make a dough and then ritually offered – 'waved before the LORD' – before a handful was burned on the altar. The rest was given back to the priests for their own use.[6] The firstfruits consecrated the whole harvest.

There were several types of wave offering, including the high priest presenting the new Levites as a 'wave offering' (Num. 8.5–22). This account, as we have seen,[7] was part of the lectionary reading for the third Passover in the cycle, and at the last supper Jesus has already washed his new Levites. After being washed, the Levites were offered and then handed back to the high priest for serving in the tabernacle/temple.

> Aaron shall offer the Levites before the LORD as a wave offering from the people of Israel, that it may be theirs to do the service of the LORD ...

---

[3] *Damascus Document*, CD III.
[4] *Apocalypse of Moses* 20.1–2; 28.4.
[5] Equivalent to about 23 litres.
[6] Mishnah *Menaḥoth* 10.1–4; A. Edersheim, *The Temple. Its Ministry and Services*, Grand Rapids, MI: Eerdmans, 1987.
[7] See above, p. 378.

> And after that the Levites shall go in to do the service at the tent of meeting, when you have cleansed them and offered them as a wave offering. For they are wholly given to me from among the people of Israel; instead of all that opens the womb, the first-born of all the people of Israel, I have taken them [the Levites] for myself. (Num. 8.11, 15–16)

The offering of the firstfruits was the token offering of the new priesthood: Jesus was the offering, and the rest were handed back for service. This was the scene in Revelation 5, where the heavenly host praised the Lamb on the throne who had himself been sacrificed such that others were released for service:

> Worthy art thou to take the book and to open its seals,
> For thou wast slain and by thy blood didst ransom men for God
> From every tribe and tongue and people and nation,
> And hast made them a kingdom and priests to our God,
> And they shall reign on earth. (Rev. 5.9–10)

The people were tying the *'ōmer*, then cutting it and taking it to the temple a few hours after Jesus died.

The anointed king emerging from the holy of holies, the restoration of Adam and the offering of firstfruits are three of the elements underlying John's Easter story. There is also a fourth: the story of Enoch's first and second ascents to heaven. This can be seen in *2 Enoch*, a text whose age and provenance cannot be agreed upon, but which undoubtedly has roots in Hebrew tradition since it is an expansion of Genesis 5.21–24. Enoch and his family are the priesthood before Noah's flood, and the end of *2 Enoch* describes how Noah's younger brother Nir, Enoch's great-grandson, became the priest.[8] Nir, who is not mentioned in Genesis, had no child, but at the time of her death, his wife was found to be miraculously pregnant. Her son was born after she died. The baby was Melchi-Zedek, whom Gabriel took to paradise until the flood was past, so that he could be the future head of priests who would reign over a royal people serving the LORD.[9] The story in *2 Enoch* is telling how the older priesthood of the first temple survived. Noah's flood represented the Babylonian invasion of Judah in the early sixth century and the subsequent scattering and destruction of the people. Isaiah had made this comparison only a generation after the events (Isa. 54.9–10), and scholars have shown recently how the Priestly writers of the second

---

[8] *2 Enoch* 70.14, 20.
[9] *2 Enoch* 71.37.

temple ('P') also used Noah's flood to describe the disaster of the exile and the building of the second temple as the new sanctuary emerging from the flood.[10] On the other hand, those who regarded the second-temple priests as apostate – the Enoch tradition[11] – would have been sympathetic to the hopes in the Qumran *Melchizedek* text: that certain teachings/teachers had been kept secret (during the flood and its aftermath) but would return when Melchi-Zedek returned.[12]

The material in *2 Enoch*, however it was transmitted and wherever it was finally written down, relates to the claims of the first-temple priests and their Melchi-Zedek. The Christians claimed that Jesus was Melchi-Zedek returned. It is likely, then, that the priestly ascents described in *2 Enoch* were known to the early Christians who stood broadly within this tradition, even if they did not know this particular text. A defining characteristic of the group led by 'Isaiah' who left Jerusalem – that thinly veiled picture of the Jerusalem Christians – was their belief in the Ascension into heaven,[13] and so the account of Enoch's two ascents is of great interest. On his first ascent (in Genesis 5 this is 'Enoch walked with God') he stood before the heavenly throne and was anointed and transformed into an angel. He was dressed in garments of the glory of God,[14] and one of the angels instructed him in all the secrets of heaven and creation. Then he returned to earth: 'And now, therefore, my children, I know everything, either from the lips of the LORD or else my eyes have seen from the beginning even to the end and from the end to the recommencement …'[15] This is very similar to John's reassurance to Christians: 'You have been anointed by the Holy One and you know all things' (1 John 2.20, my translation); and to his reflection on the teaching of Jesus: 'He bears witness to what he has seen and heard, yet no one receives his testimony … for he whom God has sent utters the words of God …' (3.32, 34). In *2 Enoch* the LORD then gave Enoch the heavenly books and told him to return to earth and teach his family what he had learned and what was in the books. Then the angels would come and take him back to heaven. When the time came for him to return to heaven, the

---

[10] J. Blenkinsopp, 'The Structure of P', *Catholic Biblical Quarterly* 38 (1976), pp. 275–92, esp. pp. 283–6.

[11] *1 Enoch* 93.9: 'in the seventh week shall an apostate generation arise …'.

[12] *Melchizedek*, 11QMelch II.5 as reconstructed in *Discoveries in the Judaean Desert* XXIII, ed. F. Garcia-Martinez, Oxford: Oxford University Press, 1998.

[13] *Ascension of Isaiah* 2.9.

[14] *2 Enoch* 22.5–10.

[15] *2 Enoch* 40.1.

elders of the people blessed Enoch and said to him: 'The LORD has chosen you ... the one who reveals, who carries away our sins.'[16] In Genesis 5.24 this is 'He was not; for God took him.' Enoch as the revealer and the redeemer could hardly have originated with a Christian scribe, but the picture of Enoch the priest ascending to heaven to be transformed into an angel, returning to earth to teach and then going back to heaven leaving no grave is very similar to John's picture of Jesus as 'the one who reveals, who carries away our sins' and who left an empty tomb.

## 20.1–10: The empty tomb

All the canonical Gospels describe the open tomb; the stone had moved from the entrance, perhaps due to an aftershock of the earthquake that Matthew described (Matt. 27.54). All the canonical Gospels also record that the tomb was empty, but no other New Testament text mentions it. Matthew, Luke and John tell of resurrection appearances, and the ending of Mark's Gospel is little more than a list of resurrection appearances. Paul does not mention the empty tomb, even though he speaks of the resurrection of the Anointed One; and Luke, who does describe the empty tomb in his Gospel, can nevertheless attribute to his characters in Acts speeches about the resurrection that do not mention the empty tomb: Peter's words at Pentecost (Acts 2.14–36); Peter's words to the council (Acts 4.8–12; 5.29–32); Peter's words to Cornelius (Acts 10.34–43); and Paul's address in the synagogue in Pisidian Antioch (Acts 13.16–41). In each of these cases, the hearers were Jews, and had they been told about the empty tomb, it would have been easy for them to repeat the story that Matthew reports: '"His disciples came by night and stole him away" ... and this story has been spread among the Jews to this day' (Matt. 28.13, 15). The emphasis, then, was not on the empty tomb but on the resurrection appearances. From the beginning, however, the Christians did proclaim the empty tomb in another way: they used Psalm 16 as a proof text, especially verse 10: 'You will not let your Holy One see corruption'[17] (Acts 2.27, 31; 13.35, my translation), understanding this to mean: 'the resurrection of Christ, that he was not abandoned to Hades, nor did his flesh see corruption' (Acts 2.31). This was the empty tomb, but expressed in another way: no dead body remained.

---

[16] *2 Enoch* 64.5.
[17] Luke quotes the LXX form of the psalm.

## John 20

The Christian community remembered which rock tomb had been the place of resurrection. John has a clear memory of the tomb and its location: it was in a garden near the place of crucifixion, which was outside the city (19.20, 41). This agrees with Hebrews 13.12, that Jesus died outside the gate of the city. Some ten years later, however, the walls of the city were extended by Herod Agrippa to enclose an area to the north and west, and after this, the site of the crucifixion and the tomb was within the city. John wrote his Gospel after the site of the tomb had been enclosed within the new walls, but he remembered accurately that the place of crucifixion and the tomb had been outside the walls. Despite this Gospel evidence, Melito was quite emphatic when he addressed the Jews in about 160 CE, that the site was (by his time) within the walls:

> You killed your LORD *in the midst of* Jerusalem ... An extraordinary murder has taken place *in the centre of Jerusalem*, in the city devoted to God's law ... in the middle of the *plateia*, even *in the centre of the city*, while all were looking on, the unjust murder of this just person took place.[18]

According to Eusebius, Melito had travelled to the east and visited 'the place where it all happened',[19] and so this was how he had seen the site of the crucifixion. He would have been in Jerusalem some 25 years after Hadrian began to rebuild the city as Aelia Capitolina, the time when, according to Eusebius, the site of the tomb was buried under a paved area (perhaps Melito's *plateia*, which can mean a square) where a temple to Aphrodite was built. People must have remembered the site of the tomb, and when Constantine had the area cleared, Eusebius said that the cave tomb, 'the holy of holies', came forth again to the light.[20] The empty tomb was part of the original proclamation, as was Eusebius' description of the tomb as the holy of holies.

John presents the Easter scene as the new Eden. The tomb is in a garden, *kēpos* (19.41),[21] and the time, in all four canonical Gospels, is not 'the third day'.[22] Nor is it 'the first day' as usually translated, but it is Day

---

[18] Melito, *On the Pasch* 93, 94.
[19] Eusebius, *History* 4.26.
[20] Eusebius, *Life of Constantine* 26, 28.
[21] 'The ecclesiastical interpretation of the Johannine scene as paradisal was surely built on more than pious fancy in the early Church ... C. K. Barrett's remark that had John intended to evoke Eden he would have used *paradeisos* instead of *kēpos* is prosaic. The point was to hint, to suggest, to lead the mind of the reader to this conclusion without spelling it out.' N. Wyatt, '"Supposing him to be the Gardener" (John 20.15). A Study of the Paradise Motif in John', *Zeitschrift für die neutestamentliche Wissenschaft* 81 (1990), pp. 37–8.
[22] The two on the road to Emmaus mention the third day (Luke 24.21).

One (20.1). This is the new creation, the new Day One (Gen. 1.5), on which light was created to dispel the chaos and darkness. Mary Magdalene comes to the tomb while it is still dark, but only John mentions the darkness. In the other canonical Gospels the women went to the tomb towards the dawn (Matt. 28.1); very early (Mark 16.2); at early dawn (Luke 24.1). For John, the darkness must be significant, perhaps to emphasize that the '*ōmer* has not yet been 'waved' in the temple. In the other canonical Gospels the women went to the tomb with spices, but John says this had already been done on the Friday evening (19.38–40). Mary Magdalene has no reason to go to the tomb. She then sees the open tomb and draws her own conclusion. She reports to Peter and the beloved disciple: 'They have taken the LORD out of the tomb, and we do not know where they have laid him' (v. 2). '*We* do not know' suggests that Mary was not alone when she went to the tomb, even though John does not mention anyone with her. The other Gospels name her companions as 'the other Mary' (Matt. 28.1); 'Mary the mother of James, and Salome' (Mark 16.1); and 'Joanna and Mary the mother of James and the other women with them' (Luke 24.10). Or the 'we' could indicate the start of another story involving several women, inserted into the original which described Mary coming to the tomb on her own.

In the inserted story (vv. 2–10) – if such it was – Mary Magdalene goes to tell Peter and the beloved disciple, who then run to the tomb, and the unnamed disciple arrives first. He stoops to look into the tomb and sees the linen cloths, but he does not go in. Was he perhaps a priest concerned for ritual purity? Then Peter arrives, goes into the tomb and sees just the linen cloths, with the piece of linen for the head lying separately. The unnamed disciple then goes into the tomb, perhaps when he knows there is no body there. John implies a contrast between the Easter event and the raising of Lazarus: people had to take away the stone from Lazarus' tomb (11.41), and he came forth still wrapped in his grave clothes, with a separate piece around his head (11.44). Lazarus, like the son of the widow of Nain and Jairus' daughter (Luke 7.11–17; 8.49–56), was restored to physical life, but not resurrected. The unnamed disciple at Jesus' tomb 'saw and believed'. The others – 'they' – apparently did not yet know the scripture that he must rise from the dead, but the text implies that the unnamed disciple did.

Mary Magdalene assumes there have been tomb robbers (v. 13), but John Chrysostom has left a vivid account of why this could not have been the case:

> When then she came and said these things, they hearing them, draw near with great eagerness to the sepulchre, and see the linen clothes lying, which was a sign of the Resurrection. For neither, if any persons had removed the body, would they before doing so have stripped it; nor if any had stolen it, would they have taken the trouble to remove the napkin, and roll it up, and lay it in a place by itself; but how? They would have taken the body as it was. On this account John tells us by anticipation that it was buried with much myrrh, which glues linen to the body not less firmly than lead; in order that when you hear that the napkins lay apart, you may not endure those who say that He was stolen. For a thief would not have been so foolish as to spend so much trouble on a superfluous matter. For why should he undo the clothes? And how could he have escaped detection if he had done so? Since he would probably have spent much time in so doing, and be found out by delaying and loitering. But why do the clothes lie apart, while the napkin was wrapped together by itself? That you may learn that it was not the action of men in confusion or haste, the placing some in one place, some in another, and the wrapping them together. From this they believed in the Resurrection.[23]

What they saw would not have been simple linen cloths, but linen impregnated with two highly perfumed resins, presumably as oils.

Only John names the spices used for Jesus' burial: myrrh and aloes, and so this detail is significant. The robes of the newly anointed Davidic king had been perfumed with myrrh, aloes and cassia (Ps. 45.8), and it was an oil blended from myrrh that conferred resurrection in the temple. The anointed ones who emerged from the holy of holies, perfumed with myrrh, were already transformed into sons of God and angels; they lived the life that Jesus said awaited the dead after they had risen: 'They are equal to angels and are sons of God, being sons of the resurrection' (Luke 20.36). This is what John 'saw and believed'. The miracle of the empty tomb confirmed the earlier spiritual resurrection when Jesus was taken up to heaven and shown all that he had to teach when he returned to earth. The Baptist knew of Jesus' ascent experiences (3.31), and so they must have preceded his public ministry. When John saw the empty tomb, he knew it was the time for the Anointed and Resurrected One to return to heaven. The *Gospel of Philip* has preserved this earliest understanding of the resurrection, the pre-death ascent of the LORD, but also of the baptized.

---

[23] John Chrysostom, *On John*, Homily 85.

Those who say that the LORD died first and rose up are in error, for he rose up first and died. If one does not first attain the resurrection, will he not die? As God lives, he would be [dead] ...

Those who say they will die first and then rise are in error. If they do not first receive the resurrection while they live, when they die they will receive nothing. So also when speaking about baptism they say: 'Baptism is a great thing, because if people receive it they will live.'[24]

'As yet they did not yet know the scripture, that he must rise from the dead' (v. 9). This is another example of the disciples' failure to understand events at the time. They had not understood Jesus' first resurrection saying: 'Destroy this temple and in three days I will raise it up' (2.19), nor the significance of Jesus choosing to ride a young donkey into Jerusalem (12.14), of which John observed on each occasion that the disciples understood only after Jesus had been raised from the dead (2.19; 12.16). Luke shows this in the story of the two disciples on the road to Emmaus. He has Jesus 'interpreting in all the scriptures the things concerning himself' (Luke 24.27). It seems that not all the disciples had known who Jesus was, nor did they recognize him until their eyes were opened and he vanished from their sight (Luke 24.31). Peter said much the same to Cornelius: '... God raised him on the third day, and made him become visible, not to all the people but to us who were prepared beforehand as witnesses ...' (Acts 10.40–41, my translation).

John captures Jesus' sense of frustration over this in his saying to Philip at the last supper: 'Have I been with you so long, and yet you do not know me, Philip?' (14.9). It was the Easter event that enabled the disciples fully to realize who Jesus was. The gift of the Paraclete was to help the disciples understand: 'The Paraclete, the Holy Spirit whom the Father will send with my Name, he will teach you all things and bring to your remembrance all that I have said to you' (14.26, my translation). But the Paraclete was the risen LORD returning to teach his disciples the meaning of what they had already seen and heard. The very similar saying in 16.13 – 'When the spirit of Truth comes, he will guide you into all the truth ... he will declare to you the things that are to come' – is another role of the Paraclete: to interpret the visions of Jesus and show when they had been fulfilled. This was the role of the angel of the LORD who made the visions known to John (Rev. 1.1b).

There is nothing in the current text of the Hebrew Scriptures which shows that the Anointed One suffered and then entered his glory, but the

---

[24] *Gospel of Philip*, CG II.3.56, 73.

## John 20

Qumran version of Isaiah's fourth Servant song could be read that way. It has *mšḥty*, 'anointed', for *mšḥt*, 'disfigured', in 52.14,[25] and since the Targum has 'my servant the Anointed One' at 52.13, the Targumist knew a text where the servant was the Anointed One. Further, the Qumran texts have an extra word in 53.11: *'wr*, 'light',[26] as does the LXX, giving: 'After the suffering of his soul he will see light ...' The Qumran version of Isaiah, then, could have been the text that Luke's Jesus said was fulfilled.

Which scripture did John have in mind when he wrote: 'They did not yet know the scripture that he must rise from the dead'? This comment, together with Luke's story of the disciples on the road to Emmaus, suggests that in the period between Passover and Tabernacles the disciples began to experience the presence of the Paraclete, the risen LORD returning and enabling them to understand who he was. Luke's story shows Jesus presenting himself as the Servant, and this initial recognition by the disciples would later be woven through the Gospels of Matthew and John.[27] But the fourth Servant song, as usually translated, does not depict a resurrected Servant. The opening line describes him as *prospering, exalted* and lifted up (Isa. 52.13), as was the Davidic king who was *exalted* and anointed (Ps. 89.19–20). In temple discourse, such exaltation was more than the gift of high status; it was the moment when the human king was transformed. 'Prospered' is *śākhal*, which more usually means 'have understanding', and so the Servant was given knowledge just as the human Enoch was instructed by the archangel after he had been anointed and transformed into a glorious heavenly being.[28] The LXX translated this verb as *suneidō*, 'see/understand'. This was all part of the Servant's resurrection experience, which Jesus received at his baptism,[29] and which was confirmed by the Easter event.

In his first letter to Corinth, written in 53/54 CE, Paul offers the earliest evidence for how the first Christians understood Jesus' resurrection. He contrasted the physical body and the spiritual body: 'Flesh and blood cannot inherit the kingdom of God' (1 Cor. 15.44, 50). It was not necessary to die in order to attain the state of resurrection: 'We shall not all sleep, but we shall all be changed ... the dead will be raised ... and we shall be changed' (1 Cor. 15.51, 53). This was written when the *parousia*

---

[25] 1QIsa$^a$.
[26] 1QIsa$^a$, 1QIsa$^b$, 1QIsa$^d$.
[27] See my book *Temple Mysticism. An Introduction*, London: SPCK, 2011, pp. 167–9.
[28] *2 Enoch* 22.9–10, and then the instruction in cc. 23—35.
[29] See above, p. 117.

was still thought to be imminent. It was only two or three years since Paul had written:

> The LORD himself will descend from heaven with a cry of command ... and the dead in Christ will rise first; then we who are alive, who are left, shall be caught up together with them in the clouds to meet the LORD in the air ...
> (1 Thess. 4.16–17, my translation)

Paul contrasted the man of dust, which was the human state, with the man of heaven which he would become. 'We shall [or 'Let us'] bear the image of the man of heaven' (1 Cor. 15.49). At about the same time, Paul had written to the Philippians: 'From [heaven] we await a Saviour ... who will change our lowly body to be like his glorious body ...' (Phil. 3.20–21). Paul associated the resurrection with regaining all the glory of Adam.

Paul gave a list of those who had seen the risen LORD, and he included in that list his own experience on the Damascus road (1 Cor. 15.5–8):[30] 'A light from heaven flashed about him, and he fell to the ground and heard a voice ...' (Acts 9.3–4).[31] This was Luke's report: Paul himself said that the gospel came to him 'through a revelation of Jesus Christ' when God revealed 'his Son *in* me' (Gal. 1.12, 16). Zechariah had described his experience of the guiding angel in the same way; he spoke *within* him [RSV 'talked with me'] (Zech. 1.9, 14, 19; 2.3). John would have described this experience as the work of the Paraclete 'who dwells with you, and will be in you' (14.17). Paul described him variously as 'the Spirit of his Son' (Gal. 4.6); 'the Spirit of Jesus Christ' (Phil. 1.19); and as the Spirit who enabled people to understand the writings of Moses:

> To this day whenever Moses is read a veil lies over their minds; but when a man turns to the LORD the veil is removed. Now the LORD is the Spirit, and where the Spirit of the LORD is, there is freedom. And we all, with unveiled faces, beholding/reflecting[32] the glory of the LORD, are being changed into his likeness, from one degree of glory to another; for this comes from the LORD who is the Spirit.
> (2 Cor. 3.15–18, my translation)

This is how Paul experienced the resurrection. It was for him the moment of realization when he was aware of the Paraclete, the ongoing and transforming presence of 'the LORD who is the Spirit'. It was when he

---

[30] But not the appearance to Mary Magdalene, although this is mentioned in the longer ending of Mark as the first resurrection appearance (Mark 16.9).

[31] Also Acts 22.6–7 and 26.13–14. All accounts mention the light and the voice, but in Acts 9 his companions heard the voice but saw no light and in Acts 22 they saw the light but heard no voice.

[32] The middle voice of *katoptrizō* can mean both of these.

## John 20

began to read 'Moses' differently, and so was able to write of 'one God, the Father ... and one Lord, Jesus Christ ...' (1 Cor. 8.6, my translation).

Paul had received this teaching when he first became a Christian and he had also learned that 'the Anointed One died for our sins in accordance with the Scriptures' (1 Cor. 15.3, my translation; cf. Acts 17.2; 20.28; 26.23). He was referring to the fourth Servant song that Luke's Jesus expounded on the road to Emmaus. This, in the pre-Christian Qumran version, is the only text that describes the death of the Anointed One to take away sins, and this was how John, in the stylized introduction to his Gospel, had the Baptist introduce Jesus: 'Behold the Lamb of God/the Servant of the Lord who takes away the sin of the world' (1.29, my translation). The death of Jesus was understood as the atonement sacrifice of the Servant.

Luke reflects this in his account of Peter's address in Solomon's porch, which happened a little while after Pentecost, when many had joined the followers of Jesus. The subject of the address – 'repent ... that your sins may be blotted out' (Acts 3.19) – suggests that the Day of Atonement was imminent, and Peter's words interpret the death of Jesus as the atonement sacrifice. 'You denied the Holy and Righteous One ... and killed the Author of life, whom God raised from the dead.' Peter then speaks of fulfilling the same prophecy about the Servant, 'that his Anointed One should suffer' (Acts 3.18, my translation). This, he says, was foretold by the mouth of *all the prophets*. Those texts no longer exist, and indeed, the text which shows the Servant as the Anointed One only exists in the pre-Christian Qumran scroll. Peter invites the people to repent that their sins may be blotted out – Day of Atonement imagery – so that the Anointed One may be sent (back) from heaven where he is to stay until the prophecies are fulfilled. And when the prophecies were fulfilled, the Anointed One would return. These prophecies – or at least some of them – now form the Book of Revelation, and when most of them had been fulfilled, the Lord did return to John to give him the revelation that prompted his Gospel.

Luke's record of the early teaching in the Jerusalem church has preserved some interesting details: 'God, having *raised up* his servant, sent him to you first' (Acts 3.26) implies that Jesus was raised up before he began his ministry and was put to death. The verb is *anistēmi*, which is used to mean 'resurrect'. In the light of this example, another may also be describing the same sequence: 'The God of our fathers *raised* Jesus whom you killed by hanging him on a tree. God exalted him at his right hand ...' (Acts 5.30). The verb here, *egeirō*, also means 'resurrect', and John used it for Jesus' saying about rebuilding the temple: 'Destroy this temple, and in three days I will *raise* it up' (2.19). These two show that the sequence in the *Gospel of Philip* – resurrection before death – was the original belief.

## 20.11–18: Mary Magdalene sees Jesus

John tells the story of Mary Magdalene seeing the risen LORD; Matthew and Luke do not, and in Mark the event is only mentioned in the long ending that was added later. Her experience must be part of the case John is making that Jesus is the Messiah, the Son of God, and that by 'believing you may have life in his name'. In this final section of the Gospel, however, John (or maybe a later writer if John himself did not write chapter 21) is also concerned with authority and roles within the Christian community. The criterion for being an apostle was having seen the LORD, and so Paul protested: 'Am I not an apostle? Have I not seen Jesus our LORD?' (1 Cor. 9.1, my translation). This must mean that he had seen the *risen* LORD, because countless people had literally seen Jesus before he died. Mary Magdalene made the same claim: 'I have seen the LORD' (v. 18, my translation). As John tells the story, Mary is the first to see the risen LORD, and *yet most other sources do not mention her*. Luke implies that Peter was the first to see the risen LORD (Luke 24.34), Paul names Peter first in his list of those who had seen the risen LORD (1 Cor. 15.5), and Mark, whose Gospel is a record of what Peter had taught, has either lost its original ending or never included any resurrection appearances.[33] The ending that was added later does say that Mary Magdalene was the first to see the risen LORD (Mark 16.9). The two claims – that Peter was the first to see the risen LORD, and that Mary Magdalene was the first to see the risen LORD – could imply two rival claims to authority in the early community: there was Peter, along with Paul and Luke; and there was Mary Magdalene, whose story is included by John in the last of the canonical Gospels to be written and so the last word on the subject of who first saw the risen LORD.

The story of Mary Magdalene at the tomb is therefore significant. First, her name. No place named Magdala existed at that time, and so her title had another meaning. The Jewish tales told about Jesus included information that his mother was Mary/Miriam the hairdresser, $m^e gadd^e la$.[34] This is clearly the same title as underlies the Greek

---

[33] Eusebius, *History* 2.15.
[34] Babylonian Talmud *Shabbat* 104b.

*magdalēnē*, and so two women named Mary have been confused by the storytellers. The form of the word suggests that the original was a passive participle formed from the root *gādhal*, 'be great', and that her title was not 'hairdresser' but *mᵉguddᵉlâ*, 'the one who has become/been made great'. When she is listed with the other women disciples, Mary's name is first (Matt. 27.56; 28.1; Mark 15.40, 47; 16.1; Luke 8.2; 24.10), which could imply a special status.

The 'exalted Mary' would fit well her role in the later Gnostic texts, and account for the rival claims to seeing the LORD. Mary Magdalene (Mariam) was a key figure in some Gnostic texts. In the *Dialogue of the Saviour*[35] Mary, Matthew and Judas question the risen LORD about his teachings.

> She spoke as a woman who knew the All.
> [Mariam said] 'Lord, you are fearful and wonderful and [ ] from those who do not know.'
> [Mariam said] 'Tell me, Lord, why I have come to this place; to benefit or to suffer loss?' The Lord said, 'Because you [singular] reveal the greatness of the revealer.'
> [Mariam said] 'I want to know how all things exist.'
> [Mariam said] 'There is one word that I will [ ] to the Lord concerning the mystery of the truth, this in which we have stood.'[36]

So too in the *Wisdom of Jesus Christ*, Mary (here Mariamne) asks Jesus questions, along with other disciples.[37]

In the *Pistis Sophia*, Mary is the main speaker in the dialogue with Jesus, and she asks most of the questions even though the male disciples are present. Jesus says to her: 'Mary, thou blessed one, whom I will perfect in all mysteries of those of the height, discourse in openness, thou whose heart is raised to the kingdom of heaven more than all thy brethren.'[38]

Mary is depicted in the *Pistis Sophia* as someone who is afraid to speak because of the male disciples, but Jesus encourages her: 'Discourse in openness and fear not; all things on which thou questionest, I will reveal to thee.'[39] Towards the end of the book, we read:

> Peter said,[40] 'My Lord, let the women cease to question, in order that we also may question.'

---

[35] One damaged copy of this was found at Nag Hammadi.
[36] *Dialogue of the Saviour*, CG III.5.139, 140, 143.
[37] *Wisdom of Jesus Christ*, CG III.4.98, 117.
[38] *Pistis Sophia* 17.
[39] *Pistis Sophia* 19.
[40] Note that it is Peter who speaks.

Jesus said unto Mary and the women, 'Give opportunity to your men brethren that they also may question.'[41]

The *Gospel of Mary*[42] depicts the same leading figure. The scene is Jesus' appearance to the disciples on Easter evening, after Mary had joined them (19.18–23). Jesus speaks his words of farewell, gives them his peace and sends them out to preach. The male disciples are bewildered and afraid: if the Man had suffered, how would they be spared? Mary assumes the role of leader and exhorts them: 'Let us praise his greatness, for he has prepared us and made us into men.' This latter must be the temple usage, where a 'man' meant an angel, and explains the closing words of the *Gospel of Thomas* which have been read as hostile to Mary and indeed to women:

> Jesus said: 'I myself shall lead her in order to make her male [i.e. a 'man'], so that she too may become a living spirit like you males. For every woman who will make herself male will enter the kingdom of heaven.'[43]

This is about becoming angels in the kingdom. Paul described the risen LORD, the last Adam, as a life-giving Spirit (1 Cor. 15.45). Peter then asks Mary to reveal to them the teaching that Jesus gave to her but not to them, and Mary answered:

> 'What is hidden from you I will proclaim to you.' And she began to speak to them these words: 'I saw the Lord in a vision, and I said to him, "Lord, I saw you today in a vision." He answered and said to me, "Blessed are you that you did not waver at the sight of me ..."'

The text breaks at this point, and resumes when Mary has been describing an ascent experience. Andrew and Peter scorn her words, and Peter says: 'Did he really speak privately with a woman [and] not openly to us? Are we to turn about and all listen to her? Did he prefer her to us?'

Mary is distressed at his reaction, but Levi defends her: 'If the Saviour made her worthy, who are you indeed to reject her?'[44]

This is Mary Magdalene in the early years of Christianity; the *Dialogue of the Saviour* and the *Gospel of Mary* are as early as any written evidence for the existence of the New Testament Gospels, and the text of *Pistis*

---

[41] *Pistis Sophia* 146.
[42] One of the four texts in the Berlin Gnostic Codex, known since 1896, which has been dated to the early fifth century. A Greek fragment has been found, possibly from the early third century.
[43] *Gospel of Thomas* 114.
[44] *Gospel of Mary* 9, 10, 17, 18.

## John 20

*Sophia* has been dated to the fourth or fifth century CE, although some have argued that it was composed by Valentinus in the second century. All this is speculation, but the exalted role given to Mary Magdalene is clear in John's account of the resurrection appearances. She was the first to see the risen LORD, and she told both Peter and the beloved disciple what she had seen. *They saw the empty tomb; but she saw the risen LORD.*

Mary stands weeping, and then stoops to look into the tomb. She sees not white grave clothes but two angels in white – perhaps where the two piles of grave clothes had been left, since John says that the headcovering was in a separate place by itself (v. 7). There was one angel at the head and one at the foot of the place where Jesus' body had been. Matthew and Mark say there was one angel, but Luke also knew of two within the tomb. *Neither Peter nor the beloved disciple saw the angels in the tomb*, according to John. This suggests that the two men saw just the empty tomb, whereas Mary had a vision which later passed into the Easter story. A 'man in white' (Mark 16.5) or men in shining clothes (Luke 24.4) were always angels: Enoch was taken up by four white men when he saw his visions;[45] Ezekiel saw a man in (white) linen coming to mark the faithful before the avenging angels brought judgement on Jerusalem (Ezek. 9.2); as he stood by the river Tigris, Daniel had a vision of a fiery man clothed in (white) linen (Dan. 10.4–6) and later he saw another man in (white) linen, or perhaps it was the same figure again (Dan. 12.6); Luke described two men in white robes who appeared when Jesus was taken into heaven (Acts 1.10); and John saw the seven archangels emerging from heaven, all clad in pure bright linen (Rev. 15.6).

Mary saw angels in white in the tomb. For her this was a vision into the place of resurrection, and what she 'saw' were the two heavenly beings over the empty mercy seat, the place where the LORD had spoken to Moses (Exod. 25.22) and where he appeared to the high priests on the Day of Atonement (Lev. 16.2). This is where the bloodstained body of Jesus had been placed, fulfilling the blood offering on the Day of Atonement which in the tabernacle/first temple was sprinkled on the mercy seat (Lev. 16.14–15); and in the second temple, after the mercy seat had been taken away, was sprinkled on the place where the mercy seat had been.[46] The Christians made this link long before John wrote his Gospel: Paul described Jesus himself as the mercy seat – 'whom God set forth as the mercy seat' (Rom. 3.25, translating literally); and the writer of Hebrews

---
[45] *1 Enoch* 87.2.
[46] Mishnah *Yoma* 5.2–3.

said that when Jesus died, 'he entered once for all into the Holy Place, taking not the blood of goats and calves but his own blood, thus securing an eternal redemption' (Heb. 9.12). When Jesus died he literally entered the rock tomb clothed in linen, but this was interpreted as entering the holy of holies as the high priest clothed in linen to make his own blood the atonement offering. 'Seeing' the tomb as the holy of holies with the bloodstained mercy seat restored could well have been Mary's vision at the tomb. The atonement offering had been made, and the high priest had been raised into garments of glory. She could have been the originator of all the imagery that was later used, but John just says she saw the two angels.

The angels ask Mary why she is weeping and she says: 'Because they have taken away my LORD and I do not know where they have laid him.' Such a dialogue with angels is often reported in visionary experiences: Ezekiel talked with the angel who showed him the vision of the temple (e.g. Ezek. 43.6–7); Daniel talked with the angel he saw by the river Tigris (e.g. Dan. 10.18–21); Mary talked with Gabriel (Luke 1.26–38); and here Mary Magdalene talks to the angels in the tomb/the holy of holies.

Something prompts her to turn round, and she sees a man whom she does not recognize, reminiscent of the Baptist's words: 'Among you stands one whom you do not know' (1.26). When he says, 'Woman, why are you weeping? Whom do you seek?', Mary thinks he is the gardener, an Eden motif and John's irony. Or maybe Mary's inspiration? She is looking at the new Adam. The 'gardener' gave rise to later rumours about who had taken away the body of Jesus. Tertullian would later take issue with the Jews who were spreading these tales:

> [Jesus] is that carpenter's or hireling's son, that Sabbath-breaker, that Samaritan and devil-possessed! This is He whom you purchased from Judas! This is He whom you struck with reed and fist, whom you contemptuously spat upon, to whom you gave gall and vinegar to drink! This is He whom His disciples secretly stole away, that it might be said He had risen again, or the gardener removed, that his lettuces might come to no harm from the crowds of visitors.[47]

Jesus as the new Adam is another important image of the resurrection, used by Paul (1 Cor. 15.22, 45) but nowhere attributed to Jesus in the Gospels. Did this also originate with Mary's vision of the gardener?

---

[47] Tertullian, *On Spectacles* 30.

## John 20

When Jesus speaks her name, Mary recognizes him, one of his sheep who know his voice (10.4). Jesus addresses her as Mariam, and she responds *'Rabbouni'*, 'Teacher'.[48] She was then sent with a message for the disciples (v. 17), the usual sequence in a theophany. John himself had a similar experience: he heard a loud voice behind him, and when he turned round to see who was speaking, it was the risen LORD (Rev. 1.10-18). He saw him standing in the temple by the menorah, a radiant figure who said he was the Living One who had died and was now alive for ever. John too was given a message – 'letters' – to send to the churches. Both incidents bear a strong resemblance to an enigmatic prophecy in Isaiah:

> Yea, O people in Zion who dwell in Jerusalem; you shall weep no more. He will surely be gracious to you at the sound of your cry of distress. And though the Lord give you the bread of adversity and the water of affliction, your teacher will no more be hidden [under the wings], and your eyes will see your teacher. And your ears shall indeed hear a word behind you, saying: 'This is the way, walk in it; both if you turn to the right and if you turn to the left.' (Isa. 30.19-21, my translation)

The verb 'be hidden', *kānap*, is only found here and derives from the word 'wing', implying that the teacher has been hidden and kept safe in the holy of holies: 'Hide me in the shadow of thy wings' (Ps. 17.8; also 57.1; 61.4; 63.7; 91.4).[49] The weeping Mary hears someone behind her who has come from the holy of holies and she addresses him as 'Teacher'.

What follows is one of the most mysterious lines in the entire Gospel: 'Do not cling to me, for I have not yet ascended to the Father' (v. 17, my translation). 'Do not *cling*', *haptō*, renders the Hebrew *dābhaq*,[50] which was a key concept in Jesus' Passover discourse. Being joined to the LORD, remaining in him and he in them (15.4), is what prompted Mary's attempted action (we assume she was trying to take hold of Jesus), but this was not the right moment. In this respect, the scene is reminiscent of Matthew's account of the Transfiguration, where Peter tried to capture and keep the moment, but the vision faded (Matt. 17.4). John does not say how the scene in the garden ended; did Jesus vanish from Mary's sight

---

[48] There has been much debate about whether this exchange was in Hebrew or Aramaic, but no satisfactory conclusion has been reached. See R. E. Brown, *The Gospel According to John XIII—XXI*, Anchor Bible 29a, New Haven and London: Yale University Press, (1970) 2008, pp. 990-2.
[49] The same image is found in *1 Enoch* 39.7; the Chosen One under the wings of the Lord of Spirits.
[50] LXX has *proskollaō* at Gen. 2.24, Ps. 102 (101).5, but LXX has *hapto* twice for *dābhaq*; see Brown, *Gospel According to John*, n. 48 above, pp. 992-3.

when she recognized him, as he did at the house in Emmaus (Luke 24.31)? It has been suggested that 'Do not cling to me', *mē mou haptou*, was originally 'Do not fear', *mē ptoou*, the word used for the disciples' fear in Luke 24.37. All the synoptic Gospels mention the fear of the women at the tomb, and so such a suggestion is possible although there is no ancient evidence for it.[51]

Mary cannot cling to the LORD because he has not yet ascended to the Father (v. 17). Here, John shows that he understood the post-resurrection period very differently from Luke. He has no 40 days of resurrection appearances (Acts 1.3) followed by Jesus being taken from the disciples' sight. Rather, he presents the resurrection and Ascension as one process, and Mary is privileged to glimpse the process. She sees the LORD ascending and has to tell the disciples that she has seen the risen and ascending LORD. The glimpse may have coincided with events in the temple that morning, the moment when the firstfruits were lifted up to the LORD, and then given back to the priests. Jesus as the firstfruits also became part of early Christian discourse (Rom. 11.16; 1 Cor. 15.20, 23). When he was given back to his new Levites, he returned to give them his Spirit (v. 22). But it was Mary who saw the LORD about to be lifted up on Easter morning, and so was this image another that originated in her vision?

Mary heard Jesus say: 'I am ascending to my Father and your Father, to my God and your God.' The question here is: does Jesus imply that he has a different relationship with the Father from that enjoyed by his disciples? Barrett, along with many other scholars,[52] opted for a difference :

> Here John emphasises that the relation between Jesus and God is different from that between the disciples and God, even though it is described in the same terms and the disciples are said to be his brothers. Jesus eternally is the Son of God; he gives to those who believe in him the power to become children of God (1.11).[53]

The more natural reading is that Jesus was emphasizing the very opposite, that his Father and God would from that time also be the Father and God of his disciples. The form of the saying is a Hebrew idiom, as in Ruth's words to Naomi: 'Your people shall be my people, and your God my God' (Ruth 1.16). This extension of the divine family had been announced in the Prologue: 'But to all who received him, who believed in his name, he

---

[51] J. H. Bernard, *The Gospel According to St John*, vol. 2, Edinburgh: T&T Clark, 1928, p. 670.
[52] Listed in Brown, *Gospel According to John*, n. 48 above, p. 1016.
[53] C. K. Barrett, *The Gospel According to St John*, London: SPCK, (1955) 1970, p. 471.

## John 20

gave power [the Paraclete] to become children of God ... who were born ... of God' (1.12–13). It was also told to Nicodemus: those born of water and the Spirit would enter the kingdom (3.5). The risen LORD speaks of his disciples as 'my brethren' (v. 17), and although it is possible that Jesus' human family were meant – those who had not supported him in the early part of his ministry – the context makes it more likely that the disciples were meant. With the gift of his Spirit, Jesus would make them all sons of God and give them eternal life: 'I will not leave you orphans, I will come to you. A little while and the *kosmos* will no longer see me, but you will see me, because I live and you will live' (14.18–19, translating literally).

Jesus extending the status of Sonship to include his disciples is a natural development from his teaching in the Passover discourse based around the Shema', namely that he, the LORD, was a unity with his disciples. What he was by nature, they would become by grace. And so he ascended to their Father and their God. Paul knew this teaching: 'All who are led by the Spirit of God are sons of God ... that he might be the Firstborn among many brethren ...' (Rom. 8.14, 29). So too the writer of Hebrews, who argued that Jesus brought many sons to glory: 'That is why he is not ashamed to call them brethren ...' (Heb. 2.10, 11). The family had one Father and also one Mother: the son snatched up to the throne in heaven was the child of the Woman clothed with the sun, who also had other children (Rev. 12.17). Hence, perhaps, the enigmatic sayings in the *Gospel of Philip*: 'When we were Hebrews we were orphans and had only our mother, but when we became Christians, we had both father and mother.'[54] The Hebrews were all children of the Lady, but now enabled to return to their Father. And 'The Father makes a son, and the Son has not the power to make a son. For he who has been begotten has not the power to beget, but the Son gets brothers for himself, not sons.'[55]

Mary was alone when she saw the LORD. She was granted a vivid and complex vision of the risen LORD newly emerged from the holy of holies into the garden of Eden, of his ascending at the time when the firstfruits were lifted up and offered, and of his returning to the Father and the disciples becoming like him, his brothers. She reported this to the disciples and thus sowed the seeds of all subsequent resurrection imagery. This could have been the basis for all the later elaborations of what the

---

[54] *Gospel of Philip* 52.
[55] *Gospel of Philip* 58.

## Temple Theology in John's Gospel

risen LORD revealed to her, but she is not credited with this resurrection inspiration. Typical would be the words of Brown:

> The vehicle for this reinterpretative dramatization of the resurrection is the appearance to Magdalene, a story that has come down from early times, but was not part of the official preaching ...
>
> This use of the Magdalene appearance as a vehicle for Johannine theological interpretation ...[56]

John was, apparently, putting his ideas into her mouth. This is very different from the words in the *Gospel of Mary*.

> 'What is hidden from you I will proclaim to you.' And she began to speak to them these words: 'I saw the Lord in a vision, and I said to him, "Lord, I saw you today in a vision." He answered and said to me, "Blessed are you that you did not waver at the sight of me . . ."'[57]

By telling this story of Mary's vision, John was emphasizing the role of Mary in the resurrection tradition.

The communities for whom John was reinterpreting the life and teaching of Jesus may have known Luke's picture of Jesus appearing for 40 days after Easter and then departing in a cloud, with two angels telling the onlookers that he would return in the same way (Acts 1.9–11). Yet the memory persisted, as we have seen, that Jesus taught his disciples for some 18 months after his resurrection. This resurrection had been the spiritual resurrection at Jesus' baptism, and he taught his disciples for some 18 months after that.[58] Paul considered that his experience on the road to Damascus was a resurrection appearance, and so he cannot have recognized that Jesus only appeared for 40 days; and John himself received visions of the risen LORD (Rev. 1.17–19) who was the Spirit speaking to the churches (e.g. Rev. 2.7). John wrote his Gospel some time after he had received the vision of the letters, to show that the future hope had already been fulfilled in the life of Jesus: he had ascended and he had already returned. Ascension, Pentecost and *parousia* had all occurred on the day of resurrection. Barnabas, writing at the end of the first century, knew that Jesus had ascended on the day of resurrection: 'We too rejoice in celebrating the eighth day, because that was when Jesus rose from the dead, and showed himself again, and ascended into heaven.'[59]

---

[56] Brown, *Gospel According to John*, n. 48 above, p. 1014.
[57] *Gospel of Mary* 10.
[58] See above, p. 517.
[59] *Letter of Barnabas* 15. Although attributed to Paul's companion on the first missionary

## John 20

John shows how the words of the Passover discourse were fulfilled: 'If I do not go away, the Paraclete will not come to you; but if I go I will send him to you' (16.7). So too, Jesus' earlier teaching: 'What if you were to see the Son of man ascending where he was before? It is the spirit that gives life, the flesh is of no avail' (6.62–63).

### 20.19–25: The disciples see the LORD

Both Luke and John tell how Jesus appeared to his disciples in Jerusalem during the evening of Easter Day. Luke sets the story after the two had returned from Emmaus where Jesus had joined them, but as they recognized him, he vanished from their sight. The disciples in Jerusalem confirmed that the LORD had appeared to Simon (Peter). Then Jesus himself 'stood among them' (Luke 24.36). The ancient versions of Luke are longer at this point, the oldest having also 'and he said to them "Peace be with you"'.[60] Jesus showed them his hands and feet, he invited them to touch him to show that he was not a ghost, and he ate a piece of fish as further proof. Then he spoke to them, showing that he had fulfilled the scriptures that the Christ should suffer and rise from the dead on the third day, and that 'repentance and forgiveness of sins should be preached in his name to all nations'. The disciples, he said, were witnesses of this, and he would send them what the Father had promised. They were to stay in Jerusalem until the power from on high clothed them. Then he led them out to Bethany and was taken up into heaven, apparently late on Easter Day, although Luke gives no indication in his Gospel of when Jesus taught the disciples or when he was taken up from them.

John sets the same story on the evening of Easter Day but does not mention the two who returned from Emmaus, nor that Peter had seen the risen LORD, nor that Jesus ate food to show he was not a ghost. The disciples were together behind closed doors for fear of the Jews, and Jesus came and stood in the midst. For John, this is the return that Jesus promised his disciples in the Passover discourse: 'a little while, and you will see me again' (16.19, translating literally), the time when they would receive the Spirit of truth (14.16–17). Through them he would convince

---

journey (Acts 13.2), the letter is now thought to come from a later author. It was written after 70 CE, and was known to Clement of Alexandria who died about 215 CE.

[60] Thus Sinai Codex, Alexandrinus and Vatican Codex. B. D. Ehrman, *The Orthodox Corruption of Scripture*, Oxford: Oxford University Press, 1993, p. 221, concluded that all these were examples of early additions to the text to counter docetism. The words are not in the Western text, which he says is the purer form.

the world of sin and righteousness and judgement (16.7–8). John describes how the disciples were given Holy Spirit (there is no 'the') and sent out to forgive or retain sins. Thus Jesus sent into the world those whom he had consecrated as sons of God to continue his role as the high priest, just as he himself had been consecrated and sent out (10.36). With the gift of the Spirit, he gave 'to all who received him, who believed in his Name, the power to become children of God' (1.12, my translation; cf. Rom. 8.14).

John does not say how many disciples were present, only that Thomas was not there. Luke says that the Eleven and some others were assembled (Luke 24.33). Nor does John say that Jesus passed miraculously through the closed doors, only that he *came* and stood among them, an allusion to the promise that Jesus would go away and then come again (14.18, 28). Jesus showed the disciples the wounds in his hands and side. None of the New Testament Gospels mentions how Jesus' hands were wounded. It may be that pierced hands were implied by crucifixion. Luke says that Jesus' feet were also wounded, which may be an allusion to 'They have pierced my hands and feet' (Ps. 22.16), especially as the Hebrew of this verse is now unreadable, and this is often a sign that it had become a Christian proof text. The current Hebrew is 'Like a lion, $k^{ea}rî$, my hands and my feet', whereas the LXX has $\bar{o}ruxan$, 'pierced through', from the Hebrew $ko^a rû$, 'they mutilated'.[61] Only John mentions the spear when Jesus died, and so here he mentions the wound in Jesus' side. Psalm 22 was recognized by the first Christians as a prophecy of the crucifixion. Justin showed this in detail, describing the psalm as 'a parable of mystery': they pierced his hands and feet, they parted his garments, and then the one who had suffered stood in the midst of the assembly:

> I will tell of thy name to my brethren;
> In the midst of the congregation I will praise thee.
> (Ps. 22.22)

This, said Justin, was fulfilled when the risen LORD appeared to his assembled disciples,[62] and for John, it was the moment when the One whom they had pierced was seen again.

The disciples saw the LORD, and twice he said to them, 'Peace be with you' (vv. 19, 21). This could have been just the customary greeting, or it could have been the fulfilment of the high-priestly blessing: 'May the

---

[61] In the written text, this means changing $w$ to $y$, a very small change.
[62] Justin, *Trypho* 97, 106.

## John 20

LORD favour you with the light of his face and give you peace', the gist of Numbers 6.26–27. John knew this as the future hope, when the servants would see the face of God-and-the-Lamb and reign with him (Rev. 22.3–5), but here John shows that the climax of the future hope had already been fulfilled. The appearance on the evening of the resurrection was a theophany, the promised return of the LORD, but John does not say if this was the spiritual body or the physical body. Luke emphasized the physical reality of the risen LORD (Luke 24.39–43), perhaps because there were already in his time people teaching that Jesus had not been fully human, and that the disciples had known only a phantom both before and after his death. Ignatius, who could have known John, drew on Luke's account when he emphasized the physical reality of the resurrection:

> For my own part, I know and believe that he was in actual human flesh, even after his resurrection. When he appeared to Peter and his companions, he said to them, 'Take hold of me, touch me, and see that I am no bodiless phantom.' And they touched him then and there, and believed, for they had had contact with the flesh and blood reality of him. That is how they came by their contempt for death, and proved themselves superior to it. Moreover, he ate and drank with them after he was risen, like any natural man, though even then he and the Father were spiritually one.[63]

John does not say what the disciples saw; Jesus appeared to them, and they said they had seen the LORD.

John's Jesus had said he would return as the Paraclete, the Spirit of the LORD. John emphasized the reality of the Incarnation, both in the Gospel (1.14) and in his first letter: 'Every spirit which confesses that Jesus Christ has come in the flesh is of God ...' (1 John 4.2); but he saw the risen LORD as the Spirit speaking to the churches (e.g. Rev. 2.7), albeit with a transfigured human form: seven stars in his right hand, eyes like fire, feet like burnished bronze (Rev. 2.1, 18). Paul emphasized that the resurrection body was a glorious body (Eph. 3.21), a spiritual body that was the physical body transformed into another state (1 Cor. 15.44). This is what the disciples experienced when they saw the LORD. He was clothed in garments of glory, a state that the ending of Mark called 'another form' (Mark 16.12). The LORD gave a message and a commission to those who saw him: Moses (Exod. 24.9–12); Isaiah (Isa. 6.8–10); Ezekiel (Ezek. 3.4); John (Rev. 1.11; 10.8–11); Enoch.[64] This was the nature of a theophany,

---

[63] Ignatius, *To the Smyrnaeans* 3.
[64] *1 Enoch* 15.1–2.

and so here, the disciples are given a message – the forgiveness of sins – and sent out to teach it.

The meaning of vanishing from sight and passing through closed doors is also the meaning of the linen grave clothes. Lazarus had emerged from his grave still wrapped in a shroud, whereas Jesus had left the linen clothes behind. This was the sign of resurrection into the spiritual state, as Thomas' Jesus explained. He gave another context and meaning for the saying 'Do not be anxious about your life, what you shall eat or what you shall drink, nor about your body, what you shall put on ...' (Matt. 6.25// Luke 12.22).

> Jesus said, 'Do not be concerned from morning until evening and from evening until morning what you shall wear.'
>
> His disciples said, 'When will you become revealed to us, and when shall we see you?'
>
> Jesus said, 'When you disrobe without being ashamed and take up your garments and place them under your feet like little children and tread on them, then [will you see] the Son of the Living One and you will not be afraid.'[65]

The garments were the symbol of earthly life and its limited perceptions. So too Philip's Jesus, following the saying that the LORD rose up first and then died:

> Some are afraid lest they rise naked. Because they wish to rise in the flesh, and [they] do not know that it is those who wear the [flesh] who are naked. [It is] those who [ ] unclothe themselves who are not naked. Flesh [and blood shall] not [be able] to inherit the kingdom [of God] ...
>
> In this world, those who put on garments are better than the garments. In the kingdom of heaven, the garments are better than those who have put them on.[66]

The allusion here is to Adam and Eve knowing they were naked when they lost their original garment of wisdom/glory and were driven from Eden in physical bodies/garments of skin.[67] The disciples saw the risen LORD as the new Adam in garments of glory.

In temple discourse, linen was the fibre that symbolized the earth because it came from a plant that grew in the earth,[68] but it also became the shining garments of the angels and so the high priest wore linen in the

---

[65] *Gospel of Thomas* 36, 37.
[66] *Gospel of Philip*, CG II.3.56, 57.
[67] *Genesis Rabbah* XX.12.
[68] Josephus, *War* 5.213.

## John 20

holy of holies (Lev. 16.4), 'because fine linen, is not, like wool, produced by creatures that die'.[69] Linen represented matter that could be and was transformed. When Enoch described his moment of resurrection/ transformation, he said that Michael took from him his earthly clothing and gave him the garments of the glory of the LORD.[70] A resurrected high priest such as Enoch wore the shining linen garments of the holy of holies, and that is how John himself described the figure he saw and recognized as the risen LORD (Rev. 1.13). *This is the only description of the post-Easter risen LORD in the New Testament; he was the shining figure of the Transfiguration, and John had received this vision before he wrote his Gospel.* John saw the Man wearing the *podērēs* (Hebrew *maḥ⁽a⁾lāṣâ*), the long flowing garment of a high priest (LXX Zech. 3.4) and also the garment of an angel (LXX Ezek. 9.2), where the Greek has *podērēs* for the Hebrew 'clothed in linen', *badh*. John saw the Man wearing the golden girdle that was only worn by a high priest.[71] 'Isaiah' saw in heaven the robes, crowns and thrones that were waiting for the faithful.[72] These were the white garments of the great multitude in heaven (Rev. 7.9), and the wedding garments needed to enter the kingdom of heaven (Matt. 22.11–14).

The risen LORD then breathed onto the disciples the gift of his Spirit. This was the Spirit that made the Davidic king the LORD and gave him gifts of wisdom, understanding, counsel, might, knowledge and the fear of the LORD (Isa. 11.2). The Spirit imparted to the king the fragrance of the anointing oil (Isa. 1 1.3),[73] and the Christians knew that they carried this fragrance with them (2 Cor. 2.14–15). John used different words for the same idea: Jesus had promised that the Spirit of truth would dwell in his disciples (14.16–17) and would guide them into all truth (16.7–14). Luke implies that the truth learned in the earliest resurrection appearances was a new understanding of the Hebrew Scriptures: on the road to Emmaus the risen LORD interpreted the Scriptures to the two disciples (Luke 24.27); and when the risen LORD came to other disciples on the same evening he opened their minds to understand the Scriptures (Luke 24.45). John mentions this in the Gospel – that it was only after the resurrection that the disciples came to realize who Jesus was (2.22; 12.16). The earliest evidence for this new understanding is the seven letters which the risen

---

[69] Philo, *Special Laws* I.84.
[70] *2 Enoch* 22.9.
[71] Josephus, *Antiquities* 3.159.
[72] *Ascension of Isaiah* 9.24–26.
[73] Isa. 11.3, translating literally, is 'His fragrance shall be the fear of the LORD.'

LORD – 'the Spirit speaking to the churches' – gave to John. He saw the risen LORD as the high priest, and the letters, which are a tightly woven fabric of allusions to the Hebrew Scriptures, show that the faithful Christian had to be like his high priest: the One among the seven lamps would remove the lamp of the unfaithful church (Rev. 2.1, 5); the One with the two-edged sword would judge false teaching with the sword of his mouth (Rev. 2.12, 16).[74]

The risen LORD then sent his disciples out, just as he had been sent by the Father (v. 21). Jesus had prayed for their mission: 'As thou didst send me into the world, so I have sent them into the world' (17.18). Clement, who also could have known John, summarized thus:

> Now the Gospel was given to the apostles for us by the Lord Jesus Christ; and Jesus Christ was sent from God. That is to say, Christ received his commission from God, and the apostles theirs through Christ. The order of these two events was in accordance with the will of God. So thereafter, when the apostles had been given their instructions, and all their doubts had been set at rest by the resurrection of our Lord Jesus Christ from the dead, they set out in the full assurance of the Holy Spirit to proclaim the coming of God's kingdom ... As they went through the territories and townships preaching, they appointed their first converts, after testing them by the Spirit, to be bishops and deacons for the believers of the future.[75]

Theophanies often included physical sensations on the part of those receiving them: Isaiah felt a hot coal purifying his mouth so that he could be the LORD's messenger (Isa. 6.6–7); Jeremiah felt the LORD touch his mouth to make him his messenger (Jer. 1 9); Ezekiel was told to eat the scroll and thus become the LORD's messenger (Ezek. 3.3–4); John himself had the same experience (Rev. 10.8–11). So too, the LORD breathed on the disciples and Thomas was invited to touch the wounds. The scene here is like the creation of Adam, when he was changed from a man of dust into a living being by the breath of the LORD God (Gen. 2.7), but all the Targums agree that this inbreathing not only gave Adam life; it also gave the power of speech. Jesus had promised that the Spirit would flow from the hearts/minds of those who believed (7.37–38), and that the Spirit of truth would come and dwell in his disciples (14.17). John had reassured the young men of his church that the Logos of God dwelt within them (1 John 2.14), and Mark's Jesus had told his disciples not to be anxious when

---

[74] For detail, see my book *The Revelation of Jesus Christ*, Edinburgh: T&T Clark, 2000, pp. 102–13.

[75] *1 Clement* 42.

*John 20*

they were put on trial, because the Holy Spirit would speak through them (Mark 13.11).

The Davidic priest-kings who were anointed and raised up were given the Spirit of the LORD and they spoke words from the LORD:

> The Spirit of the LORD speaks by/in me,
> His word is upon my tongue.
> (2 Sam. 23.2)

Thus the disciples received the power to teach and also to forgive sins (v. 23), as Jesus had done. The Jews said that this could only be done by God (Mark 2.5–8//Matt. 9.2–8; Luke 5.20–24). The synoptic Gospels have differing accounts of Jesus' last commission: Matthew's Jesus commands the disciples to baptize and teach (Matt. 28.19–20); the long ending of Mark has Jesus command the disciples to preach the gospel to all creation (Mark 16.15); Luke's Jesus showed the disciples how he had fulfilled the Scriptures, and so repentance and forgiveness in his name should be preached to all nations (Luke 24.45–49); and he taught about the kingdom of God, and promised them the gift of the Spirit (Acts 1.3–5). Only John emphasizes the disciples receiving the Spirit so that they could forgive sins.

Forgiving sins was the role of the royal high priests on the Day of Atonement, and the underlying Hebrew would have been *nāśâ*, 'to bear' or 'forgive'. Wearing the Name protected him as he bore way the sins (Exod. 20.7).[76] Just as the high priest carried the sins and thus bore them away because he was the presence of the LORD, so too the disciples were given not great power and status, but rather the role of high-priestly sin-bearers. John had seen their atonement blood under the great altar at the time of the fifth seal (Rev. 6.9–11), and he had learned the true meaning of the blood of the Lamb establishing a kingdom of priests on earth (Rev. 5.9–10). This was the role of the disciples who received the Spirit of the LORD. They bore his Name and so received the high-priestly blessing: the LORD had shown them the light of his presence and put his Name upon them (Num. 6.24–27).

## 20.24–29: Thomas sees the LORD

The other disciples kept telling Thomas[77] that they had seen the LORD, and presumably they spoke of the wounds they had seen. Thomas would not believe without proof; unless he could see and touch the wounds he

---

[76] This was the original meaning of the commandment; the high priest 'carried' the Name which protected him, but only if he took this role reverently.
[77] The verb is imperfect and implies continuous action.

would not believe (v. 25). Such physical proof would receive more and more emphasis in the struggle against docetism which denied the physical reality of the Incarnation. The *Epistle of the Apostles*, a second-century text to refute docetism, had Peter putting his finger onto the mark of the nails, Thomas putting his finger onto the mark of the spear, and Andrew checking that Jesus left footprints, all of which proved that he was not a ghost.[78] When Luke wrote, he claimed the authority of eyewitnesses (Luke 1.2), but John made a different claim for a later generation. 'Blessed are those who have not seen and yet have believed' (v. 29).

A 'letter' attributed to James contrasted those who had seen and not believed with those who had not seen and yet had believed:

> Henceforth, waking or sleeping, remember that you have seen the Son of Man, and spoken with him in person, and listened to him in person. Woe to those who have seen the Son of Man. Blessed will they be who have not seen the Man and who have not consorted with him, and they who have not spoken with him and they who have not listened to anything from him: yours is life ...
>
> As long as I am with you, give heed to me and obey me; but when I depart from you, remember me. And remember me because I was with you (and) you did not know me. Blessed will they be who have known me; woe to those who have heard and not believed. Blessed will they be who have not seen and yet [have believed].[79]

On the first day of the next week – 'eight days later' – Jesus comes again to his disciples when the doors are shut, and Thomas is with them. Again, Jesus greets them: 'Peace be with you', and then he invites Thomas to touch his wounds and believe. John does not say that Thomas *did* touch the wounds, or how Jesus knew that Thomas had expressed his doubts. Presumably Thomas sees the wounds in the theophany and then he believes. 'Do not be faithless but believing' are the words of the Paraclete within him. Thomas then utters the climax of the entire Gospel; he recognizes that the risen LORD is 'My LORD and my God' (v. 28, my translation), the two names by which Yahweh had been known in the Hebrew Scriptures. The Hebrew Scriptures show that 'the LORD' and 'my God' were both titles of the Davidic king:

> ... the processions of my God, my King into the sanctuary ...
> Bless God in the great congregation, the LORD, O you who are of
> Israel's fountain.                                    (Ps. 68.24, 26)

---

[78] *Epistle of the Apostles* 11.
[79] *Apocryphon of James*, CG I.2.3, 12.

Isaiah saw 'the King, the LORD of Hosts' (Isa. 6.5); Solomon sat on the throne of the LORD as king, and his people worshipped the LORD-and-the-king (1 Chron. 29.20, 23). John's near contemporary Philo said that the double invocation indicated the twofold power: 'LORD' was the royal power and 'God' was the creative power;[80] but for the Christians, 'LORD' and 'God' were synonymous: 'Our God and Saviour Jesus Christ' (2 Pet. 1.1); or 'Our LORD and Saviour Jesus Christ' (2 Pet. 1.11, my translation). Thomas, like Isaiah, had recognized that Jesus was the King, the LORD of Hosts, and this led John to his final statement: 'These [things] are written that you may believe that Jesus is the Christ, the Son of God, and that believing you may have life in his name' (v. 31). But 'The grammar of the Greek suggests that it *should* be translated, "the Christ, the Son of God, is Jesus."'[81]

## The day of the LORD

All three stories in this chapter take place on the first day of the week: Mary goes to the tomb, Jesus comes to the disciples, and then one week later he comes again to speak to Thomas. 'Eight days' later is just the Hebrew way of counting, including the day at each end of the period, just as Jesus rose on the third day when to our way of reckoning Friday to Sunday would be two days. Sunday became known as 'the day of the LORD'; thus Bishop Ignatius, writing about 100 CE, could say: '[Hebrew Christians] have given up keeping the Sabbath, and now order their lives by the LORD's day instead, the day when life first dawned for us, thanks to Him and his death.'[82] The Christian 'first day of the week' probably began as an extension of the Sabbath which ended at sunset.

In the New Testament, however, and so for the first generation of the Church, the day of the LORD was the day of judgement, the time when the LORD would return at some time in the near future. As late as his letter to the Romans, Paul could write that the day of the LORD was at hand (Rom. 13.12), something he had taught throughout his life as a Christian (1 Cor. 1.8; 5.5; 2 Cor 1.14; Phil. 1.6, 10; 1 Thess. 4.2). The author of Hebrews, who wrote as though the temple was still standing, knew that the day was drawing near (Heb. 10.25). In the synoptic Gospels, it was the day when the Son of Man would come in clouds with great power and glory (Mark

---

[80] Philo, *Questions on Genesis* II.51; IV.87.
[81] R. Griffith Jones, *Beloved Disciple*, New York: HarperCollins, 2008, p. 246, n. 4.
[82] Ignatius, *To the Magnesians* 9.

13.26-27//Matt 24.30; Luke 21.27). It was proverbial that the day would come like a thief in the night (2 Pet. 3.10; Rev. 16.15).

John begins Revelation by saying that he was 'in the Spirit on the day of the LORD'; in other words, he received visions about the day of the LORD's coming in judgement. He saw the risen LORD (Rev. 1.10), but the purpose of his Gospel was to show that the day of the LORD had already happened with the resurrection, and so after John's new understanding of the day of the LORD, it became the custom to call the first day of the week the day of the LORD, *the day when the LORD returned to his churches*. This was the context for *Maran atha*, 'Our LORD has come', and it also explains the origin of the *epiklēsis* prayer in the Eucharist. John has already shown that the LORD returned as the Paraclete, *paraklētos*, the one who was summoned, and the prayer to summon him came to be called the *epiklēsis*, the summons. The two verbs *parakaleō* and *epikaleō* are synonymous, being two independent translations of a Hebrew original. The earliest form of *epiklēsis* was 'Come', addressed to Christ, and then 'Let your Logos come and dwell', addressed to the Father. The development was:

- *Christ* is requested to *come* and manifest his presence;
- the Father is requested that the *Son* or Spirit come upon the oblation;
- the Father is requested to *send* the Spirit to *make* the bread and wine the body and blood of Christ.[83]

The earliest *epiklēses* were prayers for the LORD himself to return, just as John's Jesus had said he would, but in the form of the Paraclete.

There was one dissenting voice in the New Testament. The writer of 2 Thessalonians – and people have long suspected that this was not Paul but one of his later disciples[84] – warned people not to believe that the day of the LORD had already come (2 Thess. 2.2). There must have been a degree of friction between Paul and John as can be seen from their reciprocal statements: Paul claimed that he too had received a vision of the risen LORD (Acts 9.3-9; Gal. 1.15-16), whereas John compared this to Balaam's vision (Num. 23.11-12) and declared Paul to be a false prophet who taught people that they could eat meat that had been offered to idols (Rev. 2.14). This Paul undoubtedly did (1 Cor. 8.1-3). The followers of Paul, it seems, did not accept John's teaching that the LORD had already returned.

---

[83] B. D. Spinks, 'The Consecratory Epiklesis in the Anaphora of St James', *Studia Liturgica* 11.2 (1976), pp. 18-39, p. 28.

[84] Most recently B. D. Ehrman, *The New Testament. A Historical Introduction to the Early Christian Writings*, New York: Oxford University Press, 2003, p. 385.

It was Paul and his companion Luke who chose 'remembrance', *anamnēsis*, as the meaning of Jesus' word at the last supper (1 Cor. 11.24; Luke 22.19). This must have been a form of *zākhar*, which means both 'invoke' and 'remember', but the meaning *epiklēsis*, 'invocation', only survived in liturgical usage.

# John 21

This chapter shows signs of being a later addition to the Gospel, written perhaps by John or by a disciple whom he directed. It is unlikely that the last chapter was written independently of John, but if he wrote the Gospel in old age, any addition would have been made in extreme old age. J. H. Bernard wisely observed that the small amount of material in this chapter – only 25 verses – is not enough to establish stylistic differences or otherwise from the main Gospel.[1] There are some obvious links to the Gospel: the name Tiberias rather than Galilee (v. 1; cf. 6.1); a disciple named Nathanael (v. 2; cf. 1.45); Simon Peter as a double name, found in Matthew 16.16 and Luke 5.8 but otherwise only in John (1.40; 6.8, 68; 13.6, 9, 24, 36; 18.10, 15, 25; 20.6); the beloved disciple and his association with Simon Peter (v. 7; cf. 18.15; 20.2, 4); and Thomas who is only called Didymus by John (11.16; 20.24). On the other hand, John has never before mentioned the sons of Zebedee (v. 2) – not even by name as James and John – and the group of seven disciples in this episode is distinct from the Twelve in the Gospel. There is some different vocabulary, but since much of this is about fishing that was not needed elsewhere in the Gospel, the difference is not significant; and the presentation is different from the rest of the Gospel. There is no discourse based on the great catch of fishes nor around the breakfast on the shore, but there is a mysterious number – 153 – reminiscent of the number in Revelation 13.18, of which John wrote: 'This calls for wisdom: let him who has understanding reckon the number of the beast.' The people who read this Gospel must have known the meaning of the number 153.

The context of the final chapter was probably the situation in Ephesus where John spent his last years; and the final assurance – 'we know that his testimony is true' (v. 24) – could have been the testimony of the leaders of the church in Ephesus. There can be no certainty. The context of the Gospel is the Temple Theology of Jesus and his circle, found in a primitive form in Revelation, but reinterpreted as realized eschatology

---

[1] J. H. Bernard, *The Gospel According to St John*, vol. 2, Edinburgh: T&T Clark, 1928, p. 687.

## John 21

after John's vision of the mighty angel (Rev. 10.1–11). The content of the final chapter is very different, and the situation of the church in Ephesus is as likely a context as any, a city where several Christian teachers had worked, and differing emphases and even rivalries had emerged. John has already reinstated Mary Magdalene as the first to see the risen LORD, after others – Paul and those who instructed him – had omitted her from their list of those who had seen the risen LORD (1 Cor. 15.4–7). She it was who summoned Peter and John, the two leaders who are the subject of this chapter, the two men who saw the empty tomb but not, at first, the risen LORD. Mary told the assembled disciples that she had seen the risen LORD (20.18), and yet Paul forbad women to speak in such assemblies of the saints (1 Cor. 14.33–35).

There was more than one leading figure in the early Church with the name John, or so it seems. Polycrates, bishop of Ephesus at the end of the second century, knew that John the beloved disciple was buried in his city and that he had been a high priest: 'John, who leant back on the Lord's breast, and who became a priest wearing the *petalon*, a witness and a teacher, he sleeps at Ephesus.'[2] The *petalon* was the gold seal bearing the Name which the high priest wore on his forehead (LXX Exod. 28.32 = MT Exod. 28.36), suggesting that the Christians had their own temple-style hierarchy with John as a high priest. There are several indications in the Gospel that its author was of a priestly family: he knew what Caiaphas had said in the Sanhedrin (11.49–50); he knew the high priest's household (18.16; 26); and he hesitated to go into a tomb (20.5).

Papias, bishop of Hierapolis in the early second century, knew of two Johns among the disciples: one, listed with James, who must have been the son of Zebedee; and another, 'the elder John', whom he had known and heard.[3]

> Whenever anyone came who had been a follower of the elders, I enquired into the words of the elders, what Andrew or Peter had said, or Philip or Thomas or James or John or Matthew, or any other disciple of the Lord, and what Aristion and the elder John, disciples of the LORD, were still saying. For I did not imagine that things out of books would help me as much as the utterance of a living and abiding voice.

Eusebius said Papias had only known John the elder, but he also knew a story that there had been two leaders named John, because there were two tombs of John in Ephesus. It is possible, though, that there were two

---

[2] Eusebius, *History of the Church* 3.31.
[3] Eusebius, *History* 2.15; 3.39.

tombs claiming to be the burial place of John, rather than two Johns buried in Ephesus. There is some early evidence that both the sons of Zebedee were killed by the Jews. Jesus' prophecy to the sons of Zebedee points to this: they would both drink the cup that he had to drink, and receive the same baptism (Mark 10.35–40//Matt. 20.20–23). Herod did kill James the brother of John (Acts 12.2). Philip of Side, a church historian working in the early fifth century, knew the lost five-volume work of Papias. In the second volume, he noted, Papias said that both the sons of Zebedee had been killed by the Jews. If this is correct, then all the books attributed to John must have been written by John the elder. Eusebius considered that Revelation was written by John the elder,[4] and when John wrote himself into Revelation, he called himself the 'elder' who interpreted the visions (Rev. 5.5; 7.14). He introduced himself in his letters in the same way (2 John 1; 3 John 1).

John the elder was a prophet in the Jerusalem church. He was known as a pillar of the Church, along with James and Peter (Gal. 2.9), but this title could be given to any faithful Christian (Rev. 3.12). Jesus entrusted to John the interpretation of his visions and prophecies, and he was the channel through whom the LORD continued to speak to the churches (Rev. 2—3). The risen LORD gave John a letter for the angel of the church in Ephesus, perhaps its bishop or more likely the personified community there, praising its endurance in the face of false apostles (Rev. 2.1–7). He warned them to return to the earlier loving ways from which they had fallen and he praised them for resisting the Nikolaitans. Since the letter is couched in temple imagery – the seven golden lamps, eating again from the tree of life in the Paradise of God – the recipients in Ephesus must have been Hebrew Christians, and so the name Nikolaitan probably derived from the Hebrew or Aramaic *nkl*, 'deceive'. There were false and deceiving teachers in Ephesus. The letters to six other churches suggest strongly that the deceiver was Paul, described as Balaam the false prophet (Rev. 2.14), and that the seven churches of Asia were the communities of Hebrew Christians who had not been evangelized by Paul and who resisted his way of teaching Christianity.[5] Paul could well have had John's claims in mind when he wrote to his followers in Galatia: 'I did not receive [my teaching] from man, nor was I taught it, but it came through a revelation of Jesus Christ, *apokalupsis Iēsou Christou*' (Gal. 1.12), the

---

[4] Eusebius, *History* 3.39.
[5] For detail, see my book *The Revelation of Jesus Christ*, Edinburgh: T&T Clark, 2000, pp. 98–102.

## John 21

very words that John used to describe what he received from Jesus (Rev. 1.1). The final chapter of John's Gospel, then, probably addressed this situation of the divided Church, especially in Ephesus.

Of all the seven churches of Asia named in the letters, Ephesus is the only one where Paul had taught. He was there for two years (Acts 19.1–20), but on his final journey to Jerusalem he did not visit his followers there but rather had them come to him in Miletus (Acts 20.17). He warned them that after his departure fierce wolves would attack the flock and false teachers would arise from their own community (Acts 20.29–30). His teaching had led to strife in the city from the outset; the silversmiths who made objects for the cult of Artemis had lost business as the result of Paul's making converts, and there was a riot (Acts 19.23–41). This was doubtless one reason why Paul did not return, but there were others. He spoke of fighting wild beasts at Ephesus (1 Cor. 15.32), by which he meant people there who had made his life difficult – 'the plots of the Jews' (Acts 20.19; cf. Acts 19.33). When he first came to Ephesus, Paul had found not only disciples of the Baptist but also Christians who had been instructed by Apollos of Alexandria. Luke says that Apollos had spoken accurately about Jesus, but knew only the baptism of the Baptist, as did those whom he converted (Acts 18.25; 19.1–5). Paul's fellow workers Priscilla and Aquila 'expounded to him the way of God more accurately', and so he became a Pauline Christian (Acts 18.26; Rom. 16.3), and Timothy, one of Paul's converts (2 Tim. 1.2), was the first bishop of Ephesus.[6] Paul had been a major influence in Ephesus.

Then there were the seven sons of Skeva, a Jewish high priest, itinerant Jews who exorcised in the name of the LORD Jesus (Acts 19.13) as did Paul, another itinerant Jew in Asia Minor (Acts 19.12; cf. 16.18). Paul's friend Luke tells the story to ridicule them, but seven sons sounds like a group of disciples rather than a family, and so perhaps these men were the disciples of a Jewish high priest in or near Ephesus. Skeva is not known elsewhere as a name, but it could have been a title 'the watcher',[7] and a high-priestly 'watcher' with seven sons who exorcised in the name of the LORD Jesus is someone we should like to know more about. As a result of this conflict with the exorcists, many who practised magic in Ephesus burned their books and became Christians. A few years after the final chapter of John's Gospel was written, Ignatius bishop of Antioch wrote to the church in Ephesus. He exhorted them to acknowledge the authority of

---

[6] Eusebius, *History* 3.4.
[7] Hebrew *śkh* or Aramaic *sk'*.

their bishop Onesimus and the clergy – there must have been divisions even then – and he praised them for resisting the pernicious teaching of certain men from another place. He remembered Paul with reverence, and wrote of the defeat of magic and superstition.[8]

Ephesus, then, was a church with a troubled past that had been influenced by many teachers: John, Paul, and possibly Peter too, since the first letter attributed to him was an encyclical to 'the exiles in the Dispersion in Pontus, Galatia, Cappodocia, Asia and Bithynia'. It is not known where Peter travelled, but Paul implies that he had baptized in Corinth (1 Cor. 1.11–15), and his name must have been recognized by those in Asia Minor who received the encyclical. The church in Corinth was divided into the followers of Paul, of Peter and of Apollos, and the situation in Ephesus could have been similar, divided into the followers of John, of Apollos/Paul and Peter. The final chapter of John's Gospel clarifies the roles of Peter and John, but being set in the days immediately after Easter, any mention of Paul would not have been appropriate.

## 21.1–14: Breakfast by the Sea of Tiberias

There are two distinct episodes in this chapter: one is a resurrection appearance in Galilee and the other an incident that clarifies the roles of Peter and the beloved disciple. The resurrection appearance returns the story to the opening scenes of the Gospel in Galilee. The location of the appearance is not given, beyond that it was the shore of the Sea of Tiberias, but Jesus again calls the disciples and they recognize who he is. In both scenes there are two unnamed disciples (1.35; 21.2), although one of the unnamed men is soon identified as Andrew (1.40). In both scenes Peter and Nathanael are mentioned (1.41, 45; 21.2). The first scene where Jesus first showed, *phaneroō*, his glory, was the wedding feast at Cana where he performed the miracle of the wine; the final scene where Jesus again revealed himself, *phaneroō*, was at the meal on the shore, where he came to the disciples, took the bread and gave it to them. Both scenes evoke the Eucharist. The other episode set in this area was the discourse about bread in the synagogue at Capernaum. Here too, Jesus had just revealed his identity – 'I AM. Do not be afraid' (6.20, my translation) – and he had spoken of the Son of Man ascending to where he was before and of the Spirit giving life (6.62–63). After this, many disciples deserted Jesus, and he asked the Twelve if they also wished to leave him. Again, Peter was

---

[8] Ignatius, *To the Ephesians* 2–4, 9–10.

## John 21

the disciple named as spokesman, and he said they would stay: 'Lord, to whom shall we go? You have the words of eternal life; and we have believed, and have come to know, that you are the Holy One of God' (6.68–69).[9]

Breakfast by the Sea of Tiberias is a resurrection and meal appearance in Galilee where Peter is prominent. Mark and Matthew report such appearances: the angel at the tomb told the women that Jesus would be seen in Galilee: 'Tell his disciples and Peter that he is going before you to Galilee; there you will see him, as he told you' (Mark 16.7//Matt. 28.7, 10). The 11 disciples saw Jesus on a mountain there (Matt. 28.16), and Matthew's Jesus had already told his disciples that he would go before them to Galilee, after he was raised up (Matt. 26.32). The *Gospel of Peter* has the angel tell Mary Magdalene and the other women that the crucified one has risen and departed. The women were afraid and fled, and when the feast of Unleavened Bread was over – one week after Passover – the grieving disciples went home. Then Peter, Andrew and Levi son of Alphaeus went back to their fishing. At this point the surviving text breaks. The *Gospel of Peter* implies no resurrection appearances in the week after Passover, but we can guess that the missing text described the LORD appearing to Peter, possibly the story recorded by John. Paul knew a list of resurrection appearances: first to Peter, then to the Twelve, then to 500, then to James, then to all the Apostles, and finally to himself (1 Cor. 15.4–6). He does not say how soon the appearances began, whereas Luke and John have them starting on the day after the Passover Sabbath, on the first day of the week. Luke must have known Paul's list of appearances, because he said the LORD had appeared first to Peter before he appeared to the disciples in the evening after the first day of the week. Luke does not give details of the appearance to Peter, nor do his angels at the tomb tell the women to go to Galilee. Luke's Jesus appears only in Jerusalem, but there was an established tradition that Jesus appeared in Galilee, a tradition linked to Peter.

The women in John's Gospel ('we', 20.2) received no message about going to Galilee. It may be that John or his disciple appended the story of an appearance in Galilee even though it did not fit the main pattern of the Gospel. The appearance to Peter was too important to omit, and it became the means whereby John could include in his Gospel the main point of his

---

[9] James, the leader of the church in Jerusalem, also ate with the LORD after the resurrection. The *Gospel of the Hebrews*, quoted by Jerome, *On Illustrious Men* 2, says the LORD appeared to James and told him to bring a table and bread. The risen LORD then took the bread, blessed it, broke it, and gave it to James as a sign that the Son of Man had risen from the dead.

Epilogue: the relative status of Peter and himself in the Church. The additional story of Peter seeing the LORD in Galilee 'after this' (v. 1) (which could mean at the end of the seven days mentioned in the *Gospel of Peter*) would be one of the 'many other things which Jesus did' (v. 25). There is a similar collection of additional material at the end of Revelation: everything after Revelation 22.6 is detached oracles, some of which are duplicates of material elsewhere in the main text: e.g. Rev. 22.8–9 duplicates 19.10; Rev. 22.13 duplicates 21.6.[10] The key to the final formation of Revelation lies in the oracles that are not duplicated elsewhere, the oracles of the imminent return of the LORD: 'Behold, I am coming soon' (Rev. 22.7, 12, 20). The warning of the imminent return was kept in the seven letters because they had already been circulated (Rev. 2.16, 25; 3.11), but when John assembled the collection of prophecies into their final form, the return of the LORD was no longer expected in the future because he had already returned.

Some of the disciples had resumed their former occupation as fishermen. They took their boat out at night but caught nothing. A figure on the shore whom they did not at first recognize asked about the catch, and then told them to cast their net on the right side of the boat, where there were fish. The net was filled, but it did not break, and they brought ashore 153 large fish. There has been endless speculation about this number,[11] but John has elsewhere used gematria to conceal a reference to the name Neron Caesar, 666 being 'the name of the beast or the number of its name' (Rev. 13.17).[12] The Hebrew Christians in the same passage are described as the other children of the Woman clothed with the sun and crowned with stars (Rev. 12.17), and by gematria, the number of the name of the Woman's children is 153: 'children of a queen', *bny mlk'*,[13] gives B(2) + N(50) + Y(10) + M(40) + L(30) + K(20) + '(1) = 153. These were dragged from the sea in an unbroken net, an interesting image in view of the ruling from the contemporary teachers R. Gamaliel and R. Jose, that any object bearing the figure of the sun, the moon or the dragon – images associated with the Woman clothed with the sun – should be broken and either scattered or thrown into the sea.[14] The unbroken net was John's hope for the Church, especially in divided

---

[10] For detail see my book *The Revelation*, n. 5 above, pp. 369–71.
[11] For a good selection, see R. E. Brown, *The Gospel According to John XIII–XXI*, Anchor Bible 29a, New Haven and London: Yale University Press, (1970) 2008, pp. 1074–6.
[12] The letters are N (50) + R (200) + W (6) + N (50) + Q (100) + S (60) + R (200), = 666.
[13] Spelled thus at Qumran.
[14] Mishnah *Abodah Zarah* 3.2.

## John 21

Ephesus. Matthew's community knew this story as a parable of the kingdom of heaven: a net full of fish was dragged to the shore, and then sorted into the good and the bad (Matt. 13.47–50).

Luke knew this story, but set it in another place. The main features of Luke's story are the same as John's, and he has preserved some important details, but there are difficulties with Luke's context which favour John's setting as the original: that this was a resurrection appearance. Luke's story begins with Jesus standing by Lake Gennesaret. He saw two boats and asked Simon to put one of them out a little from the land so that he could teach the crowd from the boat (Luke 5.1–3). Matthew 13.1–2 and Mark 4.1 both describe Jesus teaching from a boat when he tells the parable of the sower, but Luke does not mention his being in a boat when Jesus tells this parable (Luke 8.4). Then Luke's Jesus told Simon to put down his nets for a catch, and, after protesting that he had caught nothing all night, he did as Jesus said. The men caught a shoal big enough to fill both boats, and their nets were breaking. When Simon Peter saw this, he fell down before Jesus, saying 'Depart from me, for I am a sinful man, O Lord' (Luke 5.4–8). James and John, who were fishing with him, were also astonished. Then Jesus said to Simon: 'Do not be afraid; henceforth you will be catching men.' Simon Peter, James and John then left their fishing and followed Jesus. Andrew is not mentioned. Mark, followed by Matthew, described the call of the first disciples with no mention of the great haul of fish, no special emphasis on Peter, and Jesus speaks to them all, not just to Peter, when he says 'I will make you fishers of men' (Matt. 4.18–25; Mark 1.16–20). If Luke knew the full original story and its setting, then Mark, followed by Matthew, has dismembered the story, left out the great haul of fish, left out the special emphasis on Peter, and made Jesus teach from a boat on the wrong occasion. Now Mark is said to have taken his material from Peter and so is unlikely to have omitted his part in the story,[15] and John claims to have been an eyewitness (21.24). Luke, however, collected other people's stories (Luke 1.1–4). He is more likely to have separated elements in the story and put them into different places.

### 21.15–23: Peter and John

John's story of the great catch of fish was the resurrection appearance to Peter, which – who knows? – could have been in the lost ending of Mark. Luke sets the story at the start of Jesus' ministry, and then has no detail of

---

[15] Eusebius, *History* 2.15.

the resurrection appearance to Peter, even though he knew there had been an appearance. John presents the story not as the call of Peter but as his recall, Jesus reinstating him after his threefold denial. After the meal Jesus asks Peter three times: 'Simon, son of John, do you love me?', adding after the first question, '[Do you love me] more than these?' Some have suggested that 'these' refers to the tools of his fishing trade, but it is more likely that Jesus was asking if he loved him more than other disciples did. Peter had protested at the last supper that he would follow Jesus and lay down his life for him, but Jesus warned him that before cock crow, he would have denied him three times (13.37–38). Matthew sets this exchange after the last supper, when Jesus warned that the flock would be scattered when the shepherd was struck, but after he was raised up, he would go before them to Galilee. Peter insisted that he would never desert Jesus, even if everyone else did, and Jesus warned that he would betray him before cock crow (Matt. 26.30–35). There was a pattern that linked Peter's threefold denial to a resurrection appearance in Galilee.

And so Jesus asked Peter the same question three times. Different verbs are used: *agapaō* in verses 15 and 16; *phileō* in verse 17; but, as we have seen, these two verbs meaning 'love' are used interchangeably in the Gospel.[16] Peter affirms his love for the LORD, and seems hurt by the repeated questioning. Jesus then tells him to care for his flock. Again, two synonymous verbs are used: 'Feed/pasture/act like a shepherd, *boskō*' (vv. 15 and 17); and *poimainō* (v. 16), which has the same range of meanings. Philo explained the distinction between the two verbs as he used them: 'Those who feed us, *boskō*, supply nourishment ... those who tend us, *poimainō*, have the power of rulers and governors ...'[17] The Septuagint, however, used both verbs to translate *rāʿâ*, a verb that was used literally of a shepherd – Moses was shepherding his flock (Exod. 3.1); and figuratively of a king – the Davidic king shepherded the nations with a rod of iron (Ps. 2.9, translating literally). Jesus, then, entrusts to Peter his own role as the shepherd of his flock.

Two, or perhaps three, words are used for the flock; *arnion, probation* and *probaton*. Of these, *arnion*, 'lamb', a diminutive form, is found 29 times in Revelation but only here in the Gospel; *probation*, 'little sheep', another diminutive form, occurs nowhere else in the New Testament; and *probaton*, 'sheep' or 'goat', is a common word. The ancient versions differ in their use of *probaton* and *probation*, but it is likely that the diminutive

---

[16] See above, p. 393.
[17] Philo, *The Worse Attacks the Better* 25.

## John 21

form *probation* was used in both verses 16 and 17, in parallel with *arnion*. These were the little ones, entrusted to Peter as their shepherd. In Luke's version of the story, this was Jesus' assurance to Peter that he would become a fisher of men.

Jesus then prophesied how Peter would die, and before this chapter was actually written, Peter would have died a martyr in Rome. Jesus' words begin 'Truly, truly ...', *amēn, amēn*, the double form that John (only) has him use throughout the Gospel (e.g. 1.51; 3.3, 11; 5.19, 24, 25); and they have the parallel form of a traditional wisdom saying:

> When you were younger, you girded yourself and walked where you would.
> When you grow old, you will stretch out your hands,
> And another will gird you, and carry you where you do not wish to go.
> (v. 18, my translation)

Jesus then said to Peter: 'Follow me' (v. 19), perhaps to be understood literally, but more likely an indication that he would follow Jesus in the way he died. He too would be crucified and he too would lay down his life for his friends (15.13). 'Stretching out the hands' meant crucifixion. Barnabas cited texts in the Old Testament which used the phrase and which, he said, foreshadowed the crucifixion.

> The Spirit, speaking inwardly to Moses, prompted him to make a representation of the cross and Him who was to suffer on it ... He spread his two arms out wide, and Israel began to gain the victory [Exod. 17.8–13].
> Thus he says in another of the prophets: 'All day long I stretched out my hands to a faithless people ...' [Isa. 65.2].[18]

Then Peter turned and saw the beloved disciple following them. He asked Jesus about him, presumably about his role and his destiny, just as he had learned about his own role and destiny. Jesus said that this was not Peter's concern: 'If it is my will that he remain until I come, what is that to you?' (vv. 22, 23). There was a rumour abroad that John would not die before the *parousia*. Many of the first generation had expected to live until the LORD returned:

> We shall not all sleep, but we shall all be changed ... (1 Cor. 15.51)

> The dead in Christ will rise first; then we who are alive, who are left, shall be caught up together with them in the clouds to meet the LORD in the air; and so we shall always be with the LORD. (1 Thess. 4.16–17, my translation)

---

[18] *Letter of Barnabas* 12. Justin also cited both passages as prophecies of the crucifixion: Exod. 17.8–13 in *Trypho* 90, and Isa. 65.2 in *Apology* 1.35.

As time passed and the LORD did not literally return, John was given a new understanding of the *parousia* that prompted him to write his Gospel. Not everyone accepted this, and whoever wrote 2 Thessalonians was one of them:

> Concerning the coming of our LORD Jesus Christ and our assembling to meet him, we beg you, brethren, not to be quickly shaken in mind or excited, either by spirit or by word, or by a letter purporting to be from us, to the effect that the day of the LORD has come.
>
> (2 Thess. 2.1–2, my translation)

John the elder outlived the other close disciples of Jesus; Papias had only known their followers, but the elder John he had met. Perhaps the old man had this final chapter written when he knew he was about to die, since he knew that his death – the last of those who had known the LORD in the flesh – would bring a crisis of faith. Or there could have been a misunderstanding that arose from John's own vision of the LORD returning. The conviction that he had seen the *parousia* was being understood as an assurance that he would live to see the *parousia*.

The Gospel ends for the second time with another witness statement, similar to the testimony to the spear wound at 19.35. John was adding important details that others either did not know, or had not written about, or had recorded incorrectly. The great catch of fish was a resurrection appearance, not the story of Peter's original call; Peter had been restored after his denials, and Jesus had appointed him as the shepherd of the sheep. John would not live until the *parousia*, and Jesus had given him a different role: he was the last eyewitness and the one to whom the LORD revealed and entrusted his own visions. At the beginning of Revelation John claimed to be the servant who bore witness to the Logos of God and to the witness/evidence of Jesus the Anointed One, to the things that he (Jesus) had seen. John was told to write what he saw (Rev. 1.19). At the end of his Gospel he makes the same claim: he bears witness to these things, and he has written them down. The Logos in the bosom, *kolpos*, of the Father made him known (1.18), and John, who had been in the bosom, *kolpos*, of Jesus at the last supper (13.23), made him known.[19]

The writings of John are the primary New Testament witness to the mind of Christ and to the Temple he came to restore.

---

[19] The reference to John being on the LORD's breast in 21.20 uses a different word for breast, *stēthos*.

# Index of canonical and deuterocanonical texts

**Genesis**
1.1 79, 165
1.2 159, 183
1.5 570
1.9 489
1.9–13 63
1.14 46
1.24–31 63
1.26 239
1.31 235, 556
2—3 249
Lxx 2.1 557
2.2 234
2.4 517
2.7 293, 590
2.15 50
2.17 250, 278, 284
2.24 47, 403, 489, 581
2.25 438
3.6 50
3.14–15 366
3.17–19 435
5.21–24 566
5.24 568
7.17 202
9.12–17 43
12.6–7 36, 48, 178
14.18 48, 59, 70, 73, 293, 466
14.18–23 432
14.19 171, 494
14.22 71
15.1–21 43, 432, 466
15.12–21 388
15.15 331

16.7–14 73, 411, 460
16.13 48
17.1 48
18.1–2 162, 463
18.1–15 462
18.9–10 463
18.22 463
22.2 163, 384, 402, 511
22.6 544
22.10 411
22.11–14, 19 48
22.12 163, 462
22.15 411
22.15–18 280
22.16 163
24.7, 40 411
26.23–25 48
27.36 185
27.38 489
28.3 48, 426
28.10–22 154, 155
Lxx 28.12 185
28.18 48
33.18 215
35.1–7 48
35.11 48
43.14 48
48.3 48, 427
48.15–16 411
49.1–27 387, 426
49.9–11 57, 423, 427, 428
49.11 435
49.20 252
49.25 48

**Exodus**
3.1 604
3.2 411
3.7–8 388
3.8 101
3.12 101, 251
3.13–15 49
3.14 101, 168, 250, 287, 388, 499, 502
3.15 456
3.16 404
6.2–3 49
11—16 249
12.1–20 542
12.21–27 543
12.23 210
12.43—13.16 483
12.46 562
14.19 411
15.1–18 32
15.11 68
15.13 394, 400
15.17 400, 434
16.4 249, 255
16.14–27 255
17—18 32
17.7 234
17.8–13 605
19—24 32
19.1 150
19.5–6 392, 483, 561
19.16 133, 483
19.19 133
20.6 396
20.7 351, 448, 507, 591

20.11 44
20.24 458
23.14–17 99, 149, 230
23.16 45
23.20–21 411, 462, 467
24.1 467
24.4–8 143, 392
24.9–10 31, 47, 178, 406, 541
24.9–12 587
24.10–11 509
Lxx 24.11 514
24.16–17 483
25.8 172
25.17–22 63
25.20 63
25.22 456, 546, 579
25.23–30 59
25.29–30 251
25.31–39 37, 42
25.32 93
26.6 489
26.31 137
26.32 212
28.2 96
28.5–6 137, 138, 212
28.31 440
28.31–35 548
Lxx 28.32 597
28.36 597
28.36–38 59, 254, 507
28.38 350
28.41 138–9, 315

607

## Index of canonical and deuterocanonical texts

29.9, 33, 35  138
30.11–16  192
30.15–16  192
30.26–30  509
30.29  252
30.30  315
30.32  259
30.33  76
31.15  263
31.18  80
32—34  32
32.1–12  92
32.30–33  337
32.32–33  92
32.34  411
33.1–2  411
33.11  405
33.14  103, 462
33.15  467
33.19, 20  162, 405
34.18–23  99, 149
34.24  99
40.7, 11, 30–32  63
40.17  63
40.19, 21, 23  64
40.24–25  37
40.25, 27, 29, 32  64
Lxx 40.33  557
40.34  172
40.35  135

### Leviticus
4.5–15  260
4.8–10  553
6.10  259
8—9  59
8.1–36  64
8.7  440
9.6  103
10.3  508
14.9  259
15.13, 16  259
16.1–28  44–5
16.2  63, 112, 456, 546, 579

16.4  259, 560, 563, 589
16.8  473
16.11  496
16.14–16  91, 563, 579
16.15  496
16.15–19  192
16.19  559–60
16.20–22  364
16.27  546
17.11  259, 445, 560
19.10  430
19.18  142
20.10  269
20.27  313
21.9  209
21.10  548
21.11  383
21.12  80
23.1–44  45, 149
23.10–11  565
23.33–36  542
23.37–44  149
23.39  265
24.5–9  58
24.8–9  252
24.11–16  539
24.16  312
25.5–8  251
25.8–12  258

### Numbers
3.32  341
3.40–45  482
4.1–5  18
Lxx 5.8  480
5.19–22  270
6—14  249
6.22–27  339, 362, 591
6.24–26  97, 140, 154, 156, 159, 273, 484, 587
6.27  231, 484

7.89  339
8—11  378
8.5–22  565–6
8.7  378
8.14–19  339
8.17–19  378
9.1–5  378
9.12  339, 562
10—14  32
11.24–30  412
12.1, 9  342
12.1–15  49, 339
13.8, 16–24  400
14.11  339
15.32–35  312
16.41–48  507
18.7  11, 65
18.16  482
20.1–2  49, 232
20.13  234
20.16  411
21.6–9  202
22.21–35  411
22.24  73
Lxx 22.24  546
22.31  460
23.11–12  394
Lxx 23.17  538
24.17  138, 201, 538
Lxx 24.17  201
25.10–13  380, 444
28—29  45
29.11  553
31.6  424

### Deuteronomy
1.1  387
1.1–5  390
1.5  268
1.21  399
1.22  400
1.30  399
1.33  399, 402
2.14  49, 232
4.4  438

4.5–6  43, 44, 207, 375, 403, 438
4.10  390
4.12–13  47, 96, 100, 178, 245, 284, 363, 410, 515
4.12–15  391, 405
4.19  35
4.34  445
5.3  398
5.5–6  216
5.10  396
5.15  44
5.24  391
5.28–29  218
5.33  398, 403
6.3  398
6.4–5  142, 167, 465, 489
6.4–6  398
6.6–8  203, 340
6.13  442
6.20–24  32, 445
7.6  398, 445
7.9  162, 396, 442, 445
7.12  162, 394, 396, 398, 445
7.19  446
8.1  374
8.3  254, 374
8.6  390, 398
10.12–13  442
10.20  47, 438, 442
11.8–9  43
11.22  438
12.1–14  34
12.2  35
12.3  48
12.5, 11  100
13.1–5  313, 381, 414
13.4  399, 438, 442
13.9  526
13.13  415

608

## Index of canonical and deuterocanonical texts

13.14 47
14.1 69, 237, 399
14.1–21 200
14.1–29 392
16.1–17 45, 99, 149, 258
16.16 99
17.14–20 42
17.18–19 80
18.11 331
18.15–22 84, 381
18.18–19 412
18.18–22 218
19.15 245, 273
21.22–23 526, 557
22.20–21 270, 271
22.22 269
23.3–4 73
24.13 442
26.5–9 32
27.1–8 218
28.52 47
29.9 328
29.29 11, 43, 207, 281, 328, 334, 375, 399, 403, 494
30.11 328
30.11–14 44, 85, 281, 407
30.19–20 328
31—34 212, 385
31.2 390, 393
31.3 399
31.6 399
31.8 399
31.9–11 153
31.29 403
31.30 53
32—33 481
32.1 328
32.1–43 131, 242, 318, 483–5
32.3 502
32.3–6 486
32.4 395

32.6 171
32.7–9 71, 161, 243, 497
32.8 79, 292, 333
Lxx 32.8 493
32.9 486
32.15 133
32.19–22 486
32.28–29 487, 508
32.32–33 431, 487
32.39 102, 328
32.39–43 211
32.40–41 319, 488
32.43 54, 125, 132, 203, 204, 209, 212, 276, 284, 297, 332, 333, 385, 469, 481, 485, 488, 504
Lxx 32.43 114, 488
32.46–47 375
33.1 328
33.2–3 328, 332, 333, 485, 508, 514
33.2–5 98, 132, 160, 187
33.2–29 30, 131, 153, 318, 482–4
33.3 31, 264
33.4–5 98, 133, 264, 266, 481, 488
33.26 133
34.4 387

**Joshua**
7.19 296
10.1, 3 81
24.2–13 32
24.26 36
24.29–30 329
24.32 215
24.33 329

**Judges**
2.1, 4 411
3.10 412
5.23 411
6.11–24 411
6.34 412
13.3–20 411

**Ruth**
1.14 47, 438
1.16 582

**1 Samuel**
1.3 149
2.22 239
3.4 361
8.18 40
9.9 243
10.4 252
10.6, 24 412
14.20 460
15.1 82
16.1 138, 160
16.13–14 412–14
17.6 6
23.7 331

**2 Samuel**
1.18 34
3.33 232
6.22 36
7.12 78
7.14 78, 114, 125, 162, 316
7.15 395
7.19 128
23.1–2 107, 332, 405, 413, 419, 460, 475, 591
23.1–4 374, 399
24.15–17 412

**1 Kings**
1.33–40 427
1.38–40 57, 81, 341

1.44–45 349
2.35 326
3.3–14 85
4.1–4 81
4.29, 33–34 89
5.13–18 40
6.20 66
6.22 554
6.23–28 63
6.29 49
7.49 37
8.2 149, 262
8.6–7 63
8.10–11 135, 149, 172
8.23 396
8.27 465
8.64–66 149
9.10–14 40
10.19 355
11.32 427
11.41 34
12.1–20 40
15.2 41
15.3 40
15.9–15 41
15.13 41
16.23–28 41, 214
22.13–23 414
22.42 41

**2 Kings**
4.42–44 247
10.13 41
11.12, 14 80
12.1 41
14.2 41
16.1–4 41, 48
16.5–9 293
17.29–30 216
18.1–8 41
18.4 202, 371
18.22 371
19.15 35
20.1, 4–5 371
20.1–7 41

609

## Index of canonical and deuterocanonical texts

21.18, 26  562
23.6  271
23.7  514
23.8–20  34
23.10  48
23.11  36
23.14, 15  48
23.21–23  193
23.24  331
24.3–4  293

### 1 Chronicles
15.28  135
16.3  248
16.4  456
16.42  135
17.17  128, 201
18.15  457
24.1–3  326, 341
28.18  63, 64
29.1  53
29.20  82, 104, 341, 593
LXX 29.20  297
29.22  82
29.23  82, 83, 593

### 2 Chronicles
3.10–13  63
5.3  262
6.1–3, 12–13  83
7.5, 7  83
9.29  34
15.1  412
20.14  413
24.20–22  413
26.1–23  292
26.16–21  342
29.23  395
30.1–27  193
33.10–13  511
34.3  42
35.23  561
35.25  39

### Ezra
1.3  192
3.1–6  149
3.2  389
4.1–3  217

### Nehemiah
8.1–18  149
8.8  51
9.9–15  32
9.20  412
9.38—10.10  192
13.15–22  234
13.28  217

### Esther
2.5  26

### Job
1.8  554
2.6–8  414
6.14  394
10.21  331
14.12  107
19.25–26  333
31.23  86
38.5  86
38.7  75, 171
38.33  237
42.2  85

### Psalms
2.1–2  108, 112, 113, 365, 414, 481
2.1–11  316
2.6  136
2.6–9  77
2.7  42, 108, 114, 123, 124, 125, 358, 386, 405, 460, 497
2.8–9  109, 126, 539, 604
2.10–12  123, 341
4.1, 6  97
4.3  396
6.4  394
8.1  103
16.10  568
17.8  581
17.15  98, 410
18.4  415
19.13  554
20.1, 2, 7, 8  457
21.7  394
22.11  510
22.16  586
22.18  547
22.22  586
22.23  364
23.1  300
23.5  515
24.3  304
24.6  274, 521
24.7–10  302
25.4–5  403
25.10  177, 523, 403
25.17  510
27.1  98, 273
27.2  522
27.8–9  98, 521
27.11  403
29.1  79
LXX 29.1  151
30.4  396
31.16  98
31.23  396, 522
33.4–5  396, 521
33.18, 22  396
34.7  411
34.19–21  562
35.4  522
36.7–9  267, 273
37.9  485
37.28  396
38.21–22  456
40.10–11  177, 522
41.8  415
41.9  380
42.1  44
43.3  273
45.6–7  77, 114, 133, 440, 467, 497
45.8  571
45.9  133
46.4  267
50.5  396
50.12–14  251
51.6–12  441
51.11  516
52.9  396
54.1  506
56.9  522
56.13  273
57.1  581
57.3  177
58.1–11  68
58.1  79
61.4  581
61.7  177, 522
63.1  259
63.7  581
68.8–18  390
68.24–26  42, 80, 302, 592
69.21  552
69.25–28  505
70.1, 5  457
72.1–4  95, 313
73.3, 16, 17  243
73.16–20  4
74.2  171
77.11  457
77.20  30
78.7  523
78.72  554
80.1  98
80.2–3  54, 300
80.8  56
80.8–11  428, 433
80.8–18  400
80.14–19  56, 433–5, 437
80.16  424
80.17  435

*82.1* 68, 73, 189, 282
*82.1–7* 313
*82.2* 503
*82.5–7* 68, 79, 87, 314
*85.10* 177
*86.11* 403
*86.15* 177
*88.10* 107
*88.20* 332
*89.1, 2, 5* 177, 394
*89.6* 53
*89.14* 162, 177, 395
*89.15* 273, 395
*89.19–20* 107, 128, 202, 397, 573
*89.19–28* 237
*89.20* 80, 147, 373
*89.21* 434
*89.24* 178, 373, 395
*89.25* 139
*89.26–27* 80, 136, 147, 358, 543, 561
*89.28* 178, 373, 395
*89.33* 178, 373, 395
*89.34* 395
*89.41* 442
*89.49* 178, 373, 395
*90.1* 30
*91.4* 581
*91.11–12* 125
*92.5–6* 86
*94.1* 98
*94.8* 86
*95.7–11* 234
*95.11* 389
*96.10* 435
*97.7* 488
*97.10* 397
*99.6* 30
*101.1* 395
*101.3* 415
*102.5* 438, 581
*103.7* 30
*104.1–4* 7, 50
*104.4* 412
*104.29–30* 159
*105.9–11* 280
*105.26* 30
*105.45* 523
*106.16, 23, 32* 30
*109.8–9* 506
*110.1–2* 31, 109, 114, 142, 360, 539
*110.1–7* 205
Lxx *110.3* 74
*110.3–4* 60, 74, 77, 83, 94, 108, 109, 138, 142, 147, 162, 186, 293, 315, 345, 358, 517, 539, 555
*113—118* 152, 558
*118.19–20* 302, 349
*118.22* 360, 558
*118.25* 348
*118.25–27* 140, 152, 302
*118.26* 506, 558
*118.27* 349
*118.28* 202
*119.1–176* 523
*119.2* 522
*132.7* 341
*132.9, 16* 397
*133.2–3* 75
*135.3* 364
*136.10–22* 32
*143.10* 412
*146.7–8* 288
*149.1, 5, 9* 397

**Proverbs**
*1.1* 85, 301
*1.6* 301
*1.20–33* 207
*1.23* 96, 342
*2.7* 554
*2.16* 207
*3.15–18* 206
*3.18* 75
*8.23* 38
Lxx *8.30* 394, 438
*8.36* 477
*9.1–6* 59
*9.5–6* 58
Lxx *9.5–6* 58
*9.6* 259
*10.1* 85
*13.6* 554
*24.22* 88
Lxx *24.22* 88
*25.1* 85
*30.1–4* 85, 87
*30.2* 86
Lxx *30.2* 86
*30.4* 88
*31.26* 393

**Ecclesiastes**
*5.6* 462

**Isaiah**
*1.3* 170
*1.8* 208
*1.12* 99
*1.13* 85
*1.21* 81, 182, 206
*1.21–26* 121
*1.27–31* 506
*1.31* 282
*2.2–4* 151
*3.10* 523
*4.2–4* 151
*5.1* 373
*5.1–7* 120, 314, 425, 434, 436
*5.2* 423, 437

*6.1* 91
*6.1–5* 65, 118, 286, 406, 546
*6.1–13* 289, 372
*6.5* 35, 83, 96, 162, 178, 207, 593
*6.6–7* 50, 590
*6.8* 361, 587
*6.9–10* 5, 96, 204, 227, 285, 291, 340, 587
*6.9–13* 119, 207
*6.11–12* 290, 487
*6.13* 175, 435
*7.1–14* 41
*7.3* 231
*7.10–14* 293, 300
*7.10–17* 138, 231
*7.11* 78
*7.14* 78, 94, 110, 206, 340, 410, 460
Lxx *7.14* 78
*8.5–8* 290, 293
*8.8* 292
*8.16* 34
*8.22* 510
*9.1–2* 111, 407
*9.2* 15, 110, 137, 346
Lxx *9.6* 167, 238, 253, 323, 464
*9.6–7* 15, 78, 94, 137, 206, 464
*10.18* 259
*10.32* 208
*11.1* 75, 175, 206, 425, 429
*11.1–9* 94
*11.2* 15, 60, 175, 206, 413, 460, 465, 509, 589
*11.3* 342, 589
*11.4* 88
*11.33–35* 313
*12.2–3* 151, 440

*Index of canonical and deuterocanonical texts*

13—14 238
14.4–21 331
14.12–20 238
14.19 436
18.5 554
19.11 86
19.18 51
Lxx 19.20 538
22.22 306
24.4 232
24.4–6 43
24.16 17, 84
24.23 17, 363, 391
26.3 522
26.14 107
26.19 107, 108
27.3 522
30.19–21 581
30.27 103
32.1–2 95
32.4 96
32.17 96
33.14–17 86, 98
34.16 81
35.1–2 392, 440
35.5–6 264
35.10 392, 440
36.3 457
36.7 310
37.16 35
37.22 208
38.1–8 91
40.1–2 182
40.3 130, 174
40.3–5 181
40.5 174, 307, 363
40.9 174, 257
40.10–11 182, 257, 300, 307
40.21–24 4, 66, 163, 243
41.4 274
41.8 280
41.23–24 68
42.1 108, 121, 297, 327, 413

42.1–4 90, 93, 139, 386
42.4 297
42.6 110, 120, 273, 327, 444, 513, 522
42.7 297, 327, 444
42.14–17 174
43.8–10 176, 446
43.10 102, 176, 275
43.12–13 70, 102, 128, 275
43.25 102, 275
43.26 457
44.2 133
44.3 413
44.6 470
45.22 70
48.12 102, 275, 470
49.1 110
49.1–6 90
49.2 88, 210, 328
49.3 186, 327, 392
49.4 110
49.5 327, 337, 357
49.6 110, 273, 357, 523
49.8 444, 513, 522
49.9–11 327
49.12 357
50.1 208
50.4 328
50.4–9 90
50.6 536
50.8–9 110, 328
51.1–3 277, 440, 521
51.11 440
52.1–2 208
52.7 73, 189, 257, 282, 503
52.13 85, 94, 120, 202, 573
Lxx 52.13 573

52.13–15 91, 94, 277
52.13—53.12 74, 90, 205, 367, 443
52.14 573
52.15 478, 560
53.1 91, 109, 372, 478
53.2 75, 91
Lxx 53.2 238
53.4 139
53.5 92, 95, 110, 513
53.6 110
53.7–8 119
53.9 92, 110
53.10 91, 92, 95, 143, 328, 337, 501, 560, 562
53.11 15, 81, 84, 85, 92, 94, 95, 113, 116, 121, 328, 336, 337, 351, 377, 391, 394, 410, 437, 479, 573
Lxx 53.11 92
53.11–13 478
53.12 92, 94, 109, 143, 240, 546, 560
54.4–17 271
54.8–10 396
54.11–12 196, 208
54.13 229, 249
55.6 274, 522
56.3–8 151
56.7–8 194
56.10–12 298, 307
57.1 394
57.3 135, 173
58.2 274, 537
60.1 363, 392
60.21 429, 437

61.1–2 189, 195, 258, 276, 288, 327, 413, 444, 451, 466
61.2–3 282, 440
61.4 124
61.5–7 440
61.5–11 283
61.6 32, 180
61.8 19, 451
61.10 440
62.4–5 208, 290
62.6 457
62.11–12 24
63.1–6 425
63.3–6 149
63.7 457, 458
63.8–9 103, 336, 458
63.9 411, 460, 462
Lxx 63.9 462, 464, 467
63.10 115, 516
63.11 115, 458, 516
63.11–12 30
63.14 115
65.1–2 239, 522, 605
65.13–25 283
65.15 28, 32
65.18–19 440
66.1, 3 298
66.1–4 195
66.1–6 151
66.1–14 454
66.5, 8, 14 298
66.5–6 284, 331, 333
66.6 361
66.7–9 510
66.10 440
66.18 364
66.18–21 151

*Index of canonical and deuterocanonical texts*

## Jeremiah

1.1  42
1.2  42
1.9  590
1.11-12  42
1.18  42
2.8  285
2.11-13  232
2.20-21  434
2.21  56, 423, 428
2.36  271
3.1  271
4.31  271, 510
8.7  44
8.8-9  43, 240, 285
11.19  248
13.18  41
14.7-9  233
15.1  30
17.13-14  233, 270
22.5  320
22.13-19  40
23.5-6  83, 301, 346
23.21-22  243
29.2  41
31.23  81
33.14-16  301, 346
34.5  562
36.4  431
36.27-32  39
41.4-5  216
44.16-19  40, 59
50.7  81
Lxx 52.28, 30  26

## Lamentations

1.15  425
1.19  271
2.1  208
2.13-14  271
3.1-66  39
3.42  40
4.11-13  271

## Ezekiel

1.1-28  118, 363
1.3  47, 263
1.4  173
1.4-25  9, 303
1.5, 13, 16  104
1.10  181
1.26  238, 284, 541
1.26-28  47, 103, 104, 123, 239, 515
1.28  173, 320
2.9—3.3  12, 515
3.1-3  320
3.3-4  587, 590
8.2  104
8.16-18  150
8.17  345
9.2  538, 579
Lxx 9.2  589
9.4  60, 276, 346-7, 447
10—11  118, 303
10.1  104
10.3-4  135, 173
10.15  118
10.16  202
10.17  118
10.22  104
11.22-23  173
15.1-8  434
19.1-9  56, 425
19.10-14  56, 175, 425, 426
20.37  377
20.41-42  508
28.12-19  102, 513
28.13  120
28.22, 25  508
34.2-3  307
34.4-31  299
34.23-30  311
36.23  443, 508
37.1-12  267, 334
37.4  323
37.12-14  311

37.24-27  311
38.16  508
39.27-28  508
40—47  195
40.1  303
40.1—43.5  363
43.1-5  173, 182, 263
43.4  307
43.6-7  580
44.1-2  303, 305
44.15-16  26, 45, 81, 303, 326, 379
44.15-19  348
44.20  378
45.18-25  193, 359, 542
47.1-2  218
47.1-12  559
48.35  381, 421, 468

## Daniel

7.9-14  69, 118
7.13  238
7.13-14  316, 333, 363, 555
7.14  112
7.25, 27  69
9.20-22  87, 201
9.21  538
9.24  189, 257, 554
9.24-27  120, 181, 352, 555
10.4-9  286, 579
10.4-21  68
10.5  538
10.5-14  320
10.18-21  580
12.2  108, 334
12.3  333
12.6-7  320, 579

## Hosea

4.14  272

5.10  26
5.15—6.3  330
6.6-7  64, 284, 394

## Joel

2.27-29  520
2.31, 33  520
3.1-10  520
3.13  425
3.17  520
3.18  268, 559

## Amos

3.4, 6  44
3.7  243
5.4, 6  274
5.25  267
9.1  361

## Micah

4.8  304
4.9-10  428
5.2-4  257, 300
5.3  78
6.4  30
6.7-8  443
7.1-2  430
7.18  178, 351
7.20  178, 351, 394

## Nahum

1.15  415

## Habakkuk

2.1-3  66
2.2  361, 485
Lxx 3.2  546
3.6  319

## Haggai

1.1-5  389
1.7  36
1.8  36, 363
2.5  412, 475

## Index of canonical and deuterocanonical texts

**Zechariah**
1.7–11  36
1.9  419, 475, 574
1.14  419, 574
1.19  419, 574
2.1–5  363
2.3  419, 574
3.1–5  460
3.1–9  389, 412
Lxx 3.4  589
3.8  346, 425
3.9  512
4.1–3  36
4.10–14  36
5.11  207
6.1–8  36
6.11–12  389
6.12  346, 425, 537–8
Lxx 8.23  26
9.9  57, 83, 140, 207, 209, 351, 367, 428
11.12–13  505
12.10  561
13.1  559
13.2–6  414
13.7–9  455
14.5–9  150, 347
14.6–7  153, 272
14.8  218, 267
14.8–17  194
14.9  246
14.16–17  151, 152, 246, 347
14.21  151, 152, 193, 347

**Malachi**
1.7  58
1.9  253
1.11  58, 253
1.14  253
2.4–9  248
2.7  93, 463
3.1  179, 186, 194, 263
3.2, 3  180, 194
3.5  333
4.2  150, 157
4.5–6  181

**Tobit**
12.15  465

**Wisdom**
6.12  312
6.21  78, 209
7.17–22  89
7.25, 26, 29, 30  209
8.1–2  209
10.10  155
10.17  174
15.3  513
18.15–16  210
18.22, 24  507

**Ben Sira**
Prologue  223
7.31  248
15.2  207
15.3  259
24.1–34  266
24.4  174
24.10  342
24.13–17  401
24.16–18  38, 57, 429
24.21  59
24.21–27  218
24.30–34  294
45.2  201
47.17  301
48.10  181
50.3  231
50.5  297, 557
50.5–7  483
50.7  423
50.15  557
50.17  297, 341
50.18–19  557
50.25–26  217
51.23–26  223

**1 Maccabees**
4.36–59  315
4.46  219
10.21  155
13.51  345

**2 Maccabees**
2.4–8  172
6.1–2  217

**1 Esdras**
9.8  296

**Prayer of Manasseh**
3  101

**2 Esdras**
2.42–48  348, 465
5.23  431
10.44  141
13.25–26  437

**Matthew**
1.6  160
1.18  115
1.22–23  110, 138, 290
2.1  160
2.2  54, 138, 296, 346
2.23  75, 290, 436, 547
3.3  130, 290
3.7  278
3.7–10  281
3.11  38
3.12  220, 425
3.15–16  127, 173
3.17  290, 516
4.3, 6  365
4.4  374
4.15–16  111, 290
4.17  189
4.18–25  603
5.3–12  283
5.4  290
5.5  424
5.6  268, 290
5.10–12  451
5.17  230
5.17–19  241
5.18  225
5.21, 22  230
5.35  290
6.10  139
6.12  504
6.25  588
7.9  123
7.16, 19–20  435
7.28–29  229, 230
8.2  296
8.5–13  220
8.9  405
8.17  110, 139
8.23–27  139
9.2–8  591
9.10  247
9.22  357
9.27  139
10.3  383
10.5–7  214, 509
10.24–25  376
10.28, 32  336
10.34  210, 520
10.38  447
11.10  179
11.15  13
11.19  266
11.29–30  222
12.9  224
12.9–21  110, 139
12.18  113
12.29  418
12.46–50  550
13.1–2  603
13.1–32  359
13.9  13

## Index of canonical and deuterocanonical texts

13.10-17  301
13.11  139
13.14-15  372
13.24-30  281, 301, 424
13.24-43  326
13.30  220, 520
13.36-43  111, 281, 424
13.41-43  13, 220
13.47-50  603
13.55  550
14.22-33  139
14.27  250, 251
14.33  296
15.3, 13  298
15.22  139
15.25  296
16.1-4  340
16.13-20  499
16.16  140, 596
16.17  261, 316
16.21  357
16.22-23  261
17.1-8  451
17.4  581
17.5  108, 129, 135, 173
17.22-23  451
18.2  201
18.15  477
18.20  459
19.28  111, 140
20.17-19  451
20.20-23  598
20.29-34  288
20.30  139
21.5  140
21.9  141
21.11  315
21.13  194
21.15  191
21.17  326
21.23  360
21.23-46  314
21.28-32  141, 436

22.1-14  141
22.11-14  589
22.23  330
22.41-46  109, 315
23.1-36  228
23.2-4  223
23.13-15  142, 281, 298
23.16, 31, 33  298
23.37-38  191, 290
24.1-2  333, 360
24.3  224, 319, 521
24.4-42  196
24.8  452
24.9  510
24.12  452
24.27  319
24.30  594
24.37, 39  319
25.31-46  299, 301, 332, 477
26.6-7  326, 341
26.14-16  381
26.20  383
26.20-29  381
26.25  228
26.28  143, 512
26.30  495
26.30-35  604
26.31  455
26.32  601
26.39  523
26.49  228
26.53  533
26.60-63  144, 193
26.61  196
26.75  527
27.1  525
27.3-10  505
27.4  552
27.11  316, 531
27.15-17  535-6
27.26  541
27.28  536
27.32  544
27.37  546

27.39-54  544
27.45  551
27.45-53  557-8
27.48  552
27.51  121
27.54  568
27.55  549
27.56  577
27.61  544
27.62-66  523
28.1  570, 577
28.7, 10  601
28.9  296, 341
28.13, 15  568
28.16  601
28.18-20  227, 591

**Mark**
1.2  179
1.10  60, 121
1.11  123, 386, 516
1.14-20  185
1.15  189
1.16-20  603
1.21  224
1.24  546
1.39  224
2.5-8  591
3.21  550
3.22  282
3.27  418
3.31-35  550
4.1  603
4.10  52, 119, 222
4.11-12  5, 16, 17, 84, 199, 237, 301, 321, 372
4.18  124
4.26-29  326
4.34  52
6.1-6  124
6.2  224
6.3  262, 532, 550
6.7  509
6.30—8.38  260
6.34  299, 301

6.50  250, 251
7.1-5  188
7.1-23  260
7.13  224
8.15  260
8.17  260
8.27-29  261, 499
8.28  181, 315
8.29  316
8.31  202, 357
8.34  185, 447
9.2-8  451
9.7  108, 129, 135
9.12-13  451
9.30  262
9.31  202, 451
10.5  224
10.17  198
10.33-34  202, 451
10.35-40  598
10.46-52  288
10.51  228
11.1  326
11.3  344
11.9  141
11.11-12  326, 352
11.17  151, 194
11.18  191
11.27  360
11.27-33  141
11.27—12.12  120
11.27—12.44  314
12.1-12  141, 171, 425, 436
12.3-37  315
12.12  315
12.17  531
12.18-27  142, 216
12.29-31  142
12.35-37  203
12.36  109
12.37  142, 539
13.1-2  119, 197, 315, 360
13.1-4  340

## Index of canonical and deuterocanonical texts

13.3–4  224, 354, 521
13.5–37  196, 354
13.8  452
13.9–13  295, 452
13.11  591
13.24–25  520
13.26  321, 473, 594
13.27  594
13.30  451
14.2  338
14.3  326, 341
14.3–9  143
14.10–11  381
14.17  383
14.17–25  381
14.18–21  380
14.26–27  455, 495
14.32–36  361
14.36  523
14.43  144
14.54  527
14.57–61  195
14.58  196
14.59  524
14.61  144, 316
14.62  109
14.62–64  539
14.64  144
14.67  527, 546
14.72  527
15.1  525
15.2  316, 531
15.6–8  535
15.15  541
15.21  544
15.23  551–2
15.24  541
15.26  546
15.29–32  544
15.33  358, 544, 551
15.33–39  544, 557–8
15.36  552
15.38  121
15.40  549, 577
15.44  544
15.47  544, 577
16.1–2  570, 577
16.4  450
16.5  579
16.7  601
16.9  574, 576
16.12  453, 587
16.15  591

### Luke

1.1–2  282, 592
1.1–4  603
1.4  353
1.5  179
1.13  361
1.17  60, 134
1.26–38  580
1.32–33  60, 78, 131, 311, 313
1.32–35  283
1.35  134
1.51  283
1.54–55  60, 283
1.68–79  283, 388
1.69  60, 283, 311
1.71  283, 311
1.72  394
1.73  60, 283
1.77  93
1.78–79  110, 346
1.80  179
2.4  160
2.8–12  174
2.11  54, 160
2.12  136
2.14  203
2.19  134
2.26  183
2.29–33  90
2.32  110
2.46  226
2.49  402
2.51  134
3.10–14  179
3.16  38
3.17  220
3.31  160
3.38  87
4.3  123, 365
4.4  374
4.5  126
4.9  365
4.16–21  189, 413, 440
4.16–30  124
4.18–19  115, 276, 290, 444
4.21  224, 258, 451, 466
5.1–8  603
5.8  596
5.20–24  591
5.21  467
6.40  377
7.1–10  220
7.11–17  317, 570
7.35  266, 365, 493
7.36–38  341
7.39  253
8.2  577
8.3  221
8.4  603
8.10  372
8.19–21  550
8.40–56  317, 570
9.2  509
9.10  247
9.18–21  499
9.20  316
9.28–36  451
9.31  387
9.35  108, 129, 135
9.44  451
9.51  261
9.51–54  214
10.16  366
10.18  111, 134, 365, 519
10.19  365
10.30–37  215
11.46  223
11.47–48  290
11.49  253
11.52  142, 305
12.22  588
13.34  191
14.16–24  141
14.27  447
15.4–7  299, 301
16.24  331
16.29–31  326
18.31–33  451
18.35–43  288
19.29  326
19.41–44  141, 275, 347
19.44  456
19.46  194
19.47  191, 226, 360
19.47—21.4  314
20.9–17  436
20.36  142, 317, 571
20.41–44  315
20.42–43  109
21.8–36  196
21.15  452
21.27  594
21.37–38  269, 360
22.3–6  381, 505
22.10  191
22.14–38  381
22.19  380, 595
22.21  380
22.27  376
22.28–30  379
22.37  110
22.41–44  361
22.42  523
22.51  523
22.54  525
22.55  527
22.61  527
22.67  144, 525

*Index of canonical and deuterocanonical texts*

22.69  109
22.70  525
23.2  530
23.3  316, 531
23.6–11  536
23.12  108
23.25  541
23.26  544
23.27–31  354, 544
23.34–37  544, 576
23.36  552
23.38  546
23.40–47  544
23.44  551
23.44–46  557–8
23.45  121
23.46–48  544
23.49  549
23.55  544
24.1  570
24.4  538, 579
24.10  570, 577
24.21  569
24.23  538
24.25–27  203, 227, 367, 478
24.26  15, 391
24.27  116, 572, 589
24.31  572, 582
24.33  586
24.35  323
24.36  585
24.37  582
24.39  564
24.39–43  587
24.45  589
24.45–49  591
24.50  326
24.51  370

**John**
1.1  240
1.1–14  164
1.1—2.11  157
1.2–3  496
1.3  235, 490
1.3–5  168
1.4–5  162, 325, 368
1.5  472, 498
1.6–9  162, 177
1.9  325, 346, 368
1.10–12  158, 170, 476, 503
1.11  235, 316, 317, 498, 582
1.12  497, 514, 586
1.12–13  12, 167, 172, 199, 282, 312, 325, 326, 368, 392, 461, 583
1.14  166, 172, 174, 231, 240, 257, 263, 264, 364, 368, 372, 391, 406, 474, 480, 519, 587
1.15  177, 185, 190
1.15–18  165
1.17  47, 162, 373, 391, 393, 441, 476
1.18  127, 162, 240, 404, 502, 606
1.19  157, 177, 180, 383
1.19–20  531
1.19–28  325
1.20–21  180
1.23  54
1.26  182, 580
1.28  342, 370
1.29  157, 182, 325, 327, 575
1.29–34  158, 368
1.29–51  476
1.30  54, 185, 190, 325
1.32  60, 177, 183

1.32–34  229, 296, 327
1.33  473
1.34  167, 177, 182, 325, 516
1.35  157, 327, 600
1.35–37  382
1.36  325, 376
1.37–40  188
1.38  228
1.40  382, 596
1.41  325, 600
1.43  116, 157
1.44  247
1.45  596, 600
1.46  185
1.49  228, 325, 343
1.51  186, 605
2.1  549
2.4  47, 357, 542
2.11  181, 190, 264, 325, 340, 364, 502
2.12  191
2.12—10.42  158
2.13  222, 325, 358
2.16  151, 347
2.18  222
2.19  196, 525, 572, 576
2.20  222, 525
2.21  196, 370
2.22  321, 370, 472, 525, 589
2.23  46, 148
3.2  228
3.3  548, 604
3.3–8  172, 204, 473
3.5  583
3.5–8  213
3.6  199
3.8  200
3.10  198, 312
3.11  213, 604
3.12  201, 213, 519

3.13  213, 409
3.13–15  204
3.14–15  203, 366, 478
3.15–19  204, 213
3.16–17  204, 213, 394, 397, 503
3.16–21  297
3.17–18  477, 557
3.19  315, 393
3.19–21  198
3.28–29  205, 209, 441
3.31–32  5, 9, 89, 183, 187, 213, 237, 516, 519, 533, 571
3.31–36  209, 213, 409
3.32  236, 327, 409, 476, 567
3.34  213, 229, 328, 476, 567
3.35  393, 397
3.36  213
4.5, 6  215
4.9  214
4.14  223
4.15  255
4.22  219
4.25  196
4.27  220
4.31  228
4.35  520
4.38  220
4.44–45  220
5.1  148, 222
5.2  33
5.14  233
5.14–47  222
5.17  234–5, 525
5.18  237, 525
5.19  229, 235, 605
5.19–30  243–4
5.20  393
5.21  334

## Index of canonical and deuterocanonical texts

5.22–29  245, 335
5.24, 25  605
5.26–27  229
5.27  184
5.28  337
5.30  229
5.30–35  245
5.33  229, 476
5.36  502
5.37  229, 285, 476
5.39  224, 227, 241, 476
5.39–40  198
5.42  397
5.43  229, 476, 502
5.46–47  240, 245
6.1  370, 596
6.1–15  222
6.4  46, 148, 358
6.5  247
6.8  596
6.11  255
6.14  261, 315
6.15  355, 531
6.17  248
6.20  250, 600
6.25  228
6.27  254
6.30–34  193
6.31–40  249
6.32  380
6.33  255
6.34  279
6.35  255, 256
6.37  250
6.40  255, 256
6.42  258
6.43–51  249
6.45  229, 258, 328
6.48–50  258
6.50  250
6.51  256, 258
6.52  259
6.53  254
6.53–58  249

6.56  254, 380, 443, 475
6.59  254
6.62  254, 261, 409, 585, 600
6.63  259, 261, 473, 585, 600
6.64  380
6.65–71  261
6.67–69  375
6.68–69  596, 600
7—9  263
7.1  263
7.1–3  345
7.1–52  264
7.2  148, 358
7.2–8.59  222
7.5  550
7.6  357
7.7  476
7.8  357
7.10  287
7.13  263
7.16–17  476
7.19  273
7.23  263
7.25  263
7.25–27  540
7.27  409
7.30–31  263, 265, 357, 542
7.33–34  393, 453, 478
7.35  357
7.36  269
7.37–38  151, 218, 223, 265, 300, 590
7.39  266
7.40  315
7.40–51  268
7.43  312
7.44  263
7.51  198
7.52  315
8.2  226

8.5  226, 530
8.6–8  285
8.7  226
8.11  270
8.12  327
8.14  453
8.19–20  274, 357, 542
8.21  393, 453
8.25  276
8.28  202, 276, 366, 478
8.31–38  279, 533
8.39  280
8.39–42  534
8.40  284
8.41  519
8.42  393
8.44  280, 281, 285, 432
8.46  477
8.47  285, 477, 534
8.48  281
8.50  364
8.51  420
8.56  286
8.58  286, 525
8.59  525, 534
9.1–7  57
9.2  228
9.3  299
9.5  272
9.7  267, 327
9.9  294
9.16  312
9.24  296, 299
9.28, 34  296
9.35–37  366
9.38  203
9.39  297
10.1–18  257
10.2  305
10.3–4  301, 388, 445, 581
10.6  301
10.7–9  306

10.8  307
10.10–17  309
10.11  378
10.15  312, 378
10.16  194, 311, 327, 357
10.17–18  357, 378, 393, 397
10.19  312
10.22  148
10.22–39  222
10.24–26  315, 524, 531, 539
10.27  312
10.30  167, 274, 312, 455
10.31–39  525
10.33–34  313
10.34–38  241
10.36  167, 315, 496, 508–9, 516, 548, 586
10.36–38  372
10.37–39  476
10.38  314, 475
10.39–42  316
10.40  317, 370
11—12  158
11.1–16  329
11.3  393
11.4  325, 364
11.5  397
11.8  228
11.10  325
11.14–15  330
11.16  596
11.17–37  329, 330
11.23–26  324
11.25–26  325, 335, 336
11.27  325
11.31–37  325
11.36  325, 393
11.37  325
11.38–44  329
11.40  325, 364

## Index of canonical and deuterocanonical texts

11.41  570
11.44  327, 336, 570
11.45–46  325, 330
11.46–54  325, 526
11.47–53  383
11.48  527, 531
11.49–50  597
11.53  337, 521, 525–6
11.54  329, 521, 526
11.55  358, 370, 379
11.57  325
12.1  148, 222, 325, 370
12.4–5  340, 548
12.8  343
12.9–11  325
12.10  325
12.12  340, 378
12.12–16  151, 152, 222, 343, 558
12.13  373, 458, 531–2
12.14  572
12.15  57, 207, 209
12.16  321, 341, 344, 350, 351–2, 370, 472, 475, 572, 589
12.18  340
12.19  325
12.20  356
12.20–23  151
12.23  339, 357, 362, 391, 478, 542
12.25  393
12.27–29  521
12.28  251, 339, 362, 364, 391
12.29  341, 391
12.30  361

12.31  364, 452, 503
12.31–33  480
12.32–34  202, 366
12.34  368, 478
12.35–36  170, 368, 453, 472
12.37–43  176, 204, 222, 293, 358
12.37–50  253, 286, 339
12.38  109, 478
12.39–40  5, 227, 340, 406, 473
12.41  286, 372
12.42  293, 325, 352
12.43  373, 393
12.44–50  213, 373, 374, 474
12.45–46  474, 476
12.46–48  204
13—17  158
13.1  357, 378, 393, 397, 478, 495
13.2  9, 495
13.3  378, 453, 495
13.6  596
13.7, 8  379
13.9  596
13.10  379, 380, 441
13.16  240, 376
13.17  377
13.18  402, 495, 511
13.19  381
13.21  380
13.22  399, 420
13.23  382, 393, 606
13.24  596
13.27  9, 380, 495
13.29  343
13.30  521

13.31–32  391, 495
13.31—16.33  436
13.33  393, 453
13.34  393, 420, 510
13.34–36  390, 392
13.36–38  393, 453, 527, 604
14.1–3  400
14.4, 5  453
14.6  400, 402, 429, 476
14.7–8  404, 474
14.8  116, 500, 501
14.9  410, 474, 572
14.10  413
14.11  405
14.12  478
14.15  393, 405, 420
14.15–17  456, 459
14.16  474
14.16–17  8, 418–20, 452, 460, 461, 474, 475, 476, 574, 585, 589–90
14.18–19  453, 461, 583, 586
14.20  420
14.21  393
14.26  456, 475, 572
14.23, 24  393, 420
14.26  8, 321, 420, 471, 472, 474, 559
14.27  559
14.27–29  400
14.28  393, 453, 478, 586
14.30  503
14.31  393
15.1  424
15.1–6  55, 400, 401

15.1–11  377
15.2  437
15.3  441
15.4  439, 450, 581
15.4–10  437
15.7–17  439
15.9  393
15.9–10  441
15.10  420
15.11  441
15.12  393, 420
15.13  605
15.14  443
15.15  441, 442
15.16  402, 511
15.17  393, 420
15.18–19  393, 402, 422, 445, 511
15.20  420
15.22–24  445
15.26–27  456, 474, 476
16.1–2  293, 444, 447
16.4  452
16.5  453
16.7–8  8, 420, 461, 471, 474, 541, 585–6
16.7–11  503, 556
16.7–14  456, 589
16.8–11  477, 479
16.10  453
16.12–13  8, 448, 474, 476, 559
16.13  572
16.13–15  472
16.14  480
16.16  453
16.17  399, 453
16.19  453, 585
16.21  452, 510
16.22  454
16.25–33  393
16.27  393

619

## Index of canonical and deuterocanonical texts

16.28 478, 510
16.29 390
16.32 454, 455
16.33 448, 450, 510
17.1 495
17.1–8 496
17.1–26 52, 67, 79
17.2 495
17.3 55, 499
17.4 327, 495, 502, 552
17.5 165, 251, 409, 478, 495–6, 510
17.6 7, 55, 486, 502
17.8 502
17.9 502
17.9–19 496
17.11 55, 294, 495, 506, 511
17.12 448, 495, 505–6, 523
17.14 507, 509
17.15 55, 495, 504
17.18 509, 590
17.19 55, 508
17.20 510
17.20–26 496
17.21 55, 384, 510
17.21–23 513, 514
17.23 393, 510, 552
17.24 55, 66, 129, 255, 348, 360, 389, 393, 474, 496, 510, 559
17.26 55, 393, 512–13
18.1 519
18.2 520, 541
18.4 521
18.5 522, 547
18.6 250, 522
18.7 521–2, 547
18.8 522–3

18.10 383, 596
18.11 523
18.13 309, 353
18.15 353, 382, 383, 596
18.15–18 527
18.16 597
18.18 549
18.19 524
18.20 223
18.21 527
18.25 596
18.25–27 527, 549
18.26 523, 597
18.28 383, 527
18.30–32 530
18.31 541
18.33 316
18.35–37 531, 533
18.39 541
19.5 87, 473, 534, 539, 541, 561
19.7 516, 539
19.8–11 540
19.11 479
19.12–16 540–3
19.13 33, 528, 534
19.14 473
19.14–16 558
19.16–18 544
19.17 33, 544
19.19 19, 522, 547
19.20 569
19.22, 23 547
19.26–27 382, 383, 393, 547
19.30 9, 235, 541, 552
19.31–37 46
19.34 489
19.35 382, 547, 560, 606
19.36 143, 193, 339
19.37 560
19.38 562–40, 570

19.39 198
19.41 563, 569
20.1 570
20.1–10 382
20.2 393, 570, 596, 600
20.2–10 570
20.4 596
20.5 597
20.6 336, 596
20.7 579
20.8 576
20.9 572
20.15 569
20.17 478, 581–3
20.18 597
20.19 296, 586
20.19–23 508, 578
20.21 562, 586, 590
20.22 582
20.24 596
20.25 592
20.28 562, 592
20.29 592
20.30–31 147, 157, 263, 288, 340, 446, 516, 539, 593
21.1 596, 602
21.2 188, 382, 596, 600
21.7 393, 596
21.15–17 393, 604
21.18–19 605
21.20 393
21.22–23 605
21.24 226, 382, 596, 603
21.25 269, 602

**Acts**

1.3 517, 582
1.3–5 591
1.6 115, 551

1.9–11 174, 320, 584
1.10 579
1.14 550
1.15–26 505
1.21–22 185
1.23–26 384
2.1–4 39
2.14–36 568
2.16–21 520
2.22 547
2.27, 31 568
2.31–33 107
2.34 109
2.36 541
2.45 384
3.6 547
3.11–22 261
3.12–26 115, 227, 248
3.13 377
3.14 16, 82, 302, 310, 470, 478, 556
3.15 168, 244, 541, 556
3.18–19 575
3.19–21 264, 310, 536, 556
3.21 478
3.26 107, 113, 378, 575
4.1–8 264
4.8–12 568
4.10 547
4.25–26 108, 365, 378
4.25–30 114
4.30 378
4.36 536
5.17–18 295
5.29–32 568
5.30 575
5.33 295
5.36–37 181
6.1 27

## Index of canonical and deuterocanonical texts

6.7  12, 295, 352, 558
6.11–12  530
6.14  195, 547
7.1  262
7.53  483
7.55–56  106
7.58  530
8.1–3  295
9.1–2  7, 295, 404
9.3–4  574
9.3–9  419, 594
9.17–18  294
9.26, 39  470
9.59  262
10.3, 12–15, 19  471
10.28  529
10.34–43  568
10.38  115, 124
10.40–41  262, 453, 572
11.19  510
11.28  354, 471
11.54  262
12.1–3  295
12.2  598
12.6–11  471
13.1–3  28, 221, 536, 585
13.16–41  568
13.33  108
13.35  568
13.37  110
15.10, 28  223
16.6–10  471
16.18  599
17.2  575
17.7  540
18.25–26  599
19.1–5  599
19.1–20  599
19.9  404
19.12–13  599
19.23  7
19.23–41  599

19.33  599
20.17  599
20.19  599
20.28  575
20.29–30  599
22.3  447
22.6–7  574
22.8  547
23.8  330
24.5  295, 523, 547
26.3  575
26.13–14  574
26.23  110
26.90  547
27.23  471
28.17–28  227
28.26–28  372

**Romans**
1.1–4  516
1.3–4  115, 160
3.25  579
4.3  43
5.5  115
5.12–14  278
6.3–4  518
6.4–5  117
7.7–12  279
8.2  279
8.14  514, 583, 586
8.14–16  163, 413, 419, 461
8.16–17  380, 461
8.19  514
8.20–21  421
8.29  163, 172, 294, 514, 543, 583
8.33  110
10.16  109
10.13  520
11.16  582
11.16–21  435
12.1–2  259
12.10  458
12.12  510
13.1–7  540

13.12  593
16.3  599

**1 Corinthians**
1.2  458, 514
1.8  593
1.11–15  600
1.24  8, 76, 161, 493
2.7–8  408
3.16  196
5.5  593
5.7  143, 358, 556
8.1–3  594
8.6  236
9.1  576
11.23–25  323
11.24  252, 595
12.3  160, 295
12.27  196
14.33–35  597
15.3–4  105
15.4–7  597, 600
15.5–8  574, 576
15.20  482, 582
15.20–28  335
15.22  284, 580
15.23  318, 482, 582
15.25  109
15.32  599
15.42–44  10, 334, 359, 573, 587
15.45  284, 578, 580
15.49  284, 574
15.50  10, 573
15.51–53  10, 318, 332, 489, 573, 605
16.22  317, 458

**2 Corinthians**
1.1  514
1.14  593
2.14–15  342, 589

3.15–18  470, 574
11.14  371
11.22, 24  27
12.1–4  106
12.4  12

**Galatians**
1.12  574, 598
1.13–14  27, 447
1.15–16  110, 419, 574, 594
1.17  28
2.9  598
2.14  27
2.20  20
3.6  43
3.16–18  28
3.19  483
3.27  13
4.4–7  279
4.6  470, 574
5.1  223
5.22–23  435

**Ephesians**
1.9–10  7, 168, 493
1.20–22  109
2.20–21  196, 587
3.17–19  176
4.2–3  393, 438
4.11–13  176
5.2  541
5.8  369
5.19  458

**Philippians**
1.6, 10  593
1.9–10  513
1.19  470, 574
2.5–7  313, 362, 560
2.5–11  110, 113, 238, 239, 378, 391, 556
2.7–8  92, 143, 160
2.9–11  469

## Index of canonical and deuterocanonical texts

2.11  160
2.16  110
3.5  27, 227
3.6  227
3.20–21  105, 574

**Colossians**
1.15  79
1.15–17  490
1.15–20  513
1.16  236
1.19  175
1.19–20  490
2.9  175
2.15  408
3.1–3  13, 109, 117, 518
3.14  392

**1 Thessalonians**
3.13  318, 409
4.2  593
4.13–18  318, 332
4.16–17  574, 605
5.5  369

**2 Thessalonians**
1.5–10  318, 332
1.7–8  409, 471, 485
2.1–2  606
2.1–4  505
2.2  594
2.3  416
2.9–12  505
3.3  504

**2 Timothy**
1.2  599

**Hebrews**
1.1–4  362, 470, 556
1.3  109, 183
1.3–13  114, 227
1.4  27, 183

1.5  108
1.5–13  123
1.6  54, 131, 136, 203, 242, 276, 284, 318, 386, 481, 488, 543, 555
1.11  110
1.13  109
2.2  483
2.10–11  583
3—4  339
3.1  308
3.7—4.13  252
3.19  235
4.2, 6  235
4.8–10  389
4.9  235
4.14  19
4.14–16  389, 501
5.5–6  109
5.7–10  362
5.10  109
6.4  294
6.20  109
7.1–28  11, 27, 114
7.2  81, 362
7.11  107, 109
7.11–17  144, 201, 466
7.11–25  67
7.12  292
7.15  19, 109
7.15–17  107
7.16  334
7.21  109
8.8–12  227
9.3–5  17
9.4  27, 37
9.5  11
9.11–12  92
9.11–14  114, 258, 356, 536, 545, 558
9.12  47, 563, 580
10.1  356

10.12–13  109, 356
10.19–22  404, 413, 559
10.20  137, 389
10.22  560
10.25  593
10.32  294, 308
10.34  308
11.17  163
11.17–19  545
12.2  109
12.23  136, 172, 339, 482
13.11–12  546, 569

**James**
1.1  311
1.17  511
1.18  482
2.21  545
5.4  308

**1 Peter**
1.1  311, 379
1.12  348
1.18  348
2.5  118, 196, 306, 348, 370, 458
2.9  231, 322, 348, 379, 392, 401
2.21–25  110
3.22  408

**2 Peter**
1.1  593
1.11  593
1.17  108
3.4  319
3.10  594

**1 John**
1.1  103
1.1–3  406
1.7  8, 198, 272, 369
2.1–2  336, 480

2.5  420, 552
2.10–11  9, 420
2.13–14  450, 504, 590
2.20  19, 117, 256, 369, 476, 509, 567
2.21  476
2.26  476
2.27  19, 117, 256, 476
3.1  421
3.2  369
3.8  281
3.11–18  445
3.13  392, 422, 510
3.14  324, 369, 378, 421–2, 510, 519
4.2  587
4.4  450
4.6  369
4.7  421
4.12  552
4.16  421
4.17–18  552
4.18–19  390
5.4–5  450, 503
5.6–8  560
5.19  364, 503
5.20  369

**2 John**
1  598
2  475
5–6  421

**3 John**
1  598

**Jude**
14  28

**Revelation**
1.1–2  111, 224, 276, 280, 321, 340, 472, 489,

## Index of canonical and deuterocanonical texts

533, 550, 572, 599
1.5–6 392, 561
1.7 320, 561, 564
1.8 564
1.10 594
1.10–18 581
1.11 587
1.12 211
1.12–16 68, 386
1.12–19 448
1.13 385, 432, 589
1.14 210
1.16 88, 210, 328, 450
1.17–18 275, 385, 470, 584
1.19 606
2—3 320, 385, 598
2.1 469, 587, 590
2.1–7 598
2.2 211
2.5 469, 590
2.6 211, 448
2.7 13, 38, 51, 248, 249, 401, 448, 470, 501, 504, 584, 587
2.8 335, 469, 470
2.9 211, 449
2.10–11 335, 448, 465, 470, 504
2.12 328, 469, 590
2.13–14 211, 449, 594, 598
2.15 211, 448
2.16 211, 469, 564, 590, 602
2.17 448, 470, 504, 512
2.18 469, 587
2.20 211
2.20–23 469
2.25 211, 469, 602
2.26–28 109, 171, 448, 504
2.27 469
2.29 470
3.1 469
3.3 469
3.5 448, 504
3.6 470
3.7–8 305, 469
3.9 211, 449, 469
3.11 211, 385, 469, 564, 602
3.12 381, 421, 448, 468, 504, 512, 598
3.13 305, 470
3.14 469
3.21 289, 448–9, 468, 504
3.22 470
4.1 4, 69, 432
4.1—5.14 7, 60, 63, 119, 122
4.2 391, 402, 432
4.2–8 39, 112
4.5 65, 211
4.8 54, 112, 151, 168, 184, 275, 287, 336, 458, 469, 494
4.11 168, 494, 512
5.1–5 354
5.1–7 502
5.1–10 81, 449
5.5 56, 122, 425, 532, 537, 598
5.6 15, 175, 244, 350, 460, 468, 537
5.6–10 183, 184
5.8–10 171, 392, 591
5.10 483
5.13–14 130, 187, 391, 460
6—7 196
6.1–7 36
6.1–17 111, 224
6.6 354
6.9–11 295, 354, 377, 445, 504, 591
6.11 377
6.12–17 354, 520
6.17 265
7.1–8 55, 275, 312, 482–4
7.1–12 60
7.2–3 138, 156, 346, 418, 421, 461, 482, 506
7.3–4 6
7.9 6, 510, 589
7.9–12 156, 347
7.9–17 151
7.10 130
7.13–14 295, 598
7.15 173
7.16–17 327
8.3–4 461, 465
8.13 424
9.7 239
10.1–2 174, 320, 418, 453, 461, 469, 473, 483, 515
10.1–4 319
10.1–11 148, 355, 382, 597
10.4 320
10.5–6 488
10.7 227, 280, 320, 485
10.8–11 515, 587, 590
10.9 12
10.11 323, 473
11.1–2 353
11.7 551
11.8 387, 449
11.15 112, 129, 130, 156, 160, 237
11.15–18 297, 318, 319, 353
11.15—12.6 174, 210
11.17–18 132, 204, 280, 282
11.18 408
11.19 39, 121, 133, 355
11.19—12.5 365
12—13
12.1–6 39, 76, 121, 122, 129, 208, 299, 318, 340, 355, 415, 472, 503, 519
12.4 202
12.5 109, 267
12.7–17 364, 415
12.9 9, 50, 111, 134, 211, 285
12.13–17 202
12.14 493
12.17 9, 134, 267, 295, 299, 365, 422, 452, 476, 493, 503–4, 514, 523, 550, 583, 602
13.1–4 371
13.1–9 540
13.5 414
13.11–19 505
13.13–17 280
13.16 203
13.17–18 13, 410, 602
14.1 348, 381, 421, 482, 533
14.1–5 6, 199, 416
14.4 130, 172, 370
14.14–16 111, 220, 281, 326, 339
14.14–20 149
14.17–20 424

*14.19* 425
*15.1* 551
*15.1-8* 175
*15.5-8* 465
*15.6* 59, 579
*16.15* 594
*17—18* 121
*17.1* 297
*17.1-6* 209
*17.6* 182, 293, 298, 504
*17.9* 182
*17.13-14* 449
*17.17* 551
*18.1* 418, 461
*18.11-17* 193
*18.20* 297
*19.1-4* 182
*19.2* 209, 298, 504
*19.6-9* 141, 182, 441
*19.7-8* 208, 459
*19.9* 360
*19.10* 602
*19.11* 305, 476
*19.11-16* 6, 76, 199, 449, 472, 539
*19.11-21* 210, 370, 416, 533
*19.11—20.3* 211
*19.12* 210
*19.13-14* 348, 459, 476, 477
*19.15* 88, 109, 210, 328, 450, 469
*19.16* 6, 476
*19.19* 477, 505
*19.20* 480, 505
*20.1-3* 282, 477
*20.1—22.5* 335
*20.2* 211
*20.3* 552
*20.4* 111, 297, 318
*20.5* 552
*20.6* 289, 336
*20.7* 552
*20.11-15* 143, 336
*20.14* 336
*21.2* 481
*21.3* 148, 173
*21.6* 602
*21.8* 308, 336, 370
*21.9-11* 209, 211
*21.9-27* 6, 182
*21.15-18* 66
*21.16* 209
*21.17* 87, 201, 538
*21.22-26* 151
*21.25, 27* 209
*22.1-2* 38, 39, 151, 208, 218, 249, 267, 372, 401, 429, 432, 480, 498
*22.1-5* 66, 105, 121, 129, 348, 360
*22.3* 160, 265
*22.3-5* 55, 110, 130, 231, 256, 282, 302, 377, 389, 429, 474, 496, 510, 587
*22.4* 559
*22.5* 209, 272
*22.6* 602
*22.7* 564, 602
*22.8-9* 602
*22.12* 105, 275, 564, 602
*22.13* 470, 602
*22.14* 38, 51, 249, 335, 401, 427
*22.15* 190, 308, 335, 370
*22.16* 56, 75, 91, 105, 345, 381, 425, 483, 504, 532
*22.17* 208, 218, 265, 473, 480, 498
*22.20* 105, 317, 458, 564, 602

# Index of other texts

### PSEUDEPIGRAPHA

**Apocalypse of Abraham**
9—32  72
10.3-4  466, 475
10.16  466
11.3  466
23.1-14  432
31.6-8  432

**Life of Adam and Eve**
12—16  122
32—39  502

**Testament of Adam**
3.6  139

**Apocalypse of Moses**
20.1-2  565
28.4  565
29  138

**Ascension of Isaiah**
1.4  386
1.8-9  417
2.1-2  417
2.1-12  291
2.5  417
2.7-11  106
2.9  567
3.1-12  521
3.6  406
3.7-10  406, 515
3.10  406
3.13  386, 406, 409
3.17  386
3.18  386, 409
4.3, 9  386
4.4-8  410
4.6  386, 408
4.14  409
4.18, 21  386
4.21-22  406
5.1  417
5.15  417
6—11  407
6.1  515
7.9  417
7.11  106
7.17, 23  386
8.18, 25  386
9.12  386
9.16  517
9.24-26  589
10—11  161
10.7  106, 475
10.11-16  408
10.19  475
10.30  417
11.4  475
11.13  409
11.19  406
11.23-33  408
11.24, 26  409
11.33  475

**Assumption of Moses**
10.1-3  212, 386

**Letter of Aristeas**
100  297
112  344

**1 Enoch**
2.1  44
5.4  44
9.1  464
14—16  119
15.1-2  200, 587
20.1-8  465
22.1-14  331
24.4-5  249
25.3-5  37, 38
25.6  401
26.1-2  41
37.5  301
39.1-7  402
39.7  581
40.1-9  464
40.2  11, 67
40.8  237
41.1  67, 237
42.2-3  207
45—57  479, 498
45.1  479
46.1-4  480
46.5  479
46.8  479
47—51  113
47.1-3  67, 445, 556
47.10  67
48.1  218, 267, 480, 498
48.2  67, 480, 498
48.3  498
48.5-10  556
48.10  480
51.3  67, 480
53—56  480
54.1  480
69.9-10  11
69.13-15  88
69.16-25  512
71.14  366
80.2  542
80.2-8  359
81.1-6  200
85—89  194
87.2  579
89.1  87, 201, 538
89.36  87, 538
89.50  305
89.51-67  291
89.54  305
89.54-56  487
89.55  543
89.56  28, 195, 305, 314
89.59  292
89.72-74  253, 535
90.5-6  292
90.24-26  299
90.25  314
90.28-29  299, 314, 402
90.28-38  144, 195, 305
93.3-7  29
93.5  175
93.6  133, 483
93.8  119, 289, 292, 406, 487
93.9  28, 454, 464, 535, 567
93.10  51, 175, 250
98.14-15  52
98.14—99.2  225
99.2  52
104.10-11  52, 225

**2 Enoch**
8.4  37

## Index of other texts

22  255
22.5-10  567
22.8-10  75, 136, 160, 509, 573
22.9  589
23—25  573
40.1  567
64.5  568
70—73  30
70.14, 20  566
71.37  566

### 3 Enoch
14  468
16  468
45  4, 126
48D  466

### Jubilees
1.15, 17  155
1.26  155
2.1  462
2.2  65
7.34-39  29
16.1  462
16.19-31  154
18.9  462
20—22  387
21.1-26  29
32.1-2, 16-29  154
36.7  511

### 2 Baruch
39.7  431
59.4-12  90

### 3 Baruch
4.15  433

### Pseudo-Philo
12.8-10  434
13.7  153

### Psalms of Solomon
2.3  307
15.6  507

### Testament of Levi
5.1-2  154
8.1-11  59, 64, 154
9.1-14  29
14—18  190
14.1  361
17.11  190, 307
18.2-13  191
18.6-8  308, 361
18.10-11  308

### Testament of Judah
24.4  429

### QUMRAN TEXTS

### Damascus Document, CD
I  26, 303, 487
III  5, 45, 81, 193, 303, 326, 359, 542, 547, 565
IV  26, 81, 326, 371, 379
V  329
VI  26
VII  276
VIIB  507
VIII  5, 26, 347, 449, 487
X  227
XIII  227

### Hymns, 1QH
III  106
X  211
XI  6, 244, 331
XII  15, 98, 244, 449
XIV  429
XV  244
XVI  266, 429
XX  46

### War Scroll, 1QM
I  6, 26, 370, 415
II  532
IV  6
VII  6, 370, 415
XI  343
XII  199, 532
XIII  6, 199, 370, 383, 416
XVII  370

### Community Rule, 1QS
I  384, 392, 415, 420
II  97, 273, 282, 363, 415, 484
III–IV  8, 190, 198, 227, 273, 282, 369, 414, 475, 560, 564
V  81
VI  383, 384
VIII–IX  196, 369, 379, 384
X  5, 415
XI  3, 6, 7 5
XIII  504

### 1QSa
I  227

### 1QSb
IV  6, 106, 413

### 1QpHab
II  227
VII  227, 320, 326, 485
IX  307, 326
X  211, 326, 449
XI  359
XII  307

1QIsa$^a$  90, 135, 225, 391, 437, 479, 560, 573

1QIsa$^b$  429, 573

1QIsa$^d$  573

1Q14  211

1Q20  72

3Q15
XI  232

4Q164  196

4Q169  309

4Q171  485

4Q174  196

4Q184  208

4Q280  414

4Q286  371

4Q403  196

4Q405  196

4Q417  244, 404

4Q418  244, 404, 495

4Q491  256, 334

4Q521  264, 288

4Q543-8  8

4QphylN  431, 487

## Index of other texts

**4QBer<sup>a</sup>**
1.2  102

**4QDeut<sup>j</sup>**  71, 242, 486

**4QDeut<sup>q</sup>**  125, 132, 242, 470, 481, 488

**4QEn<sup>c</sup>**  37

**4QEn<sup>e</sup>**  37

**4QEn<sup>g</sup>**  175

**4QSam<sup>a</sup>** 332

**11QMelch**  8, 11, 52, 72, 181, 258, 313, 371, 414, 502, 553, 567

**11QPs<sup>a</sup>**  159, 443

**11QTemple**
29  155

### JEWISH TEXTS

**Philo**
*Allegorical Interpretation*
I.5  234
II.86  169
III.82  73, 81, 188

*Cherubim*
3  73, 460
35  73, 460

*The Worse Attacks the Better*
25  604

*Tongues*
41  73
62–63  236
96  103
97  73
146  236

*Migration*
174  461

*Heir*
79  255
191–3  255
215  103

*On Flight*
12  103, 236
108–10  79, 135, 212
118  73, 103

*Dreams*
I.215  73, 103
I.229  166
I.239  73

*Abraham*
235  73

*Life of Moses*
I.158  31, 405

*Special Laws*
I.184  589

*Contemplative Life*
75  228, 390, 398
76  390
78  228, 390

*Embassy to Gaius*
299  528
301–2  529

*Questions on Genesis*
II.51  593
II.62  103
IV.87  593

*Questions on Exodus*
II.13  461
II.85  137, 413, 559

**Josephus**
*Antiquities*
1.146  25
1.180  72, 81
1.196  538
1.198  463
3.159–161  68, 548, 589
3.183  559
4.176  268
8.101  150, 342
8.106  263
9.288  216
11.173  25
11.344  27
13.256  217
14.34–36  425
15.136  483
15.319–322  309
15.380  197
15.395  423
17.199  562
18.26  309
18.85  219
18.94  309
18.116  180
20.118  214
20.179–81  308
20.198  524
20.207  308
20.248  309

*War*
1.48–53  424
1.364–370, Slavonic text  181
2.142  87
2.301  528
2.328  528
4.317  557
5.51  541
5.188  304
5.201  304
5.212–13  137, 212, 413, 588
5.222  304
5.272  319
6.4  319
6.110  354
6.289–94  352
6.311–13  353
6.424–6  338
7.323  278

*Life*
1  353
52  214

**Mishnah**
*Berakoth*
4.2  226
4.3  244

*Shabbat*
7.2  234
19.2  264

*Pesaḥim*
3.1  529
5.1  358

*Shekalim*
1.3  192

*Yoma*
3.3  379
3.3–6  560
3.8  511
4.2  496

## Index of other texts

5.2–3  579
5.3–4  192
5.6  92, 445
6.1  536
6.2  101, 511, 522
6.8  356, 474

*Sukkah*
3.1–3  156
3.9  348
4.5  152, 156, 265, 349
5.2–4  272
5.4  150

*Megillah*
4.10  97, 231, 484

*Mo'ed Katan*
3.4  51, 240

*Ḥagigah*
2.1  119, 200

*Ketuboth*
2.9  245

*Sotah*
2.2  270
7.6  101
9.9  430
9.12  229

*Baba Kamma*
7.7  527

*Sanhedrin*
1.5  525
5.4  524
6.4  526
7.1  530
7.5  539

*Aboth*
1.4  223
1.5  215

2.7  241
3.5  226
4.11  464

*Abodah Zarah*
3.2  602

*Horayoth*
3.4  524

*Menaḥoth*
6.7  553
10.1–4  565
11.5  144
11.7  46, 252

*Bekhoroth*
8.7  482

*Tamid*
3.7  303

*Middoth*
1.3, 4  303
3.8  423
4.2  303
5.4  528

*Kelim*
10.1  188

*Oholoth*
18.7  529

*Zabim*
1.5  232

**Tosefta**
*Kippurim*
2.15  38

*Sukkah*
3.15  434

*Ḥagigah*
2.2  127

**Jerusalem Talmud**
*Ta'anit*
4.5  28

*Ḥagigah*
2.1  127

**Babylonian Talmud**
*Shabbat*
104b  576

*Pesaḥim*
57a  308

*Yoma*
21b  37
39b  356, 473

*Ḥagigah*
14b  127, 438
15a  468

*Gittin*
56a  197

*Baba Metzia*
86b  463

*Sanhedrin*
38b  467
43a  381, 526, 551
64a  438, 489
70a  431

*Abodah Zarah*
8b  528

*Horayoth*
12a  37, 507

*Menaḥoth*
100a  553

**Targums**
*Neofiti*

Gen. 14.8  30
Exod. 3.8  101
Exod. 3.12  101, 251
Exod. 3.14  168, 336
Lev. 24.7  252
Num. 6.24–26  484

*Pseudo-Jonathan*
Gen. 4.15  507
Gen. 14.8  30
Gen. 22  48
Exod. 3.8  101
Exod. 24.4–8  143
Num. 6.24–26  484
Num. 24.17  138
Num. 24.23  461
Deut. 31.6  461
Deut. 32.39  103

*Onkelos*
Exod. 24.4–8  143
Lev. 24.7  252

*Jonathan*
Isa. 5.2  120
Isa. 8.14  461
Isa. 24.16  17
Isa. 52.13  368
Isa. 53.2  368
Isa. 53.5  368
Isa. 65.1  461

*Psalms*
2.6–7  124
87.4–6  124
118.24–26  349

**Midrash Rabbah**
*Genesis*
III.8  65
XV.7  431
XX.6  229
XXXII.10  215
XLIII.6  59

## Index of other texts

XLVIII.9 464
L.2 463
LXVIII.12 130, 155
LXVIII.13 186
XCVIII.9 427
XCIX.8 428

Exodus
XLVIII.4 49

Leviticus
XXV.6 30

Numbers
XV.10 37

Merkavah
Hekhalot Rabbati (Schäfer's numbering)
170 465
201 237
202-3 226
206 464
228 226

Hekhalot Zutarti
496 237

Ma'asseh Merkavah
565 466

Merkavah Rabbah
680 273

CHRISTIAN AND GNOSTIC TEXTS

Athanasius
On the Incarnation
40 120

To the Baptized 322

Aphrahat
Demonstrations
5.21, 23 69

Epistle of the Apostles
11 592
13 161

Arabic Infancy Gospel
19 137

Barnabas, Letter of
5 455
6 523
7 46, 144, 545, 552, 562
8 435
12 605
15 235, 584
16 28, 195, 557
18 369, 416
18—20 8

Basil
On the Holy Spirit
66 322

Clement of Alexandria
Miscellanies
1.1 15
1.28 225
1.66 227
5.10 17, 84, 496
6.7 15, 119
7.17 15, 305

Excerpts from Theodotus
12 490

23, 24 454
36 167, 490

Clement of Rome
To the Corinthians
36 27, 260
42 590

Clementine Homilies
1.39 507
19.20 17, 84, 496

Clementine Recognitions
1.32-34 72
1.39 281
1.44-48 77
1.54 181
1.60 181
1.66-70 290

Cyril of Jerusalem
Catecheses
22.5 58

Didache
1 416
1-6 8
8 55
9 3, 53, 114, 163, 254, 377, 401, 424, 433, 495, 500
10 3, 53, 55, 114, 163, 254, 377, 496, 500, 506, 508, 509, 513
14 58, 253

Didascalia Apostolorum
II.32 117

Dionysius
Divine Names
592B 16

Celestial Hierarchy
137AB 10

Ecclesiastical Hierarchy
472C-485B 76

Ephrem
On the Diatessaron
IV.5 127

Epiphanius
Panarion
1.29.4 16, 308, 548
1.30.16 106
1.33.4 225

Egeria's Travels
68, 71 224

Eugnostos, CG III.3
74 492
77-78 494
83 492
90 7, 491

Eusebius
Church History
2.1 12
2.15 576, 597, 603
2.23 16, 290, 291, 308, 370, 548
2.25 106
3.4 282, 599
3.12 532
3.19-20 532
3.24 13, 262, 343, 525
3.31 16, 308, 370, 383, 548, 597

629

## Index of other texts

3.39 269, 597–8
4.26 545, 569
6.6 119

Preparation
9.29 31

Proof of the Gospel
I.5 286
IV.15 77, 468, 497

Life of Constantine
26, 28 569

Germanus
On the Divine
   Liturgy
29 364

Hebrews, Gospel
   of the 135, 601

Hermas
Mandate
6.2 9, 369, 416

Similitudes
8.2 156
9.7 538
9.12 306, 538

Hippolytus
On Daniel
17 555
24 286, 320, 538

Hypostasis of the
   Archons, CG
   II.4
87 291
94 417

Ignatius
Ephesians
2–4 600
9–10 600

17 14, 371
19 450

Magnesians
9 593

Trallians
5 14

Romans
7 259

Philadelphians
4 259
9 14, 306, 380

Smyrnaeans
3 587
7 259

Irenaeus
Demonstration
3 321
32–33 279
44 286, 463

Against Heresies
I.3 518
I.24 493
IV.5 544
V.2 322
V.21 279

James,
   Apocryphon of,
   CG I.2
2 517
3, 12 592

James, Infancy
   Gospel of
10 136
19 174

Jerome
On Isaiah

9 550
11 121, 173, 183

Illustrious Men
2 523, 601

Jesus Christ,
   Wisdom of, CG
   III.4
91 7
98 577
102 494
117 577
118 7, 36, 38, 493

John, Acts of
94 50
96 84, 321

John, Apocryphon
   of, CG II.1
18 417

John Chrysostom
Homilies on John
85 544, 571

Justin
Trypho
8 182
16–17 533
41 58, 253
53 455
56 286, 463, 538
71 241
73 435
88 127
90 605
97 586
106 586
110 436
126 238, 463, 538
127 238, 286

Apology
1.35 522, 537, 605

1.52 561
1.61 16, 117, 201, 294
1.63 170
1.65 117

Mary, Gospel of
9 578
10 578, 584
17–18 578

Melchizedek, CG
   IX.1
27 11

Melito
On Genesis 544

On the Pasch
fr. 9 544
72 545
93 569
94 545, 569

Novatian
On the Trinity
18 286

Origen
Against Celsus
2.5 527
2.9 526
6.6 12, 320, 515
6.43 45

Homilies on
   Genesis
8 544

Homilies on
   Numbers
4 18
5 18, 321

*Index of other texts*

*Homilies on*
  *Jeremiah*
*15* 550

*Homilies on*
  *Ezekiel*
*1* 118

*Commentary on*
  *Matthew*
*11* 322

*Commentary on*
  *John*
*2.12* 550
*2.14–17* 166, 186
*2.31* 130

*Paul, Apocalypse*
  *of* 304

*Peter, Gospel of*
*6–9* 537
*8* 523

*Philip, Gospel of,*
  *CG* II.3
*3* 324
*52* 583
*53* 498

*54* 350
*55* 134
*56* 116, 324, 518, 572, 588
*57* 588
*58* 172, 583
*63* 166
*67* 76
*69* 400
*71* 76, 127
*72* 278
*73* 324, 518, 572
*74* 278
*75* 24

*Pistis Sophia*
*17, 19* 577
*146* 578

*Saviour, Dialogue*
  *of, CG* III.5
*139, 140, 143* 577

*Serapion's Prayer*
  *Book,*
  *Bishop* 322

*Silvanus, Teaching*
  *of, CG* VII.4
*89* 136, 549

*Solomon, Odes of*
*8.10* 84, 321
*8.11–13* 18
*12.3* 18
*17.12, 13* 18
*36.1, 2, 6* 256
*36.3, 5* 509

*Sozomen*
  *History*
*2.4* 463

*Tertullian*
  *On Spectacles*
*30* 580

*Thomas, Acts of*
*47* 287

*Thomas, Gospel of*
*1* 286
*13* 169, 265, 287
*18* 402
*34, 35* 499
*36, 37* 588
*40* 435
*49* 402
*50* 8, 402, 511
*75* 402
*114* 578

*Tripartite*
  *Tractate, CG*
  I.5
*116* 490

*Truth, Gospel of,*
  *CG* I.3
*16* 500
*17* 534
*18–19* 500, 535
*20, 24–25* 501
*36* 502
*38* 501–2

**Diodorus of Sicily**
*XL.3.5–6* 297, 467

**Tacitus**
  *History*
*V.5* 423

**Pliny**
  *Natural History*
*V.15* 179
*V.58* 354
*XIII.26, 44, 45* 344
*XVIII.167–8* 354

# Index of names and subjects

Writers and writings mentioned in the other indexes are not included here.

abiding 438, 441
Abraham 48, 67, 105, 154, 286; children of 81, 277–87; representing first temple 277
Adam 49, 123, 134, 138, 238, 303, 494, 501, 512, 566; enthroned 122, 277; fall of 122; as high priest 65; as Man 87, 538
*agrapha* 84, 225
Akiba, Rabbi 438, 489
angel(s) hosts of heaven 35; angelic worship 5; of covenant 263; emanation of 7, 79, 103; fallen 119; of great counsel 78, 91, 206, 253; hierarchy of 10; in holy of holies 65; mother of 7, 38; of nations 68; seven(fold) 59; seventy shepherds 291; a unity 490
angel of the LORD 166, 460; as angel of Name 462; not in Deuteronomic or priestly texts 412; as Paraclete 472; as Spirit of the LORD 412–13
angel of presence 6, 336, 458; as archangels 463; giving wisdom 465; multiform 462; names of and meanings 463–4
Annas 309, 524

Annunciation 134
anointed/disfigured 573
anointing 13, 90, 315, 509, 573; of Jesus 340–1; oil, 'dew' 75, 517; from tree of life 76, 315
apostasy 52
Arabia 28
archetypes 236, 239
ark of covenant 38, 134
arrest of Jesus 519–27
ascent 86, 106, 119, 127–8, 161, 291, 362, 406, 509, 516; as characteristic of Christians 567; of Enoch 566
Asherah 35; *see also* Lady of the temple
Ashratah 39, 132
Asia, seven churches of 598–9
atonement 192, 310, 337; Day of 44–6, 73, 143, 161, 210, 255, 364; imagery at crucifixion 545; offering eaten by priests 553; renewal of creation 557
authority 314, 373
Azazel 45, 282, 350, 506

baptism 13, 200; fire in Jordan 127; as illumination 117; of Jesus 54, 60, 115, 127, 516; as resurrection 117, 517

Barabbas 535–6
Basil, Saint 322
Basilides 492
Beatitudes 451
Belial 415; meaning lawlessness 415
beloved, meaning of 163, 204, 384, 454; Jesus as 386; pierced 560
beloved disciple 381–6; identity of 382; linked to Peter 382; possibly a priest 383
Bethany 180, 326, 340–2, 370
Bethel 48, 155, 185, 427
Bethesda 222–3
'birth' 15, 199, 497; of Christian 162; in holy of holies 136–7, 172–4, 366, 498; of king 74–81, 124, 128–9; into kingdom 201
blasphemy 167, 313–16, 524, 539
blessing of high priests 97, 156, 159, 230, 275, 318, 362, 392, 481–4, 507, 587, 591
blindness 195, 207, 285, 288–92, 409, 534; of Pharisees 298
Boethus, high priest 309
bones broken 562
'Branch' 236, 346, 538; of vine 425
bread: barley 247; broken 55; feeding miracle 248;

## Index of names and subjects

of life 254–60; Passover 380; polluted 55; of presence 58–9, 250–3, 260, 426; teaching about 248–9
'Bride' 205, 265, 459; in Isaiah 206
'Bridegroom' 205, 441; as Messiah 209
burial: of Jesus 144, 557–63; of Lazarus 336

Caesar as king 543
Caiaphas 337, 524
calendar 98; 490 years 189, 353, 554; in Deuteronomy 45; in Exodus 45; second temple 47, 150, 359, 542; solar 45, 359, 556
Capernaum 220; sermon in synagogue 249
capital punishment 530
children of God 171
Chosen one(s)/lot 24, 502
cloud 135, 149, 151, 263, 320; sons of 173
coming one 184, 323, 458
commandment, new 390, 514
community: pre-Christian 111; as unity 384, 402; withdraws from Jerusalem 291, 338, 370
completion 554
conflict 450, 503–4
conquest 448–50
consecration 315–16, 496, 508
covenant: with Abraham 388; blood of 392, 444; everlasting/eternal 17, 42–3, 252, 310; of ḥesedh 392, 396, 419, 510; Mosaic 42; of peace 512; for the

people 444; renewing 93, 556, 560
creation, six days 63–4, 235, 236
Creator, Logos as 168
creatures: of throne 122; wild 122
cross 447
crucifixion 544–57

dābhaq 47, 200, 403, 420, 437–8, 489, 581
Damascus 5; road 574
darkness 65, 169, 327, 368, 570; angel of 199, 504; powers of 210; as Romans 532; as second-temple Jews 532
David: last words of 373–5; vine of 424
Dawn 236, 275, 346, 364, 482
day of the LORD 150, 189, 193, 211, 276, 318, 561, 593; later became Sunday 594
Day One 65–6, 510, 570
death 331–6; of Jesus in Jewish tradition 526
departure of Jesus 453–6
Deuteronomists 101; deny vision 199, 245, 405
Deuteronomy 11, 34; basis of Passover discourse 398–9
devil see Satan
diaspora 327, 357
disciples in the temple 352, 356
divine origin 513
door 302–7
double identity 112, 129–30, 135, 160, 186, 318, 391, 510
Dura Europos 425–6

earthquake 568
Ebionites 127
Eden 49, 580; new 569; story of 50, 250, 279
egō eimi 251, 275, 336, 522, 524
Eighteen Benedictions 330
ekklēsia 53, 55, 422, 445, 514
El 48, 67, 69; as the LORD 70
El Elyon 238, 404; begetter of heaven and earth 171, 494; sons of 131, 134
El'azar ben 'Arakh, Rabbi 126
Elijah 150, 182
Elisha ben Abuyah 468
'emeth 373, 384
Enoch 11; as redeemer and revealer 568
enthronement 117–29, 391, 469, 537; symbolism at crucifixion 546
Ephesus 1, 596–7
epiklēsis 322, 594
'error' 3, 285, 369, 500, 534
Essenes 179
Eucharist/thanksgiving 60, 259; prayers at 163, 247
exile 26, 106, 151
exodus 387, 400
eyewitness detail 521, 606
Ezekiel the prophet: his chariot vision 280; his Passover 193, 359
Ezekiel the tragedian 32
Ezra 51

Father 3, 285, 312, 491–2; hidden 501; lost knowledge of 534

*Index of names and subjects*

fear 442
fire in Jordan 127
Firstborn 67, 136, 203, 481, 543
firstfruits 565; Levites offered as 565
flesh 258–9
footwashing 376–81
foreign woman 207; from Babylon 207
forgiveness 591
friends/companion 442–6
fullness 175

Gamaliel, Rabbi 602
gardener 580
garments of Jesus 547–8, 588
gates of temple 302–4; golden gates 303–4; liturgy before 349; Nicanor gate 303
*gematria* 410, 602
Gerizim, Mount 218–19
Gethsemane 361, 521
Gihon spring 267
glory 15, 36, 128, 165, 173–4, 181, 190; comes to temple 263–4, 303, 364; Jesus returns to pre-creation glory 496
gnosis *see* knowledge
Gnosticism 1, 14, 490–3
good tidings 257
grace 47, 162
grapes: gathering as study 430; poisonous 431, 487; as wisdom 430
Greeks 356, 391

Hagar 73
*Hallelujah* 98
handing over 541, 552
Hanukkah 148, 222, 312, 315
harvest 220, 281

Hebrews 2, 26–7, 311
Hellenists 1, 27
Hellenization 313
Herod 179–80, 309, 451
ḥesedh 47, 177–8, 373, 384, 393–7, 419–22, 441; represents both *phileō* and *agapaō* 393, 604
Hezekiah 192, 371
hierarchy: of angels 10, 405, 418, 492; of emanations 495–7; of evil 421, 540; of ḥesedh 421
high priests 144; Christians as 308; garments of 547–8; James as 16, 106, 369; Jesus as 315; John as 16, 106, 369, 524, 597; as seal of creation 102; tenants of temple 314
Ḥisda, Rabbi 551
history: alternative/ Enochic 29, 133, 194; Deuteronomic 37, 40–1
Ḥiyya, Rabbi 186
Ḥiyya ben Ashi, Rabbi 551
holiness, revealing 508
holy of holies 4, 66, 74, 121, 159, 165, 329; opened at death of Jesus 558; tomb of Jesus as 563
Holy Week, John and Synoptics differ 525
hostility to Jesus 263

Ignatius of Antioch 371
Immanuel 147, 160, 410
Incarnation 170–2, 187, 362, 405, 450, 497, 587
invocation 252, 323, 456–8

irony 337
Isaac 48, 163; as atonement 545; prefiguring Jesus 544, 552
Isaiah, importance of for Christians 290
Ishmael, Rabbi 4, 126, 273, 438, 465, 489
Ishmael ben Fabi, high priest 308

Jabneh 126
Jacob, blessing of 426
James, bishop of Jerusalem 106, 161, 290
Jehoash 80
Jehoshaphat, valley of 520
Jeremiah 30–40
Jerusalem: as bride 182; as Egypt 449–50; as harlot 182, 193, 504; in Isaiah 206–8; new 258; as Wisdom 209
Jewish Christians 27
Jews 23–33; their accounts of Jesus' death 526–7
Johanan ben Zakkai, Rabbi 126–7, 271
John the Baptist 93, 178–87; disciples of 181, 185
Jonathan, Rabbi 215
Jose ben Johanan, Rabbi 215
Joseph of Arimathea 562
Joshua 388–9
Joshua, Rabbi 229
Josiah 3, 34, 39, 63, 70, 101, 192, 561
joy 439–40, 491, 499
Jubilee 24, 181
Judan, Rabbi 65
Judas 381–2, 504–6; as agent of Satan 521
judgement, day of 54, 149, 180, 245, 282, 297, 314,

## Index of names and subjects

332, 477; first and second 335; in valley of Jehoshaphat 520

Kabbalah 79, 458–9
*kenōsis* 240
king 141, 153; Davidic 52, 57, 80; Deuteronomic ideal 41, 80; myth of 95; resurrection of 108; sacral 12, 42, 139–40, 147; as shepherd 309–11; as son of the LORD 405; titles of 184, 206; wise 89; worship of 82
kingdom 66, 200, 237; secrets of 15
kingship, nature of 360, 531
knowledge 86, 119, 377

Lady of the temple 24, 76, 130, 153; betrayed 271; birth of son 422; driven from temple 207, 289; in labour 452–4; not in second temple 206
Lamb of God 15, 112, 171–2, 184, army of 421
last supper 358; in holy of holies 509; like Qumran meal 383; restoring eternal covenant 512
Lazarus 324–31; as Eleazar 326, 341
lectionary 249, 328, 339, 565
Levi as high priest 154
Levites 378
light 65, 169; Jesus as 272–4, 368; Prince of 198; seeing 15, 391; sons of 6, 198, 227, 369–71, 401; in temple courts 153

linen 68, 210, 348, 376, 459, 562, 570, 588–9
lion imagery 56, 425
Lithostrōtos 541
Living One 118
Logos 6, 164; as firstborn 73, 236; as high priest 73, 79; as the LORD 189; a Man 236; as *memra* 103; as Paraclete 461–2; as warrior 370, 449
love *see* ḥesedh

Magharians 2
Magi 138
magic 450; charge against Jesus 526
Malchus 523, 527
Mamre 462–3, 538
Man/son of Man 67, 68, 87, 91, 187, 201, 245, 254, 296, 332, 362; as angel 538; as Messiah 538
Manasseh 417
Mandaeism 1
manna 255
*Maranatha* 54, 317, 459, 474
Marcellus of Ancyra 534
Martha 324, 335, 342
martyrs 182, 209, 504
Mary, Virgin 39
Mary of Bethany 329, 342
Mary Magdalene 550, 570, 576, 597; key figure in non-canonical texts 577–9; name meaning 'exalted' 577
Meir, Rabbi 431
Melchi-Resha‘ 8
Melchi-Zedek 8, 30, 59, 70–3, 81–5, 91, 114, 147, 161, 181, 188, 292, 315, 362; as good spirit 414; Jesus as 189, 368,

555; as manifestation of the LORD 71–3, 466
*memra* 99–104, 165; as divine presence 101, 250–3, 327, 460–1, 498
menorah 37, 93; Man amid 211; position of 65
Metatron 466–8, 497; Jesus as 468
*miqveh* 233
Minim 295
miracles as magic 313
Miriam 49, 232
Morning Star 75, 238, 345, 504
Moses 29, 49, 60, 62, 73, 101; absence of 30; *Blessing of* 131, 318, 160, 481; disciples of 296; as king 31, 49, 483; law of 162, 264, 273, 374; *Song of* 131, 242, 318, 481
Mother: of king 75, 133; of the LORD 130
Mount of Olives 223, 520
mysteries *see* secrets
mystics, Merkavah 466

Nag Hammadi 3–8
Name 55, 287, 294, 336, 362; called out 101; giving power 88; manifesting 462, 498, 502; meaning of 168; protection by 448, 506–7, 511; seal of creation 101–2, 511; secret 210; sign of baptism 381, 421; sign of high priesthood 448; as X 6, 60, 156, 350, 421, 447
Nathanael 185
Nazorene, keeper 295, 436, 522–3, 546

## Index of names and subjects

Nehemiah, Rabbi 427
Nehunyah, Rabbi 226
net of fish 602; Luke's version of 603
Nicodemus 98, 334, 562
Nicolaitans 448

oath/bond of creation 511-12
One and many 313

palms 152, 343; 'branches' 345; symbol of Judah 344; vision of 347
Papias 597
parables 5, 237, 301, 326, 359-60; visions as 301
Paraclete 410-19, 456-90, 471, 560; as angel of the LORD 411; as atonement offering 480; does not mean comforter 418; as Jesus returning 454, 572, 587; 'the one called upon' 456; only in John 456; as Spirit of the LORD 470
*parousia* 148, 605; delay of 317, 452; John's vision of 319, 453, 551; realized 564
Passover 46, 148, 191-3, 222, 338; discourse 386-480; Ezekiel's 542; lamb 339; on Sabbath 542
Paul/Saul of Tarsus 27-8, 43, 447, 599
peace 203
perception *see* sight
perfumed oil 341-2
persecution: of Christians 23, 295, 336, 447-52, 533; of Jews 532
Peter 527, 586; address in Solomon's porch 113, 556, 575; confession at Caesarea Philippi 261; by sea of Tiberias 601; made shepherd of the flock 604
Philip 116, 404, 500, 518
phylacteries 203
piercing Jesus 559; wounds of 586
pilgrimage to temple 230, 234, 344
Platonism 10, 494
Polycrates 597
Pontius Pilate 219; trial of Jesus 527-43
'poor' 343, 548
powers of darkness 210, 521
Praetorium 528
prayer, high priestly 495-515
priest(s): Aaronite 11, 67, 107, 334; fallen 119, 135, 190, 194, 307-8; Melchi-Zedek 19, 67, 107, 334; new 378, 566; restored 348
prophecy fulfilled by Jesus 119, 124, 140, 351, 381, 572; not in Hebrew Scriptures 354, 360; false 449
purification 289, 379, 528, 559
Pythagoras 494

Qumran 1, 78, 92, 227, 307; covenant of *ḥesedh* there 419-20

rabbi, Jesus as 223-30, 581
Rabbinic Judaism 1
rabbis *see individual names*
rainbow 174
raising up 202, 366, 368, 546, 575
*raz nihyeh* 4, 10, 66, 77, 159, 243, 404, 495
redemption from Egypt 482
remembrance 323
repentance 179
resurrection 12, 107, 142, 318, 322, 324-36; as Ascension 582, 584; at baptism 117; not post mortem 108-9, 116, 378, 518, 572; as *theōsis* 12
Revelation, Book of 147
Righteous One(s) 15, 17, 72, 81-5, 113, 209, 367; number of 445; *see also* Zadok
rooms 402

Sabbath 44, 234, 288, 501
sacrifice 48; animal 64; of king 69, 92; of lamb 350
Samaritans 25, 214; five nations of 216; temple of 216-18
Sanhedrin 524, 527
sapphire throne 363, 541
Satan 9, 55, 134, 285; fall of 122, 364, 452; children of 281; deceit of 371; defeat of 503
Saviour 500
scattering of flock 455
scribes 51, 191
Scriptures: changes to 30, 50-2, 69, 85, 99, 124, 131-2, 200, 203, 225, 230, 240-2, 284, 481, 572; corrupted 74, 82-3, 88, 205, 332, 349, 367, 486, 488-9, 517, 586; Hebrew 24, 30, 34, 40, 48, 62; hidden

## Index of names and subjects

meanings 36, 106; Jesus' interpretation of 222, 240, 316, 390, 589; Jewish 2; Samaritan 25, 217–18; Septuagint 24
seal 156, 254; of creation 513
sealed book 160, 243; as book of life 501; opening of 319
Second God 67, 103, 162, 178, 238, 277, 286
secrets 5, 13–14, 43, 67–8, 118, 237, 258, 303, 320, 329, 380, 403–4, 494; restored 73, 323, 503
seeing God 404–10
seeking the LORD 521–2
Servant 90–6, 112–14, 184, 328, 371, 376–7; Jesus as 3, 54, 60, 203, 478; Lamb as 13, 327; of the LORD 23; oracles of 94–6, 110; resurrected 391, 510; songs of 90–4, 109–10, 327, 443; suffering like abuse of Jesus 536–7; as wise 85
sevenfold presence 175; light 244, 391
Shechem 215
sheep: blinded 305, 535; entrusted to Peter 604; and goats parable 332; in other folds 311; returning 327
Shekinah 438–9, 459
Shemaʿ 481, 489, 514, 583
Sheol 331
Shepherd (good) 257, 300–2, 309, 455, 533
shepherd angels 291–2, 299, 305; evil 305–12, 388; as high priests 293

Shiloaḥ/Siloam 57, 152, 265, 288
Shittim 268
sight 95, 293
signs 231, 288, 340–1; before fall of Jerusalem 319, 351–5, 473
Simon of Cyrene 544
Simon the leper 342
sin-bearer 367, 371
sixth day 235
snake 50, 202; bite/mark of 202–3; children of 179; as law of Moses 278; poison of 487
solitary one 402
Solomon, enthroning of 82, 103
Son(s) of God 13, 79, 294, 404, 509, 514, 539–40; a Hebrew term 313
son of lawlessness 415–16
sonship 78, 108, 124, 237, 281, 315, 492, 583
Spirit(s): birth from 200; distinct from Logos/Paraclete 471; gifts of 176; given to disciples 589; holy 38, 115, 134, 322, 516; of the LORD 257, 460, 470; as mother 121, 184; poured out 96; resting 183; two 8–9, 371, 414; sevenfold 183; as Wisdom 96
stoning 270, 286, 312
suffering 451
sun 51, 147; children of 202; goddess at Ugarit 35; woman clothed with 39, 123, 129–30, 267, 365
Sun of Righteousness 150
sunrise ritual 150

Sychar 215
synagogue teaching 254–60; expulsion from 295, 373

tabernacle 62, 148, 172; as symbol of creation 63
Tabernacles, feast of 140, 148–57, 222, 262, 347; palms at 344
Taheb 219
temple: cleansing 191–6; dedication of 149, 262; destruction 586 BCE 28, 406; destruction 70 CE 137, 142; first 3, 28, 62, 494; living 196, 370; lost furnishings 37; measurements of 303; of Messiah 194–6, 219, 524; myth of 501; new 144; restored furnishings 39; second 29, 93, 151, 348, 500; tax 192; as tower 304; veil of 212
temptations of Jesus 123–6, 365
testament literature 386–7; Deuteronomy as 387
theophany 133, 391; physical sensation with 590
*theōsis* 12, 75, 87, 91, 130, 160, 254–5, 330–2, 343, 497, 538
Therapeuts 227, 389, 398
thieves, symbolism of 546
Thomas 10, 324, 499, 586; seeing the LORD 591–3; touching wounds 590
throne, heavenly 31; cherubs of 35, 38, 98; sharing 77; teachings about 63
Tiberias, sea of 596

## Index of names and subjects

'time' 357
title on cross 546
tombs: empty 568; of Jesus 563; memory of location 569; of prophets 290; vision of holy of holies 579
tradition: hidden/oral 11, 12, 16, 119; post-resurrection 12–13, 517
Transfiguration 7, 116, 128, 203, 261, 367, 451, 581, 589
tree: of life 36–8, 501; as menorah 36, 93; restored 121, 372, 400–1; sacred 48
trial by high priests 524–7
truth 47, 162, 369, 403, 533–4; angel of 369

Ugarit 35, 41, 69
unity 67, 166–7, 243, 312, 384, 392, 455, 489; as harmony 438, 514; shows divine origin 513–14
Uzziah 292, 372

Valentinus 454, 490, 499
veil of temple 66, 389; as flesh of Jesus 559
Vespasian 532
vine 54–6, 377, 423–35; choice 427; false 435; as forbidden tree 431–3; golden over temple 423; symbol of Lady 425, 429; wild 436
vinedresser 437

vinegar 552–5
vineyard parable 120, 141, 314, 436
Virgin 78, 206, 285; her son 293
vision of throne, *merkavah* 47, 111, 118, 126, 183; of enthronement 69; of the LORD 97, 116, 178, 230, 404, 515
visions: seen by: Daniel 555; Ezekiel 60, 118; Isaiah 406–8; Jesus 39, 111, 117, 121, 126, 148, 183, 186, 201, 276, 473, 485, 519, 533; John 39, 105, 385; Mary Magdalene 576, 583; second Isaiah 243; visions fulfilled 472
voice from heaven 360; in the temple 361

watchmen 299
water as symbol of Wisdom 294, 498; bitter 271; libation 152; living 218, 265; from rock 232; from temple 195, 267
way 5, 7, 403–4; of Messiah 162; of two spirits 415
willow branches 156
wine 188, 380; with myrrh 551
Wisdom 56, 85–90, 155; abandoned 44, 96, 199, 204–7, 286, 372;

changes to 43; clothing disciples 549; feeding disciples 253, 259; as Jerusalem 209; linked to ḥesedh 394; as mother 57–9, 166, 365, 493; myth of 2; returning to temple 372; teaching through her messengers 266, 290; as vine 429
witness 176–7
women at the cross 549–50
Word *see* Logos
wordplay 120, 258, 292, 437
world, *kosmos* 204, 503
worship 19, 82; of high priest 297; of Jesus 296–7, 341
wounds of Jesus 592
wrath: age of 486–7; winepress of 424, 521


Yahwehel/Yahoel 72, 466
Yannai, Rabbi 186
Yeb, temple at 64, 67
yoke of teaching 227


Zaddik 81, 93
Zadok 72, 302, 366; sons of 26, 45, 303, 326, 565
Zadok, Rabbi 197
Zebedee, sons of 596; both killed by Jews 598
Zered, brook of 49, 232

www.ingramcontent.com/pod-product-compliance
Lightning Source LLC
Chambersburg PA
CBHW070753300426
44111CB00014B/2395